W9-BRZ-448

PARAGUAY

GARLAND REFERENCE LIBRARY
OF SOCIAL SCIENCE
(VOL. 51)

PARAGUAY
A Bibliography

David Lewis Jones

GARLAND PUBLISHING, INC. • NEW YORK & LONDON
1979

Library of Congress Cataloging in Publication Data

Jones, David Lewis.
Paraguay, a bibliography.

(Garland reference library of social science ; v. 51)
Includes index.
1. Paraguay—Bibliography. I. Title.
Z1821. J66 016.9892 77-83382
ISBN 0-8240-9825-0

Printed on acid-free, 250-year-life paper
Manufactured in the United States of America

CONTENTS

INTRODUCTION

The considerable difficulties which face the bibliographer of Latin America are increased in the case of Paraguay, a country whose complex history includes two major wars and several coups d'etat. A rapid survey of the first pages of this work will show the limitations, until recent years, of Paraguayan bibliography.

The primary concern of the author in compiling this work has been to present a fairly comprehensive list of works relating to Paraguay for the use of students in other countries. The author naturally hopes that it will be found useful by librarians and scholars within Paraguay.

The method of selection has been as follows. All books, in European languages or Guarani, which could be traced and for which complete bibliographical details could be established, have been included. There is no firm rule regarding the years covered; the earliest imprint is from the sixteenth century while the latest Paraguayan imprint is from 1977. However, as details of Paraguayan books often take a number of years to reach Europe, the coverage of the period 1975–78 is not very full. The author hopes that it will be possible to produce a supplement to this work, and he would be grateful to receive details of any additions or corrections to the present work.

Articles from Paraguayan periodicals are included where the periodicals are reasonably accessible in British, United States and Canadian libraries. Articles from non-Paraguayan periodicals are included except where they were less than three pages long. Articles from scientific periodicals were omitted unless they appeared to be of general interest.

All works cited in this bibliography have been arranged by subject and in alphabetical order within each subject category except for literary works, where the writer's work and critical studies of his work are arranged under each writer. Paraguayan books are frequently reprinted; to avoid making this work excessively long, only the first edition is described in detail, with other editions briefly listed with only changes of editor, imprint or collation shown. As there was some delay between the final preparation of the original text and its publication, the author decided to make certain additions to the text. These additions were inserted in the relevant sections and are indicated by a, b, etc.

Brief annotations have been provided to indicate either outstanding or misleading works.

Anyone who compiles a bibliography enters into many debts to friends and colleagues. The present writer is grateful to the following libraries for permitting access to their collections: The British Library, London; the Institute of Historical Research and the Institute of Latin American Studies, both part of the University of London; and the University of London Library. The task was made easier because my former employers, the University College of Wales Library, Aberystwyth, possess a good collection of reference works and bibliographies. Mr. Robert Cooper, my former colleague at Aberystwyth, was very patient in obtaining Paraguayan material on inter-library loan. Srta. Alicia Moguilevsky gave much help and encouragement in the preparation of this work, while Mrs. R.E. Thompson helped considerably in the final preparation of the manuscript.

Finally, I must offer my thanks to those unseen colleagues who preceded me in the field of Paraguayan bibliography.

David Lewis Jones
Christmas/Nadolig, 1978

ABBREVIATIONS

A. General

A.	Asunción
B.A.	Buenos Aires
c.	circa
CPDS	Centro Paraguayo de Documentación Social
CPES	Centro Paraguayo de Estudios Sociologicos
ed., eds.	edition; editions
Edit.	Editorial
IDIA	Instituto de Desarrollo Integral
illus.	illustrations
Imp.	Imprenta
n.d.	no date
n.p.	no place
n.s.	nova série; new series
N.Y.	New York
nac.	nacionales, nacional
rev.	revised
Tall.	Talleres
trans.	translation; translated by

B. Periodicals

AAAFH	Americas - Academy of American Franciscan History (Washington)
AAE	Archivo per l'antropologia e la etnologia (Florence)
AAIP	Anales de la Asociación Indigenista del Paraguay
AAN	American anthropologist (Washington)
ABBA	Anales de la Biblioteca Buenos Aires
ABNRJ	Annaes - Bibliotheca Nacional do Rio de Janeiro
AC	Antropologica (Caracas)
ACO	L'Agricoltura coloniale (Florence)

ACP	Anales cientificos paraguayos (A.)
ACQR	American Catholic quarterly review (Philadelphia)
AEA	Anuario de Estudios Americanos (Seville)
AEAR	Archivio Español de Arte (Madrid)
AESC	Annales: economies, sociétés, civilization (Paris)
AFSJ	American foreign service journal (Washington)
AH	Agricultural history (Chicago)
AHA	Anuario de historia argentina (B.A.)
AHSJ	Archivium historicum societatis Jesu (Rome)
AI	América indígena (Mexico)
AIAAIE	Anales del Instituto de Arte Americana e Investigaciones Esteticas (B.A.)
AIEA	Anales del Instituto Etnografia Americano (Cuyo)
AJ	Arbitration journal (New York)
AJIL	American journal of international law (New York)
AJO	American journal of Orthopsychiatry (Menasha, Wisc.)
AJPA	American journal of physical anthropology (Philadelphia)
AL	América Latina (Rio de Janeiro)
ALH	América (Havana)
ALS	Anthropological linguistics (Bloomington, Ind.)
ALT	Annali Lateranensis (Rome)
AMH	América (Havana)
AMLP	Anales del Museo de La Plata
AMNBA	Anales del Museo Nacional de Buenos Aires
AN	Anthropos (Stuttgart, etc.)
ANEP	American Neptune (Salem)
ANYAS	Annals of the New York Academy of Sciences
AP	Aportes (Paris)
APAU	Americas - O.A.U. (Washington)
AR	Archeologia (Paris)
ARP	Archipum - revista de la junta de historia eclesiástica Argentina
AS	Aggiornamenti sociali (Milan)
ASCA	Anales de la sociedad cientifica Argentina (B.A.)
ASGHG	Anales de la sociedad de geografia e historia de Guatemala (Guatemala)
ASR	Archives de sociologie des rêligions (Paris)
AT	Atenea (Concepción, Chile)
ATL	Atlas (Paris)
AUCE	Anales - Universidad Central del Ecuador (Quito)
AV	Archiv für Völkerkunde (Vienna)

B	Biblioteca (B.A.)
BAAL	Boletín de la Academia Argentina de letras (B.A.)
BACH	Boletín Academia Chilena de la historia (Santiago)
BANHA	Boletín de la Academia Nacional de historia, Argentina (B.A.)
BANHE	Boletín de la Academia Nacional de historia, Ecuador (Quito)
BANHV	Boletín de la Academia Nacional de historia, Venezuela (Caracas)
BAV	Boletín de la Academia Venezolana (Caracas)
BBAA	Boletín bibliográfico de antropologia americana (Mexico)
BBAN	Boletín de la biblioteca y archivo nacional (Tegucigalpa)
BBMP	Boletín de la Biblioteca Menendez Pelayo (Santander)
BCB	Boletín cultural y bibliografia (Bogota)
BF	Boletín de filologia (Montevideo)
BFDCS	Boletín de la Facultad de Derecho y Ciencias Sociales (Cordoba, Arg.)
BFIASEE	Banque française et italienne pour l'Amerique du Sud. Etudes économiques (Paris)
BFLS	Bulletin de la Faculté des Lettres de Strasbourg
BFT	Bois et forêts des tropiques (Paris)
BG	Boletim geográfico (Rio de Janeiro)
BHAC	Boletín de historia y antigüedades (Bogota)
BI	Boletín indigenista (Mexico)
BIB	Bibliographica (London)
BICUAER	Bulletin of the International Commission on Urgent Anthropological and Ethnological Research (The Hague)
BIGA	Boletín del Instituto Geográfico Argentina (B.A.)
BIIAPI	Boletín del Instituto Internacionale Americana de Proteccion a la Infancia (Montevideo)
BIIH	Boletín del Instituto de Investigaciones Historicas (B.A.)
BINF	Boletín Informativo (B.A.)
BJNHA	Boletín de la junta de historia y numismatica americana (B.A.)
BKA	Books abroad (Norman, Okl.)
BL	Berichte über Landwirtschaft (Hamburg)
BMNA	Boletim do Museu Nacional - Antropologia (Rio de Janeiro)
BMNB	Boletim do Museu Nacional (Rio de Janeiro)
BMRE	Boletín del Ministerio de Relaciones Exteriores (La Paz)
BNAP	Boletín naval armada paraguaya (A.)

BPAU	Bulletin of the Pan American Union (Washington)
BRAH	Boletín de la Real Academia de la Historia (Madrid)
BS	Bulletin Salésien (Nice)
BSAB	Boletín. Sociedad argentina de botánica
BSAL	Bulletin de la Société d'Anthropologie de Lyon
BSBP	Boletín de la Sociedad Bolivariana del Paraguay (A.)
BSCP	Boletín de la Sociedad Cientifica del Paraguay y del Museo Etnográfico (A.)
BSGI	Bolletino della Societá Geografico Italiana (Rome)
BSGL	Bulletin de la Société de Géographie de Lille
BSGS	Boletín, Sociedad Geografica de Madrid
BSN	Bolletino della Societá di Naturalisti (Naples)
BSSA	Bulletin de la Société Suisse de Americanistes (Geneva)
BTJ	Board of Trade journal (London)
BVF	Beiträge zur völkerkundliche Forschung (Cologne)
C	Combate (San José)
CA	Cuadernos americanos (Mexico)
CB	Cuadernos brasilenos (B.A.)
CH	Cuadernos hispanoamericanos (Madrid)
CHA	Chasqui (Williamsburg)
CHR	Catholic historical review (Washington)
CI	Cahiers internationaux (Paris)
CINA	Cuadernos del Instituto Nacional de Antropologia (B.A.)
CINIF	Cuadernos del Instituto Nacional de Investigaciones Folklóricas (B.A.)
CIV	Civilisations (Brussels)
CLA	Casa de la Americas (Havana)
CM	Comentario (B.A.)
CMHL	Cahiers du monde hispanique et luso-bresilien - Caravelle (Toulouse)
COM	Cahiers d'outre-mer (Bordeaux)
COR	Contemporary review (London)
CP	Cultura politica (Rio de Janeiro)
CR	Cuadernos republicanos (A.)
CRAS	Comptes rendus de l'Académie de sciences (Paris)
CS	Ciencias sociales (Medellin)
CSS	Cultura (San Salvador)
CU	Cuadernos (Paris)
CUA	Current anthropology (Chicago)
CUH	Current history (Philadelphia)
CUN	Cultura Universitaria (Caracas)

DA	Der deutsche Auswanderer (Berlin)
DAI	Documentación administrativa (Madrid)
DHR	Duquesne hispanic review (Pittsburgh)
DM	Das Munster (Munich)
DSB	Department of State Bulletin (Washington)
E	Europe (Paris)
EA	Estudios Americanos (Seville)
EALP	Estudios de la Academia Literaria del Plata (B.A.)
EB	Economia Boliviana: revista de economia y finanzas (La Paz)
EBA	Estudios (B.A.)
EC	Espiral (Bogota)
EG	Europäische Gespräche (Hamburg)
EK	Ekistics (Athens)
EM	España Misionera (Madrid)
EOR	El escarabojo de oro (B.A.)
EP	Estudios paraguayos (A.)
EPA	Economista paraguayo (A.)
ER	Erde (Berlin)
ERM	Economie et realités mondiales (Paris)
ES	Economia Salvadoreña (San Salvador)
ESC	Estudios sobre el comunismo (Santiago de Chile)
ET	Ethnology (Pittsburgh)
ETH	Ethnos (Stockholm)
ETL	Explicacion de Textos Literarios (Sacramento)
EUS	Education and urban society (Beverly Hills)
F	Formaçao: revista brasileira de eduçacao (Rio de Janeiro)
FA	Foreign affairs (New York)
FAI	Freedom at issue (N.Y.)
FAM	Folklore americano (Lima)
FBA	Filologia (B.A.)
FI	Foro internacional (Mexico)
FM	Fraser's magazine (London)
FMQ	Foreign minerals quarterly (Washington)
FO	Focus - American geographical society (New York)
FPAIS	Foreign Policy Association information service (New York)
FPR	Foreign policy review (New York)
FQR	Foreign quarterly review (London)
FRB	Federal Reserve bulletin (Washington)
G	Géographie (Paris)
GC	Growth and change (Lexington, Ky.)
GE	Geografia (Sao Paulo)

GFT	Geografiska förenings tidskrift (Helsingfors)
GJ	Geographical journal (London)
GL	Globus (Brunswick)
GM	Geographical magazine (London)
GR	Geographical review (New York)
GRSGA	Gaea: revista de la Sociedad Geografica Argentina (B.A.)
GUA	Guarania (A.)
GW	Geographische Wochenschrift (Breslau)
H	Hispania (Washington)
HAHR	Hispanic American historical review (Baltimore)
HAM	Hispamerica (Takoma Park, Md.)
HB	Historical bulletin (St. Louis)
HBA	Historia (B.A.)
HBAM	Historiografia y Bibliografia Americanista (Seville)
HF	Hispanofila (Chapel Hill, N.C.)
HI	Historian (Allentown, Pa.)
HLAS	Handbook of Latin American studies (Miami, Fla.)
HM	Homme (Paris)
HNA	Historia de la nación argentina, ed. by Ricardo Levene. B.A., Imp. universidad, 1937 (vol. 2)
HO	Hoy (Mexico City)
HP	Historia Paraguaya (A.)
HR	Hispanic review (Philadelphia)
HU	Humanidades (La Plata)
IA	Ibero-amerikanische Archiv (Bonn)
IAE	Internationales Archiv für Ethnographie (Leyden)
IAEA	Inter-American economic affairs (Washington)
IALR	Inter-American law review (New Orleans)
IARB	Inter-American review of bibliography (Washington)
IB	Information bulletin: supplement to the World Marxist Review
IC	International conciliation: documents for the year ... (New York)
IE	Investigaciones y ensayos (B.A.)
ILR	International labour review (Geneva)
IM	Internatsional molodezhi
IMFSP	International Monetary Fund staff papers (Washington)
IN	Insula (Madrid)
INT	International affairs (London)
IRM	International review of missions (Edinburgh)

JAF	Journal of American folklore (Boston)
JAI	Journal of the Anthropological Institute of Great Britain and Ireland (London)
JCS	Journal of church and state (Waco, Tx.)
JDA	Journal of developing areas (Macomb, Ill.)
JE	Journal des economistes (Paris)
JF	Journal of forestry (Washington)
JFI	Jornal de filologia (Sao Paulo)
JGWSGL	Jahrbuch für Geschichte von Staat, Wirtschaft und Gesellschaft Lateinamerikas (Cologne)
JIAS	Journal of inter-american studies (Gainesville, Fla.)
JNH	Journal of negro history (Washington)
JSA	Journal de la société des américanistes (Paris)
K	Kosmos (Stuttgart)
KFLQ	Kentucky foreign language quarterly (Lexington)
LA	Lasso (B.A.)
LALR	Latin American literary review (Pittsburgh)
LARR	Latin American research review (Austin, Tx.)
LATR	Latin American theatre review (Lawrence, Ks.)
LB	Los libros (B.A.)
LC	Letras (Curitiba)
LD	La diligencia
LH	Louisiana history (New Orleans)
LI	Linguistics (The Hague)
LL	Letras (Lima)
LLN	Les langues néolatines (Paris)
LN	Landscape (Santa Fe, New Mexico)
LNOJ	League of Nations official journal (Geneva)
LS	Lebende Sprachen (Berlin)
LUA	Luzernische Auswanderung (Lucerne)
MA	Miscelánea americanista (Madrid)
MAB	Meteorological abstracts and bibliography (Lancaster, Pa.)
MDM	Migrations dans le Monde (Geneva)
MGG	Mitteilungen der geographischen Gesellschaft (Berlin)
MH	Missionalia Hispanica (Madrid)
MIA	Mid-America (Chicago)
MIG	Migration news (Geneva)
MIOG	Mitteilungen des Instituts für österreichische Geschichtsforschung (Vienna)
MJ	Mining journal

MLJ	Modern language journal (New York)
MLR	Monthly labour review (Washington)
MM	Mariner's mirror (London)
MN	Mundo nuevo (Paris)
MQR	Mennonite quarterly review (Goshen, Ind.)
MR	Military review (Fort Leavenworth, Ks.)
MRB	Marine Rundschau (Berlin)
MSGI	Memorie della societá geografica italiana (Rome)
NC	Nineteenth century (London)
NED	Notes et études documentaires (Paris)
NGM	National geographic magazine (Washington)
NMN	New monthly magazine (London)
NNI	Novaia i noveishaia istoriia (Moscow)
NNH	Nueva narrativa hispanoamericana (Madrid)
NP	Neophilologus (The Hague)
NR	Norte: revista hispanica de Amsterdam
NRFH	Nueva revista filológica hispanica (Mexico)
NS	Nueva sociedad (Costa Rica)
P	Pesquisas: anuario de Instituto Anchietano de Pesquisas (Porto Alegre)
PA	Panoramas (Mexico City)
PAPS	Proceedings of the American Philosophical Society (Philadelphia)
PH	Palabra y el hombre (Mexico City)
PM	Petermanns geographische Mitteilungen (Gotha)
POL	Politica (Caracas)
PR	Progreso (Mexico City)
PRDIA	Pan-América: revista de derecho internacional americana (Montevideo)
PSA	Papeles de son armadans (Madrid)
PSN	Peasant studies newsletter (Pittsburgh)
PSQ	Political science quarterly (Boston)
PX	Phoenix (B.A.)
QR	Quarterly review (London)
RA	Revista de antropologia (Sao Paulo)
RABA	Revista americana de Buenos Aires
RABC	Revista de América (Bogotá)
RAL	Re: arts and letters (Nacogdoches, Tx.)
RAMSP	Revista do Arquivo Municipal do Sao Paulo
RAP	Revista del Ateneo Paraguayo (A.)
RASP	Revista de antropologia (Sao Paulo)
RBA	Revista de Buenos Aires

RBC	Revista bimestre Cubana (Havana)
RBNA	Revista banco nacional argentino (B.A.)
RBNBA	Revista de la Biblioteca Nacional (B.A.)
RBNC	Revista Biblioteca Nacional (Havana)
RBPI	Revista brasileira de politica internacional (Rio de Janeiro)
RC	Revue contemporaine (Paris)
RCE	Revista de ciencias económicas (B.A.)
RCECE	Revista centro estudiantes de ciencias economicas (A.)
RCHG	Revista Chilena de historia y geografia (Santiago)
RCIAS	Revista del Centro de Investigacion y Accion Social (B.A.)
RDF	Revista Dominicana de filosofia (Santo Domingo)
RDHL	Revista de derecho, historia y letras (B.A.)
RDISDP	Revue de droit internationale de sciences diplomatiques et politiques (Geneva)
RDM	Revue des deux mondes (Paris)
RDN	Revue de défense national (Paris)
RE	Revista de las Españas (Madrid)
REABA	Revista eclesiástica del arzobispado de Buenos Aires
RED	Revista de educación (La Plata)
REF	Revue économique française (Paris)
REMP	Bulletin - Research group for European migration problems (The Hague)
REP	Revista de estudios politicas (Madrid)
RF	Razón y fe (Madrid)
RFH	Revista de filologia hispanica (B.A.)
RFMSN	Rivista di fisica, matematica e scienza naturali (Naples)
RG	Revista Guarania (A.) (no. 239)
RG	Revue de géographie (Paris) (no. 2591)
RGA	Revista geográfica americana (B.A.)
RGDIP	Revue génerale de droit international public (Paris)
RGIPGH	Revista geográfica del instituto pan-americano de geografia e historia
RGPS	Revue géographique des Pyrénées et Sud-Ouest (Toulouse)
RHA	Revista de historia de America (Mexico City)
RHB	Revista de historia (Brazil)
RHES	Revue d'histoire économique et sociale (Paris)
RHM	Revista hispanica moderna (New York)
RI	Revista iberoamericana (Pittsburgh)
RIB	Revista interamericana de bibliografia (Washington)

RIHGB	Revista do Instituto historico e geographico Brasileiro (Rio de Janeiro)
RIHGMG	Revista do Instituto historico e geographico de Minas Gerais (Belo Horizonte)
RIHGU	Revista del Instituto historico y geográfico del Uruguay (Montevideo)
RIL	Revista iberoamericana (Pittsburgh)
RIM	Revista de Indias (Madrid)
RIP	Revista del Instituto Paraguayo (A.)
RISS	Revista iberoamericana de seguridad social (Madrid)
RJ	Revista Javeriana
RJB	Revista del jardin botánico (A.)
RJEHM	Revista de la Junta de estudios historicos de Mendoza (Mendoza, Arg.)
RL	Revista do livro (Rio de Janeiro)
RLM	Revista de literaturas modernas (Mendoza, Arg.)
RM	Revista meteorológica (Montevideo)
RMA	Revista del Museo Americanista (Lomas de Zamora, Arg.)
RMG	Revista militar (Guatemala)
RMJ	Revista de Museu Julio de Castilhos e Arquivo Histórico do Rio Grande do Sul (Porto Alegre)
RMLP	Revista del Museo de La Plata
RMN	Revista militar y naval (Montevideo)
RMP	Revista do Museu Paulista (Sao Paulo)
RNBA	Revista nacional (B.A.)
RNC	Revista nacional de cultura (Caracas)
RNCP	Revista nacional de cultura (A.)
RNM	Revista nacional (Montevideo)
ROMF	Romanische Forschungen (Erlangen)
RP	Revue de phonétique
RPARA	Revista Paraguaya
RPM	Revista Paraguaya de microbiologia
RPOL	Review of politics (Notre Dame, Ind.)
RPP	Revue du psychologie des peuples (Paris)
RPS	Revista Paraguaya de sociologia (A.)
RS	Réforme sociale (Paris)
RSAA	Revista de la Sociedad de Amigos de la Arqueologia (Montevideo)
RSAAT	Revista Sociedad Argentina Antropologia (B.A.)
RSBEE	Revue société belge d'études et d'expansion (Brussels)
RSBV	Revista de la Sociedad Bolivariana de Venezuela (Caracas)
RSCI	Rivista di storia della chiesa in Italia (Rome)
RSCP	Revista de la Sociedad Cientifica del Paraguay (A.)

RSH	Revue des sciences humaines (Paris)
RSW	Research studies - Washington State University (Seattle)
RTA	Revue des travaux de l'Académie des Sciences Morales et Politiques et Comptes Rendus de ses Séances (Paris)
RUBA	Revista de la Universidad de Buenos Aires
RUNP	Revista de la Universidad Nacional de La Plata
RUZ	Revista de la Universidad del Zulia (Maracaibo)
RY	Revista Yvytyrusu
SA	Suplemento antropológico (A.)
SAMM	South American missionary magazine (London)
SE	Sciences ecclésiastiques (Montréal)
SET	Sovietskaia etnografiia (Leningrad)
SEUL	Seul (Brussels)
SGM	Scottish geographical magazine (Edinburgh)
SIA	Survey of international affairs - Royal Institute of International Affairs (London)
SIR	Survival International Review (London)
SJA	Southwestern journal of anthropology (Santa Fe, New Mexico)
SM	Saeculum (Freiburg)
SMAE	Sbornik - Muzei antropologii i etnografii, Akademiia nauk SSSR (Leningrad)
SMU	Sovietskaia muzyka (Moscow)
SOCA	Sociological analysis (San Antonio)
SS	Seguridad Social (Mexico)
SSF	Studies in short fiction (Newbury, S.C.)
SSP	Sociologia (Sao Paulo)
SU	Sudamerika
SUR	Sur (B.A.)
T	Temas (Montevideo)
TA	Terra ameriga (Genoa)
TAM	Terre, air, mer: la géographie (Paris)
TC	Trabajos y comunicaciones - Universidad Nacional de La Plata, Departamento de historia
TE	Trimestre económico (Mexico City)
TF	Tierra firme (Madrid)
TILAS	Travaux de l'Institut d'études latinoaméricaines de l'Université de Strasbourg
TKNAG	Tijdschrift van het Koninklijk Nederlandsch aardrijkskundig genootschap Amsterdam
TL	Taller de letras (Santiago de Chile)
TLR	Tulane law review (New Orleans)
TP	Tropenpflanzer (Berlin)
TR	Tradición (Cuzco)

U	Universidad (Santa Fe, Arg.)
UN	Unasylva (Washington)
UNI	L'Universo (Florence)
US	United Service (New York)
UZK	Uchenye zapiski - Kalininsk ped. inst.
VE	Véritas (B.A.)
VGE	Verhandlungen der Gesellschaft für Erdkunde (Berlin)
VI	Voprosy istorii (Moscow)
VM	Vie del mondo (Milan)
VR	Voina i revoliutsiia (Moscow)
VRU	Verfassung und Recht in Ubersee (Hamburg)
VSW	Vierteljahrschrift für Sozial und Wirtschafts-geschichte (Leipzig)
VU	Vivant univers
WMR	World Marxist review (Toronto)
WTISER	World Trade Information Service. Economic reports
WW	Wissen und Wehr (Berlin)
ZAE	Zeitschrift für Allgemeine Erdkunde (Berlin)
ZAL	Zeitschrift für Auslandische Landwirtschaft (Frankfurt)
ZE	Zeitschrift für Ethnologie (Brunswick)
ZFE	Zeitschrift für Eingeborensprachen (Berlin)
ZG	Zeitschrift für Geopolitik (Bad Godesburg)
ZGW	Zeitschrift für Geschichtwissenschaft (Berlin)
ZKT	Zeitschrift für Katholische Theologie (Innsbruck)
ZV	Zeitschrift für Völkerrecht (Breslau)
ZWI	Zeitschrift für wissenschaftliche Insektenbiologie (Berlin)

I. BIBLIOGRAPHY AND REFERENCE WORKS

A. Bibliographies

1 AMERICAN GEOGRAPHICAL SOCIETY. A catalogue of the maps of Hispanic America. Vol. III: Maps of Venezuela, The Guianas, Brazil and Paraguay. N.Y., American Geographical Society, 1933. 217p. (Map of Hispanic America, Publication no. 3)

1a ARNDT, Karl John Richard; OLSON, May E. The German language press of the Americas, 1732-1968: history and bibliography. Volume 2: Argentina, Bolivia, Brazil, Canada, Chile, Colombia, Costa Rica, Cuba, Dominican Republic, Ecuador, Guatemala, Guyana, Mexico, Paraguay, Peru, U.S.A. (addenda), Uruguay, Venezuela. Pullach/Munich, Verlag Dokumentation, 1973. 708p.

2 AYROSA, Plinio. Apontamientos para a bibliografia da língua tupí-guaraní. Sao Paulo, 1943. 303p. (Universidade de Sao Paulo. Faculdade de Filosofia, Ciências e Letras, boletim no. 33. Etnografia e Tupí-Guaraní, no. 4)

3 AYROSA, Plinio. Apontamientos para a bibliografia da língua tupí-guaraní. 2. ed. Sao Paulo, 1954. 261p. (Universidade de Sao Paulo. Faculdade de Filosofia, Ciências e Letras, boletim no. 169. Etnografia e Tupí-Guaraní, no. 29)

4 BIBLIOGRAFIA: Estudios y documentos sobre la política en el Paraguay. RPS 5, no. 13 (1968) 155-59.

5 BIBLIOGRAFIA: La población en el Paraguay. RPS 5, no. 12 (1968) 136-40.

6 BIBLIOGRAFIA sobre la sociedad rural en el Paraguay. RPS 5, no. 11 (1968) 129-34.

7 BIBLIOTECA NACIONAL. ASUNCION. Bibliografía paraguaya: catálogo de la biblioteca paraguaya "Solano Lopéz". A., Tall. nac. de H. Kraus, 1906. 984p.

8 BINAYAN, Narciso. Bibliografía de bibliografías Paraguayas. HU 3 (1922) 449-57.

9 BRAZIL. MINISTERIO DA MARINHA. SERVICO DE DOCUMENTACAO GERAL DA MARINHA. Exposiçao comemorativa do centenário do término da Guerra do Paraguai, 1870-1970: acervo da Biblioteca Rio-Grandense, Coleçao José Arthur Montenegro. Rio Grande do Sul, 1970. 41p.

10 CARVALHO NETO, Paulo de. Bases bibliográficas para el estudio sistemático de la antropologia paraguaya. BBAA 13 (1950) 1, 179-210.

11 CARVALHO NETO, Paulo de. Bibliografía afro-paraguaya. Informe preliminar. BBAA 18 (1955) 1a, 164-70.

12 CARVALHO NETO, Paulo de. Bibliografía crítica del folklore paraguayo. RMP n.s. 11 (1959) 178-232.

13 CENTRO PARAGUAYO DE DOCUMENTACION SOCIAL. Bibliografia de las publicaciones del Centro Paraguayo de Estudios Sociológicos y del Centro Paraguayo de Documentacion Social. A., CPDS y CPES, 1973. 15p.

14 CHASE SARDI, Miguel. An annotated bibliography of works on "The Indian problem" published in Paraguay. *In* no. 2659, 423-30.

15 CHRISTMAN, Calvin Lee. The Chaco War: a tentative bibliography of its diplomacy. AAAFH 26 (1969) 54-65.

16 CLAGETT, Helen L. A guide to the law and legal literature of Paraguay. Washington, Library of Congress, 1947. 59p.

17 CORVALAN, Grazziella. Bibliografía sobre estudios socíolinguísticos en el Paraguay. A., Centro Paraguayo de Estudios Sociologicos, 1973. 10p.

17a CORVALAN, Grazziella. Estudios socíolinguísticos en el Paraguay. 2 ed. A., CPES y CPDS, 1976. 32p.

18 DALRYMPLE, Alexander. Catalogue of authors who have written on Rio de la Plata, Paraguay and Chaco. London, Printed by Ballantine & Law, 1807. 22p.

19 DECOUD, José Segundo. Biblioteca de José Segundo Decoud, estadista del Paraguay; catálogo detallado en secciones, conteniendo el nombre de los editores, número de páginas, clase de encuadernación. B.A., Spinelli, 1912. 462p.

20 DECOUD, José Segundo. A list of books, magazine articles, and maps relating to Paraguay. Books, 1638-1903. Maps, 1599-1903. A supplement to the Handbook of Paraguay, published in September, 1902, by the International Bureau of the American Republics. Washington, Government Printing Office, 1904. 53p.

21 DIAZ PEREZ, Viriato. Obras y manuscritos referentes al Paraguay que se encuentran en algunas bibliotecas españolas. RIP no. 54 (1906) 233-44.

22 DIAZ PEREZ, Viriato. Sobre una bibliografía de bibliografías paraguayas. RPARA 2, no. 2 (1926) 26-37.

23 FERNANDEZ-CABALLERO, Carlos F.S. Arandukã ha kuatiañeẽ paraguai rembiapocué. The Paraguayan bibliography. A retrospective and enumerative bibliography of printed works of Paraguayan authors. A., Washington, Paraguay Arandú Books, 1970. iii, 143p.

24 FERNANDEZ-CABALLERO, Carlos F.S. Paraguái tai hume. Tove Paraguái arandu taisarambi ko yvy apere. The Paraguayan bibliography. Vol. 2. Amherst, Mass., Seminar on the Acquisition of Latin American Library Materials, University of Massachusetts Library, 1975. xvii, 221p. (SALALM Bibliography, 3).

These two bibliographies cover works on Paraguay and works by Paraguayan authors. Vol. 2 contains an index to both vols.

24a FERRARO, Oscar Humberto. Datos y estudios sobre educación en el Paraguay. A., CPES, 1976. 71p.

25 GARRETT, Richard. Paraguayan and Argentine bibliography. BIB 1 (1895) 262-73.

26 GEOGHEGAN, Abel R. Bibliografía sobre Ludovico A. Muratori y su obra sobre las Misiones Jesuiticas del Paraguay, 1743-1749. ARP 4 (1960) 276-96.

27 HAMBURG. WELT-WIRTSCHAFTS-ARCHIV. BIBLIOTHEK. Paraguay-Uruguay; Stand: Januar 1959. Hamburg, 1959. 88p. (Auslandskunde; Literaturnachweis über die Gebeite Wirtschaft und Politik, Recht und Technik. Länder-Abteilung, no. 18).

28 HEISECKE, Guillermo. La bibliografía sociológica en el Paraguay. A., Centro Paraguayo de Estúdios Sociológicos, 1965. 23p.

29 HEISECKE, Guillermo. La bibliografía en el Paraguay. RPS 1, no. 2 (1965) 57-53.

30 HISTORIA y bibliografía de las primeras imprentas rioplatenses, 1700-1850; misiones del Paraguay, Argentina, Uruguay, por Guillermo Furlong and others. B.A., Edit. Guaranía, 1953-
Vol. 1, La imprenta en las reducciones del Paraguay, 1700-1727, etc. 1953. 596p.

31 KALLSEN GINI, Margarita. Referencias bibliográficas de la historia paraguaya; guerra contra la Triple Alianza, guerra del Chaco. EP 1, no. 1 (1973) 85-138.

32 MARESKI, Sofía; FERRARO, Oscar Humberto. Bibliografía para el estudio de los mensajes presidenciales del Paraguay. A., CPDS, 1974. 20p.

33 MARESKI, Sofía; FERRARO, Oscar Humberto. Bibliografía sobre datos y estudios económicos en el Paraguay. A., CPDS, 1972. 82p.

34 MARESKI, Sofía; FERRARO, Oscar Humberto. Bibliografía sobre datos y estudios etnográficos y antropológicos del Paraguay. A., CPDS, 1972. 143p.

35 MEDINA, José Toribio. Bibliografía de la lengua guaraní. B.A., Peuser, 1930. 93p. (B.A. Universidad nacional. Facultad de filosofia y letras. Publicaciones del Instituto de Investigaciones históricas, num. 51)

36 MEDINA, José Toribio. Historia y bibliografía de la imprenta en el antiguo virreinato del Río de la Plata. La Plata, Tall. de publicaciones del Museo; B.A., F. Lajouane; London, B. Quaritch, 1892. 4pt. in 1v.
Pte. 1. Historia y bibliografía de la imprenta en el Paraguay (1705-1727). Reprinted: Amsterdam, N. Israel, 1965.

36a MELIA, Bartomeu. Bibliografía sobre el bilingüismo en el Paraguay. EP 2, no. 2 (1974) 72-82.

36b MELIA, Bartomeu; PALAU, Tomás. Producción sociológica sobre el Paraguay: relevamiento bibliográfico de los últimos años. EP 3, no. 1 (1975) 147-89.

37 MESA, Rosa Quintero. Latin American serial documents: a holdings list, vol. 9: Paraguay. Ann Arbor, Xerox University Microfilms, 1973. xxxii, 61p. (Documents of government agencies)

38 MOSCOV, Stephen C. Paraguay: an annotated bibliography. Buffalo, Council on International Studies, State University of New York at Buffalo, 1972. 104p. (Special Studies, no. 10)

38a OLAVARRIA ARANGUREN, José; SCHELLHORN, Maria. La Cuenca del Plata y su proceso de integración: referencias bibliograficas sobre la Cuenca del Plata. B.A., FLASCO, Facultad Latinoamericano de Ciencias Sociales, 1976. vi, 326p.

38b OSUNA, Mauricio. Bibliografías paraguayas y bolivianas sobre la Guerra del Chaco. A., Centro Cultural Paraguayo-Americano, 1974. 26p.

38c RAMIREZ ESCARCEGA, Alejandro. Bibliografía de ciencias sociales en America del Sur: Bolivia, Brasil, Paraguay y Peru. Mexico, Escuela Nacional de Biblioteconomia y Archivonomía, 1976. 344p.

38d RAMOS, R. Antonio. Una selección de libros, folletos y articulos por autores nacionales publicados en 1950. RIB 1 (1950) 219-21.

39 RAPHAEL, Maxwell Isaac; FORD, Jeremiah Denis Matthias. A tentative bibliography of Paraguayan literature. Cambridge, Mass., Harvard University Press, 1934. xi, 25p.

40 RICE, Mary L. Selective annotated bibliography on the climates of Paraguay, Uruguay and Argentina. MAB 3 (1952) 3, 243-90.

41 RIVAROLA, Domingo M. Estudios y datos sobre la población en el Paraguay; bibliografía. A., Centro Paraguayo de Estudios Sociológicos, 1970. 27p.

41a RIVAROLA, María Magdalena. Datos y estudios sobre la vivienda en el Paraguay. A., CPES, 1976. 35p.

42 SOCIEDAD TIPOGRAFICA DEL PARAGUAY. La Sociedad tipográfica del Paraguay en el primer Congreso americano de bibliografía e historia. Tucuman, 1816-1916. A., 1916. 38p.

43 UNITED STATES. OFFICE OF INTER-AMERICAN AFFAIRS. RESEARCH DIVISION. Preliminary bibliography of Paraguay, compiled from the Strategic Index of the Americas. Washington, 1943. 32p.

44 UNIVERSIDAD CATOLICA DE ASUNCION. CONSEJO DE PLANIFICACION. Bibliografía básica sobre desarrollo socio-económico del Paraguay, 1950-1973. A., U.C.A., 1974. 31p. (Informe preliminar de discusión, no. 7)

45 UNIVERSITY OF TEXAS LIBRARY. LATIN AMERICAN COLLECTION. Recent Paraguayan acquisitions. No. 1 1962/ Mar. 1967. Austin, n.d.
No more published.

46 VELAZQUEZ, Rafael, Eliado. Informaciones bibliograficas americanas: Paraguay. AEA 18 (1961) 715-27.

47 VELAZQUEZ, Rafael Eliado. Paraguay. AEA 15 (1958) 675-86.

47a ZARATE, T. Bibliografía sobre los estudios sociales en el Paraguay. n.p., Instituto Latinoamericano de Relaciones Internacionales, 1971. 60p.

48 ZIMMERMAN, Irene. Current national bibliographies of Latin America: a state of the art study. Gainesville, Center for Latin American Studies, University of Florida, 1971. x, 139p.
Paraguay = p. 50-4.

49 ZINNY, Antonio. Bibliografía histórica del Paraguay y de Misiones. RNBA 4 (1887) 87-96, 179-91, 372-83; 5 (1887) 82-96, 168-80, 264-88, 364-84; 6 (1888) 373-83; 7 (1888) 67-94, 185-92; 8 (1888) 272-88, 369-83; 9 (1889) 342-83; 10 (1889) 67-93.

B. Collected biography

50 BIOGRAFIA de nuestros artistas. n.p., 1959. 49p. (Colección Ocara poty cué mi, 1)
Musicians

51 ALBUM paraguayo. A., Editorial Guaraní, 1955-

52 BORDON, F. Arturo. Liberales ilustres. A., Sociedad 18 de Octubre, 1966-

53 BRAY, Arturo. Hombres y épocas del Paraguay; prólogo del Doctor Higinio Arbo. B.A., Edit. Difusam, n.d. 178p.
Contents: Francia; Carlos Antonio López; Solano López; Bernardino Caballero; Patricio Escobar;

Juan B. Egusquiza; Manuel Gondra; Eligio Ayala.
2. ed. B.A., Edit. Ayacucho, 1943. 186p.
3. ed. B.A., Ediciones Nizza, 1957-

54 CIRCULO PARAGUAYO. Argentina-Paraguay, homenajes a San Martin. B.A., Colaboradores Paraguayos, 1950. 32p.

55 GALERIA de paraguayos ilustres. A., Edit. Bosco, 1968?- 1-

56 MARTINEZ, Sindulfo. Hombres y pasiones. A., Edit. El Gráfico, 1966. 184p.
Includes essays on Estigarribia, José Gill, Justo Pastor Benitez, Juan Martincich, Juan Francisco Recalde, Andres Barbero, Domingo Montanaro, Luis A. Riart, Cesar Vasconcellos, Enrique L. Pinho, Felipe Molas Lopez, Vicente Lamas, Joel Estigarribia, Francisco Brizuela.

57 MOSQUEIRA, Silvano. Nuevas semblanzas. Civilización arábiga. A., La Colmena, 1937. 160p.

58 MOSQUEIRA, Silvano. Semblanzas paraguayas. A., Tall. nac. de H. Kraus, 1908. 209p.

59 MOSQUEIRA, Silvano. Siluetas femininas. Los españoles en el Paraguay. El ocaso de los grandes hombres. A., La Colmena, 1930. 142p.

59a ORTELLADO ROJAS DE FOSSATI, María Antonia. Buscando a los que fueron. A., Graf. Zamphirópolos, 1970. 147p.

60 OXILIA, Héctor. Oratorio de Nuestra Señora de la Asunción y Panteón Nacional de los Héroes. A., 1969. 83p.

61 PARKER, William Belmont. Paraguayans of to-day. B.A., N.Y., The Hispanic Society of America, 1920. xv, 315p. (Hispanic notes & monographs; essays, studies, and brief biographies, issued by the Hispanic Society of America, 6)
Another impression issued in London and N.Y., 1921.
Reprinted: N.Y., Kraus Corporation, 1967.

62 QUIEN es quién en el Paraguay? B.A., F. Monte Domecq, 1941- 1-

62a RECALDE A., Sergio. Crónica de una estirpe prócer, (los precursores). A., 1976. 298p.

63 VERON de ASTRADA, Manuel. Hombres en la vida y en la muerte. A., Zamphirópolos, 1975. 112p.

64 WHO'S who in Latin America: a biographical dictionary of notable living men and women of Latin America; ed. by Ronald Hilton. 3rd ed. Stanford: Stanford University Press, 1945-51. 7 vols.
Pt. 5: Argentina, Paraguay & Uruguay.
Reprinted: Detroit, B. Ethridge, 1971, 2 vols.

65 ZUBIZARRETA, Carlos. Cien vidas paraguayas. B.A., Ediciones Nizza, 1961. 201p.

C. Libraries and archives

66 AVEIRO LUGO, Eusebio. Organización de biblioteca: informe que elevó el 30 de septiembre de 1933 al Señor Ministro de Relaciones Exteriores y Culto Dr. J.P. Benitez el director de la Biblioteca y Archivo. A., Imp. Nac., 1933. 16p.

67 FURLONG CARDIFF, G. Las bibliotecas de las Reducciones del Paraguay. EBA 38 (1925) 469-75; 39 (1925) 52-55.

68 McCARTHY, Cavan. Developing libraries in Brazil, with a chapter on Paraguay. Metuchen, N.J., Scarecrow Press, 1975. 207p.

69 RODRIGUEZ ELIAS, Avelino. El museo de Bellas Artes y la Biblioteca Americana Juan Silvano Godoi. A., Imp. Nac., 1940. 82p.

70 CASTAÑEDA, Carlos Eduardo; DABBS, Jack Autrey. The Manuel E. Gondra collection. HLAS 6 (1940) 505-517.

71 DIAZ PEREZ, Viriato. Para escribir una historia del Archivo Nacional. I. El documento más antiguo. RIP no. 62 (1909) 813-19.

72 HAHNER, June E. The Archivo Nacional in Asunción, Paraguay: addendum. LARR 6 (1971) no. 3, 131-132.
See also no. 83.

73 PARAGUAY. ARCHIVO NACIONAL. Catálogo de los documentos de la Sección historica de los años 1534-1871 del Archivo Nacional de Asuncion, por José Doroteo Bareiro. A., 1935. 46p.
Also published in GUA, nos. 17-37, 1935-36.

74 PARAGUAY. ARCHIVO NACIONAL. Catálogo de testamentos y codicilos del Archivo nacional por el paleógrafo José Doroteo Bareiro. A., Imp. Nac., 1936. 70p.

75 PARAGUAY. ARCHIVO NACIONAL. Documentos de 1534 á 1600 que se conservan en el Archivo nacional. Primer ensayo de indice. A., 1909. 18p.
Prepared by Viriato Díaz-Pérez.

76 PARAGUAY. ARCHIVO NACIONAL. Informes del Cabildo y de los gobernadores del Paraguay, ordenados y publicados por José Doroteo Bareiro. GUA (1935-36) no. 20, 27-33; no. 21, 31-36; no. 22, 31-33; no. 23, 3-5; no. 25, 29-31; no. 26, 35-37; no. 27, 27-29.

77 PARAGUAY. ARCHIVO NACIONAL. Libros de la Real Hacienda; documentos inéditos del Archivo de Asunción. A.?, 19--. 352p.

78 PARAGUAY. ARCHIVO NACIONAL. Lista de contenido de los volumenes microfilmados del Archivo Nacional de Asunción (Paraguay). Redactado por Francisco Sevillano Colom. A.?, 1965? 77p. (Mision de Unesco en el Paraguay. Publ. 22)

79 PEREZ ACOSTA, Juan Francisco. Los archivos de la Asunción del Paraguay. B.A., Coni, 1923. 42p. (Buenos Aires. Universidad Nacional. Publicaciones del Instituto de investigaciones históricas, 15)

80 SEVILLANO COLOM, Francisco. Lista de contenido de los volúmenes microfilmados del Archivo Nacional de Asunción. HAHR 38 (1958) 1, 59-120.

81 SEVILLANO COLOM, Francisco. Trabajos de la UNESCO en el Archivo de Asunción. HP 1 (1956) 115-20.

82 UNIVERSITY OF TEXAS. LIBRARY. Calendar of the Manuel E. Gondra manuscript collection, the University of Texas Library, prepared by Carlos Eduardo Castañeda and Jack Autrey Dabbs. Mexico, Edit. Jus, 1952. xxii, 467p.

83 WILLIAMS, John Hoyt. The Archivo Nacional in Asuncion, Paraguay. LARR 6 (1971) 1, 101-18.
See also no. 72.

D. General and Miscellaneous

84 CAMPOS, Arturo R. Significado etimológico de Paraguay y Uruguay. A., 1953. 14p.

85 ENDLICH, Rud. Zur Etymologie des Wortes 'Paraguay'. GL 77 (1900) 191-93.

86 INSTITUTO PARAGUAYO, ASUNCION. Himno nacional del Paraguay, su letra y su música; encuesta. B.A., Comité Paraguayo, 1933. 56p.

87 SCARONE, Arturo. La letra del himno del Paraguay; contribución a una encuesta iniciada por el Instituto Paraguayo. Montevideo, Renacimiento, 1924. 11p.

87a VARGAS PENA, Benjamín. La bandera del Paraguay, en su día, 1812 - 15 de agosto - 1946, aporte al esclarecimiento de su origen. B.A., Tall. gráf. Padilla y Contreras, 1946. 61p.

88 BENITEZ, Justo Pastor. Diagrama de las ideas en el Paraguay. RDF 2 (1956) 58-62.

89 SAGUIER ACEVAL, Emilio. El drama del siglo; dedicado a los trabajadores del Paraguay. A., El Pais, 1963. xvi, 306p.

90 CENTRO PARAGUAYO, MONTEVIDEO. Pro-patria; contribución a la paz y a la concordia, 25 de noviembre de 1922. Montevideo, Imp. Latina, 1922. 33p.

91 GILL AGUINAGA, Juan Bautista. Catálogo de la primera exposición de numismática hispano americano y paraguaya: colección Juan Bautista Gill. 12 de octubre de 1956. A., 1956. 64p.

92 INSTITUTO DE NUMISMATICA Y ANTIGUEDADES DEL PARAGUAY. Estatutos, aprobados en la asamblea constituyente del 11 de agosto de 1943. A?, 1944? 10p.

92a PENA, Enrique. Moneda y medallas paraguayas. A., Instituto Paraguayo, 1900. 51p.

92b SEPPA, Dale Allan. Paraguayan paper money. Chicago, Obol International, 1973. 50p.

93 ESCOBAR, Horacio. Páginas de gloria del deporte paraguayo. A., El Arte, 1955. 207p.

94 FERREIRA GUBETICH, Hugo. Lecciones de moral deportiva; manual del árbitro de fútbol. A., La Colmena, 1961. 101p.

95 MALDONADO, Julio César. Fútbol paraguaya y mundial. Ed. Complementaria de la primera de 1967. A., 1971. 59p.

96 MALDONADO, Julio César. Medio siglo de fútbol paraguayo. A?, El Arte, 1951. 172p.

97 SANCHEZ, Nicolás. Atletismo paraguayo; origenes, evolución, juegos colegiales, universitarios, estadisticas anuales, récords nacionales, olimpicos, mundiales y sudamericanos. A., Ediciones "Circulo de Periodistas Deportivas del Paraguay", 1957. 145p.

97a KNEITSCHEL, Víctor. Catálogo de los sellos postales de la Republica del Paraguay y sus derivados. B.A., 1947. 188p.

II. RELIGION

97b ALMONTE, Nemesio. Moñs. Emilio Sosa Gaona. A., Edit. Don. Bosco, 1970? 18p. (Galería de paraguayos ilustres, 3. Celeste)

98 ANDREA, Migual de. Oración patriotica pronunciada por monseñor doctor Miguel de Andrea, con motivo de la misa por la paz en la Catedral de la Asunción del Paraguay, el Domingo de Pascua, 7 de abril de 1912. A., Impresa por la Comisión de damas argentinas en obsequio á la Comisión de damas paraguayas, 1912. 24p.

98a BELZA, Juan E. Luís Lasagna, el obispo misionero: introducción a la historia Salesiana del Uruguay, el Brasil y el Paraguay. B.A., 1968. 457p.

99 BENITEZ, Justo Pastor. El lucero del Paraguay. Monseñor Juan Sinforiano Bogarín. *In* no. 159, 73-108.

100 BERINO MARTINEZ, Ignacio Amado. Ofertorio a Nuestro Señor de los Milagros, venerable patrono de Piribebuy; historia y leyenda. A., El Arte, 1960. 74p.

101 BOGARIN, Juan Sinforiano. Cartas pastorales, 1895-1949. Cuernavaca, Centro Intercultural de Documentación, 1969. 2 vols. (Sonedos no. 29, 30)

102 CADOGAN, León. Curuzú Yeguá: apostilla a la interpretación psicoanalítica del Culto a la Cruz en el folklore paraguaya. RA 9 (1961) 39-50.

103 CARRON, Juan Maria. El cambio social y el clero en el Paraguay. RPS 4, no. 8-9 (1967) 129-32.

104 CATHOLIC CHURCH IN PARAGUAY. CONCURSO DEL CLERO NACIONAL. Documentos referentes al Concurso del clero nacional paraguayo. A., Imp. de "El Comercio", 1877. 10p.

105 CATHOLIC CHURCH IN PARAGUAY. BISHOPS. Las exigencias de la doctrina social cristiana ante el insuficiente desarrollo del país; pastoral colectiva del Episcopado

Paraguayo. A., Secretariado Permanente de la Conferencia Episcopal Paraguayo, 1963. 31p. (Hablan los Obispos del Paraguay, 1)

105a CATHOLIC CHURCH. TREATIES. I concordati di Giovanni XXIII e dei primi anni de Paolo VI, 1958-1974; Austria, Germania, Jugoslavia, Spagna, Svizzera, Argentina, Bolivia, Colòmbia, Paraguay, El Salvador, Tunisia, Venezuela; a cura di Pio Ciprotti ed Elisa Zampetti. Milan, A. Giuffre, 1976. 152p.

106 COLAGNO, José W. El Templo de la Merced y nuestra historia. La Orden de Nuestra Señora de la Merced en el Paraguay. HP 4/5 (1960) 67-73.

106a CORDOBA, Antonio Santa Clara. Los franciscanos en el Paraguay (1537-1937); ensayo histórico. B.A., Imp. Lopez, 1937. xii, 226p.

107 CORREA, Domingo. Delegación indígena en viaje a Montevideo; Vicariato Apostólico del Chaco Paraguayo Boreal. B.A., 1961. 36p.

108 FARINI, L. La mission du Chaco Paraguayen. BS 56 (1934) 337-40.

109 GONZALEZ, Gustavo. El ciclo legendario de Fray Luis de Bolaños, La Virgen de Ka'akupé y El lago Ypakarai: leyendas y tradiciones. Con un glosario etimológico de voces guaraníes y modismos españoles del Paraguay. A., La Colmena, 1964. 66p.

110 GUILLEN-ROA, Miguel Angel. La Virgen de Caacupé; su historia, su leyenda. A., Emasa, 1966. 108p.

111 HENRIKSEN, A. Paraguay Mission. SAMM 22 (1888) 242-6, 268-73; 23 (1889) 18-21, 37-8, 53-8, 102-8, 133-8, 219-22.

112 HICKS, Frederick. Politics, power, and the role of the village priest in Paraguay. JIAS 9 (1967) 2, 273-82.

113 HICKS, Frederick. Politica, poder, y el papel del cura de pueblo en el Paraguay. SA 4 (1969) no. 1, 35-44.

113a HOMENAJE de gran veneración y recuerdo imperecedero al Excmo. y Rvdmo. Monseñor Juan Sinforniano Bogarín, 1er Arzobispo de Asunción en el 60 aniversario de su fallecimiento. A., Edit. El Grafico, 1954. 87p.

114 LIVIERES BANKS, L. Notas para la comprensión de la función socio-histórica de la Iglesia Católica Apostólica Romana en el Paraguay. RPS 7, no. 17 (1970) 123-32.

115 MAIZ, Fidel. Monseñor Bogarín; rasgos de su vida de digno prelado al par que distinguido ciudadano. A., Los Principios, 1913. 21p.

116 MAIZ, Fidel. La Virgen de los Milagros. A., 1883. 30p.

117 MAIZ, Fidel. La Virgen de los Milagros de Caacupé; su origén, su santuario y su pueblo; manojito de notas y apuntes espigador en el campo de la tradición y de la historia, por un misionero diocesano. A., Tall. nac. de H. Kraus, 1898. 193p.

118 MORA MERIDA, Luis. Notas al episcopologio paraguayo. AEA 30 (1973) 317-36.

119 NOGUES, Alberto. El provisor Roque Antonio Céspedes Xeria. A., Instituto Paraguayo de Investigaciones Históricas, 1960. 22p.

120 NUNEZ, Secundino. Nueva imagen del sacerdote rurale. RPS 5, no. 11 (1968) 93-6.

121 PANE, Ignacio Alberto. Las debilidades individuales y la religión de los fuertes. La Comisión del Circulo católico del Paraguay á sus obreros y pueblo trabajador. A., Tall. gráf. "La Unión", 1908. 12p.

121a PARAGUAY: the church confronted by a country in evolution. Brussels, Pro Mundi Vita, Centrum Information, 1971. 87p.

122 PARAGUAY. CONGRESO NACIONAL. CAMARA DE DIPUTADOS. Arzobispado; debates a su respecto, agosto 30 a setiembre 5 de 1928. A., Imp. Nac., 1929. 79p.

123 PARAGUAY. MINISTERIO DE JUSTICIA, CULTO E INSTRUCCION PUBLICA. Cuestión religiosa en el Paraguay; espediente ajustado con motivo de una nota bajo el nombre de monseñor Miguel Ferrini, encargado que fué de los negocios de la Santa Sede en el Brasil, y reproducida por monseñor César Ronsotti, internuncio y delegado apostólico en la misma corte. Motivos y razones de su retención por el gobierno de la república del Paraguay. A., Imp. de "El Comercio", 1877. 39p.

123a PAROLA, Luis. Historia contemporánea de la Compañía de Jésus en el Paraguay, 1927-1969. A., 1973. xxi, 608p.

124 La SALESIANOS en el Paraguay; reseña historica, 1896-1960; homenaje filial al Rvmo. P. Renato Ziggiotti. A., 1960? 115p.

125 SANCHEZ LABRADOR, José. Los indios pampas, puelches, patagones, según Joseph Sánchez Labrador, S.J.; monografia inédita prologada y anotada por Guillermo Furlong Cárdiff, S.J. B.A., Viau y Zona, 1936. xlvii, 251p.

126 SANCHEZ LABRADOR, José. El Paraguay católico, homenaje de la Universidad nacional de la Plata al XVII Congreso internacional de los americanistas en su reunión de Buenos Aires, en mayo 16 á 21 de 1910. B.A., Imp. de Coni hermanos, 1910-17. 3 vols.

127 WESTHUES, Kenneth. Curses versus blows: tactics in church-state conflict. SOCA 36 (1975) 1-16.

128 WESTHUES, Kenneth. The established church as an agent of change. SOCA 34 (1973) 106-23.

128a ZINNY, Antonio. Cronología de los Obispos del Paraguay. B.A., Imp. Europe, 1887. 29p.

III. HISTORY

A. General studies

129 ACEVAL, Benjamin. República del Paraguay: apuntes geográficos e históricos. A., Imp. de la "Democracia", 1893. 45p.

130 ADLER, Walterio Mercado. Paraguay: contradicción hecha destino. C 24 (1962) 39-46.

131 AGUIRRE, José de Jesus. Carácter e inteligencia; un estudio de tipologia paraguaya. A., "El Ateneo", 1966. 305p.

132 ALONSO CRIADO, Matias. La République du Paraguay. Traduit de l'espagnol par Max Winsweiler. Bordeaux, R. Coussau & F. Coustalat, 1889. 9p.

133 ALVERADO GARCIA, Ernesto. Impresiones sobre algunos paises del Caribe y el Paraguay. BBAN (1939) 9-16, 65-68.

134 AYALA QUEIROLO, Víctor. Historia de la cultura en el Paraguay. A., Imp. Zamphirópolos, 1966. 241p.

135 AYALA QUEIROLO, Víctor. Historia de la cultura en el Paraguay. A., Escuela Tecnica Salesiana, 1969. 249p.

136 BAEZ, Cecilio. Cuadros históricos y descriptivos. A., Tall. nac. de H. Kraus, 1906. 344p.

137 BAEZ, Cecilio. El Paraguay moderno; ó sea, El Paraguay estudiado del punto de vista geográfico, agrícola, industrial, comercial y estadístico, etc. Trabajo realizado por el doctor Cecilio Baez, con la cooperación del Señor Don José Rodriguez Alcalá. Gaudencio Yubero, iniciador y editor propietario de la obra. A., Tall. nac. de H. Kraus, 1915. 408p.

138 BAEZ, Cecilio. La Paraguay, son évolution historique et sa situation actuelle. Paris, F. Alcan, 1927. 123p.

139 BAEZ, Cecilio. Resumen de la historia del Paraguay desde la época de la conquista hasta el año 1880, seguido de la historia particular de la instrucción pública desde el gobierno de Domingo Martínez de Irala hasta nuestros días. A., Tall. nac. de H. Kraus, 1910. 256p.

140 BALEN, Chr. van. De toekomst van Paraguay. TKNAG, 2 ser., 51 (1934) no. 6, 889-92.

141 BAREIRO SAGUIER, Rubén; GARAVITO, Julian. Chronologie historique et littéraire. E 48, no. 494 (1970) 156-68.

142 BAREIRO SAGUIER, Rubén. Guarani; proud mark of the Paraguayan. APAU 16 (1964) no. 3, 6-10.

143 BAREIRO SAGUIER, Rubén. Le Guarani. E 48 no. 494 (1970) 133-39.

144 BAREIRO SAGUIER, Rubén. Le Paraguay; traduit de l'espagnol par Jean-Paul Duviols. Paris, Bordas, 1972. 128p. (Coll. Etudes 201. Sér. Espagnol)

145 BARRETT, Rafael. El dolor paraguayo. Lo que son los yerbales. B.A., B. Fueyo, 1909? 143p.

146 BARRETT, Rafael. El dolor paraguayo. Montevideo, Tall. graf. "El Arte", O.M. Bertani, 1911. 226p.

147 BARRETT, Rafael. Lo que son los yerbales. Montevideo, O.M. Bertani, 1910. 43p.

148 BARRETT, Rafael. Lo que son los yerbales paraguayos. Semblanzas de Barrett, por Ramiro de Maeztu y Emilio Frugoni. Montevideo, C. García, 1926. 52p.

149 BAZAN, Juan F. Algunos comentarios sobre la obra "Donde esta el Paraguay?" *In* no. 152, p. 114-22.

150 BAZAN, Juan F. Donde esta el Paraguay? A., 1955. 97p.

151 BAZAN, Juan F. Formación social del pueblo paraguayo. *In* no. 152, p. 50-73.

152 BAZAN, Juan F. Sobre política, y otros ensayos. A., 1958. 112p.

153 BAZAN, Juan F. La tercera dimension del hombre Paraguayo. *In* no. 152, p. 75-89.

154 BAZAN, Juan F. Tres problemas que no son Tres Leyes de la Historia Paraguaya. *In* no. 152, p. 29-41.

155 BEJARANO, Ramón César. "Somos lo que fuimos, seremos lo que somos". Patria y patriotismo; símbolos de la patria. A., 1964. 50p.

156 BELTRAN, L. Sulla condizione fisiche e sociali della Republica del Paraguay. BSGI 26 (1889) 197-206.

157 BENITEZ, Justo Pastor. Bajo el alero asunceño. Rio de Janeiro, Ministério da Educaçao e Cultura, Serviço de Documentaçao, 1955. 108p. (Coleçao "Aspectos" 18.)

158 BENITEZ, Justo Pastor. Formación social del pueblo paraguayo. A., Edit. América-Sapucai, 1955. 227p.
2. ed. A., Ediciones Nizza, 1967. 239p.

159 BENITEZ, Justo Pastor. Mancebos de la tierra. B.A., 1961. 100p.

160 BENITEZ, Justo Pastor. Páginas libres. A., El Arte, 1956. 171p.

161 BENITEZ, Justo Pastor. Panorama político e social do Paraguai. Rio de Janeiro, Associaçao Brasileira do Congreso pela libertade da cultura, 1960. 16p.

162 BENITEZ, Justo Pastor. El solar guaraní, panorama de la cultura paraguaya en el siglo XX. Prólogo de Max Henriquez Ureña. B.A., Edit. Ayacucho, 1947. 254p.
2. ed. A., Ediciones Nizza, 1959. 216p.

163 BENITEZ, Justo Pastor. El Paraguay y su ciudadanía. ALH 43 (1954) 16-22.

164 BENITEZ, Justo Pastor. La ruta; texto de lectura para las escuelas primarias, adoptado por decreto n. 8.862 de 1 de setiembre de 1938. A., Imp. nac., 1939. 115p.

165 BENITEZ, Luis G.; BAEZ, Jorge. Historia cultural; reseña de su evolución en el Paraguay, de acuerdo al programa de la signatura, para el 6. curso del bachillerato en humanidades y comercial. A., El Arte, 1962. 232p.

166 BENITEZ, Luis G. Historia cultural; reseña de su evolución en el Paraguay. A., El Arte, 1966. 307p.
Also: A., El Arte, 1969. 237p.

167 BENITEZ, Luis G. Manual de historia paraguaya para el primer curso del ciclo básico. A., El Arte, 1963. 134p.
Also: A., El Arte, 1970. 141p.

168 BERTONI, Guillermo T.; GORHAM, J. Richard. The people of Paraguay: origin and number. *In* no. 474, p. 109-40.

169 BOURGADE LA DARDYE, Emanuel de. Le Paraguay. Paris, E. Plon, Nourrit et cie, 1889. 460p.

170 BOURGADE LA DARDYE, Emanuel de. Paraguay: the land and the people, natural wealth and commercial capabilities. English ed., edited by E.G. Ravenstein. London, G. Philip, 1892. xiii, 243p.

171 BRIZUELA, Juan J. Ojeada histórica sobre el Paraguay, seguida del vapuleo de un traidor; dividida en varias azotainas, administradas al extraviado autor de las producciones contra el Paraguay; conocido vulgarmente por el nombre de Luciano el Zonzo. Escrita en verso y prosa por el ciudadano paraguayo Juan J. Brizuela. B.A., 1856. 86p.

172 BROWNING, Webster E. The River Plate republics; a survey of the religious, economic and social conditions in Argentina, Paraguay and Uruguay. London, N.Y., World Dominion Press, 1928. 139p.

173 BRUYSSEL, Ernest Jean van. La république du Paraguay. Brussels, C. Muquardt, 1893. 219p.

174 BUTLER, William Mill. Paraguay: a country of vast natural resources, delightful climate, law-abiding people, and stable government, rightly called the paradise of South America. Philadelphia, The Paraguay Development Company, 1901. 60p.

175 CABANELLAS, Guillermo. Figuras, paisajes y leyendas guaraníes; prólogo de Jóse Santiago Villarejo. B.A., Edit. Heliasta, 1974. 170p.

176 CABRERA, Gaspar Natalicio. Parâcua'y: geología, arqueología, antropología, lingüística. A., Edit. E. Gráfico, 1954. xix, 129p.

177 CAPDEVIELLE, Bernardo. Historia del Paraguay desde los orígenes hasta nuestros días. A., Tall. nac. de H. Kraus, 1927. 463p.

178 CAPDEVIELLE, Bernardo; OXIBAR, C. Historia del Paraguay. A., Colegio de San José, 193? 331p.
Reprinted: 1935?; 1939?; 1942; 1948; 1953.

179 CARDOZO, Efraím. Apuntes de historia cultural del Paraguay. 6. curso. A., Colegio de San José, 1963? 2 v. in 1.

180 CARDOZO, Efraím. Breve historia del Paraguay. B.A., Edit. Universitaria de B.A., 1965. 169p. (Biblioteca de América. Libros del tiempo nuevo, 33)

181 CARDOZO, Efraím. Efemérides de la historia del Paraguay. "Hoy en nuestra historia". A., Ediciones Nizza, 1967. 517p.
A daily chronicle of historical events.

182 CARDOZO, Efraím. La historia del Paraguay como creación del espiritu. BRAH 136 (1955) no. 1, 111-30.

183 CARDOZO, Efraím. El Paraguay en la epopeya americana. B.A., Edit. R. Monte Domecq, 1952. 48p.

184 CARDOZO, Efraím. Paraguay independiente, por Efraím Cardozo; Uruguay independiente, por J.E. Pivel Devoto. Barcelona, Salvat, 1949. 637p. (Historia de America y de los pueblos americanos, 21)

185 CARDOZO, Efraím. El sentido de nuestra historia. A., La Colmena, 1953. 27p.

186 CARDUS HUERTA, Gualberto. Arado, pluma y espada. Barcelona, Imp. Domensch, 1911. 691p.

187 CARONI, Carlos A. Paraguay, formación y supervivencia. A., Escuela Técnica Salesiana, 1975. 162, 10p.

188 CELLIEZ, Adélaïde. Histoire du Paraguay. Paris, Librarie international-catholique, 1877. 175p.

189 CHARTRAIN, François. La République du Paraguay. Paris, Berger-Levrault, 1973. 82p. (Enclycopédie politique et constitutionelle. Série Amérique)

190 CHAVES, Julio César. El aislacionismo en el alma paraguaya. B.A., Edit. Ayacucho, 1948. 30p.

191 CHAVES, Julio César. Compendio de historia paraguaya; adaptado al nuevo programa del primer curso del ciclo básico. B.A., 1958. 265p.
3. ed. B.A., Tall. Gráf. Lumen Noseda, 1962. 239p.

192 CHAVES, Julio César. Historia general del Paraguay. A., Ediciones Nizza, 1968-
Vol. 1. Descubrimiento y conquista del Rio de la Plata y el Paraguay. 395p.

192a CHAVES, Osvaldo. La formación del pueblo Paraguayo. B.A., Ediciones Amerindia, 1976. 178p.

193 COSTAGUTA, Raffaele. Cenni storici, commerciali e geografici sul Paraguay. Genova, Stabilimento artisti tipografi, 1901. 82p.

194 CREYDT, Oscar A. Formación histórica de la nación paraguaya. n.p., 1963. 55p.

195 CRIST, Raymond E. Paraguay. FO 7 (1956) no. 3. 6p.

196 DEMARIA, Alfonso. Paraguay, heroico y romántico. Santiago de Chile, 1947. 133p.

197 DEMERSAY, Alfred. Historia geral de Paraguay desde a sua descoberta até nossos dias ... seguida de uma Noticia geographica de estado actual do Paraguay, pelo dr. J.M.L. Rio de Janeiro, Typographia Perseverança, 1865. 237p.

198 DENIS, Ferdinand. Résumé de l'histoire de Buenos Aires, du Paraguay et des provinces de la Plata, suivi du résumé de l'histoire du Chili. Paris, Lecointe et Duray, 1827. 321p.

199 DIAZ de ARCE, Omar. Paraguay. Havana, Casa de las Américas, 1967. 53, (30)p. (Colección Nuestros países)

200 DOMINGUEZ, Manuel. El alma de la raza. Prólogo de Juan E. O'Leary. A., C. Zamphirópolos, 1918. 340p. (Biblioteca paraguaya del Centro estudiantes de derecho, 1)
Another ed: B.A., Edit. Ayacucho, 1946. 278p.

201 DOMINGUEZ, Manuel. Causas del heroismo paraguayo. A., Tall. nac. de H. Kraus, 1903. 46p.

202 DOMINGUEZ, Manuel. Estudios históricos y literarios. A., Edit. Emede, 1956. 235p.
First ed. under the title: El milagro de lo eterno.

203 DOMINGUEZ, Manuel. El milagro de lo eterno y otros ensayos; estudios históricos y literarios. B.A., Edit. Emede, 1948. 223p. (Ediciones paraguayes)

204 DOMINGUEZ, Manuel. La nación. A., Tall. nac. de H. Kraus, 1908. 24p.

205 DOMINGUEZ, Manuel. La sierra de la Plata; primeros pasos de la conquista. A., Tall. nac. de H. Kraus, 1904. 56p.

206 DOMINGUEZ, Manuel. La traición a la patria y otros ensayos. A., Dirección de Publicaciones de las Fuerzas Armadas de la Nación, 1959. 295p.

207 ELLIOTT, Arthur Elwood. Paraguay: its cultural heritage, social conditions, and educational problems.

N.Y., Bureau of Publications, Teachers College, Columbia University, 1931. xiv, 210p.
Reprinted: N.Y., AMS Press, 1972.

208 EMELIANOW, Nicolás. El Paraguay; su presente y su porvenir. A., Imp. Militar, 1934. 26p.

209 FALEGEAU, Xavier. Les pays du Rio de la Plata. RDN 27 (1971) no. 1, 45-59.

210 FERGUSON, John Halcro. The River Plate Republics: Argentina, Paraguay, Uruguay, by J. Halcro Ferguson and the editors of Life. N.Y., Time Inc., 1965. 160p. (Life World Library)
Other eds: 1968, 1971.

211 FERGUSON, John Halcro. Las repúblicas del Rio de la Plata: Argentina, Paraguay, Uruguay, por J. Halcro Ferguson y los redactores de Life en español. Mexico, Offset Multicolor, 1966. 160p. (Biblioteca universal de Life en español)

212 FERNANDEZ, Carmen S. Inquietudes de la hora. La Paz, Bolivia, Edit. "Sport", 1940? 164p.

213 FISCHER-TREUENFELD, Richard Friedrich Eberhard von. Paraguay: ein historischer Abriss. Brunswick, Druck von A. Limbach, 1905. 43p.

214 FISCHER-TREUENFELD, Richard Friedrich Eberhard von. Le Paraguay décrit et illustré; étude sur le progrès économique du pays. Brussels, Typ. E. Guyot, 1906. 81p.

215 FISCHER-TREUENFELD, Richard Friedrich Eberhard von. Paraguay in Wort und Bild. Eine Studie über den wirtschaftlichen Fortschritt des Landes. 2. Aufl. Berlin, E. Mittler, 1906. viii, 379p.

216 FOGEL, Gerardo; GALCANO, Oscar Santacruz; FOGEL, Ramón; VELA, Ruth de. Paraguay: realidad y futuro, una aproximación al presente del país y sus perspectivas. A., IDIA, 1970? 133p.

217 FOURNIAL, Georges. Brève histoire du Paraguay. E 48, no. 494 (1970) 5-14.

218 FREIRE ESTEVES, Gomez. Historia contemporanea del Paraguay; lucha de cancillerias en el Plata. B.A., 1921. xv, 140p.

219 FREIRE ESTEVES, Luis; GONZALEZ PENA, Juan C. El Paraguay constitucional, 1870-1920. B.A., Empresa gráf. del Paraguay, G. Peña y cía, 1921. xxxi, 336p.

220 GAONA, Francisco. Introducción a la historia gremial y social del Paraguay. A., Edit. Arandú, 1967. Vol. 1 -
Valuable.

221 GARAY, Blas. Breve resumen de la historia del Paraguay. Madrid; A., Libreria y casa edit. A. de Uribe y cía, 1897. 142p.

222 GARAY, Blas. Colección de documentos relativos á la historia de América y particularmente á la historia del Paraguay. A., Tall. nac. de H. Kraus, 1899-1901. 2 vols.
Also published in RIP, vols. 2-3.

223 GARAY, Blas. Compendio elemental de historia del Paraguay. Madrid; A., Libreria y casa editora A. de Uribe y cía, 1896. 297p. (Biblioteca paraguaya)
Also: A., Tall. graf. "La Colmena", 1915. xiii, 228p.
4. ed. A., Imp. militar., 1928. 252p.

224 GARAY, Blas. Pequeña biblioteca histórica. A., Tip. "La Opinión", 1895. 3v. in 1.
A collection of sources.

225 GARAY, Blas. Tres ensayos sobre historia del Paraguay; prólogo de J. Natalicio González. A., Edit. Guarania, 1942. 336p. (Biblioteca paraguaya)

226 GARCIA y MELLID, Atilio. Proceso a los falsificadores de la historia del Paraguay. B.A., Ediciones Theoria, 1963-64. 2 vols. (Biblioteca de estudios históricos) (Liberalismo en el Rio de la Plata, 2)

227 GIMENEZ, Pastor. El miedo de escribir la historia; conferencia auspiciada por el Instituto Cultural Paraguay Brasil; acto realizado en el local de la misma entidad cultural el 28 de abril de 1954. A., El Arte, 1954. 18p.

228 GODOI, Juan Silvano. Bibliografía. "Ensayos" por Silvano Mosqueira, septiembre 10, 1902. A., Tall. nac. de H. Kraus, 1903. 20p.

229 GOEHRING, Maurizio. Il Paraguay. Milan, Società italiana di esplorazioni geografiche e commerciali, 1916. 94p.

230 GOMEZ, Tristan. Des eaux et des déserts. E 48, no. 494 (1970) 15-18.

231 GOMEZ RIOS, Emiliano. El Paraguay y su historia; obra ajustada a los programas oficiales del bachillerato. A., 1952. 224p.
2 ed: A., Mimeografía "Alcora", 1958. 162p.
3 ed: B.A., 1963. 253p.
2 & 3 eds: "del bachillerato y ciclo básico".

232 GOMEZ SERRATO, Darió. Visión de la patria. A., Dirección General de Turismo, 1971. 64p.

233 GONDRA, Manuel. Hombres y letrados de América; prólogo de J. Natalicio González. A., Edit. Guarania, 1942. 296p. (Biblioteca paraguaya)

234 GONZALEZ, Juan Natalicio. Bases y tendencias de la cultura paraguaya. CA 1, no. 5 (1942) 87-106; RG 1, no. 1 (1942) 3-25.

235 GONZALEZ, Juan Natalicio. El estado servidor del hombre libre. Mexico, Edit. Guarania, 1960. 326p.

236 GONZALEZ, Juan Natalicio. La formación de un pueblo. *In* ENSAYOS sobre la historia de Nuevo Mundo. Mexico, Instituto Panamericano de Geografía e Historia, 1951. (Publ. no. 118). pp. 431-59.

237 GONZALEZ, Juan Natalicio; YNSFRAN, Pablo Max. El Paraguay contemporáneo. Paris; A., Edit. de Indias, 1929. 196p.

238 GONZALEZ, Juan Natalicio. El Paraguay eterno. A., Edit. "Guarania", 1935. 204p.

239 GONZALEZ, Juan Natalicio. Paraguay y la cultura Rioplatense. RG 1, no. 2 (1942) 118-28.

240 GONZALEZ, Juan Natalicio. Proceso y formación de la cultura paraguaya. A., B.A., Edit. Guarania, 1938 (-1940) -
2 ed.: 1948-
Reprinted: A., Instituto Colorado de Cultura, 1976. 416p.

241 GORHAM, J. Richard. Portraits of Paraguay. *In* no. 474, 209-75.

242 GRUELUND, Kirsten. Paraguay. Copenhagen, Dansk Unicef Komite, Billedvej 5, 1968. 37p.

243 HANFF, Helene. Paraguay and Uruguay; prepared with the co-operation of the American Geographical Society. Garden City, N.Y., Doubleday, 1967. 63p. (Around the world program)

244 HELMER, M. A propos des origines de la conscience nationale au Paraguay. BFLS 44 (1965-66) 814-17.

245 HIRSCH, Leo. Die geistige und wirtschaftliche Entwicklung der Republik Paraguay ... Vienna; Leipzig, C. Fromme, 1913. 41p.

246 HISTORIA politica del Paraguay. n.p., Ateneo Liberal, 195-? 32p.

247 HOPKINS, Edward Augustus; CRIST, Raymond E.; SNOW, William P. Paraguay, 1852 and 1968. N.Y., American Geographical Society, 1968. 64p. (Occasional publications, 2)

248 HORNOS, Axel. Argentina, Paraguay & Uruguay. Camden, N.J., T. Nelson, 1969. 224p. (World neighbours)

249 IBARRA, Alonso. Cien años de vida polĩtica paraguaya posterior a la epopeya de 1865 al 70. A., 1973. 92p.

250 IBARRA, Alonso. Episodios nacionales de la vida politica y social del Paraguay de antes y de ahora. A., 1956. 63p.

251 INTERNATIONAL BUREAU OF THE AMERICAN REPUBLICS. Paraguay: a handbook. Washington, Government Printing Office, 1895. vi, 146p. (*Its* Bulletin, no. 54, 1892)

252 INTERNATIONAL BUREAU OF THE AMERICAN REPUBLICS. Paraguay. 2. ed., rev. by José Segundo Decoud with a chapter on the native races by J. Hampden Porter. Washington, Government Printing Office, 1902. 182p.

253 KOEBEL, William Henry. Paraguay. London, T.F. Unwin, 1917. 348p. (The South American series, 13)
2d. impression in 1919.

254 KOEBEL, William Henry. The romance of the river Plate. London, H. Ponsonby, 1914. 2 vols.

255 KOLINSKI, Charles J. Historical dictionary of Paraguay. Metuchen, N.J., Scarecrow Press, 1973. vi, 282p. (Latin American historical dictionaries, 8)

256 KRIER, Hubert. Tapferes Paraguay. Würzburg, Marienburg-Verlag, 1973. 127p.

257 LAMBEL, Alexander Pierre François, *comte* de. Le Paraguay. Tours, A. Mame et fils, 1878. 237p.
2 ed. 1881. 239p.

258 LAND und Volk von Paraguay. GL 2 (1862) 65-76.

259 LANTEUIL, Henri de. O Paraguai intelectual. Rio de Janeiro, Ediçao do autor, 1939. 24p. (Biblioteca pan-americana, 1)

260 LOPEZ DECOUD, Arsenio. Albúm gráfico de la República del Paraguay 1811-1911. B.A., Tall. graf. de la Companía General de Fósforos, 1911. 360, xlix, cxxxvip.
A general survey covering all aspects of Paraguayan life. It includes a good series of photographs of people and places.

261 MALDONADO, Silvio. El Paraguay: aspecto político, recursos humanos, recursos económicos, hechos e ideas. Mexico, Fondo de Cultura Económica, 1952. 169p. (Colección Tierra firme, 52)

262 MANGELS, Heinrich. Wirtschaftliche, naturgeschichtliche und klimatologische Abhandlungen aus Paraguay. Munich, F.P. Datterer, 1904. viii, 364p.
2 ed. 1919. 255p.

263 MANZONI, Cosme J. Un factor de progreso para el Paraguay. B.A., Tall. de la Casa Garcia & Dasso, 1912. 19p.

264 MARBAIS DU GRATY, Alfred Louis Hubert Ghislain, *baron*. La république du Paraguay. Brussels, Librairie européenne de C. Muquardt; London, Trubner, 1862. xxvii, 407, 200p.
2 ed. 1865.

265 MARBAIS DU GRATY, Alfred Louis Hubert Ghislain, *baron*. La república del Paraguay, por Alfredo M. du Graty. Traducida del francés al español por Carlos Calvo. Besanzón, Imp. de J. Jacquin, 1862. xlii, 364, 169p.

266 MARCOS, José. Linea de pensamiento 1811-1969; conferencias. A., Edit. El Arte, 1969. 141p.

267 MENDEZ CALDERON, Rafael. El Paraguay que he visto; apuntes de crítica social política y moral. Cochabamba, Edit. "El Mercurio", 1933. 122p.

268 MEULEMANS, Auguste. La république du Paraguay, étude historique et statistique. Paris, E. Dentu, 1884. 33p.

269 MÖLLER, Georg. Paraguay im Rahmen Südamerikas. ZG 16 (1939) no. 6, 432-36.

270 MONTALTO, Francisco Américo. Panorama de la realidad histórica del Paraguay; proceso y formación social y cultural del pueblo paraguayo a los fines nutricionales. A., 1967-
Vol. 1, pt 1 -

271 MONTE DOMECQ', Raul. La República del Paraguay en su primer centenario, 1811-1911. B.A., Compañia Sud-Americana de Billetes de Banco, 1911. 472p.
A very useful general survey with good photographs.

272 MONTE DOMECQ', Raul. La republica del Paraguay en su sesquicentenario 1811-1961; albúm gráfico del Paraguay. A., Edit. F. Monte Domecq', 1961. 276p.
Also useful, especially pp. 261-73: "Sintesis biográficas".
2. ed. 1964. 303p.

273 MORITAN, Santiago. Argentina y Paraguay; porque no constituyeron una sola nación. B.A., 1947. 23p.

274 MORTON, Clement Manly. Paraguay: the inland republic. Cincinnati, Powell & White, 1926. 177p.

275 MOSQUEIRA, Silvano. Ensayos. I. A., Tall. nac. de H. Kraus, 1902. 178p.

276 MOSQUEIRA, Silvano. Ideales: discursos y escritos sobre temas paraguayos. Washington, R. Beresford, 1913. 249p.

277 MULHALL, Michael George; MULHALL, Edward T. Handbook of the river Plate republics. Comprising Buenos Ayres and the provinces of the Argentine republic and the republics of Uruguay and Paraguay. London, E. Stanford; B.A., M.G. & E.T. Mulhall, 1875. viii, 432p.

278 MULHALL, Michael George; MULHALL, Edward T. Handbook of the river Plate, comprising the Argentine republic, Uruguay, and Paraguay. 5. ed. B.A., M.G. & E.T. Mulhall; London, Trubner, 1885. x, 732p.
6. ed. 1892. 686p.

279 MULHALL, Michael George; MULHALL, Edward T. Manual de las repúblicas del Plata; datos topográficos, históricos y económicos, sobre los productos, colonias, empresas, comercio, rentas nacionales, deuda publica, inmigración, ciudades, provincias, instituciones, ferro-carriles, bancos, escuelas y literatura de las repúblicas Argentina, Oriental y Paraguay. B.A., Imp. del "Standard"; London, E. Stanford, 1876. viii, 403p.

280 MULHALL, W.F.; FREUND, P.A. Letters from Paraguay, extracted from "The Standard", Buenos Aires. B.A., The Standard printing-office, 1888. 36p.

281 MUNOZ, Félix. Cómo somos los paraguayos. A., 1974. 133p.

282 O'LEARY, Juan Emiliano. Apostalado patriótico; conferencia dada en la ciudad de Pilar el 12 de octobre de 1930; prólogo de Arsenio López Decoud. A., 1930. 80p.

283 O'LEARY, Juan Emiliano. Discurso pronunciada por Juan E. O'Leary en el acto de entrega de las reliquias históricas del Paraguay por el presidente de la República Argentina, General Juan Perón, 16 de agosto de 1954. n.p., Presidencia de la Nación Argentina, Secretaria de Prensa y Difusion, 1954? 8p.

284 O Paraguay. Seu passado, presente e futuro. Por um Estrangeiro que residio seis annos naquelle Paiz. Obra publicada sob os auspicios da legaçao do Paraguay na córte do Brazil. Rio de Janeiro, Typ., imp. e const. de J. Villeneuve e comp., Rua do Ouvidor, 1848. 77p.

285 OVEN, Wilfred von. Argentinien, Paraguay, Uruguay: Land am Silberstrom die La Plata Länder. Nuremberg, Glock und Lutz Verlag, 1969. 391p.

286 PAN AMERICAN UNION. Paraguay. Washington, Pan American Union, 1927. 30p.

286a PAN AMERICAN UNION. Paraguay. Rev. ed. Washington, Pan American Union, 1942. 32p. (American nations series, 16)

286b PAN AMERICAN UNION. Paraguay. Washington, 1950. 32p.

286c PAN AMERICAN UNION. DEPARTMENT OF PUBLIC INFORMATION. Paraguay. Washington, Pan American Union, 1965. 47p. (American Republics series, 17)

287 PANE, Ignacio Alberto. Cuestiones paraguayas. A., Imp. Brossa, 1914. 68p.

288 PANE, Ignacio Alberto. El Paraguai intelectual; conferencia leída en el Ateneo de Santiago, el 26 de noviembre de 1902. Santiago, Imp. Mejia, 1902. 30p.

289 PARAGUAY 1524-1963. A., 1963? 15p.

290 PARAGUAY. CONSULADO. BUENOS AIRES. Paraguay: "nación bilingüe", el país de los ríos; publicación

del Consulado General del Paraguay en Buenos Aires. B.A.,? 195-. 20p.

291 PAREDES, Augusto. Album gráfico de la república del Paraguay. A., Artes graf. Rem, 1941. 288p.

292 PASTORE, Carlos. La lucha por la tierra en el Paraguay; proceso histórico y legislativo. Montevideo, Edit. Antequera, 1949. 191, xxxvp.
Another ed. 1972. xvi, 526p.
An important work.

293 PENA, Manuel de la. El ciudadano paraguayo. B.A., 1866. 22p.

294 PENAS, Agustín R. Alma y espíritu del Paraguay. Soul and spirit of Paraguay. A?, 1954? 11, 10p.
In Spanish and English.

295 PENDLE, George. Paraguay; a riverside nation. London; N.Y., Royal Institute of International Affairs, 1954. vi, 115p.
2 ed. 1956. 120p.
3 ed. London, N.Y., issued under the auspices of the Royal Institute of International Affairs by Oxford University Press, 1967. ix, 96p. One of the better English-language surveys of Paraguay.

296 PENDLE, George. The lands and peoples of Paraguay & Uruguay. London, A. & C. Black, 1959. 113p.; New York, Macmillan, 1959. 95p. (Lands and Peoples)

297 PEREIRA SALAS, E. América del Sur: Perú, Bolivia, Paraguay, Argentina, Chile. Período nacional. Mexico, Instituto Panamericano de Geografia e Historia, 1956. 68p.

298 PEREZ ACOSTA, Juan Francisco. Fechas y emblemas patrios del Paraguay; 14 de mayo, 15 de agosto, 25 de noviembre, simbolos nacionales. B.A., Ferrari hños, 1939. 104p.

299 PEREZ ACOSTA, Juan Francisco. El Paraguay y América: bosquejo histórico presentado al 2º Congreso Cientifico Panamericano por el delegado del Instituto Paraguayo. Washington, 1916. 4p.

300 PLA, Josefina. Apuntes para una historia de la cultura paraguaya. A., Tall. de Artes Graf. Zamphirópolos, 1967. 73p.
First published as part of no. 2239.

301 PLA, Josefina; FERNANDEZ, M.A. Aspectos de la cultura paraguaya. CA 21 (1962) 1, 68-103.

302 PLA, Josefina. Español y guaraní en la intimidad de la cultura paraguaya. CMHL 14 (1970) 7-21.

303 PRIETO, Justo. Paraguay, la provincia gigante de las Indias; análisis espectral de una pequeña nación mediterranea. B.A., Librería "El Ateneo", 1951. 243p.

304 QUENTIN, Ch. A verdade sobre o Paraguay. Rio de Janeiro, B.L. Garnier, 18--. 67p.

305 RIGUAL, Miguel. Apuntes de historia del Paraguay y nociones de la general, adaptados estrictamente al programa de las escuelas superiores. V grado. A., 19--. 123p.

306 RIQUELME, Andrés. Apuntes para la historia política y diplomatica del Paraguay. A., Edit. Toledo, 1960-61. 2 vols.

307 RODAS, C. El Paraguay; bosquejo sobre su estado económico, político y social. B.A., Imp. y est. de Buffet & Bosch, 1888. 67p.

308 ROLON MEDINA, Anastasio. Al margen de nuestra historia; puntualizaciones, comentarios y rectificaciones sobre hechos históricos del Paraguay. A., Imp. "La Humanidad", 1955. viii, 201p.

309 ROLON MEDINA, Anastasio. Temple y estirpe; ensayo histórico-apologéticos sobre la raza guaraní y el criollo paraguayo. A., 1953. 258p.

310 SANCHEZ, Santiago. Manual de informaciones sobre el Paraguay, para maestros y alumnos. A., Escuela Técnica Vocacional, 1961. xi, 270p.

311 SANCHEZ QUELL, Hipólito. Falando do Paraguai ao Brasil; 6 conferencias. Rio de Janeiro, Biblioteca do Exército, 1958. 86p. (Coleçao Taunay)

311a SANCHEZ QUELL, Hipólito. El tiempo que se fue. A., Ediciones Comuneros, 1976. 173p.

312 DON BOSCO (SOSA GAONA, Emilio) Ensayo de historia patria. A., Tall. nac. de H. Kraus, 1912. 61p.

313 STEWARD, Julian H. El pueblo Paraguayo. HP 1 (1956) 90-102.

314 TERAN Y GAMBA. Compendio de historia del Paraguay. 14 ed. A., Tip. y Encuad. de J. Quell, 1904. 114p.

315 TERAN Y GAMBA. Compendio de historia del Paraguay. 16 ed., rev. by Héctor F. Decoud. A., Tip. Quell & cía., 1920. 143p.

316 URBIETA ROJAS, Pastor. Camino de la hispanidad. A., Colección Paraguay, 1965. 160p.

317 URBIETA ROJAS, Pastor. Estampas paraguayas; prólogo por Enrique de Gandía. B.A., Edit. Difusam, 1942. 113p.
2. ed. A., Colección Paraguay, 1957. 117p.

318 URBIETA ROJAS, Pastor. La mujer en el proceso cultural del Paraguay; prólogo del doctor Eduardo Crespo. B.A., Edit. Ayacucho, 1944. 54p.

319 URBIETA ROJAS, Pastor. Paraguay: destino y esperanza. B.A., Ediciones Colección Paraguay, 1968. 172p.

320 VALDOVINOS, Arnaldo. La incógnita del Paraguay. B.A., Edit. Atlántida, 1945. 159p.

321 VARGAS PENA, Benjamin. Los ideales del Paraguay, y otros ensayos. Corrientes, La Edit. Corrientes, 1954. 89p.

322 VASCONSELLOS, Víctor Natalicio. Lecciones de historia paraguaya; con ilus. de Oscar Ferreiro. Responde al programa del primer curso del ciclo básico. A., 1959. 222p.
2 ed. A., 1962. 251p.
4 ed. A., 1966. 252p.
7 ed. A., 1970. 253p.

323 VELAZQUEZ, Rafael Eliado. Breve historia de la cultura en el Paraguay. A., 1965. 328p.
2 ed. A., Ediciones Universitarias Criterio, 1968. 311p.

324 VELLARD, J. Les hommes et leurs travaux au Paraguay (Amérique du Sud). BSGL 58 (1937) 171-83.

325 VILLALBA, Rufino A. Tipos y caracteres. A., Tall. nac. de H. Kraus, 1911. 67p.

326 VITTONE, Luis. La mujer paraguaya en la vida nacional. A., 1968. 70p.

327 WARREN, Harris Gaylord. Paraguay, an informal history. Norman, University of Oklahoma Press, 1949. xii, 393p.
The most recent narrative history in English.

328 WASHBURN, Charles Ames. Historia del Paraguay, con notas de observaciones personales y reminiscencias de algunas dificultades diplomáticas. B.A., Impresos con tipos de propiedad de la Revista del Paraguay, 1892-98. 3 v.
Not a complete translation of the English original.

329 WASHBURN, Charles Ames. The history of Paraguay, with notes of personal observations and reminiscences of diplomacy under difficulty. Boston, Lee, Shepard and Dillingham, 1871. 2 vols.
Reprinted: N.Y., AMS Press, 1973. 2 vols.

330 WEIL, Thomas E., and others. Area handbook for Paraguay. Washington, U.S. Government Printing Office, 1972. xiv, 316p.

331 ZINNY, Antonio. Historia de los gobernantes del Paraguay, 1535-1867. B.A., Imp. y librería de Mayo, 1887. xvi, 515, 5p.

B. Description and travel

1. *Before 1810*

332 AZARA, Félix de. Descripción é historia del Paraguay y del Rio de la Plata. Obra póstuma ... La publica su sobrino y heredero el señor don Agustín de Azara, marqués de Nibbiano ... bajo la dirección de don Basilio Sebastian Castellanos de Losada. Madrid, Imp. de Sanchiz, 1847. 2 vols.
Reprinted: A., A de Uribe y cía, 1896. 2 vols.
B.A., Edit. Bajel, 1943. xiii, 383p.
Madrid, Imp. nac., 1973. 2 vols.
A., Imp. nac., 1973. 638p.

333 AZARA, Félix de. Reise nach Süd Amerika von Don Felix von Azara in den Jahren 1781 bis 1801. Aus dem Spanischen mit Anmerkungen und einer Nachricht von dem Leben des Verfassers herausgegeben von Walkenaer. Aus dem Französischen übersetzt von Ch. Wenland. Berlin, Vossischen Buchhandlung, 1810. xxvi, 479p.

334 AZARA, Félix de. Sketches of South America. *In* MACKINNON, Lauchlan B. Steam warfare in the Parana ... London, Charles Ollier, 1848. Vol. 2, p. 121-281.

335 AZARA, Félix de. Viaggi nell'America meridionale di D. Felice di Azara, commisario e comandante de'confini nel Paraguay fatta da lui tra il 1781 ed il 1801 e publicata sulla scorta de'suoi manoscritti dal Sig. C.A. Walckenaer, tradotti dal Sig. Prof. Gaetano Barbieri con tavole in rame colorate. Milan, dalla Tip. Sonzogno e Comp., 1817. 2 vols.
Also: Turin, Dalla stampiera Alliana, 1830. 5 vols in 3.

336 AZARA, Félix de. Viajes por la América del Sur de Don Félix de Azara, Comandante de la Comisión de Límites Española en la Sección del Paraguay. Desde 1789 hasta 1801, en los cuales se dá una descripción geográfica, politica y civil del Paraguay y del Rio de la Plata: la historia del descubrimiento y conquista de dichos paises, con numerosos detalles sobre la historia natural y sobre los Pueblos Salvajes, que habitan en la expresada región, a la que se acompaña una exposición de los medios empleados dos por los Jesuitas para sujetar y civilizar los naturales de la citada sección de la América. Todo ello arreglado a los manuscritos de su autor, con una noticia sobre su vida y sus escritos, publicada por C.A. Walckenaer. Con notas de G. Cuvier. Montevideo, 1845-46. 260p. (Biblioteca del Comercio del Plata, 2)
Also: Montevideo, 1850. 2,318,2p. (Biblioteca del Comercio de Plata, 9)

337 AZARA, Félix de. Viajes inéditos de d. Félix de Azara desde Santa-Fe á la Asunción, al interior del Paraguay, y á los pueblos de Misiones, con una noticia preliminar por el general d. Bartolomé Mitre y algunas notas por el doctor d. Juan María Gutiérrez. B.A., Imp. de Mayo, 1873. 254p.
Selections from Viajes por la América Meridional.

338 AZARA, Félix de. Viajes inéditos de Azara. (Manuscrito en la colección de documentos del doctor Estanislao S. Zeballos, precedido de una introducción escrita por este y anotado por Luis M. Torres. RDHL 28 (1907) 193-212; 363-85; 509-31.

339 AZARA, Félix de. Viajes por la América Meridional contienen la descripción geográfica política y civil del Paraguay y del Río de la Plata; la historia del descubrimiento y conquista de estas regiones; detalles numerosos sobre su historia natural y sobre los pueblos salvajes que las habitan; el relato de los medios

empleados por los Jesuitas para someter y civilizar a los indígenas ... publicados con arreglo a los manuscritos del autor, con una noticia sobre su vida y sus escritos, por C.A. Walckenaer; enriquecidos con notas por G. Cuvier; traducida del frances por Francisco de las Barras de Aragón. Madrid, Calpe, 1923. 2 vols. (Viajes clasicos, 27-28)

Also: Madrid, Espasa-Calpe, 1941. 2 vols.
Madrid, Espasa-Calpe, 1969. 326p.
Another Spanish translation has the title: Viajes por la América del Sur (no. 336)

340 AZARA, Félix de. Voyage dans l'Amérique méridionale contenant la déscription géographique, politique et civile du Paraguay et de la rivière de la Plata; l'histoire de la découverte et de la conquête de ces contrées; des détails nombreux sur leur histoire naturelle, et sur les peuples sauvages qui les habitent; le récit des moyens employés par les Jésuites pour assujétir et civiliser les indigènes ... Publiés d'après les manuscrits de l'auteur, avec une notice sur sa vie et ses écrits par C.A. Walckenaer; enrichies de notes par G. Cuvier ... Suivis de l'histoire naturelle des oiseaux du Paraguay et de La Plata, par le même auteur, traduite d'après l'original espagnol, et augmenté d'un grand nombre de notes, par M. Sonnini; accompagnés d'un atlas de vingt-cinq planches. Paris, Dentu, 1809. 4 vols.

Vols. 3-4 are translated from no. 4230.

341 BAUCKE, Florian. Hacia allá y para acá (una estada entre los indios mocobíes, 1749-1767) traducción castellana por Edmundo Wernicke. Primera edición completa de la obra. Tucumán-B.A., 1942. 3 vols. in 4. (Universidad nacional de Tucumán. Departamento de investigaciones regionales. Publicaciones especiales del Instituto de antropologia (v). En colaboración con la Institución cultural argentino-germana, Buenos Aires. Publicación no. 11). (Universidad nacional de Tucumán. Publicación no. 324)

342 BAUCKE, Florian. Hin und her. Hin süsse und vergnügt, her bitter und betrübt: das ist: Treu gegebene Nachricht durch einem im Jahre 1748 aus Europa in West-America, nahmentlich in die Provinz Paraguay abreisenden und im Jahre 1769 nach Europe zurückkehrenden Missionarium. Zwettler-Codex 420. Hrsg. von Etta Becker-Donner unter Mitarbeit von Gustav Otruba. Vienna, W. Braumüller, 1959-66. 2 vols. (Veröffentlichungen zum Archiv für Völkerkunde, Bd. 4)

343 BAULNY, Olivier. Le Paraguay de Félix de Azara. TILAS 9 (1969) 519-36, 542-46.

344 BRAUMANN, Franz. Unternehmen Paraguay. Nach den Aufzeichnungen des Jesuitenpaters Anton Sepp, 1691-1703. Vienna, Herder, 1967. 226p.

345 The CONQUEST of the River Plate. I. Voyage of Ulrich Schmidt to the rivers La Plata and Paraguay. From the original German edition, 1567. II. The commentaries of Alvar Nuñez Cabeza de Vaca. From the original Spanish edition, 1555. Both translated with notes and an introduction by L.L. Dominguez. London, Hakluyt Society, 1891. xlvi, 282p. (Hakluyt Society Publications, 1st ser., 81)
Reprinted: N.Y., B. Franklin, c. 1964.

346 DAVIE, John Constanse. Letters from Paraguay: describing the settlements of Montevideo and Buenos Ayres; the presidencies of Rioja Minor, Nombre de Dios, St. Mary and St. John etc., etc., with the manners, customs, religious ceremonies etc. of the inhabitants. Written during a Residence of seventeen months in that country. London, G. Robinson, 1805. vii, 293p.
A work of little value.

347 DOMINGUEZ, Manuel. Las Amazonas y El Dorado. A., Tall. nac. de H. Kraus, 1902. 19p.

348 FURLONG CARDIFF, Guillermo. Cartografia jesuítica del Río de la Plata. B.A., Tall. s.a. Casa Jacobo Peuser, 1936. 228p. (Buenos Aires. Universidad nacional. Publicaciones del Instituto de investigaciones históricas 71)

349 MAACK, Reinhard. Sôbre o itinerário de Ulrich Schmidel através do sul do Brasil, 1552-1553; uma pesquisa histórico-geográfica. En lengua portuguesa e alemã. Curitiba, 1959. 64p. (Universidade de Paraná. Faculdade de Filosofia, Ciências e Letras. Curso de geografia e história. Geografia física, no. 1)

350 QUIROGA, José. Breve noticia del viage que hizo el padre José Quiroga por el rio Paraguay con la partida que fué á poner el marco en la boca de Jaurú (1753-1754). (Copia moderna de otra del original de su mano.) *In* COLECCION de documentos inéditos para la historia de España por el Marques de la Fuensanta del Valle. Madrid, Imp. de José Perales y Martinez, 1892. Vol. 104, 407-48.

351 QUIROGA, José. Descripción del Rio Paraguay desde la boca de Xaurú hasta la confluenca del Paraná. *In* no. 666 (1910), Vol. 2, p. 361-71.

352 SCHMIDEL, Ulrich. Abenteuer in Südamerika 1534 bis 1554; nach den Handschriften bearbeitet von Curt Cramer. Leipzig, F.A. Brockhaus, 1922. 158p.

353 SCHMIDEL, Ulrich. Crónica del viaje a las regiones del Plata, Paraguay y Brasil. Reproducción y version paleográfica del manuscrito de Stuttgart traducido al castellano por Edmundo Wernicke, con anotaciones críticas, precedido todo de estudios publicados en Alemania y Argentina. B.A., Tall. Peuser, 1948. clxxvi, 536p.

353a SCHMIDEL, Ulrich. Der erste Deutsche am Rio de la Plata, Utz Schmidl von Straubing; zur vierhundertjährigen wiederkehr seiner ausfahrt aus der deutschen heimat, hrsg. und bearbeitet von Max Tepp. B.A., Die Umwelt, 1934. 96p. (Die umwelt des auslandsdeutschen in Sudamerika. 1 reihe: Bücherei zur landeskunde Sudamerikas, 3)

354 SCHMIDEL, Ulrich. Derrotero y viaje a España y las Indias; traducido del alemán, según el manuscrito original de Stuttgart, y comentado por Edmundo Wernicke; prólogo de Josué Gollan h. Santa Fe, Instituto social, Universidad nacional del litoral, 1938. 245p.

355 SCHMIDEL, Ulrich. Derrotero y viaje a España y las Indias, traducido del alemán según el manuscrito original de Stuttgart por Edmundo Wernicke ... Prólogo de Enrique de Gandia. 152p. B.A., Mexico, Espasa-Calpe argentina, 1944. (Colección austral)

356 SCHMIDEL, Ulrich. Histoire véritable d'un voyage curieux, fait par Ulrich Schmidel de Straubing, dans l'Amérique ou le Nouveau monde, par le Brésil, et le Rio de la Plata, depuis l'année 1534 jusqu'en 1554. Où l'on verra tout ce qu'il a souffert pendant ces dix-neuf ans, et la description des pays et des peuples extraordinaires qu'il a visités. Ouvrage écrit par lui-même, et publié de nouveau, après corrections des noms de villes, de pays et de rivières, par Levinus Hulsius. Nuremberg, Aux frais de L. Hulsius, 1599. Paris, A. Bertrand, 1837. viii, 264p.

357 SCHMIDEL, Ulrich. Historia y descubrimiento del Rio de la Plata y Paraguay. Con una introducción y

observaciones críticas por M.A. P(elliza). B.A., Imp. y librería de Mayo, 1881. 266p.

358 SCHMIDEL, Ulrich. Reise nach Süd Amerika in den Jahren 1534 bis 1554. Nach der Münchener Handscrift hrsg. von Dr. Valentin Langmantel. Tübingen, 1889. 162p.

359 SCHMIDEL, Ulrich. Ulrich Schmidels reise nach Süd Amerika in den Jahren 1534 bis 1554. Nach der Stuttgarter Handschrift hrsg. von Johannes Mondschein. Programm zum Jahresberichte der K. Realschule Straubing für 1892. Straubing, Al. Attenkoffer'sche Buchdruckerei, 1893. 60p.

360 SCHMIDEL, Ulrich. Viaje del Rio de la Plata y Paraguay. *In* no. 666 (1910), vol. 2, p. 273-333.

361 SCHMIDEL, Ulrich. Viaje al Rio de la Plata (1534-1554). Notas bibliográficas y biográficas por Bartolome Mitre; prólogo, traducción y anotaciones por Samuel A. Lafone Quevedo. B.A., Cabaut y cía, 1903. xv, 499p. (Biblioteca de la Junta de historia y numismática americana, t.1)

362 SCHMIDEL, Ulrich. Viaje al Rio de la Plata. B.A., Emecé, 1942. 109p.

362a SCHMIDEL, Ulrich. Wahrftige Historie einer wunderbaren Schiffhart, welche Ulrich Schmidel von Straubing von 1534 bis 1554 in Amerika oder Neuewelt bei Brasilia oder Rio della Plata ... Munich, Im Verlas von Albert Langen, 192? 173p.

363 SCHMIDEL, Ulrich. Wahrhaftige Historien einer wunderbaren Schiffart. Graz, Akademische Druck- u. Verlagsanstalt, 1962. xxvii, 103p. (Frühe Reisen und Seefahrten in Originalberichten, 1)

Facsimile reproduction of the 1602 ed. Schmidel's narrative was first published at Frankfurt am Main in 1567 under the title "Warhafftige vnd liebliche Beschreibung etlicher fürnamen indianischen Landtschaften."

364 SEPP, Anton. An account of a voyage from Spain to Paraquaria; performed by the Reverend Fathers Anthony Sepp and Anthony Behme, both German Jesuits, the first of Tyrol upon the River Eth, the other of Bavaria: containing a description of all the remarkable things, and the inhabitants, as well as of the missionaries residing in the country, taken from the letters of the

said Anthony Sepp, and published by his own brother Gabriel Sepp. *In* CHURCHILL, Awnsham; CHURCHILL, John. A collection of voyages and travels ... London, 1704. Vol. 4, p. 633-64.

365 SEPP, Antonio. Continuation oder Fortsetzung der Beschreibung Deren denckwüdigeren Paraquarischen Sachen selbiger Landschaft Völckern und Arbeit deren sich alldort befindenden RR. im PP. Missionarium Soc. Jesu. Insondereheit aber Wie R.P. Antonius Sepp, Auss wohlgemelter Societat in Paraquaria Missionarius den Christlichen Glauben unter anderen Völckern noch weiter fortzupflanssen sich bearbeitet und bemühet. Foderist zu grösserer Ehr und Lob Gottes alsdann auch zu sonderen Wohlgefallen Lust und Eergozzlihkeit eines geugeten Lessers. Ingolstatt, Joh. Andreas de la Haye, 1710. 490p.

366 SEPP, Antonio. Continuatio Laborum Apostolicorum, quos R.P. Antonius Sepp, Soc. Jesu Missionarius Apostolicus in Paraquaria ab Anno Christi 1693, usque ad annum 1701 Exantlevit, Ubi describuntur illius barbarae Gentis mores, ingenium et docilitas in rebus practicis, et mechanicis ... Contra in specultativis, et metaphysicis ruditas; aliaque plurima Euroepeais admiranda. Ingolstatt, Sumptibus Joannis Andreae de la Haye, Typis Thomae Grass, 1709. 174p.

367 SEPP, Antonio. Erster Theil der Reisebeschreibung RR. PP. Antonii Sepp, Und Antonii Bohm Der Societät Jesu Priestern Teutscher Nation, deren der erste aus Tyrol und der Etsch der ander auss Bayrun gebürting. Wie nemlichen dieselbe auss Hispanien in Paraquariam kommen; Und Kursser Bericht der denckwürdigsten Sachen selbiger Landschaft Völckern und Arbeitung der sich alldort befindenden PP. Missionariorum, gezogen Auss denen durch R.P. Sepp, Soc. Jesu mit eigener Hand geschrieben Briefen zu mehrern Nussen. Ingolstatt, Johann Andreas de la Haye, 1712. 263p.

368 SEPP, Antonio.. Viagem ás missoes jesuiticas e Trabalhos apostólicos. Introduçao e notas por Wolfgang Hoffman Harnisch; traduçao de A. Reymundo Schneider e alunos da Companhia de Jesús, am Pareci; fotografias de Wolfgang Hoffman Harnisch Junior. Sao Paulo, Livraria Martius, 1943. 256p.

369 SEPP, Antonio. RR. PP. Antonii Sepp und Antonii Bohm der Societät Jesu Priestern Teutscher Nation, deren der erste aus Tyrol an der Etsch der ander aus Bayrn

gebürtig Reisebeschreibung wie dieselbe aus Hispanien in Paraquariam Kommen. Und Kursser Bericht der dencrwürdigsten Sachen Selbiger Landschaft Volckern und Arbeitung dersich alldort befindenden PP. Missionarium, gezogen Aus denen durch R.P. Sepp. Soc. Jes. mit eigener Hand geschriebenen Briefen zu mehrern Nussen. Nürnberg, Joh. Hoffmann, 1696. 333p.

2. 1811-1939

370 ADAMS, Harriet Chalmers. River-encircled Paraguay. NGM 63 (1933) no. 4, 385-416.

371 AMORIM, Annibal. Viagens pelo Brazil; do Rio ao Acre, aspectos da Amazonia, do Rio a Matto Grosso. Com oitenta gravuras. Rio de Janeiro, Livraria Garnier, 1911? 505p.

372 ARROYOS Y ESTEROS, PARAGUAY. ESCUELA. Pequeña geografía (para los niños de la Escuela de Arroyos y Esteros). A., Imp. de la Democracia, 1886. 134, vii p.

373 BAGNET, A. Rio Grande do Sul et le Paraguay: précedé d'une notice historique sur la découverte du Brésil. Anvers, N. Ernest, 1884. 200p.

374 BAILLIE, Alexander F. A Paraguayan treasure: the search and the discovery. London, Simpkin, Marshall, 1887. 368p.
A novel, but valuable for its observations on the country. Baillie was associated with the 'Lincolnshire Farmers'.

375 BARSZCZEWSKI, Stefan. Na ciemnych wodach, Paragwaju. Wspomnienia z podróżzy. Lwów, Książnica Atlas, 1931. 126p.

376 BERMEJO, Ildefonso Antonio. Repúblicas americanas. Episodios de la vida privada, politica y social en la república del Paraguay. Madrid, R. Labajos, 1873. 283p. (Biblioteca histórico-recreativa)
2. ed. A., J. Quell, 1908. 189p. (Biblioteca histórico-recreativa)
3. ed. A., Quell y Garron, 1913. 205p.

377 BERMEJO, Ildefonso Antonio. Vida paraguaya en tiempos del viejo López. B.A., Edit. Universitaria de Buenos Aires, 1973. 205p.
Originally published as Repúblicas americanas, no. 376.

378 BERMUDEZ, Washington Pedro. Estampas de viaje, un crucero estudiantil. Montevideo, Edit. Ad astra, 1939. 175p.

378a BLADH, C.E. Resa till Montevideo och Buenos Ayres, jemte beskrifning öfver Plata-floden och de forenta provinserna af samma namn, Paraguay, Misiones och Republiken Orientel del Uruguay, eller Cisplatina. Stockholm, Tryckt hos. L.J. Hjerta, 1839. 400p.

379 BORDON, F. Arturo. Paraguay; guia geográfica de turismo. A., La Colmena, 1932. 434p.

380 BOSSI, Bartolome. Viaje pintoresco por los rios Paraná, Paraguay, San Lorenzo, Cuyabá y el Arino tributario del grande Amazonas; con la descripción de la provincia de Mato Grosso bajo su aspecto fisico, geografico, mineralojico y sus producciones naturales. Paris, Librairie parisienne; Dupray de la Moherie, 1863. xi, 153p.

381 BOZZO, Emmanuele. Notizie storiche sulla Republica del Paraguay e la guerra actuale con la descrizione de un viaggio nel fiumi Paraná e Paraguay. Genova, Tip. del Comercio, 1860. 88p.

382 BURGER, Otto. Paraguay, der "Garten Südamerikas"; ein Wegweiser für Handel, Industrie und Einwanderung. Leipzig, Dieterich, 1927. viii, 280p.

383 CARPENTER, Frank George. Along the Paraná and the Amazon, Paraguay, Uruguay, Brazil. Garden City, N.Y., Doubleday, Doran, 1925. xiv, 310p. (Carpenter's world travels)

384 CARRASCO, Gabriel. Cartas de viaje por el Paraguay, los territorios nacionales del Chaco, Formosa y Misiones y las provincias de Corrientes y Entre Rios. B.A., La Plata, Imp. litogr., y encuadernación de J. Peuser, 1889. 319p.

385 CARTE générale et vues de la République du Paraguay. Brussels, Etablissement géographique de Ph. van der Maelen et lithographie de Simonau et Toovey, 1862. 20 plates.

386 CASSAGNE SERRES, Alberto. Excursión al Paraguay. (Buenos Aires - Asunción). RGA 1936, 351-58.

387 CHAVES, Manuel Wenceslao. El Paraguay ilustrado. B.A., Tall. Rosso, 1918. 284p.
Another ed: A., 1920. 280p.

388 CLARK, Edwin. A visit to South America; with notes and observations on the moral and physical features of the country, and the incidents of the voyage. London, Dean, 1878. 355p.

389 CLEMENS, Eliza Jane McCartney. La Plata countries of South America. Philadelphia, J.B. Lippincott, 1886. 511p.

390 CRAIG, Charles William Thurlow. Paraguayan interlude. N.Y., F.A. Stokes, 1935. 319p.
Also: London, Arthur Barker, 1935. 319p.

391 DADANYI, György. Csordás voltam Paraguayban. Budapest, Stadium, 1939. 336p.

392 DEISS, Edouard. De Marseille au Paraguay; notes de voyage. Paris, Cerf, 1896. 227p.

393 DEMERSAY, L.M. Alfred. Fragments d'un voyage au Paraguay, executé par ordre du gouvernement. Paris, 1854. 31p.

394 DENIS, Ferdinand. Buenos Aires et le Paraguay, ou histoire, moeurs, usages et coutumes des habitants de cette partie de l'Amérique. Paris, Nepreu, Librarie, Passage des Panoramas, 1823. 2 vols.

395 DETAILS intimes sur l'état des lieux, des hommes et des choses au Paraguay. Marseille, Joseph Clappier, 1868. 46p.

395a FABRICIUS, Johan Wigmore. Gringo: een reis naar het Paraguay van 1922. The Hague, Leopold, 1976. 157p.

395b FRACCAROLI, Arnaldo. Splendori e ombre del Paraguay. Milan; Romes, Treves-Treccani-Tumminelli, 1932. 200p.

396 FRESCURA, Bernardino. Le Repubbliche del Rio de la Plata: Paraguay, Uruguay, Argentina. Prefazione di Olinto Marinelli. Milan, Fratelli Treves, 1926. viii, 171p.

397 FROBEL, Julius. Geographisch-statistische Beschreibung der Argentinischen Republik oder die Freistaaten vom Rio de la Plata, des Freistaats vom Uruguay und des Staats Paraguay. Weimar, Im Verlag des Geographischen Instituts, 1832. xxvi, 248p. (Vollständiges Handbuch der neusten Erdbeschreibung, 5 Abth., 5 Bd.)

397a GONZALEZ, Gonzalo. Uruguay, Paraguay; apuntes de un reporter andariego. Santa Fe (Arg.) Casa Editora de Ramón Ibañez, 1907. 209p.

398 GRAHAM, Robert Bontine Cunningham. Relatos del tiempo viejo. Selección y prólogo de Antonio Aita. B.A., Ediciones Peuser, 1955. 400p.

398a GUIBERT RIERA, Fernando David. Un retrato equivocado de J.P. y G.P. Robertson. B.A., 1975. 20p.

399 HADFIELD, William. El Brasil, el rio de la Plata y el Paraguay. Ilustraciones de Sir W. Gore Ouseley y de Sir Charles Hotham. B.A., Edit. Difusam, 1943. 213p. (Colección Viajeros en el Plata, 1)

400 HADFIELD, William. Brazil, the River Plate, and the Falkland Islands; with the Cape Horn route to Australia. Including notices of Lisbon, Madeira, the Canaries and Cape Verde. Illustrated, by permission, from the South American sketches of Sir W. Gore Ouseley ... and, by permission, from the drawings of Sir Charles Hotham. London, Longman, Brown, Green and Longmans, 1854. vi, 384p.

401 HILLEKAMPS, Karl Heinz. Das romantische Südamerika: Ecuador, Paraguay, Bolivien, Peru. Reichenau/Sa., R. Schneider, 1938. 98p. (Völker und Staaten)

402 HILLS, John Waller; DUNBAR, Ianthe. The golden river; sport and travel in Paraguay. London, P. Allan, 1922. 187p.
Also: N.Y., F.A. Stokes, 1922. 187p.

403 JERRMANN, Ludwig. Der Unterlauf des Igatimi und der Gran Salto Guayrá des Alto Paraná. Hamburg? 19--. 28p.

404 JOHNSON, K. Recent journeys in Paraguay. GM 2 (1875) 264-73, 308-13, 342-45.

405 KENDE, Oskar. Paraguay und Uruguay. Berlin, Safari, 1926. 103p. (Taschenbücher des Auswanderers)

406 KERST, G.S. Paraguay. ZAE 2 (1854) 1-41.

407 LANDABURU, Bernardo. De Asunción a Posadas (de la capital del Paraguay a la capital de Misiones, Argentina). RGA 1946, 151-60.

408 LECEA Y NAVAS, Julio de. La república del Paraguay. Acción de la Orden militar y hospitalaria de San Juan de Acre en la misma. Madrid, Academia heráldica, 19--. 14p.

409 LEITE, Mario. Do Brasil ao Paraguai. Impressoes de viagem e de costumes. Sao Paolo, Empresa gráfica de "Revista dos tribunais", 1940. 185p.

410 LEVERGER, A. Roteiro de Navegaçao do Rio Paraguay desde a Foz de Sao Lourenço ate o Parana. RIHGB 25 (1862) 211-84.

410a LEVEY, George Collins. A handy guide to the River Plate, including the Argentine Republic, Uruguay and Paraguay, their physical features, resources and railways. 2 ed. London, Hutchinson, 1890. 240p.

411 LO que es Paraguay en la actualidad. RGA 1934, 261-74.

412 MACDONALD, Alexander K. Picturesque Paraguay, sport, pioneering, travel; a land of promise, stockraising, plantation, industries, forest products, commercial possibilities. London, O.H. Kelly, 1911. 498p.

413 MANSFIELD, Charles Blachford. Paraguay, Brazil and the Plate. Letters written in 1852-1853. With a sketch of the author's life, by the Rev. Charles Kingsley, jun. Cambridge, Macmillan, 1856. xxi, 504p.
Reprinted: N.Y., AMS Press, 1971.

414 MANTEGAZZA, Paolo. Río de la Plata e Tenerife, viaggi e studi. Milan, G. Brigola, 1867. 731p.
2. ed., 1870. 670p.

415 MASTURZI, Giovanni. Il Paraguay. UNI, 11 (1930) no. 12, 1253-72.

416 MEVERT, Ernst. Ein Jahr zu Pferde. Reisen in Paraguay. Wandsbeck, A. Mencke, 1883. 151p.

417 MOLINS, Wenceslao Jaime. Paraguay: crónicas americanas. B.A., Impr. A. Molinari, 1915. 234p.
2. ed. B.A., Estab. graf. "Oceana", 1916. 307p.
3. ed. B.A., 1919. 204p.

417a MULHALL, Marion McMurrough. From Europe to Paraguay and Matto-Grosso. London, E. Stanford, 1877. 115p.

418 MULHALL, Marion McMurrough. Between the Amazon and Andes or ten years of a lady's travels in the pampas, Gran Chaco, Paraguay and Matto Grosso. London, E. Stanford, 1881. xl, 340p.

419 MUNCK af ROSENSCHOLD, Eberhard. Algunas cartas del naturalista sueco don Eberhard Munck af Rosenschöld, escritas durante su estadía en el Paraguay, 1843-1869, con una introd. del Dr. Magnus Mörner. Traducción del sueco por Ernesto Dethorey. Estocolmo, 1955. 30p.
Letters to C.J. Sundervall.

419a MUZIO, Carlo. Paraguai. Milan, Casa Ed. Sonzogno, 1923. 28p. (Mundus; le contrade mondiali illustrate nell'ambiente fisico, suolo, clima, flora, fauna, genti, con cenni storici; monografia 27a)

420 NAGY, Arturo; PEREZ-MARICEVICH, Francisco. Paraguay, imagen romántica, 1811-1853. Selección, traducción y notas de Arturo Nagy y Francisco Pérez-Maricevich. A., Edit. del Centenario, 1969. 218p. (El Paraguay en la opinión mundial, 1)

421 NEWBOULD, Charles Edmund. A padre in Paraguay. London, Society for Promoting Christian Knowledge, 1929. 192p.

422 NUNEZ, José Ramón. De Corrientes a la Asunción. RGA 19, no. 115 (1943) 181-86.

423 NUNEZ, José Ramón. Viajando por el Río Paraná. RGA vol. 19, no. 112 (1943) 11-28, 85-104.

424 OLLEROS, Mariano L. Alberdi a la luz de sus escritos en cuanto se refieren al Paraguay. Editor: Juan E. Quell. A., Tip. "El Civico", 1905. 349p.

425 PAGE, Thomas Jefferson. La Plata, the Argentine Confederation, and Paraguay. Being a narrative of the exploration of the tributaries of the river La Plata and adjacent countries during the years 1853, '54, '55 and '56, under the orders of the United States government. N.Y., Harper & brothers, 1859. xxii, 632p.
Also: London, Trübner, 1859. xvi, 632p.

426 PAGE, Thomas Jefferson. Le Paraguay et les républiques de La Plata. Paris, Au Bureau de la Revue des deux mondes, 1851. 48p.
Also published in RDM 1851.

427 PALACIO DE LIBARONA, Agustina. Aventuras y desgracias de la señora de Libarona en el Gran Chaco. Santiago de Chile, Zig-zag, 1946. 108p. (Biblioteca Zig-zag; serie Ocre 58)

428 PARAGUAY and its lands. A short description of the resources of the country, collected for the use of travellers and immigrants, from the most recent sources of information. London, Printed by Wertheimer, Lea & Co., 1889. 76p.

429 PASOS, Ignacio de. Diario de una navegación y reconocimiento del río Paraguay, desde la ciudad de la Asumpción, hasta los presidios portugeses de Coimbra y Albuquerque. *In* no. 666 (1910) vol. 3, 555-94.

430 PATIÑO, Domingo. Diario de um viage por el Paraná desde al puerto de la Villa Encarnación hasta el Salto de Guairá por el teniente Domingo Patiño, con un prefacio por J (Juan Antonio Jara). A., 1881, 29p.

431 PLATE, Enrique. Notes on Paraguay. B.A., A.L. Samson, 1899. 36p.
2. ed. 1899. 42p.

432 PLATE, Enrique. Notices sur le Paraguay. 2. ed. B.A., A.L. Samson, 1899. 39p.

433 POSADA, Adolfo. La República del Paraguay, impresiones y comentarios. Madrid, V. Suárez, 1911. 274p.

434 RECLUS, Elisée. Paraguay; capítulos entresacados de la Nueva geografía universal; prólogo, traducción y notas por Ramón de Olascoaga. A., A. de Uribe, 1896. xliii, 101p.

435 REID, William Alfred. In yerba mate forests of South America. Washington, Pan American Union, 1926. 23p. (Commodities of Commerce series, 4)

436 RENGGER, Johann Rudolph. Reise nach Paraguay in den Jahren 1816 bis 1826; aus des Verfassers handschriftlichen Nachlasse. Aarau, H.R. Saeurlaender, 1835. xxxxvi, 495p.
Text in French and German.

437 La REPUBLIQUE du Paraguay (Amérique du Sud). Notice sur ce pays et ses ressources, avec le catalogue officiel et détaillé des produits qu'il expose. Braine-Le-Comte (Belgium), Imprimerie Lelong, successeurs Zech & Cornet, 1885. 67, 17p.

438 REY DE CASTRO, Carlos. El Paraguay; rápidas notas de viajero. B.A., Imp. de J.A. Alsina, 1901. 28p.

439 RIO ZAÑARTU, Pedro del. Nuevos viajes. Navegación de los rios La Plata, Paraná i Paraguai al través de las provincias de Santa Fé, Entre-Rios, Corrientes, territorios del Chaco, república del Paraguai, Asunción su capital, i villa de Concepción, centro de yerbales. Santiago de Chile, Imp. i encuadernación Barcelona, 1897. xiii, 60p.

440 ROBERTSON, John Parish; ROBERTSON, William Parish. La Argentina en los primeros años de la revolución; traducción de Carlos A. Aldao. B.A., Imp. de La nación, 1916. 287p. (Biblioteca de La nación)

441 ROBERTSON, John Parish; ROBERTSON, William Parish. La Argentina en la época de la revolución, cartas sobre el Paraguay: comprendiendo la relación de una residencia de cuarto años en esa República, bajo el gobierno del Dictador Francia. B.A., Administración general Vaccaro, 1920. 269p.

441a ROBERTSON, John Parish; ROBERTSON, William Parish. Dr. Francia, dictator von Paraguay, geschildert wahrend eines vierjahrigen Aufenthalts in dieser Republik, nebst den nothigen Erlauterungen uber die sudamerikanische Revolution. Quedlinburg und Leipzig, Druck und Verlag von Gottfr. Basse, 1839. 3 vols.

442 ROBERTSON, John Parish; ROBERTSON, William Parish. Four years in Paraguay: comprising an account of that republic, under the government of the dictator Francia. Philadelphia, E.L. Carey & A. Hart, 1838. 2 vols.
First published under the title: Letters on Paraguay.

442a ROBERTSON, John Parish; ROBERTSON, William Parish. Francia's reign of terror, being a sequel to Letters on Paraguay. Philadelphia, E.L. Carey & A. Hart, 1839. 2 vols.
Also published as vol. 3 of Letters ... (see following item)

443 ROBERTSON, John Parish; ROBERTSON, William Parish. Letters on Paraguay: comprising an account of four years' residence in that republic, under the government of the dictator Francia. London, John Murray, 1838-39. 3 vols.
2. ed. 1839. 3 vols.
Reprint of 2. ed. N.Y., AMS Press, 1970. 3 vols.

444 RODRIGUEZ ALCALA, José. El Paraguay en marcha. A., M.W. Chaves, 1907. 560p.
Another ed. A., El País, 1907. 558p.

445 ROLON MEDINA, Anastasio. Estampas de mi terruño. Prólogo del Dr. Juan Stefanich. A., 1930. 140p.

445a RUSCH, Johann Baptist. Die Paraguayer. Rupperswil, Gasser, 1929. 128p.

446 SAN MARTIN, Manuel de. Un viaje al Salto Guayrá. A., Tall. nac. de H. Kraus, 1897. 33p.

447 SANTOS, Carlos R. La república del Paraguay. A., H. Kraus, 1897. vii, 146p.

2. ed. A., Escuela tipográfica salesiana, 1898. iv, 120p.

448 SCHMIDT, Hans. Meine Jagd dem Glück in Argentinien und Paraguay; Reise-, Arbeits- und Jagdabenteur; mit 63 Abbildungen nach eigenen Photographien und einer Karte. Leipzig, R. Voigtländer, 1921. 208, 24p.

449 SCHMIDT, Hans. Vom rio de la Plata zum rio Alto, Paraguay; 2300 km nordwärts auf südamerikanischen Riesenströmen. 2. ed. San Andreas, F.C.C.A., H. Schmidt, 1939. 287p.

450 SCHUSTER, Adolf N. Paraguay: Land, Volk, Geschichte, Wirtschaftsleben und Kolonisation. Stuttgart, 1929. 667p.
A very important survey.

451 SMITH, L. Le Paraguay. RC 2 ser., 45 (1865) 593-623.

452 SPAIN. MINISTERIO DE ESTADO. CENTRO DE INFORMACION COMERCIAL. Informe sobre la república del Paraguay. Madrid, Imp. del Ministerio de estado, 1913. 18p.

453 SUAREZ, Luis. De Tupambaé al Apa. Montevideo, "Casa A. Barreiro y Ramos", 1932. 333p.

454 THOMPSON, Reginald William. Land of tomorrow: a story of South America. London, Duckworth, 1936. 459p.

455 TOEPPEN, Hugo. Hundert Tage in Paraguay. Reise ins innere Paraguay im Hinblick auf deutsche Kolonisations-Bestrebungen. Hamburg, L. Friederichsen, 1885. 264p.

456 TOLTEN, Hugo. Kampf um die Wildnis: die letzten Tage einer Rasse. Frankfurt am Main, Rütten & Loening, 1935. 286p.

457 TOLTEN, Hugo. Enchanting wilderness: adventures in darkest South America. Translated by Ferdi Loesch. London, Selwyn & Blount, 1936. 285p.

458 TOURING CLUB ITALIANO. Argentina. Paraguay. Uruguay. Milan, T.C.I., 1932. iv, 582p. (Las Guias azules)

458a TRUQUIN, Norbert. Mémoires et aventures d'un proletaire á travers la révolution: l'Algerie, la République Argentine et le Paraguay; introd. de Paule Lejeune. Paris, F. Maspero, 1977. 278p.

459 VALLENTIN, Wilhelm. Paraguay, das Land der Guaranís. Berlin, H. Paetol, 1907. viii, 323p.

460 WAPPAUS, Johann Eduard. Die Republik Paraguay, geographisch und statistisch dargestellt von Dr. J.E. Wappäus. Leipzig, J.C. Hinrichs, 1867. x, 1137-1201p.
Reprinted from: Handbuch der Geographie und Statistik, von Stein und Hörschelmann. 7. ed., vol. 1, pt. 15.

461 XAVIER DE BRITO, Pedro Torquato. Noticia historica geographica e estatistica da republica do Paraguay. Rio de Janeiro, B.L. Garnier, 1865. 67p.

462 ZUBIZARRETA, Carlos. Acuarelas paraguayas. B.A., Mexico, Espasa-Calpe argentina, 1940. 248p.
3. ed. B.A., Ediciones Nizza, 1959. 140p.

3. 1940-

463 ABRAMO, Livio. Paraguay: siete dibujos. Texto preliminar de Miguel Angel Fernández. A., Ediciones Diálogo, 1964. 7 illus. (in portfolio). (Colección Imago)

464 ANDIA, Ernesto Daniel. En el país de los héroes. B.A., El Ateneo, 1947. 178p.

465 BRUGADA GUANES, Alejandro. Qué es el turismo? A.?, 1966? 16p.

466 AMIGAS NORTEAMERICANAS DEL PARAGUAY. Land of lace and legend; an informal guide to Paraguay. A., La Colmena, 1958. 128p.
2. ed. 1960. 162p.
4. ed. 1969. 208p.

467 AMIGAS NORTEAMERICANAS DEL PARAGUAY. Tierra de leyendas y ñanduties; bosquejo turístico e histórico del Paraguay. A., 1970. 210p.

467a BRITISH OVERSEAS TRADE BOARD. Paraguay. London, 1976. 45p.
For earlier eds. see no. 474a.

468 CAVALCANTI, Mário de Barros. Paraguai. RGIPGH 5-8, nos. 13-24 (1949) 105-15.

469 DE SHERBININ, Betty. The River Plate republics: Argentina, Uruguay, Paraguay. N.Y., Coward-McCann, 1947. xii, 276p. (Invitation to travel series)

470 DURRELL, Gerald. The drunken forest. London, Hart-Davies, 1956. 238p.

471 EHRSTROM, Inga. Annu blommar våra träd; med jeep genom Argentina och Paraguay. Stockholm, Forum, 1963. 202p.

471a FAIRFAX, Jan. Vagabundos bajo el sol. B.A., Edit. Stilcograf., 1957. 240p.

471b FERNANDEZ, Miguel Angel. Paraguay. English trans. by Ralph E. Dimmick. Washington, Pan American Union, 1969. 18p.

472 GIMENEZ CABALLERO, Ernesto. Revelación del Paraguay. Madrid, Espasa-Calpe, 1958. 310p.

473 GOISON, Christopher H. Through Paraguay and southern Matto Grosso. NGM 84 (1943) no. 4, 459-88.

474 GORHAM, John Richard. Paraguay: ecological essays, edited by J. Richard Gorham. Introd. by Jesse D. Perkinson. Miami, Fla., Academy of the Arts and Sciences of the Americas, 1973. 296p.

474a GREAT BRITAIN. BOARD OF TRADE. Hints to businessmen visiting Paraguay. London, 1954. 16p.
New ed. 1961. 20p.; Later ed. no. 467a.

475 GREENBIE, Sydney. Republics of the pampas: Argentina, Uruguay, Paraguay. Evanston, Ill., N.Y., Row, Peterson and company, 1943. 84p. (The good neighbor series)

476 HALLEY MORA, Gerardo. Imágenes de un tiempo en fuga. A., Edit. La Voz, 1971. 195p.

477 HALLEY MORA, Gerardo. La palabra y los días. A., Edit. La Voz, 1970. 166p.

478 HANZELKA, Jiri; ZIKMUND, Miroslav. Südamerika zwischen Paraná und Rio de la Plata. Deutsch von Adolf Langer. Berlin, Verlag Volk und Welt, 1956. 422p.

479 HANZELKA, Jiri. Tam za rekou Argentina. 3. ed. Prague, Nakl. politické literatury, 1964. 376p.

480 HAVERSTOCK, Nathan A.; HOOVER, John P. Paraguay in pictures. N.Y., Sterling Publ. Co., 1975. 64p. (Visual geography series)
Also: 1977.

481 KASTBERG, Nils Ivan. I Guarani-indianeras land. Upplevelser i Paraguay. Stockholm, Filadelfia, 1960. 82p.

481a KRIER, Hubert; PONEMUNSKI, Gerhard. Paraguay: Herzland Sudamerikas: Reisefuhrer mit Landeskunde. 2 ed. Buchenhain vor Munchen, Verlag Volk und Heimat, 1977. 78p.
See also no. 501 (1. ed.)

481b LATEINAMERIKA anders: Argentinien, Paraguay, Guatemala, Mexiko. Vienna, Leo M. Gabriel, 1976. 51p.

482 LEPECKI, Mieczyslaw. W selwasach Paragwaju. 2. ed. Warsaw, Wiedza Powszechna, 1962. 269p.

483 McADAMS, John. Guarani spoken here. Washington, Pan American Union, 1950. 7p. (Club and study series)

484 MAHE, Marcel. Méfiez-vous des paradis, aventures et mésaventures d'un Français au Paraguay. Paris, Amiot-Dumont, 1954. 252p. (Toute la ville en parle)

485 MAKOTO, Simón. Manual turístico del Paraguay. A., 1972. 94p.

486 MARFAING, Victor M. Pampa de agua. B.A., 1959. 100p.

487 MARTINI, Virgilio. Paraguay, la terra del Guarani. UNI, 37 (1957) 1, 41-48.

488 MARTINIS, B. Il Paraguay. VM 21 (1959) no. 11, 1181-96.

489 MEYER, Gordon. The river and the people. London, Methuen, 1965. 223p.

490 MIRANDA, Mário Botelho de. Um brasileiro no Paraguai. Sao Paulo, Editora do Escritor, 1975. 174p. (Coleçao Depoimento, 3)

491 NISSEN, Tage. Kvindens land; rejseskildringer fra Paraguay. Copenhagen, Wangel, 1959. 180p.

492 OLIVENCIA MARQUEZ, Roberto. Curuguaty, una aldea perdida en la selva; notas de viaje, mayo-junio de 1951. Montevideo, Impresora L.I.G.U., 1952. 55p.

493 OLROG, Claës Chr. Landet västor om floden. Stockholm, Bonnier, 1949. 145p.

494 ORGANIZATION OF AMERICAN STATES. Image of Paraguay. Washington, 1974. 16p. (Image series)
Also: Imagen de Paraguay. 1974. 16p. (Serie de imagenes)

495 PAN AMERICAN UNION. TRAVEL DIVISION. Visit Paraguay. Washington, P.A.U., 1955. 32p.

496 PARAGUAY: una obra con fotografías en colores. Dirección artística y fotografías tomados con cámaras Leica a cargo de Adolfo María Friedrich. Prólogo: Cirilo Zayas. A., Dirección General de Turismo, 1968? 33p.

497 PARAGUAY. DIRECCION GENERAL DE TURISMO. Guia de turismo. A., 1958. 231p.

498 PARAGUAY. MINISTERIO DE HACIENDA. El Paraguay de hoy; el valor económico de la paz. A., 1965. 47p.

499 PARAGUAYAN TRADE CENTRE. Paraguay today: information handbook. London, 1971? 50p.

500 PITAUD, Henri. Paraguay, terre vierge. Paris, F. Chambriand, 1950. 196p. (Regards sur le monde)

501 PONEMUNSKI, Gerhard. Paraguay. Mit Stadtführer Asunción und Reiserouten. Buchenhain vor München, Verlag Volk und Heimat, 1967. 88p. (Mai's Weltführer, 11)

502 RAINE, Philip. Paraguay. New Brunswick, N.J., Scarecrow Press, 1956. 443p.

503 SCHRODER, Enrique A. Una excursión fluvial al Paraguay, agosto de 1949, y un poco de historia artiguista, crónicas de viaje. Montevideo, 1949. 46p.

504 SERMET, Jean. Le Paraguay. COM 3 (1950) no. 9, 28-65.

505 SMITH, Willard H.; SMITH, Verna Graber. Paraguayan interlude; observations and impressions. Scottdale, Pa., Herald Press, 1950. xii, 184p.

506 THOMPSON, Reginald William. Germans and Japs in South America, being a record of my search for El Dorado and of those who have sought and found new lives. London, Faber & Faber, 1942. 360p.
First published as Voice from the wilderness.

507 THOMPSON, Reginald William. Voice from the wilderness: being a record of my search for El Dorado and of those who have sought and found new lives. London, Faber & Faber, 1940. 360p.

508 THOMPSON, Reginald William. Voice from the wilderness. Rev. ed. London, Macdonald, 1947. 238p.

509 UNITED STATES. OFFICE OF INTER-AMERICAN AFFAIRS. Paraguay, country of rivers. Washington, United States Government Printing Office, 1944. 12p.

510 VOSS-GERLING, Wilhelm. Argentinien, Uruguay, mit Paraguay. Munich, Polyglott-Verlag, 1973. 63p. (Polyglott-Reiseführer)

511 WARREN, Carlos A. Paraguay. Montevideo, Edit. Ceibo, 1946. 366p.

512 WARSVSKA, S. Le Paraguay; notes de voyage (1958). REF 72 (1959) no. 2, 19-24.

512a WEISNER, Benno. Si yo fuero paraguayo: artículos aparecidos y charlas pronunciadas en el Paraguay por Benjamín Varón. A., Edit. del Centenario, 1972. 204p.

513 WILHELMY, Herbert; ROHMEDER, Wilhelm. Die La Plata Länder: Argentinien, Paraguay, Uruguay. Brunswick, G. Westermann, 1963. 584p.

514 The WORLD and its peoples: Paraguay, Argentina, Chile, Falkland Islands. N.Y., Greystone Press, 1966. 216p.
Reprinted: 1968.

515 YNSFRAN, Pablo Max. Paraguay. APAU 3 (1951) no. 8, 16-20, 46.

515a ZENDEGUI, Guillermo de. Image of Paraguay. APAU 27 (1975) no. 2, S1-24.

C. Historiography

516 ACADEMICOS del Instituto Paraguayo de Investigaciones Historicas. HP 2 (1957), 103-09; 3 (1958) 127-31.
Biographies of members.

517 ALPEROVICH, M.S. Istoriia Paragvaia v osveshchenii noveishei burzhuaznoi istoriografii. VI 1965 no. 1, 66-78.

518 BARAGER, Joseph R. The historiography of the Rio de la Plata area since 1830. HAHR 39 (1959) no. 4, 588-642.

519 BARROSO, Gustavo. O Brazil em face do Prata. Rio de Janeiro, Imprensa nacional, 1930. 452p.

520 BAZAN, Juan F. Influencias y deficiencias de nuestros historiografos. *In* no. 152, 49-55.

520a BENITEZ, Justo Pastor. El historiador de Asunción. *In* no. 162(2 ed.) 107-10.

521 CARDOZO, Efraím. Historiografía paraguaya. Mexico, 1959- (Instituto Panamericano de Geografia e Historia. Publicación no. 221. Comisión de Historia. Publicaciones, 83. Historiografías, 5)
Vol. 1 only published: Paraguay indigena, española y jesuita. 610p.

522 CHAVES, Julio César. Doctor Justo Pastor Benitez. HP 8-10 (1963-65) 25-27.

523 DAVALOS, Juan Santiago. Cecilio Baéz, como ideólogo. A., Escuela Técnica Salesiana, 1967. 14p.

524 DAVALOS, Juan Santiago; BANKS, Lorenzo Livieres. El problema de la historia del Paraguay. RPS 4 no. 8-9 (1967) 108-14.

525 FURLONG-CARDIFF, Guillermo. Los Jesuítas y la historiografía rioplatense. EBA 63 (1940) 129-46.

526 GRANDE de la historiografia nacional: Dr. Cecilio Baéz. HP 2 (1957) 11-14.

527 GRANDE de la historiografía nacional: Fulgencio R. Moreno. HP 3 (1958) 11-14.

528 IRALA BURGOS, Adriano. Nueves corrientes de la historiografía Paraguaya. IARB 18 (1968) 2, 125-41.

529 LEHMANN-NITSCH, Robert. Ulrich Schmidel, der erste Geschichtsschreiber der Plata-Länder. B.A., G. van Woerden, 1909. 38p.
2. ed. Munich, M. Müller, 1912. 37p.

530 LOPEZ, Vicente F. De algunos historiadores y publicistas de los misiones del Paraguay. EBA 57 (1937) 159-70.

530a MARIN IGLESIAS, Alejandro. Interpretación de Efraím Cardozo. A., Academia Paraguaya de la Lengua Española, 1974. 15p.

531 MIEMBROS del Instituto Paraguayo de Investigaciones Historicas. HP 6-7 (1962) 97-101.

532 PENA VILLAMIL, Manuel. La ciencia de la Historia. HP 3 (1958) 88-91.

533 RODRIGUEZ ALCALA, Hugo. Efraím Cardozo y la interpretación espiritualista de nuestra historia. HP 13 (1969-70) 99-106.

534 UZCATEGUI, Emilio. Historiadores de Bolivia, Ecuador y Paraguay. BANHE 50 no. 110 (1967) 205-13.

535 VELAZQUEZ, Rafael Eliado. Los estudios historicos en el Paraguay. EA 11, no. 52 (1956) 65-79.

536 WILLIAMS, John Hoyt. "De calor al frío": una visión personal de la historiografía paraguaya. EP 1, no. 1 (1973) 139-63.

D. Diplomatic history

1. *Treaties*

537 PARAGUAY. TREATIES. Colección de tratados celebrados por la república del Paraguay. Publicación oficial. A., Imp. de "El Orden", 1885. 136p.
Other eds.: A., Tip. de El Paraguayo, 1890. 91p. A., Tall. de tip. y encuadernación de H. Kraus, 1895. 57p.

538 PARAGUAY. TREATIES. Colección de tratados históricos y vigentes, recopilados por Oscar Pérez Uribe y Eusebio A. Lugo bajo la dirección del subsecretario de relaciones exteriores y culto d. Ernesto Egusquiza. Publicación ordenado por el ministro de relaciones exteriores y culto, d. Justo Pastor Benitez, Vol. 1: América. A., Imp. nac., 1934. 730p.
No more published.

538a PARAGUAY. TREATIES. Manual de tratados, convenios y acuerdos internacionales con los países limítrofes. A., Organización Labor, 1975? 257p.

539 PARAGUAY. TREATIES. Tratados y protocolos firmados entre la república del Paraguay, el imperio del Brasil y la República argentina desde 1872 hasta 1878. A., Imp. de La Reforma, 1878. 155p.

2. *General Surveys*

540 BAEZ, Cecilio. Historia diplomática del Paraguay, precedida de un estudio sociológico de los pueblos mediterráneos que concurrieron a la formación de la nación española; le acompaña un mapa de América. A., Imp. nac., 1931-32. 2 vols.

541 BELMONT, Andrés de. Situación internacional del Paraguay. A., Tip. la Colmena, 1912. 19p.

542 BENITEZ, Justo Pastor. La politica internacional Paraguaya 1850-1862: las gestiones de José Berges. *In* no. 1093, p. 93-121.

543 BENITEZ, Luis G. Historia diplomática del Paraguay. Prólogo del Dr. Ezequiel González Alsina. A., 1972. 496p.

544 BROSSARD, Alfred de. Considérations historiques et politiques sur les républiques de La Plata dans leurs rapports avec la France et l'Angleterre. Paris, Guillaumin, 1850. 471p.

545 CALVO, Cárlos. Una página de derecho internacional; 6, La América del Sur ante la ciencia del derecho de gentes moderno. Paris, Librería de A. Durand, 1864. xii, 307p.

546 CODAS, L. Eugenio. La libertad de navegación de los rios. El caso de los cañoneros "Paraguay" y "Humaitá"; conferencias pronunciadas con motivo de la sublevación en la rada de Buenos Aires, de los cañoneros paraguayos "Paraguay" y "Humaitá". A., Tall. Gráf. de la Edit. El País, 1947. 38p.

547 GONZALEZ, Luis J. Paraguay: prisionero geo-policito. B.A., Ediciones Nogal, 1947. 273p.

548 IRALA, Antolin. La causa de aliada en el Paraguay. A., Tall. Zamphirópolos, 1919. 26p.

549 INSTITUTO PARAGUAYO, ASUNCION. El Instituto paraguayo y su representación en el Congreso panamericano de Washington. A., Imp. La Mundial, 1917. 10, 4, 19p.

550 LA POEPE, Claude de. La politique du Paraguay; identité de cette politique avec celle de la France et de la Grand-Bretagne dans la Rio de La Plata. Paris, E. Dentu, 1869. 348p.

551 PARAGUAY. MINISTERIO DE RELACIONES EXTERIORES. Cuerpo consular paraguayo y extranjero. A., Tall. gráficos La Colmena, 1913. 43p.

552 PARAGUAY. MINISTERIO DE RELACIONES EXTERIORES. Reglamento para los cónsules de la república del Paraguay. A., Imp. de "La Reform", 1877. 14p.

553 PRIETO, J. El problema del Paraguay mediterráneo. PRDIA 1 (1946) 29-45.

554 SALUM-FLECHA, Antonio. Historia diplomática del Paraguay de 1869 a 1936. A., EMASA, 1972. 215p.

555 SANCHEZ QUELL, Hipólito. La diplomacia paraguaya de Mayo a Cerro-Cora. 3. ed. B.A., Edit. G. Kraft, 1957. 252p.
First published as Política internacional del Paraguay.
4. ed. 1964. 243p.
5. ed. A., Casa América, 1973. 282p.

556 SANCHEZ QUELL, Hipólito. Politica internacional del Paraguay (1811-1870). A., Imp. nac., 1935. 174p.

557 SANCHEZ QUELL, Hipólito. Politica internacional del Paraguay; la Junta de 1811, Francia y los López. 2. ed. B.A., Edit. Tupa, 1945. 247p.

558 SCHMITT, Peter Adolf. Começo e desenvolvimento das relaçaos diplomaticas entre o Paraguai e as potencias Europeias (1811-1870). RHB 22 no. 46 (1961), 345-67.

559 SCHMITT, Peter Adolf. Paraguay und Europa; die diplomatische Beziehungen unter Carlos Antonio López und Francisco Solano López, 1841-1870. Berlin, Colloquium Verlag, 1963. 366p. (Bibliotheca Ibero-Americana, 4)

560 SCHMITT, Peter Adolf. Las relaciones diplomaticas entre el Paraguay y las potencias europeas (1840-1870). HP 3 (1958), 65-87.

561 SOLER, Juan José. Pacifismo internacional del Paraguay. A., Imp. Ariel, 1924. 31p.

561a SOUZA, José Antonio Soares. José Berges, sua vida e seu diário. RIHGMG 292 (1971) 130-55.

562 STEFANICH, Juan. La diplomacia de la revolución. B.A., Edit. El Mundo nuevo, 1945. 127p. (Capítulos de la revolución paraguaya, 2)

563 VIDAURRETA de TJARKS, Alicia. Diario de viaje al Plata de José Berges, 1851-52. TC 19 (1969), 205-69.

3. *Argentina*

564 ALCORTA, Sinforiano. Antecedentes historicos sobre los tratados con el Paraguay. B.A., Establecimiento tip. de Moreno y Nuñez, 1885. xix, 247p.

565 ARGENTINA. MINISTERIO DE RELACIONES EXTERIORES Y CULTOS. La política argentina en la guerra del Chaco. B.A., Guillermo Kraft, 1937. 2 vols.

566 ARGENTINA. MINISTERIO RE RELACIONES EXTERIORES. La paz de la república argentina. Colección de los documentos oficiales relativos a este fausto acontecimiento. Publicación oficial. Paraná, Imp. de "El nacional argentino", 1860. 49p.

567 BAREIRO, Francisco L. El Paraguay en la República argentina. La condonación de la deuda de guerra. Nobles iniciativas. B.A., Imp. de J.A. Alsina, 1900. 48p.

568 BIANCO, José. Negociaciones internacionales; los tratados de 1876; gestiones administrativas. De la revista Estudios. B.A., Coni hermanos, 1904. 254p.

569 CENTURION, Carlos R. Relaciones diplomáticas entre el Paraguay y la Argentina, 1811-1863. HBA 9, no. 32 (1963) 67-111.

570 CHAVES, Julio César. Historia de las relaciones entre Buenos Ayres y el Paraguay, 1810-1813. B.A., J. Menéndez, 1938. 269p.
2. ed. A., Ediciones Nizza, 1959. 231p.

571 CIANCIO, Pedro N. La condecoración del gobierno paraguayo a s.e. rvma. el sr. obispo de Temnos monseñor dr. Miguel de Andrea. Entrega oficial del diploma en la "Casa de la empleada", en solemne acto público, por el comisionado especial de la Cancillería paraguay. B.A., 1942. 22p.

572 COMITE PARAGUAYO. BUENOS AIRES. Memoria y reorganización. Asamblea del 30 de octobre de 1932. B.A., 1932? 23p.

573 CORRESPONDENCIA confidencial entre el Excmo. Sr. Presidente de la República del Paraguay y el de la Confederación Argentina en 1863 y 1864. A., 1867. 74p.
Reprinted: A., La Democracia, 1881. xxxii, 74p.

574 DEUDA argentino-paraguaya; petición presentada al honorable Congreso nacional abris sus sesiones en 1901. B.A., Establecimiento tip., 1901. 17p.

575 HERRERA, Luis Alberto de. La diplomacia oriental en el Paraguay; correspondencia oficial y privada del doctor Juan José de Herrera, ministro de relaciones

exteriores de los gobiernos de Berro y Aguirre. Montevideo, Tall. A. Barreiro y Ramos, 1908-27. 5 vols.

576 HERRERA, Luis Alberto de. La diplomacia oriental en el Paraguay. El mariscal Francisco Solano López. B.A., M. Rodriguez Giles, 1912. 46p.
Chapter 15 of vol. 2. of no. 575.

577 IRALA, Antolin. Negociaciones paraguayo-argentino; sus antecedentes. A., Tall. de Zamphiropolos, 1912. 70p.

578 JORGUENSEN, Marcos. Limite argentino-paraguayo en la zona del Pilcomayo. RGA 24, no. 143 (1945) 71-76.

579 LANUSSE, Alejandro Agustín. Entrevista de los presidentes de la Argentina y Paraguay, teniente general D. Alejandro Agustín Lanusse y general de ejército D. Alfredo Stroessner. B.A., Presidencia de la Nacion, 1971. 51p.

580 LANUSSE, Alejandro Agustín. Segunda entrevista de los presidentes de la Argentina y Paraguay. B.A., Presidencia de la Nacion, 1972. 23p.

581 MOSCARDA, Andrés. Las tierras de madama Lynch, 1865-1920; un caso de prescripción contra el fisco. A., Imp. "Trujillo", 1920? 78p.
2. ed. 192? 93p.

582 O'LEARY, Juan Emiliano. El Paraguay en la unificación argentina. A., Imp. y librería La Mundial, 1924. 173p.

582a O'LEARY, Juan Emiliano. El Paraguay en la unificación argentina; La Guerra de la Triple Alianza. A., Instituto Colorado de Cultura, 1976. 521p. (Biblioteca Clásicos Colorados, 4)

583 PARAGUAY. MINISTERIO DE RELACIONES EXTERIORES. Documentos oficiales de la mediación pacifica de la republica del Paraguay en la disidencia armada entre los exmos. gobiernos de la Confederación argentina y Buenos Aires. Publicación oficial. A., Imp. de la República, 1860. 123p.

584 PARAGUAY. MINISTERIO DE RELACIONES EXTERIORES. Documents officiels rélatifs à la médiation pacifique de la république du Paraguay dans le différend existant entre les gouvernements de la Confédération Argentine et de Buenos-Ayres. Paris, Imp. S. Racon, 1860. 259p.

585 PARAGUAY. SUBSECRETARIA DE INFORMACIONES Y CULTURA. El abrazo de los pueblos. A., 1969. 26p.

586 PEREZ, Juan F. Confraternidad Argentino-Paraguaya. I. Una Mediación histórica. II. La Misión del General Guido. A., La Colmena, 1928. 39p.

587 PEREZ ACOSTA, Juan Francisco. Simbiosis argentino-paraguaya, fundación e independencia. Mexico? 1961? 3p.

588 PEREZ ACOSTA, Juan Francisco. Vieja fraternidad; Argentina, Paraguay. B.A., Imp. Ferrari hnos, 1939. 133p.

589 QUESADA, Ernesto. Historia diplomática nacional. La política argentino-paraguaya. B.A., Libreria Brédahl, 1902. xxi, 302p.

590 RAMOS, R. Antonio. El reconocimiento de la independencia del Paraguay por la Argentina. RHA 32 (1951), 1-20.

591 SALMON BALDIVIESCO, Luis. El Paraguay provincia argentina. Breve estudio de las relaciones paraguayo-argentinas a través de la historia. La Paz, Imp. Artistica, 1935. viii, 93p.

592 STEFANICH, Juan. Alberdi, la Argentina y el Paraguay. A., Tall. nac. de H. Kraus, 1920. 199p. (Biblioteca paraguaya del Centro Estudiantes de Derecho, 7)

593 URQUIZA, Eduardo de. El pacto de unión nacional, la gestión general Solano López, 1859: conferencia. B.A., 1963. 13p.

594 VARGAS PEÑA, Benjamin. Paraguay-Argentina; correspondencia diplomática 1810-1840. B.A., Edit. Ayacucho, 1945. 324p.

595 VILA, M. La ley social en la Argentina. A., Imp. Grabow Schauman, 1910. 32p.

4. *Bolivia*

596 AVILA, Federico. Bolivia en el concierto del Plata. Mexico, Edit. Cultura, 1941. vi, 341p.

597 GONDRA, César. La diplomacia de los tratados; Paraguay y Bolivia. B.A., F. Lajouane, 1906. 239p.

598 GUACHALLA, Luis Fernando. Misión en el Paraguay, mayo, 1930-julio, 1931. La Paz, Univ. Mayor de San Andrés, 1971. 287p.

599 PARAGUAY. MINISTERIO DE RELACIONES EXTERIORES. Paraguay-Bolivia, tratados y protocolos. A., Imp. nac., 1927. 20p.

600 SOLIZ RIVERO, Gonzalo. Ecos de una visita al Paraguay. Santa Cruz, Bolivia, 1961. 167p.

5. Brazil

601 BRAZIL. MINISTERIO DAS RELAÇOES EXTERIORES. Correspondencia trocada entre o governo imperial e o da Republica argentina relativa aos tratados celebrados entre o Brazil e a republica do Paraguay, e à desoccupaçao da ilha do Atajo. Rio de Janeiro, Typ. nac., 1872. 73p.

602 BRUGADA, Ricardo. Brazil-Paraguay. Rio de Janeiro, Typ. lith. de L. Malafaia, junior, 1903. 288p.

603 COLECCION de piezas oficiales concernientes á las cuestiones paraguayo-brasileras. A., Imp. de la República, 1855. 64p.

604 CORREIO MERCANTIL. RIO DE JANEIRO. Negocios do Rio da Prata relativos ao Brasil. Rio de Janeiro, Typ. philantropica, 1851. 103p.

605 DOCUMENTS oficiales concernientes a la ruptura de relaciones entre el gobierno de la república del Paraguay y el del imperio del Brasil a consecuencia de la ocupación a mano armada del territorio de la república oriental del Uruguay por fuerzas brasileras. Ed. particular. A., Tip. y encuadernacion "El Paraguayo", 1890. 55p.

606 DOCUMENTOS officiels rélatifs au conflit existant entre le Brésil et les gouvernements de Montevideo et de l'Assomption. Montevideo, Imp. de "La Tribuna", 1865. 18p.

607 FRANÇA, Mario Ferreira. O reconhecimento da independencia do Paraguai pelo imperio (a missao Pimenta Bueno). RIHGB 292 (1971) 3-129.

608 GODOI, Juan Silvano. Mi misión a Río de Janeiro. B.A., F. Lajouane, 1897. 100p.

609 MEIRA, L. Brasil-Paraguai: uma experiencia de cooperaçao administrativa. RBPI 1 (1958) no. 2, 5-17.

610 OJEADA retrospectiva sobre las cuestiones paraguayo-brasileras, desde la retirada de la escuadra del Brasil de las Tres Bocas. A., Imp. nac., 1858. 151p.

611 ONETO Y VIANA, Carlos. La diplomacia del Brasil en el Rio de la Plata. Montevideo, Libreria de la Universidad, 1903. 387p.

612 PARAGUAY y Brazil, polémica histórica sostenida entre Historicus y Veritas en la ciudad de La Paz, Bolivia. A., Tall. Graf. "La Tribuna", 1918. 55p.

613 PAREDES, José D. Paraguay-Brasil: jornadas de amistad. Centenario de la epopeya nacional 1864-1870. A., 1964? 86p.

614 RAMOS, R. Antonio. Correa da Cámara en Asunción. BIIH 26 no. 89-92 (1942) 57-81.

615 RAMOS, R. Antonio. El Paraguay y el Brasil durante la dictadura de Francia. BIIH 27 no. 93-96 (1942-43) 254-98.

616 RAMOS, R. Antonio. La política del Brasil en el Paraguay (bajo la dictadura de Francia). B.A., Edit. Ayacucho, 1944. 258p.
2. ed. B.A., Ediciones Nizza, 1959. 232p.

617 RAMOS, R. Antonio. La primera misión diplomática del Paraguay en el Brasil. Relaciones con el Brasil. HP 4/5 (1959-60) 45-66.

618 RAMOS, R. Antonio. El reconocimiento de la independencia del Paraguay por el Brasil; misión Pimenta Bueno. Conferencia pronunciada el 7 de agosto de 1952, en el Salón de Actos del Instituto Cultural Paraguay-Brasil. A., 1953. (Publicaciones del Instituto Cultural Paraguay-Brasil, 1)

619 RAMOS GIMENEZ, Leopoldo. Paraguay-Brasil: profecia cumplida del canciller Aframio (sic) de Mello Franco. A., Edit. "El Arte", 1961. 67p.

620 RIBERIO, Pedro Freire. A Missao Pimento Bueno 1843-1847. Rio de Janeiro?, Divisao de Documentaçao, Seçao de Publicaçoes, 1965- (Coleçao "Documentos diplomáticos").

621 ROLON, Raimundo. Algunos aspectos del Brasil con relación al Paraguay. A., Imp. militar, 1940. 88p.

622 SOSA ESCALADA, Jaime. Negociaciones diplomáticas entre el Brasil, la República argentina y el Paraguay; misión del ciudadano paraguayo Jaime Sosa á Rio de Janeiro. B.A., Imp. de la Tribuna, 1875. 108p.

623 SOUZA, José Antonio Soares de. A Missao Bellegarde ao Paraguai (1849-1852). Rio de Janeiro, Divisao de Documentaçao, Seçao de Publicadade, 1966-70. 3 vols. (Coleçao "Documentos diplomáticos")

624 WARREN, Harris G. Brazil's Paraguayan policy, 1869-1876. AAAFH 28 (1972) no. 4, 388-406.

6. Chile

625 BRUGADA, Ricardo. El Paraguay y Chile. A., Tall. nac. de H. Kraus, 1902. 52p.

626 CRUCHAGA OSSA, Alberto. Centenario de un reconocimiento. BACH 9 no. 23 (1942) 55-62.

7. France

627 LE LONG, John. Révélations à la France. Les négotiations au Rio-de-la-Plata. Paris, Impr. de Madame de Lacombe, 1851. 107p.

628 SANCHEZ QUELL, Hipólito. Jornadas paraguayas junto al Sena. Paris, 1962. 100p.

8. Great Britain

629 DECOUD, José Segundo. Informe del comisinado especial, Ministro de Relaciones Exteriores don José S. Decoud, al gobierno de la República del Paraguay, dando cuenta de su misión a Londres para el arreglo de la deuda procedente de los emprestitos de 1871 y 1872. A., Imp. "El Orden", 1886. 37p.

630 DECOUD, José Segundo. Report of Don José Segundo Decoud, special commissioner of the Paraguayan Government, and Secretary of Foreign Relations, giving an account of his mission to London for the arrangement of the foreign debt proceeding from the loans of 1871 and 1872. A., 1886. 37p.

631 MATEEVA, N.R. Kolonialnaia ekspansiia Anglii v Paragvae. UZK 26 (1962) 215-50.

632 PARAGUAY. LEGACION. GREAT BRITAIN. Cuestión Canstatt. Documentos oficiales cambiados entre la Legación de la república del Paraguay y el gobierno de Su Majestad británica, sobre la referida cuestión, aun pendiente. Besanzón, Imp. de J. Jacquín, 1861. 198p.

633 PARAGUAY. LEGACION. GREAT BRITAIN. Cuestión Canstatt. Documentos oficiales cambiados entre le Legación de la republica del Paraguay y el gobierno de Su Majestad británica con motivo de dicha cuestión, que terminó por la convención firmada en la Asunción el 14 de octubre de 1862. Besanzón, 1864. 198p.

634 QUESTION Anglo-Paraguayenne: recueil d'articles, traduits du Sèminario "Journal de l'Assomption". Paris, 1860. 168p.

9. Portugal

635 RAMOS, R. Antonio. La política do Portugal y la Independencia del Paraguay. La corte de Lisboa en América. JGSWGL 10 (1973) 251-97.

10. Spain

636 COMISION PATRIOTICA ESPAÑOLA DEL PARAGUAY. Incidente entre la razón y la fuerza. A., Imp. de "La Democracia", 1898. 90p.

11. United States

637 AGETON, Arthur A. Good partnership in Paraguay. DSB 35 (1956) 847-54.

638 BLISS, Porter Cornelius. Historia secreta de la misión del ciudadano norte americano Charles A. Washburn, cerca del Gobierno de la República del Paraguay. n.p., 1868. 323p.

639 CORRESPONDENCIAS cambiadas entre el Ministro de Relaciones exteriores de la República y el Señor Charles A. Washburn, Ministro residente de los Estados Unidos de América sobre la conspiración fraguada contra la patria y el Gobierno en combinación con el enemigo: y el atentado de asesinato á la persona del exmo. Señor Mariscal López por Nacionales y Extranjeros. Luque, Imp. nac., 1868. 124p.

640 CORRESPONDENCIA diplomática entre el Gobierno del Paraguay y la Legación de los Estados Unidos de América y el Cónsul de S.M. el Emperador de los franceses, publicada en el "Seminario" de la Asunción. B.A., Imp. de B.A., 1863. 23p.

641 Un EXEMPLE du Point IV: le Paraguay. CI 5 no. 44 (1953) 79-82.
U.S. foreign aid.

642 FLICKEMA, Thomas O. "Sam Ward's bargain": a tentative reconsideration. HAHR 50 (1970) no. 3, 538-42.

643 FLICKEMA, Thomas O. The settlement of the Paraguayan-American controversy of 1859: a reappraisal. AAAFH 25 (1968) no. 1, 49-69.

644 GONDRA, Manuel. Paraguay and the United States of America; address by Mr. Manuel Gondra, envoy extraordinary and minister plenipotentiary of Paraguay at the luncheon given in his honor by the Pan American Society of the United States at the Bankers' Club, New York, January 30, 1919. N.Y.? 1919? 4p.

645 HISTORIA documentada de las cuestiones entre el gobierno del Paraguay y el de los Estados Unidos. A., Imp. nac., 1858. 131p.

646 McKANNA, Clare V. The "Water Witch" incident. ANEP 31 (1971) no. 1, 7-18.

647 TURNER, William. Trabajos y servicios del illustro señor John N. Ruffin, cónsul de los Estados Unidos de América en Asunción, en el establicimento de relaciones comerciales entre Paraguay y la América del Norte. n.p., 1901? 24p.

648 UNITED STATES. CONGRESS. HOUSE COMMITTEE ON FOREIGN AFFAIRS. Report of the Committee on foreign affairs on the Memorial of Porter C. Bliss and George F. Masterman, in relation to their imprisonment in Paraguay. House of Representatives, May 5, 1870. Washington, Government Printing Office, 1870. xxx, 314p. (U.S. 41st Congress, 2d. session. House Report, no. 65)

649 YNSFRAN, Pablo Max. La expedición norteamericana contre el Paraguay, 1858-1859. México, Edit. Guarania, 1954-58. 2 vols.

650 YNSFRAN, Pablo Max. Sam Ward's bargain with President López of Paraguay. HAHR 34 (1954) 313-31.

12. Uruguay

651 ALONSO CRIADO, Matías. Carta al dr. d. José Z. Caminos, agente confidencial del Paraguay. Montevideo, Imp. latina, 1905. 13p.

651a BORDABERRY, Juan María. La visita del presidente Bordaberry a Paraguay, 13-16 de mayo de 1975. Montevideo, República Oriental del Uruguay, Presidencia de la República, 1975. 39p.

652 CARDOZO, Efraím. Afinidades entre el Paraguay y la Banda Oriental en 1811. Montevideo, 1963. 57p.

653 GRANADA, Nicolás. De patria á patria. Narración del viaje de la Comisión uruguaya encargada por el gobierno de la República Oriental del Uruguay de devolver los trofeos adquiridos por esta nación en la guerra de la Triple alianza a la República del Paraguay. Montevideo, Imp. a vapor de la Nacion, 1886- vols.

654 IRALA, Adriano; BARBIERI, Santino. Paraguay-Uruguay; las fiestas de confraternidad celebradas en Asunción con motivo de la peregrinación uruguaya al solar de Artigas. B.A., Cia. Sud-Américana de Billetes de Banco, 1913. 180p.

655 MARTINEZ, José Luciano. Devolución de los trofeos de guerra al Paraguay. RNM 3 no. 25 (1940) 102-10.

656 PARAGUAY y Uruguay, dos pueblos unidos en la gesta fraterna de la solidaridad americana: visita del Excmo. señor consejero nacional de gobierno del Uruguay, doctor don Eduardo Víctor Haedo, y de su ilustre comitiva al Paraguay, julio, 1960, Asunción, Paraguay. A., Sub-Secretaria de Informaciones y Cultura, 1960. xix, 302p.

657 TOURING CLUB PARAGUAYO. Touring club paraguayo a la Embajada uruguaya, homenaje. A., ? 193-? 12p.

13. Vatican

658 SANGUINETTI, Manuel Juan. La representación diplomática del Vaticano en los paises del Plata. B.A., 1954. 127p.

14. Venezuela

659 RAMOS, Antonio. El reconocimiento de la independencia del Paraguay por Venezuela. La revolución paraguaya. *In* ROUND TABLE ON THE ORIGINS OF THE SPANISH-AMERICAN EMANCIPATION MOVEMENT, CARACAS, 1960. El movimiento emancipador de Hispanoamérica. Actas y ponencias. Caracas, 1961. Vol. 4, 411-52. (Mesa redonda de la Comisión de Historia del Instituto Panamericano de Geografía e Historia, 1-4)

E. Military history

660 BEJARANO, Ramón César. Vencer o morir; formación guerrera del pueblo paraguayo antes de 1932. A., Edit. Toledo, 1970. 92p. (Serie Guerra del Chaco, 5)

661 PANE, Justo Alejandro. Episodios militares. A., Tall. R. Monte Domecq' & cia., 1908. 164p.

662 SPERATTI, Juan. Historia de la Armada Nacional en el período 1925-1937. A., Tall. Gráf. de la Escuela Técnica Salesiana, 1972. 133p.

663 VITTONE, Luis. Las fuerzas armadas paraguayas en sus distintas épocas; la Infantería paraguaya y su patrono. A., Edit. El Gráfico, 1969. xiii, 233p.

664 VITTONE, Luis. Tres guerras, dos mariscales, doce batallas. A., Edit. El Gráfico, 1967. 457p.

F. 1527-1811

1. General

665 AGUIRRE, Juan Francisco. Discurso historico que comprende el discubrimiento, conquista y establecimiento de los españoles en las provincias de la Nueva Vizcaya, generalmente conocidas por el nombre de Rio de la Plata. B.A.-Mexico, Espasa-Calpe Argentina, 1947. 214p.

666 ANGELIS, Pedro de. Colección de obras y documentos relativos á la historia antigua y moderna de las provincias del Rio de la Plata. B.A., Imp. del estado, 1836-37. 6 vols.
Reprinted: B.A., Libreria Nac. de J. Lajouane, 1910. 5 vols.

667 BAEZ, Cecilio. Historia colonial del Paraguay y del Río de la Plata. A., Zamphiropolos, 1926. viii, 193p.

668 BECKER-DONNER, Etta. Problemas de aculturación entre los indigenas del viejo Paraguay en los siglos XVII y XVIII. ASGHG 35 (1965) 93-99.

669 BERUTTI, Juan Manuel. Gobernadores del Paraguay desde 1620 hasta 1785, y Obispos del Paraguay hasta 1779. RBNBA 13 (1945) 487-90.

670 BORDON, Clotilde. Historia del Paraguay; epoca de la colonización española. A., Tall. gráf. El Arte, 1928. 104p.

671 CACERES ZORRILLA, Cirilo. Cronología historica de la antigua Provincia del Guairá. A., Edit. "El Grafico", 1962. 35p.

672 CARDOZO, Efraím. El Paraguay colonial; los raices de la nacionalidad. Prólogo de Justo Pastor Benitez. B.A., Ediciones Nizza, 1959. 231p.

673 CARDOZO, Ramón Indalecio. La antigua provincia del Guairá y la Villa Rica del Espíritu Santo. B.A., J. Menéndez, 1938. 195p.
2. ed. A., El Arte, 1970. 195p.

674 ESTRADA, José Manuel. Historia del Paraguay, Río de la Plata y Tucumán, por el P. José Guevara, don Pedro de Angelis y don Félix de Azara. RBA 1 (1863) 154-56, 302-12, 634-45.

675 FUNES, Gregorio. Ensayo de la Historia civil del Paraguay, Buenos Aires y Tucumán. B.A., Ganderillas Benavente y Imp. de Niños Expositos, 1816-17. 3 vols.
2. ed. B.A., Imp. Bonaerense, 1856. 2 vols.
3. ed. Biografia y retrato del autor con notas de D. José Arturo Scotto. B.A., Tall. gráf. de L.J. Rosso, 1910-11. 2 vols.

676 GONZALEZ de la LLANA, Manuel. Historia de las repúblicas de La Plata. (Paraguay, Uruguay y Confederación argentina.) (1512-1810) Madrid, Impr. de J. de Rojas, 1863. 267p.

677 GUEVARA, J.M. de. Historia del Paraguay, Río de la Plata y Tucumán. *In* no. 666 (1836), vol. 2. vii, 212, 11p.

678 GUEVARA, J.M. de. Historia de la conquista del Paraguay, Rio de la Plata, y Tucumán, con introducción por Andrés Lamas. Tomo primero. B.A., S. Ostwald, 1882. xl, 431p.
No more published. Also published under title Historia del Paraguay ... (no. 677).

679 LASTARRIA, Miguel. Colonias orientales del Río Paraguay ó de la Plata; con introducción de Enrique del Valle Iberlucea. B.A., Compañía sud-americana de billetes de banco, 1914. xxvi, 506p. (Documentos para la historia argentina, III.) (Buenos Aires. Universidad Nacional. Facultad de filosofia y letras. Sección de historia. Publicaciones)

680 LOZANO, Pedro. Historia de la conquista del Paraguay, Rio de la Plata y Tucuman, ilustrada con noticias del autor y con notas y suplementos por Andrés Lamas. B.A., Casa editora "Imp. popular", 1873-75. 5 vols. (Biblioteca del Rio de la Plata, t. 1-5)

681 MATEO PIGNATARO, Tomás. La integración jurídico-política de España en América (Emancipación del Paraguay). Madrid, Edit. Gráf. Torroba, 1971. 149p.

681a MILLE, Andres. Crónica de la Orden Franciscana en la conquista del Peru, Paraguay y el Tucumán y su conventu del antiguo Buenos Aires, 1212-1800. B.A., Emecé Editores, 1961. 501p.

682 MOGRO MORENO, Antonio. La provincia del Paraguay y el Chaco. La Paz, Lit. e imp. Unidas, 1937. 288, iip.

683 MOLAS, Mariano Antonio. Descripción histórica de la antigua provincia del Paraguay. Correjida, aumentada y anotada por el doctor Anjel Justiniano Carranza. B.A., Imp. de Mayo de C. Casavalle, 1868. 388p.
3. ed. Pref. y notas de Oscar Ferreiro. A., Ediciones Nizza, 1957. 159p.

684 MOLINA, Raúl A. La obra franciscana en el Paraguay y Rio de La Plata. MH 11, no. 32 (1954) 329-400; no. 33 (1954) 485-522.

685 MORA MERIDA, José L. La demografía colonial paraguaya. JGSWGL 11 (1974) 52-77.

686 MORENO, Fulgencio R. El Paraguay colonial y las provincias meridionales. RCHG 36 (1920) 426-66.

687 NAGY, Arturo; PEREZ-MARICEVICH, Francisco. Tres encuentros con América. A., Edit. del Centenario, 1967. 103p. (Colección "Paraquaria", 2)
Contents: N. del Techo: Relación de la gente Caaiguá que se empezó a convertir; B. Ximémez, Misión a los tobatines; M. Dobrizhoffer: Relación de la expedición al Mbaéverá.

688 NEYRA, Domingo de. Ordenanzas, actas primeras de la moderna Provincia de San Agustín de Buenos Ayres, Thucumán y Paraguay. n.p., c. 1742. 292p.
Another ed.: Introducción de Jorge M. Furt. B.A., Tall. s.a. Casa Jacobo Peuser, 1927. xxiv, 292, 21p. (Biblioteca argentina de libros raros americanos, 5)

689 NUÑEZ, Ignacio Benito. Noticias históricas, políticas y estadísticas, de las Provincias Unidas del Rio de La Plata, con un apendice sobre la usurpación de Montevideo por los gobiernos portugues y brasilero. London, R. Ackermann, 1825. xi, 323p.

690 PEÑA VILLAMIL, Manuel. Espíritu de la legislación española de indias. A., Instituto Paraguayo de Investigaciones Históricas, 1956. 22p.

691 RELA, Walter. Celebraciones teatrales y fiestas en el Paraguay colonial. RIL 1, no. 1 (1969) 65-88.

692 SANCHEZ QUELL, Hipólito. Estructura y función del Paraguay colonial; obra elegida por el Ateneo paraguaya para el Concurso latinoamericano de Nueva York. A.?, 1943. 188p.

693 SANCHEZ QUELL, Hipólito. Estructura y función del Paraguay colonial. B.A., Edit. Tupá, 1944. 197p.
2. ed. B.A., Edit. Tupá, 1947. 214p. (Colección Amerindia)
3. ed. B.A., G. Kraft, 1955. 240p. (Colección Cúpula)
4. ed. B.A., G. Kraft, 1964. 236p.
5. ed. A., Casa América, 1972. 264p.

694 SOUTHEY, Robert. Historia do Brazil; traduzida ... pelo Dr. Luiz Joaquim de Oliveira e Castro e annotada pelo conego Dr. J.C. Fernandes Pinheiro. Rio de Janeiro, Livraria de B.L. Garnier; Paris, Garnier, 1862. 6 vols.
Another ed.: Bahia, Aguiar & Souza, 1948-54. 6 vols.

695 SOUTHEY, Robert. History of Brazil. London, Longman etc., 1817-22. 3 vols.
Reprinted (i) N.Y., Greenwood Press, 1969. 3 vols.; (ii) With a new preface and biography by Herbert Cahn. N.Y., B. Franklin, 1970. 3 vols.

695a SUSNIK, Branka J. Aproximación a la realidad vivencial y al ethos existencial en el Paraguay colonial (ambiente rural). EP 3 no. 2 (1975) 157-74.

696 SUSNIK, B.J. El Guaraní en la vida socio-económica colonial. RPS 1, no. 1 (1964) 30-48.

696a SUSNIK, Branka J. El rol de la iglesia en la educación indigena colonial. EP 3 no. 2 (1975) 147-56.

697 TOMMASINI, Gabriel. La civilización cristiana del Chaco. B.A., Librería Santa Catalina, 1937. 2 vols.

698 VELAZQUEZ, Rafael Eliado. Navegación paraguaya de los siglos XVII y XVIII. EP1, no. 1 (1973) 45-82.

699 VOGT, Federico. Estudios históricos: la civilización de los guaranies en los siglos XVII y XVIII. B.A., Imp. de Guadalupe, 1903. 88p.

700 WHITE, Richard Alan. The political economy of Paraguay and the impoverishment of the missions. AAAFH 31 (1975) 417-33.

2. *16th and 17th centuries*

701 ALVAREZ LOPEZ, Enrique. Comentarios y anotaciones acerca de la obra de don Félix de Azara. MA 3 (1952) 9-61.

702 ANGELIS, Pedro de. Fundación de la ciudad de Buenos Aires por D. Juan de Garay, con otros documentos de aquella época. *In* no. 666, (1910) vol. III, 9-30.

703 AZAROLA GIL, Luis Enrique. El proyecto de fundación de la villa de Nueva Estepe. B.A., Librería y editorial "La Facultad", Bernabé y cía., 1936. 15p.

704 BAEZ ALLENDE, Amadeo. Fray Hernando de Trejo y Sanabria, paraguayo y fundador de la Universidad de Córdoba. A., Imp. nac., 1942. 40p.

705 BRUXEL, Arnaldo. O sistema de Propriedade das Reduçoes Guaranticas. P 3 (1959) 29-198.

705a CALZADA, Isidoro. Paí Tucú: biografía de fray Luis Bolaños. A., Ediciones Franciscanas, 1975. 211p.

706 CARDOZO, Efraím. La fundación de la ciudad de N.S. de la Asunción en 1541. *In* SEGUNDO congreso internacional de historia de América reunido en Buenos Aires en los días 5 a 14 de julio de 1937. B.A., 1938. Vol. 2, 110-120.

707 CARDOZO, Ramón Indalecio. Ruy Díaz de Melgarejo: fundador de la ciudad de la Villa Rica del Espíritu Santo. A., La Colmena, 1939. 152p.

708 CHAVES, Julio César. Las ordenanzas de Ramirez de Velazco, Hernandarias y Alfaro. HP 13 (1969-70) 107-20.

709 DIAZ de GUZMAN, Ruy. Argentina. Historia del descubrimiento, conquista, población del Río de la Plata; escrita por Rui Diaz de Guzman el año 1612. B.A., C. Casavalle, 1882. 210p.

710 DIAZ de GUZMAN, Ruy. Historia argentina del descubrimiento, población y conquista del Rio de la Plata. *In* no. 666 (1836) Vol. I, 1-140.
Another ed: B.A., Imp. de la Revista, 1854. 3 vols.

711 DIAZ de GUZMAN, Ruy. Historia del descubrimiento, conquista y población del Río de la Plata. Escrita por Rui Diaz de Guzman, conquistador, el año 1612. A., Imp. de la República del Paraguay, 1845. 160p.

712 DOMINGUEZ, Manuel. Prólogo de la relación de Hernando de Ribera. RIP, no. 36 (1902) 41-47.

713 DOMINGUEZ, Manuel. Schmidl. Estudio crítico sobre la historia y descubrimiento del Río de la Plata y Paraguay. RIP 2 (1900) 1-16.

713a DOMINGUEZ, Manuel. Schmidl. *In* no. 203, 87-105.

714 DOMINGUEZ, Manuel. Viajes y muerte de Ayolas. RIP 2, no. 16 (1899) 146-56.

714a FERNANDEZ, J.B. Alvar Núñez Cabeza de Vaca: the forgotten chronicler. Miami, Universal, 1975. 144p.

715 FERNANDEZ de BURZACO y BARRIOS, Hugo. El maestre de campo, don Juan José Diez de Andino, gobernador del Paraguay, del Tucumán y del Río de la Plata (1624-1683). B.A., Academia Nacional de la Historia, 1973. 24p. (Investigaciones y ensayos, 15)

716 FURLONG CARDIFF, Guillermo. Apuntamiento sobre Félix de Azara. BANHA 44 (1971) 377-83.

717 GANDIA, Enrique de. Francisco de Alfaro y la condición social de los indios: Río de la Plata, Paraguay, Tucumán y Perú, siglos XVI y XVII. B.A., Librería y edit. "El Ateneo", 1939. 572p.

718 GANDIA, Enrique de. Historia de la conquista del Río de la Plata y del Paraguay: los gobiernos de don Pedro de Mendoza, Alvar Núñez y Domingo de Irala, 1535-1556. B.A., A. García Santos, 1932. 311p.

719 GANDIA, Enrique de. Indios y conquistadores en el Paraguay. B.A., A. García Santos, 1932. 160p.

720 GANDIA, Enrique de. Información genealógica de Juan Ortiz de Zárate. *In* HOMENAJE de la Universidad de Chile a su ex. rector Don Amunátegui Solar en el 75 aniversario de su nacimiento. Santiago de Chile, Imp. universitaria, 1935. Vol. 1, p. 331-40.

721 GANDIA, Enrique de. Jaime Rasquín y su expedición del año 1559. BIIH 18 (1935) 241-322.

722 GANDIA, Enrique de. Nuevos datos para la biografía de Juan de Garay. B.A., La Facultad de J. Roldán, 1928. 85p.

723 GANDIA, Enrique de. El primer clérigo y el primer obispo del Rio de la Plata. B.A., García Santos, 1935. 204p.

723a GARMENDIA, José Ignacio. El casamiento de doña Juana Ortiz de Zárate; crónica histórica colonial. B.A., 1916. 106p.

724 GONZALEZ, Juan Natalicio. Vida, pasión y muerte de Güyra-Verá. B.A., Tall. gráf. "Augusta", C. Marello, 1942. 45p. (Colección Problemas Americanos, 8).

725 GONZALEZ, Julio César. Don Félix Azara, apuntes bio-bibliográficos. B.A., Edit. Bajel, 1943. 125p.

726 GONZALEZ ODDONE, Beatriz R.A. Roque Gonzales de Santacruz: protomatir Paraguayo. HP 13 (1969-70) 65-81.

727 GRENON, Pedro. Las renuncias de bienes en la provincia del Paraguay. Siglo XVII. AHSJ 24 (1955) 402-17.

728 GUZMAN, Augusto. El kolla mitrado. Biografía de un obispo colonial, Fray Bernardino de Cárdenas. La Paz, Edit. Juventud, 1954. 169p.

729 HABIG, Marion A. The Franciscan provinces of South America: IX, Provincia de la Asunción de Nuestra

Señora del Río de la Plata, 1612. AAAFH 2 (1946) no. 4, 461-81.

729a LACALLE, Carlos. Noticia sobre Alvar Núñez Cabeza de Vaca; hazañas americanas de un caballero andaluz. Madrid, Instituto Cultura Hispánica, 1961. 156p.

730 LACONICH, Marco Antonio. Caudillos de la conquista; romance de una cédula real. B.A., Edit. Yegros, 1948. 154p.
2. ed. n.p., Ediciones Nizza, 1961. 136p. (Obras paraguayas)

731 LAFUENTE MACHAIN, Ricardo de. Alonso Riquelme de Guzmán. B.A., Tall. graf. de S. de Amorrortu, 1942. 96p. (Los Capitanes de acero)

732 LAFUENTE MACHAIN, Ricardo de. Conquistadores del Río de la Plata; prólogo de Juan B. Téran. B.A., Tall. graf. de S. de Amorrortu, 1937. xiv, 696p.
2. ed. B.A., Edit. Ayacucho, 1943. 705p.

733 LAFUENTE MACHAIN, Ricardo de. El gobernador Domingo Martínez de Irala. B.A., Librería y edit. "La Facultad", Bernabé y cia., 1939. xi, 568p. (Biblioteca de la Sociedad de historia argentina, 10)

734 MOLINA, Raúl A. Fray Martín Ignacio de Loyola. EBA 79 no. 427 (1948) 131-48; no. 428 (1948) 206-21.

735 MOLINA, Raúl A. Hernandarias, el hijo de la tierra. B.A., Edit. Lancestremere, 1948. 523p.

736 MORA MERIDA, José Luis. Historia social de Paraguay, 1600-1650. Prólogo por el Dr. D. Luis Navarro García Seville, Consejo Superior de Investigaciones Científicas. Escuela de Estudios Hispano-Americanos, 1973. xvi, 366p. (Publicaciones de la Escuela de Estudios Hispano-Americanos de Sevilla, 214)

737 MORA MERIDA, José Luis. La sociedad paraguaya hacia 1625. AEA 28 (1971) 57-81.

738 NECKER, L. La réaction des Indiens guarani à la conquête espagnole du Paraguay, un des facteurs de la colonisation de l'Argentine à la fin du XVIe siècle. BSSA 38 (1974) 71-80.

738a NIETO, Alejandro. Hernandarias. A., Edit. Don Bosco, 1970? 11p. (Galería de paraguayos ilustres, 10. Verde)

738b NIETO, Alejandro. Juan de Ayolas. A., Edit. Don Bosco, 1970? 12p. (Galería de paraguayos ilustres, 11. Verde)

738c NIETO, Alejandro. Juan de Garay. A., Edit. Don Bosco, 1970? 14p. (Galería de paraguayos ilustres, 18. Verde)

739 NODENSKIÖLD, E. The Guarani invasion of the Inca empire in the sixteenth century: an historical Indian migration. GR 4 (1917) 103-21.

740 NUÑEZ CABEZA DE VACA, Alvar. Commentaires d'Alvar Núñez Cabeca de Vaca, adelantade et gouverneur du Rio de la Plata, rédigés par Pero Hernandez, notaire et secrétaire de la province Valladolid, 1555. Paris, A. Bertrand, 1837. 507p.

741 NUÑEZ CABEZA DE VACA, Alvar. Comentarios de Alvar Núñez Cabeza de Vaca, adelantado y gobernador del Río de la Plata. A., Tall. nac. de H. Kraus, 1902. 143p.

742 NUÑEZ CABEZA DE VACA, Alvar. Naufragios, texto restaurado, prologado y anotado por Justo García Morales. Madrid, M. Aguilar, 1945. 463p. (Colección Crisol, 98)
 3. ed. B.A.-Mexico, Espasa-Calpe argentina, 1947. 262p. (Colección austral, 304)

743 NUÑEZ CABEZA DE VACA, Alvar. Relación de Alvar Nuñez Cabeza de Vaca. B.A., Tall. de la Casa J. Peuser, 1907. 70p.

743a OPISSO, Alfredo. Los martirios de Alvar Núñez; escenas históricas de la conquista del Plata. Barcelona, Maucci, n.d. 206p.

743b ORO, Buenaventura, *Fray*. Fray Luís Bolaños, apóstol del Paraguay y Río de la Plata, homenaje al XXXII Congreso eucarístico internacional de Buenos Aires. Cordoba, Imprenta de la Universidad, 1934. xii, 169p.

743c OTAROLA, Alfredo J. Antecedentes históricos y genealógicos el conquistador don Domingo Martínez Irala, símbolo y espina dorsal de la conquista del Río de la Plata, precursor y fundador de la Américа del Sur, excepto Chile; su numerosa y distinguida descendencia. B.A., Casa Pardo, 1967. 185p.

743d OTAROLA, Alfredo J. Cunas de ilustres linajes; descendencia de Domingo Martínez de Irala y otros de la época de la conquista, orígenes de primitivas dinastías medievales. B.A., Casa Pardo, 1970. 213p.

743e OTAROLA, Alfredo J. Datos y linajes; nuevos estudios históricos genealógicos milenarios: Domingo Martínez de Irala; Ruy Díaz de Guzmán, el general Miguel Estanislao Soler. Con palabras preliminares por Enrique de Gandía. B.A., Casa Pardo, 1970. 187p.

743f PARAGUAY. ARCHIVO NACIONAL. Bandeirantes no Paraguai, século XVII; documentos inéditos. Sao Paulo, Divisao do Arquivo Historico, 1949. 702p. (Coleçao Departamento de Cultura, 35)

744 PEÑA VILLAMIL, Manuel. La casa del cabildo durante el siglo dieciseis. HP 8-10 (1963-65) 65-74.

745 ROLON MEDINA, Anastasio. Arquetipos de la raza: Hernando Arias de Saavedra, Roque González de Santa Cruz, Jose Félix Bogado. A., Imp. Militar, 1962. 70p.

746 RUBIO, Julián María. Exploración y conquista del Río de la Plata, siglos XVI y XVII. Barcelona-B.A., Salvat editores, 1942. xii, 844p. (Historia de América y de los pueblos americanos, 8)

746a SANABRIA FERNANDEZ, Hernando. Ñuflo de Chavez; el caballero andante de la seva. La Paz, Edit. Don Bosco, 1966. 317p.

746b SANABRIA FERNANDEZ, Hernando. Ulrico Schmidel: el alemán de la aventura española. La Paz, Edit. Los Amigos del Libro, 1974. 159p.

747 SANZ Y DIAZ, J. Irala, fundador del Paraguay. Madrid, Publicaciones Españolas, 1963. 31p. (Temas Españolas, 443)

748 SERVICE, Elman Rogers. The encomienda in Paraguay. HAHR 31 (1951) no. 2, 230-52.

749 SERVICE, Elman Rogers. Spanish-Guarani relations in early colonial Paraguay. Ann Arbor, University of Michigan Press, 1954. 106p. (Anthropological papers, Museum of Anthropology, University of Michigan, 9)
Reprinted: Westport, Conn., Greenwood Press, 1971.

749a TISCORNIA, Ruth. Hernandarias estadista: la política económica rioplatense de principios del siglo XVII. B.A., EUDEBA, 1973. 257p.

749b VALLE LERSEUNDI, Fernando del; LAFUENTE MACHAIN, Ricardo de. Irala; algunos documentos inéditos relativos al gobernador Domingo Martínez de Irala, a sus padres y hermanos. Madrid, Tip. de Archivos, 1932. 228p.

750 VARGAS UGARTE, Rubén. Fray Bernardino de Cárdenas, Obispo del Paraguay. BIIH 8 (1930) 81-102, 531-33.

751 VELAZQUEZ, Rafael Eliado. La población del Paraguay en 1682. PPS 9 no. 24 (1972) 128-48.

752 VELAZQUEZ, Rafael Eliado. La rebelión de los indios de Arecayá en 1660; reacción indigena contra los excesos de la encomienda en el Paraguay. RPS 1, no. 2 (1965) 21-56.
Also: A., Centro Paraguayo de Estudios Sociológicos, 1965. 42p.

753 VELILLA, Benjamin. El gobernador Irala. A., Edit. "Dagre", 1955. 27p.

754 XARQUE, Francisco. Ruiz de Montoya en Indias (1608-1652); ed. by P. Vindel. Madrid, Victoriano Suarez, 1900. 5 vols. (Colección de Libros Raros y Curiosos que tratan de América, 17-20)

755 ZUBIZARRETA, Carlos. Capitanes de la aventura; Cabeza de Vaca el infortunado; Irala, el predestinado. Madrid, Cultura Hispánica, 1957. 394p.

3. *18th century*

756 AGUIRRE, Juan Francisco. Diario del Capitan de fragata, D. Juan Francisco Aguirre. RBNBA 17 nos. 43-44 (1947) 7-497; 18 nos. 45-46 (1948) 9-534; 19 nos. 47-48 (1948) 561-1192; 20 nos. 49-50 (1949) 15-745.
Also: B.A., Imp. de la Biblioteca Nacional, 1949. 536p.

757 ALVAREZ AZCUE, Maria Luisa. La revolución comunera del Paraguay. RBC 58 (1951) 119-54.

758 BENITEZ, Justo Pastor. Los comuneros del Paraguay, 1640-1735. Prólogo del Dr. Enrique Bordenave. A., Imp. nac., 1938. 55p.

759 BENITEZ, Justo Pastor. La revolución de los comuneros en el Paraguay. RBNC 6 (1955) 95-102.

760 BLUJAKI, Agustín. Un gran paraguayo: presbitero Juan Francisco Amancio González y Escobar. Prólogo por Roberto Quevedo. A., Escuela Técnica Salesiana, 1972. 237p.

761 BRUXEL, Arnaldo. Bicentenario de um Rei Gaúcho em 1956? RMJ 7 (1958) no. 9, 103-43.

762 CARLOS V, el Paraguay y el Río de la Plata: trabajo presentado por el Instituto Paraguayo de Investigaciones Históricas al III Congreso de Cooperación Intelectual reunido en España. HP 2 (1957) 19-35.

763 CHAVES, Julio César. Acto en la Academia Nacional de la Historia. Conferencia del Doctor Julio César Chaves sobre "La revolución Paraguaya de los Comuneros". HP 6-7 (1961-62) 69-81.

764 CHAVES, Julio César. Carlos V, el Paraguay y el Río de la Plata. CH 36 nos. 107-108 (1958) 129-43.

765 CHAVES, Julio César. Caudillos e ideología de la revolución comunera del Paraguay. *In* TERCER CONGRESO Internacional de Historia de América. B.A., 1960. Actas. B.A., Academia Nacional de la Historia, 1961. Vol. 1, 155-76.

766 CORONA BARATECH, Carlos E. Notas para un estudio de la "Sociedad en el Río de la Plata durante el virreinato". AEA 8 (1951) 59-109.

767 DABBS, Jack Autrey. A Messiah among the Chiriguanos. SJA 9 (1953) no. 1, 45-58.

768 DIARIO de los particulares que precedieron desde el 6 de agosto de 1724. RIP 3 (1899) 254-72; 331-33.

769 DIAZ PEREZ, Viriato. Las "comunidades peninsulares" en su relación con los levantamientos "comuneros" americanos y en especial con la "revolución comunera del Paraguay". A., 1930. 288p.

770 DIAZ PEREZ, Viriato. La revolución comunera del Paraguay. Antecedents hispanicos. Desarrollo. 2. ed. Palma de Mallorca, Imp. Mossén Alcover, 1973. 2 vols.

771 ESTRADA, José Manuel. Ensayo histórico sobre la revolución de los comuneros del Paraguay en el siglo XVIII, seguido de un apéndice sobre la decadencia del Paraguay y la guerra en 1865. B.A., Imp. de la Nación argentina, 1865. x, 366p.

772 FURLONG CARDIFF, Guillermo. Las regiones rioplatenses, a mediados del siglo XVIII, según noticias de Florian Baucke. GRSGA 4 (1935) 209-29.

773 GROUSSAC, Pablo. Noticia biográfica de don Juan Francisco Aguirre y examen crítico de su Diario. ABBA 4 (1905) ix-xl.

774 HISTOIRE de Nicolas I, roy du Paraguai, et empereur des Mamelus. Saint Paul, 1756. 117p.
Fictitious imprint.

775 HISTOIRE de Nicolas I, roy du Paraguai, et empereur des Mamelus. Ediçao fac-similar; anotaçoes de Rubens Borba de Moraes e Augusto Meyer. Rio, Z. Valverde, 1944. xxii, 117p.

776 HISTORIA de Nicolás Primero, rey del Paraguay y emperor de los Mamelucos. Traducción, edición y notas por Arturo Nagy y Francisco Perez-Maricevich. A., Ed. del Centenario, 1967. 77p.

777 La INTENDENCIA del Paraguay en las invasiones inglesas. AHA 1940, 318-40.

778 KAHLE, Gunter. Los catecismos políticos a fines de la era colonial. HP 6-7 (1961-62) 53-59.

779 KEGLER KRUG, Anneliese. La población del Paraguay. A través de los censos de Azara y Aguirre (1782-1792). RPS 11 no. 30 (1974) 179-213.

780 LATORRE, Manuel Antonio. Razón que de su visita general. REABA 5 (1905) 390-98, 481-86, 571-77, 620-34, 688-98.

781 LOPEZ, Adalberto. The revolt of the Comuneros, 1721-1735: a study in the colonial history of Paraguay. Cambridge, Mass., Schenkman, 1976. 214p.

782 LOZANO, Pedro. Historia de las revoluciones de la Provincia del Paraguay en la América meridional, desde el año de 1721 hasta el de 1735. B.A., Imp. de "La Nación", 1892. (Biblioteca de la "Revista del Paraguay")
Another ed.: B.A., Cabaut y cia, 1905. 2 vols. (Biblioteca de la Junta de historia y numismática americana, 2-3)

782a MAEDER, Ernesto J.; BOLSI, Alfredo S. La población de las misiones guaraníes entre 1702-1767. EP 2 no. 1 (1974) 111-37.

782b MAEDER, Ernesto J. La población del Paraguay en 1799: el censo del gobernador Lázara de Ribera. EP 3 no. 1 (1975) 63-86.

782c MORA MERIDA, José Luis. Cedulario para la gobernación de Paraguay (1700-1716). AEA XXXI (1974) 1031-47.

782d MORA MERIDA, José Luis. Iglesia y sociedad en Paraguay en el siglo XVIII. Seville, Escuela de Estudios Hispanoamericanos de Sevilla, 1976. x, 162p.

783 NOGUES, Alberto. El castillo de Arecutacua. HP 8-10 (1963-65) 53-64.

784 O'SHEA, J.J. Portugal, Paraguay and Pombal's successors. ACQR 33 (1908) 239-52.

785 PEREZ, Juan Francisco. Repercusión de las invasiones inglesas en el Paraguay. BIIH nos. 58-60 (1933-34) 142-50.

786 PINEDO, Agustín Fernando de. Memorial que el gobernador Pinedo elevó en 1777 al Rey. RIP 6 (1906) no. 51, 337-52; no. 52, 3-31.

787 QUEVEDO, R. Antequera: historia de un silencio. A., Edit. La Voz, 1970. 112p.

788 RAINE, Philip. Rebeliones de los comuneros paraguayos. CA 49 (1950) 181-91.

788a RIO DE JANEIRO. BIBLIOTECA NACIONAL. Antecedentes do Tratado de Madri; Jesuítas e bandeirantes no Paraguai, 1703-1751. Introduçao, notas e sumario por Jaime Cortesao. Rio de Janeiro, Biblioteca Nacional, Divisao de Obras Raros e Publicaçoes, 1955. 328p. (Manuscritos de coleçao De Angelis, 6)

789 RIO DE JANEIRO. BIBLIOTECA NACIONAL. De tratado de Madri a conquista dos sete povos, 1750-1802. Introd., notas e sumario por Jaime Cortesao. Rio de Janeiro, Biblioteca Nacional, Divisao de Publicaçoes e Divulgaçao, 1969. 495p. (Manuscritos da coleçao De Angelis, 7)

790 SAEGER, James Schofield. Institutional rivalries, jurisdictional disputes, and vested interests in the viceroyalty of Peru: José de Antequera and the rebellion of Paraguay. AAAFH 32 (1975) 92-116.

791 SAEGER, James Schofield. Origins of the rebellion of Paraguay. HAHR 52 (1972) no. 2, 215-29.

792 TORMO SANZ, Leandro. Paraguay en el siglo XVIII. CH 41 no. 122 (1960) 191-203.

793 URQUIJO, José M. Los Guaraníes después de la expulsión de los Jesuítas. EA 6 no. 25 (1953) 324-30.

794 VELAZQUEZ, Rafael Eliado. Un antecedente próximo de la revolución comunera del Paraguay. La desposición

del gobernador Escobar y Gutierrez en 1705. HBA 3 no. 10 (1951) 56-70.

795 ZAVALA, Francisco Bruno de. Informe del estado de las antiguas reducciones guaranies, 1784. BIIH 25 (1941) 161-84.

4. Jesuit missions 1609-1769

a) Works written before 1800

796 ANGLES Y GORTARI, Matías de. I Gesuiti del Paraguai. Documento autentico di D. Mattia D'Angles e Gortari Generale e Governatore del Potosí. Dedicato al P. Zaccaria Soavissimo Che serve anelia de Parte seconda all'Appendice alle Rifflesioni del Portoghese. Lugano, Nella Stamperia Privilegiata della Suprema Superiorità Elvetica nelle Prefetture Italiane, 1767. 136p.

797 ANGLES Y GORTARI, Matías de. Los Jesuitas en el Paraguay. Copia del informe que hizo el general D. Mathias De Anglís y Gortari Corregidor de Potosí sobre los puntos que han sido causa de las discordias sucedidas en la ciudad de la Asunción, de la provincia del Paraguay, y motivaron la persecución de Joseph de Antequara, de parte de los Regulares de la Compañía. Reimpresa según la edición de 1769. Hecha en Madrid en la Imprenta Real de la Gaceta. A., Librería y Casa Editora de A. de Uribe y Cía, 1896. 245p.

798 APENDICE de documentos pertenecientes á las controversias de los Regulares de la Compañía en el Paraguay, contra el venerable Obispo don fray Bernardino de Cardenas. Madrid, En la Imp. Real de la Gazeta, 1768. 71p.

799 ARROYO, Pedro de. Alegato en justicia á favor de los Indios Guaraníes que, en treinta Pueblos en la Provincia del Paraguay. n.p., n.d.

800 BAUCKE, Florian. Bilder aus der Alten Indianermission von Paraguay. Nach dem Auszeichnungen Bauckes neu bearbeitet von Augustin Bringmann. Freiburg im Breisgau, Herdesche Verlagshandlung, 1968. ix, 140p.

801 BAUCKE, Florian. Iconografia colonial rioplatense, 1749-1767; costumbres y trajes de españoles, criollos e indios; introducción por Guillermo Furlong. B.A., Viau y Zona, 1935. 21p. 43plates.

802 BAUCKE, Florian. Misiones del Paraguay. Memorias del P. Florian Paucke. Misionero de la Compañía de Jesús (1748 a 1767) por A.V. B.A., Imp. Encuadernación y Estereotipia de Leo Miran, 1900. vi, 161p.

803 BAUCKE, Florian. P. Florian Baucke, ein deutscher Missionär in Paraguay (1749-1768). Nach den Aufzeichnungen Bauckes neu bearbeitet von Augustin Bringmann. Freiburg im Breisgau, Berlin, Herdersche Verlagshandlung, 1908. vii, 139p.

804 BAUCKE, Florian. Pater Florian Baucke ein Jesuit in Paraguay 1748-1766. Nach dessen eigenen Auszeichnungen von A. Klober. Regenstburg, N.Y., Cincinatti, 1870. xi, 712p.

805 BAUCKE, Florian. P. Florian Pauckes Reise in die Missionen nach Paraguay und Geschichte der Missionen St. Xavier und St. Peter. Ein Beytrag zur Geschichte der Jesuiten in Paraguay. Aus der Handschrift Paukes herausgegeben von P. Johan Trast. Vienna, Anton Edlem von Schmidt, 1829. viii, 164p.

806 CARDIEL, José. Declaración de la verdad: obra inédita del p. José Cardiel, religioso de la Compañía de Jesú, con una introd. por Pablo Hernandez. B.A., Imp. de J.A. Alsina, 1900. 491p.

807 CHARLEVOIX, Pierre François Xavier de. Geschichte von Paraguay und dem Missionwerke der Jesuiten in diesen Lande aus dem Französischen des P. Franz Xavier de Charlevoix von der Gesellschaft Jesu. Nuremberg, Gabriel Nicolaus Raspe, 1768. 40, 390p.
Another, abridged, translation: Vienna, Verlag der Mechitaristen-Congregations-Buchhandlung, 1830-31. 2 vols. This translation was reprinted, 1834-35. 2 vols.

808 CHARLEVOIX, Pierre François Xavier de. Histoire du Paraguay. Paris, Desaint & Saillant, 1756. 3 vols.
Also: Paris, Desaint, 1757. 6 vols.

809 CHARLEVOIX, Pierre François Xavier de. Historia del Paraguay, con las anotaciones correcciones latinas del p. Muriel; tr. al castellano por el p. Pablo Hernandez. Madrid, V. Suárez, 1910-16. 6 vols. (Colección de libros y documentos referentes á la historia de América, 11-13, 15-16, 18)

810 CHARLEVOIX, Pierre François Xavier de. Historia Paraguajensis Petri Francisci-Xavierii de Charlevoix ex Gallico Latina, cum animadversionibus et supplemento. Venetiis, Apud F. Sansoni, 1779. 608p.

811 CHARLEVOIX, Pierre François Xavier de. The history of Paraguay. Containing amongst many other new, curious and interesting particulars of that country, a full and authentic account of the establishments formed there by the Jesuits, from among the savage natives, in the very center of barbarism: establishments allowed to have realized the sublime ideas of Fénélon, Sir Thomas More and Plato. London, L. Davis, 1769. 2 vols.
An abridged translation.
Also: Dublin: Printed for P. & W. Wilson, 1769. 2 vols.

812 COLECCION general de documentos, tocantes a la persecución, que los regulares de la Compañía suscitaron y siguieron tenázmente por medio de sus jueces conservadores, y ganando algunos ministros seculares desde 1644 hasta 1660 contro el Ilmo. y Rmo. Sr. Fr. D. Bernardino de Cardenas, religioso antes del ordén de S. Francisco, obispo del Paraguay, expeliendole tres veces de su obispado á fuerza de armas, y de manejos de dichos regulares de la Compañía, por evitar que este prelado entrase ni visitase sus misiones del Paraná, Uruguay, e Itatí. Ván añadidos en esta edición muchos documentos inéditos, y un prólogo que sirve de introducción. Madrid, Imp. real de la Gaceta, 1768-70. 4 vols.

Contents:

Vol. I
(i) Memorial y Defensorio de D. Fray Bernardino de Cardenas. p. 1-245.
(ii) Memorial del P. Julian de Pedraza. p. 245-83.
(iii) Discurso de la vida, méritos y trabajor del obispo del Paraguay por Fr. Juan S. Diego Villalon. p. 323-87.

Vol. II
(i) Papel en verso sobre el recibimiento del V. Obispo Bernardino, y persecuciones que le suscitaron los de la Compañía, p. 20-31.

(ii) Requerimiento en que se hace relación de la trayción, y alzamiento executado en el Paraguay contra la Iglesia y el Rey por las Armas, consejos y asistencia de los Religiosos de la Compañía ... por Fr. Gaspar de Arteaga. p. 32-49.
(iii) Respueta que dió Fr. Gaspar de Arteaga, a unos Cargos maliciosos que los Padres de la Compañía hicieron contra el dicho ante su Provincial. p. 59.
(iv) Continuación de lo sucedido al Obispo del Paraguay, desde donde lo dexó Fr. Juan de Villalon en su Memorial. p. 68-71.
(v) Discursos juridicos en defensa de la consagración de Fray Don B. de Cárdenas, Obispo del Paraguay, por Alonso Carrillo. 126p.
(vi) Consulta que hizo Fr. J. de S. Diego y Villalon sobre la consagración de Fr. B. de Cárdenas; y Dictámenes que sobre ella dieron los más celebres Catedrálicos. p. 127-237.
(vii) Noticia de las resoluciones ... de Alexandro VII y Phelipe IV, en los negocios del Obispo del Paraguay, por A. Carrillo.

Vol. III
(i) Memorial ajustado de D. Joseph de Antequera. 239p.
(ii) Cartas del Sr. D. Joseph de Antequera y Castro al Maestro Fr. Joseph de Palos, Obispo Taliense, y Coadjutor del Paraguay. 374p.
(iii) Copia del informe que hizo el General D. Mathias de Anglés y Gortesi, corregidor del Potosí, sobre los puntos que han sido causa de las discordias sucedidas en Asunción del Paraguay, y motivaron la persecución de D. J. de Antequera de parte de los Regulares. 64p.

Vol. IV
(i) Pruébase la existencia del Reyno Jesuitico, y muéstranse los medios, con que se logró su secreto, y conservación por siglo y medio, por Bernardo Ibanéz de Echevarri. 241p.
(ii) Efemérides de la guerra de los Guaranies desde el 1754, o Diario de la Guerra del Paraguay, por el P. Tadeo Henis. 113p.

813 DECADES, virorum illustrium Paraguariae Societatis Iesu ex historia eiusdem Societatis Gallo Belga insulensi. Cum synopsi chronologica Historia Paraguariae. Tyrnaviae (Trnava), Typis Academicis Societatis Jesu, 1759. 375, 173p.

814 DURAN, Nicolas. Relation des insignes Progrez de la religion chrestienne, faits au Paraguai, Province de l'Amérique Méridionale & dans les vastes Régions de Guair & d'Uraig. Nouvellement découverte par les Pères de la Compaigne de Jésus, les années 1626 & 1627. Envoyée au R.P. Mutio Vitelesci Général de la mesme Compaigne, par le R.P. Nicolas Duran, Provincial en la Province de Paraguai. Et traduite de Latin en français par un Père de la mesme Compaigne. Paris, Sebastian Cramoisy, 1638. 162p.

815 FERNANDEZ, Juan Patricio. Ertrauliche und angenehme Geschichten der Chiquitos, und anderer von denen patribus der Gesellschaft Jesu in Paraguaria neubekehrten Völcker; samt einem ausführlichen Bericht von dem Amazonen-Strom, wie auch einigen Nachrichten von der Landschaft Guiana, in der Neuen Welt. Alles aus Spanisch- und Französischen in das Teutsche übersetzt, von einem aus erwehnter Gesellschaft. Vienna, P. Straub, 1729. 774p.

816 FERNANDEZ, Juan Patricio. Historica relatio de apostolicis missionibus Patrum Societatis Jesu apud Chiquitos, Paraquariae populos, primó hispano idiomate conscripta a P. Joan Patricio Fernandez, dein ad Typum promoto a P. Hieronymo Herran, procuratore generali provinciae Paraquariae, utroque Societatis Jesu sacerdote, anno MDCCXXVI. Hodie in linguam latinam translata ab alio eiusdem Societatis Jesu sacerdote. Augustae Vindelicorum (Augsburg), sumptibus Mathiae Wolff, 1733. 276p.

817 FERNANDEZ, Juan Patricio. Relación historial de las misiones de los Indios, que llaman Chiquitos, que estan a cargo de los padres de la Compañía de Jesús de la provincia del Paraguay. Sacada a luz por el Padre Gerónimo Herrán, procurador general de la misma provincia. Madrid, Por Manuel Fernandez, 1726. 452p.
Reprinted: Madrid, V. Suárez, 1895. 2 vols. (Colección de libros raros o curiosos que tratan de América, 12-13). A., A. de Uribe, 1896. 282p.

818 FERNANDEZ, Juan Patricio. Relazione istorica della nuova christianitá degli Indiani detti Cichiti scritta in spagnuola dal P. Gio Patrizio Fernandez, e tradotto in italiano da Gio. Battista Memuci, ambidue della Compagnia di Gesú. Coll'aggiunta d'un'indice delle cose piú notibili. Rome, per Antonio de Rossi, 1729. 233p.

819 FERRUFINO, Juan Bautista. Relación del martirio de los Padres Roque González de Santa Cruz, Alonso Rodríguez, Juan del Castillo, de la Compañía de Jesús, padecido en el Paraguay a 16 de Noviembre de 1628. Madrid, Real, hacia 1629. 29p.
Pseudonym of Ayora y Sotomayor, Fernando de. Reprinted in no. 754, vol. 4, p. 259-308.

820 FURLONG CARDIFF, Guillermo. Diario del viaje o entrada que hizo el Padre José Jolis, de la Compañía de Jesús a lo interior del Chaco. Año de 1767. EBA 18 (1920) 480-500.

821 FURLONG CARDIFF, Guillermo. Domingo Muriel, S.J., y su "Relación de las misiones" (1766). B.A., Libreria del Plata, 1955. 220p. (Escritores coloniales rioplatenses, 7)

822 FURLONG CARDIFF, Guillermo. José Cardiel, S.J., y su Carta-relación (1747). B.A., Librería del Plata, 1953. 216p. (Escritores coloniales rioplatenses, 2)

823 FURLONG CARDIFF, Guillermo. José Manuel Peramás y su Diario del Destierro (1768). B.A., Librería del Plata, 1952. 226p. (Escritores coloniales rioplatenses, 1)

824 FURLONG CARDIFF, Guillermo. Pedro Juan Andreu y su carta a Mateo Andreu (1750). B.A., Librería del Plata, 1953. 150p. (Escritores coloniales rioplatenses, 3)

825 IBAÑEZ DE ECHAVARRI, Bernardo. Le gouvernement du Paraguay sous les Jésuites. Ouvrage où l'on expose les moyens que les Jésuites ont employés pour maintenir leur royauté dans le Paraguay, et l'y tenir secrète pendant un siècle et demi. Madrid, 1771. 3 vols.

826 IBAÑEZ DE ECHAVARRI, Bernardo. Histoire du Paraguay sous les Jésuites et de la Royauté qu'ils y ont exercée pendant un siècle et demi; ouvrage, qui renferme des détails très intéressants et qui peut servir de suite à l'histoire philosophique et politique des établissements et du commerce des Européens dans les deux Indes. Amsterdam & Liepzig, Arkstée & Merkus, 1780. 3 vols.

827 IBAÑEZ DE ECHAVARRI, Bernardo. Jesuiti Reich in Paraguay, durch Original documente der Gesellschaft Jesu bewiesen von dem auss dem Jesuitenorden verstossenen Pater Ybagnez. Cologne, Peter Mateau, 1774. 264p.

828 IBAÑEZ DE ECHAVARRI, Bernardo. Regno Gesuitico del Paraguay; dimostrato co' documenti più classici de' medesimi padri della Compagnia, i quali confessano, e mostrano ad evidenza la regna sovranità del R.P. Generale con independenza, e con odio verso la Spagna anno 1760. Lisbon, Stamperia Reale, 1770. xix, 167p.

829 IBAÑEZ DE ECHAVARRI, Bernardo. Das Reich der Jesuiten in Paraguay. Aus zuverlässichen Urkunden der Vater der Gesellschaft selbst erwiesen von P. Ibagnez, Priester der Gesellschaft Jesu. Aus dem Spanischen in das Lateinische, aus diesem ins Deutsche übersetzt. Frankfurt & Leipzig, 1783. 235p.

830 KURTZE Nachricht von der Republique, so von denen R.R.P.P. der Gesellschaft Jesu der Portugiessisch und Spanischen Provinzen in den über meer gelegenen diesen zweyen Mächten gehörigen Königreichen aufgerichtet worden. Und von dem Krieg welchen gemelde Patres Jesuiten wider Spanien und Portugall geführet und ausgehalten haben. Diese Nachricht ist aus der geheimen Registratur der zweyen Bevollmächtigten respective Principal-Commissarien, und bewährten Urkunden gezogen, aus der Portugiessischen in die Welsche, und von dieser in die Teutsche Sprache übersetzt werden. Lisbon, 1760. 67p.
Trans. of no. 857.

831 LITTERAE annuae Provinciae Paraquariae Societatis Iesu ad admodum R.P. Mutium Vitellescum eiusdem Societatis Praepositum Generalem Missae a R.P. Nicolao Duran Paraquariae Praesiposito Provinciali, eius nomine ac inssu scriptae a P. Iacobo Rançonier Belga eiusdem Societatis. Antwerp, Typis Ioannis Mevisi, 1636. 168p.

832 LITTERAE annuae provinciae Paraquariae Societatis Jesu ad admodum R.P. Mutium Vitellescum eiusdem societatis prepositum generalem missae a R.P. Jacob de Beroa Paraquariae praeposito provinciali, ex hispanico autographo latine redditae a P. Francisco de Hamal. Insulia, Typis T. Le Clercq, 1642. 347p.

833 LOZANO, Pedro. Carta del P. Pedro Lozano, de la Compañía de Jesús, de la provincia de Paraguay, escrita al P. Bruno Morales, de la misma Compañía, y provincia, existente en esta corte de Madrid. Madrid, 1747? 56p.

834 LOZANO, Pedro. Copia de carta, escrita por un misionero de la Compañía de Jesús del Paraguay, al padre

Juan Joseph Rico, procurador general de dicha provincia en esta corte, en que le refiere el estado presente de aquella provincia, y sus missiones, assi antiguas, como nuevas, entre christianos, y gentiles. Cordoba? 1740?

835 LOZANO, Pedro. Descripción chorographica del terreno, rios, arboles, y animales de las dilatadissimas provincias del Gran Chaco, Gualamba: y de los ritos, y costumbres de las innumerables naciones barbaras, è infieles, que le habitan: con una cabal relación historica de lo que en ellas han obrado para conquistarlas algunos governadores, y ministros reales: y los missioneros Jesuitas para reducirlas à la fé del verdadero Dios. Cordoba, En el Colegio de la Assumpción, 1733. 485p.

836 LOZANO, Pedro. Historia de la Compañía de Jesús en la provincia del Paraguay. Madrid, Imp. de la viuda de M. Fernández y del supremo Consejo de la inquisición, 1754-55. 2 vols.
Reprinted: Farnborough, Gregg International Publishers, 1970. 2 vols.

837 LOZANO, Pedro. Relación de la vida y virtudes del venerable martyr P. Julian de Lizardi de la Compañía de Jesús de la Provincia del Paraguay. Salamanca, Antonio Villagordo, 1741. 218p.
Reprinted: San Sebastian, Imp. de Ignacio Ramón Baroja, 1857. 210p.
Madrid, Imp. de Uriarte y Lavajos, 1862. xviii, 186p.

838 MACHONI, Antonio, *de Cerdeña*. Las siete estrellas de la mano de Jesús. Tratado histórico de las admirables vidas, y resplandores de virtudes de siete Varones Ilustres de la Compañía de Jesús, naturales de Cerdeña, y Misioneros Apostólicos de la Provincia del Paraguay de la misma Compañía. Cordoba, Impreso en la Colegio de la Assumpción por Joseph Santos Balbao, 1732. 472p.

839 MESSIS Paraquariensis a patribus societatis Jesu per sexenium in Paraquaria collecta, annis videlicet MDCXXXVIII. XXXIX. XL. XLI. XLII. XLIII. Conscripta a P. Adamo Schirmbeck Societatis eiusdem sacerdote. Permissu superiorum. Monachii, Formis Strarbii, Impensis Joannis Wagneri, Ciuis & Bibliop., 1649. 366p.

840 MURATORI, Lodovico Antonio. Il cristianesimo felice nelle missioni de' Padri della Compagnia de Jesú nel Paraguai. Venice, Presso Giambatista Pasquali, 1742-49. 2 vols.
Reprinted: 1752. 2 vols.
Turin, dalla Tipografia Bianco, 1824. 2 vols.
Naples, Stabilimento Tip. di P. Androsio in S. Sebastiano, 1852. 256p.
Turin, Typ. e Libreria Salesiana, 1880. xv, 404p. (Biblioteca della gioventú italiana)

841 MURATORI, Lodovico Antonio. Das glückliche Christenthum in Paraguay, unter den Missionarien der Gesellschaft Jesu. Vienna, Prague, Trieste, Johann Thomas Trattnern, 1758. 2 vols.

842 MURATORI, Lodovico Antonio. The Jesuit's travels in South America, Paraguay, Chili, etc.... with the relations of Father Cajetan Cattaneo. London, Jeffery and Sael, 1788. xvi, 294p.

843 MURATORI, Lodovico Antonio. Relation des missions du Paraguai. Paris, Bordelet, 1754. xxiv, 402p.

844 MURATORI, Lodovico Antonio. Rélation des missions du Paraguai. Traduit de l'Italien de M. Muratori suivi de 3 lettres du P. Caetan Cattaneo, missionaire de la compagnie de Jesús à M. Joseph Cattaneo, son frère sur les missions à Buenos-Ayres. Paris, Bordelet, 1757. xxiv, 402p.
Reprinted: Louvain, Valinthout et Vandenzande, 1822. xvi, 218p.
Paris, La Société Catholique des Bons Livres, 1826. 302p.

845 MURATORI, Lodovico Antonio. A relation of the missions of Paraguay wrote originally in Italian, by M. Muratori, and now done into English from the French translation. London, J. Marmaduke, 1759. xvi, 294p.

846 MURIEL, Domingo. Historia del Paraguay desde 1747 hasta 1767, obra latina del P. Domingo Muriel ... tr. al castellano por el P. Pablo Hernandez. Madrid, V. Suarez, 1918. 659p. (Colección de libros y documentos referentes a la historia de América, 19)

847 NEUE Nachrichten von den Missionen der Jesuiten in Paraguay, und von andern damit verbundenen vorgangen in der Spanischen Monarchie. Aus dem Spanischen. Hamburg, In Comiszion bey der typographischen Gesell-

schaft, 1768. xxiii, 307p.
Works by Juan de Escandón and Bernardo Nusdorfer relating to the Guarani wars.

848 NIEREMBERG, Juan Eusebio. Vidas exemplares y venerables memorias de algunos claros Varones de la Compañía de Jesús de los quales es este. Madrid, A. de Paredes, 1647. 12, 787, 9p. (Varones ilustres de la Compañía de Jesús, 4)

849 Le PARAGUAY jésuitique; ou description des terres dont les Jésuites Espagnoles se sont emparés dans l'Amérique meridionale en y portant la Foi, les productions naturelles du pays, les moeurs des peuples qui habitent, l'esclavage honteux où ils se trouvent réduits sous la domination despotique des Curés, etc. le tout extrait des mémoires du sieur Bravet, ingénieur à la Martinique, que ces Pères firent généralissme de leurs Troupes dans la guerre contre les Xaraïes en 1718. Amsterdam, 1768. 55p.

850 PERAMAS, José Manuel. De vita et moribus sex sacerdotum paraguaycorum. Faventiae (Barcelona), Ex typographia Archii, 1791. 299p.

851 PERAMAS, José Manuel. De vita et moribus tredecim virorum paraguaycorum. Faventiae (Barcelona), Ex typographia Archii, 1793. 462p.

852 PERAMAS, José Manuel. Una página de la historia moderna, Clemente Baigorri o fidelidad hasta la muerte por el P. Vicente Agustí de la Compañía de Jesús. Barcelona, Librería y typografía Católica, 1895. 88p.

853 PERAMAS, José Manuel. La república de Platon y los Guaraníes. B.A., Emecé, 1946. 124p.
Trans. of no. 851, p. 1-162.

854 PERAMAS, José Manuel. Vida y obra de seis humanistas. Traducción de Antonio Ballus. Prólogo de Guillermo Furlong. B.A., Edit. Huarpes, 1946. 300p. (Biblioteca americana de escritores coloniales, 1)
Trans. of no. 850.

855 PERAMAS, José Manuel. Vie du R.P. Ygnace Chomé de la Compagnie de Jésus missionaire au Paraguay d'après ses lettres et les détails que nous a laissés le P. Peramás, missionaire comme lui au Paraguay. Douai, Dechristé, 1864. 151p.

856 RECUEIL des decrets apostoliques et des ordonnances du roi de Portugal concernant la conduite des jésuites

dans le Paraguai etc. Le tout traduit conformément à la collection imprimée en 1759. Avec les mandemens des evêques de Portugal, traduit sur les originaux imprimés en ce royaume & autres pièces autentiques, rélatives à la même affaire. Amsterdam, M. Rey, 1760-1761. 3 vols.

857 RELAÇAO abbreviada da republica, que os religosos jesuitas das provincias de Portugal, e Hespanha, estabelecerao nos dominios ultramarinas das duas monarchias, e da guerra, que nelles tem movido, e sustenado contra os exercitos hespanhoes e portuguezes; formada pelos registos das secretarias dos dous respectivos principaes commissarios, e plenipotenciarios; e por outros documentos autenticos. Lisbon? 1757? 85p.
See no. 830, 861.

858 RELACION del glorioso Martyrio de los Padres Roque Gonçalez, Alonso Rodriguez y Juan del Castillo de la Compañía de Jesús, que la predicación del Santo Evangelio, y defensa de nuestra Santa Fe Catolica murieron a manos de los Indios infieles de la Provincia del Uruay, el mes de Noviembre de 1628 años. Compuesta por el P. Francisco Crespo, Procurador General de la Compañía de Jesús de la Indias. Madrid, por Andrés de Parra, 1630. 16p.

859 RELACION del martirio de los Padres Roque Gonçalez de Santacruz, Alonso Rodriguez, Juan del Castillo, de la compañía de Jesús. Padecido en el Paraguay a 16 de noviembre de 1628. Al Rey Don Felipe N.S. El P. Juan Baptista Ferrufino Procurador General de la Provincia del Paraguay. Seville, 1633. 30p.

860 RELATIO gloriosi martyrii patrium Rochi Gonzalez, Alphonsi Rodriguez, et Joannis de Castillo, Societatis Jesu Sacerdotum, qui ob praedicationem Evang.: et defensionem Fidei Catholicae occisi sunt ab Indis, Provinciae Urvayae, Mense Novemb. Ann. 1628. Ex Hispanico, Matristi excuso, in Gallicum idioma per Franciscum Crespum, eiusdem Soc. Proc.: Gen in Indis occid: translata, et Insulis denuo typis Gallicis impressa, ac demum per alium eiusdem Soc: Patrem Latinae reddita. Vienna, ex Typographia Mathaer Formicae, 1631. 24p.

861 RELATION abregée, concernant la république que les religieux, nommés Jésuites, des provinces de Portugal & d'Espagne, ont établie dans les pays & domaines d'outremer de ces deux monarchies, & de la guerre qu'ils y ont excitée & soutenue contre les armées espagnoles &

portugaises: dressée sur les registres de sécretariat des deux commissaires respectifs principaux & plenipotentiaires des deux couronnes, & sur d'autres pièces autentiques. Traduites du portugais. Le Haye, 1758. 68p.

See no. 857.

862 RELATION du glorieux martyr du Pères Roch Gonzalez, Alphonse Rodriguez et Juan de Castillo, de la Compagnie de Jésus, massacrés par les Indiens de la Province d'Uruay, au mois de novembre de l'an 1628. Traduit de l'espagnol du P. François Crespo, procureur des Indes Orientales. Lille, P. de Roche, 1630. 40p.

863 RELATION von der Blutigen Schlacht, welche den 1 October 1759 in Paraguay zwischen den Jesuiten einer Seits, und den Spaniern und Portugiesen andern Theils, vorgefallen; sammt der Beylage einem Schreibung von einem Spanischen Minister an Pabst Clemens XIII. Aus dem Spanischen ins italianischen, und aus diesem in das deutsche übersetzt. n.p., Gedruckt im Jahre, 1760. 36p.

864 RELAZIONE breve della Repubblica, che i religiosi Gesuiti delle provincie de Portogallo e de Spagna anno stabilita ne' domini oltramarini delle due monarchie e della guerra, che in esse hanno mossa, e sostenuta contro gli eserciti Spagnuoli e Portoghesi. Lisbon, 1757. 48p.

865 RELAZIONE della Battaglia del di 1 de Ottobre 1759. Seguita nel Paraguay trai Gesuiti, e gli spanuoli e portughesi. Si aggiunge una Lettera di un Ministro di Spagna con la traduzione dallo spagnuolo nell'Italiano del signor Bernardo. Naples, Presse Giustino Ferri, 1760. 34p.

866 Die REPUBLIK der Jesuiten, oder Das umgestürzte Paraguay, welches eine richtige erzehlung des Krieges enthält, den diese geistliche gegen die monarchen Spaniens und Portugalls in America zu führen gewaget. Nach den secretariats-aufsätzen der beiderseitigen königl. commissarien und bevollmächtigten der zweyen kronen. Auf besondere ausdrücklichen befehl des portugiesischen hofes an das licht gestellt. Amsterdam, 1758. 68p.

867 La REPUBLIQUE des Jésuites, ou Paraguay renversée contenant une relation authentique de la guerre que ces religieux ont osé soutenir contre les monarques d'Espagne & de Portugal en Amérique: dressée sur les régistres de secrétariat des deux commissaires respec-

tifs principaux & plenipotentiaires des deux couronnes & sur d'autres pièces authentiques. Traduit de l'original portugais, publié par ordre de la cour de Portugal. Amsterdam, Aux dépens de la compagnie, 1758. 64p.

868 RESTIVO, Paulo. Manuale ad usum Patrium Societatis Jesu qui in Reductionibus Paraquariae versantur. Ex Rituali Romano ae Toletano decerptum. Laureti, Typis PP. Societatis Iesu, 1721. 266, 40p.

869 RUIZ DE MONTOYA, Antonio. Aba Reta y Caray ey baecue Tupa Upe ynemboaguiye uca hague Pay de la Comp.a de IHS. Poromboeramo Ara Cae P. Antonio Ruiz Icaray ey baê Mongetapi hare oiquatia caray Nee Rupi Yma Cara Mbohe Hae Pay Ambuae Ogueroba Aba Nee Rupi Año de 1733 Pipe. S. Nicolas Pe. Ad Majorem Dei Gloriam Primera catechese dos Indios Selvagens feita pelos Padres da Companhia de Jesus. Originariamente escripta em hispanhol (em lingua europea) pelo padre Antonio Ruiz Antigo Instructor do Gentio e depois vertida em abaneenge (em lingua indigena) por outro Padre 1733 S. Nicolas ad Majorem Dei gloriam. ABNRJ 6 (1878-79) 91-366.

870 RUIZ DE MONTOYA, Antonio. Conquista espiritual hecha por los religiosos de la Compañía de Jesús en las Provincias del Paraguay, Parana, Vruguay, y Tape. Escrita por el Padre Antonio Ruiz de la misma Compañía. Dirigida A. Octavio Centurion, Marqués de Monasterio. Madrid, Imp. del Reyno, 1639. 103p.
Reprinted: Bilbao, Imp. del Corazón de Jesús, Muelle de Marzana, 7, 1892. 309p.

871 TECHO, Nicolás del. Epítome de la vida del V.P. Iuan de Vianna de la Compañía de Jesús, Missionero Apostólico de la América: sacado de la Historia Latina que de su Provincia del Paraguay escribío el R.P.M. Nicolás de Techo de la misma Compañía. Con una addición de otros cinco Jesuitas Originarios, y naturales Paysanos del P. Viana. Viana (Vienna), Por Joseph Oachin Martínez, 1716. 384p.

872 TECHO, Nicolás del. Historia de la provincia del Paraguay de la Compañía de Jesús, por el p. Nicolás del Techo; versión del texto latino, por Manuel Serrano y Sanz, con un prólogo de Blas Garay. Madrid, Librería y casa edit. A. de Uribe, 1897. 5 vols. (Biblioteca paraguaya)

873 TECHO, Nicolás del. Historia Provinciae Paraguariae Societatis Jesu. Leodii (Lieja), Joan Mathiae Hovii, 1673. 390p.

874 TECHO, Nicolás del. The history of the provinces of Paraguay, Tucuman, Rio de la Plata, Paraná, Guaira and Urvaica and something of the Kingdom of Chili, in South America. *In* CHURCHILL, Awnsham; CHURCHILL, John. A collection of voyages and travels ... London, 1704. Vol. 4, p. 663-750.

875 TECHO, Nicolás del. Relati o triplex de rebus Indicis: I. R.P. Cornelii Beudinii, dicti Godinez, Martirium. II. Caaigarum gentis mores, coepta conuercio. III. R.P. Adriani Knudde, dicti Crespi, Elogium. Antwerp, Apud Iacobum Mevrsium, 1654. 70p.

876 VAZQUEZ TRUXILLO, Francisco. Información fecha por el P. Francisco Vazquez Truxillo, provincial de la Compañía de Jesús en la provincia del Paraguay, sobre la destrucción y daños que los portugueses de San Pablo han fecho en seis reducciones de las que la Compañía tiene por orden de S.M. en las provincias del Guayra. *In* COLECCION de documentos inéditos para la historia de España por el Marqués de la Fuensanta del Valle. Madrid, Imp. de José Perales y Martinez, 1892. Vol. 104, 307-43.

877 XARQUE, Francisco. Insignes missioneros de la Compañía de Jesus en la Provincia del Paraguay. Estado presente de sus Misiones en Tucumán, Paraguay y Río de la Plata, que comprehende su Distrito. Pamplona, Juan Micón, 1687. xxiv, 432p.

878 XARQUE, Francisco. Vida apostólica del venerable Padre Josef Cataldino, uno de los primeros, y más insignes Conquistadores de la delatadas Provincias, y barbaras Naciones del Guayrá, valeroso soldado de la Minima, y Máxima Compañía de Iesu. Zaragosa, Por Juan de Ybar, 1664. 264p.

879 YAPUGUAI, Nicolás. Explicación de el Catechismo en lengua Guaraní, por Nicolás Yapuguai, con dirección del P. Paulo Restivo de la Compañía de Jesús. En el Pueblo de S. María La Mayor, 1724. 4, 152, 22, 228, 55p.

880 YAPUGUAI, Nicolás. Sermones y exemplos en lengua Guaraní. En el Pueblo de S. Francisco Xavier, 1727. 165p.

b) Works written after 1800

881 ARANGO VIEIRA, Antonio. Las reducciones de los jesuítas en el Paraguay. RJ 16 (1941) no. 8, 318-27.

882 ARMANI, Alberto. Sull'origine e sviluppo del'ordine politico e sociale nelle reduzioni del Paraguay. AHSJ 24 (1955) 379-401.

883 ARMANI, Alberto; LACOMBE, Robert. Les institutions politiques et sociales dans les Réductions au Paraguay. SE 13 (1961) 401-7.

884 ATTERIDGE, A.H. The Paraguayan missions. *In* EYRE, Edward. European civilization, its origins and developments. N.Y., Oxford University Press, 1934-39. Vol. 6, p. 719-40.

885 BALEN, Chr. van, jr. Het Jesuitenrijk in Paraguay. TKNAG 2. ser., 52 (1935) no. 5, 730-38.

886 BAREIRO SAGUIER, Ruben; CLASTRES, Hélène. Aculturación y mestizaje en las misiones jesuiticas del Paraguay. AP 14 (1969) 6-27, 62-66.

887 BARRIO, Maximo de. Las colecciones de las misiones del Paraguay existentes en el Museo de la Plata. RUNP 33 (1931) 195-205.

888 BARRIO, Maximo de. Misiones jesuiticas del Paraguay. *In* LA PLATA. UNIVERSIDAD NACIONAL. MUSEO DE HISTORIA NATURAL. Guía para visitar el Museo de La Plata. La Plata, 1927. p. 311-21.

889 BAUDIN, Louis. Une théocratie socialiste: l'Etat jésuite du Paraguay. Paris, M.-T. Génin, 1962. 69p.

890 BAYLE, Constantino. Los nuevos beatos mártires del Paraguay, simiente de la Reducciones. RF 104 (1934) 145-61.

891 BECKER, Franz. Geschichtliche und sociale Entwicklung des Reiches der Jesuiten in Paraguay in siebzehnten und achtzehnten Jahrhundert. PX 20 (1934) no. 1-2, 7-34.

892 BEGUIRIZTAIN, Justo. E. P. Juan Pastor y su inédita Historia de la Provincia del Paraguay. EBA 75 (1946) 147-55.

893 BEGUIRIZTAIN, Justo. Una versión portuguesa de las obras del P. Sepp, S.J. EBA 71 (1944) 427-41.

894 BERNARDI, Mansueto. O governo temporal das missoes e o Padre Antonio Sepp. P 2 (1958) 21-54.

895 BERTHET, Elie. Les Missionaires du Paraguay. Paris, 1855.

896 BLANCO, José María. Historia documental de la vida y gloriosa muerte de los padres Roque Gonzalez de Santa Cruz, Alonso Rodríguez y Juan de Castillo de la Compañía de Jesús, martires del Caaro y Yjuhí. B.A., Sebastian de Amorrortu, 1929. 742p.

897 BLANCO, José María. Los mártires del Caaró e Yjuhí: compendio de la historia de los padres Roque González de Santa Cruz, Alonso Rodríguez y Juan de Castillo, primeros mártires de las misiones guaraniticas. B.A., Edit. "Surgo", 1931. 161p.

898 BLANCO VILLALTA, Jorge Gastón. Montoya: apóstol de los Guaraníes. B.A., G. Kraft, 1954. 181p. (Colección Cúpula)

899 BRAVO, Francisco Javier. Colección de documentos relativos á la expulsión de los Jesuitas de la República Argentina y del Paraguay en el reinado de Carlos III, con introducción y notas. Madrid, Establecimiento tip. de José María Perez, 1872. cxi, 404p.

900 BRAVO, Francisco Javier. Inventarios de las misiones jesuíticas del Paraguay, Mojos y Chiquitos. Relaciones documentales. AIAAIE 14 (1961) 112-19; 15 (1962) 128-36.

900a BRUXEL, Arnaldo. Padre Roque: a epopeia libertaçao guarani. Sao Paulo, Edicoes Loyola, 1977. 283p.

901 BUENOS AIRES. UNIVERSIDAD NACIONAL. INSTITUTO DE INVESTIGACIONES HISTORICAS. Iglesia; cartas anuas de la provincia del Paraguay, Chile, y Tucumán, de la Compañía de Jesús, con advertencia de Emilio Ravignani e introducción del p. Carlos Leonhardt. B.A., Tall. s.a. Casa Jacobo Peuser, 1927-29. 2 vols. (Documentos para la historia argentina, 19-20)

901a CABRAL, Jorge. Conferencias sobre las misiones jesuíticas en el Rio de la Plata, pronunciadas en el Instituto de la Universidad de Roma. B.A., Tall. s.a. Casa Jacobo Peuser, 1934. 240p.

902 CADDELL, Cecilia Mary. Historia de las misiones en el Japon y Paraguay, escrita en inglés por C.M. Cadell, tr. directamente por d. Casimiro Pedregal. 2. ed. Madrid, S. Sanchez Rubio, 1857. 390p. (Biblioteca instructiva)

903 CADDELL, Cecilia Mary. A history of the missions in Japan and Paraguay. London, Burns and Lambert; N.Y., Sadlier, 1856. xvii, 180, iv, 102p.
Reprinted: 1879; 1881; N.Y., F.J. Kenedy, 1896. 102p.

904 CAPDEVIELLE, Bernardo. Misiones jesuíticas en el Paraguay. A., 1921? 82p.
2. ed. A., Imp. y librería "La Mundial", 1923. 262p.

905 CARAMAN, Philip. The lost paradise: an account of the Jesuits in Paraguay 1607-1768. London, Sidgwick & Jackson, 1975. vii, 341p.
Also: N.Y., Seabury Press, 1976.

906 CHAUNU, Pierre. Au point d'impact de deux colonisations: l'état jésuite du Paraguay, un empire du maté. AESC 10 (1955) no. 4, 559-64.
A review of no. 994.

907 CONSTATT, O. Das indianische Bevölkerung der alten Jesuiten reductionen in Südamerika. ZE 37 (1905) 882-98.

908 CONZELMANN, Paulwalter. Wirtschaftwachstum und -entwicklung im Jesuitenstaat von Paraguay. Inaugural Dissertation der Wirtschafts- und Sozialwissenschaftlichen Fakultät der Universität zu Köln, 1958. Cologne, 1959. 152p.

909 DECHRISTE, Louis Ferdinand. Vie du R.P. Ignacio Chomé, de la Compagnie de Jésus, missionaire au Paraguay; d'après les lettres et les détails que nous a laissé le P. Peramas, missionaire comme lui au Paraguay. Douai, Dechristé, 1864. 156p.

910 DECOBERT, J. Les missions jésuites du Paraguay devant la philosophie des Lumières. RSH 149 (1973) 17-46.

911 DELATTRE, Pierre; LAMALLE, Edmond. Jésuites wallons, flammands, français missionaires au Paraguay 1608-1767. AHSJ 16 (1947) 98-176.

912 DESCOLA, Jean. Quand les Jésuites sont au pouvoir. Paris, A. Fayard, 1956. 191p. (Cahiers missionaires, 1)

913 DUHR, Bernard. Ungedruckte Briefe zur Geschichte des sogenannten Jesuiten-Krieges in Paraguay. ZKT (1898) 688-708.

914 EGUIA RUIZ, Constancio. Algo sobre la Compañía de Jesús y las lenguas indigenas. EBA 61 (1939) 245-64.

915 EGUIA RUIZ, Constancio. España y sus misioneros en el antiguo Paraguay. EM 1 (1944) 489-506.

915a EGUIA RUIZ, Constancio. España y sus misioneros en los países del Plata. Madrid, Ediciones Cultura Hispánica, 1953. 634p.

916 EGUIA RUIZ, Constancio. El espíritu militar de los jesuitas en el antiguo Paraguay español. RIM 5, no. 16 (1944) 267-319.

917 EGUIA RUIZ, Constancio. Mártires Jesuitas en la antigua provincia paraguaya, hoy argentina. EBA 67 (1942) 110-28, 210-15.

918 FASSBINDER, Maria. Der "Jesuitenstaat" in Paraguay. Halle, Niemeyer, 1926. (Studien über Amerika und Spanien, Völkerkundlich-geschichtliche Reihe, 2)

919 FREIBERG, C. Deutsche Missionarbeit im Chaco. IA 11 (1937) 92-97.

919a FURLONG CARDIFF, Guillermo. Antonio Ruíz de Montoya y su carta a Comental, 1645. B.A., Ediciones Theoria, 1964. 174p. (Escritores coloniales rioplatenses, 17)

920 FURLONG CARDIFF, Guillermo. De la Asunción a los Chiquitos por el Río Paraguay. Tentativa frustada en 1703. "Breve relación" inédita del P. José Francisco de Arce. AHSJ 7 (1939) 54-79.

921 FURLONG CARDIFF, Guillermo. En defensa del Padre Ruiz de Montoya. EBA 65 (1941) 225-34, 431-42.

922 FURLONG CARDIFF, Guillermo. La enciclopedia Rioplatense de José Sanchez Labrador S.J. RSAA 1931, no. 5, 263-307.

923 FURLONG CARDIFF, Guillermo. Entre los abipones del Chaco; según noticias de las misioneros jesuitas, Martín Dobrizhoffer, Domingo Muriel, José Brigniel, Joaquín Camaño, José Jolis, Pedro Juan Andreu, José Cardiel y Vicente Olcina. B.A., Tall. gráf. "San Pablo", 1938. 188p.

924 FURLONG CARDIFF, Guillermo. El expulso Bernardo Ibañez de Echavarri y sus obras sobre las Misiones del Paraguay. AHSJ 2 (1933) 25-35.

925 FURLONG CARDIFF, Guillermo. Un gran humanista de la época colonial: José Manuel Peramás (1732-1793), su

vida, su labor, su gloria. EBA 29 (1925) 337, 30 (1926) 43, 140, 209, 292, 452; 31 (1926) 125.

925a FURLONG CARDIFF, Guillermo. Joaquín Camaño, S.J. y su "Noticia del Gran Chaco (1778)". B.A., Librería del Plata, 1955. 181p. (Escritores coloniales rioplatenses, 8)

925b FURLONG CARDIFF, Guillermo. José Sánchez Labrador, S.J., y su "Yerba Mate" (1774). B.A., Librería del Plata, 1960. 121p. (Escritores coloniales rioplatenses, 10)

926 FURLONG CARDIFF, Guillermo. José Solis. Misionero e historiador (1728-1790). EBA 46 (1932) 82-91, 178-88.

927 FURLONG CARDIFF, Guillermo. Misiones y sus pueblos de Guaraníes. B.A., Ediciones Theoria, 1962. 788p.

928 FURLONG CARDIFF, Guillermo. Nicolás del Techo, historiador. EBA 83 (1950) 17-30, 163-88.

929 FURLONG CARDIFF, Guillermo. El P. Francisco Javier Miranda S.J. EBA 44 (1931) 350-58; 45 (1931) 47-62.

930 FURLONG CARDIFF, Guillermo. El Padre Nicolás de Techo, S.J. EBA 82 (1950) 141-52.

931 FURLONG CARDIFF, Guillermo. El P. Martin Dobrizhoffer, S.J., filólogo e historiador. BIIH 6 (1928) no. 35, 417-81.

932 FURLONG CARDIFF, Guillermo. El P. Pedro Lozano, S.J. Su personalidad y su obra, bio-bibliografía. Montevideo, Imp. "El siglo ilustrada", 1930. 104p.
Also: RSAA 1 (1930) 241-53.

932a FURLONG CARDIFF, Guillermo. Pedro Lozano, S.J. y su "Observaciones a Vargas" (1750). B.A., Librería del Plata, 1959. 176p. (Escritores coloniales rioplatenses, 9)

933 FURLONG CARDIFF, Guillermo. La tradición histórico-literaria del martirio de los Padres Roque González de Santa Cruz, Alonso Rodriguez y Juan del Castillo. EBA 36 (1928) 209-21.

934 GAMBON, Vicente. A través de las Misiones Guaraníticas. B.A., Angel Estrada, 1904. 139p.

935 GANDIA, Enrique de. Las misiones jesuíticas y los bandeirantes paulistas. B.A., Edit. "La Facultad", Bernabé y cia, 1936. 92p.

936 GARAY, Blás Manuel. El comunismo de las misiones de la Compañía de Jesús en el Paraguay. Madrid, M. Tello, 1897. 191p.
Reprinted: A., La Mundial, 1921. 118p.

936a GARAY, Blás. El comunismo de las misiones. La revolución de la independencia del Paraguay. A., Instituto Colorado de Cultura, 1975. 252p. (Biblioteca Clasicos Colorados)

937 GARRAGHAN, G.J. The martyrs of the Reductions. HB 13 (1935) 43-57.

938 GARSCH, Bruno. Der Einfluss der Jesuiten-Missionen auf den Wandel der Naturlandschaft zur Stromgebiet des Paraguay-Parana während des 17 und 18 Jahrhunderts. Breslau, 1934. 150p.

939 GAY, Juan Pedro. Historia da Republica Jesuitica do Paraguay desde o descobrimento do Rio da Prata atê nossos dias, anno de 1861. RIHGB 26 (1863) 5-120, 185-268, 361-447, 589-838.
Also: Rio de Janeiro, D.L. dos Santos, 1863. 484, 65, vip.
2. ed. Rio de Janeiro, Imprensa nac., 1942. xii, 644p.
N.B. The author is also known as Joao Pedro Gay and Jean Pierre Gay.

940 GEER, Johann Sebastian. Der Jesuitenstaat in Paraguay; Staatswirtschaftform und Entwickelungsgeschichte. Nuremberg, Krische, 1928. 112p.

940a GENELIN, Placidus. Die Reunionen der Jesuiten in Paraguay. Vienna, Norbertus, 1895. 38p.

941 GONZALEZ, Julio C. Notas para una historia de los treinta pueblos de Misiones. AHA (1942-43) 273-347; (1943-45) 141-85.

942 GONZALEZ PINTADO, Gaspar. Los mártires jesuitas de las Misiones del Paraguay: Roque Gonzâlez de Santa Cruz, Alfonso Rodríguez y Juan del Castillo. Bilbao, Imp. y encuadernación "La Vizcaina", 1934. 239p.

943 GOTHEIN, Eberhard. Der christlich-sociale Staat der Jesuiten in Paraguay. Leipzig, Duncker & Humboldt, 1883. viii, 68p.

944 GRAHAM, Robert Bontine Cunninghame. A vanished Arcadia; being some account of the Jesuits in Paraguay, 1607-1767. London, W. Heinemann, 1901. xvi, 294p.
Reprinted: (1) 1924. (2) N.Y., Haskell House, 1968.

944a GRAZIUSSI-GROZZOTTI, Delia. L'opera dei gesuiti nelle riduzioni del Paraguay. Rome, Abete, Az Beneventana Tip. ed., 1951. 10p.

945 GROH, John E. Antonio Ruiz de Montoya and the early reductions in the Jesuit province of Paraguay. CHR 56 (1970) 501-33.

946 GROUSSAC, Pablo. Noticia biográfica de don Diego de Alvear y examen crítico de su Diario. ABBA 1 (1900) 195-261.

947 GROUSSAC, Pablo. Noticia del P. José Guevara y estudio de la Historia del Paraguay. ABBA 6 (1908) ix-lxxxvi.

948 GROUSSAC, Pablo. Ruy Díaz de Guzmán. Noticia sobre su vida y su obra. ABBA 9 (1914) ix-liii.

949 GUTIERREZ, Ramón. Estructura socio-politica, sistema productivo y resultante espacial en las misiones jesuiticas del Paraguay durante el siglo XVIII. Resistencia, Dpto. de Historia de la Arquitectura, Fac. de Arquitectura, 1974. 39p.
Also: EP 2 no. 2 (1974) 83-140.

950 GWYNN, Aubrey Osborn. Father Thomas Fields, S.J. A pioneer of the Church in Paraguay 1549-1625. Dublin, Irish Messenger, 1924. 24p. (Sheaf Mission Series, 2)

951 HAFKEMEYER, J.B. Zür Geschichte der Jesuiten Krieges in Paraguay; eine kritische Studien. ZKT 32 (1908) 673-92.

952 HAUBERT, Maxime. Indiens et Jésuites au Paraguay. Rencontre de deux messianismes. ASR 14, no. 27 (1969) 119-33.

953 HAUBERT, Maxime. L'oeuvre missionaire des jésuites au Paraguay, 1585-1768; genèse d'un "paradis". Paris, EPHE, 1966. 2 vols.

954 HAUBERT, Maxime. La vie quotidienne au Paraguay sous les Jésuites. Paris, Hachette, 1967. 319p.

955 HERNANDEZ, Pablo. El extrañamiento de los jesuitas del Río de la Plata y de las misiones del Paraguay por decreto de Carlos III. Madrid, V. Suarez, 1908. 420p. (Colección de libros y documentos referentes a la historia de América, 7)

956 HERNANDEZ, Pablo. Misiones del Paraguay. Organización social de las doctrinas guaraníes de la Compañía de Jesús. Barcelona, G. Gili, 1913. 2 vols.

957 HERRAN, Jerónimo. Misiones Jesuíticas en el Paraguay. EBA 19 (1921) 382-456; 20 (1921) 63-66, 135-147.

958 JACOBSEN, Jerome V. Dobrizhoffer, Abipón missionary. MIA 29, n.s. 18, (1947) 139-84.

959 JAEGER, Luís Gonzaga. La compañía de Jesús en el antiguo Guairá (1585-1631). Localización de sus trece reducciones. P 1 (1957) 93-121.

959a JAEGER, Luís Gonzaga. Os bem-aventurados, Roque Gonzalez, Afonso Rodríguez e Joao del Castillo, martires do Caaro e Pirapo. 2. ed. melhorada. Porto Alegre, Livraria Selbach, 1951. 389p. (Jesuitas no Sul do Brasil, 1)

960 KOEBEL, W.H. In Jesuit land, the Jesuit missions of Paraguay. London, S. Paul, 1912? 381p.

961 KONETZKE, Richard. Zur Geschichte der Jesuiten-reduktionen in Paraguay. VSW 47 (1960) 232-44.
On the Zwettler Codex of Florian Paucke.

962 LABURU, José A. de. Organización social, urbanismo y arte en las reducciones guaranies. EBA 67 (1942) 240-79.

963 LACOMBE, Robert. Sur la terre comme au ciel: l'expérience économique des Jésuites au Paraguay. SE 7 (1955) 293-318.

964 LACOMBE, Robert. Trois documents Français du début du xviii siècle sur les Jésuites du Paraguay. RHES 42 (1964) 27-73.

965 LAFUENTE MACHAIN, Ricardo de. Los parientes del beato padre Roque Gonzãlez de Santa Cruz. EBA (1934) 81-138.

966 LEITE, Serafim. Jesuitas do Brasil no fundaçao da Missao do Paraguay. AHSJ 6 (1937) 1-24.

967 LEONHARDT, Carlos. El Cardenal Federico Borromeo, protector de las antiguas misiones del Paraguay. AHSJ 1 (1932) 308-31.

968 LEONHARDT, Carlos. Los mártires del Chaco: PP. Gaspar Osorio y Antonio Ripario. EBA 67 (1942) 297-312.

969 LEONHARDT, Carlos. El padre Antonio Sepp, S.J., insigne misionero de las reducciones guaranísticas del Paraguay 1691-1733. EBA 27 (1924) 214-19, 285-86, 370-76, 451-53; 28 (1925) 127-31, 327-28, 387-88.

970 LEONHARDT, Carlos. El Padre Julián Lizardi. EBA 52 (1935) 92-99.

971 LEONHARDT, Carlos. El Padre Roque Gonzãlez y compañeros, mãrtires de la Compañĩa de Jesũs, segũn documentos contemporãneos. EBA 36 (1928) 193-208.

972 LEONHARDT, Carlos. Roque Gonzãlez de Santa Cruz. EBA 63 (1940) 305-11.

973 LOBO, Eulalie Maria Lahmeyer. Caminho de Chiquitos as missoes guaranis de 1690 a 1718. Sao Paulo, 1960. 84p. (Coleçao da "Revista de histõria", 20)
Also in RHB 11, no. 41 (1960) 85-90; no. 42, 413-33.

974 LUGON, Clovis. La rẽpublique communiste chrẽtienne des Guaranis (1610-1768). Paris, Les Editions Economie et Humanisme, 1949. 293p.

974a LUGON, Clovis. La rẽpublique des Guaranis (1610-1768): les jẽsuites au pouvoir. Paris, Editions Economie et Humanisme, Les Editions Ouvrières, 1970. 244p.

974b LUGON, Clovis. A Republica Comunista Crista dos Guaranis, 1610-1768. Traduçao de Alvaro Cabral. Rio de Janeiro, Paz e Terra, 1968. 353p.

974c LUGON, Clovis. Chrzescijanska komunistyczna republica Guaranow 1610-1768. Przedmore napisal Mieczyslaw Zywczynski. Warsaw, Pax, 1956. 352p.

975 LUGONES, Leopoldo. El imperio jesuĩtico; ensayo histõrico. B.A., Compañĩa sud-americana de billetes de banco, 1904. 332p.
2. ed. B.A., A. Moen y hermano, 1907. 300p.
3. ed. B.A., La Comisiõn Argentina de Fomento Interamericano, 1945. 289p.

976 MARTIN DE MOUSSY, Jean Antoine Victor. Mẽmoire historique sur la dẽcadence et la ruine des missions des Jẽsuites dans la bassin de la Plata; leur ẽtat actuel. Paris, C. Douniol, 1864. 88p.

977 MARTINEZ MENDIETA, Marcos. El imperio jesuĩtico y la Ciudad del Sol. FI 3 (1962) no. 2, 277-305.

978 MARTIRES jesuĩtas en la antigua provincia Paraguay, hoy Argentina. EBA 67 (1942) 110-28, 201-15.

979 MARYGROVE COLLEGE, DETROIT. A spiritual conquest: the Jesuit reductions in Paraguay 1610-1767. Detroit, Mich., Marygrove College, 1942. vi, 73p.

980 MATEOS, Francisco. La anulaciõn del Tratado de Limites con Portugal de 1750 y las Misiones del Paraguay. MH 11 (1954) 523-64.

981 MATEOS, Francisco. Cartas de indios cristianos del Paraguay. MH 6 (1949) 547-72.

982 MATEOS, Francisco. La guerra guaranítica y las misiones del Paraguay. MH 8 (1951) 241-316; 9 (1952) 75-121.

983 MATEOS, Francisco. Nuevos incidentes en las misiones del Paraguay hasta el final de la demarcación de límites, 1757-1760. MH 11 (1954) 135-92.

984 MATEOS, Francisco. Pedro de Cevallos, gobernador de Buenos Aires, y las misiones del Paraguay. MH 10 (1953) 313-75.

985 MATEOS, Francisco. El tratado de límites entre España y Portugal de 1750 y las misiones del Paraguay (1751-1753). MH 6 (1949) 319-78.
Also in MA 3 (1952) 531-73.

986 METRAUX, A. The contribution of the Jesuits to the exploration and anthropology of South America. MIA 15 (1944) 183-91.

986a MICO, Tomás L. Roque Gonzalez de Santa Cruz. A., Edit. Emasa, 1977. 99p. (Colección Cultura Paraguaya)

987 MIGRAY, Jozsef. Egy keresztényszociális állam története. A Jesuiták Köztársasága Paraguayban (1609-1768). Budapest, Népszava, 1923. 71p.

988 MILLE, Andrés. Derrotero de la Compañía de Jesús en la Conquista de Perú, Tucumán y Paraguay y sus iglesias del antiguo Buenos Aires, 1567-1768. B.A., Emecé, 1968. 539p.

989 MIRANDA, Francisco Javier. Vida del venerable sacerdote don Domingo Muriel, religioso un tiempo de la abolida Compañía de Jesús y último provincial de su Provincia del Paraguay, escrita por un disipulo suyo. Córdoba, Arg., 1916. ix, 547p.

990 MOLINA, Raúl A. Las primeras reducciones franciscanas y jesuíticas. La enorme gravitación de Hernandarias de Saavedra en sus fundaciones y legislación. EBA 80 (1948) 93-117, 263-283.

991 MONNER SANS, Ricardo. Misiones guaraníticas, 1607-1800; pinceladas históricas. B.A., "La Argentina Sociedad Cooperativa de Libreria", 1892. 232p.

991a MÖRNER, Karl Robert Stellan. Framstallning af Paraguays och dithörande Jesuitermissioners historia, fran landets upptäckande till 1813. Upsala, Wahlstrom, 1858. 102p.

992 MÖRNER, Magnus. The Guarani missions and the segregation policy of the Spanish Crown. AHSJ 30 (1961) 367-86.

993 MÖRNER, Magnus. Misiones guaraníticas de los jesuitas. *In* La CORONA Española y los foraneos en los pueblos de Indios de America. Stockholm, Almqvist & Wiksell, 1970. p. 315-25. (Instituto de Estudios Ibero-Americanos, Estocolmo. Publicaciones Ser. A. Monografias Num. 1)

994 MÖRNER, Magnus. The political activities of the Jesuits in the La Plata region. The Hapsburg era. Stockholm, Library and Institute of Ibero-American Studies, 1953. 254p.

995 MÖRNER, Magnus. Un procurador jesuita del Paraguay ante la corte de Felipe V. HBAM 15 (1971) no. 3, 367-443.

996 MÖRNER, Magnus. La vida económica de los Indios en las Reducciones Jesuiticas. EBA 78 (1948) 22-34.

997 MULHALL, Marion McMurrough. Explorers in the New World before and after Columbus and the story of the Jesuit Missions of Paraguay. London, Longmans, Green, 1909. xiii, 313p.

998 O'NEILL, George. Golden years on the Paraguay: a history of the Jesuit missions from 1660 to 1767. L., Burns, Oates & Washbourne, 1934. xii, 267p.

999 OTRUBA, Gustavo. Der Anteil österreichischer Jesuitenmissionäre am "heiligen Experiment" von Paraguay. MIOG 63 (1955) 430-45.

1000 OTRUBA, Gustavo. Der Jesuitenstaat in Paraguay. Idee und Wirklichkeit. Vienna, Bergland, 1962. 189p. (Österreich-Reihe, 157-59)

1001 OTRUBA, Gustav. Die Wirtschaftsverfassung des "Jesuitenstaates" in Paraguay nach dem Zwettler Cod. 420 (P. Florian Baucke). AV 11 (1956) 116-34.

1001a El P. ANTONIO Ruiz de Montoya, su vida y su obra, by Raul Alvarez and others. Posadas (Arg.), Instituto Superior del Profesorado Antonio Ruiz de Montoya, Departamento de Historia, 1974. xxi, 103p.

1002 PASTELLS, Pablo. Historia de la Compañía de Jesús en la provincia del Paraguay (Argentina, Paraguay, Uruguay, Perú, Bolivia y Brasil) según los documentos originales del Archivo General de Indias. Madrid, V. Suarez, 1912-49. 8 vols.

1003 PEREZ ACOSTA, Fernando. Las misiones del Paraguay. Recuerdos históricos de una vida feliz entre los indios guaranies. Palamós, L. Castelló, 1920. 53p.

1004 PFOTENHAUER, J. Die Missionen der Jesuiten in Paraguay. Ein Bild aus der älteren römischen Missionsthätigkeit zugleich eine Antwort auf die Frage nach dem Werte römischer Mission, sowie ein Beitrag zur Geschichte Südamerikas. Gütersloh, C. Bertelsmann, 1891-93. 3 vols.

1005 PLA, Josefina. Las misiones jesuíticas guaranies. La circumstancia histórica. Organización social y económica. Ambiente y obra cultural. CA 22 (1963) 131-61.

1005a POPESCU, Oreste. El sistema económico en las misiones jesuitícas. Bahia Blanca, Edit. Pampa Mar, 1952. 125p.
2. ed. El sistema económico en las misiones jesuíticas: un vasto experimento de desarrollo indoamericano. Barcelona, Ediciones Ariel, 1967. 198p.

1006 QUELLE, O. Das Problem des Jesuitenstaates Paraguay. Ein Beitrag zur Geschichte Südamerikas und des dortigen Deutschtumes. IA 8 (1934) 260-82.

1007 RADA, Andrés. Dos cartas inéditas del Padre Andrés de Rada acerca de las Reducciones del Paraguay. Años 1666 y 1667. BRAH 37 (1900) 301-17.

1008 RASTOUL, Amand. Une organisation socialiste chrétienne: les Jésuites au Paraguay. Paris, Bloud, 1907. 61p. (Science et religion, études pour le temps présent. Vol. 420. Question de sociologie.)

1009 RELACIONES documentales. Inventario de las misiones Jesuíticas de Paraguay, Mojos y Chiquitos, recopiladas por Francisco Javier Bravo. AIAAIE 14 (1961) 112-19.

1010 RICHTER, Friedrich Wilhelm. Die sieben Missionen, eine kulturhistorische Skizze vom Aufsteig und Niedergang der Jesuitenmissionen bei den Guarany-indianern Süd-Amerikas. Porto Alegre, Typ. do Centro, 1930. 55p.

1011 RIEGO, Manuel Luis de. El imperio jesuítico del Paraguay. AMH 17 (1943) 27-30.

1012 ROJAS, Alberto. Los Jesuítas en el Paraguay (y otros artículos). A., 1936. 140p.

1013 ROJAS, Antonio. Un conquistador paraguayo: Beato Roque González de Santa Cruz. 3. ed. A., 1964. 42p.

1014 ROJAS, Antonio. Trayectorias de un corazón. A., 1960. 16p.
On the Jesuit martyrs of 1628.

1014a ROQUE González de Santa Cruz, colonia y reducciones en el Paraguay de 1600, by Rafael E. Velázquez and others. A., 1975.

1015 ROSA, Enrico. Primize di martiri dell'America Latina; i beati Rocco Gonzalez de S. Cruz, Alfonso Rodriguez e Giovanni del Castillo di C. de G. Rome, Tip. della Pontifica Universitá gregoriana, 1934. 216p.

1016 RUIZ MORENO, Aníbal. La lucha antiacohólica de los Jesuitas en la época colonial. EBA 62 (1939) 339-52, 423-46.

1017 RUIZ MORENO, Aníbal. El urbanismo en las misiones jesuíticas; trabajo del segundo año de adscripción a la cátedra de historia de la medicina de la Facultad de ciencias médicas de Buenos Aires. B.A., Tall. de la Edit. de A. Moly, 1940. 48p.

1018 SAGOT, François. Le communisme au nouveau monde: Réductions du Paraguay. Sociétés communistes des Etats Unis. Dijon, L. Venot, 1900. vi, 235p.

1019 SALVA, Jaime. Semblanzas misioneras. El P. Pedro Juan Andreu, S.J. Provincial del Paraguay. MH 4 (1947) 65-136.

1020 SANABRIA-FERNANDEZ, Hernando. Cristóbal de Mendoza, un misionero cruceño en tierras guaraníticas. Santa Cruz de la Sierra, Bolivia, Edit. Santa Cruz, 1947. 76p.

1020a SANABRIA-FERNANDEZ, Hernando. Cristóbal de Mendoza, el apóstol de los guaraníes. La Paz, Biblioteca del Sesquicentenario de la República, 1976. 132p.

1021 SCHMIDT, Franz. Der christlich-soziale Staat der Jesuiten in Paraguay in wirtschaftlicher und staatsrechtlicher Bedeutung. Glabach, Volksvereins-verlag, 1913. 60p.

1022 SOSSON, A. Egalité, fraternité, prosperité. VU 264 (1969) 2-21.

1022a STERZA, Andrea. Il comunismo dell'antica Sparta, della primitiva chiesa e del Paraguai sotto la direzione dei Gesuiti. Parma, Premiata Tipografia Grazioli, 1895. 154p.

1022b STORNI, Julio Juan de Mata Santiago. El comunismo jesuítico guaraní en las regiones del Plata. Tucumán, Edit. La Raza, 1940. 91p.

1023 SUAREZ, Sofia. El fenómeno sociológico del trabajo industrial en las misiones jesuíticas. B.A., 1920. 400p.

1024 SVIATLOVSKY, Vladimir Vladimirovich. Kommunisticheskoe gosudarstvo iezuitov v Paragvae v XVII i XVIII st. Petrograd, Put' k znaniiu, 1924. 53p.

1025 TEPP, Max. Die Indianreduktion in Jesuitenstaat. SU 3 (1953) 568-73.

1026 TESCHAUER, Carlos. Vida e obras de Venerável Roque Gonzãlez de Santa Cruz, primero apostolo do Rio Grande do Sul. Contribuiçao a historia da civilizaçao do Brasil. 2 ed. Rio Grande do Sul, Ediçao da Livraria americana, 1913. 191p.

1027 TISSERA, Ramón. De la civilización a la barbarie: la destrucción de los misiones guaraníes. Prólogo de Arturo Jauretche. B.A., A. Peña Lillo, 1969. (Colección El Ensayo americano, 21)

1028 TORRE REVELLO, José. Informe sobre las Misiones de Indios existentes en la segunda mitad del siglo XVIII, en las provincias del Paraguay. BIIH 13 (1931) 99-123.

1028a TORRES, Santiago. Vida del P. Juan Saloni, de la Compañía de Jesús, primer superior de la Missión del Paraguay. Barcelona, 1893. 112p.

1029 VON DER HEYDTE, Friedrich A. Las reducciones del Paraguay. EA 6 no. 27 (1953) 561-69.

1030 WAGNER, Richard. Die Mojosindianer; eines Jesuitenmission im 18 Jahrhundert und ihre spätere Entwicklung. PM 77 (1931) 77-81.

1031 ZUBILLAGA, Felice. Muratori storice delle missioni americane della Compagnie di Gesú "Il Cristianesimo Felice". RSCI 4 (1950) 70-100.

5. *War of independence*

1032 ABADIE-AICARDI, Aníbal. Acerca de los orígenes históricos de la conciencia nacional paraguaya. RIB 8 (1968) 38-57.
Review of no. 1064.

1032a AUTOS de la Revolución del Paraguay del 15 de mayo de 1811: copia facsimilar. A., Academia Paraguaya de la Historia, 1976. 406p.

1033 BENITES, Gregorio. La revolución de mayo, 1814-1815. A., Establecimiento tip. de Jordán & Villamil, 1906. 142, vip.

1034 BENITEZ, Justo Pastor. Algunos congresistas del 20 de junio de 1811. *In* no. 159, p. 21-42.

1035 BENITEZ, Justo Pastor. Una etapa de la emancipación paraguaya. BJHNA 10 (1937) 127-39.

1036 BENITEZ, Justo Pastor. Progenie de los próceres de Mayo. *In* no. 159, p. 13-20.

1037 BENITEZ, Justo Pastor. La revolución de mayo. A., Imp. Nac., 1940. 7p.

1038 BENITEZ, Justo Pastor. La revolución paraguaya del 15 de mayo de 1811. Ensayo de interpretación. RHA 43 (1957) 114-28.

1039 BENITEZ, Justo Pastor. Uno de los documentes de la doctrina de Mayo. *In* no. 159, p. 43-52.

1040 BLANCO SANCHEZ, Jesús L. El capitán don Antonio Tomás Yegros, prócer de la independencia nacional; conferencia. A., Instituto Paraguayo de Investigaciones Históricas, 1961. 28p.

1041 BRICE, Angel Francisco. Bolívar, conquistador del Paraguay. RSBV 23 no. 79 (1964) 352-65.
Also in BANHV 47 no. 185 (1964) 18-26.

1042 CARDOZO, Efraím. El Paraguay y Buenos Aires en 1811. BANHA 14 (1941) 297-316.

1043 CARDOZO, Efraím. La Princesa Carlota Joaquina y la independencia del Paraguay. RIM 14 no. 57-58 (1954) 359-83.

1044 CARDOZO, Efraím. La revolución de la independencia: las journadas de Mayo de 1811. *In* no. 272, p. 33-47.

1045 CARDOZO, Efraím. Una conferencia inédita en Tacauri. HP 1 (1956) 57-65.

1046 CENTURION, Carlos R. Precursores y actores de la independencia del Paraguay. A., Edit. Alas, 1962. 63p.

1047 CHAVES, Julio César. Belgrano y el Paraguay. La Plata, 1960. 52p.

1048 CHAVES, Julio César. Belgrano y el Paraguay. El Paraguay frente a la revolución. TC 9 (1960) 47-98.

1049 CHAVES, Julio César. Discurso. HP 2 (1957) 137-43.
Reflections on the independence of Paraguay.

1050 CHAVES, Julio César. Ideologia de la revolución Paraguaya del 14 y 15 de Mayo de 1811. HP 8-10 (1963-65) 151-62.

1051 CHAVES, Julio César. Paraguayos con San Martin. Conferencia pronunciada bajo los auspicios de la Casa Argentina en su local social el 7 de julio de 1955, en el acto de homenaje a la Argentina con motivo de la fiesta de julio. A., 1957. 28p.

1052 CHAVES, Julio César. La revolución del 14 y 15 de mayo, resumén. A., Librería Nizza, 1957. 80p. (Biblioteca histórica paraguaya de cultura popular, 1)

1053 CHAVES, Julio César. La revolución del 14 y 15 de mayo: sesquicentenario, 1811-1961. Relato y biografías de los próceres; introd., comentarios y notas. A., Edit. Asunción, 1961. 104p.

1054 COONEY, Jerry W. Paraguayan independence and Doctor Francia. AAAFH 28 (1972) 407-28.

1055 DECOUD, José Segundo. Recuerdos históricos; homenaje a los próceres de la independencia paraguaya. A., 1894. 20p.

1056 DOCUMENTOS. HP 1 (1956) 147-165.
11 letters, 1810-11.

1057 DOCUMENTOS. Independencia (documentos del año 1810). HP 3 (1957) 138-52.

1058 DOCUMENTOS. Reconstrucción del Congreso del 17 de junio. HP 2 (1958) 125-36.

1059 "EXPEDIENTE formado sobre el apresamiento de la Balandra Sn. Joseph y Animas de Dn. Manuel Doldan, procedente del Paraguay por el bergantín de S.M. El Parana". Juzgado de Presas, año 1811. Montevideo, año de 1811. HP 6-7 (1961-62) 105-25.

1060 GANDIA, Enrique de. Los prolegómenos de la independencia en el Paraguay. RIM 22, nos. 87-88 (1962) 30-40.

1061 GARAY, Blas. La revolución de la independencia del Paraguay. Madrid, Est. tip. de la viuda é hijos de Tello, 1897. 214p.
See no. 936a for reprint.

1062 GILL AGUIÑAGA, Juan B. Un documento inédito sobre la revolución de 14 y 15 de mayo de 1811. HP 6-7 (1961-62) 21-30.

1063 JORNADAS de Historia del Sesquicentenario de la Revolución Paraguay del 14 y 15 de mayo de 1811. HP 6-7 (1961-62) 82-88.

1064 KAHLE, Günter. Grundlagen und Anfänge des paraguayischen Nationalbewusstseins. Cologne, Universität zu Köln, 1962. 362p.

1065 LACONICH, Marco Antonio. Dos doctors de Cordoba frente a frente: José Gaspar de Francia y Pedro Somellera en la independencia del Paraguay. HP 8-10 (1963-65) 49-52.

1066 MOLAS, José Agustín de. Conferencia que tuvo el capellán del Exército del Paraguay D. José Agustín de Molas, con el General D. Manuel Belgrano, el dia 10 de mayo de 1811, en el Arroyo de Taquarí. Montevideo, Imp. de la Ciudad, 1811. 8 p.
Reprinted: Montevideo, 1951.

1067 MORENO, Fulgencio Ricardo. Estudio sobre la independencia del Paraguay. Tomo I. A., Tall. nac. de H. Kraus, 1911. 256p.
No more published.

1067a MORENO, Fulgencio Ricardo. Geografía etnográfica del Chaco; Estudio sobre la independencia del Paraguay. A., Instituto Colorado de Cultura, 1975. 498p. (Biblioteca Clasicos Colorados, 3)

1068 MOSQUEIRA, Silvano. Discurso del consul paraguayo don Silvano en el Centro paraguayo de Rosario al conmemorarse el 128 aniversario de la independencia nacional. Rosario de Santa Fé, Casa editora librería Alvarez, 1939. 15p.

1069 ORNSTEIN, Leopoldo R. El proceso al general Belgrano por el fracaso de la expedición al Paraguay. IE (1970) no. 9, 245-64.

1070 PEREZ ACOSTA, Juan Francisco. Les contingentes paraguayos de 1806 y 1807 (invasiones inglesas); relación nominal de jefes, oficiales y tropa, planillas, listas, gastos, vestuario, sanidad, etc. BIIH 26 nos. 89-92, (1942) 150-90.

1071 PEREZ ACOSTA, Juan Francisco. Quinta columna en Buenos Aires y Asunción, 1811 y 1812; peligrosas actividades. B.A., S. Peuser, 1944. 22p.
Also: BIIH 27 nos. 93-96 (1942-43) 155-72.

1072 PRIETO, Justo. Causas de la emancipación Paraguaya. RY 1 (1961) 3-12.

1073 PRIETO, Justo. Elementos ideológicos de la emancipación americana. A., Imp. Atalaya, 1975. 68p. (Ediciones de biblioteca popular, 1)

1074 QUEVEDO, Roberto. Paraguay, año 1806: juras al deseado Fernando VII. A., 1970. 16p.

1075 RAMOS, R. Antonio. Juan Andres Gelly en la revolución de Mayo de 1810. HP 1 (1956) 77-87.

1075a RAMOS, R. Antonio. La independencia del Paraguay y el imperio del Brasil. Rio de Janeiro, Conselho Federal de Cultura, 1976. 586p.

1076 La REVOLUCION del 15 de mayo, ilustrada para niños. A., Edit. Asunción, 1961. 31p.

1077 SALAS RAMIREZ, Jesús. Sobre la independencia de América; Bolivar y Paraguay. RUZ 9 no. 30 (1965) 71-81.

1078 SARAVI, Mario Guillermo. El cabildo del periodo revolucionario: un aporte para su estudio. HBA 9 no. 36 (1964) 3-21.

1078a SOSA ESCALADA, Juan Manuel. Caballero en ocasión del centenario paraguayo, 1811 - 15 de mayo - 1911. B.A., 1911. 24p.

1078b STEFANICH, Juan. El Paraguay en la emancipación americana. EP 3 no. 2 (1975) 7-44.

1079 VARGAS PEÑA, Angel. El mayor general José Ildefonso de Machain; ¿traidor o prócer? B.A., 1933. 58p.

1081 VELAZQUEZ, Rafael Eliado. El Paraguay en 1811. *In* no. 272, p. 16-32.

1082 VELAZQUEZ, Rafael Eliado. El Paraguay en 1811; estado político, económico y cultural en las postrimerías del período colonial. A., 1965. 104p.

1082a VELAZQUEZ, Rafael Eliado. La sociedad paraguaya en la época de la independencia. RPS 13 no. 35 (1976) 157-69.

1083 VITTONE, Luis. El Paraguay en la lucha por su independencia. A., Imp. Militar, 1960. 217p.

1084 WILLIAMS, John Hoyt. El gobernador Velasco y los portugueses. HP 13 (1969-70) 121-30.

1085 WILLIAMS, John Hoyt. Governor Velasco, the Portuguese and the Paraguayan revolution of 1811: a new look. AAAFH 28 (1972) 441-49.

G. 1811-1870

1. *General studies*

1086 ALPEROVICH, M.S. Arkadiia novogo sveta (neizvestnye materialy o Paragvae 20kh godov XIXv.) NNI 13 (1969) 112-24.

1087 AMARILLA FRETES, Eduardo. Independencia del Paraguay. A., "El Arte", 1943. 26p.

1088 AVALOS, José del Pilar. Romance del libertador: el glorioso coronel José Félix Bogado. A., Ministerio de Defensa Nacional, 1961. 41p. (Paraguayo histórico, 5)

1089 BAEZ, Cecilio. La tiranía en el Paraguay; sus causas, caracteres y resultados; colección de artículos publicados en "El Civico". A., Tip. de "El País", 1903. 291p.

1090 BARRA, Federico de la. Narraciones, 1845-1846-1847. B.A., Imp. litografía y encuadernación de J. Peuser, 1897. 270p.

1091 BEALER, Lewis W. Francia, supreme dictator of Paraguay; Carlos Antonio Lopez, organizer and dictator of the Paraguayan republic; Francisco Solano Lopez, a dictator run amuck. *In* WILGUS, A. Curtis. South American dictators during the first century of independence. Washington, The George Washington University Press, 1937. p. 58-77; p. 136-72.

1092 BENITEZ, Justo Pastor. Independencia y organización del estado, 1811-1870. *In* LEVENE, Ricardo. Historia de América. B.A., W.M. Jackson, 1940-41. Vol. 5, 295-332.

1093 BENITEZ, Justo Pastor. Temas de la cuenca del Plata. Montevideo, Imp. "El Siglo ilustrado", 1949. xiv, 121p.

1094 BENITEZ, Luis G. La Junta Superior Gubernativa y el sesquicentenario de la proclamación de la república, 1813-1963. A., El Arte, 1964. 16p.

1095 EL CORONEL Bogado. *In* no. 3776, 19-52.

1096 BUENOS AIRES. MUSEO MITRE. Contribución documental para la história del Río de la Plata. B.A., Imp. de Coni hermanos, 1913. 5 vols.

1097 CARDOZO, Efraím. Artigas y el Paraguay. RIHGU 19 (1952) 11-52.

1098 CARDOZO, Efraím. Bolívar y el Paraguay. *In* SEGUNDO congreso internacional de historia de América reunido en Buenos Aires en los días 5 a 14 de julio de 1937. B.A., 1938. Vol. 4, p. 133-40.

1099 CARDOZO, Efraím. Tensiones en la ideologia de la revolución emancipadora. RCHG 128 (1960) 11-56.

1100 CARRANZA, Adolfo P. El coronel José Felix Bogado en las guerras de la independencia. A., Zamphirópolos, 1963? 27p.

1101 CARRANZA, Carlos Alberto. Polonia y Paraguay. B.A., El Comercio, 1912. 54p.
A comparison of Paraguayan history with Polish history.

1102 CARRASCO, Gabriel. La población del Paraguay, antes y después de la guerra; rectificación de opiniones generalmente aceptadas. A., Tall. nac. de H. Kraus, 1905. 26p.

1103 CENTURION, Carlos R. La obra de la primera junta gubernativa. HP 6-7 (1961-62) 37-52.

1104 COONEY, Jerry W. Abolition in the Republic of Paraguay: 1840-1870. JGSWGL 11 (1974) 149-66.

1105 DECOUD, Hector Francisco. El Campamento de Laurelty. Montevideo, El Siglo Ilustrado, 1930. 19p.

1106 DIAZ, Antonio. Historia política y militar de las repúblicas del Plata desde el año de 1828 hasta el de 1866. Montevideo, Imp. de "El Siglo", 1877-78. 12 vols. in 6.

1107 DIAZ PEREZ, Viridiato. La remuneración del trabajo en el viejo Paraguay. RAP 3 (1945) 24-31.

1108 DOMINGUEZ, Manuel. El Paraguay, sus grandezas y sus glorias. B.A., Edit. Ayacucho, 1946. 245p.

1109 EZCURRA MEDRANO, Alberto. La independencia del Paraguay; história de una desmembración argentina. B.A., Tall. gráf. de Ediciones católicas argentinas, 1941. 101p.

1110 GELLY, Juan Andrés. El Paraguay; lo que fue, lo que es, y lo que será. Prólogo de J. Natalicio González. Paris, Edit. de Indias, 1926. 165p.

1111 GELLY, Juan Andrés. El Paraguay, lo que fue, lo que es y lo que será. Por un extranjero que residió seis años en aquel país. Obra publicada bajo los auspicios de la Legación del Paraguay en la corte del Brasil. A., Imp. de la República, 1949. 63p.

1112 (GELLY, Juan Andrés). Paraguay, in zijnen vroegeren en legenwoordigen toestand, met een blik op zijne teokomst. n.p., 1848. 96p.

1113 (GELLY, Juan Andrés). Le Paraguay. Son passé, son présent et son avenir. Par un étranger qui a résidé six ans dans ce pays. Ouvrage publié sous les auspices de la légation du Paraguay au Brésil. Rio de Janeiro, Typ. imp. e const. de J. Villeneuve e comp., 1840. 81p.

1114 (GELLY, Juan Andrés). Le Paraguay; son passé, son présent et son avenir, par un étranger qui a vécu longtemps dans ce pays, ouvrage publié à Rio-Janeiro en 1848, et reproduit en France par le général oriental Pacheco-y-Obes. Paris, Imp. de Madame de Lacombe, 1851. 78p.

1115 (GELLY, Juan Andrés). O Paraguay. Seu passado, presente e futuro. Por um estrangeiro que residio seis annos naquelle paiz. Obra publicada sob os auspicios da Legaçao do Paraguay na corte do Brazil. Rio de Janeiro, Typ. imp. e const. de J. Villeneuve e comp., 1848. 77p.
This work, first published anonymously, is a series of essays in the form of letters.

1116 GRATTY, Alfredo M. du. La República del Paraguay, traducida del francés al castellano por Carlos Calvo. Encargado de negocios del Paraguay cerca de los gobiernos de Francia y de la Gran Bretaña, etc. Besanzon, 1862. xlii, 364, 169p.

1117 HOPKINS, Edward Augustus. La tirania del Paraguay, a la faz de sus contemporáneos. B.A., Imp. argentina de El Nacional, 1856. iii, 27p.

1117a KEGLER DE GALEANO, Anneliese. Alcance histórico-demográfico del censo de 1846. RPS 13 no. 35 (1976) 71-121.

1118 MAIZ, Fidel. Desagravio. A., Imp. La Mundial, 1916. 135p.

1119 MAIZ, Fidel. Etapas de mi vida: contestación a las imposturas de Juan Silvano Godoy. A., Imp. La Mundial, 1919. 232p.

Reprinted: A., Impreso por la Oficina de Prensa del Ministerio de Hacienda, 1970. 232p.

1120 MASSARE DE KOSTIANOVSKY, Olinda. José Berges, malogrado estadista y diplomático. A., Tall. gráf. de la Penitenciaría Nacional, 1969. 40p.

1121 MASSARE DE KOSTIANOVSKY, Olinda. El Vice Presidente Domingo Francisco Sánchez. A., 1972. 196p.

1122 NAGY, Arturo; PEREZ-MARICEVICH, Francisco. Paraguay: imagen romántica, 1811-1853. A., Edit. del Centenario, 1969. 218p. (El Paraguay en la opinión mundial, 1)

An anthology from contemporary sources.

1123 PARAGUAY. CONGRESO NACIONAL. Monumento a Artigas. A., Imp. nac., 1926. 59p.

1124 NOTAS biográficas de Manuel Pedro de Peña (el ciudadano paraguayo) conmemorando el centenario de su nacimiento, 1811-1911. A., Robles, Herrando & cia, 1911? 52p.

1125 ODDONE, Rafael. Esquema político del Paraguay. B.A., Edit. Asunción, 1948. 223p.

1126 PEREZ ACOSTA, Juan F. Una gestión de don Pedro de Angelis en el Paraguay. BIIH 25 nos. 85-88 (1941) 188-91. (Plans for a cathedral in Asunción, 1842.)

1127 PETERSON, Harold F. Edward A. Hopkins: a pioneer promoter in Paraguay. HAHR 22 (1942) 245-61.

1128 PLA, Josefina. Los británicos en el Paraguay: 1850-1870. RHA 70 (1970) 339-91; 71 (1971) 23-65.

1129 PLA, Josefina. The British in Paraguay 1850-1870; translated by Brian Charles MacDermot. Richmond (Eng.), Richmond Publishing Co., in association with St. Antony's College, Oxford, 1976. xxv, 277p.

1130 POUCEL, Benjamin. Le Paraguay moderne et l'intérêt général du commerce fondé sur les lois de la géographie et sur les enseignements de l'histoire, de la statistique et d'une saine économie politique. Marseille, Typographie M. Olive, 1867. 336, ccxiiip.

1131 QUENTIN, Charles. An account of Paraguay: its history, its people and its government from the French of M. Ch. Quentin. London, Trübner, 1865. 90p.

1132 QUENTIN, Charles. Le Paraguay. Paris, Garnier frères, 1865. 104p.

1133 RAMOS, R. Antonio. Discurso del Presidente de la Sociedad Bolivariana del Paraguay. RSBV 19 no. 64 (1960) 522-26.
Includes a brief sketch of José Felix Bogado.

1134 RAMOS, R. Antonio. Gestiones del Brasil, en América y Europe para el reconocimiento de la independencia del Paraguay. *In* no. 272, p. 53-58.

1135 RAMOS, R. Antonio. Gestiones en Alemania para el reconocimiento de la independencia del Paraguay. JGSWGL 5 (1968) 235-63.

1136 RAMOS, R. Antonio. Gestoes do Brasil, na América e na Europa, para o reconhecimento da independencia do Paraguai. RIHGB 244 (1959) 300-17.

1137 RAMOS, R. Antonio. Juan Andrés Gelly. B.A., The Author, 1972. 514p.
An important biography.

1138 RAMOS, R. Antonio. Juan Andrés Gelly y la primera legación del Paraguay en Europa. Misión del general López. RIM 16 no. 65 (1956) 413-33.

1139 RAMOS, R. Antonio. El Paraguay y San Martín: conferencia pronunciada en el paraninfo de la Universidad Nacional el 25 de febrero de 1950. A., Imp. "Paraguay", 1950. 12p.

1140 SOCIEDAD BOLIVARIANA DEL PARAGUAY. Sesquicentenario de la batalla de Carabobo. A., 1971. 61p.

1140a TRIAS, Vivian. El Paraguay de Francia el Supremo a la guerra de la Triple Alianza. B.A., Crisis, 1975. 79p.

1141 VELILLA, Benjamin. Parentesco de Bernardo de O'Higgins con los yegros del Paraguay. HP 6-7 (1962) 31-36.

1142 WARREN, Harris G. Dr. William Stewart in Paraguay, 1857-1869. AAAFH 25 (1969) 247-64.

1143 WILLIAMS, John Hoyt. Esclavos y pobladores: observaciones sobre la historia parda del Paraguay en el siglo XIX. RPS 11 no. 31 (1974) 7-27.

1143a WILLIAMS, John Hoyt. Foreign técnicos and the modernization of Paraguay, 1840-1870. JIAS 19 (1977) 233-58.

1144 WILLIAMS, John Hoyt. Observations on the Paraguayan census of 1846. HAHR 56 (1976) 424-37.

1145 WILLIAMS, John Hoyt. Paraguay's nineteenth-century "Estancias de la República". AH 47 (1973) 206-15.

2. José Gaspar Rodriguez Francia

1146 AYALA, Elias. El Dr. Francia: apologia en el primer centenario de su fallecimiento 20-x-40. A., Imp. Militar, 1942. 11p.

1147 BAEZ, Cecilio. Ensayo sobre el Dr. Francia y la dictadura en Sud-América. A., H. Kraus, 1910. 198p.

1148 BAEZ, Cecilio. En torno al General Artigas. RNM 25 no. 74, (1944) 210-19.

1149 BALLARDE BIGAIRE, Luis. José Gaspar Rodríguez de Francia, primer dictador perpetuo sud americano. B.A., Edit. "Urbe", 1942. 216p.

1150 BENITEZ, Justo Pastor. José Gaspar de Francia dictator of Paraguay. BPAU 74 (1940) 737-42.

1151 BENITEZ, Justo Pastor. La vida solitaria del dr. José Gaspar de Francia, dictador del Paraguay. Montevideo, Imp. "El Siglo Ilustrado", 1938. 17p.

1152 BENITEZ, Justo Pastor. La vida solitaria del dr. José Gaspar de Francia, dictador del Paraguay. B.A., Librería y edit. "El Ateneo", 1937. 275p.

1153 BENITEZ, Justo Pastor. Un perfil de Dr. José Gaspar de Francia. RNC 18 no. 114 (1956) 113-17.

1154 BOLIVAR, Francia y Bonpland. BSBP 2 (1957) 35.
A letter from Bolívar to Francia, 1832.

1155 CABANELLAS, Guillermo. El dictador del Paraguay, Dr. Francia. B.A., Edit. Claridad, 1946. (Biblioteca de grandes biografias. Ser. B, 12)
The standard biography of Francia.

1156 CARDOZO, Efraím. El plan federal del Dr. Francia; discurso de incorporación en la Academia Nacional de la Historia de Buenos Aires. B.A., 1941. 24p.

1157 CARLYLE, Thomas. Dr. Francia. FQR 31 (1843) 544-89.
Reprinted in the various editions of Carlyle's collected essays.

1158 CARLYLE, Thomas. El dictador de Francia. B.A., Guarania, 1937. 138p.

1159 CHAVES, Julio César. Los restos mortales del Doctor José Gaspar Rodríguez de Francia. A., Ministerio del Interior, 1962. 77p.

1160 CHAVES, Julio César. El supremo dictador, biografía de José Gaspar de Francia. B.A., Edit. Difusam, 1942. 402p.
2. ed. B.A., Edit. Ayacucho, 1946. 427p.
3. ed. B.A., Ediciones Nizza, 1958. 456p. (Obras paraguayas, 8)
4. ed. Madrid, Edit. Atlas, 1964. 488p.

1161 FRANCIA, the dictator. NMN 43 (1835) 417-29; 44 (1835) 34-43, 183-89.

1162 FRANKL, Víctor. El jusnaturalismo tomista de fray Francisco de Vitoria como fue e del plan de Confederación hispanoamericana del Dr. José Gaspar de Francia. RHA 37-38, (1954) 163-204.

1163 GARAY, Blás Manuel. Descripción de las honras fúnebres que se hicieron al Excmo. Sr. Dr. D. José Gaspar Rodríguez de Francia, supremo dictador perpetuo de la República del Paraguay. A., Tall. nac. de H. Kraus, 1898. 71p.

1164 IBARRA, Alonso. José Gaspar de Francia; el supremo defensor del Paraguay. A., Trujillo, 1961. 121p.
Uncritical.

1164a IRALA BURGOS, Adriano. La ideología del Dr. Francia. A., I.D.I.A., 1975. 91p.

1164b IRIGOYEN DUPRAT, Eduardo. Las Heras, Bolívar y el Paraguay; capitulo de una tesis profesoral. B.A., Plantié, 1956. 18p.

1165 KAHLE, Günter. Die Diktatur Dr. Francias und ihre Bedeutung für die Entwicklung des paraguayischen Nationalbewusstseins. JGSWGL 1 (1964) 238-82.

1166 KAHLE, Günter. Ein südamerikanischer Diktator, Dr. Francia von Paraguay, im Spiegel der europäischen Geschichtschreibung. SM 15 (1964) 249-59.

1166a LAFUENTE MACHAIN, Ricardo de. Muerte y exhumación del supremo dictador perpetuo del Paraguay. B.A., Tall gráf. de S. de Amorrortu e hijos, 1943. 22p.

1166b LLANOS, Julio. El Dr. Francia. A., Moen y hermano, 1907. 11-81p.

1167 MORENO, Fulgencio R. Origen del Dr. Francia. HP 3 (1958) 15-19.

1168 MIROSHEVSKY, V. Khose Gaspar Francia, vozhd paragvaiskoi revoliutsionnoi demokratii, 1814-1840. VI 1946, no. 4, 68-81.

1169 A NARRATIVE of facts connected with the change effected in the political condition and relations of Paraguay, under the directions of Dr. Thomas (sic) Francia, by an individual who witnessed many of them, and obtained authentic information respecting the rest. London, W. Mason, 1826. 56p.

1170 NAVARRO, Ramón Gil. Veinte años en un calabozo, ó sea la desgraciada historia de veinte y tantos argentinos muertos ó envejecidos en los calabozos del Paraguay. Rosario, Imp. de El Ferro-Carril, 1863. 87p.
Reprinted: A., Edit.-Tall. gráf. Zamphirópolos, 197? 133p.

1171 NOGUES, Alberto. La iglesia en la época del Dr. Francia; discurso de incorporación al Instituto Paraguayo de Investigaciones Históricas, leído el 22 de abril de 1960. A., El Gráfico, 1960. 32p.

1172 NOGUES, Alberto. El provisor Roque Antonio Céspedes Xeria. HP 3 (1958) 45-64.

1172a O'CONNOR d'ARLACH, Tomás. Rozas, Francia y Melgarejo. La Paz, González y Medina, 1914. iv, 142p.

1173 PACIELLO, Oscar. Inspiración romana en el pensamiento del Dr. Francia: trabajo presentado al Primer Congreso Latinoamericano de Derecho Romano. A., 1976. 72p.

1174 PEREZ ACOSTA, Juan Francisco. El doctor Francia y la influencia de Córdoba. Breves comentarios a Ramos Mejía. *In* SEGUNDO congreso internacional de historia de América reunido en Buenos Aires en los días 5 a 14 de julio de 1937. B.A., 1938. Vol. 2, 396-409.

1175 PEREZ ACOSTA, Juan Francisco. Francia y Bonpland. Con apéndice documental. B.A., Tall. s.a. Casa Jacobo Peuser, 1942. 58, xv, 3p. (Publicaciones del Instituto de investigaciones históricas, 79)

1176 PEREZ ACOSTA, Juan Francisco. Gaspar Rodríguez de Francia y Pedro Ferré. BIIH 24 no. 81-84 (1940) 112-36.

1176a RAMOS, R. Antonio. Falsedades en la historia del Dr. José Gaspar Rodriguez de Francia. A., 1975. 31p.

1177 RENGGER, Johann Rudolph; LONCCHAMP, Marcelin. Il Dottor Francia ed il Paraguay. Milan, Tip. Pirotta, 1837. 252p.

1178 RENGGER, Johann Rudolph; LONGCHAMP, Marcelin. Ensayo histórico sobre la revolución del Paraguay, y el gobierno dictatorio del doctor Francia, traducido al castellano por D.J.C. Pagès. Paris, Imp. de Moreau, 1828. xxxii, 309p.
Reprinted: A., Imp. de "La Reforma", 1882. vii, 88p.
Edición especial precedida de la biografía del tirano Francia, y continuada con algunos documentos y observaciones históricas, por M.A. Pelliza. B.A., C. Casavalle, 1883. 258p. A., Imp. de "La Democracía", 1897. xv, 128p.

1179 RENGGER, Johann Rudolph; LONGCHAMP, Marcelin. Essai historique sur la révolution du Paraguay, et le gouvernement dictatorial du docteur Francia. Paris, H. Bossange, 1827. xxxv, 300p.
2. ed. 1827.

1180 RENGGER, Johann Rudolph; LONGCHAMP, Marcelin. Historischer Versuch über die Revolution von Paraguay und die Dictatorial-Regierung von Dr. Francia. Ein Abschnitt der Reise nach Paraguay von J.R. Rengger und M. Longchamp. Stuttgart, J.G. Cotta, 1827. xx, 168p.

1181 RENGGER, Johann Rudolph; LONGCHAMP, Marcelin. The reign of Doctor Joseph Gaspard Roderick de Francia, in Paraguay; being an account of six years' residence

in that republic, from July 1819- to May, 1825. London, Hurst, E. Chance and co., 1827. xvi, 208p.
Reprinted: Washington, Documentary Publications, 1970. 208p.
Port Washington, N.Y., Kennikat Press, 1971. xvi, 208p.

1185 SAGUIER ACEVAL, Emilio. El Supremo. A., 1970. 617p.

1186 SORIA, Pablo. Informe del comisionado de la Sociedad del Rio Bermejo á los señores accionistas. B.A., Imp. del Estado, 1831. 60p.
On his imprisonment.

1187 TOBAL, Federico. El Dictador Francia ante Carlyle. B.A., 1893. 106p.

1188 VAZQUEZ, José Antonio. El doctor Francia, visto y oído por sus contemporáneos. A., Fondo Edit. Paraquariae, 1961. 928p.
A collection of contemporary documents.
Reprinted: B.A., Eudeba, 1975. 420p.

1188a VIOLA, Alfredo. Facetas de la política gubernativa del Dr. Francia. A., Cuadernos Republicanos, 1975. 33p.

1189 WILLIAMS, John Hoyt. The "Conspiracy of 1820" and the destruction of the Paraguayan aristocracy. RHA 75-76 (1973) 141-55.

1189a WILLIAMS, John Hoyt. Deadly selva: Paraguay's northern Indian frontier. AAAFH 33 (1976) 1-24.

1190 WILLIAMS, John Hoyt. Dictatorship and the Church: Doctor Francia in Paraguay. JCS 15 (1973) 419-36.

1190a WILLIAMS, John Hoyt. El Dr. Francia ante la Iglesia paraguaya. EP 2 no. 1 (1974) 139-54.

1190b WILLIAMS, John Hoyt. From the barrel of the gun: some notes on Dr. Francia and Paraguayan militarism. PAPS 119 (1975) no. 1, 73-86.

1191 WILLIAMS, John Hoyt. Paraguayan isolation under Dr. Francia: a re-evaluation. HAHR 52 (1972) 102-22.

1192 WILLIAMS, John Hoyt. Woodbine Parish and the "opening" of Paraguay. PAPS 116 (1972) 343-49.

1193 (WISNER, Enrique). El dictador del Paraguay, doctor José Gaspar Rodríguez de Francia. Concordia (E. Rios), 1923. 177p.

2. ed. Prólogo y notas de Julio César Chaves. B.A., Edit. Ayacucho, 1957. 170p.
Wisner was commissioned by Solano López to collect material on Francia.

1194 VARGAS PEÑA, Benjamin. "Vencer o morir": la próceres de la independencia, el doctor Francia, su política de aislamiento. A., La Colmena, 1933. 158p.

3. Carlos Antonio López

1195 BENITEZ, Justo Pastor. Carlos Antonio López, first constitutional president of Paraguay. BPAU 75 (1941) no. 3, 168-73.

1196 BENITEZ, Justo Pastor. Carlos Antonio López, estructuración del Estado Paraguayo. Prólogo de Julio César Chavez. B.A., Edit. Ayacucho, 1949. 298p.

1197 BENITEZ, Justo Pastor. Perfil de Carlos Antonio López. HP 4-5 (1960) 31-44.
Also in no. 272, 49-52.

1198 CHAVES, Julio César. Después de caseros: importante correspondencia entre el presidente Carlos Antonio López y el canciller Soares de Sousa, vizconde de Uruguay. HP 1 (1956) 103-9.

1199 CHAVES, Julio César. El presidente López: vida y gobierno de don Carlos. B.A., Edit. Ayacucho, 1955. 364p.
2. ed. B.A., Ediciones Difusam, 1968. xvi, 368p.
The best biography of López.

1200 LOPEZ, Carlos Antonio. La emancipación paraguaya; prólogo de J. Natalicio González. A., Edit. Guarania, 1942. 312p. (Biblioteca paraguaya)
Also in RABA, Mar.-Dec. 1942, 1-312.

1201 LOPEZ, Carlos Antonio. Mensajes de Carlos Antonio López, primer presidente constitucional de la república; primera edición autorizada por s.e. el señor ministro de justicia, culto e instrucción pública, dr. Justo Pastor Benítez, en la Resolución ministerial no. 685. A., Imp. nac., 1931. 139p.

1202 O'LEARY, Juan Emiliano. La alianza de 1845 con Corrientes; aparición de Solano López en el escenario del Plata; A., Imp. Militar, 1944. 295p. (Biblioteca de la "Revista de las FF. AA. de la Nación, 6)

1203 EL PARAGUAY y su gobierno. Refutación al folleto publicado por Hopkins, bajo el título de Tiranía del Paraguay. B.A., Imp. de la "Tribuna", 1856. 103p.

1204 PEREZ ACOSTA, Juan Francisco. Carlos Antonio López, obrero máximo, labor administrativa y constructiva. A., Edit. Guarania, 1948. 691p. (Biblioteca paraguaya)

1205 PEREZ ACOSTA, Juan Francisco. Gestiones de Carlos Antonio López ante Juan Manuel de Rosas, 1842-1844. BIIH, 28, no. 97-100 (1943-44) 34-61.

1206 PRIETO, Juan Pastor. Carlos Antonio López y la independencia del Paraguay. BJHNA 10 (1937) 43-58.

1207 PRIETO, Justo. 2 vidas ejemplares. B.A., Tall. graf. A. Plantie, 1939. 79p.

4. *Francisco Solano López*

1208 BARRETT, William E. Una amazona; biografía de Francisco Solano López y Elisa Lynch; traducida por Alejandro A. Rosa. B.A., Compañía editora del Plata, 1940. 382p.

1209 BARRETT, William E. Woman on horseback: the biography of Francisco Lopez and Elisa Lynch. N.Y., Frederick A. Stokes, 1938. xi, 362p.
Also: London, Peter Davies, 1938. 352p.
Reprinted: N.Y., Doubleday, 1952. xi, 362p.

1210 BLOMBERG, Héctor Pedro. La dama del Paraguay. B.A., Editora Inter-americana, 1942. 178p.
A biography of Eliza Lynch.

1211 BRAY, Arturo. Solano López, soldado de la gloria y del infortunio. B.A., Ed. Guillermo Kraft, 1945. 402p.
2. ed. A., 1958. 283p.
A fairly impartial biography of López.

1212 BRODSKY, Alyn. Madame Lynch & friend: a true account of an Irish adventuress and the dictator of Paraguay, who destroyed that American nation. N.Y., Harper & Row, 1975; London, Cassell, 1976. xx, 312p.
A very anti-Lynch study.

1213 CANET, J.P. Pancha Garmienda; el libro que no debe faltar en ningún paraguayo y cristiano. n.p., 1957. 59p.

1213a CALZADA, Isidoro. Solano López: mariscal del Paraguay. A., Edit. Don Bosco, 1970? 20p. (Galería de paraguayos ilustres, 6. Naranja)

1214 CANCOGNI, Manlio; BORIS, Ivan. Il Napoleone del Plata. Milan, Rizzoli, 1970. 248p.

1214a CANCOGNI, Manlio; BORIS, Ivan. El Napoleón del Plata; historía de una héroica guerra sudamericana. Barcelona, Edit. Noguer, 1972. 286p.

1215 CARDOZO, Efraím. Donde estan los restos del Mariscal López? HP 13 (1969-70) 29-45.

1215a CASCUDO, Luis da Camara. López do Paraguay. Natal (Brazil), Typ. d'"A Republica", 1927. 114p.

1216 COVA, Jesús Antonio. Solano López y la epopeya del Paraguay. Carátula y dibujo de Guevara. B.A., Edit. Venezuela, 1948. 258p. (Biblioteca indoamericana, 7)

4. ed. Caracas, Sociedad Hispano-Venezolana de Ediciones, 1956. 231p.

1217 DECOUD, Héctor Francisco. Elisa Lynch de Quatrefages. B.A., Librería "Cervantes", J. Suárez, 1939. 323p.

Profoundly anti-Lynch.

1218 GODOY, Juan Silvano. El barón de Rio Branco; La muerte del Mariscal López; El concepto de la Patria. A., Tall. nac., 1912. 299p.

1219 GONZALEZ, Juan Natalicio. Solano López y otros ensayos. Paris, Edit. de Indias, 1926. 167p.

1220 GONZALEZ, Juan Natalicio. Solano López, diplomático. Prólogo de Juan Frederico Garay. A., Imp. Militar, 1948. 121p. (Biblioteca de las FF. AA. de la Nación, 7)

1221 GRAHAM, Robert Bontine Cunningham. Portrait of a dictator: Francisco Solano López (Paraguay 1865-1870). London: Heinemann, 1933. 283p.

Anti-López, but a fairly balanced account.

1221a GRAHAM, Robert Bontine Cunningham. Retrato de un dictador, Francisco Solano López (Paraguay 1865-70). B.A., Inter-Americana, 1943. 271p.

1222 LOPEZ, Francisco Solano. Con la rúbrica del Mariscal: documentos. Compilador: Juan I. Livieres Argaña. A., Escuela Técnica Salesiana, 1960-

6 vols. were published by 1971, covering the years 1845-60. An important collection of documents.

1223 LOPEZ, Francisco Solano. Pensamiento político. Estudio preliminar: Francisco Solano López y el Paraguay nacionalista por Rodolfo Ortega Peña y Eduardo L. Duhalde. B.A., Edit. Sudestada, 1969. 214p. (Colección Pensamiento político)

1224 LOPEZ, Francisco Solano. Proclamas y cartas del mariscal López. B.A., Edit. Asunción, 1957. 203p.

1225 NAGY, Arturo; PEREZ-MARICEVICH, Francisco. El mariscal de la epopeya. A., Edit. del Centenario, 1970. 36p.

1226 NOGUES, Alberto. El General Lopez en Roma. HP 13 (1969-70) 47-63.

1227 O'LEARY, Juan Emiliano. Bolívar y Solano López. BSBP 5 (1965) 5-8.

1228 O'LEARY, Juan Emiliano. El héroe del Paraguay en el LX aniversario de su gloriosa muerte. Montevideo, Tall. gráf. Prometeo, 1930. 105p.

1229 O'LEARY, Juan Emiliano. El mariscal López. A., Tall. gráf. "La Prensa", 1920. 374p.
2. ed. Madrid, Imp. de F. Moliner, 1925. 403p.
A., Junta Patriótica Paraguaya, 1926. 460p.
3. ed. A., Casa América-Moreno Hnos., 1970. 452p.
O'Leary's study makes a national hero of López.

1230 EL PARAGUAYO independiente. 2. ed. A., Imp. de la República, 1859. 2 vols.
3. ed. A., Imp. nac., 1930. 2 vols.
A reprint of the Asunción periodical, no. 1 (April 26, 1845) - no. 118 (Sept. 18, 1852)

1231 EL PARAGUAYO independiente. Asunción, 1850. Reproducción facsimilar. Dirección: Ariosto D. Ganzález; prólogo: Carlos Pastore; bibliografía: Arturo Scarone. Montevideo, Imp. "El Siglo Ilustrado", 1950. 40p.
A reprint of no. 96 (Sept. 28, 1850).

1232 PEÑA, Manuel Pedro de. Cartas del ciudadano Manuel Pedro de Peña dirigidas á su querido sobrino Francisco Solano López. B.A., Imp. de la Sociedad tip. Bonaerense, 1865. 224p.

1233 PEREYRA, Carlos. Solano López y su drama. B.A., Ediciones de la Patria Grande, 1962. 169p.

1234 RAMOS GIMENEZ, Leopoldo. En el centenario del mariscal Francisco Solano López: refutaciones al sr. Lindolfo Coller. Sao Paulo, 1927. 62p.

1235 RAMOS GIMENEZ, Leopoldo. Los mensajes del mariscal Francisco Solano López a la posteridad. A., 1966. xii, 113p. (Anales de Paraguay, año 1, no. 3)

1236 RAMOS, R. Antonio. El vice-presidente Sánchez. HP 12 (1967-68) 27-36.

1237 REBAUDI, Arturo. Un tirano de Sudamérica, Francisco Solano López. B.A., Serantes hnos, 1925. 84p.

1238 RECALDE, Luciano. Carta primera al presidente López del Paraguay. B.A., Imp. de "El Orden", 1857. x, 30p.

1239 SODRE, Alcindo. Solano López, imperador. RIHGB 182 (1944) 105-15.

1240 (VARELA, Héctor Florencio). Elisa Lynch, por Orión. Precedida de una semblanza del autor, por Emilio Castelar. B.A., Imp. de la Tribuna, 1870. xvi, 419p.
Reprinted: B.A., Imp. de B.J. Rosso-Doblas, 1884. 363p.
B.A., 1934. 363p.
Varela is critical of Elisa Lynch.

1241 YNSFRAN, Pablo Max. Sam Ward's bargain with President López of Paraguay. HAHR 34 (1954) 313-31.

1242 YOUNG, Henry Lyon. Eliza Lynch, regent of Paraguay. London, Anthony Blond, 1966. 196p.
A rather slight work,

5. *The War of The Triple Alliance 1865-1870*

a) General accounts

1243 ALBUM de la guerra del Paraguay. t. 1-2 (entrega 1-45); 1 Feb. 1893-1896. Buenos Aires, 1893-96.
Published by the Asociación guerreros del Paraguay.

1244 ALMEIDA, Antonio da Rocha. Efemérides dos principais fatos relacionados com a Campanha. Porto Alegre, Pontifica Universidade Católica do Rio Grande do Sul, 1965. 124p.

1245 AMERLAN, Alberto. Bosquejos de la guerra del Paraguay; edición ilustrada por A. Methfessel. Con un apéndice de la Memoria militar del general Bartolomé

Mitre, publicada en "La Nación" del 22 y 23 de setiembre de 1903. B.A., Editores H. Tjarks y co., 1904. 111, 98p.
See no. 1467.

1246 AMERLAN, Albert. Nächte am Rio Paraguay: Krieges-bilder und Charakter-skizzen. B.A., H. Tjarks, 1886. 123p.
2. ed. 1890. 169p.
3. ed. 1898. 175p.

1247 AMERLAN, Albert. Nights on the Rio Paraguay; scenes of war and characterscetches (sic). With illus. by A. Methfessel. Trans. from the German by Henry F. Suksdorf. B.A., H. Tjarks, 1902. 158p.
A valuable account of the conflict.

1248 AMOITE Cerro Corá pe; ed. especial dedicada al centenario de la epopeya nacional. A., ABC color, 1970. 47p.

1249 BAPTISTA PEREIRA, Antonio. Civilisaçao contra barbarie, conferencia feita na Faculdade de direito de Bello Horizonte a 15 de abril de 1928. Sao Paulo, Rossetti & Camara, 1928. 174p.

1250 BAPTISTA PEREIRA, Antonio. Civilización contra barbarie; traducido del portugués por Luis Terán Gómez. La Paz, Imp. Arnos hños, 1935. viii, 216p.

1251 BARRETO, José Francisco Paes. Historia da Guerra do Paraguay. Recife, Typ. de F. Boulitreau, 1893. v, 136p.

1252 BARRETTO, Mario. "A campanha lopezguaya". Rio de Janeiro, Officinas graphicas de Archivo nacional, 1928-

1253 BENITES, Gregorio. Anales diplomático y militar de la guerra del Paraguay. A., Establecimiento tip. de Muñoz hnos, 1906. 2 vols.

1254 BEVERINA, Juan. La Guerra del Paraguay, 1865-1870; resumen histórico. B.A., 1943. 207p. (Círculo Militar. Biblioteca del suboficial, 118)
2. ed. 1973. 288p.

1255 BONIFAZI, Walter. Rugidos de leones. Dibujos de Walter Bonifazi, escritos de Juan A. Meza. A., 1968. 68p.

1256 BRITTO, José Gabriel de Lemos. Solano López e a guerra do Paraguay; replica ao livro de igual titulo do escriptor mexicano D. Carlos Pereyra. Rio de Janeiro, Typ. da Escola 15 de Novembro, 1927. 306, xp.

1257 BRUGADA, Ricardo. Uruguay-Paraguay; la guerra de la triple alianza. Córdoba (Arg.), Est. tip. "Los Principios, 1915". 16p.

1258 CARCANO, Ramón José. Guerra del Paraguay; acción y reacción de la Triple alianza. Ilustraciones de Ana Inés Cárcano. B.A., D. Viau y cía, 1941. 2 vols.

1259 CARDOZO, Efraím. Hace cien años; crónicas de la guerra de 1864-1870 publicadas en "La Tribuna" de Asunción en el centenario de la epopeya nacional. Mapas de Roberto Thompson. A., Ediciones EMASA, 1967-
7 vols. published by 1972, covering the years 1864-67.

1260 CARVAJAL, Alberto. Héroes y fundadores; ensayos de historia americana. Barcelona, Araluce, 1930. 240p.

1261 CARVAJAL, Alberto. Héroes y fundadores. Ed. modificada. Cali, Colombia, 1957. 178p.

1262 CARVALHO, Alberto Marquez de. Réponse aux articles de la "Patrie" sur la guerre du Paraguay. Paris, Typ. Hennuyer et fils, 1869. 40p.

1263 CARVALHO, Humberto Feliciano de. A guerra do Paraguai, A. Praça da Rendiçao, E os brasileiros desalmados. 2. ed. Uruguaiana (RGS) Novidade, 1954. 101p.

1264 EL CENTINELA; colección del semanario de los paraguayos en la guerra de la Triple Alianza, 1867. Prólogo de José Antonio Vázquez. A., Fondo Edit. Paraquariae, 1964. 1 vol. (unpaged).
A reprint of the weekly journal (no. 1-36: 1867) published in Asunción.

1265 CENTURION, Juan Crisóstomo. Memorias del coronel Juan Crisóstomo Centurión; ó sea, Reminiscencias históricas sobre la guerra del Paraguay. B.A., Imp. de J. Berra, 1894-1901. 4 vols.
Reprinted: Prólogo de J. Natalicio González, notas del mayor Antonio E. González. A., Edit. Guarania, 1944-45. 4 vols.

1266 (CENTURION, Juan Crisóstomo). Viaje nocturno de Gualberto, o Recuerdos y reflecciones de un ausente, por el paraguayo J.C. Roenicunt y Zenitram. N.Y., Imp. de E. Pérez, 1877. 64p.

1267 COUTO, Antonio Correa de. Disertación sobre el actual gobierno de la República del Paraguay, seguida de la descripción de Coimbra, del Pan de Azúcar y otros lugares; de los actos de vandalismo practicados en la provincia de Matto-Grosso, por su ordén: de la contestación á su pretendido derecho á la parte del territorio du dicha provincia, y de la indicación de los medios de poder hacérsele la guerra de desagravio de las atrocidades é insultos cometidos por sus oficiales y soldados. Rio de Janeiro, Imperial Instituto Artistico, 1865. 104p.

1268 CUNHA, Maurilio da. Guerra da tríplice aliança contra o governo do Paraguai. Rio de Janeiro, Escola de Aeronáutica, Campo dos Afonsos, 1946. 456p.

1269 DALLEGRI, Santiago. El Paraguay y la guerra de la Triple Alianza. B.A., Instituto Amigos del Libro Argentino, 1964. 272p.

1270 DIAS DA CRUZ LIMA, José. Réponse à un article de la Revue des deux mondes sur la guerre du Brésil et du Paraguay. Rio de Janeiro, Imprimerie universelle de Laemmart, 1869. 47p.
Reply to an article written by Elisée Reclus.

1270a DOMINGUEZ, Manuel. Paraguayos y Argentinos ante un héroe, 25 de mayo de 1907: discurso pronunciado por el Dr. Manuel Dominguez en la Recoleta al ser depositada por la Delegación Argentina sobre la tumba del General José E. Díaz una corona de bronce. *In* no. 203, 113-15.

1271 DUPRAT da LASSERRE, Dorothea. Guerra do Paraguay; memorias de Mme. Dorothea Duprat da Lasserre. Rio Grande, Livraria americana, 1893. 50p.

1272 EXPILLY, Charles. Le Brésil, Buenos Aires, Montevideo et le Paraguay devant la civilisation. Paris, H. Willems, 1866. 157p.

1273 EXPILLY, Charles. La vérité sur la conflit entre le Brésil, Buenos Aires, Montevideo et le Paraguay. Paris, Dentu, 1865. 32p.

1274 FIX, Nathanaël Théodore. La guerre du Paraguay. Paris, C. Tanera, 1870. viii, 222p.

1275 FIX, Nathanaël Théodore. Historia da guerra do Paraguay. Traduzida do francez por A.J. Fernando dos Reis. Rio de Janeiro, Livraria Garnier, 1872. 255p.

1276 (GARCIA, Manuel). Paraguay and the alliance against the tyrant Francisco Solano Lopez. General remarks-reliable documents. N.Y., Hallet & Breen, 1869. 40p.

1277 GIMENEZ VEGA, Elias S. Actores y testigos de la Triple Alianza. B.A., A. Peña Lillo, 1961. 96p. (Colección La Siringa, 20)

1278 GODOI, Juan Silvano. Monografias históricas. 1. série. B.A., F. Lajouane, 1893. xvi, 216p.
Includes studies of J.E. Diaz and F.S. López.

1279 GREAT BRITAIN. FOREIGN OFFICE. Correspondence respecting hostilities in the River Plate, etc. *British Parliamentary Papers* 1865, LVII, 199-398 (Papers-command 3463, 3514, 3552); 1866, LXXVI, 65-94 (3630); 1867, LXXIV, 647-714 (3795, 3945); 1867-68, LXXIII, 691-784 (3984, 3984-i).

1280 HOMENAJE de La Tribuna al centenario de la epopeya nacional. A., 1970. 24p.

1281 KENNEDY, Andrew James. La Plata, Brazil, and Paraguay, during the present war. London, E. Stanford, 1869. viii, 273p.

1282 KOLINSKI, Charles J. The death of Francisco Solano López. HI 26 (1963) 75-91.

1283 KOLINSKI, Charles J. Independence or death? The story of the Paraguayan War. Gainesville, University of Florida, 1965. xvi, 236p.

1284 GONZALEZ, Juan Natalicio. La guerra al Paraguay; imperialismo y nacionalismo en el Rio de la Plata. Prólogo a la nueva edición de las "Cartas Polemicas" de Bartolomé Mitre y Juan Carlos Gómez. A.-B.A., Edit. Guarania, 1940? 91p.
First published as a prologue to no. 1294.
Reprinted: B.A., Edit. Sudestada, 1968. 104p.

1285 LIMA, Luiz Flamarion Barreto. Guerra do Paraguai. Rio de Janeiro, Escola de Comando e Estado-Maior do Exército, 1967. 88p.

1286 MAC MAHON, Martin. La guerra en el Paraguay. HP 3 (1958) 20-44.
The English original is in Harper's New Monthly Magazine XI (1870) no. 239.

1286a MAGNASCO, Silvano. Guerra del Paraguay. B.A., "Argos" Imp., 1906. iv, 95p.

1287 MAIZ, Fidel. Discurso del pbro. Fidel Maiz, pronunciado hace 21 años en Piribebuy, é inédito entonces hoy se publica por no dejar de tener aun su actualidad. A., "Los Principios", 1912. 21p.

1288 MANNEQUIN, Théodore. A propos de la guerre contre le Paraguay par la Confédération argentine, l'Uruguay et le Brésil. Paris, Librairie de Guillaumin, 1866.
Reprinted from Journal des économistes, août 1866.

1289 MARQUES DE CARVALHO, Alberto. Réponse aux articles de La Patrie sur la guerre du Paraguay. Paris, Typ. Hennuyer et fils, 1869. 40p.

1290 MASTERMAN, George Frederick. Seven eventful years in Paraguay. A narrative of personal experience amongst the Paraguayans. London, S. Low, 1869. xv, 356p.
2. ed. 1870. xvi, 332p.

1291 MASTERMAN, George Frederick. Siete años de aventuras en el Paraguay. Traducido al español por David Lewis, Aumentada con notas rectificativas. B.A., Imp. Americana, 1870. 501p.
Reprinted: anotadas por el profesor Ubaldo de Dovitiis. Con ilustraciones y vistas del Paraguay. B.A., J. Palumbo, 1911. iv, 423p.

1292 MILTOS, Cuyo. Guerre du Paraguay. Mensonge et vérité. Paris, Dentu, 1867. 31p.

1292a MITRE, Bartolomé. Guerra del Paraguay. B.A., Biblioteca de "La Nación", 1911. 5 vol. (Archivo del General Mitre, t. II - t. VI)

1293 MITRE, Bartolomé. Cartas polémicas sobre la triple alianza y la guerra del Paraguay. B.A., Imp. de la Sociedad Anónima, 1871. 91p.

1294 MITRE, Bartolomé. Cartas polémicas sobre la guerra al Paraguay, prólogo de J. Natalicio González. A.-B.A., Edit. Guarania, 1940. 415p.

1295 MITRE, Bartolomé. Páginas históricas, polémica de la triple alianza, correspondencia cambiada entre el Gral. Mitre y el dr. Juan Carlos Gómez, con una introducción del dr. Jacob Larrain. La Plata, Imp. La Mañana, 1897. xxxi, 135p.

1296 MONTENEGRO, J. Arthur. Fragmentos históricos; homems e factos da guerra do Paraguay. 1a serie. Rio Grande, Typ. da Livraria Rio-Grandense, 1900. viii, 114p.

1297 MOSQUEIRA, Silvano. General José Eduvigis Díaz. B.A., Tall. S. Ostwald, 1900. 29p. (Galería Paraguaya, 1)

1298 NABUCO, Joaquim. La guerra del Paraguay. Versión castellana de Conzalo (sic) Reparaz. Paris, Garnier hermanos, 1901. 397p.
Reprinted: 1909.

1299 ORIGEN de la Guerra del Paraguay con las potencias aliadas del Rio de la Plata y Brasil; elementos de los beligerantes, organización de sus ejércitos y puntos estratégicos que ocupan. Barcelona, Gaspar, 1865. 31p.

1300 OROÑO, Nicasio. Opiniones y discursos sobre la libertad y la paz. B.A., Imp. y librería Boullosa, 1899. 345p.

1301 PALOMEQUE, Alberto. Conferencias históricas. Montevideo, Serrano & Berro, 1909. ii, 244p.

1301a PALOMEQUE, Alberto. La Guerra del Paraguay. Montevideo, n.d. 244p.

1302 PARAGUAY. A concise history of its rise, and progress; and the causes of the present war with Brazil. London, E. Wilson, 1867. 67p.

1303 PARAGUAY. CONGRESO NACIONAL. CAMARA DE DIPUTADOS. El mariscal López en la Cámara de Diputados; una sesión histórica, Agosto de 1926. A., Imp. nac., 1927. 68p.

1304 PARDO TOVAR, Andrés. El sacrificio de un pueblo. A., Comando en Jefe de las FF.AA. de la Nación, Dirección de Publicaciones, 1970. 23p.

1305 PEREYRA, Carlos. Francisco Solano López y la guerra del Paraguay. Madrid, Edit.-América, 1919. 270p. (Biblioteca de la juventud hispano-americana, 13)
Reprinted: B.A., Ediciones San Marcos, 1945. 208p.
B.A., 1953. 229p.
Solano López y su drama. B.A., Ediciones de la Patria Grande, 1962. 169p.
A very favorable account of Lopez.

1306 PHELPS, Gilbert. The tragedy of Paraguay. London, C. Knight; N.Y., St. Martin's Press, 1975. xvi, 288p.

1307 PEREGRINO, Umberto. A guerra do Paraguai, na obra de Machado de Assis. Joao Pessoa, Universidade Federal da Paraiba, Departamento Cultural, 1969. 37p. (Coleçao Ensaios contemporâneos, 3)

1308 POMER, Léon. La guerra del Paraguay: gran negocio! B.A., Ediciones Caldén, 1968. 428p. (Colección Procesos, 5)

1309 POMER, Léon. La guerra del Paraguay. B.A., Centro Editor de América Latina, 1971. 113p. (La Historia popular, 34)

1310 PROCESO a la Guerra del Paraguay por Carlos Guido y Spano et al. Prólogo de Léon Pomer. B.A., Ediciones Caldén, 1968. 222p. (Colección Procesos, 4)

1311 RAMOS GIMENEZ, Leopoldo. "Resurgiras Paraguay". Una oda histórica de Martin MacMahon. A., 1963. 127p. (Anales del Paraguay, 1)

1312 REBAUDI, Arturo. Guerra del Paraguay; la conspiración contre S.E. el presidente de la República, mariscal Don Francisco Solano López. B.A., Imp. "Constancia", 1917. vii, 157p.

1313 REBAUDI, Arturo. Guerra del Paraguay, un episodio. B.A., Imp. "Constancia", 1918. 188p.

1314 REBAUDI, Arturo. El Lopizmo; trozos selectos de la obra "Viajos en América y la guerra Sud Americana", por el mayor prusiano Max von Versen. B.A., 1923. 53p.

1315 REBOLLO PAZ, León. La guerra del Paraguay; historia de una epopeya, 1865-1965. B.A., Tall. gráf. Lombardi, 1965. 141p.

1316 RESQUIN, Francisco Isidoro. Datos históricos de la guerra del Paraguay con la Triple Alianza, escritos por Francisco Isidoro Resquín, el año 1875. Publicados por Dr. Angel M. Veneroso el año 1895. B.A., Compañía Sud-Americana de Billetes de Banco, 1895. 187p.
Reprinted: A., Dirección de Publicaciones de las FF.AA. de la Nación, 1971. iv, 156, 42p.

1317 RIVERA, Enrique. José Hernández y la guerra del Paraguay. B.A., Edit. Indoamérica, 1954. 121p. (Biblioteca de la nueva generación, 4)

1318 ROLON MEDINA, Anastasio. El lustro terrible. Versión cronográfica de la guerra del Paraguay contra la

Triple alianza, en el primer centenario de la hectacombe. A., Imp. "La Humanidad", 1964. 245p.

1319 SAGUIER ACEVAL, Emilio. La lucha por la libertad ... prólogo del dr. Justo Pastor Benitez. A., Imp. nac., 1940. 141p.

1319a SARMIENTO, Domingo Fidel. Correspondencia de Dominguito en la guerra de Paraguay: estudio preliminar, selección y notas de Andrés M. Carretero. B.A., Ediciones Librería El Lorraine, 1975. 107p.

1320 SCHNEIDER, Louis. A guerra da triplice allianca (Impero do Brazil, República Argentina e República Oriental do Uruguay) contra o governo do República do Paraguay, 1864-1870. Traduzido do allemao por Manoel Thomas Alves Nogueira. Annotado por J.M. da Silva Paranhos. Rio de Janeiro, Typ. americana, 1875-76. 2 vols.
Reprinted: Rio de Janeiro, H. Garnier, 1902-
Rio de Janeiro, 192?
Sao Paulo, Ediçoes Cultura, 1945. 2 vols.

1321 SCHNEIDER, Louis. Der Krieg der Triple-Allianz (Kaiserthum Brasilien, Argentinische Conföderation und Republik Banda Oriental del Uruguay) gegen die Regierung der Republik Paraguay. Berlin, B. Behr, 1872-1875. 3 vols.

1322 SEEBER, Francisco. Cartas sobre la guerra del Paraguay, 1865-1866. B.A., L.J. Rosso, 1907. 181p.

1323 SENA MADUREIRA, Antonio de. Guerra do Paraguay. Resposta ao sr. Jorge Thompson, auctor de - "Guerra del Paraguay" - e dos annotadores argentinos D. Lewis e A. Estrada. Rio de Janeiro, Typ. do Imperial instituto artistico, 1870. 183, xxx, 106p.

1324 SOARES, Alvaro Teixeira. O drama de Tríplice Aliança, 1865-1876. Rio de Janeiro, Brand, 1956. 359p.

1324a SOUSA, Eusebio de. Anedotario da guerra da Triplice Aliança, 1865-1870. Rio de Janeiro, Grafica Laemmert, 1944. 159p.

1325 SOUSA, Octaviano Pereira de. Historia da Guerra do Paraguai. Rio de Janeiro, Imprensa Nac., 1930. 497p.

1326 TALAVERA, Natalicio. La guerra del Paraguay; correspondencias publicadas en El Semanario. B.A., Ediciones Nizza, 1958. 137p.

1327 TEIXEIRA MENDES, Raymundo. A guerra do Paraguai á luz do criterio historico positivo; extracto da biographia de Benjamin Constant. Recife, Emp. d'A. Provincia, 1899. 58p. (Republica ocidental, 2)
Reprinted: Extrato de esboço biografico de Benjamin Constant sobre a guerra do Paraguai. Ediçao de Joaquim Bagueira Leal. Rio de Janeiro, Typ. Martins de Araujo, 1920. 39p.

1328 THOMPSON, George. A guerra do Paraguay, com uma resenha historica do paiz o seus habitantes. Traduzido do inglez por Antonio Augusto da Costa Aguiar. Rio de Janeiro, E. & H. Laemmert, 1869. 198p.

1329 THOMPSON, George. La guerra del Paraguay, acompañada de un bosquejo histórico del pais y con notas sobre la ingenieria militar de la guerra. B.A., Imp. americana, 1869. 403, cxxxvip.
Reprinted: Juicio crítico del Dr. Osvaldo Magnasco. B.A., Editor J. Palumbo, 1910. 241p. Anotada y aumentada con un apéndice en que se refutan algunas apreciaciones del autor y con los partes oficiales de los generales del ejército aliado. 2. ed. profusamente ilustrada y enriquecida con nuevas notas por José Arturo Scotto. B.A., Tall. gráf. de L. Rosso, 1910-11. 2 vols.

1330 THOMPSON, George. The war in Paraguay, with a historical sketch of the country and its people, and notes upon the military engineering of the war. London, Longmans, Green, 1869. x, 347p.

1331 VAZ, Antonio Alvarez Guedes; DIAS, V. Apontamentos biographicos para a historia das campanhas do Uruguay e Paraguay desde 1864. Rio de Janeiro, Typ. Perseverança, 1866. 228p.

1332 VERSEN, Maximilian von. Historia da guerra do Paraguay e episodios da viagem na America do Sul; trad. do Dr. Manoel Thomas Alves Nogueira. Notas sobre este trabalho, pelo General E.A. Cunhas Mattos. Rio de Janeiro, 1914. 270p.

1333 VERSEN, Maximilian von. Reisen in Amerika und der Sudamerikanische Krieg. Breslau, M. Mälzer, 1872. iv, 220p.

1334 VICENCIO, Jacinto V. Dictadura del mariscal López; ó sea, Un cúmulo de episodios históricos del Paraguay y de las naciones limítrofes, conexos con los intereses de las repúblicas sudamericanas y del Brasil en forma de cartas epistolares. B.A., 1874. xiv, 210p.

1335 VIDAURRETA de TJARKS, Alicia. Al margen de la guerra del Paraguay. TC 18 (1968) 243-61.

1336 VITTONE, Luis. Calendario histórico de la guerra de la Triple Alianza contra el Paraguay; homenaje al centenario de la epopeya nacional, 1864-1870, 1964-1970. A., 1970? 61p.

1337 VITTONE, Luis. Conferencia patriótica pronunciada por Luis Vittone, con motivo del centenario de la muerte heroica del mariscal Francisco Solano López en Cerro Corá, 1870 - 1 de marzo - 1970. A., Imp. Militar, 1970. 44p.

1338 VITTONE, Luis. Guerra de la Triple Alianza contre el Paraguay. A., Imp. Militar, 1962. 557p.

1339 WARREN, Harris Gaylord. The Paraguayan image of the war of the Triple Alliance. AAAFH 19 (1962) 3-20.

b) Diplomatic history

1340 ACUÑA, Angel. Antecedentes de la guerra con el Paraguay (conferencia leída en la escuela General Roca, el 26 de abril de 1930, bajo los auspicios del Centro positivista argentino). B.A., Espiasse, 1930. 31p.

1340a ALBERDI, Juan Bautista. Las disensiones de las repúblicas del Plata y las maquinaciones del Brasil. Montevideo, Imp. Tip. a Vapor, 1865. 73p.

1341 ALBERDI, Juan Bautista. El imperio del Brasil ante la democracia de América; colección de artículos escritos durante la guerra del Paraguay contra la Triple alianza. A., Edición especial de "El Diario", 1919. xxvii, 183p.
Reprinted as: El Brasil ante la democracia de América, las disensiones de las repúblicas del Plata y las maquinaciones del Brasil. B.A., ELE, 1946. 460p.
Historia de la guerra del Paraguay. B.A., Ediciones de la Patria Grande, 1962. 247p.

1342 ALBERDI, Juan Bautista. Los intereses Argentinos en la guerra del Paraguay con el Brasil. Cartas dirigidas á sus amigos y compatriotas por el Dr. Juan B. Alberdi. Gualeguaychú, Imp. del Porvenir, 1865. 50p.
2. ed. Paris, Impresión privada, 1865? 30p.

1343 ALONSO PIÑEIRO, Armando. La misión diplomática de Mitre en Rio de Janeiro - 1872. B.A., Institución Mitre, 1972. 139p.

1344 AMARILLA FRETES, Eduardo. La liquidación de la guerra de la triple alianza contra el Paraguay (negociaciones diplomáticas). A., Imp. militar, 1941. 140p.

1345 ANGIO, José. A propósito de la devolución de los trofeos de la guerra del Paraguay. Paraná, 1954. 8p.

1345a ARGENTINA. Documentos relativos a la declaración de guerra del gobierno argentino al del Paraguay. B.A., Imp. de la Nación argentina, 1864. 42p.

1346 BOX, Pelham Horton. Los origenes de la guerra del Paraguay contra la triple alianza, versión castellana de Pablo M. Ynsfrán, hecha con permiso del autor y de la Universidad de Illinois y revisada por el prof. J.R. Carey. A., La Colmena, 1936. 371p.
2. ed. B.A., Ediciones Nizza, 1958. 321p. (Obras paraguayas, 9)

1347 BOX, Pelham Horton. The origins of the Paraguayan war. Urbana, The University of Illinois, 1930. 345p.
Reprinted: N.Y., Russell & Russell, 1967.

1348 BUENOS AIRES. BIBLIOTECA NACIONAL. Guerra del Paraguay. (Archivo de Félix Frias; correspondencia con Mariano Balcarco). RBNBA 1943, 466-81.

1349 CARCANO, Ramón José. Guerra del Paraguay, orígenes y causas; ilustraciones de Luis Seoane. B.A., D. Viau, 1939. 506p.

1350 CARDOZO, Efraím. El imperio del Brasil y el Río de la Plata; antecedentes y estallido de la Guerra del Paraguay; B.A., Librería del Plata, 1961. 566p.

1351 CARDOZO, Efraím. Urquiza y la guerra del Paraguay. IE 2 (1967) 141-65.

1352 CARDOZO, Efraím. Vísperas de la guerra del Paraguay. B.A., El Ateneo, 1954. 340p.

1352a CRESTO, Juan José. La correspondencia que engendró una guerra: nuevos estudios sobre los orígenes de la guerra con el Paraguay. Prólogo de Enrique de Gandía. B.A., Ediciones Convergencia, 1974. 59p.

1353 CUNHA, Francisco Xavier da. Propaganda contra o imperio, reminiscencias na imprensa e na diplomacia, 1870 a 1910. Rio de Janeiro, Imprensa nac., 1914. xxi, 903p.

1354 DANIERI, Leonardo. Leque e lenço da Aliança uruguaio-argentino-brasileira. RMJ 5 (1955) 123-47.

1355 DOCUMENTOS relativos á la reclamación norte-americana. A., Imp. de "El Paraguayo", 1887. 23p.

1356 FLORES, Venancio. La Guerra del Paraguay y la alianza oriental. Montevideo, Imp. "El Siglo Ilustrado", 1921. 36p.

1356a GARMENDIA, José Ignacio. Del Brasil, Chile y Paraguay, gratas reminiscencias. B.A., J. Roldán, 1915. 295p.

1357 GUIDO Y SPANO, Cárlos. El gobierno y la alianza; consideraciones politicas. n.p., Imp. de Buenos Aires, 1866. 114p.

1358 HERRERA, Luis Alberto de. Antes y despuēs de la Triple Alianza. Montevideo, Impresora Adroher, 1951-52. 2 vols.

1359 HERRERA, Luis Alberto de. El drama del 65: la culpa mitrista. Montevideo, A. Barreiro y Ramos, 1926. 435p.
2. ed. 1927. (Vol. V of "La diplomacia oriental en el Paraguay").
B.A., Ediciones Homenaje, 1943. 533p. (Obras completas de Luis Alberto de Herrera, 3)
La culpa mitrista; el drama de 65. Ed. de homenaje. B.A., Ediciones Pampa y Cielo, 1965. 2 vols. (El Drama de América)

1360 LE LONG, John. L'alliance du Brésil et des républiques de la Plata contre le gouvernement du Paraguay. Paris, Imprimerie Schiller, 1866. 80p.

1361 LE LONG, John. Les républiques de la Plata et la guerre du Paraguay. Le Brésil. Paris, E. Dentu, 1869. 96p.

1362 LOBO, Helio. Antes da guerra (a missao Saraiva ou os preliminares do conflicto com o Paraguay). Rio de Janeiro, Imprensa ingleza, 1914. 260p.

1363 LOBO, Helio. As portas da guerra (do ultimatum Saraiva, 10 de agosto de 1864, á convençao da Villa Uniao, 20 de fevereiro de 1865). Rio de Janeiro, Imprensa nac., 1916. vii, 270p.

1364 NEGOCIACION de paz bajo la mediación de la República del Paraguay, representada por el brigadier general don Francisco Solano López. Publicación oficial. B.A., Imp. de La Tribuna, 1859. 32p.

1365 "OS PREJUDICADOS". A divida paraguaya. Sao Paulo, Typ. Espindola, Siqueira & comp., 1905. 11p.
On war damages-compensation.

1366 PAPELES del tirano del Paraguay, tomados por los aliados en el asalto de 27 de diciembre de 1868. B.A., Imp. "Buenos Aires", 1869. 140p.
Translated: The WAR in Paraguay. President López, official papers taken by the allies, in the assault of December 27, 1868, and other authentic documents. With an introduction. Translated and published by order of the Argentine government. B.A., Standard Printing, 1869. xxii, 26p.

1367 PAPELES de López; o, El tirano pintado por si mismo y sus publicaciones. Papeles encontrados en los archivos del tirano. Tablas de sangre y copia de todos los documentos y declaraciones importantes de los prisioneros, para el proceso de la tiranía; incluso la de madame Lasserre. B.A., Imp. americana, 1871. 166p.

1368 PARAGUAY. MINISTERIO DE RELACIONES EXTERIORES. Correspondencia cambiadas entre el Ministerio de relaciones exteriores de la República y el Señor Charles A. Washburn, ministro residente de los Estados Unidos de América, sobre la conspiración fraguada contra la patrie y el gobierno en combinación con el enemigo; y el atentado de asesinato a la persona del Exmo. Señor Mariscal López por nacionales y estrangeros. Luque, Imprenta nac., 1868. 124p.

1369 PARAGUAY. MINISTERIO DE RELACIONES EXTERIORES. Correspondencia diplomática entre el gobierno del Paraguay y la legación de los Estados Unidos de América y el cónsul de s.m. el emperador de los Franceses, publicada en el Seminario de la Asunción. Horrendes crímenes del tirano paraguayo, declaraciones arrancadas por la tortura. López declarada enemigo del genero humano por le ministro Washburn. Circular de este cuerpo diplomático. B.A., Imp. "Buenos Aires", 1868. 24, xxiii p.

1370 PARAGUAY. MINISTERIO DE RELACIONES EXTERIORES. Documentos diplomáticos; correspondencia diplomática entre el gobierno del Paraguay y la Legación de los Estados Unidos de América y el cónsul de los franceses. A., La Unión, 1930. 154p.

1371 PARAGUAY. PRESIDENTE, 1862-70. Documentos oficiales relativos al abuso de la bandera nacional paraguayo. Por los gefes aliados. Piribebul, Imp. nac., 1869. 23p.

1372 The PARAGUAYAN question. The alliance between Brazil, the Argentine Confederation and Uruguay, versus the dictator of Paraguay. Claims of the republics of Peru and Bolivia in regard to this alliance. N.Y., Hallet & Breen, 1866. 56p.

1373 PARTES oficiales y documentos relativos a la guerra del Paraguay. B.A., Imp. Americana, 1871. 128p.

1374 PEÑA, David. Alberdi, los mitristas y la Guerra de la Triple Alianza. Con un estudio preliminar de Rodolfo Ortega Peña y Eduardo Luis Duhalde. B.A., A Peña Lillo, 1965. 155p. (Colección "Los Hombres y el tiempo".)

1375 PERU. MINISTERIO DE RELACIONES EXTERIORES. Correspondencia diplomática relativa a los cuestión del Paraguay. Publicado por orden de S.E. el jefe supremo provisorio par ser presentada al Congreso constituyente. Lima, Imp. de "El progreso", 1867. 158p.

1376 PERU. MINISTERIO DE RELACIONES EXTERIORES. Protestation du Pérou et de ses alliés du Pacifique contre les tendances de la guerre que le Brésil, la Confédération argentine et l'Uruguay font au Paraguay. Texte du traité secret des alliés et commentaire de ce traité. Paris, Dentu, 1866. 38p.

1377 PETERSON, Harold F. Efforts of the United States to mediate in the Paraguayan war. HAHR 12 (1932) 2-17.

1378 PINHEIRO, Raimundo Teles. Aspectos politicos da Guerra do Paraguai. Fortaleza, Imp. Universitaria do Ceará, 1967. 40p.

1379 Une QUESTION du droit des gens: M. Washburn, exministre des Etats-Unis à l'Assumption, et la conspiration Paraguayenne. Paris, Impr. de Dubuisson, 1868. 96p.

1379a QUEZADA, Ernesto. La declaración de la Guerra de la República de Paraguay a la Republica Argentina; Misión Luis Cannings; Misión Cipriano Ayala; Declaración de Isidro Ayala. B.A., Ed. Serantes, 1924. 296p.

1380 REBAUDI, Arturo. La declaración de guerra de la República del Paraguay a la República Argentina;

misión Luis Caminos, misión Cipriano Ayala, declaración de Isidro Ayala. B.A., Serantes hnos, 1924. 334p.

1381 REFUTACION al memorandum que el ministro de relaciones exteriores de la República argentina, dr. d. Rufino de Elizalde, dirijió á los agentes de la misma república en circular de 8 de abril de 1867. A., Imp. nac., 1867. 12p.

1382 REVELATIONS on the Paraguayan war and the alliances of the Atlantic and the Pacific. N.Y., Hallet & Breen, printers, 1886. 48p.

1383 SOUZA DOCCA, Emilio Fernandes de. Causas da guerra com o Paraguay, nufores e responsaveis. Porto Alegre, Cunha, Reutzsch, 1919. 229p.

1384 TASSO FRAGOSO, Augusto. A paz com o Paraguai depois da Guerra da Triplice Aliança. RIHGB 174 (1939-40) 1-334.

1385 TATSCH, Alberto. A verdade sobre as apolices paraguayas emmittidas em virtude do Tratado de paz firmado a 9 de janeiro de 1873 (i.e. 1872). Montevideo, 1908. 58p.

1386 TORRENTS, Leonardo Severo. Divida e trophéos paraguayos e a propaganda no Brazil; contendo algunos documentos e factos pouco conhecidos no Brazil. Rio de Janeiro, Typ. Montenegro, 1899. xix, 241p.

1387 VASCONCELLOS, Zacarias de Góes e. Discursos proferidos no debate do voto de graças de 1865. Rio de Janeiro, Typ. Perseverança, 1865. 136p.

1388 VASCONCELLOS, Zacarias de Góes e. Discursos proferidos no debate do voto de graças de 1868. Rio de Janeiro, Typ. de J.I. da Silva, 1868. xvi, 329p.

1389 VASCONCELLOS, Zacarias de Góes e. Discursos proferidos no debate do voto de graças e do orçamento do imperio de 1870. Rio de Janeiro, Typ. de J.I. da Silva, 1871. xxix, 276p.

1390 VERISSIMO, Inacio José. Antecendentes diplomáticos de guerra do Paraguai. CP 1942, 235-48.

1391 YNSFRAN, Pablo Max. Gestiones hecha por el gobierno del Perú, en 1866, para poner término a la guerra del Paraguay; conferencia leida en la Escuela de Comercio el 28 de julio de 1919. A., Imp. La Mundial, 1919. 27p.

1391a ZARZA, Idalia Flores G. de. Juan Bautista Alberdi y la defensa del Paraguay en la guerra contra la Triple Alianza. B.A., 1976. 420p.

1392 ZEBALLOS, Estanislao Severo. El tratado de alianza; esposición hecha en la Universidad de Buenos Aires el 30 de agosto de 1872. B.A., Imp. de J.E. Cook, 1872. 53p.

c) Military history - general

1393 APONTE BENITEZ, Leandro. Hombres ... armas ... y batallas: de la epopeya de los siglos. A., Imp. Comuneros, 1971. 242p.

1393a ASSIS, Anatólio Alves de. Milagre em Diamantina. Belo Horizonte, Editora Littera Maciel, 1974.

1394 AVIERO, Silvestre. Memorias militares, 1864-1870. A., Ediciones Comuneros, 1970. 106p.

1395 AZEVEDO, Manuel Duarte Moreira da. Rio da Prata e Paraguay; quadros guerreiros. Rio de Janeiro, E. & H. Laemmert, 1871. 199p.

1396 BAEZ, Adolfo I. Yatayty-Corá, una conferencia historica (recuerdo de la guerra del Paraguay). B.A., Imp. J. Perrotti, 1929. 42p.

1397 BECKER, Klaus. Alemaes e descendentes do Rio Grande do Sul na guerra do Paraguai. Canoas, Ed. Hilgert, 1968. 204p.

1398 BEJARANO, Ramón César. Panchito López: homenaje al cumplirse 100 años de su holocausto 1870 - 1 de marzo - 1970. A., Edit. Toledo, 1970. 77p.

1399 BENITES, Gregorio. Guerra del Paraguay; las primeras batallas contra la Triple Alianza. A., Tall. gráf. del Estado, 1919. 289p.

1400 BENITES, Gregorio. La Triple Alianza de 1865; escapada de un desastre en la guerra de invasión al Paraguay. A., Lasagna, 1904. 111p.

1401 BENITEZ, Justo Pastor. La causa nacional, ensayo sobre los antecedentes de la guerra del Paraguay (1864-70); prólogo de Juan S. Chaparro. A., Imp. y librería La Mundial, 1919. 117p. (Biblioteca paraguayo del Centro e. del derecho, 5)

1402 BENITEZ, Justo Pastor. El vencedor de Curupayty. *In* no. 159, p. 53-72.

1403 BEVERINA, Juan. La guerra del Paraguay, las operaciones de la guerra en territorio argentino y brasileño. B.A., Ferrari Hnos, 1921-33. 7 vols.
Reprinted: B.A., 1932-43. 5 vols.

1404 BOITEUX, Lucas Alexandre. A Provincia de Santa-Catarina nas guerras do Uruguai e do Paraguai. (Notas e apontamentos). Florianópolis, Imp. da Universidade Federal de Santa Catarina, 1972. 199p.

1405 BORMANN, José Bernardino. Historia da guerra do Paraguai, pelo coronel do estado maior do exercito José Bernardino Bormann. Curityba, J. Lopes, 1897. 3 vols.

1406 BRAZIL. EXERCITO. Campanha do Paraguay. Diarios do exercito em operaçoes sob o commando em chefe do exm. sr. marechal do exercito marquez de Caxias. Rio de Janeiro, Typ. nac., 1868-69. 4 pts.

1407 BRAZIL. EXERCITO. Exercito em operaçoes na republica do Paraguay (anteriormente, exercito em operaçoes na provincia de S. Pedro do Sul.) Segundo corpo sob o commando em chefe do exm. sr. tenente-general Manoel Marques de Souza, conde de Porto Alegre. Ordens do dia. Rio de Janeiro, Typ. de F. Alves de Souza, 1877. 2 vols.

1408 BRAZIL. EXERCITO. Exercito em operaçoes na republica do Paraguay. Primeiro corpo sob o commando em chefe do exm. sr. general Manoel Luiz Osorio, marquez do Herval. Ordens do dia. Rio de Janeiro, Typ. de F. Alves de Souza, 1877. 2 vols.

1409 BRAZIL. EXERCITO. Exercito em operaçoes na republica do Paraguay. Primeiro corpo sob o commando em chefe do exm. sr. general Polydoro da Fonseca Quintanilha Jordao, visconde de Santa Thereza. Ordens do dia (comprehendendo as de n. 1 a 22) 1866 a 1867. Rio de Janeiro, Typ. de F. Alves de Souza, 1877. 390, lvip.

1410 BRAZIL. EXERCITO. Exercito em operaçoes na republica do Paraguay sob o commando em chefe de todas as forças de s. ex. o sr. marechal do exercito, Luiz Alves de Lima e Silva, duque de Caxias. Ordens do dia. Rio de Janeiro, Typ. de F. Alves de Souza, 1877. 4 vols.

1411 BRAZIL. EXERCITO. Exercito em operaçoes na republica do Paraguay sob o commando em chefe interino de s. ex. o sr. marechal de campo Guilhermo Xavier de

Souza. Ordens do dia (comprehendendo as de n. 1 a n. 13) 1869. Rio de Janeiro, Typ. de F. Alves de Souza, 1877. 235, lxxxi p.

1412 BRAZIL. EXERCITO. Exercito em operaçoes na republica do Paraguay sob o commando em chefe do todas as forças, de sua alteza o senhor principe marechal do exercito, Luiz Felippe Fernando Gastao de Orleans, conde d'Eu. Ordens do dia (comprehendendo as de n. 1 a 47) 1869 a 1870. Rio de Janeiro, Typ. de F. Alves de Souza, 1877. 902, ccxxxii p.

1413 BRAZIL. EXERCITO. Campanha do Paraguay. Diarios do Exercito em operaçoes sob o commando em chefe do exm. sr. marechal do exercito marquez de Caxias. (Acampamento em Tuyuty, marcha para Tuyu-cuê) Julho-setembro, 1867. Rio de Janeiro, 1867. 3 pts.
Also: RIHGB for 1922 (1926) 9-673.

1414 BRUGADA, Arturo. Laudatoria al general Caballero en ocasión de su muerte. A., 1939. 92p.

1415 BURTON, *Sir* Richard Francis. Letters from the battlefields of Paraguay. London, Tinsley, 1870. xix, 491p.

1416 CALMAN DU PIN LISBOA, Miguel. Memorias da campanha do Paraguay, pelo capitao Miguel Calman. 1 vol. Para, Typ. de A.F. da Costa, 1868. 143p.
No more published.

1416a CALZADA, Isidoro. General Díaz. A., Edit. Don Bosco, 1970? 12p. (Galería de paraguayos ilustres, 7. Naranja)

1417 CARNEIRO, Daví. O Paraná na guerra do Paraguai. Curitiba, D. Plaisant, 1940. 367p.

1418 CERQUEIRA, Dionisio Evangelista de Castro. Reminiscencias da campanha do Paraguay, 1865-1870. Tours, E. Arrault, 1910. viii, 360p.
2. ed. Rio de Janeiro, F. Briguiet, 1929. viii, 360p.
4. ed. Rio de Janeiro, Biblioteca do Exercito, 194? 461p.
Reprinted: Rio de Janeiro, Grafica Laemmert, 1958? 412p. (Biblioteca militar, vol. cxxv, cxxvi)

1419 CERRI, Daniel. Compaña del Paraguay: tomo de la ciudad de Corrientes 25 de mayo 1865; movimientos y combates después de Curupaití; espedición al Chaco en el sitio de Humaitá 1 de mayo de 1868. B.A., Tip. "Del Pueblo", 1892. 91p.

1420 CHAVES, Julio César. La conferencia de Yataity-Corá; resumen. A., B.A., 1958. 53p. (Biblioteca histórica paraguaya de cultura popular, 2)

1421 CHAVES, Julio César. El general Díaz. Biografía del vencedor de Curupaity. Prólogo de Justo Pastor Benitez. B.A., Ediciones Nizza, 1957. 143p.

1422 DAMIANOVICH, Eleodoro A. Algunos datos sobre la organización del Cuerpo de Sanidad en la campaña del Paraguay, en las guerras civiles y frontera desde 1865 a 1895. Ed. intima. B.A., Imp. Frascoli y Bindi, 19--. 123p.

1423 DE MARCO, Miguel Angel. La Guardia Nacional argentina en la guerra del Paraguay. IE 3 (1967) 215-41.

1424 ESCRAGNOLLE TAUNAY, Alfredo de. Campanha do Paraguay. Commando em chefe de s.a.o. sr. marechal de exercito, conde d'Eu. Diario de exercito. Rio de Janeiro, Typ. nac., 1870. 404p.

1425 ESCRAGNOLLE TAUNAY, Alfredo de. Cartas da campanha: a Cordilheira, agonia de López, 1869-1870. Sao Paulo, Editôra Companha Melhoramentos de S. Paulo, 1921. 199p.

1426 ESCRAGNOLLE TAUNAY, Alfredo de. Diário do exército. Sao Paulo, Comp. Melhoramentos de S. Paulo, 1926? 2 vols.

1427 ESCRAGNOLLE TAUNAY, Alfredo de. Diário do exército, 1869-1870: A campanha da cordilheira; De Campo Grande a Aquidaba. 2. ed. Sao Paulo, Ediçoes Melhoramentos, 1958. 306p. (*His* Obras, v. 3)

1428 ESCRAGNOLLE TAUNAY, Alfredo de. Días de guerra e de sertao. 3. ed. Sao Paulo, Comp. Melhoramentos de Sao Paulo, 1927? 156p.

1429 ESCRAGNOLLE TAUNAY, Alfredo de. Em Matto Grosso invadido, 1866-1867. Sao Paulo, Editora comp. Melhoramentos de Sao Paulo, 1929? 152p.

1429a ESCRAGNOLLE TAUNAY, Alfredo d'. Relatorio geral da Comissao de engenheiros junto as forcas em expediçao para a Provincia de Matto Grosso 1865-1866. RIHGB XXXVII, pt. 2 (1874) 79-177; 209-339.

1430 EU, Louis Philippe Marie Ferdinand Gaston d'Orleans, *Comte* d'. Viagem militar ao Rio Grande do Sul (agosto o novembre do 1865) com prefacio o 19 cartas do principe Gastao de Orleans, commentadas por Max Fleiuss. Sao Paulo, Companhia editora nac., 1936. 290p. (Bibliotheca pedagogica brasileira, Ser. 5a: Brasiliana, v. 61)

1430a FERNANDES DE SOUZA. A invasao Paraguaya em Matto-Grosso. Ediçao commemorativa ao bi-centenario da fundaçao da cidade de Cuyabá. Cuiabá, Typ. J. Pereira Leite, 1919. 136p.

1431 FLORO, Leozitor. Manual de história militar geral e do Brasil. Belo Horizonte, Imprensa Oficial do Estado de Minas Gerais, 1972. 238p.

1431a FRAGOSO, Augusto Tasso. Historia da guerra entre a Tríplice Aliança e o Paraguai. Rio de Janeiro, Imp. do Estado-maior do Exercito, 1934. 5 vol.

1432 FRAGOSO, Augusto Tasso. História da guerra entre a Triplice Aliança e o Paraguai. 2. ed. preparada e organizada pelo major Francisco Ruas Santos. Rio de Janeiro, Livraria Freitas Bastos, 1956-60. 5 vols.

1433 FRANCO, Victor I. Coronel Florentín Oviedo. A., Academia Paraguaya de la Historia, 1971. 45p.

1434 GARCIA Y PEREZ, Antonio. Reseña histórico-militar de la campaña del Paraguay (1864 á 1870). Burgos, Imp. de A. Diez y compañía, 1900. iv, 162p.

1435 GARMENDIA, José Ignacio. La cartera de un soldado (bocetos sobre la marcha). B.A., J. Peuser, 1889. vii, 407p.
3. ed. 1890.
4. ed. 1890. vii, 411p.
5. ed. 1891. vii, 411p.
6. ed. B.A., Circulo Militar, 1973. 366p. (Biblioteca del oficial, vol. 640-651. Colección historico-militar.)

1436 GARMENDIA, José Ignacio. Recuerdos de la Guerra del Paraguay. B.A., Peuser, 1883-84. 120, 188p.
2. ed. 1885. 128p.
4. ed. 1890. 518p.
5. ed. 1890. 518p.

1436a GARMENDIA, José Ignacio. Recuerdos de la guerra del Paraguay: batalia del Sauce, combate de Yataytí Cora,

Curupaytī, campaña del Pikiciri. 3. ed. B.A., J. Peuser, 1889. 508p.

1437 GARMENDIA, José Ignacio. Recuerdos de la guerra del Paraguay. Campaña del Pikiciry, con un plano é ilustrada por el distinguido artista Alfredo Paris. B.A., Imp. y casa editora de J. Peuser, 1884. 188p.

1438 GARMENDIA, José Ignacio. Recuerdos de la guerra del Paraguay; campaña de Corrientes y de Río Grande. Con cuatro planos. B.A., Imp., litografía y encuadernación de J. Peuser, 1904. xxix, 707p.

1439 GAY, Jean Pierre. Invasao paraguaya na fronteira brazileira do Uruguay, desde seu principio até seu fin (de 10 de junho a 18 de setembro de 1865). Rio de Janeiro, Typ., imperial e constitucional de J. Villeneuve, 1867. 44p.

1440 GILL AGUINAGA, Juan B. Datos biográficos del capitán Pedro V. Gill. RNCP 1 (1957) no. 1, 47-58.

1441 GODOI, Juan Silvano. El asalto a los acorazados; el comandente José Dolores Molas. A., 1919. xxix, 89p.

1442 GODOI, Juan Silvano. Ultimas operaciones de guerra del jeneral José Eduvigis Diaz, vencedor de Curupaitī; su horoscope. B.A., F. Lajouane, 1897. 178p.

1443 GONZALEZ, José Guillermo. Reminiscencias históricas de la Guerra del Paraguay; pasaje de Ypecuá. A., La Democracia, 1897. 15p.
Reprinted: A., Tall. nac. de H. Kraus, 1914. 15p.

1444 GONZALEZ, Juan Natalicio. Cincuentenario de Cerro Corá. A., La Prensa, 1920. 201p.

1445 GONZALEZ ALSINA, Ezequiel. A cien años de Cerro Corá. A., Edit. de Centenario, 1970. 111p.

1446 GUERRA, Ubaldo Ramón. La defensa de Montevideo y la guerra del Paraguay; discursos de los diputados Ubaldo Ramón Guerra y Julio María Sosa. Montevideo, Imp. Artistica de Dornaleche y Reyes, 1907. 108p.

1447 La GUERRE du Paraguay et les belligérants. La République argentine - La République de Paraguay - Le Brésil - Le Paraguay. Brussels, Librairie de l'office de publicite, 1866. 65p.

1448 GUERRE du Paraguay. Faits authentiques de l'occupation d'une province brésilienne par les paraguayens. Paris, Paul Dupont, 1867. 17p.

1449 GUIMARAES, Francisco Pinheiro. Um voluntário de pátria; fôlha dos serviços prestados pelo general Dr. Francisco Pinherio Guimarâes às classes armades. 2. ed. Rio de Janeiro, J. Olympio, 1958. (Coleçao Documentos brasileiros, 94)

1450 GUIMARAES, Jorge Maia de Oliveira. A invasao de Mato Grosso. Ed. comemorativa de lo centenario da guerra do Paraguai. Apreciaçao e comentarios: Raul Silveira de Mello. Organizaçao e preparo dos originais: Elber de Mello Henriques. Rio de Janeiro, Biblioteca do Exercito, 1964. 322p. (Coleçao General Benício 33). (Biblioteca do Exercito, 238)

1451 HUTCHINSON, Thomas Joseph. The Paraná; with incidents of the Paraguayan war, and South American recollections, from 1861 to 1868. London, Edward Stanford, 1868. xxvii, 424p.

1452 HUTCHINSON, Thomas Joseph. A short account of some incidents of the Paraguayan war: read before the Liverpool Literary and Philosophical Society. Liverpool, David Marples, 1871. 15p.

1453 JACEGUAY, Arthur Silveira da Motta, barao de. Reminiscencias da guerra do Paraguay (con um prefacio do contra-almirante Raul Tavares). Rio de Janeiro, impreso nas. Off. de obras Graph. da S.A.A. Noite, 1935. 321p.

1454 JAEGGLI, Alfredo L.; BORDON, F. Arturo. Cartografia explicada de la Guerra contre la Triple Alianza. A., 1961. 1 vol. (unpaged).

1455 JOURDAN, Emilio Carlos. Guerra do Paraguay. Rio de Janeiro, Typ. Perceverança, 1871. 157p.
Reprinted: 1890. 252p.

1456 JOURDAN, Emilio Carlos. Histoire des campagnes de l'Uruguay, de Matto-Grosso et des Paraguay, Brésil, 1864-1870. Rio de Janeiro, Imp. nac., 1893-

1457 LACONICH, Marco Antonio. El mariscal Francisco Solano López. Réplica al coronel Arturo Bray. A., Revista de las FF. AA. de la Nación, 1946. 96p. (Biblioteca de la Revista de las FF. AA. de la Nación, 8)

1458 LEITE DE CASTRO, Joao Vicente. Diccionario geographico e historico das campanhas do Uruguay e Paraguay. Rio de Janeiro, Imprensa nac., 1892. 104p.
Only pt. 1 published.

1459 LEMOS BRITTO, José Gabriel de. Guerra do Paraguay; narrativa histórica dos prisioneiros do vapor "Marquez de Olinda" prefacio do dr. Arlindo Fragoso. Bahia, Litho-typ. e encadernaçao - Reis, 1907. 41, 96, iii p.

1460 LOPACHER, Ulrich. Die Abenteuer eines Reisläufers: Ulrich Lopachers Söldnerleben in päpstlichen und argentinischen Diensten, 1860-1870. Geschrieben von (Alfred) Tobler. Trogen, Buchdruckerei F. Meili, 1967. 80p.

1461 LOPACHER, Ulrich. Un suizo en la Guerra de Paraguay por Tobler/Lopacher. Traducción y nota preliminar de Arturo Nagy y Francisco Pérez-Maricevich. A., Edit. del Centenario, 1969. 82p. (Colección Paraquaria, no. 3)
A trans. of chapters 3-5 of no. 1460.

1462 LOPEZ, Cándido. A Campanha do Paraguai de Corrientes a Curupaiti vista pelo tenente Cándido López; apresentaçao de Marcos Tamoyo. Rio de Janeiro, Distribiúdora Record, 1973? 14p. 48 plates.

1462a MAIA DE OLIVEIRA GUIMARAES, Jorge. A invasao de Mato Grosso. Ediçao comemorativa do lo centenario da guerra do Paraguai. Rio de Janeiro, Biblioteca do Exercito, 1964. 328p. (Coleçao Gen. Benício, vol. 33, publ. 238)

1463 MARACAJU, Ruñno Eneas Gustavo Galvao, *visconde de*. Campanha do Paraguay (1867 a 1868). Rio de Janeiro, Imp. militar, Estado-maior do exercito, 1922. 226p.

1464 MARTIN, María Haydee. La juventud de Buenos Aires en la guerra con el Paraguay. TC 19 (1969) 145-76.

1465 MEDINA, Pedro P. Estampa del guerrero, "Gral. José Diaz", (De Romerocué a Curupayty). Prólogo de Jorge Solano López. A., Tall. Gráf. Emasa, 1962. 47p.

1466 MEDINA, Pedro P. Recopilación de hechos de armas, 1864-1870, 1932-1935. A?, 1962? 149p.

1467 MITRE, Bartolomé. Guerra del Paraguay; memoria militar sobre el estado de la guerra con el Paraguay en 1867, y sobre los planes de campaña y operaciones é ejecutar, demostrando la probabilidad de forzar el paso de Humaitá (con los documentos comprobantes). B.A., Imp. de "La Nación", 1903. vii, 183p.

1468 MOSQUEIRA, Silvano. General José Eduvigis Dias. B.A., Tall. S. Ostwald, 1900. 29p. (Galería Paraguaya, 1)

1469 O'LEARY, Juan Emiliano. El centauro de Ybycui; vida heroica del general Bernardino Caballero en la guerra del Paraguay; prólogo de Carlos Pereyra. Paris, Edit. "Le livre libre", 1929. 455p.
Reprinted: A., Oficina de Prensa del Ministerio de Hacienda, 1970. 467p.

1470 O'LEARY, Juan Emiliano. Frente al pasado. A., Tall. de "Ariel", 1916. 75p.
On General Elisardo Aquino.

1471 O'LEARY, Juan Emiliano. El libro de los héroes; páginas históricos de la guerra del Paraguay. A., Librería La Mundial, 1922. 515p.
Reprinted: A., Oficina de Prensa del Ministerio de Hacienda, 1970.

1472 O'LEARY, Juan Emiliano. Nuestra epopeya (guerra del Paraguay). Juicio de José Enrique Rodó. A., Imprimeria y librería La Mundial, 1919. 648p. (Biblioteca paraguaya del Centro estudiantes del derecho)
See also no. 582a.

1473 O'LEARY, Juan Emiliano. Páginas de historia. A., Zamphirópolos, 1916. 37p.

1474 PAGE, Robert W. The Paraguayan war. MR 43 (1963) no. 9, 89-96.

1475 PALLEJA, Leon de. Diario de la campaña de los fuerzas aliadas contra el Paraguay. Montevideo, Imp. de el Pueblo, 1865-66. 2 vols.
Reprinted: Montevideo, Ministerio de Instrucción Pública y Previsión Social, 1960. 2 vols. (Biblioteca Artigas. Colección de clásicos uruguayos, v. 20-30).

1476 PAOLI, Pedro de; MERCADO, Manual Gregorio. Proceso a los montoneros y guerra del Paraguay: aplicación de la justicia social de clases, Aurelio Zalazar, Ambrosio Chumbita, Carlos Angel, Francisco y Carlos M. Alvarez, José A. Gimenez. B.A., Edit. Universitaria de B.A., 1973. 217p. (Historia de las luchas sociales del pueblo argentino).

1477 PIMENTEL, Joaquim Silveiro de Azevedo. Guerra del Paraguay; episodios militares. Rio de Janeiro, 1887. viii, 208p.

2. ed. Rio de Janeiro, Papelaria e typographia L. Macedo, 1897. xxii, 197p.

1478 PIMENTEL, Joaquim Silveiro de Azevedo. O onze de voluntarios da patria (depois 42. corpo da mesma denominaçao); sua fé de officio e relatorio dos serviços militares prestados na campanha de 1865 a 1870. Rio de Janeiro, Officinas Gráphicas do Jornal do Brasil, 1909. 147p.

1479 (PEREIRA DA COSTA, Francisco Felix). Historia da guerra do Brasil contra as republicas do Uruguay o Paraguay contendo consideraçoes sobre o exercito do Brasil e suas campanhas no sul até 1852. Campanha do estado oriental em 1865. Marcha do exercito pelas provincias argentinas. Campanha do Paraguay. Operaçoes do exercito e da esquadra. Acompanhada do juizo critico sobre todos os acontecimentos que tiveram lugar nosta memoravel campanha. Rio de Janeiro, Livraria de A.G. Guimaraes, 1870-71. 4 vols.

1480 REBOUÇAS, Andre Pinto. Diário: a guerra do Paraguai (1866). Introduçao e notas de Maria Odila Silva Dias. Sao Paulo, Instituto do Estudos Brasileiro, Universidade de Sao Paulo, 1973. 173p. (Publicaçoes do Instituto do Estudos Brasileiros, 27)

1481 ROLON MEDINA, Anastasio. El general Bernardino Caballero; homenaje al Prócer en el centenario de la epopeya nacional (1865-1965). A., La Humanidad, 1965. 173p.

1482 ROTTJER, Enrique I. Mitre militar. B.A., "Coni", 1937. 444p.

1483 RUEDA, Pedro. Biografía militar del general don Pedro Duarte, ministro de Guerra y Marina de la República del Paraguay. A., El Paraguayo, 1890. 18p.

1484 SANCHEZ QUELL, Hipolito. Pedro Juan Caballero y el sesquicentennial Paraguayo. HP 6-7 (1961-62) 17-20.

1485 SANTOS XAVIER DE AZEVEDO, Carlo Frederico. Historia medico-cirugica da esquadra brasileira nas campanhas do Uruguay e Paraguay do 1864 a 1869. Rio de Janeiro, Typ. nac., 1870. 523p.

1486 (SENNA MADUREIRA, Antonio de). Manuscrito do mil oitocentos e sessenta e nove; ou, Resumo historico das operaçoes militares dirigidas pelo marechal d'exercito, marquez de Caxias na campanha do Paraguay.

Rio de Janeiro, Typ. e lithographia popular de Azeredo Leite, 1872. 174p.
Also attributed to NEVES GONZAGA, José Basileu das.

1487 SHIPPEN, E. Recollections of the Paraguay Expedition. US 2 (1880) 328-49.

1488 SILVA, José Luiz Rodriguez da. Recordaçoes da campanha do Paraguay. Sao Paulo, Comp. Melhoramentos, c. 1924. 128p.

1489 SOUZA, Luis de Castro. A medicina na guerra do Paraguai. Rio de Janeiro?, 1972. 171p.

1490 SPALDING, Walter. A invasao Paraguaia no Rio Grande do Sul e a rendiçao de Uruguaiana. RIHGB 294 (1972) 222-36.

1491 SPALDING, Walter. A invasao Paraguaia no Brasil (prefacio e notas com muita documentaçao inédita). Ed. ilustrada. Sao Paulo, Companhia editora nac., 1940. xlix, 633p. (Biblioteca pedagogica brasileira. 5a ser: "Brasiliana", v. 185)

1492 VILLAMAYOR, José Marcos. El célebre guerrero del 65 al 70: Sixto Britez (a) alferez Ñanduá. Concepción, Imp. Minerva, 1932. 39p.

d) Military history - naval

1493 COSTA, Didio Iratym Affonso da. Marcilio Dias, imperial-marinheiro. 2. ed. Rio de Janeiro, Serviço do Documentaçao da Marinha, 1947. 141p.
5. ed. Rio de Janeiro, 1959. 107p.

1494 GILL AGUINAGA, Juan Bautista. Un marino en la Guerra de la Triple Alianza. A., Imp. "Paraguay", 1959. 19p.

1495 GONCALVES, Alberto Augusto. Antônio Joaquim. Rio de Janeiro, Imp. Naval, 1953. 148p.

1496 JACEQUAY, Arthur Silveira da Motta, *barão* de; OLIVEIRA, Vidal de. Quatro seculos de actividade maritima: Portugal e Brasil. Rio de Janeiro, Imp. nac., 1900. vii, 258p.
2 pte: A guerra do Paraguay.

1497 LAING, E.A.M. Naval operations in the War of the Triple Alliance, 1864-70. MM 54 (1968) 253-80.

1498 MACEDO SOARES, José Eduardo de. O contra-almirante Luiz Philippe de Saldanha da Gama; sua vida e sua epoca. Sao Paulo, Typ. Espindola, 1906-

1499 MEIRELLES DA SILVA, Theotonio. A marinha de guerra brasileira em Paysandá e durante a campanha do Paraguay; resumos históricos. Rio de Janeiro, Typ. theatral e comercial, 1876. 287p.

1500 MEISTER, Jürg. Die Flussoperationen der Triple-Allianz gegen Paraguay; 1864-1870. MRB 69 (1972) 594-616; 660-75.

1501 OTAÑO, Juan B. Datos para la historia del "Tacuarí". A., 1932. 197p.

1502 OTAÑO, Juan B. Origen, desarrollo y fin de la Marina desaparecida en la guerra de 1864-70. A., La Colmena, 1942. 20p.

1503 OTAÑO, Juan B. "Ypora". A., Imp. militar, 1941. 19p.

1504 OURO PRETO, Affonso Celso de Assis Figueiredo, *visconde de.* A marinha d'outr'ora. Subsidios para a historia. Rio de Janeiro, D. de Magalhaes, 1894. xi, 467p.

1505 RUFFIN, John N. The "Temerario" at Asunción. AFSJ 1944, 612-13, 636, 664.

1506 SILVADO, Americo Brazilio. A nova marinho; resposta á "Marinha d'outr'ora" do sr. Affonso Celso de Assis Figueiredo (ex-visconde de Ouro Preto). Rio de Janeiro, Typ.-lith. C. Schmidt, successor de H. Lombaerts, 1897. 232p.

1507 TOMB, James Hamilton. As experiencias do capitao James H. Tomb na Marinha brasileira, 1865-1870; documento editado pelo Prof. Robert C. Cotner. Traduçao e algunas notas sobre o documento, de Eulália N.L. Lobo. Rio de Janeiro, Serviço de Documentaçao Geral da Marinha, 1964. 16p.
Also in: Revista maritima brasileira, 1964.

1508 VICTORINO DE BARROS, Antonio José. Guerra do Paraguay. O almirante visconde de Inhaúma. Rio de Janeiro, Typ. do Imperial instituto artistico, 1870. viii, 446p.

e) Military history - individual battles

1509 AGUIAR, Adriano M. Yatebó; episodio de la guerra del Paraguay. Montevideo, Imp. y Lib. de Vázquez Cores y Montes, 1899. 60p.

1509a BAEZ, Adolfo I. Tuyuty. B.A., Tall. graf. Ferrari hnos., 1929. 148p.

1510 CINCUENTENARIO de Cerro Corá. Por Benjamin Velilla et al. Aparece bajo la dirección J. Natalicio González. A., Tall. de la Prensa, 1920. 203p.

1511 COMISION ORGANIZADORA DE LA PEREGRINACION AL RIACHUELO. Peregrinación al Riachuelo; homenaje de confraternidad internacional a los que cayeron en el combate naval de 11 de junio 1865-1913. Corrientes? 1913. 122p.

1512 CONMEMORACION del primer centenario da la batalla de Cerro Corá. BHAC 57 no. 663-665 (1970) 55-71.

1513 CORREIA, Jonas. Perfil histórico de uma batalha. Tuiuti. RIHGB 294 (1972) 255-89.

1514 COSTA, Didio Iratym Affonso da. Riachuelo. 6. ed. Rio de Janeiro, Serviço de Documentaçao de Marinha, Secçao de História Maritima do Brasil, 1949. 38p.
7. ed. 1952. 32p.

1515 CUNHA, Francisco Manoel da. Guerra do Paraguay. Tujuty: ataque de 3 de novembre de 1867. Rio de Janeiro, Imp. "Mont' Alverne", 1888. 40p.

1516 ESCRAGNOLLE TAUNAY, Alfredo de. A retirada da Laguna; episodio da guerra do Paraguay. Tr. da 3. ed. franceza pelo Dr. B.T. (sic) Ramiz Galvao. Rio de Janeiro, Paris, Garnier, 1915. xxxv, 291p.

1517 ESCRAGNOLLE TAUNAY, Alfredo de. A retirada da Laguna; episodio da guerra do Paraguay. Tr. da quinta ediçao franceza por Affonso d'Escragnolle Taunay. 10. ed. brasileira illustrada e acrecisda de avultada documentaçao. Sao Paulo, Comp. Melhoramentos de S. Paulo (Weiszflog irmãos incorporada), 1935? xviii, 272p.
12. ed. 1942. 256p.
14. ed. 1957. 202p.
16. ed. 1963. 202p.

1518 ESCRAGNOLLE TAUNAY, Alfredo de. La retraite de Laguna. Imprimé par ordre de vicomte de Rio Branco,

ministre de la guerre. Rio de Janeiro, Typ. nat., 1871. 224p.
2. ed. Paris, Plon, 1879. xx, 268p.
3. ed. Paris, Plon, 1891. 266p.

1519 FONSECA, Ignacio Joaquim da. Estudo. A batalha de Riachuelo. Rio de Janeiro, Lombaerts, 1883. xvi, 191p.

1520 GARMENDIA, José Ignacio. Campaña de Humaytá: pasaje del río Paraná el 16 de abril de 1866 - batalla del Estero Bellaco el 2 de mayo de 1866 - combate del Paso Sidra el 20 de mayo de 1866 - batalla de Tuyuti el 24 de mayo de 1866. B.A., Casa editora de J. Peuser, 1901. xxiii, 262p.

1521 GILL AGUINAGA, Juan Bautista. La Batalla del Riachuelo, narrada por prácticos incorporadas a la Escuadra Brasileña. A., Academia Paraguay de la Historia, 1968. 16p.

1522 LACONICH, Marco Antonio. La campaña de Amambay. HP 13 (1969-70) 15-22.

1523 O'LEARY, Juan Emiliano. Curupayty; discurso pronunciado en 22 de septiembre de 1912, con motivo de la peregrinación patriótica. B.A., Tall. gráf. M. Rodríguez Giles, 1912. 13p.

1524 O'LEARY, Juan Emiliano. Lomas Valentinas; conferencia dada en Villeta el 25 de diciembre de 1915. A., 1916. 48p.

1525 O'LEARY, Juan Emiliano. 24 de Mayo: Tuyuty, Estero Bellaco. Prólogo del dr. Ignacio A. Pane. A., Tip. "La Tarde", 1904. 75p. (Recuerdos de gloria)
Reprinted: 1924. 75p.

1526 OZORIO, Fernando Luiz. Discurso de Fernando Ozorio sobre o quadro; Batalha do Avahy de Pedro America, pronunciada na Camara dos senhores deputados, em sessao de 30 de agosto de 1877, contendo o resumo da opiniao européa o nacional sobre o mesmo quadro. Rio de Janeiro, Typ. de J. Villeneuve, 1877. 29p.

1527 REBAUDI, Arturo. Lomas Valentinas. A., Serantes, 1924. 31p.

1528 ROLON, Raimundo. La batalla de Curupayty, en el centenario de la epopeya nacional. A., Edit. La Patria, 1966. 24p.

1528a TUYUTY DE OLIVEIRA FREITAS, Osorio. A invasao de San Borja. Porto Alegre, Livraria do Globo, Bercellos, Bertaso, 1935. 166p.

1529 (VARELA, Hector Florencio). Orión a Ságita. El asalto de Curupaiti. n.d., 30p.

1529a VASCONCELLOS, Armando Batista de. Uma testemunha da Batalha de Tuiuti (1866); apontamentos sobre a batalha de Tuiuti, o General Cabeleira e Episódios da Guerra do Paraguai. Recife, Arquivo Público Estadual, 1966. 58p.

1530 VIANNA, José Feliciano Lobo. A epopéa da Laguna. Rio de Janeiro, Estado-Maior do Exercito, Imp. Militar, 1920. 125, 69p.

1531 VITTONE, Luis. Alocución patriótica con motivo del centenario de la batalla de Piribebuy, 1869 - 12 de agosto - 1969. A., Imp. Militar, 1969? 35p.

1532 VITTONE, Luis. Alocución patriótica pronunciada por Luis Vittone, jefe de publicaciones de las FF. AA. de la Nación, con motivo del centenario de las batallas de las Lomas Valentinas, 27 de diciembre de 1968. A., Imp. Militar, 1968? 22p.

f) Other aspects

1533 BOVIER, Victor Simón. El periodismo combatiente del Paraguay durante la guerra contra la Triple Alianza. HP 12 (1967-68) 47-115.

1534 BUENOS AIRES. BIBLIOTECA NACIONAL. Guerra de la Triple Alianza contra el Paraguay. RBNBA 21 no. 51 (1949) 265-96; 21 no. 52 (1949) 465-633; 22 no. 53 (1950) 147-237; 22 no. 54 (1950) 348-462.
Documents relating to the Paraguayan emigrants.

1535 DECOUD, Héctor Francisco. Los emigrados paraguayos en la guerra de la Triple Alianza, prólogo de José Juan Biedma. B.A., Tall. gráf. argentinos L.J. Rosso, 1930. 156p.

1536 DECOUD, Héctor Francisco. Guerra del Paraguay; las masacre de Concepción ordenada por el mariscal López. Contiene un apéndice con documentos importantes referentes a los acontecimientos producidos durante la guerra, entre los cuales figura una parte del famoso proceso de San Fernando. B.A., Imp. Serantes, 1926. 414p.

1536a DOMINGUEZ, Manuel. El patriota y el traidor. *In* no. 203, 117-24.
On the Lopezguayos and the Legionarios.

1537 FRUTOS N., Cristóbal A. Condecoraciones en la Guerra del Paraguay contra la Triple Alianza. A?, 1966. 29p.

1538 GAONA, Silvio. El clero en la guerra del '70. A., Dagre, 1957. 142p.
2. ed. enriquecida con nuevos documentos. A., El Arte, 1961. 168p.

1539 GILL AGUINAGA, Juan Bautista. La Asociación Paraguaya en la guerra de la triple alianza. Prólogo de R. Antonio Ramos. B.A., Tall. Gráf. Lumen, 1959. 202p.

1540 GODOI, Juan Silvano. Documentos históricos; al fusilamiento del obispo Palacios y los tribunales de sangre de San Fernando. A., Imp. "El Liberal", 1916. 259p.

1541 GONDRA, César. La deuda de la guerra de 1865. A., El Pais, 1903. 16p.

1542 LELONG, John. Le Paraguay: la dynastie des Lopez avant et pendant la guerre actuelle. RC, 2 ser., 61 (1868) 321-47.

1543 MASSARE DE KOSTIANOVSKY, Olinda. La cultura en la epopeya nacional. A., Instituto de Investigaciones Históricas, 1967. 33p.

1544 MASSARE DE KOSTIANOVSKY, Olinda. La mujer paraguaya; su participación en la Guerra Grande. Prólogo de R. Antonio Ramos. A., 1970. 123p.

1545 MILET, Henrique Augusto. Le Brésil pendant la guerre du Paraguay (1865 a 1870); mémoire lu au Congrès du Havre (section d'économie politique, 24 août 1877). Paris, Librairie Guillaumin, 1877. 47p.

1546 OLARAN CHANS, Justo. El Paraguay y la condonación de su deuda de guerra con los paises de la Triple Alianza. B.A., 1941. 23p.

1547 O'LEARY, Juan Emiliano. Los legionarios. A., Edit. do Indias, 1930. 235p.

1548 PUSINERI SCALA, Carlos Alberto. Las monedas que circularon en el Paraguay durante la Guerra de la Triple Alianza. HP 12 (1967-68) 117-34.

1549 ROSA, José Maria. La guerra del Paraguay y las montoneras argentina. B.A., A Peña Lillo, 1964. 354p.
3. ed. 1968.
4. ed. 1974.

H. 1870 - 1938

1. *General studies*

1550 ALMANAQUE de escritorio para el año 1896. Especial de la Guia general de la República del Paraguay. B.A., Compañía Sud Americana de Billetes y Banco, 1896. 340p.

1551 ALMANAQUE nacional del Paraguay para el año de 1884-1886. Año I - II. A., Curutchet, 1884-86. 2 vols.

1552 ARBO, Higinio. Política paraguaya. B.A., Colegio Libre de Estudios Superiores, 1947. 64p.

1553 ARTAZA, Policarpo. Ayala, Estigarribia y el Partido Liberal. B.A., Edit. Ayacucho, 1946. 255p.
2. ed. 1946. 261p.

1554 ARTAZA, Policarpo. ¿Que hizo el Partido Liberal en la oposición y en el gobierno? B.A., Lucania, 1961. 80p.
A history of the Liberal Party.

1555 AUDIBERT, Alejandro. Sobre elecciones presidenciales en el XI periodo constitucional. A., Tall. de "El Nacional", 1912. 70p.

1556 AYALA, Elías. Pro-inundados. A., Tall. de "El Diario", 1905. 28p.

1557 AYALA, Eusebio. Discurso del señor presidente de la república, dr. Eusebio Ayala, ante la convención del Partido Liberal, 20 de enero de 1935. A?, 1935. 25p.

1558 AYALA, Eusebio. Patria y libertad; selección de discursos, artículos y documentos. B.A., Comisión de Homenaje, 1952. 401p.

1559 BAEZ, Jorge. Politica paraguaya de la pre-guerra. A., Cía. Edit. Nac., 193-? 11p.

1559a BARRIOS, M. Virgilio. La gira internacional del doctor Guggiari. A., 1929. 7-90p.

1559b BAZAN, Francisco. Eligio Ayala, el pensador. A?, Edit. Curupí, 1976. 186p.

1560 BENITES, Gregorio. Las imposturas de Juan Bautista Gill y el Informe del Comité del Parlamento de Inglaterra en la cuestión Empréstito del Paraguay. Montevideo, Imp. de "El Siglo", 1876. 58p.

1560a BENITEZ, Justo Pastor. Un agitador des ideas. *In* no. 162, 2 ed., 113-14.
On Ignacio A. Pane.

1561 BENITEZ, Justo Pastor. 18 de Octubre de 1891. *In* no. 1903, p. 84-87.
On the Liberal Party.

1561a BENITEZ, Justo Pastor. El estadista del Paraguay moderno. *In* no. 162, 2 ed., 125-29.
On Eligio Ayala.

1562 BENITEZ, Justo Pastor. Frederico Garcia, el penultimo aloniano. *In* no. 1903, p. 106-9.

1562a BENITEZ, Justo Pastor. Gondra o la tentative de perfección espiritual. *In* no. 162, 2 ed., 75-100.

1563 BENITEZ, Justo Pastor. Historia contemporánea del Paraguay a partir del 1870. *In* LEVENE, Ricardo. Historia de América. B.A., W.M. Jackson, 1940-41. Vol. 9, 265-330.

1563a BENITEZ, Justo Pastor. Un hombre del renacimiento pasa. *In* no. 162, 2 ed., 111-13.
On Arsenio López Decoud.

1563b BENITEZ, Justo Pastor. Manuel Dominguez, el animador. *In* no. 162, 2 ed., 70-75.
Also in no. 203, 5-10.

1563c BENITEZ, Justo Pastor. El presidente de la victoria. *In* no. 162, 2 ed., 122-25.
On Eusebio Ayala.

1564 BENITEZ, Justo Pastor. Progenie de los Liberales. *In* no. 1903, p. 80-83.

1565 BENITEZ, Justo Pastor. Un tribuno del pueblo: Lisandro Diaz Leon. *In* no. 1903, p. 102-5.

1565a BENITEZ, Justo Pastor. Una tribuna libre. *In* no. 162, 2 ed., 62-70.
On Cecilio Baez.

1565b BENITEZ, Justo Pastor. Una vida novelesca. *In* no. 162, 2 ed., 43-57.
On Juan Silvano Godoi.

1566 BERINO MARTINEZ, Ignacio Amado. Doctor Ramōn Fermīn Zubizarreta, jurisconsulto y educador, en el LXI aniversario de su muerte. A., El Arte, 1963. 140p.

1567 BERTONI, Guillermo Tell. Bosquejos sobre politica econōmica del Paraguay. San Lorenzo (Paraguay), Imp. y ediciones Guaranī, 1936- (Instituto de investigaciones informes y publicidad. Museo, archivo y biblioteca Bertoni. Boletīn, 1)

1568 BORDON, F. Arturo. La vida romāntica de Alōn, Juan de la Cruz Ayala, mārtir de la democracia paraguaya. A., 1966. 20p.
Also in no. 52.

1568a BORDON, F. Arturo. Historia polītica del Paraguay: era constitucional. A., Orbis, 1976-

1569 BREGAINS, Carlos. Episodio de la revoluciōn colorada de 1910: Livoria y Renē. A., Edit. El Grāfico, 1947. 31p.

1570 BRUGADA, Arturo. Dr. Benjamin Aceval; su actuaciōn polītica. A., Asilo, 1925. 295p.

1570a CALZADA, Isidoro. General Bernardino Caballero. A., Edit. Don Bosco, 1970? 12p. (Galerīa de paraguayos ilustres, 8. Naranja)

1571 CALZADA, Rafael. Rasgos biogrāficos de Josē Segundo Decoud. Homenaje en 4. aniversario de su fallecimiento. 4 de marzo de 1909. B.A., 1913. 152p.

1572 CARDOZO, Efraīm. 23 de octubre; una pāgina de historia contemporānea del Paraguay. B.A., Edit. Guayra, 1956. 389p.
On the uprising in 1931.

1573 CARDUS HUERTA, Gualberto. Discursos polītico. A., 1922. 40p.

1574 CARRERAS, Fernando. Las elecciones del norte; colecciōn de documentos, antecedentes y artīculos de la prensa, relacionados con las mismas: fraudes, abusos y violencia del poder oficial. A., La Democracia, 1901. 152p.

1575 CENTURION, Carlos R. Blas Garay. A., Imp. militar, 1935. 55p.

1576 CENTURION, Carlos R. Los hombres de la Convención del '70. A., Tall. gráf. "El arte", 1938. 31p.

1577 CENTURION, Carlos R. El libro como expresión del Partido Liberal del Paraguay. B.A., Edit. Asunción, 1950. 62p.

1578 CENTURION, Carlos R. Manuel Domínguez, el abogado de la patria. B.A., Edit. Asunción, 1950. 62p.

1579 CENTURION, Carlos R. Partido liberal; jornadas opositoras. A., Imp. "Ariel", 1935. 27p.
Reprinted: A., 1954. 28p.

1580 CENTURION, Carlos R. Sarmiento en Paraguay. HU 37 (1961) 27-58.

1580a CENTURION, Juan Crisostomo. Mocedades. Los sucesos de Puerto Pacheco. A., Instituto Colorado de Cultura, 1975. 169p. (Biblioteca Clasicos Colorados, 1)

1581 CHAMORRO NOCEDO, Victor. De la revolución la contrarevolución. CR 6 (1973) 93-149.

1582 EL CIVICO, *Asunción*. El gran chantago contra el general y doctor Don Benigno Ferreira, candidato del Partido Liberal a la presidencia de la república del Paraguay. A., Tall. de "El Cívico", 1906. 157p.

1583 COLLE, Ello M.A. El drama del Paraguay; estudio sobre la bancarrota social, política y económica de un pueblo sometido a la penetración imperialista. B.A., Edit. Claridad, 1936. 157p. (Colección Claridad "Estudios sociales")

1584 DAHL, Victor O. The Paraguayan "Jewel Box". AAAFH 21 (1965) 223-42.

1585 DECOUD, Héctor Francisco. Dos páginas de sangre año 1877, 12 de abril - 29 de octubre. A., Tall. nac. de H. Kraus, 1925. 67p.

1586 DECOUD, Héctor Francisco. Sobre los escombros de la guerra: una década de vida nacional, 1869-1880. A., Tall. nac. de H. Kraus, 1925. 426p.

1587 DECOUD, Héctor Francisco. La revolución del comandante Molas. B.A., Tall. Gráf. de J. Perrotti, 1930. 120p.

1588 DECOUD, José Segundo. Cuestiones políticas y económicas. A., 1877. 27p.

1589 DECOUD, José Segundo. Exposición presentada por José S. Decoud a la Honorable Cámara de Diputados a própo- sito de la investigación iniciada en virtud de una denuncia falsa de anexión. A., H. Kraus, 1898. 7p.

1590 DECOUD, José Segundo. La historia de una administra- ción ó sea las dilapidaciones de Salvador Jovellanos, ex-Vicepresidente de la República del Paraguay. Corrientes, 1877. 42p.
2. ed. Corrientes, 1906. 44p.

1591 DECOUD, José Segundo. La patria, fragmento de una obrita en preparación titulada: "El evangelio de los pueblos libres". A., H. Kraus, 1904. 18p.

1592 DECOUD, José Segundo. El patriotismo, fragmento de una obrita en preparación titulada: "El evangelio de los pueblos libres". A., H. Kraus, 1905. 23p.

1593 DOMINGUEZ, Manuel. Menéndez y Pelayo. Cartas al Dr. Cecilio Baez. A., Imp. de "La Juventud", 1899. 66p.

1594 ESTRADA, Victor Emilio. Vida de un hombre: Emilio Estrada. Guayaquil, (Imp. A.G. Senefelder), 1942. 260p.

1595 FRANCO, Rafael. Mensaje al pueblo del presidente provisional de la República Coronel Rafael Franco, 17 de febrero de 1937. A., Imp. Nac., 1937. 20p.

1596 FREIRE ESTEVES, Gomez. Historia contemporánea del Paraguay. B.A., 1921. 140p.

1597 GAONA, Juan Bautista. Colección de datos referentes a su arbitraria destitución de la presidencia de la República. A., Tall. de "El Diario", 1906. 38p.

1598 GODOI, Juan Silvano. El coronel don Juan Antonio Es- curra, presidente electo de la república del Paraguay. A., Tall. nac. de H. Kraus, 1903. 32p.

1599 GONZALEZ, Juan Gualberto. Manifiesto del presidente de la república del Paraguay, d. Juan G. González, as sus conciudadanos. B.A., Tip. de El Correo español, 1894. 17p.

1600 GONZALEZ, Juan Natalicio; MORINIGO, Victor. Bajo las bombas del malón. A., Edit. Guarania, 1947. 77p.

1601 GONZALEZ, Juan Natalicio. Cuestiones políticas: con- ferencia dada el 11 de marzo de 1926, en el Club Re- publicano. A., 1926? 10p.

1602 GONZALEZ, Teodosio. Infortunios del Paraguay. B.A., Tall. gráf. argentinos L.J. Rosso, 1931. 577p.

1603 GORI, Pedro. La anarquía ante los tribunales. A., 1924. 32p. (Biblioteca de la Agrupación "El Combate", 4)

1603a GREAT BRITAIN. FOREIGN OFFICE. Reports by Her Majesty's Secretaries of Embassy and Legation on the manufactures, commerce, &c., of the countries in which they reside. Part I. *British Parliamentary Papers* 1883, LXXI, 83-160 (Papers - command C3472).
This contains, in pp. 83-160, a report by A.G. Vansittart on the commerce, finance, &c. of Paraguay. It is an important source.

1604 HOMENAJE al Dr. Eusebio Ayala en el X aniversario de su deceso. B.A., 1952. 40p.

1605 IBARRA, Alonso. La revoluciones paraguaya en letras de molde, de 1870 a 1949. A., Edit. Popular, 1949. 67p.

1606 ISASI, Carlos Luis. Política; tesis presentada para optar al título de doctor en derecho y ciencias sociales. A., Imp. de El Civico, 1902. 52p.

1607 JACQUET, Alfredo J. Problemas de las tras-guerra, con un prólogo del dr. Adolfo Aponte. A., S. Puigbonet, 1935. 166p.

1608 JAEGGLI, Alfredo L. Albino Jara, un varón metéorico. B.A., 1963. 357p.

1609 LACONICH, Marco Antonio. El Paraguay mutilado. Montevideo, Edit. Paraguay, 1939. 94p.

1610 LIGA NACIONAL INDEPENDIENTE. La nueva política; acta-programa de constitución de la Liga Nacional Independiente y memoria del presidente del Consejo Directivo. A., 1930. 29p.

1610a LOPEZ DE DECOUD, Adelina. Biografía de Don Hector Francisco Decoud; in memoriam. B.A., J. Suarez, 1937. 399p.

1611 LUMSDEN, E.W.H. Fascist Paraguay in which South America's poorest, most isolated, most backward republic takes a plan from Europe. CUH (1936) 61-65.

1612 MAIZ, Fidel. Carta del padre Fidel Maíz al director de "La Democracia" a prósposito de las conferencias

del doctor Wood en el Ateneo Paraguayo. A., Imp. de "La Democracia", 1886. 65p.
On church-state relations.

1613 MIRANDA, Blas. Ligeras disquisiciones. A., Tall. nac. de H. Kraus, 1902. 67p.

1614 MIRANDA, Blas. Una figura contradictoria y sombría. A., 194? 29p.
Arturo Bray.

1615 MOSQUEIRA, Silvano. Juan Silvano Godoi, su vida y su obra. A., La Colmena, 1935. 117p.

1616 MOSQUEIRA, Silvano. Páginas sueltas. A., H. Kraus, 1907. 113p.

1617 MUÑOZ, Ramón P. Inquietudes nacionales, la idealidad paraguayista. A., Tall. gráf. "El Arte", 1926. 87p.

1618 LA NACION, BUENOS AIRES. Reclamación temeraria; las pretendidas 3,105 leguas de tierras publicas en el Paraguay de madam Linch y de sus subrogantes, consideradas ante la razón y el derecho. Artículos jurídicos publicados en "La Nación" sobre esta cuestión.... Fallo del Superior tribunal de justicia. A., Tip. de "La nación", 1888. 35p.

1618a NIETO, Alejandro. Silvio Pettirossi. A., Edit. Don Bosco, 1970? 8p. (Galería paraguayos ilustres, 2. Celeste)

1619 El NUEVO ideario nacional; manifiesto á los trabajadores y hombres jóvenes de todos los partidos. A., La Colmena, 1929. 66p.

1620 O'LEARY, Juan Emiliano. Apoteosis del general Bernardino Caballero. A., Imp. Militar, 1949. 16p.

1621 O'LEARY, Juan Emiliano. Bernardino Caballero; discurso pronunciada en Ybycuí el 20 de mayo 1939 en el grandioso homenaje a la memoria del gran soldado y reconstructor de la patria, en el centenario de su nacimiento. A., Tall. "El Arte", 1939. 43p.

1622 O'LEARY, Juan Emiliano. Ildefonso A. Bermejo, falsario, impostor y plagiario. A., 1953. 74p. (Biblioteca de la FF. AA. de la Nación, 10)

1623 O'LEARY, Juan Emiliano. El legado cívico del héroe. A., Biblioteca "Blas Garay", 1944. 21p.

1624 ORIHUELA, E. Leyendas falsas: por la verdad histórica, por los fueros del partido liberal. B.A., Edit. Poguasu, 1961. 51p.

1625 ORTIZ PACHECO, Nicolás. La justicia contra el machete: réplica al libro "Bajo el signo del marte" del Canciller paraguaya Justo Pastor Benítez. La Paz, Ed. Renacimiento, 1935. 220p.

1625a PAIVA, Armando. Dr. Félix Paiva. A., Edit. Don Bosco, 1966? 16p. (Galería de paraguayos ilustres, 1)

1626 PALOTES, Perico de los, *pseud.* Historia del General Avestruz, ex-Presidente de la República del Paraguay, escrito en verso jocoserio. n.p., 1889. 62p.

1627 PARAGUAY: a note as to its position and prospects. n.p., 1871. 8p.

1628 PARAGUAY. CONGRESO NACIONAL. CAMARA DE DIPUTADOS. Juicio político, iniciado a pedido de S.E. el Señor Presidente de la República Dr. José P. Guggiari, con motivo de los sucesos del 23 de octubre de 1931. A., Imp. nac., 1932. 142p.

1629 PARAGUAY. CONVENCION NACIONAL CONSTITUYENTE. Actas de la Convención nacional constituyente del año 1870. República del Paraguay. A., Tip. del Congreso, 1897. 158p.

1630 PARAGUAY. MINISTERIO DE RELACIONES EXTERIORES. Circular del Ministerio de relaciones exteriores, república del Paraguay. A., Imp. de La Nación paraguaya, 1873. 14p.
On the revolt led by Caballero and Barreiro.

1631 PARAGUAY. PRESIDENTE, 1880-1886. Discurso del jeneral don Bernardino Caballero al recibirse de la presidencia de la república ante el honorable Congreso de la nación el 25 de noviembre de 1882. A., Imp. de "La Reforma", 1882. 5p.

1632 PARAGUAY. PRESIDENTE, 1880-1886. Discursos pronunciada por el señor general don Bernardino Caballero en el acto de la transmisión del mando supremo de la república y por el señor general don Patricio Escobar al recibirse de él, el día 25 de noviembre de 1886. A., Imp. de "El Orden", 1886. 7p.

1633 PARAGUAY. PRESIDENTE, 1886-1890. Discursos del general don Patricio Escobar en el acto de prestar juramento ante el Congreso legislativo como presidente de la república del Paraguay en el 5. período constitucional, 25 de noviembre, 1886. A., Imp. de La Democracia, 1886. 9p.

1634 PARAGUAY. PRESIDENTE, 1890-94. Discours prononcé au Congrès national par le citoyen Jean G. González en prêtant serment à la Constitution le 24 novembre 1890. Assomption, Imprimerie et Atelier de Reliure "El Paraguayo", 1890. 8p.

1635 PARAGUAY. PRESIDENTE, 1890-1894. Manifiesto del presidente de la república del Paraguay, d. Juan G. González, a sus conciudadanos. B.A., Tip. de El Correo español, 1894. 17p.

1636 PARAGUAY. PRESIDENTE, 1890-1894. Mensaje del gobierno y proyectos de ley relativos al arreglo de la garantía del Ferro-carril central. 24 de mayo de 1893. A., Tall. nac. de H. Kraus, 1896. 15p.

1637 PARAGUAY. PRESIDENTE, 1890-1894. Mensaje y discursos leidos al Congreso Nacional el 25 de noviembre de 1890 en ocasión del juramento à la Constitución prestado por el nuevo Presidente de la República, ciudadano Juan G. Gonzalez. A., Tip. y Encuadernación "El Paraguay", 1890. 9p.

1638 PARAGUAY. PRESIDENTE, 1894-1898. Discursos pronunciados por el señor general d. Juan Bautista Eguzquiza al prestar al juramento ante el h. Congreso de la nación el 25 de noviembre de 1894 y por el señor don Marcos Morínigo en el acto de la transmisión del mando supremo de la república. A., 1894. 8p.

1639 PARAGUAY. PRESIDENTE, 1894-1898. Discursos pronunciados por el general Juan B. Egusquiza en el acto de la transmisión del mando supremo de la república y por el ciudadano don Emilio Aceval al recibirse de él, el dia 25 de noviembre de 1898. A., Escuela tip. salesiana, 1898. 15p.

1640 PARAGUAY. PRESIDENTE, 1894-1898. Mensaje del presidente de la República al honorable Congreso de la Nación al abrir sus sesiones, abril de 1898. A., Tip. de "La Opinión", 1898. 31p.

1641 PARAGUAY. PRESIDENTE, 1898-1902. Mensaje del presidente de la República del Paraguay al abrir las sesiones del Congreso de la Nación en 1900. A., Tip. "La Tribuna", 1900. 26p.

1642 PARAGUAY. PRESIDENTE, 1902-1904. Coronel Juan A. Escurra, presidente de la repúblíca, su manifiesto al pueblo paraguayo. A., Tip. "El Pais", 1904. 15p.

1643 PARAGUAY. PRESIDENTE, 1902-1904. Discurso pronunciada por el ciudadano coronel don Juan A. Escurra al prestar el juramento ante el h. Congreso de la nación. A., Escuela artes y oficios, 1902. 8p.

1644 PARAGUAY. PRESIDENTE, 1902-1904. Mensaje al honorable Congreso Nacional al abrir sus sesiones, abril de 1904. A., Tip. "El País", 1904. 16p.

1645 PARAGUAY. PRESIDENTE, 1904-1905. Mensaje del presidente provisorio de la República al honorable Congreso Nacional al abrir sus sesiones, abril de 1905. A., Tall. de "El Diario", 1905. 18p.

1646 PARAGUAY. PRESIDENTE, 1912-1916. Mensaje del presidente de la República del Paraguay don Eduardo Schaerer, abril de 1915. A., Tall. Gráf. del Estado, 1915. 56p.

1647 PARAGUAY. PRESIDENTE, 1916-1919. Discurso-programa del exmo. señor presidente de la república, dr. dn. Manuel Franco, y otros documentos relativos a la transmisión del mando, agosto de 1916. A., Tall. gráf. del estado, 1916. 27p.

1648 PARAGUAY. PRESIDENTE, 1916-1919. Mensaje del presidente de la República del Paraguay Dr. don Manuel Franco, abril de 1917. A., Tall. Gráf. del Estado, 1917. 52p.

1649 PARAGUAY. PRESIDENTE, 1919-1920. Transmisión de mando. Discurso y programa de gobierno. 15 de agosto de 1920. Piribebul, Imp. nac., 1921. 22p.

1650 PARAGUAY. PRESIDENTE, 1920-1921. Mensaje del presidente de la República del Paraguay don Manuel Gondra, abril de 1921. A., Imp. nac., 1921. 77p.

1651 PARAGUAY. PRESIDENTE, 1920-1921. Transmisión de mando, discurso y programa de gobierno, 15 de agosto de 1920. A., Imp. nac., 1921. 22p.

1652 PARAGUAY. PRESIDENTE, 1924-1928. Mensaje del Presidente de la República del Paraguay al Congreso Nacional. A., Imp. nac., 1926. 76p.

1653 PARAGUAY. PROVISIONAL GOVERNMENT, 1869-1870. Manifiesto del gobierno provisorio. A., Typ. do Exercito, Imp. L.C.O., Guimaraes, 1869. 10p.

1654 EL PARAGUAYO. Artículos publicados en "El Paraguayo" referentes a la reclamación Coredero. A., Imp. de El Paraguayo, 1888. 56p.

1655 PARENTESIS siniestro en la democracia paraguaya. La obra de Caín librada á la luz de la civilización y del sentimiento humanitario. Proceso público de la despiadada matanza de un pueblo despotizado á la vista del augusto tribunal de la conciencia nacional. Corrientes, Establecimiento tip. B. Fages, 1910. 13p.

1656 PASTORE, Carlos. Contribución de Manuel Gondra en la paz de América. Conferencia pronunciada en la Academia Diplomatica Internacional el 12 de junio de 1953. Montevideo, Antequera, 1953. 11p.

1657 PASTORE, Carlos. Interpretación histórica del movimiento del 18 de Octubre de 1891. B.A., Ed. del autor, 1957. 12p.

1658 PEREZ, José A. Cecilio Baez, su actuación política dentro y fuera del país. A., 1907. 103p.

1659 PERSPECTIVAS que ofreceria un conflicto armado entre el Paraguay y Bolivia; estudio por el que se demuestra que el triunfo corresponderia ampliamente a las armas paraguayas. A? 192? 10p.

1660 PRIETO, Justo. 18 meses de regresión política. B.A., Tall. Gráf. A. Plantié, 1937. 110p.

1661 PRIETO, Justo. Eusebio Ayala, presidente de la victoria. B.A., Edit. Ayacucho, 1950. 60p.

1662 PRIETO, Justo. "Llenense los claros"; una omisión en el texto de libro: 23 de octubre, una página del historia contemporánea del Paraguay. B.A., Tall. Gráf. Lucania, 1957. 16p.
See no. 1572.

1663 La REVOLUCION del 17 de febrero, 1936. A., Imp. nac., 1938. 479p.
Reprinted: 1941. 476p.

1664 La REVOLUCION de febrero. A., Edit. Paraguay, 1939. 72p.

1665 RIQUELME GARCIA, Benigno. Cumbre en soledad, vida de Manuel Gondra. B.A., Ayacucho, 1951. 180p.

1666 RIVAROLA, Rodolfo Juan Nemesio. El Paraguay político. B.A., Revista argentina de ciencias políticas, 1911. 23p.

1667 RODRIGUEZ ALCALA, José. La administración del coronel Escurra; colección de los artículos editoriales publicados bajo el título de Pueblo y gobierno en la Democracia. A., Tip. "El País", 1904. 92p.

1667a ROJAS, J. Guillermo. El doctor don Benjamín Aceval en villa Encarnación. A., Imp. de la Democracia, 1896. 31p.

1668 ROMERO, Genaro. Los problemas nacionales. A., Tall. gráf. del estado, 1915. 72p.

1669 RUIZ FERNANDEZ, Antonio. Los gobernantes del Paraguay; trasmisión del poder público 25 de noviembre de 1886. A., Imp. de Obras, 1886. 36p.

1670 SAMANIEGO, Pedro P. Por los fueros de un libro. B.A., 1938. 63p.

1671 SAMANIEGO, Pedro P. Por los fueros de la justicia y en defensa de los blasones de la Facultad de derecho. B.A., 1937. 123p.

1672 SCALA, Carlos Alberto Pusineri. La moneda de 1870. HP 8-10 (1963-65) 128-50.

1673 SINTESIS política y cívica del Paraguay de 1904 a 1940. A., 1961. 9p.

1674 SOLER, Juan José. Hacia la unión nacional. Cuarenta años de vida pública. B.A., Impresora del Plata, 1943. 299p.

1675 SOSA, Antonio. Vida pública. B.A., Imp. y casa edit. de A. Grau, 1905. 173, ii p.

1676 SOSA ESCALADA, Jaime. El general Ferreira; apuntes biográficos sacados de la obra inédita: Política brasileira en el Paraguay y Rio de la Plata. A., Est. tip. de Jordan y Villaamil, 1906. 56p.

1677 STEFANICH, Juan. El Paraguay en febrero de 1936. B.A., Edit. El Mundo Nuevo, 1946. 228p. (Capítulos de la revolución paraguaya, 3)

1678 STEFANICH, Juan. Renovación y liberación, la obra del Gobierno de Febrero. B.A., Edit. El Mundo Nuevo, 1946. 324p. (Capítulos de la revolución paraguaya.)

1679 STEFANICH, Juan. La restauración histórica del Paraguay. B.A., Edit. El Mundo Nuevo, 1945. 80p. (Capítulos de la revolución paraguaya, 1)

1680 VALLE, Florentino del. Cartilla cívica; proceso político del Paraguay 1870-1950; el Partido Liberal y la Asociación Nacional Republicana (Partido Colorado) en la balanza de la verdad histórica. B.A., Tall. gráf. Lucania, 1951. 142p.

1681 VOLTA GAONA, Enrique. 23 de octubre; caireles de sangre en el alma de la patria paraguaya. 2. ed. A., El Arte, 1957. 303p.

1682 WARREN, Harris Gaylord. The golden fleecing: the Paraguayan loans of 1871 and 1872. IAEA 26 (1972) no. 1, 3-24.

1683 WARREN, Harris Gaylord. The Hopkins claim against Paraguay and "The case of the missing jewels". IAEA 22 (1968) no. 4, 23-44.

1684 WARREN, Harris Gaylord. Litigation in English courts and claims against Paraguay resulting from the War of the Triple Alliance. IAEA 22 (1969) no. 4, 31-46.

1685 WARREN, Harris Gaylord. Political aspects of the Paraguayan revolution. HAHR 30 (1950) 2-25.

1686 ZARATE, Teresa. Parcelación y distribución de las tierras fiscales en el Paraguay (1870-1904). RPS 10 no. 26 (1973) 121-40.

1687 ZULEIZARRETA, Ramón. Dictamen del doctor Ramón Zuleizarreta sobre el valor legal de los títulos de Madame Lynch en la reclamación de las 3,000 y pico de leguas. A., 1880. 40p.

2. *The Chaco War 1932-1935*

a) General accounts

1688 ALVAREZ del VAYO, J. El conflicto del Chaco y su fin. TF 1 (1935) no. 2, 25-43.

1689 APONTE BENITEZ, Leandro. Buscando la verdad histórica al margen de "Reminiscencias". A., El Arte, 1963. 46p.
See no. 1691.

1689a BAPTISTA GUMUCIO, Mariano. Historia grafica de la guerra del Chaco. 2. ed. La Paz, Ultima Hora, 1976. 254p.

1690 BARRETO, Sindulfo. Por qué no pasaron: nubes sobre el Chaco, revelaciones diplomáticas y militares. A., Escuela Técnica Salesiana, 1969. 362p.

1691 BOZZANO, José Alfredo. Reminiscencias. A., Casa Edit. Toledo, 1962. 129p. (Serie Guerra del Chaco, 3)

1692 CENTURION, César R. Breve reseña histórica de la Guerra del Chaco. A., 1970. 240p.

1693 DELGADO, Nicolás. História de la Guerra de Chaco; mis recuerdos personales. A., Imp. Militar, 193?-43. 2 vols.

1694 DE RONDE, Philip. Paraguay, a gallant little nation; the story of Paraguay's war with Bolivia. N.Y., G.P. Putnam, 1935. 123p.

1695 DE RONDE, Philip. Paraguay: el heroísmo de una pequeña nación; entretelones de la guerra entre Paraguay y Bolivia en el Gran Chaco. B.A., Imp. inglesa, 1935. 67p.

1696 DIANDERAS, Antonio. Sinopsis de la guerra del Chaco. RMG 1934, June-July, 1879-86.

1697 DIAZ ARGUEDAS, Julio. Como fué derrocado el hombre simbolo, Salamanca; un capítulo de la guerra con el Paraguay. La Paz, Empresa Editoria "Universio", 1957. 344p.

1698 DIAZ ARGUEDAS, Julio. Los elegidos de la gloria. La Paz, Imp. Intendencia General de Guerra, 1937-
Vol. 1 only published.

1699 DIAZ ARGUEDAS, Julio. La guerra con el Paraguay, resumen histórico-biográfico, 1932-1935. La Paz, 1942. vi, 402p.

1699a DIAZ MACHICAO, Porfirio. Los invencibles en la Guerra del Chaco; palabras de un combatiente contra el crimen de la guerra. B.A., Edit. Claridad, (1936). 107p.

1700 ESTIGARRIBIA, José Félix. The epic of the Chaco: Marshal Estigarribia's memoirs of the Chaco War, 1932-1935; ed. and annotated by Pablo Max Ynsfran. Austin, University of Texas Press, 1950. xiv, 221p.
Reprinted: N.Y., Greenwood Press, 1969.

1701 ESTIGARRIBIA, José Félix. La epopeya del Chaco; memorias de la Guerra del Chaco del mariscal José Félix

Estigarribia. Redacción y anotación del Dr. Pablo Max Ynsfran. A., Imp. nac., 1972. xii, 375p.

1702 GLAGOLEV, V.P. Voina v Gran Chako, 1931-1933gg; sostavleno po nemetskim i angliiskim istochnikam. VR 10 (1934) 110-15.

1703 GONZALEZ, Antonio E. La guerra del Chaco: contribución a la historia. Sao Paulo, Tip. Cupolo, 1941. 242p.

1703a GONZALEZ, Antonio E. Triptico del Chaco (la guerra, el hombre, la paz). A., Ediciones Comuneros, 1977. 306p.

1704 GUANES, Alejo H. El cuarto: honrar a padre y madre; contestando a un distinguido veterano de la guerra del Chaco que cometió la irreverencia de injuriar la memoria de su ilustre ex comandante en jefe. A., 1971. 14p.

1704a GUANES, Alejo H. Verde Olivo!! reflexiones de un lisido de guerra. n.p., 1975? 62p.

1705 GUANES MACHAIN, Luis. Recuerdos y observaciones de la Guerra del Chaco. A., El Arte, 1963. 34p.

1706 La GUERRA del Chaco Boreal vista en sus aspectos diplomático, político y militar a través de las crónicas de la epoca. A., Edit. Popular, 1949-

1706a GUERRERO, Julio C. También estuve en el Chaco; edición especial del capítulo III del libro del autor "El Chaco", o "La guerra boliviano-paraguaya", revisada y seguida de varios anexos. La Paz, Arno hnos, 1935. iii, 146p.

1707 ISLAS, Alejandro. Perfiles y relatos de la epopeya chaqueña. A., Edit. Popular, 1949. 109p.

1708 LINDSAY, J.W. The war over the Chaco: a personal account. INT, 1935, 231-40.

1709 LLORENS MORA, Alcides. Héroes y mártires de la epopeya del Chaco. A., Edit. El Gráfico, 196-? -

1710 MACIAS, Silvio. La guerra del Chaco, Paraguay versus Bolivia (1932-1935). A., Edit. "La Tribuna", 1936? 275p.

1711 MARCET, José Carlos. Datos para una reseña cronológica sobre los antecedentes, desarrollo y resultado de la Guerra del Chaco. A., Ediciones Comuneros, 1974. 113p.

1712 MOLAS, José D. Polvaredas de bronce en los caminos trágicos del Chaco Paraguayo. A., S. Puigbonet, 1934. 158p.

1713 OLIVER, M.M. La guerra en el Chaco Boreal. Cómo se defiende el Paraguay. Crónicas de la linea de fuego. B.A., Roldán, 1935. 259p.

1714 OSORIO, Juan Antonio. Entretelones de la guerra del Chaco; documentos básicos para el juicio histórico. La Paz, 1973. 122p.

1715 PARAGUAY. DEPARTAMENTO DE TIERRAS Y COLONIZACION. El Chaco Paraguayo para sus defensores; iniciativa de un proyecto para colonización en el Chaco elevado al Ministerio de Hacienda por Genaro Romero, presidente. A., Imp. nac., 1933. 11p.

1716 PEREZ ACOSTA, Ernesto. La contienda del Chaco. A., Edit. El Gráfico, 1962-64. 2 vols.
Memoirs of an army chaplain.

1717 PEREZ ACOSTA, Juan Francisco. La conducta de Bolivia a la luz de las "reversales". B.A., 1934. 10p.

1718 POZO CANO, Raúl de. Santa Cruz de la Sierra por Raúl del Pozo Cano en colaboración con universitarios cruceños. Homenaje al pueblo mártir en el 340 aniversario de su traslación y en la aurora de su libertad: 1595 - 21 de mayo - 1935. A., Tall. de valores oficiales, 1935. 80p.

1719 QUEREJAZU CALVO, Roberto. Masamaclay; historia política, diplomática y militar de la Guerra del Chaco. La Paz, 1965. 484p.

1720 RAMOS GIMENEZ, Leopoldo. Los guerrilleros de la Muerte. A., Imp. "La Comercial", 1932. 16p. (Nandeba, v. 1, 1932, no. 1)

1721 RAMOS GIMENEZ, Leopoldo. Revelaciones sobre el alma paraguaya. B.A., Ferrari, 1934. 16p.

1722 RIOS, Angel F. La defensa del Chaco; verdades y mentiras de una victoria. B.A., Edit. Ayacucho, 1950. 450p.

1722a ROLON, Raimundo. Significación histórica de la guerra del Chaco para el destino del Paraguay en el nuevo aniversario del Campo Vía, 11 de diciembre 1933-1965. A?, Centenario de la Epopeya Nacional, n.d. 7p.

1723 SALAMANCA, Daniel. Documentos para una historia de la guerra del Chaco; selecionados del archivo de Daniel Salamanca. La Paz, D. Bosco, 1951-74. 4 vols.

1723a SALAMANCA, Daniel. Mensajes y memorias póstumas. Cochabamba, Edit. Canelas, 1976. 194p.

1724 SANCHEZ BONIFATO, César L. La última guerra en Sud América (connotaciones para una historia de la Guerra del Chaco). A., Ediciones del Pueblo, 1972. 112p. (Colección Blás Garay, 3)

1725 SELAYA P, Salustio. Documentos y memorias de la guerra del Chaco. La Paz, 1972-

1725a SETARO, Ricardo M. Imagenes secretas de la Guerra del Chaco (documentos). B.A., Edit. Fegrabo, 1935. 86p.

1726 SILES SALINAS, Jorge. La literatura boliviana de la Guerra del Chaco. La Paz, Ediciones de la Universidad Católica Boliviana, 1969. 142p.

1727 SOLER, Juan José. El Partido Liberal y la defensa del Chaco. A., 1935. 32p.

1728 STEFANICH, Juan. La guerra del Chaco; su significación rioplatense y americana; conferencia pronunciada el 20 de setiembre de 1972 en conmemoración del 40 aniversario de la Batalla de Boquerón, primera gran victoria del Paraguay en la Guerra del Chaco, 1932-1935. B.A., Casa Paraguaya, 1973. 20p.

1729 STEFANICH, Juan. El 23 de octubre de 1931; primera batalla por la defensa del Chaco y primer grito de la revolución de febrero de 1936. B.A., Edit. Febrero, 1959. 287p.

1730 TABERA R., Félix. Apuntes para la historia de la Guerra del Chaco. Picuiba. La Paz, Edit. Don Bosco, 1960. 461p.

1731 TORRES, A. Voina v Chako. IM 1933, no. 1-2, 21-5; 1935, no. 3, 52-6.

1732 TORRES, Juan Manuel; SOSA VALDEZ, D.; DELGADO, J. Garcia. La guerra y la paz del Chaco a través de la operación General Eugenio A. Garay del Colegio Militar Mariscal Francisco S. López. A., EMASA, 1967. 117p.

1733 VAUDRY, J. Le conflit entre la Bolivie et le Paraguay. TAM 58 (1932) no. 5, 275-80.

1734 VERGARA VICUÑA, Aquiles. Historia de la guerra del Chaco. La Paz, Lit. e imp. Unidas, 1940-44. 7 vols.

1735 VITTONE, Luis. La guerra del Chaco; aspectos y episodios sobresalientes. A., Direcc. Publiciones, Imp. Militar, 1964? 197p.

b) Diplomatic history

1736 AYALA, Eusebio. Ante el país: discursos del Dr. Eusebio Ayala. A., Imp. nac., 1932. 87p.

1736a AYALA QUEIROLO, Víctor. Gerónimo Zubizarreta, su actuación en la Conferencia de Paz. A., Edit. Casa-Libro, 1976. 342p.

1736b BALDIVIA GALDO, José María. La guerra con el Paraguay y la diplomacia Argentina. La Paz, Imp. "Electrica", 1934. 44p.

1737 BEJARANO, Ramón César. Antecedentes de la guerra con Bolivia. A., Casa Edit. Toledo, 1959. 45p. (Guerra del Chaco, 1)

1738 BEJARANO, Ramón César. Estudio de un pacto de no agresión entre Bolivia y Paraguay: noviembre 1931-diciembre 1932. Pitiantuta (cronología). A., Edit. Toledo, 1974. 55p. (Guerra del Chaco, 6)

1739 BOLIVIA and Paraguay make peace. BPAU 72 (1938) no. 8, 450-55.

1740 BOLIVIA. MINISTERIO DE RELACIONES EXTERIORES. Bolivian-Paraguayan conflict. Violations of the practices of international law. La Paz, Imp. "Electrica", 1932. 16p.

1741 BOLIVIA. MINISTERIO DE RELACIONES EXTERIORES. Conflicto boliviano-paraguayo; violaciones a las prácticas del derecho internacional. La Paz, 1932. iii, 18p.

1741a BOLIVIA. MINISTERIO DE RELACIONES EXTERIORES. Documentos relativos a la agresión del Paraguay contra el fortín boliviano Vanguardia. La Paz, Edit. Renacimiento, 1929. v, 129p.

1742 BRADEN, Spruille. Inter-American commercial arbitration. A resumé of the role played by arbitration in the Chaco dispute. AJ 2 (1938) no. 4, 387-95.

1743 BUENOS AIRES. CHACO PEACE CONFERENCE, 1935-1939. Communication from the President of the Buenos Aires

Conference transmitting the procès-verbal containing the text of the declaration of the cessation of war and an appeal to the two Republics. Geneva, 1935. 2p. (League of Nations no. C. 455. M. 237. 1935. vii)

1744 BUENOS AIRES. CHACO PEACE CONFERENCE, 1935-1939. Conferencia de Paz; documentos y delagaciones. B.A., 1936. 51p.

1745 BUENOS AIRES. CHACO PEACE CONFERENCE, 1935-1939. La Conferencia de Paz del Chaco, 1935-1939; compilación de documentos. B.A., Grandes Tall. gráf. E.L. Frigerio, 1939. 1056p.

1746 BUENOS AIRES. CHACO PEACE CONFERENCE, 1935-1939. Dispute between Bolivia and Paraguay: communication from the President of the Peace Conference of Buenos Aires, Jan. 21, 1936. Geneva, 1936. 5p. (League of Nations no. C. 79 (a) M. 27 (a) 1936 vii)

1747 BUENOS AIRES. CHACO PEACE CONFERENCE, 1935-1939. Dispute between Bolivia and Paraguay: telegrams from the President of the Peace Conference at Buenos Aires. Geneva, 1935. 1p. (League of Nations no. C. 340. M. 215. 1936 vii)

1748 BUENOS AIRES. CHACO PEACE CONFERENCE, 1935-1939. Procès-verbal. Oct. 18, 1935. Geneva, 1935. 4p. (League of Nations no. C. 431. M. 222. 1935 vii)

1749 BUENOS AIRES. CHACO PEACE CONFERENCE, 1935-1939. Texts of the protocols signed at Buenos Aires on June 12th, 1935, by the ministers of foreign affairs of Bolivia and Paraguay together with the representatives of the mediating countries. Geneva, 1935. 5p. (League of Nations no. C. 270. M. 137. 1935 vii)

1750 BUSTAMENTE, Daniel Sánchez. La verdad sobre el conflicto del Chaco; reseña histórico-juridica. La Paz, Escuela tip. Salesiana, 1932. 43p.
Also: B.A., Comité de Defensa de los Derechos e Intereses de Bolivia, 1932. 38p.

1751 CAMPOS, Alfredo R. Misión de paz en el Chaco Boreal. Montevideo, Centro Militar, 1954. 2 vols. (Obras de la Biblioteca General Artigas, 19-20)

1752 CESSATION of war in the Chaco (protocol of June 12, 1935). BPAU 69 (1935) 518-20.

1753 The CHACO boundary award. BPAU 72 (1938) 620-22.

1754 The CHACO dispute between Bolivia and Paraguay. IC 1936, 518-44.

1755 CHARTRAIN, François. Causes de la guerre du Chaco: éléments du jugement. CMHL 14 (1970) 97-123.

1756 CIANCIO, Pedro N. La guerra del Chaco; Bolivia y el Paraguay ante la historia; América y el conflicto. B.A., Tall. gráf. de "La Vanguardia", 1933. 40p.

1757 COMITE PARAGUAYO, BUENOS AIRES. América contra la guerra, por la paz y la justicia internacional; la opinión de la prensa argentina en defensa del derecho. B.A., 1932. 16p.

1758 The CONFLICT between Bolivia and Paraguay in the Chaco Boreal. SIA for 1933 (1934) 393-438.

1758a COOPER, Russell Morgan; MATTISON, Mary. The Chaco dispute, the development and phases of the Bolivia-Paraguay conflict and League intervention. Geneva, Geneva Research Center, 1934. 25p. (Geneva special studies, vol. v, no. 2, 1934)

1759 DE WILDE, John C. South American conflicts: the Chaco and Leticia. FPR 9 (1933) no. 6, 58-68.

1760 The DISPUTE between Bolivia and Paraguay over the Chaco Boreal. SIA for 1930 (1931) 421-36; for 1936 (1937) 837-72.

1761 ELIO, Tomás Manuel. La Guerra y la Paz del Chaco. La Paz, 1970. 332p.

1762 FINOT, Enrique. La guerra del Chaco y los Estados Unidos. La Paz, Ed. América, 1935. 48p.

1763 GARNER, William R. The Chaco dispute: a study of prestige diplomacy. Washington, Public Affairs Press, 1966. 151p.

1764 GILLETTE, Michael L. Huey Long and the Chaco War. LH 11 (1970) no. 4, 293-311.

1765 GONZALEZ, Juan Natalicio. El drama del Chaco; el petróleo, la guerra y la oligarquía liberal. A., Edit. Guarania, 1938. 28p.

1766 GONZALEZ ALSINA, Ezequiel. El entregador del Chaco. A., Artes Gráficas Zamphiropolos, 1968. 145p.
An attack on Efraím Cardozo.

1767 GONZALEZ BLANCO, P. El conflicto entre Bolivia y Paraguay: El por qué de la guerra del Chaco. RE 10 (1935) 48-56.

1768 GONZALEZ BLANCO, Pedro. El conflicto beligero Boliviano-Paraguayo y la cuestión chaqueña. Madrid, Imp. Saez hermanos, 1934. 110p.

1769 La GUERRA en el Chaco y la Liga de las Naciones. Santiago de Chile, El Imparcial, 1934. 51p.

1770 GUTIERREZ, Julio A. El conflicto del Chaco; la nación agresora. B.A., Tall. Gráf. "Gadola", 1933. 57p.

1771 INTERNATIONAL CONFERENCE OF AMERICAN STATES ON CONCILIATION AND ARBITRATION, 1928-29. Proceedings of the International conference of American states on conciliation and arbitration held at Washington December 10, 1928 - January 5, 1929. English, Spanish, Portuguese and French texts. Washington, United States Government Printing Office, 1929. ix, 738p.

1772 KAIN, Ronald Stuart. Behind the Chaco War. CUH 1935, Aug., 468-74.

1773 KAIN, Ronald Stuart. The Chaco dispute and the peace system. PSQ 50 (1935) 321-42.

1774 KIRKPATRICK, Helen Paull. The Chaco dispute, the League and Pan Americanism. Geneva, Geneva Research Center, 1936. 23p. (Geneva Special Studies, vol. vii, no. 4, June 1936)

1775 LACONICH, Marco Antonio. El espíritu de Chuquisaca; proceso y desarrollo de la agresión boliviana. A., Imp. nac., 1933. 93p.

1776 LACONICH, Marco Antonio. El Iris de la paz o los mercaderes de ginebra en el Chaco Boreal. n.p., 1935. 107p.

1777 LACONICH, Marco Antonio. La paz del Chaco; un pueblo traicionado. Prólogo del coronel Rafael Franco. A?, Edit. Paraguay, 1939. 242p.

1778 (LA PRADELLE, P. du.) Le conflit du Chaco. RDISDP 12 (1933) 297-322, 645-65.

1779 LEAGUE OF NATIONS. Dispute between Bolivia and Paraguay. LNOJ (1929) Feb., 264-74; (1933) June, 752-89; Sept., 1072-80, 1082-99; Nov., 1552-93; (1934) Feb., 239-71; July, 743-867; Nov., 1539-1611. LNOJ Special Supplements: no. 124 (1934) 175p.; no. 126 (1934) 9-53; no. 134 (1935) 74p.; no. 135 (1935) 1-50.

1780 LEAGUE OF NATIONS. Documents received from the president of the Council of the League of Nations relative to certain incidents on the frontier of Bolivia and Paraguay. London, HMSO, 1929. 20p. (British Parliamentary Papers, 1928-29, xxiii, 743. -Cmd 3259)

1781 LEAGUE OF NATIONS. CHACO COMMISSION. Dispute between Bolivia and Paraguay. Geneva, 1934. 67p. (C. 154. M. 04. 1934. vii)

1782 LEAGUE OF NATIONS. DELEGATION FROM PARAGUAY. Dispute between Bolivia and Paraguay. Communication from the Paraguayan representative. Memorandum on the action of the League of Nations, and particularly of the Chaco Commission of Enquiry, in the Bolivian-Paraguayan dispute. Geneva, 1934. 14p. (C. 186. M. 75. 1934. vii)

1783 LEAGUE OF NATIONS. SPECIAL ASSEMBLY, 1934. Dispute between Bolivia and Paraguay. Report as provided for under article 15, paragraph 4, of the Covenant, drawn up by the Committee of the Assembly in pursuance of the resolution of September 27th, 1934, and adopted by the Assembly on November 24th, 1934. Geneva, 1934. 10p. (A (Extr.) 5, 1934. vii)

1784 LEAGUE OF NATIONS. ASSEMBLY. ADVISORY COMMITTEE ON THE DISPUTE BETWEEN BOLIVIA AND PARAGUAY; Dispute between Bolivia and Paraguay; report by M. de Vasconcellos (Portugal). Geneva, 1935. 2p. (A. 46. 1935. vii)

1785 LOUREIRO, Pizarro. La conferencia del paz del Chaco. Rio de Janeiro, 1936. 48p.

1786 MERCADO MOREIRA, Miguel. Historia diplomática de la Guerra del Chaco. La Paz, 1966. 287p.

1787 MOLINS, Wenceslao Jaime. Una voz argentina en el conflicto del Chaco Boreal. B.A., Comité de Defensa de los Derechos e Intereses de Bolivia, 1932. 8p.

1788 NIELSEN REYES, Federico. El conflicto del Chaco entre Bolivia y el Paraguay. BMRE 1931, Oct.-Dec., 96-124.

1789 NIETO PENA, Xesús; SAS-MURIAS, Ramiro de. El conflicto del Chaco a la luz de la historia. Madrid, Edit. Cenit, 1933. 257p.

1790 NUESTRO país suscribió tratados con Paraguay y Bolivia. RCE 1941, 148-55.

1791 ON Spruille Braden's contribution to the solution of the Chaco dispute. IAEA 14 (1960) no. 2, 104.

1792 PARAGUAY-BOLIVIA; aspectos de la guerra del Chaco. A., Imp. militar, 1934? 38p.

1793 PARAGUAY. CONGRESO NACIONAL. La paz con Bolivia ante el poder legislativo. A., Imp. nac., 1939. 99p.

1794 PARAGUAY. CONGRESO NACIONAL. Prótocolo de paz suscrito en Buenos Aires el 12 de Junio de 1935, su discusión y sanción en las cámaras legislativas. A., Imp. nac., 1935. 67p.

1795 PARAGUAY. DELEGACION A LA COMISION ESPECIAL DE LA SOCIEDAD DE LAS NACIONES. Los origenes de la guerra del Chaco; memorandum el 8 de marzo de 1934. A., Imp. nac., 1934. 28p.

1796 PARAGUAY. DELEGACION DEL PARAGUAY SOBRE CANJE Y REPATRICACION DE PRISIONEROS A LA COMISION DE LA CONFERENCIA DE PAZ. Memorandum de la Delegación del Paraguay sobre canje y repatricación de prisioneros presentado a la Comisión respective de la Conferencia de paz, Buenos Aires, 14 de octubre de 1935. A., Imp. nac., 1935. 37p.

1797 PARAGUAY. MINISTERIO DE RELACIONES EXTERIORES Y CULTO. Libro Blanco. A., Imp. nac., 1933-34. 4 vols.

1798 PARAGUAY. MINISTERIO DE RELACIONES EXTERIORES Y CULTO. Los origenes de la Guerra del Chaco. A., Imp. nac., 1943. 28p.

1799 PARAGUAY. MINISTERIO DE RELACIONES EXTERIORES Y CULTO. La responsabilité de la guerre du Chaco. The responsability (sic) for the war of the Chaco. Paris, 1935. 61p.
In French and English.

1800 RAMIREZ, Juan Isidro. El panamericanismo, el arbitraje y la agreción boliviana en el Chaco; un examen documental. Santiago de Chile, 1933. 126p.

1801 RAMIREZ, Juan Isidro. La paz del Chaco; la defensa de la linea de Hitos y el Comité de tres. B.A., Imp. Ferrari, 1942. 335p.

1802 RAMIREZ, Juan Isidro. El tratado de paz con Bolivia. Réplica al ex-canciller Luis Argaña y al ex-embajador Sr. Braden. Libertad de Prensa. B.A., 1946. 81p.

1802a RAMIREZ LOAIZA, Arturo. Position juridique du conflict du Chaco Boreal. Paris, A. Pedone, 1935. lv, 166p.

1803 RIVAROLA, Vicente. Memorias diplomáticas. B.A., Edit. Ayacucho, 1952-57. 3 vols.

1804 RODAS EGUINO, Justo. La guerra del Chaco; interpretación de política internacional americana. B.A., Librería y edit. "La Facultad", Bernabé y cia, 1938. 228p.

1805 ROUT, Leslie B. Politics of the Chaco Peace Conference, 1935-39. Austin, Published for the Institute of Latin American Studies by the University of Texas Press, 1970. xiv, 268p. (Latin American monographs, 19)

1806 SAAVEDRA, Bautista. El Chaco y la conferencia de paz de Buenos Aires. Santiago de Chile, Talleres de la Editorial Nascimiento, 1939. 291p.

1807 SAMANIEGO, Roque. Problemas nacionales. El Paraguay frente a Bolivia. A., 1932. vii, 99p.

1808 SAMPOGNARO, V. Causas geográficas de la guerra del Chaco. Leipzig, Verlag von Wilhelm Gronau, 1955. 18p.

1809 SANDELMANN, Hans. Die diplomatische Vorgeschichte des Chacokonflikts. Leiden, Sijthoff, 1936. 300p.

1810 SCHURZ, William Lytle. The Chaco dispute between Bolivia and Paraguay. FA 7 (1929) 650-55.

1811 SINANI, G. Voina v Iuzhnoi Amerike i anglo-amerikanskoe sopernichestvo. Moscow, Partizdat, 1933. 47p.

1811a SOLER, Juan José; El proyecto de la Comisión de la Liga y las aspiraciones nacionales. A., Imp. nac., 1934. 47p. (Publicación del Ateneo paraguayo)

1811b STEFANICH, Juan. La guerra del Chaco. A., 1934. 175p.

1812 Der STREITFALL zwischen Bolivia und Paraguay. ZV 19 (1935) 341-59.

1813 UNITED STATES. DELEGATION TO THE CHACO PEACE CONFERENCE, BUENOS AIRES, 1935-1939. The Chaco peace conference. Report of the delegation of the United States of America to the peace conference held at Buenos Aires July 1, 1935 - January 23, 1939. Washington, United States Government Printing Office, 1940. iv, 198p. (Dept. of State. Publication 1446. Conference series, 46)

1814 VAUDRY, J. La guerre au Chaco et la protocole de paix. G 65 (1936) 125-32.

1815 WADDELL, Agnes S. The Bolivia-Paraguay dispute. FPAIS 5 (1930) 483-90.

1816 WOOD, Bryce. The United States and Latin American wars, 1932-1942. N.Y., Columbia University Press, 1966. x, 519p.

1817 WOOLSEY, Lester Hood. The Chaco dispute. AJIL 26 (1932) 796-801.

1818 ZUBIZARRETA UGARTE, José M. La paz del Chaco. B.A., Buschi, 1974-

c) Military history - general

1819 ADORNO BENITEZ, Félix. Relato de episodios de la guerra del Paraguay con Bolivia, 1932-1935. A., El Arte, 1963. 171p.

1820 AMENDOLA DE TEBALDI, Honorato. La tragedia del Chaco Boreal, apuntes de guerra. B.A., Tor., 1935. 158p.

1821 APONTE BENITEZ, Leandro. Coronel Eugenio A. Garay, héroe del Chaco. A., Imp. Militar, 1944. 148p. (Biblioteca de las FF. AA. de la Nación, iv)
2. ed. General Garay, héroe del Chaco. A., El Arte, 1956. 249p.

1822 AYALA, Juan B. Planes de operaciones en la Guerra del Chaco. A., Tall. gráf. de la Escuela Técnica Salesiana Teniente Farmá y Capitán Figari, 1969. 64p.

1823 AYALA MOREIRA, Rogelio. Por que no ganamos la guerra del Chaco. La Paz, Tall. Gráf. Bolivianos, 1959. 375p.

1824 AZURDUY, Luis. Alto el fuego! Tres años de guerra chaqueña. B.A., Cabaut y cía, 1935. 193p.

1825 BEDOYA, Manuel. Actuación de la retaguardia en la guerra del Chaco; Junta de Aprovisionamiento, escrito a manera de memoria por su presidente Manuel Bedoya. A., Imp. Militar, 1957. 128p.

1826 BENITEZ, Justo Pastor. Bajo el signo de Marte. Montevideo, Impresora Uruguaya, 1934. 175p. (Crónicas de la guerra del Chaco)

1827 BRIZUELA, Rolando. Regimiento no. 12 "Rubio Ñú"; su actuación en la contienda del Chaco, 1932/36. A?, 1968? 31p.

1828 CABALLERO IRALA, Basiliano. Nuestros zapadores en la Guerra del Chaco. Montevideo, Libertad, 1939. 210p.

1829 CARISIMO, Atilano. El la Primera División de Infantería; diario de un combatiente. A., 1971. 569p.

1830 CASTAÑE DECOUD, Carlos. Tres acciones tácticas de la guerra del Chaco. A., Edit. El Gráfico, 1962. 83p.

1830a CESPEDES, Augusto. Crónicas heroicas de una guerra estupida. La Paz, Librería Edit. Juventud, 1975. 164p.

1831 DAVALOS, Hugo. Actuación de la marina en Guerra del Chaco. A., 1974. 219p.

1832 DIAZ LEON, Carlos. La sanidad militar paraguaya en la guerra del Chaco; historia documentada de su actuación. A., 1956-59. 3 vols.

1832a ENCINA, Eulogio. Por la senda del honor y del coraje. A., Dirección de Publicaciones de las FF. AA. NN., 1975. 153p.

1833 ESCOBAR RODAS, Cecilio. 8 dias de vida de úna patrulla: desde el 31. 10. 1934 al 7. 11. 1934, un jalón de contienda paraguayo-boliviana. A., Ediciones Comuneros, 1970. 125p.

1834 FAUPEL, W. Über Entstehung, Verlauf und Lehren des Chaco-krieges, 1932-1935. WW 70 (1936) 31-56.

1835 FERNANDEZ, Carlos José. La guerra del Chaco. B.A., A., 1955-73. 5 vols.
A work of major importance.

1836 GAGLIARDONE, César. La cirugía de guerra en la campaña del Chaco Boreal. A., El Arte, 1956. 82p.

1837 GONZALEZ, Antonio E. Preparación del Paraguay para la Guerra del Chaco. A., Edit. "El Grafico", 1957. 2 vols.

1837a KUNDT, Hans. Campaña del Chaco, el general Hans Kundt, comandante en jefe del Ejercito de Bolivia por Raúl Tovar Villa. La Paz, Edit. Don Bosco, 1961. 187p.

1838 LOPEZ, Pedro Germán. Aspectos del servicio de reabastecimiento del III Cuerpo de Ejército en la primera etapa de la guerra con Bolivia, agosto de 1932 - diciembre de 1933. A., Imp. Militar, 1942? 33p.

1838a LOPEZ VIDELA, Winsor. Documentos para la historia; sinopsis del Chaco Boreal, acciones del III Cuerpo de Ejercito, calendario de las acciones de guerra, 1932-1935. La Paz, 1977. 109p.

1839 MEDINA, Lorenzo. Algunas batallas memorables de la guerra del Chaco. A., 1972. 163p.

1840 MELGAREJO, Juan E. Transmisiones en la guerra del Chaco. A., Edit. El Gráfico, 1969. 422p.

1841 PARAGUAY. EJERCITO. Los partes del conductor, comunicados oficiales sobre la Guerra del Chaco. A., Sección Historia e Imprenta, 1950. 263p.

1842 PARAGUAY. MINISTERIO DE GUERRA Y MARINA. SERVICIO DE INFORMACION Y PROPAGANDA. Breve resumen de la campaña del Chaco. A., Imp. Militar, 1934. 22p.
Another ed.: 1935. 63p.

1842a POL, Hugo René. La campaña del Chaco; glosas y reflexiones militares zona de separación 1937 - primavera 1938. La Paz, 1945. 136p.

1842b RODRIGUEZ, Angel. Autopsia de una guerra (campaña del Chaco) (con opiniones técnicas de cinco generales de América). Santiago de Chile, Ediciones Ercilla, 1940. 9-138p.

1842c RODRIGUEZ ALCALA DE GONZALEZ ODDONE, Beatriz. Testimonios veteranos, evocando la Guerra del Chaco. A., Tall. Gráf. de Casa América, 1977. 608p.

1843 ROLON, Raimundo. La guerra del Chaco; campaña de 1934: después de Campo Via hasta el Parapití. A., Emasa, 1961-63. 2 vols.
An important work, by a leading military participant.

1843a SALDIVAR, Julio F.M. Yrendagüe y otros episodios: Guerra del Chaco, 1932-1935. A., 1975. 128p.

1844 SANIDAD del ejército en campaña durante la guerra del Chaco Boreal. RMN 1944, 185-91.

1845 VASCONSELLOS, Cándido A. Memoria de la sanidad en campaña; 1 de mayo, 1934 - 12 junio, 1935. A., La Colmena, n.d. 152p.

1846 VASCONSELLOS, Cándido A. El Regimiento de Caballeria N. 7 "General San Martín"; sus gestas gloriosas en la Guerra del Chaco. Prólogo del Dr. Laurentino Olascoaga. A., Edit. Tall. Gráf. Zamphirópolos, 1958. 110p.

1847 VIEDMA ESPINOLA, Luís. Coronel Valois Rivarola, "el jinete alado y fioro". n.p., Imp. Militar, 1955. 56p.

1848 ZOOK, David Hartzler. La conducción de la guerra del Chaco. Prólogo del dr. Charles W. Arnade. Traducción castellana del professor Pablo Max Ynsfran. B.A., Biblioteca del Oficial del Círculo Militar de la República Argentina, 1962. 463p.

1849 ZOOK, David Hartzler. The conduct of the Chaco War. Preface by Pablo Max Ynsfran. Foreword by Charles W. Arnade. N.Y., Bookman Associates, 1961. 280p.

1850 ZOTTI, Anibal. Siempre vivos; memorias de un excombatiente de la Guerra del Chaco. A., Artes Gráficas Zamphirópolos, 1972. 234p.

d) Military history - individual battles

1850a La ARTILLERÍA en las acciones de "Km 7", guerra del Chaco, by José Quiroga and others. La Paz, 1966. 64p.

1851 ARZABE REQUE, Antonio. Boquerón; diario de campaña: mes del sitio del glorioso. Oruro, 1961. 166p.

1852 AYALA QUEIROLO, Víctor. El Carmen; conferencia dictada en homenaje a los sub-teniente de la promoción Nanawa. A., Dirección de Publicaciones, 1959. 93p.

1853 AYALA QUEIROLO, Víctor. La incógnita de Platanillos, Guerra del Chaco, 1932. A., Imp. Zamphirópolos, 1965. 57p.

1853a BALBUENA ROJAS, Dionisio. Sucesos inéditos de la Batalla de "El Carmen". A., Dirección de Publicaciones de las FF. AA. NN., 1976. 270p.

1853b BARRIENTOS GUTIERREZ, Pablo H. La contraofensiva del Parapetí; guerra del Chaco. Santiago de Chile, Imp. "General Díaz", 1936. viii, 354p.

1854 BARRENECHEA TORRES, Adrian. Una verdad de la guerra; relación documentada de la gloriosa acción del 20 de febrero de 1935, defensa de Villa Montes. 2. ed. La Paz, 1960. Unpaged.

1855 La BATALLA de Gondra a través del testimonio de algunos protagonistas; Guerra del Chaco. Conferencias, disertaciones y publicaciones alusivas realizadas durante la semana de la Defensa de Gondra. A., Imp. Militar, 1959. 117p.

1856 BEJARANO, Ramón César. Boquerón; la batalla decisiva. A., 1965. 47p. (Serie Guerra del Chaco, 4)

1857 BRITOS, José Clemente. Batalla de El Carmen. A., Imp. La Humanidad, 1963. 216p.

1858 BRITOS, José Clemente. Fragmentos de la Batalla Zenteno-Gondra (Campo Via) desde el 24 de noviembre al 11 de diciembre de 1933. A., Nizza, 1966. 110p.

1859 COSTA DECOUD, José Segundo da. Batalla de Toledo (el núcleo y el martillo). Prólogo y notas del teniente coronel (S.R.) Antonio E. González. A., 1972. 384p.

1860 COSTA DECOUD, José Segundo da. El Frente oeste de la Batalla de Pampa Grande; episodios y recuerdos de la actuación de los Compañías del Regimiento de Infanteria no. 5 General Diaz, en la batalla de Pampa Grande, que demuestran que en la guerra la fortuna tanto como el valor determinan los sucesos que conducen a la victoria. A., 1968. 107, 68, 57, 153p.

1861 COSTA DECOUD, José Segundo da. Guerra del Chaco 1932-1935; batalla de Pampa Grande; setiembre de 1933; la historia del Frente Oeste. A., Imp. La Humanidad, 1969. 153p.

1862 COSTA DECOUD, José Segundo da. Guerra del Chaco 1932-1935; Yrendague de 9 de noviembre; actuación del I/R. 5; algunas reminiscencias de su ex-comandante el teniente 1 de ejército paraguayo (hoy Coronel Sr.) José Segundo da Costa Decoud. A., 1968. 239, 174, 33p.

1863 ESPINOLA, Jenaro. Nanawa, batalla del 20 al 24 de enero de 1933; primera ofensiva del ejército boliviano sobre el sector Nanawa. A., 1971. 164p.

1864 ESPINOLA, Jenaro. Nanawa, 4, 5 y 6 de julio de 1933; una batalla en la campaña defensiva de la guerra del Chaco. A., La Colmena, 1960. 155p.

1865 FLORENTIN, Heriberto. La batalla de Strongest; apuntes para la historia de la Guerra del Chaco. B.A., Edit. Asunción, 1958. 287p.

1866 FLORENTIN, Heriberto. Lo que he visto en Boquerón; apuntes para la historia de la Guerra del Chaco. B.A.; A., 1957. 254p.

1867 FLORENTIN, Heriberto. Mas allá de Boquerón; contribución para la historia de la Guerra del Chaco. Rio de Janeiro, Imprensa do Exercito, 1964. 190p.

1868 FLORENTIN, Heriberto. Victoria de Boquerón; contribución para la historia de la Guerra del Chaco. A., 1964. 49p.

1869 FRANCO, Rafael. Dos batallas de la Guerra del Chaco; Gondra y Picuibe-Yrendagué. B.A., Yegros, 1959. 77p.

1869a FRANCO, Rafael. Campo Vía y Strongest. A., El Arte, 1967. 117p.

1870 MACHUCA, Vicente. Batalla de Toledo; Guerra del Chaco. B.A., 1962. 189p.

1871 OLMEDO, Natalicio. Acciones de Pitiantua. A., Casa Edit. Toledo, 1959. 62p. (Serie Guerra del Chaco, 2)

1872 OLMEDO, Natalicio. Pitiantua; la primera historiación, corregida y ampliada, de las acciones libradas en el Fortín Carlos Antonio López (Pitiantua), el 29 junio y 15 de julio de 1932. 2. ed. A., Tall. Gráf. del Estado Mayor General, 1959. 124p.

1873 ORTIZ, J.A. "La batalla de Strongest"; réplica al libro del Cnel. (S.R.) Heriberto Florentín. A., 1959. 12p.

1874 OVANDO CANDIA, Alfredo. Lecciones de Picuiba. La Paz, Comando de Ejército, Sección III, 1961. 46p.

1875 PENAYO, Jeremías. Capitulaciones de la IV y IX divisiones bolivianos en Campo Vía y defensa del "Fortín Gondra". A., Edit. EMASA, 1967. 131p. (Colección Cultura Paraguaya)

1876 ROLON, Raimundo. La batalla general de Zenteno-Gondra-Nanawa y rendición de Campo Vía. A?, Imp. Militar, 1940? 11p.

1876a ROLON, Raimundo. Guerra del Chaco, 1932-1935, el bautismo de fuego de la artillería paraguaya en Boquerón: Boquerón, 40 años después. A., Imp. Militar de la Dirección de Publicaciones de la FF. AA. de la Nación, 1975. 95p.

1877 ROSA VERA, José. La batalla de Strongest frente a su tergiversación histórica. A., Edit. El Gráfico, 1966. 130p.

1877a SANCHEZ DOMINGUEZ, Enrique. La rendición del TCnel Marzana en Boquerón. A., Imp. Militar, 1976. 38p.

1878 SCARONE, Ernesto. Ataque y retoma del Fortín Carlos Antonio López: Pitiantua, 15 y 16 de julio de 1932. A., 1973. 252p.

1879 SCARONE, Ernesto. Contribución para la historia de la Guerra del Chaco; reconocimiento en fuerza en Pitiantuta, junio 29 de 1932. A., Imp. Militar, 1963? 126p.

1880 TABORGA T., Alberto. Boquerón (diario de campaña). La Paz, Canata, 1956. 109p.

1880a TABORGA T., Alberto. Boquerón; diario de campaña, Guerra del Chaco. 2. ed. La Paz, Edit. Juventud, 1970. 241p.

1880b TOVAR VILLA, Raúl. Maniobras de aniquilamiento en Campo Grande y Rojas Silvas, guerra del Chaco. La Paz, Edit. Don Bosco, 1966. 415p.

1881 VARESINI RUSSO, Julio. Algunos realidades par Mas allá de Boquerón. A., Edit. "El Gráfico", 1965. 132p.
See no. 1867.

1882 VEGA, Ceferino. Guerra del Chaco: Yrendagüé - Picuiba. A., 1962. 508p.

1882a VERA, Jose Rosa. La batalla de Strongest; frente a su tergiversación historica. A., 1966. 130p.

1883 VIDAL, Gerónimo A. Misión de la patrulla "Teniente Vidal" para la maniobra de "El Carmen". Prólogo: Raimundo Rolón. B.A., Artes Gráficas Negri, 1968. 193p.

1884 VYSOKOLAN, Stephan. Batalla de Nanawa; conferencia pronunciada en la Guarnición Militar de Paraguari, el dia 4 de julio de 1958. A?, Imp. Militar, n.d. 26p.

e) Other aspects

1885 AYALA QUEIROLO, Víctor. Los prisioneros de la Guerra del Chaco. A., n.d. 320p.

1886 CENTURION, Carlos R. Gabriela Mistral y la epopeya del Chaco; articulos aparecidos en "El Liberal" de Asunción. A., Imp. Militar, 1935. 29p.

1887 CRUZ del defensor; guerra con Bolivia, 1932-1935. A., Edit. Tarapi, 1958. 95p.

1888 CRUZ del Chaco; guerra con Bolivia, 1932-1935. A., Edit. Toledo, 1957. 136p.
The above 2 works describe medals.

1889 GAONA, Silvio. Capellanes de la Guerra del Chaco. (1932-1935) A., Tall. Gráf. Emasa, 1964-

1889a OSUNA, Mauricio T. La Cruz del Chaco en el Chaco: trabajo presentado a la Academia de Historia Militar del Paraguay para ser incorporado en calidad de Académia de Numero el Viernes 31 de octubre de 1975. A., Ediciones Comuneros, 1976. 80p.

1889b OSUNA, Mauricio T. La Medalla de la Defensa del Chaco; prólogo de Benigno Riquelme Garcia. A., Ediciones Comuneros, 1975. 73p.

1890 2 ANIVERSARIO de la imposición de la "condecoración Cruz del Chaco" al Batallón "General Aquino" de Zapadores No. 1. Publicación ordenada por el Sr. Comandante en jefe de la FF. AA. de la Nación, coronel don Raimundo Rolón; orden general no. 96 del 31. XII. 940. A?, Imp. Militar, 1941. 25p.

1891 VARAS REYES, Victor. Ch'ajmidas. La Paz, 1972. 327p.
Bolivian folklore relating to the Chaco War.

J. 1938 -

1892 ADUANAS Y PUERTOS. Paraguay bajo la nueva dinámica constructiva; realizaciones, 15 de agosto de 1957. A., 1957. 108p.

1893 ALBERTO, Carlos. Itinerario político del Paraguay, 1936-1949. A., 1950. 78p.

1893a ALEXANDER, Robert J. The tyranny of General Stroessner. FAI 41 (1977) 16-18.

1894 ALFREDO Stroessner; his life and thoughts. A., El Arte, 1961? 26p.

1895 ALMEIDA, Federico A. El reverso de "El valor social de la historia", réplica al Sr. Epifanio Méndez Fleitas. A?, Ediciones Polémicas, 1954? 31p. (Paraguay libre, 1)

1896 AMNESTY INTERNATIONAL. Prison conditions in Paraguay: conditions for political prisoners. A factual report. London, 1966. 34p.

1896a AMNESTY INTERNATIONAL. Paraguay. London, Amnesty International Publications, 1976. 13p.

1897 ASPECTOS del Paraguay de hoy. CU 68 (1963) 47-67.
Articles by José Antonio Ayala; José Luis Mendaro, Horacio Daniel Rodriguez, Josefina Pla.

1897a BACIU, Stefan. Justo Pastor Benitez, un paraguayo de ley. POL 5 no. 49 (1966) 61-75.

1898 BAEZ ACOSTA, Pedro. Angelillo y querubín; verídica historia de dos inocencias; la cuestión política y social del Paraguay. Santa Fé, Arg., 1959. 127p.
Also: Santa Fé, Arg., 1963. 183p.

1899 BARCENA ECHEVESTE, O. Concepción 1947, contribución a la historia política del Paraguay. A., 1948. 288p.

1900 BELLANI NAZERI, Rodolfo. Los campos de concentración en el Paraguay: el bluff periódistico mas grande de Sudamerica en el transcurse de los últimos años. A., Edit. L.F. Riolleva, 1945. 51p.

1901 BELLANI NAZERI, Rodolfo. Morínigo, un hombre de América. Santiago de Chile, Edit. "Revista de las Américas", 1946. 292, vii p.

1902 BENITEZ, Justo Pastor. Estigarribia, el soldado del Chaco. B.A., Edit. Difusam, 1943. 234p.
2. ed. B.A., Edit. Nizza, 1958. 140p.

1903 BENITEZ, Justo Pastor. El mirador de un exilado; nueve años al margen de los acontecimientos políticos del Paraguay. B.A., 1949. 109p.

1904 BENITEZ, Justo Pastor. La situación política en el Paraguay. CU 56 (1962) 69-72.

1904a BORCHE, Carlos. Campos de concentración en América (misión en Paraguay). Documentos gráficos de Alberto Rodríguez. Montevideo, Comité Nacional de Ayuda al Pueblo Paraguayo, 1945? 202p.
2. ed. Montevideo, Edit. Independencia, 1949? 202p.

1904b BORDON, F. Arturo. Morínigo, un paréntesis trágico en la vida democrática del Paraguay. A., Editora Tavare, 1975. 231p. (Colección Testimonios)

1905 CACERES, Luis Alberto. En busca de la verdad, el Paraguay de hoy. A., Aurora, 1956. 104p.

1906 La CALUMNIA al descubierto. A., 1958. 21p.

1907 La CANDIDATURA presidencial del Gral. Estigarribia. A., 1939. 144p.

1908 CARDOZO, Efraím. America at the crossroads: Parthenon, yes, firing-squad, no; translated from the Spanish by Judith Ishmael Bissett; with an intro. by Charles J. Kolinsky. Tempe, Center for Latin American Studies, Arizona State University, 1974. 25p. (Alberdi-Sarmiento Award lectures, 1974)

1909 CARLOS ALBERTO (pseud.) Itinerario del proceso político del 3/8 de mayo de 1954: documentos. A., 1954. 45p.
An extraordinary session of the governing body of the Partido Colorado.

1909a CARONI, Carlos A. Longitud, latitud y dinámica del Movimento Febrerista del Paraguay; seguido de una síntesis histórica del problema agrario en el Paraguay. B.A., Edit. Tupa, 1947? 24p. (Colección "Realidad y posibilidad")

1910 CHAVES, Osvaldo. Carta a Germán Arciniegas sobre la teoria y práctica del totalitarismo. N.Y., C. López Press, 1952. 14p.

1911 CHILCOTE, Ronald H. Dictatorship in Paraguay. COR 203 (1963), May, 242-45.

1912 CIBILS, Manuel J. Anarquía y revolución en el Paraguay; vórtice y asíntota. B.A., Edit. Americalee, 1957. 202p. (Biblioteca de cultura social. Sección 8: Ensayos e interpretaciones)

1913 CONFEDERACION PARAGUAYA DE TRABAJADORES EN EL EXILIO. Los partidos democráticos del Paraguay a través de sus lideres opinan sobre la tiranía de Stroessner. Montevideo, 1961. 46p.

1914 ESTIGARRIBIA, José Félix. Programa de gobierno del exmo. sr. presidente electo de la república, general de ejército, don José Félix Estigarribia, y discursos pronunciadas en su gira por el interior del país. A., Imp. nac., 1939. 72p.

1914a ESTIGARRIBIA DE FERNANDEZ, Graciela. Estigarribia: el gran desconocido. A., Ediciones Cabildo, 1974. 154p.

1915 FERNANDEZ, Atilio R. El Paraguay del atraso quedó atrás; discurso del diputado nacional Atilio R. Fernández. Itacurubi del Rosario, 1968. 17p.

1916 FRANCO, Carlos Hernán. Esquema del sistema represivo vigente en el Paraguay. CMHL 14 (1970) 125-38.

1916a FRUTOS N., Cristóbal A. Biografía que honra; páginas de la vida de Leopoldo Ramos Gimenez. A., Imp. nac., 1964. 29p.

1917 FRUTOS N., Cristóbal A. Stroessner; una luz en la noche; biografía. A., 1967. 105p.

1918 GAGLIARDONE, César. Organicemos una nación! Inquietudes políticas de la época presente. A., La Colmena, 1950. 166p.
2. ed. A., El Arte, 1959-

1919 GOÑI GARCETE, Lindolfo. El mariscal José Félix Estigarribia. *In* no. 272, 64-68.

1920 GONZALEZ, Agustín. Actividades generales y realizaciones de progreso cumplidas por el gobierno del presidente Alfredo Stroessner, agosto 1962-julio 1963. A., Sub-secretaria de Informaciones y Cultura de la Presidencia de la República, 1963? 78p.

1921 GONZALEZ, Antonio E. La rebelión de Concepción. B.A., 1947. 130p.

1922 GONZALEZ, Juan Natalicio. Cómo se construye una nación. A., Edit. Guarania, 1949. 238p. (Biblioteca paraguaya)

1923 GONZALEZ, Juan Natalicio. Discurso a la nación paraguaya. A., Edit. del Paraguay, 1947. 21p.

1924 GONZALEZ, Juan Natalicio. Historia de una difamación. n.p., n.d. 26p. (Biblioteca colorada, 5)

1925 GONZALEZ, Juan Natalicio. J. Natalicio Gonzâlez, presidente electo del Paraguay para el periodo 1948-1953, se dirige al pueblo de la República desde una banca de la Cámara de Representantes, 13 de mayo de 1948. A., 1948. 14p.

1926 GONZALEZ Y CONTRERAS, Gilberto. J. Natalicio González, descubridor del Paraguay. A., Guarania, 1951. 433p.

1926a HERKEN, Juan Carlos. Desarrollo capitalista expansión brasilera y condiciones del proceso político en el Paraguay. NS 17 (1977) 44-62.

1926b HIGINIO Morínigo; el soldado presidente; reseña de la visita del mandatario paraguayo a los Estados Unidos, México, Panama, Venezuela, Colombia, Ecuador, Perú, Chile y Bolivia en el año de 1943. N.Y., International Business Machines Corporation, 1944. 180p.

1926c JIMENEZ, Zenón. Paraguay en un paréntesis trágico (1947-1948). Formosa (Arg.), Ed. América Libre, 1948. 108p.

1927 JOVER PERALTA, Anselmo. El Paraguay revolucionario; significación histórica de la Revolución de Febrero. B.A., Edit. Tupä, 1946. 2 vols. (Colección "Realidad y Posibilidad", 1)

1928 KHARITONOV, Vitalii Aleksandrovich. Paragvai: voenno-politicheskaia bor'ba. Moscow, Nauka, 1970. 179p.

1929 LABREUEUX, Philippe. Paraguay: acrobacias sobre bayonetas. POL 6 no. 65 (1967) 45-59.

1929a LIGA ARGENTINA POR LOS DERECHOS DEL HOMBRE. Paraguay bajo el terror; documentos que acusan. B.A., Tall. Gráf. Poliglota, 1947. 91p.

1930 LOBO, Eulália Maria Lahmeyer. Análise do panorama politico de 1956. Rio de Janeiro, 1957. 3 vols.
Vol. 2. Bolivia, Paraguai, Uruguai.

1931 LOTT, Leo B. Venezuela and Paraguay; political modernity and tradition in conflict. N.Y., Holt, Rinehart and Winston, 1971. xviii, 395p. (Modern comparative politics series)

1932 MACIAS, Silvio. Morínigo y la horda roja. B.A., 1947. 192p.

1933 MALLAN, L. Paraguay: land of the dead. CUH 6 (1944) 486-90.

1934 (MARTINEZ ARBOLEYA, Joaquin.) Charlas con el general Stroessner, por Santicaten. 3. ed. Montevideo, 1973. 121p.

1934a MENDEZ FLEYTAS, Epifanio. Lo histórico y lo antihistórico en el Paraguay: carta a los colorados. B.A., Artes Gráficas Negri, 1976. 367p.

1935 MENDEZ FLEYTAS, Epifanio. El valor social de la históría. A., Imp. La Tarde, 1945. 37p.
2. ed. A., La Colmena, 1951. 56p.

1936 MIRANDA, José D. Barbarie colorada y cultura liberal. B.A., Edit. Democracia, 1956. 27p. (*His* Enfoques de la realidad paraguayo. Cuaderno no. 2)

1937 MONCADA, Raúl. Ocaso de una dictadura. El general Higinio Morínigo, en visperas de ser derrocado por el pueblo y el ejército del Paraguay. HO (1947) Aug. 23, 28-81.

1938 MORENO, Augusto. La época de Alfredo Stroessner; valoración política, historica y filosófica, a doce años de distancia, 15 de agosto de 1954 - 15 de agosto de 1966. Centenario de la epopeya nacional, 1864-1870. A?, 1967? 316p.

1938a NIETO, Alejandro. Mariscal Estigarribia. A., Edit. Don Bosco, 1970? 11p. (Galeria paraguayos ilustres, 4. Naranja)

1939 O'LEARY, Juan Emiliano. El hombre de la hora; o, El presidente constructor. A., 1963. 10p.

1940 EL PAIS, ASUNCION. El Paraguay en 1957. A., 1957. 192p.

1941 EL PAIS, ASUNCION. El Paraguay en 1959. A., 1959. 160p.

1942 PAMPLIEGA, Amancio. El conductor glorioso Mariscal José Félix Estigarribia. A., Artes Gráf. Zamphirópolos, 1968. 31p.

1943 PANORAMA político del Paraguay. La postguerra del Chaco (1936-1946). A?, 1946. 76p.

1944 PARAGUAY. DEPARTAMENTO NACIONAL DE PRENSA Y PROPAGANDA. Higinio Morínigo; soldado, estadista, gobernante. A., Imp. nac., 1943. 33p.

1945 PARAGUAY. MINISTERIO DEL INTERIOR. Un mensaje fraterno a través de caminos olvidados; en torno a la gira Asunción-Concepción realizada por el Ministro del Interior Doctor Edgar L. Ynsfrán, del 7 al 15 de octubre de 1959. A., Imp. nac., 1960. 72p.

1946 PARAGUAY. PRESIDENCIA. Plan nacional de desarrollo económico y social para el bienio 1965-1966. A., 1965. 2 vols.

1947 PARAGUAY. PRESIDENTE, 1937-1939. Mensaje del Presidente de la República del Paraguay, doctor Félix Paiva, al h. Congreso Nacional, octubre de 1938. A., Imp. nac., 1938. 82p.

1948 PARAGUAY. PRESIDENTE, 1937-1939. Mensaje del Presidente de la República al h. Congreso Nacional; abril de 1939. A., Imp. Nac., 1939. 50p.

1949 PARAGUAY. PRESIDENTE, 1940-1948. Mensaje del excmo. Señor Presidente de la República, gral. don Higinio Morínigo M, setiembre de 1941. A., Imp. Nac., 1941. 77p.

1950 PARAGUAY. PRESIDENTE, 1940-1948. Mensaje del excmo. Señor Presidente de la República, gral. d. Higinio Morínigo M. A., Imp. Nac., 1942. 114p.
2. ed. 1943.

1951 PARAGUAY. PRESIDENTE, 1940-1948. Mensaje presidencial, leido en el palacio de gobierno por el exco. gen. don Higinio Morínigo M. en el acto de prestar juramento para asumir la presidencia de la república par el período constitucional 1943-1948. A., Dpto. Nac. da Prensa y Propaganda, 1943. 8p.

1952 PARAGUAY. PRESIDENTE, 1940-1948. Plan quinquenal 1943-1948 de reconstrucción nacional. A., Dpto. Nacional de Prensa y Propaganda, 1944. 25p.

1953 PARAGUAY. PRESIDENTE, 1940-1948. Plan trienal, programa de gobierno del presidente Morínigo diciembre 24 de 1940. A., Imp. Nac., 1941. 21p.

1954 PARAGUAY. PRESIDENTE, 1940-1948. La reconstrucción nacional. Seis años de labor. Gobierno del general Morínigo. A?, 1946? 32p.

1955 PARAGUAY. PRESIDENTE, 1940-1948. Tetapi moatiro jhagua petai po ro'ijho aya. Plan quinquenal del gral. de div. presidente de la república del Paraguay. Traducción de Gumersindo Ayala. A., Imp. Nac., 1944. 16p.
A Guarani translation of no. 1952.

1955a PARAGUAY. PRESIDENTE, 1954- Carta del presidente Stroessner a la Sociedad Interamericana de Prensa. A., Sub-Secretaría de Informaciones y Cultura, Presidencia de la República, 1960? 43p.

1955b PARAGUAY. PRESIDENTE, 1954- Discurso pronunciado en el acto inaugural de la VI reunión de la Asamblea de Gobernadores del Banco Interamericano de Desarrollo, abril, 26 de 1965. A., Sub-Secretaría de Informaciones y Cultura de la Presidencia de la República, 1965. 11p.

1956 PARAGUAY. PRESIDENTE, 1954- Mensaje de navidad, del excmo. sr. Presidente de la República general de ejército don Alfredo Stroessner, Asunción, 24 de diciembre de 1960. A., Sub-secretaría de Informaciones y Cultura de la Presidencia de la República, 1960?

1956a PARAGUAY. PRESIDENTE, 1954- Mensaje de Navidad del presidente Stroessner al pueblo paraguayo. A., Sub-Secretaría de Informaciones y Cultura de la Presidencia de la República, 1970? 11p.

1957 PARAGUAY. PRESIDENTE, 1954- Mensaje del excelentísimo señor Presidente de la República y comandante en jefe de las FF. AA. de la Nación, general del ejército don Alfredo Stroessner al Congreso Nacional, 1 de abril de 1969. A., Sub-secretaria de Informaciones y Cultura de la Presidencia de la República, 1969. xxxviii, 769p.

1958 PARAGUAY. PRESIDENTE, 1954- Mensaje del excelentísimo señor Presidente de la República y comandante en jefe de las FF. AA. de la Nación, general de ejército don Alfredo Stroessner al Congreso Nacional, 1 de abril de 1970. A., Sub-secretaria de Informaciones y Cultura de la Presidencia de la República, 1970. xxvi, 801p.

1959 PARAGUAY. PRESIDENTE, 1954- Mensaje del Presidente de la República Alfredo Stroessner a la Cámara de Representantes, leído el 1 de abril de 1966, centenario de la epopeya nacional. A., Sub-secretaria de Informaciones y Cultura de la Presidencia de la República, 1966. xliiip.

1960 PARAGUAY. PRESIDENTE, 1954- Mensaje presidencial a la Honorable Cámara de Representantes, 1 de abril de 1960. A., Sub-secretaria de Informaciones y Cultura de la Presidencia de la República, 1960. 259p.

1961 PARAGUAY. PRESIDENTE, 1954- Mensaje presidencial a la Honorable Cámara de Representantes, 1 de abril de 1961. A., Sub-secretaria de Informaciones y Cultura de la Presidencia de la República, 1961. 287p.

1962 PARAGUAY. PRESIDENTE, 1954- Mensaje presidencial a la Honorable Cámara de Representantes, 1 de abril de 1962. A., Sub-secretaria de Informaciones y Cultura de la Presidencia de la República, 1962. 52p.

1963 PARAGUAY. PRESIDENTE, 1954- El Presidente de la República, General de División don Alfredo Stroessner contesta a cuestionarios presentados por periodistas extranjeros. A., Imp. Nac., 1955. 10p.

1963a PARAGUAY. PRESIDENTE, 1954- El presidente Stroessner ante el pueblo de Itapúa. Discurso. A., Sub-Secretaria de Informaciones y Cultura, Presidencia de la República, 1959? 26p.

1963b PARAGUAY. PRESIDENTE, 1954- Por la paz, por la democracia, y el progreso. A., Sub-Secretaría de Informaciones y Cultura, Presidencia de la República, 1960. 7p.

1963c PARAGUAY. PRESIDENTE, 1954- Veinte años de labor de un gobierno patriota y progresista. 15 de agosto de 1954 - 15 de agosto de 1974: Líder Ejecutor-General de Ejército Don Alfredo Stroessner, Presidente de la República del Paraguay, y Comandante en Jefe de las FF. AA. de la Nación. A., Imp. nac., 1974. 849p.

1964 PARAGUAY. SECRETARIA TECNICA DE PLANIFICACION. La estrategia de desarrollo nacional. A., 1967. 48p.

1965 PARAGUAY. SECRETARIA TECNICA DE PLANIFICACION. Plan nacional de desarrollo económico y social, bienio 1967-1968. Propuesta. A., 1966. 1 vol. (various pagings).

1966 PARAGUAY. SECRETARIA TECNICA DE PLANIFICACION. Plan nacional de desarrollo económico y social para el bienio 1965-1966. A., 1965-

1967 PARAGUAY. SECRETARIA TECNICA DE PLANIFICACION. Propuesta del segundo plan de desarrollo económico y social para el bienio 1967-1968. A., 1969. 255p.
Anexo I A., 1966. 136p.
Anexo II A., 1966. 93p.

1968 PARAGUAY. SECRETARIA TECNICA DE PLANIFICACION. Plan nacional de desarrollo económico y social, 1971-1975. A., 1970-

1969 PARTIDO COLORADO. El caso Estigarribia. A., Edit. "El País", 1952. 51p.

1969a PARTIDO COLORADO. Pruebas de una inconducta política: 27 de octubre de 1955 - 29 de mayo de 1959. A., 1959. 135p.

1970 PASTORE, Carlos. El Paraguay y la tirania de Morínigo. Montevideo, Edit. Antequera, 1947. 76p.

1971 PEREZ ECHEGUREN, José Antonio. Relieve y categoría de la revolución paraguaya. A., Imp. nac., 1940. 100p.

1972 PEREZ M., Sindulfo; MEO, Carlos. Stroessner. A., Offset Gráfica Asuncena, 1972-
Laudatory.

1973 EL PROCESO de Bouvier; declaración de uno de los encausados. B.A., 1959. 32p.
Issued by: Agrupación Liberal "Volveremos".

1974 RAMIREZ, Federico. La realidad del Paraguay. Posadas?, 1948? 19p.

1975 RAMOS GIMENEZ, Leopoldo. Stroessner: una linea en la perspectiva del tiempo; o el Paraguay de hoy y de mañana. A., Ed. Arte, 1967. 494p. (Anales del Paraguay, páginas documentales de la historia y para la historia, artes, ciencias y letras, año 4, num. 5)

1976 LA RAZON, ASUNCION. Batallas por la democracia. A., 1950-51. 2 vols.
Articles by Epifanio Méndez Fleytas, Osvaldo Chaves, Bacón Duarte Prado.

1977 ROA BASTOS, Augusto. Paraguay ante la necesidad de su segunda independencia. CLA 5 no. 32 (1965) 13-26.

1978 ROMERO BASTOS, Raúl. El Paraguay, entre el terror y revolución. CA 170 (1970) 29-44.

1979 SANCHEZ, Luis Alberto. Reportaje al Paraguay: el Paraguay que yo he visto. A., Edit. Cuarania, 1949. 124p.

1980 SANCHEZ QUELL, Hipólito. Alfredo Stroessner, el Programa Colorado y el desarrollo paraguayo. A., Partido Colorado, 1972. 23p.

1981 SANCHEZ QUELL, Hipólito. Proyección del general Caballero en la ruta de la patria. 2. ed. A., Partido Colorado, 1970. 164p.

1981a SELDEN, Armistead I.; MAILLARD, William S. Report of the special study mission to the Dominican Republic, Guyana, Brazil and Paraguay, comprising Armistead I. Selden, Jr. and William S. Maillard, pursuant to the provisions of H. Res. 84, 89th Congress. Washington, U.S.G.P.O., 1967. vii, 61p.

1982 STEFANICH, Juan. El Paraguay nuevo; por la democracia y la libertad hacia un nuevo ideario americano. B.A., Edit. Claridad, 1943. 186p. (Colección Claridad, 189)

1983 STROESSNER, Alfredo. Programa de gobierno del Gral. de Ejército. Alfredo Stroessner, candidato del Partido Colorado a la presidencia de la República. A., 1963. 30p.

1984 UNION NACIONAL PARAGUAYA. JUNTA CENTRAL COORDINADORA EN EL EXILIO. El tirano Stroessner ante la conciencia democrática de América. B.A., 1960. 46p.

1985 UNION NACIONAL PARAGUAYA. JUNTA CENTRAL COORDINADORA EN EL EXILIO. La tragedia paraguaya: datos para el análisis de la gestión gubernátiva del tirano Stroessner. n.p., 1961. 40p.

1985a UNITED STATES. CONGRESS, HOUSE. COMMITTEE ON INTERNATIONAL RELATIONS. SUBCOMMITTEE ON INTERNATIONAL ORGANIZATIONS. Human rights in Uruguay and Paraguay, hearings before the Subcommittee on International Organizations of the Committee on International Relations, House of Representatives, 94th Congress, 2nd session. Washington, U.S.G.P.O., 1976. vi, 228p.

1986 VARGAS PEÑA, Benjamin. Una opinión para la República. Corrientes, Impreso en el Diario "La Provincia", 1958. 45p.

1987 VELAZQUEZ, Rafael. Justo Pastor Benitez en la vida cultural de Paraguay. IARB 15 (1965) 35-43.

1988 VERITAS, pseud. Epifanio: el mayo de las finanzas. A., 1970. 84p.
An attack on Epifanio Méndez Fleytas.

1989 VILLAMAYOR, Jesús M. Stroessner y su claque; vicisitudes de un soldado. Montevideo, 1957. unpaged.

1990 YNSFRAN, Edgar Linneo. El caso Paraguay dal Castro Marxismo. A., Casa América, 1963. 24p.

1991 YNSFRAN, Edgar Linneo. ¿Crisis de crecimiento? A., 1961. 26p.

1992 YNSFRAN, Edgar Linneo. ¿Crisis de crecimiento? Tapejuasa (encrucijada); o camino de Yenan, o camino de tradición. A., Imp. Nac., 1962. 48p.

1993 YNSFRAN, Edgar Linneo. La irrupción moscovita en la Marina Paraguaya. A., 1947. 80p.

1994 YNSFRAN, Edgar Linneo. En el centenario de "El grito Paraguayo". A., Imp. nac., 1958. 16p.

1995 YNSFRAN, Edgar Linneo. La lucha por la verdad; versión de una reunión de prensa en Montevideo. A., Ministerio del Interior, 1963. 43p.

1996 YNSFRAN, Edgar Linneo. El Paraguay habló, en esta hora política de América, con su immortal espíritu de soberanía, a través del mensaje del ministro del interior doctor Edgar L. Ynsfrán. A., Sub-Secretaria de Informaciones y Cultura de la Presidencia de la República, 1959. 38p.

1997 YNSFRAN, Edgar Linneo. Tapejuasa (Encrucijada); o camino de Yenán, o camino de tradicion. A., 1961. 28p.

1998 YNSFRAN, Edgar Linneo. Tres discursos (oct. 27, 1955; enero 7, 1956; agosto 20, 1956). A., Edit. América, 1956. 39p.

1999 YNSFRAN, Edgar Linneo. Triptico republicano: democracia, agrarismo, paraguayidad; ensayos. A., Edit. América-Sapucai, 1956. 74p.

2000 YNSFRAN, Walter E. Movimiento 27 de octubre de integración partidaria; donde el partido es lo más, todo la demás es menos. Discurso pronunciado en Luque por el representante nacional. A., El Arte, 1959. 35p.

2001 ZACARIAS, Oscar. Documentos para la historia. A., Centro de Documentación del Clarín Republicano, 1971. 49p.
On the detention in 1940 of Victor Riquelme.

2002 ZACARIAS CUBILLA, Oscar. Estrategia política: estudio introductorio. A., Cromos, 1975. 253p.

K. Regional history

1. Chaco Boreal. Paraguayan Chaco

a) The boundary dispute with Bolivia

2003 AGUIRRE ACHA, José. La antigua provincia de Chiquitos, limítrofé de la provincia del Paraguay. Anotaciones para la defensa de los derechos de Bolivia sobre el Chaco Boreal. La Paz, Imp. "Renacimiento" - Flores, San Román & cía, 1933. 166p.

2004 AGUIRRE ACHA, José. The arbitration zone in the Bolivian-Paraguayan dispute through the diplomatic negotiations. La Paz, 1929. 68p.

2005 AGUIRRE ACHA, José. The boundary dispute between Bolivia and Paraguay, trans ... by Andrew Boyle. With a preface by His Excellency Señor Don Carlos Victor Aramoyo, Bolivian minister at the Court of St. James. Birmingham, Baker's Great Bookshop, 1929? 24p.

2006 AGUIRRE ACHA, José. El desacuerdo y el conflicto entre Bolivia y el Paraguay; exposición sintética para la prensa extranjera y la apreciación mundial. La Paz, Tall. "Renacimiento", 1929. 11p.

2007 AGUIRRE ACHA, José. The disagreement and conflict between Bolivia and Paraguay, a concise statement for the foreign press and the judgment of the world. N.Y., Mason Press, 1929. 18p.

2008 AGUIRRE ACHA, José. La zona del arbitraje en el litigio boliviano-paraguayo, al través de las gestiones diplomáticas. La Paz, Edit. "Renacimiento", Flores, San Román y cía, 1929. 64p.

2009 ALALZA, Miguel. Los derechos de Bolivia, sobre el oriente y el Chaco Boreal. Con 44 vistas ilustrativas y un mapa del oriente del Chaco. La Paz, Litografías e Imp. Unidas, 1928. 72p.

2010 ALVESTEGUI, David. Bolivia-Paraguay; títulos de Bolivia. La Paz, Litografías y Imp. Unidas, 1933. 2 vols.

2011 ALVESTEGUI, David. Bolivia y el Paraguay; la cuestión de limites. Cochabamba, Imp. El Mercurio de J.P. Sempértegui, 1913. 156p.

2012 ALVESTEGUI, David. Bolivia y el Paraguay; la cuestión de limites. La Paz, Imp. "Renacimiento", 1926. x, 438p.
Despite the same title, this is not the same work as no. 2011.

2013 AMARILLA FRETES, Eduardo. El Paraguay en el primer cincuentenario del fallo arbitral del presidente Hayes. A., Imp. nac., 1932. 180p.

2014 AMARILLA FRETES, Eduardo. La posesión del Paraguay en el Chaco y las pretensiones de Bolivia a través del tiempo. A., 1929. 40p.

2015 ARBO, Higinio. La cuestión del Chaco Boreal: conferencia pronunciada por el señor ministro del Paraguay en el Uruguay ... el día 29 de agosto de 1931. Montevideo, C. Garcia, 1931. 63p.

2016 ARBO, Higinio. Le conflit entre la Bolivia et le Paraguay à propos du Chaco boréal. RGDIP 36 (1929) 528-53.

2017 AUDIBERT, Alejandro. Cuestión de límites entre el Paraguay y Bolivia; artículos publicados en "La Democracia" y en "El Pueblo". A., Escuela tip. salesiana, 1901. 144p.

2018 AYALA, Elías. Paraguay y Bolivia en el Chaco Boreal. A., Imp. nac., 1929. 124p.

2019 BAEZ, Cecilio. Paraguay-Bolivia; su cuestión de límites. A., J.M. Duarte, 1917. 44p.

2020 BAEZ, Cecilio. The Paraguayan Chaco; or, A brief statement of the titles of Paraguay on the ownership of the territory of that name; accompanied by the map of Dr. De Moussy. N.Y., 1904. 66p.

2021 BALDIVIA GALDO, José Maria. La política argentina en Bolivia: reminiscencias históricas. La Paz, Imp. Eléctrica, 1933. 67p.

2022 BENITES, Gregorio. Exposición de los derechos del Paraguay en la cuestión de límites con Bolivia sobre el territorio del Chaco, presentada al plenipotenciario boliviano Dr. D. Telmo Ichazo por D. Gregorio Benites, plenipotenciario paraguayo. A., Tip. "La Opinión", 1895. 229p.

2022a BERNARDEZ, Manuel. El tratado de la Asunción. Montevideo, Imp. artistica y librería de Dornaleche y Reyes, 1894. 79p.

2023 BOGGIANI, Guido. La questione dei confini tra le Repubbliche del Paraguay e della Bolivia. Rome, 1897. 20p.

2024 BOLIVIA. MINISTERIO DE RELACIONES EXTERIORES. La conferencia de Mendoza y el conflicto del Chaco. La Paz, Imp. "Eléctrica", 1933. ii, 26p.

2025 BOLLAND, Enrique. Exploraciones practicadas en el Alto Paraguay y en la laguna Caiba por el capítan de marina Enrique Bolland, de orden y por cuenta del gobierno de Bolivia. Fundación de un puerto. B.A., Compañía sudamericana de billetes de banco, 1901. 144p.

2026 BRAVO, Francisco Javier. Oriente de Bolivia. Territorio del Chaco. Correspondencia sostenida con los gobiernos de Bolivia y Paraguay sobre los territorios del Chaco. Concesión del gobierno del Paraguay. Toma de posesión. Instrucciones dadas á las comisiones exploradas y varias noticias de ellas. B.A., Imp. de M. Biedma, 1879. 103p.

2027 BREARD, F. Omar. Conferencia sobre motivos del conflicto paraguayo-boliviano pronunciada en el Teatro Vera de la ciudad de Corrientes (R.A.) en la velada del 28 de septiembre de 1932. Corrientes, Imp. San Francisco, 1932? 33p.

2028 CANO DE LA VEGA, Emeterio. The Bolivia and Paraguay boundary dispute; brief survey of Bolivia's case. N.Y., Consulate General of Bolivia, 1927. 16p.
Reprinted: 1929. 100p.

2029 CARDOZO, Efraím. Aspectos de la cuestión del Chaco. A., Imp. nac., 1932. 126p.

2030 CARDOZO, Efraím. La Audiencia de Charcas y la Facultad de Gobierno. B.A., Imp. y casa editora "Coni", 1936. 22p.

2031 CARDOZO, Efraím. El Chaco en el régimen de las intendencias. La creación de Bolivia. Prólogo del doctor Eusebio Ayala. A., Imp. nac., 1930. xix, 162p.

2032 CARDOZO, Efraím. El Chaco y los virreyes; la cuestión paraguaya-boliviana según documentos de los archivos Buenos Aires y de Rio de Janeiro. A., Imp. nac., 1934. 200p.

2033 CENTURION, Carlos R. El conflicto del Chaco Boreal; gestiones diplomáticas. A., La Colmena, 1937. 2 vols.

2034 CHAVES S., Medardo. Dilucidaciones históricas sobre el Chaco. La Paz, Imp. Renacimiento, 1929. xii, 170p.

2035 CLEVEN, Nels Andrew Nelson. The dispute between Bolivia and Paraguay. CUH 1929, Jan., 661-63.

2036 COMMISSION OF INQUIRY AND CONCILIATION, BOLIVIA AND PARAGUAY, 1929. Actuaciones de la Comisión de investigación y conciliación boliviano-paraguayo, 13 de marzo de 1929 - 13 de septiembre de 1929. Washington, 1929. v, 1214p.

2037 COMMISSION OF INQUIRY AND CONCILIATION, BOLIVIA AND PARAGUAY, 1929. Report of the chairman submitted to the Secretary of State of the United States of America September 21, 1929, for transmission to the American Governments not represented on the Commission and appended documents. Washington, United States Government Printing Office, 1929. vi, 63p. (U.S. Dept. of State. Publication, no. 5. Latin American series, no. 1)

2038 COMMISSION OF INQUIRY AND CONCILIATION, BOLIVIA AND PARAGUAY, 1929. List of delegations and organizations of the Secretariat General. Washington, United States Government Printing Office, 1929. iii, 8p.

2039 COMMISSION OF INQUIRY AND CONCILIATION, BOLIVIA AND PARAGUAY, 1929. Proceedings of the Commission of inquiry and conciliation, Bolivia and Paraguay, March 13, 1929 - September 13, 1929. Washington, 1929. 1210p.
The English version of no. 2036.

2040 CUELLO FREYRE, Juan Andrés. Por qué estamos con Bolivia. B.A., Gleizer imprimió, 1933. 126p.

2041 DOMAICA, Angel. Conferencias sobre el Gran Chaco Boreal, dadas en Cochabamba y La Paz. Cochabamba, Comité Pro-Defensa Nacional de Cochabamba, 1928. 36p.

2042 DOMINGUEZ, Manuel. Bolivia atropelló el statu-quo y sus reconocimientos del laudo Hayes. A., Imp. nac., 1935. 24p.

2043 DOMINGUEZ, Manuel. Bolivia y sus mistificaciones. Resumen de una conferencia dada en el Teatro nacional a beneficio de las familias de los movilizados. Publicación ordenada por el señor ministro de relaciones exteriores dr. Justo Pastor Benitez. A., Imp. nac., 1932. 22p.

2044 DOMINGUEZ, Manuel. El Chaco Boreal; informe del Dr. Manuel Dominguez, miembro de la Comisión Asesora de límites, que arruina la tésis boliviana y expone los títulos del Paraguay sobre dicha zona. A., Imp. nac., 1925. 195p.

2045 DOMINGUEZ, Manuel. El Chaco Boreal fue, es y será del Paraguay. A., Imp. nac., 1927. 72p.

2046 DOMINGUEZ, Manuel. El Chaco pertenecia al obispado del Paraguay. A., Imp. nac., 1933. 16p.

2047 DOMINGUEZ, Manuel. El Chaco Boreal pertenece al Paraguay; once títulos irrefutables contra las mistificaciones de Bolivia. A., Imp. nac., 1932. 7p.

2048 DOMINGUEZ, Manuel. El dr. J. Nicolás Matienzo y la soberanía del Paraguay. A., Imp. nac., 1934. 13p.

2049 DOMINGUEZ, Manuel. Elelin; ó, "La tierra de los Césares". El Paraguay se propone conquistar y poblar regiones más alla del Chaco Austral, que caian dentro de su distrito y jurisdicción. A?, 1908. 10p.

2050 DOMINGUEZ, Manuel. Informe del plenipotenciario paraguayo dr. Domínguez acerca de las negociaciones Dominguez-Cano posteriores al ajuste Soler-Pinilla de 1907. A., Imp. nac., 1929. 61p.

2051 DOMINGUEZ, Manuel. Nuestros pactos con Bolivia. A., Imp. nac., 1928. 19p.

2052 DOMINGUEZ, Manuel. Paraguay-Bolivia. Contraréplica del Dr. Manuel Domínguez al conferencista Boliviano Dr. Cornelio Rios. Conferencias dadas en el Teatro nacional de la Asunción. A., Imp. nac., 1925. 50p.

2053 DOMINGUEZ, Manuel. Paraguay-Bolivia, cuestión de límites; conferencias dadas por el doctor Manuel Domínguez, ex-ministro plenipotenciario especial en las negociaciones de 1906 y 1907. A., Tall. gráf. del estado, 1917. 43p.

2054 DOMINGUEZ, Manuel. Paraguay-Bolivia, cuestión de límites; el derecho de descubrir y conquistar el Paraguay o río de la Plata, ruina de la 2a tesís boliviana. (2a conferencia del dr. Manuel Domínguez). A., Tall. gráf. del estado, 1918. 30p.

2055 DOMINGUEZ, Manuel. Seven kings and ten viceroys affirm the rights of Paraguay over the Chaco. Washington, Legation of Paraguay, 1937. 16p.

2056 DOMINGUEZ, Manuel. Siete reyes y diez virreyes afirman los derechos del Paraguay sobre el Chaco. A., Imp. nac., 1933. 20p.
Also: RABA 1935, June, 99-116.

2057 DOMINGUEZ, Manuel. Los títulos del Paraguay y el dr. Lindolfo Collor. A., Imp. nac., 1933. 37p.

2058 DOYLE, Henry Grattan. Bolivia and Paraguay moving toward settlement of Chaco dispute. CUH 1929 Nov., 375-78.

2059 DOYLE, Henry Grattan. Bolivia's international problems. CUH 1929 Dec., 582-84.

2060 FINOT, Enrique. Nuevos aspectos de la cuestión del Chaco. La Paz, Edit. Renacimiento, 1931. ix, 415p.

2061 GANCEDO, Alejandro. Límites entre la República de Bolivia y Paraguay. A., 1935. 106p.
From an Argentinian viewpoint.

2062 GANDIA, Enrique de. La cuestión de límites entre Paraguay y Bolivia. RABA 1932, Sept., 6-23.
Also: RE 1934, Jan.-Mar., 28-35 and RGA 1 (1934) no. 4, 239-46.

2063 GANDIA, Enrique de. Los derechos del Paraguay sobre el Chaco Boreal y las doctrinas del "uti possidetis" en el siglo XVI. B.A., Edit. L.J. Rosso, 1935. 200p.

2064 GONZALEZ-BLANCO, Pedro. Los derechos inobjectables de Bolivia al Chaco Boreal. Madrid, Saéz hermanos, 1934. 111p.

2064a GREZ PEREZ, Carlos E. Falsificaciones bolivianas; estudio documental y crítico. Santiago de Chile, 193?-

2065 GROTEWALD, C. Die Vorgeschichte des Konfliktes zwischen Bolivien und Paraguay. EG 7 (1929) 417-29.

2066 GUACHALLA, Luis Fernando. Misión en el Paraguay, mayo, 1930 - julio, 1931. La Paz, 1971. 287p.

2067 GUTIERREZ R., Victorino. Los sucesos del Otuquis. La Paz, Imp. Intendencia de Guerra, 1929. 44p.

2068 ICHASO, Telmo. Antecedentes del tratado de límites celebrado con la República del Paraguay, por el enviado extraordinario y ministro plenipotenciario de Bolivia. Sucre, Tip. "El Cruzado", 1894. 338p.
Actually published in 1896.

2069 IRAIZOS, Francisco. El sudeste de Bolivia. La Paz, Tall. tip. lit., 1901. xiii, 98p. (Asuntos internacionales 1)

2070 KANTER, Helmuth. Die neue Grenze zwischen Bolivien und Paraguay. ZG 12 (1935) 608-13.
This contains an important map, showing the vegetation cover.

2071 LAGUNA, Adolfo. La diplomacia paraguaya en la cuestión del Chaco Boreal. Mercedes, B.A., Est. Gráf. Herrero Hnos, 1932. 40p.

2072 LEMOINE, Joaquín de. Bolivia y el Paraguay, pleito y medianería. B.A., Compañía sud-americana de billetes de banco, 1898. 49p.
2. ed. Anvers, Schotte & Van Eeckhout, 191? 54p.

2073 LOPEZ MAIZ, José. Expresión de agravios presentada por don J. López Maíz en representación del doctor don Alejandro Audibert contra la sentencia del juez Gregorio Ortiz en la reclamación de sus honorarios contra el fisco. A., Imp. de "La Democracia", 1899. 158p.

2074 LOZA, Léon M. El laudo Hayos; su ineficacia en el litigio boliviano-paraguayo. La Paz, Edit. "Renacimiento", Flores, San Román & cía., 1936. 192p.

2075 MENDOZA, Jaime. Bolivia y el Paraguay: la tesis andinista; ensayos. Sucre, Imp. Bolívar, 1933. ii, 104p.

2076 MENDOZA, Jaime. El ideal pacifista; líneas adicionales al libro La tragedia del Chaco. Sucre, Imp. La Glorieta, 1933. ii, 38p.

2077 MERCADO MOREIRA, Miguel. El Chaco boliviano (anotaciones al alegato paraguayo). Cochabamba, Lopez, 1928. vii, 164p.

2078 MERCADO MOREIRA, Miguel. El Chaco Boreal (litigio boliviano-paraguayo). La Paz, Imp. Velarde, 1920. xvii, 230p.
Reprinted: La Paz, Imp. "Atenea" de Crespi hnos, 1929. ii, 181p.

2079 MERCADO MOREIRA, Miguel. Títulos de Bolivia sobre el Chaco Boreal. La Paz, Imp. Unidas, 1935. 55p.

2080 MEXICO. DELEGACION, COMISION DE INVESTIGACION Y CONCILIACION, BOLIVIA Y PARAGUAY, 1929. Comisión de investigación y conciliación para el arreglo del conflicto entre Bolivia y Paraguay. Informe que rinde a la Secretaría de relaciones exteriores el señor licenciado Fernando González Roa, delegado mexicano. Mexico, Imp. de la Secretaría de relaciones exteriores, 1930. 80p.

2081 MORENO, Fulgencio Ricardo. Cuestión de límites con Bolivia; negociaciones diplomáticas, 1915-1917. A., Ministerio de Relaciones Exteriores, 1917. 2 vols.

2082 MORENO, Fulgencio Ricardo. Diplomatie paraguayo-bolivienne; précédentes des traités des limites et causes de leur insuccès. A., La "Revue Commerciale", 1904. 34p.

2083 MORENO, Fulgencio Ricardo. Diplomacia paraguayo-boliviana; antecedentes de los tratados de límites y causas de su fracaso. A., Tall. nac. de H. Kraus, 1904. 53p.

2084 MORENO, Fulgencio Ricardo. La extensión territorial del Paraguay al occidente de su río. Breve exposición de los títulos paraguayos. A., Imp. Ariel, 1925. 38p.
2. ed. A., Imp. nac., 1933. 88p.

2085 MORENO, Fulgencio Ricardo. Paraguay-Bolivia, cuestión de límites; memorandums del plenipotenciario del

Paraguay sobre el carácter y alcance del diferendo y el uti possidetis de 1810. A., Imp. nac., 1934. 81p.

2086 MORENO, Fulgencio Ricardo. Paraguay-Bolivia, cuestión de límites; actas de las conferencias, y memórias de los negociadores Fulgencio R. Moreno, Plenipotenciario Especial del Paraguay, y Dr. don Ricardo Mujía, E.E. y Ministro Plenipotenciario de Bolivia, 1915-1916. A., 1917. 396p.

2087 MORENO, Fulgencio Ricardo. El problema de las fronteras. B.A., 1927. 78p. (Biblioteca de la Asociación Paraguaya, 2)

2088 MUJIA, Ricardo. El Chaco; monografía histórico-geográfica y los alegatos paraguayos en la cuestión de límites con Bolivia. Sucre, Imp. y litografía Salesianas, 1933. vi, 169p.

2089 MUJIA, Ricardo. Bolivia-Paraguay; exposición de los títulos que consagran el derecho territorial de Bolivia, sobre la zona comprendida entre los rios Pilcomayo y Paraguay. La Paz, Empresa edit. de "El Tiempo", 1914. 3 vols.
Anexos. 1914? 5 vols.

2090 MUJIA, Ricardo. Bolivia-Paraguay; anotaciones a la "Replica" del excelentisimo sr. ministro plenipotenciario especial del Paraguay, don Fulgencio R. Moreno. A., 1916. 394, viii p.

2091 O'LEARY, Juan Emiliano. Un abogado especial de Bolivia. A., Imp. "La Paraguaya", 1934. 12p.

2092 OROZA DAZA, Julio. Conflicto boliviano-paraguayo, páginas para la historia: los ataques a los fortines Vanguardia y Boquerón, la responsabilidad del agresor. ¿Quien tiene la razón? B.A., 1929. 128p.

2093 PARAGUAY. MINISTERIO DE RELACIONES EXTERIORES. Cuestión de límites con Bolivia; negociaciones diplomáticas, 1915-1917. A., Imp. de El Liberal, 1917. 3 vols.
2. ed. A., Imp. nac., 1928-29. 3 vols.

2094 PARAGUAY. MINISTERIO DE RELACIONES EXTERIORES. Exposición de la causa del Paraguay en su conflicto con Bolivia; presentada a la XV asamblea de la Sociedad de las naciones, reunida en setiembre de 1934. A., Imp. nac., 1934. 371p.

2095 PARAGUAY. MINISTERIO DE RELACIONES EXTERIORES. Libro blanco. Documentos relativos a las conferencias de Buenos Aires sobre la cuestión de límites paraguayo-boliviana y algunos antecedentes. 1927-1928. A., Imp. nac., 1928. 219p.

2096 PARAGUAY. MINISTERIO DE RELACIONES EXTERIORES. Paraguay-Bolivia, cuestión de límites; exposición del ministro de relaciones exteriores Don Rogelio Ibarra, ante el Congreso nacional sobre los antecedentes y estado actual del litigio. A., Imp. nac., 1924. 20p.

2097 PARAGUAY. MINISTERIO DE RELACIONES EXTERIORES. Paraguay-Bolivia, protocolos y notas cambiadas. A., Imp. nac., 1927. 40p.

2098 PARAGUAY. MINISTERIO DE RELACIONES EXTERIORES. Paraguay-Bolivia, tratados y protocolos. A., Imp. nac., 1927. 20p.

2099 PAZ, Julio. Expediciones al Chaco. Prólogo del general Carlos Blanco Galindo. Cochabamba, 1936. viii, 196p.

2100 PAZ, Román. Diferendo del Chaco, aspectos de actualidad; pro juris et honoris. Ed. autorizada por el Centro de Propaganda y Defensa Nacional. La Paz, Imp. Renacimiento, 193-. 100p.

2101 PLACE DE CHAUVAC, Marcelo de la. Gran Chaco: Chaco Austral, Chaco Boreal. A., 1916. 29p.

2102 POZO CANO, Raúl del. Paraguay-Bolivia; el Chaco paraguayo y el Vaticano. A., Imp. nac., 1927. 89p.

2103 POZO CANO, Raúl del. Paraguay-Bolivia; la audiencia de Charcas. Refutación a todos los abogados de Bolivia, que funda los hipotéticos derechos de su patria sobre el Chaco Boreal en una supuesta jurisdicción administrativa do ese alto tribunal de apelación. A., Imp. sudamericana, 1926. 70p.

2104 POZO CANO, Raúl del. Paraguay-Bolivia; continuidad del esfuerzo del Paraguay en el Chaco (1537-1811). A., Imp. Nac., 1934. 54p.

2105 POZO CANO, Raúl del. Paraguay-Bolivia. Nuevos documentos que prueban la jurisdicción del Paraguay en el Chaco, seguidos de varios testimonios de Azara, que prueban le mismo. A., Imp. nac., 1927. 57p.

2106 POZO CANO, Raúl del. Paraguay-Bolivia, la Real cédula de 1743 a la luz de la geografía de la época. A., Imp. nac., 1935. 16p.

2107 QUIJARRO, Antonio. La cuestión de límites entre Bolivia y el Paraguay; documentos de la misión confidencial desempeñada por el doctor Antonio Quijarro en enero de 1901. B.A., Compañía sud-americana de billetes de banco, 1901. 113p.

2108 RAMIREZ, Juan Isidro. Alrededor de la cuestión paraguayo boliviana. Lima, Imp. Minerva, 1930. 286p.

2109 RAMOS GIMENEZ, Leopoldo. El Chaco Boreal en la historia y en nuestro días. B.A., Tall. gráf. Ferrari hnos, 1934. 2 vols.

2110 RAMOS GIMENEZ, Leopoldo. El Chaco a través de los siglos en los mapas de la Colección Rio Branco. Rio de Janeiro, Edit. Alba, 1933. 16p.

2111 RAMOS GIMENEZ, Leopoldo. El Chaco Paraguayo; estudio presentado al Primer Congreso del Instituto Panamericano de Geografía e Historia, reunida en Rio de Janeiro. Rio de Janeiro, Edit. Alba, 1932. 80p.

2112 RAMOS GIMENEZ, Leopoldo. Historia cartográfica del Paraguay con relación al Chaco Boreal. B.A., Tall. gráf. E.L. Frigeiro, 1935. 36p.

2113 RAMOS GIMENEZ, Leopoldo. El Chaco Paraguayo y la paz de América; carta de un periodista paraguayo a la prensa del continente. Rio de Janeiro, 1932. 8p.

2114 RAMOS GIMENEZ, Leopoldo. Los rios del Gran Chaco. RGA 1 (1934) 77-84.

2115 RIOS, Cornelio. Cuestión de límites entre el Paraguay y Bolivia; conferencia pronunciada por el doctor Cornelio Ríos, en los salones del Ateneo hispanoamericano, el 22 de noviembre de 1924. La Paz, Empresa editora "La República", 1925. 47p.

2116 RIOS, Cornelio. Los derechos de Bolivia sobre el Chaco Boreal y sus límites con el Paraguay; conferencias del doctor Cornelio Ríos, en el Ateneo hispanoamericano. B.A., 1925. 138p.

2117 ROEMER, H. Die neue Grenze im Chaco Boreal. IA 12 (1939) 470-75.

2118 ROLON, Francisco. El Paraguay y Bolivia. Cuestión de límites. A., Tall. nac. de H. Kraus, 1903. 38p.

2119 SAAVEDRA, Bautista. La cuestión fronteriza con el Paraguay. La Paz, Tall. gráf. "La Prensa", 1908. 24p.

2120 SAAVEDRA, Bautista. El último jirón de la patria. Lo que para conservarlo hizo Bautista Saavedra. La Paz, Edit. Universo, 1941. iv, 132p.

2121 SANCHEZ, Zacarias. La cuestión de límites con Bolivia. A., Honorable Cámara de Diputados, 1928. 10p.

2122 SANTOS, Carlos R. Conflicto paraguayo-boliviano. B.A., 1930. 96p. (Biblioteca de la Asociación paraguaya)
2. ed. A., 1932. 126p.

2123 SOCIEDAD COLOMBISTA PANAMERICANA. Conmemoración del 446 aniversario del descubrimiento de América por Cristóbal Colón. Homenaje panamericano a las repúblicas de Bolivia y Paraguay. Havana, Imp. P. Fernandez, 1938? 89p.

2124 SOLARES, Aniceto. El problema del sudeste de Bolivia. n.p., Bolivia, 1926. 28p.

2125 SOSA ESCALADA, José Maria. Conferencias sobre límites paraguayos. A., 1891. 84p.

2126 STEFANICH, Juan. La Sociedad de las naciones y la doctrina de Monroe. ¿Tiene competencia la Sociedad de las naciones para intervenir en el litigio de límites paraguayo-boliviano? A., Tall. gráf. "La Nación", 1928. 17p. (Publ. del Centro estudiantes de derecho)

2127 TORO RAMALLO, Luis. Una síntesis del pleito boliviano-paraguayo. Santiago de Chile, Imp. Universitaria, 1932. 59p.

2128 ULLOA Y SOTOMAYOR, Alberto. Habla un maestro de derecho internacional: "el Paraguay ha sido el agresor ... " Edición de la legación de Bolivia en el Perú. Lima? 1930? 90p.

2129 UNIVERSIDAD MAYOR DE SAN FRANCISCO XAVIER. The Chaco dispute, proofs and truths; a document by the Major university of Saint Francis Xavier of Chuguisaca. Paris, Imprimerie "Le Livre libre", 1932. 20p.

2130 UNIVERSIDAD MAYOR DE SAN FRANCISCO XAVIER. Manifesto de la Universidad mayor de San Francisco Xavier central de Bolivia: litigio boliviano-paraguayo. Sucre, Imp. y lit. salesiana, 1932. 6p.
Spanish version of no. 2129.

2131 URQUIDI, José Macedonio. El uti possidetis juris y el de facto. Cochabamba, Imp. Universitaria, 1946.

224p. (Cuadernos sobre derechos y ciencias sociales, 35)

2132 VALDOVINOS, Arnaldo. Bajo las botas de una bestia rubia. 2. ed. A., Puigbonet, 1933. 106p.

2133 VIRREIRA PACCIERI, Alberto. Bolivia-Paraguay, 5 de diciembre de 1928; datos para la historia diplomática. La Paz, Imp. Eléctrica, 1932. v, 217p.

b) Other aspects

2134 ABZAC, P. d'. Sur le Grand-Chaco. BSAL ser. 2, 12 (1877) 394-96.

2135 ALARCON Y CAÑEDO, José; PITTINI, Riccardo. El Chaco paraguayo y sus tribus: apuntes etnograficos y leyendas. La misión Salesiana. Turin, Sociedad Editora Internacional, c. 1925. 118p.

2136 AMERLAN, A. Die Indianer des Gran Chaco. GL 42 (1882) 183-86; 201-2.

2137 AZARA, Félix de. Informes de D. Félix de Azara sobre varios proyectos de colonizar el Chaco. *In* no. 666 (1910) Vol. 4, p. 5-20.

2138 BENDER, Fritz. In unerschlossenen Chaco von Paraguay. K 57 (1961) no. 11, 465-73.

2139 BRADFORD, William; FISHER, Frederick. The Paraguayan Chaco. A., USAID, 1955. 250p.

2140 CAMPOS, David. De Tarija a la Asunción: expedición boliviana de 1883; informe del Doctor David Campos, Comisario Nacional y Delegado del Supremo Gobierno. Ed. oficial. B.A., Imp. de J. Peuser, 1888. xxv, 785p.

2141 CARNIER, K. Skizzen vom Paraguayischen Chaco. MGG 8 (1913) 16-32.

2142 CASTRO BOEDO, Emilio. Estudios sobre la navegación del Bermejo y colonización del Chaco. B.A., Imp., litografía y fundación de tipos de la Sociedad Anónima, 1873. 276p.

2143 COMINGES, Juan de. Obras escogidas de don Juan de Cominges, con su biografía por el doctor D. Matías Alonso Criado. B.A., Casa Editora de Juan A. Alsina, 1892. xxxix, 490p.
"Desde el Chaco paraguayo", p. 366-71.

"El Chaco y sus indios", p. 286-307.
"Exploraciones del Chaco del Norte", p. 3-249.

2144 DAGUERRE, Juan B. Notas de um viaje al Chaco Salteño. RGA 1 (1934) 409-16.

2145 DOBSON, Arthur Austin Greaves. A short account of the Leach Bermejo expedition of 1899, with some references to the flora, fauna and the Indian tribes of the Chaco. B.A., J. Smart, 1900. 74p.

2146 DOMINGUEZ, Manuel. El Chaco. RIP 6 no. 48 (1904) 14-65.

2147 DOMINGUEZ, Manuel. Expediciones del Paraguay al Chaco. A., Imp. nac., 1934. 26p.

2148 FIEBRIG, C. Was ist der Chaco? IA 11 (1937) 161-82.

2149 FONTANA, Luis Jorge. El Gran Chaco ilustrada. B.A., Imp. de Ostwald y Martinez, 1881. xxxi, 235p.

2150 FONTANA, Luis Jorge. Viaje de esploración al Rio Pilcomayo. B.A., Imp. del Departamento Nac. de Agricultura, 1883. 72p.

2151 FRIC, Alberto Vojtech. Prikliucheniia okhotnika v Gran-Chako; tr. by S. Kovalevsky. Moscow, Geografgiz, 1958. 141p. (Puteshestviia, prikliucheniia, fantastika)
Russian trans. of no. 2152.

2152 FRIC, Alberto Vojtech. Strýcek Indián; dobrodrustvi lovce v Gran Caku. Prague, Statní nakl. detské knihy, 1956. 173p.
2. ed. 1965.

2153 FRIS, Vostech. Eine Pilcomayo-Reise in den Chaco central. GL 89 (1906) 213-20; 220-39.

2154 GANDIA, Enrique de. Historia del Gran Chaco. Madrid, La Facultad de Juan Roldán y cía, 1929. 209p.

2155 GIANNECCHINI, Dorotéo. Diario de la expedición explorada boliviana al Alto Paraguay de 1886-1887. Santa Madonna degli Angeli, Tip. de la Porciúncula, 1896. 359p.

2156 GIBSON, *Sir* Christopher H. Enchanted trails. London, Museum Press, 1948. 272p.

2157 GIBSON, *Sir* Christopher H. Through Paraguay and Southern Matto Grosso. NGM 1943, Oct., 459-88.

2158 GIBSON, Meredith Herbert. Gran Chaco calling; a chronicle of sport and travel in Paraguay and the Chaco. London, H.F. & G. Witherby, 1934. 220p.

2159 GORHAM, J. Richard. The Paraguayan Chaco and its rainfall. *In* no. 474, p. 39-60.

2160 GRUBB, W. Barbrooke. Among the Indians of the Paraguayan Chaco: a story of missionary work in South America told by W. Barbrooke Grubb and his fellow-workers in the Chaco Mission of the South American Missionary Society; ed. by Gertrude Wilson. London, Charles Murray, 1904. xiv, 176p.

2161 GRUBB, W. Barbrooke. A church in the wilds: the remarkable story of the establishment of the South American mission amongst the hitherto savage and intractable natives of the Paraguayan Chaco; ed. by H.T. Morrey Jones. London, Seeley Service; N.Y., Dutton, 1914. 287p.

2162 GRUBB, W. Barbrooke. The Paraguayan Chaco and its possible future. GJ 54 (1919) 157-78.

2163 GRUBB, W. Barbrooke. An unknown people in an unknown land: an account of the life and customs of the Paraguayan Chaco, with adventures and experiences met with during twenty years' pioneering and exploration amongst them; ed. by H.T. Morrey Jones. London, Seeley; Philadelphia, Lippincott, 1911. 330p.
On the Lengua Indians.

2164 HERMANN, W. Die ethnographischen Ergebnisse der Deutschen Pilcomayo Expedition. ZE 40 (1908) 120-37.

2165 HUONDER, P.A. Die Völkergruppierung im Gran Chaco im 18. Jahrhundert. GL 81 (1902) 387-91.

2166 JOLIS, D. Giuseppe. Saggio sulla storia naturale della provincia del Gran Chaco. E sulle pratiche, e sui costumi dei popoli che l'abitano insieme con tre giornali di altrettanti viaggi fatti alle interne contrade di quei Barbari. Tomo 1. In Faenza, per Lodovico Genestri, 1788. 600p.

2167 KANTNER, Helmuth. Der Gran Chaco und seine Randgebiete. Hamburg, Friederichsen, de Gruyter & Co., 1936. xii, 376p. (Abhandlungen aus dem Gebiet der Auslandkunde, 43)

2168 KANTNER, Helmuth. Der südamerikanische Chaco und seine Flussprobleme. GW 3 (1935) 89-102.

2169 KERR, *Sir* John Graham. The Gran Chaco. SGM 8 (1892) 73-87.

2170 KERR, *Sir* John Graham. A naturalist in the Gran Chaco. Cambridge, Cambridge University Press, 1950. xi, 234p.

2171 KRIEG, Hans. Geographische Übersicht und illustrierter Routenbericht. Stuttgart, Strecker & Schroeder, 1931. xi, 95p. (Wissenschaftliche Ergebnisse der Deutschen Gran Chaco Expedition)

2172 KRIEG, Hans. Indianerland; Bilder aus dem Gran Chaco. Stuttgart, Strecker & Schroeder, 1929. viii, 140p.

2173 KRIEG, Hans. Menschen, die ich in der Wildnis traf. Stuttgart, Strecker & Schroeder, 1935. 220p.

2174 LOZANO, Pedro. Descripción corográfica del Gran Chaco Gualamba. Reedición con prólogo e indice por Radamés A. Altieri. Tucumán, Instituto de antropología, 1941. xix, 466p. (Universidad nacional de Tucumán. Publ. no. 288. Departamento de investigaciones regionales. Publicaciones especiales del Instituto de antropología)
First published in 1738.

2175 MARIN IGLESIAS, Alejandro. Meditación sobre el Chaco Boreal. A., 1956. 8p.

2176 MARRO, Giovanni. Costume ornementale precolombiano e su riscontro oggidi nel Gran Chaco. JSA n.s., 21 (1932) 259-71.

2177 MENDOZA, Jaime. El Chaco en los albores de la conquista. Sucre, Imp. salesiana, 1937. vi, 140p.

2178 METRAUX, A. Estudios de etnografia Chaquena. AIEA 5 (1944) 263-314.

2179 METRAUX, A. La obra de las misiones inglesas en el Chaco. JSA n.s., 25 (1933) 205-9.

2180 OLMEDO, Natalicio. El gran Chaco paraguayo; amparo de civilización y progreso; 1935-1965; estudio gráfico de los aspectos más resaltantes del pasado y presente de la Región Occidental. A., 1967? 266p.

2180a OLMOS, J. Leonardo. El Chaco; disertaciones sobre geografía, zoologia, botanica, maderas y su aprovechamiento, etnogafía (sic), geologia y colonización del territorio chaqueño. La Paz, Edit. Boliviana, Velarde, Bilbao y cía, 1929. 3-154p.

2181 PARTIDO COLORADO. El despertar del Chaco; una obra del coloradismo para el desarrollo nacional. A., Edit. República, 1970. 67p.

2182 PELLESCHI, Giovanni. Otto mesi nel gran Chaco; viaggio lungo il fiume Vermiglio di Giovanni Pelleschi. Firenze, 1881. 428p.

2183 REDSKOP, C. Mission in the Paraguayan Chaco. IRM 62 no. 247 (1972) 303-17.

2184 REMEDI, Joaquin. Apuntes sobre el Chaco y los indios que lo habitan. BIGA 17 (1896) 333-62.

2185 RYDEN, Stig. Chaco: en resa bland forulamningar och indianer i argentinska och bolivianska Chaco. Göteborg, 1936. 187p.

2185a SAMANIEGO, Marcial. El Chaco Paraguayo: conferencia pronunciada a los alumnos del Colegio Nacional del Guerra. A., Imp. Militar, 1976. 95p.

2186 SUSNIK, Branislava. Dimensiones migratorias y pautas culturales de los pueblos del Gran Chaco y de su periferia (enfoque etnológico). Resistencia, Universidad Nacional del Nordeste, Instituto de Historia, 1972. 31p.
Also: SA 7 (1972) 85-105.

2187 UNRUH, Robert C. Colonization and agriculture in the Paraguayan Chaco. *In* no. 474, p. 105-7.

2188 VELLARD, Jehan. Le Chaco paraguayen. BMNB 14-17 (1942) 287-301.

2189 VELLARD, Jehan. Conditions écologiques et humaines et mise en valeur du Chaco. RTA 125 (1972) no. 1, 31-45.

2189a WEWEGE-SMITH, Thomas. Gran Chaco adventure, the thrilling and amazing adventures of a Bolivian air caballero. London, Hutchinson, 1937. 288p.

2. Other regions

2190 FRANCO PREDA, Artemio. El Guaira y su aporte a la cultura paraguaya; historia cultural del Guaira. A? 1972. 460p.

2190a JORNADAS DE HISTORIA DEL GUAIRA, 1st, VILLARRICA. Primeras jornadas de Historia del Guairá, celebradas en Villarrica del 16 al 20 de Julio de 1970. Villarrica, Instituto de Numismática y Antigüedades, Filial No. 1, 1970. 189p.

3. *Boundaries*

(For the boundary with Bolivia, see III K. 1.)

2191 AUDIBERT, Alejandro. Los límites de la antigua provincia del Paraguay. Primera parte. B.A., Imp. "La Economica" de Iustoni, 1892. 388p.

2192 GARAY, Blas. Historia, observaciones críticas sobre los límites de la antigua provincia del Paraguay. A., 189? 60p.
A criticism of no. 2191.

2193 MALLORQUIN, Juan L. Los límites del Paraguay; conferencia leida en el "Instituto paraguayo" en los primeros días del mes de mayo de 1907. A., Est. tip. de "El Civico", 1907. 80p.

2194 SOSA ESCALADA, Juan Manuel. Conferencia sobre límites paraguayos. B.A., Imp. del Congreso, 1895. xx, 113p.

2195 SOSA ESCALADA, Juan Manuel. El Paraguay occidental. B.A., Imp. López, 1934. 355p.

2196 VASCONSELLOS, César Augusto. Los límites del Paraguay. A., Imp. nac., 1931-

2197 VASCONSELLOS, Víctor Natalicio. Resumen de historia del Paraguay; delimitaciones territoriales. A., 1970. 118p.

2198 VITTONE, Luis. Provincia gigante de las Indias, sus desmembraciones. A?, 1966. 232p.

a) Argentina

2199 ARGENTINA. MINISTERIO DE RELACIONES EXTERIORES Y CULTO. Antecedentes históricos y geográficos, que sirvieron de base para dar solución definitiva a los límites entre las Repúblicas Argentina y del Paraguay en el Río Pilcomayo. B.A., Tall. Gráf. del Instituto Geográfico Militar, 1956. xii, 392p.

2200 BEJARANO, Ramón César. El Paraguay en busca del mar. A., Casa Edit. Toledo, 1965. 100p.

2201 BOLIVIA. MINISTERIO DE RELACIONES EXTERIORES. Notas y el memorandum de Bolivia contra el Tratado de arbitraje argentino-paraguayo de 1876. La Paz, Escuela tip. salesiana, 1929. 64p.

2202 CUESTION de límites entre la República argentina y El Paraguay; ojeada retrospectiva por Unos Amigos de la Justicia. B.A., Imp. de F.E. Coni, 1880. 64p.

2203 PARAGUAY. INSTITUTO GEOGRAFICO MILITAR. Antecedentes históricos y solución de la cuestión de límites entre las repúblicas del Paraguay y Argentina en el Río Pilcomayo. Preparada por el Capitán de Corbeta S.R. Américo González Merzario. A., Imp. nac., 1946. 82p.

2204 PARAGUAY. INSTITUTO GEOGRAFICO MILITAR. Río Pilcomayo. Reseña hidrográfica; problemas hidráulicos estudiados en ocasión de la determinación de la línea de frontera entre la República del Paraguay y la República Argentina; por Vasilio Yakovleff. A., 1948. 74, 7, i-iii p. (*Its* Publication no. 12)

2205 PARAGUAY. MINISTERIO DE RELACIONES EXTERIORES. Chaco paraguayo; memoria presentada al arbitro por Benjamín Aceval, E. E. y ministro plenipotenciario del Paraguay en Washington. Apéndice: documentos anexos y fallo arbitral. A., Tall. nac. de H. Kraus, 1896. 327p.

2206 PARAGUAY. MINISTERIO DE RELACIONES EXTERIORES. Appendix and documents annexed to the memoir filed by the minister of Paraguay, on the question submitted to arbitration. N.Y., Evening Post Steam Presses, 1878. 367, vi p.

2207 PARAGUAY. MINISTERIO DE RELACIONES EXTERIORES. Paraguay-Argentina. La cuestión del Río Pilcomayo. A., Imp. nac., 1927. 58p.

2208 SARAVIA, Belisario. Memoria sobre los límites entre la República argentina y el Paraguay, 1867. B.A., Imp. del "Comercio del Plata", 1867. 163p.

2209 SOMELLERA, Pedro Antonio. Documento importante por la ilustración de algunas de las cuestiones de territorio entre la Confederación arjentina y el Paraguay, publicado en Buenos-Aires, en la Gazeta mercantil del 11 de febrero de 1851. Corrientes, Imp. del estado, 1855. 39p.

2210 SOSA ESCLADA, Juan Manuel. El Pilcomayo como límite argentino-paraguayo. B.A., 1939. 67p.

2211 TRELLES, Manuel Ricardo. Anexos a la Memoria sobre cuestión de límites entre la República argentina y el Paraguay. Publicación oficial. B.A., Imp. del Comercio del Plata, 1867. 310p.

2212 TRELLES, Manuel Ricardo. Cuestión de límites entre la República Argentina y el Paraguay. B.A., Imp. del Comercio del Plata, 1867. 96p.

b) Brazil

2213 ACCIOLY, Hildebrando Pompeo Pinto. Limites do Brasil, a fronteira com o Paraguay. Sao Paulo, Companhia editora nac., 1938. 149p. (Bibliotheca pedagogica brasileira. Ser. 5a: Brasiliana, 131)

2214 ALMEIDA, Mario Monteiro de. Episódios históricos da formaçao geográfica do Brasil; fixaçao das raias com o Uruguai e o Paraguai. Rio de Janeiro, Pongetti, 1951. xii, 636p.

2215 AMARILLA FRETES, Eduardo. La soberanía paraguaya en el Salto del Guairá; conferencia pronunciada en el salón de actos de Casa Paraguaya, el 11 de junio de 1964, bajo los auspicios de la Asociación de Ex-Combatientes de la Guerra del Chaco Residentes en la Argentina y el Instituto Cultural Argentino-Paraguayo. B.A., 1964. 16p.

2216 AZARA, Félix de. Correspondencia oficial e inédita sobre la demarcación de límites entre el Paraguay y el Brasil. B.A., Imp. del Estado, 1836. 68p.

2217 AZARA, Félix de. Memorias sobre el estado rural del Río de la Plata en 1801; demarcación de límites entre el Brasil y el Paraguay a últimos del siglo XVIII, é informes sobre varios particulares de la América Meridional española. Escritos postumos de Don F. de Azara ... Los pública su sobrino Don. A. de Azara, bajo la dirección de Don B.S. Castellanos de Losada. Madrid, Imp. de Sanchiz, 1847. viii, 232p.
Reprinted: B.A., Edit. Bajel, 1943. cxiv, 310p. (Biblioteca histórica colonial, 1)

2218 BLANCO SANCHEZ, Jesús L. El gran salto del Guairá o Kanendiyú; fundamentos de los derechos paraguayos al mismo. A., Edit. "El Gráfico", 1964. 33p.

2219 BRAVO, Francisco Javier. Atlas de cartas geográficas de los países de la América Meridional, en que estuvieron situadas las más importantes misiones de los Jesuitas: como también de los territorios sobre cuya posesión versaron allí las principales cuestiones entre España y Portugal; acompañado de varios documentos sobre estas últimas, y precedido de una introducción histórica por D. Francisco Javier Bravo. Madrid, Imp. y estereotipia de M. Rivadeneyra, 1872. xxiii, 51p.

2220 BRAZIL. EMBASSY (PARAGUAY). A fronteira Brasil-Paraguai. Nota no. 92, de 25 de março de 1966, da Embaixada do Brasil em Assunçao. Rio de Janeiro?, Ministério das Relaçoes Exteriores, Divisao da América Meridional, Seçao Publicaçoes, 1966. 48p.

2221 CARDOZO, Efraím. Los derechos del Paraguay sobre los saltos del Guairá. Prólogo del Excmo. y Rvdmo. arzobispo de Asunción monseñor Anibal Mena Porta. A., 1965. 279p. (Biblioteca Guaireña "Cirilo Cáceres Zorrilla", 1)

2222 CARDOZO, Efraím. 20 preguntas sin respuestas sobre los Saltos del Guairá; recopilación de articulos publicados en El Radical. A., 1971. 120p.

2223 COUTO, Antonio Correa do. Dissertaçao sobre o actual governe da República do Paraguay. Rio de Janeiro, Typ. do Imperial Instituto Artístico, 1865. 104p.

2224 DIAZ, Adolfo M. El tratado de permuta de 1750 y la actuación de los misioneros del Paraguay. EBA 60 (1938) 742-82.

2225 Les DISSENSIONS des républiques de La Plata et les machinations du Brésil. Paris, E. Dentu, 1865. 87p.

2226 IBARRA, Rogelio. El tratado de límites entre el Paraguay y el Brasil. A., Imp. nac., 1929. 31p.

2227 LACONICH, Marco Antonio. La cuestión de límites en el Salto del Guairá. A., La Colmena, 1964. 90p.

2228 PARAGUAY. CONGRESO NACIONAL. CAMARA DE DIPUTADOS. COMISION DE RELACIONES EXTERIORES. El Tratado de Río de Janeiro; dictamen por el que se aconseja a la Cámara de diputados su aprobación. A., Tall. gráf. El Arte, 1929. 65p.

2229 PARAGUAY. MINISTERIO DE RELACIONES EXTERIORES. Demarcación de límites en la región del Salto del

Guairá; nota D.P.I. no. 712, del 14 de diciembre de 1965, dirigida por la Cancillería del Paraguay al Embajador del Brasil en Asunción. A., 1965. 26p.

2230 PIMENTA BUENO, José Antonio, marqués de San Vicente. Discurso na sessao do Senado de 26 de junho de 1855, relativamente aos limites com o Paraguay discutindose a fixaçao das forças de mar. Rio de Janeiro, J. Villeneuve, 1855. 23p.

2231 RAMOS GIMENEZ, Leopoldo. Sobre el Salto del Guairá, al oído de América. A., 1966. 181p. (Anales del Paraguay; páginas documentales de la historia y para la historia, año 3, no. 4)

2232 LOS SALTOS del Guairá; cuerpo documental. Compilación ordenada por el Banco Central del Paraguay. A., 1967. 352p.

2233 SOSA, Ruperto. Contestación al folleto de Juan S. Godoy, ante la publicación de la anexión del Paraguay á la República argentina. Corrientes, Establecimiento tip. B. Fages, 1897. 27p.

2234 VARZEA, Afonso. Límites meridionaes; as fronteiras com o Uruguai, Argentina, e Paraguai, do ponto de vista de geografia social. Rio de Janeiro, Alba, 193? 219p.

c) Peru

2235 DOMINGUEZ, Manuel. Límite este del Perú en los contrafuertes andinos. A., Imp. nac., 1934. 20p.

L. Urban History

a) Areguá

2236 ORTIZ, José Concepción. Apuntes para la historia de Areguá. RAP 3 (1973) no. 5, 14-20.

b) Asunción

2237 AGRUPACION FOLKLORICA GUARANI. BUENOS AIRES. 405 aniversario de la fundación de la ciudad de Asunción. B.A., 1942. 32p.

2238 AMARILLA FRETES, Eduardo. Asunción, ciudad madre de ciudades (la fundación de Buenos Aires). A., Imp. nac., 1942. 62p.

2239 ASUNCION. DEPARTAMENTO DE CULTURA Y ARTE. Histōria edilicia de la ciudad de Asunción. A., Artes Gráficas Zamphirópolos, 1967. 397p. (Departamento de Cultura y Arte, 4)

2240 ASUNCION. DIRECCION DE CATASTRO. SECCION CATASTRO III LIBRO. Datos de la ciudad: nomenclatura, barrios, avenidas, calles, pasajes. A., 1970. 142p.

2241 ASUNCION. INTENDENCIA MUNICIPAL. Planes municipales, 1962; pavimentos, transportes, viviendas, supermercados, Palacio Municipal. A., Edit. "El País", 1962. 11p.

2242 ASUNCION. INTENDENCIA MUNICIPAL. Planes municipales, 1963; resumen de la conferencia pronunciada por el intendente municipal de la capital, César Gagliardone; con motivo de anunciar los planes municipales del año 1963. A., 1963. 14p.

2243 ASUNCION. UNIVERSIDAD NACIONAL: CENTRO DE ADIESTRAMIENTO EN SERVICIO. Guía de reglamentos municipales. Anexo: Ley no. 200 "Estatuto del funcionario público". A., 1970. 22, 10, 12p.

2244 ASUNCION, Paraguay's interesting capital. BPAU 61 (1927) no. 11, 1073-85.

2245 AYALA AQUINO, Gumersindo. Jhenoivo Tavaguasu; fundación de Asunción. Versión al español: Nabel Felipe Estruc. 2. ed. A., Edit. Avaité, 1969. 30p.

2246 BELLANI NAZERI, Rodolfo. Asunción, la ciudad de doble fisonomia; lo viejo y lo nuevo en mezola desordenada. RGA 24 no. 142 (1945) 27-33.

2246a BREVE reseña histórica de la iglesia de la santísima Asunción del Paraguay, por una comisión de dos sacerdotes nombrada por s.a. iltma don Juan Sinforiano Bogarin, obispo de la misma iglesia. Año de 1899. A., Establecimiento tip. de Jordán y Villamil, 1906. xiii, 69, xxiip.

2246b CACERES DE THOMAS, Carmen. Aportes al desarrollo de la ciudad de Asunción. A., 1977. 195p.

2246c CALZADA, Isidoro. La plateada bahía de los carios; primera biografía de Juan Salazar Espinoza, fundador de la ciudad de Asunción. A., Edit. Don Bosco, 1971. 123p. (Colección Ñanduti literario, 5)

2247 CARDOZO, Efraím. Asunción del Paraguay. HNA 3 (1937) 235-74.

2248 CARDOZO, Efraím. La fundación de la ciudad de Asunción en 1541. AHA for 1940 (1941) 145-222.

2249 GARAY, Blas. El paseo del estandarte real. HP 1 (1956) 15-22.

2250 GIMENEZ CABALLERO, Ernesto. Asunción, capital de América. Madrid, Ediciones Cultura Hispánica, 1971. 29p.
Also: REP no. 169-170 (1970) 209-18.

2251 GIRALT, Miguel. Guía de Asunción "Giralt". A., 1944. 144p.

2252 HENNING, Klaus. Asunción. A., Ediciones "El Gallo", 1970. 24p. (Paraguay pictórico, 1)
Photographs.

2252a La IMAGEN patrona de la Asunción. B.A., Tall. gráf. "La Baskonia", 1917. 15p.

2253 KALLSEN, Osvaldo. Asunción y sus calles; antecedentes históricos. A., 1974. 354p.

2254 LAFUENTE MACHAIN, Ricardo de. La Asunción de antaño; ilustrador: Roger H. Ayala. B.A., Tall. gráf. de S. de Amorrortu, 1942. 180p.
A description of Asunción before 1869.
Also: B.A., Emecé, 1943. 87p.

2255 LAFUENTE MACHAIN, Ricardo de. La casafuerte de la Asunción. Paris; B.A., Hachette, 1936. 24p. (Publicaciones de la Sociedad de história argentina, 5)

2255a LAFUENTE MACHAIN, Ricardo de. La Virgen de la Asunción y su oratorio. B.A., Tall. gráf. de S. de Amorrortu e hijos, 1940. 213p.

2255b MONUMENTOS, parques, jardines y plazas de la ciudad de Asunción; história y comentarios. Guía para el turista. A., 1967. 109p.

2256 MORENO, Fulgencio Ricardo. La ciudad de la Asunción. B.A., J. Suarez, 1926. 277p.
2. ed. A., Edit. Paraguaya, 1968. 258p.

2257 ORTELLADO ROJAS DE FOSSATI, María Antonia. Leonor de América. A., Artes Gráficas Zamphirópolos, 1971. 223p.

2258 ORTIZ MAYANS, Antonio. Evocaciones de la Asunción, 1915-1930. A., Emasa, 1967. 92p. (Colección Cultura Paraguaya)

2259 OXILIA, Héctor. Oratorio de Nuestra Señora de la Asunción y Panteón Nacional de los Héroes. A., 1969. 83p.

2260 PAN AMERICAN UNION. Asunción. Washington, 1945. 19p.

2261 PEÑA VILLAMIL, Manuel. La fundación del Cabildo de la Asunción; antecedentes históricos y juridicos. A., 1969. 183p.

2262 PUSINERI SCALA, Carlos Alberto. Asunción proclama a Carlos IV; trabajo leído en sesión pública del Instituto en diciembre. A., Instituto de Numismatica y Antigüedades del Paraguay, 1971. 11p.

2263 QUEVEDO PFANNI, Roberto. La Asunción del mil seiscientos en dos padrones inéditos. HP 8-10 (1963-65) 96-127.

2264 REID, William Alfred. Asunción, Paraguay's interesting capital. Washington, Government Printing Office, 1919. 28p.
Issued by the Pan American Union.
Reprinted: 1923. 25p.
1927. 30p.
1932. 24p.

2265 RELACION de las fiestas quese hicieron con motivo de haber aceptado el Príncipe de la Paz, el oficio de Primer Regidor Perpetuo del Cabildo de Asunción, 1804. RBA 21 (1870) 172-80.

2266 RIVAROLA, Juan Bautista. La ciudad de Asunción y la Cédula real del 12 de setiembre de 1537. Una lucha por la libertad. Asunción, Imp. Militar, 1952. 277p.
Only vol. 1 published?

2267 SANCHEZ QUELL, Hipolito. Asi fueron transcurriendo los días Asunceños. HP 2 (1957) 50-64.

2268 SANCHEZ QUELL, Hipolito. Como era Asunción alla por 1913. HP 13 (1969-70) 23-27.

2269 ZUBIZARRETA, Carlos. Historia de mi ciudad. Cubierta, viñetas y colofones de Roger Ayala. A., Edit. Emasa, 1964-.

c) Concepción

2270 CABRAL GIMENEZ, Guillermo A. Semblanzas de Concepción. A., Imp. Comuneros, 1970. 490p.

2271 CONCEPCION en las artes: la región norteña en la cultura de la nación paraguaya: exponentes de su narrativa: cuentos, relatos y páginas literarias de los escritores norteños del siglo XX. Concepción, Ediciones Futuro, 1973. 382p.

2272 OLMEDO, Natalicio. Album gráfico de Concepción. A., La Colmena, 1927. 200p.

2273 QUEVEDO PFANNI, Roberto. El Gobernador Pinedo y su fundación de Villa Real de Concepción. HP 4-5 (1959-60) 74-83.

2274 QUEVEDO PFANNI, Roberto. Villa Real de la Concepción en los días de la independencia. HP 6-7 (1961-62) 60-68.

2275 ROMERO, Genaro. El Paraguay progresa. La ciudad de Concepción. A., Tall. gráf. del estado, 1913. 82p.

2276 VILLA, Benigno. Historias, anéctodas y "casos". San Pablo (Brazil), 1968. 146p.

2276a MICO, Tomás L. Antecedentes históricos de Encarnación Itapúa. A., 1975. xi, 127p.

d) Itacurubí

2277 ALMADA, Zenón. Reminiscencias de Itacurubí de la Cordillera. A., El Arte, 1952. 22p.

e) Mbuyapey

2277a SPERATTI, Juan. Mbuyapey; origen, evolución y realidad actual. Mbuyapey, 1966. 55p.

f) Pilar del Neembucú

2278 RIQUELME GARCIA, Benigno. La villa de Nuestra Señora del Pilar del Neembucú. A., 1974. 17p.

g) San Pedro

2279 VILLALBA, Rufino A. Fiestas mayas en la villa de San Pedro, 1900. A., Tall. nac. de H. Kraus, 1900. 30p.

h) Villarrica

2280 AYALA AQUINO, Gumersindo; MARTINEZ, Eladio. Libro de oro: IV centenario de Villarrica. A., 1970? 114p.

i) Villeta

2281 VELAZQUEZ, Rafael Eliado. La fundación de la Villeta del Guarnipitan en 1714 y la población del litoral paraguayo. AEA 21 (1964) 211-46.

M. Immigration and emigration

1. *Immigration*

2281a ALEGRE, Heriberto. La colonización en el Paraguay: el eje este. RPS 14 no. 38 (1977) 135-55.

2282 AYALA, Eligio. Migraciones, ensayo escrito en Berna en 1915. Editado, en memoria de su esclarecido autor, por dos amigos, admiradores de su brillante obra gubernativa. Santiago de Chile, Imp. "La Sud-América", 1941. 74p.

2283 BAEZ, Cecilio. História del Paraguay: las leyes de extranjería. RIP 9 no. 58 (1909) 396-403.

2283a BRAIDO, Jacyr F. Inquiry into Brazilian settlers in Paraguay. MIG 21 (1970) no. 4, 12-20.

2283b BURR, Malcolm. Russians in Paraguay. NC 704 (1935) 441-48.

2284 DIE ANSIEDLUNG der deutschen Mennoniten in Paraguay. DA 31 (1935) 113-21.

2285 DROULER, C. Une colonie socialiste au Paraguay: la Nouvelle Australie. RS 3 ser., 10 (1895) 232-38.

2286 EGLER, Válter Alberto. A colonizaçao no norte da Argentina e sudoeste do Paraguai. BG 7 no. 81 (1959) 931-41.

2287 FÖRSTER, Bernhard. Dr. Bernhard Försters Kolonie Neu-Germania in Paraguay. Berlin, Comissions-Verlag der Actiengesellschaft "Pionier", 1891. 173p.

2288 FÖRSTER, Bernhard. Deutsche Colonien in dem oberen Laplata-gebiete, mit besonderer Berücksichtigung von Paraguay. 2. ed. Leipzig, G. Fock, 1886. xi, 223p.

2289 FRETZ, Joseph Winfield. Immigrant group settlement in Paraguay: a study in the sociology of colonization. North Newton, Bethel College, 1962. 194p.

2290 FRETZ, Joseph Winfield. Pilgrims in Paraguay; the story of Mennonite colonization in South America. Scottsdale, Herald Press, 1953. xv, 257p.

2291 HACK, H. Die Kolonisation der Mennoniten im paraguayischen Chaco. Amsterdam, Königliches Tropeninstitut, 1960? 232p. (Königliches Tropeninstitut, 138)

2292 HACK, H. Primavera: a communal settlement of immigrants in Paraguay. Amsterdam, Königliches Tropeninstitut, 1958. 13p.
Also: REMP 6 (1958) no. 3/4, 75-87.

2292a ILG, Karl. Pionere in Argentinien, Chile, Paraguay und Venezuela, durch Bergwelt, Urwald und Steppe erwanderte Volkskunde der deutschsprachigen Siedler. Innsbruck; Vienna; Munich, Tyrolla-Verlag, 1976. 318p.

2293 IMMIGRATION into Paraguay. BTJ 6 (1889) 552; 7 (1889) 65-66, 544; 9 (1890) 202, 703-04; 16 (1894) 219-20; 23 (1897) 214-343.

2294 JOHN, R. Paraguay: Winke für Einwanderer. A., 1919. 51p.

2295 KLIEWER, Fritz. The Mennonites of Paraguay. MQR 12 (1938) 92-97.

2296 KLIEWER, Fritz. Mennonite young people's work in the Paraguayan Chaco. MQR 11 (1937) 119-30.

2297 KOSSOK, Manfred. Die Mennonite-Siedlungen Paraguays in den Jahren 1935-1939. ZGW 8 (1960) no. 2, 367-76.

2298 KRAUSE, Annemarie Elisabeth. Mennonite settlement in the Paraguayan Chaco. Chicago, 1952. xiii, 143p. (University of Chicago. Dept. of Geography, Research paper no. 25)

2299 LIVERMORE, Harold V. New Australia. HAHR 30 (1950) 290-313.

2300 MAJAVACCA, José; PEREZ ACOSTA, Juan Francisco. El aporte italiano al progreso del Paraguay (1527-1930). B.A., Tall. gráf. Lucania, 1951. 219p.

2301 NISHIKAWA, Daijiro. A expansao dos núcleos colonials japonêses no Paraguai após a segunda guerra mundial. SSP 26 (1964) 33-81.

2302 PARAGUAY. DEPARTAMENTO DE TIERRAS Y COLONIZACION. Colonización mennonita; derechos, privilegios y concesiones a los miembros de la comunidad mennonita y a los de cualquier otra comunidad religiosa de procedencia americana o europea, que vengan a establecerse en el Chaco paraguayo - otras informaciones. Anotaciones recopiladas por Genaro Romero, presidente del Departamento de tierras y colonias. A., Imp. nac., 1933. 22p.

2303 PARAGUAY. DIRECCION GENERAL DE INMIGRACION Y COLONIZACION. Datos estadísticos sobre el movimiento de inmigración en el Paraguay desde 1882 hasta 1907. A., Tall. nac. de H. Kraus, 1908. 16p.

2304 PARAGUAY. DIRECCION GENERAL DE INMIGRACION Y COLONIZACION. Informe de la Dirección general de inmigración y colonización presentado al Ministerio de relaciones exteriores, con anexos sobre varios proyectos relativos á la colonización y propaganda. A., H. Kraus, 1906. 82p.

2305 PARAGUAY. DIRECCION GENERAL DE INMIGRACION Y COLONIZACION. Reglamento para la colonia "Nueva Italia" en el departamento de "Villeta". A., Tall. nac. de H. Kraus, 1907. 24p.

2306 PARAGUAY. MINISTERIO DE ECONOMIA. Las colonias mennonitas en el Chaco Boreal. A., Imp. nac., 1934. 64p.

2307 PARAGUAY. MINISTERIO DE RELACIONES EXTERIORES. Colonia Gaboto; organización y reglamentación. A., Escuela tip. salesiana, 1902. 9p.

2308 PARAGUAY. OFICINA GENERAL DE INFORMACIONES Y CANJES. Guide de l'immigrant au Paraguay. Assomption, Imp. du "Paraguayo", 1889. vii, 219p.

2309 PARAGUAY. OFICINA GENERAL DE INFORMACIONES Y CANJES. Noticia sobre la colonia "Presidente González" en el Departamento de Caazapá. A., Tip. y encuadernación de "La República", 1891. 24p.

2310 PARCHEVSKY, K. V Paragvai i Argentinu. Ocherki Yuzhnoi Ameriki. Paris, Les Editeurs réunis, 1937? 304p.
On Russian immigration.

2311 PATERNO, Guiseppe de Stefano. Ai ministri del'interno e dell'estero del regno d'Italia. n.p., 1899? 12p.

2312 PATERNO, Giuseppe de Stefano. Relazione sulla colonizzazione nel Paraguay del dr. Giuseppe de Stefano Paternó. Catania, Tip. Guttenberg di R. Giuntini, 1899. 68p.

2313 PIDOUX DE DRACHENBERG, Lyra. Inmigración y colonización en el Paraguay, 1870-1970. RPS 12 no. 34 (1975) 65-123.

2314 PITAUD, Henri. Les Français au Paraguay. Bordeaux, Editions Bièrs, 1955. 217p.

2315 QUIJARRO, Antonio. Navegación del Río Otuquis, fundación de un puerto y establecimiento de colonias agricolas, propuesta de la compañía inglesa "The Paraguayan development company, limited". La Paz, Imp. y litografía de El Nacional, 1890. 97p.

2316 QUIRING, Walter. Deutsche Erschliessen den Chaco. Karlsruhe, H. Schneider, 1936. 207p.
Mennonite colonies.

2316a QUIRING, Walter. Russlanddeutsche suchen eine Heimat; die deutsche Einwanderung in den paraguayischen Chaco. Karlsruhe, H. Schneider, 1938. 192p.

2317 ROMERO, Genaro. Cartilla del colono. A., Imp. nac., 1930. 40p. (Departamento de tierras y colonias, Folleto, 19)

2318 ROMERO, Genaro. Informes sobre las colonias "Trinacria", "Nueva Italia", "25 de noviembre" presentados al Ministerio de relaciones exteriores. A., Tall. tip. del estado, 1911. 51p.

2319 ROMERO, Genaro. Nociones útiles para el campesino. A., Imp. Lit. M. Brossa, 1923. 33p. (Cartilla informativa, folleto 1)

2320 ROMERO, Genaro. Notizen für Einwanderer. Trans. by Clara, Gräfin von Bülow. A., Staatsdruckerei Estrella, 1914. 40p.

2321 ROMERO, Genaro. El Paraguay como país de inmigración. A., 1926. 18p.

2322 ROMERO, Genaro. Que proporción existe entre el extranjero y el inmigrante paraguayo. A., La Paraguaya, 1934. 15p.

2323 ROMERO, Genaro. Repatriación. A., Tall. Gráf. del Estado, 1913. 54p.

2324 ROMERO, Genaro. Republik Paraguay; Handbuch für Einwanderer. A., 1914. 48p.

2324a SANDRI, Pietro. Coloni nell'Argentina e Paraguay. Merano, Tip. Editoriale Meranense, 1948. 111p.

2324b SCHLACHER, Jacob. Erlebnisse in Paraguay, von J' Sch'. Nach seinen Briefen. Zurich, Genossenschaftsdruckerei, 1922. iv, 32p.

2325 SCHNEIDER, Oscar; WILHELMY, Herbert. Deutsche Ackerbausiedlung im südamerikanischen Grasland, Pampa und Gran Chaco. Leipzig, Hirt und Sohn, 1938. 134p. (Wissenschaftliche Untersuchungen des Deutschen Museums für Länderkunde, neue folge, Bd. 6)

2326 SCHNEIDER, Gustav Adolf. Die Wahrheit über Paraguay; eine Entgegnung auf die Berichte der Herren Gensch und Jordan in der Zeitschrift "Export". A., Vorwort, 1895. 82p.

2327 SCHULTZE, C.F.E. Das Paraguayfieber. Eine koloniale-pathologisch-satirisch-kritische Abhandlung. Bremen, Commissionsverlag von C. Schünemann, 1893. 44p.

2328 SOCIETE GENERALE PARAGUAYO-ARGENTINA, BUENOS AIRES. Colonies de Villa Sana, créés en 1889, par J. Valentin. Paris, Imprimerie générale Lahure, 1891. 21p.

2329 SOUTER, Gavin. A peculiar people: the Australians in Paraguay. Sydney, Angus & Robertson, 1968. 309p.

2330 STEINBART, Otto. Die Regierungs-Kolonien "Antequera" und "Rosario Loman", Departamento Villa de San Pedro (Republik Paraguay). B.A., 1914. 16p.

2331 STEWART, N.R. Japanese colonization in eastern Paraguay. Washington, National Academy of Sciences, National Research Council, 1967. xiii, 202p.

2332 STEWART, N.R. Recent trends in Paraguayan immigration and pioneer settlement. GR 51 (1961) 431-33.

2332a VOGLER, F. Wass muss der Auswanderer von der Republik Paraguay wissen? Diessen, Huber, 1919. 48p.

2333 WARREN, Harris Gaylord. The "Lincolnshire Farmers" in Paraguay: an abortive emigration scheme of 1872-1873. AAAFH 21 (1965) no. 3, 243-62.

2334 WIADOMOSCI o Paragwaju dla ǔzytku Wychodźców. Warsaw, Syndykat Emigracyjny, 1937. 92p.
A guide-book for immigrants.

2335 WILHELMY, Herbert. Die deutschen Siedlungen in Mittelparaguay. Kiel, 1941. 40p. (Schriften des Geographischen Instituts der Universität Kiel. Bd. 11, Heft 1)

2335a WILHELMY, Herbert. Siedlung um sudamerikanischen Urwald. Hamburg, KrogersVerlagsanstalt, 1949. 104p.

2335b ZBINDEN, Karl. Die Luzerner in Paraguay. LUA (1928-29) 4 Hefte. 18p.

2. *Emigration*

2336 CENTRO PARAGUAYO, MONTEVIDEO. Estatutos del "Centro Paraguayo", fundado al 18 de julio de 1916. Montevideo, Tall. gráf. A. Barreiro y Ramos, Barreiro, 1917. 31p.

2337 CENTRO PARAGUAYO, BUENOS AIRES. Centro paraguayo bonarense, 14 de mayo 1811 - 14 de mayo 1890. Discursos pronunciados, opinión de la prensa, Memoria del Centro Paraguayo. B.A., Imp. Sud-América, 1890. 89p.

2338 CORVALAN, Grazziella. La emigración de profesionales paraguayos. RPS 11, no. 31 (1974) 91-120.

2338a ESPINOLA, Blanca R.H. Estructura de personalidad y ajuste del inmigrante paraguayo en el nordeste argentino. EP 3 no. 1 (1975) 191-200.

2339 ESPINOLA, Blanco Rosa H. de. Tipos psicológicos y aculturación de los inmigrantes paraguayos en el nordeste argentino. RPS 11 no. 31 (1974) 79-89.

2340 FLORES COLOMBINO, Andrés. La fuga de intelectuales; emigración paraguaya. Prólogo de Carlos Pastore. Montevideo, Tall. Gráf. de la Comunidad del Sur., 1972. 255p.

2341 FLORES COLOMBINO, Andrés. Reseña historica de la migración paraguaya. RPS 4 no. 8-9 (1967) 89-107.

2342 FOGEL, Gerardo. Notas sobre les migrantes paraguayos en Misiones (Argentina). EP 1 no. 1 (1973) 165-94.

2343 MOSQUEIRO, Silvano. El papel de Rosario como emporio del litoral y capital agrícola de la república en las relaciones argentino-paraguayas. Rosario de Santa Fé, Librería Alvarez, 1942. 92p.

2343a PELLEGRINI, Vicente; OLIVA, Francisco de Paula. La inmigración ilegal paraguaya, una minoria condenada? RCIAS 19 no. 192 (1970) 23p.

2344 PEREZ ACOSTA, Juan Francisco. Migraciones históricas del Paraguay a la Argentina. B.A., Tall. gráf. "Optimus", 1952. 20p.

2345 RIVAROLA, Domingo M. Aspectos de la migración paraguaya. AP 3 (1967) 25-71.
Also: RPS 4 no. 8-9 (1967) 40-88.
and: A., Centro Paraguayo de Estudios Sociológicos, 1967. 40p.

2345a ROCHCAU, Georges. Inmigrantes boliviens, chiliens et paraguayennes en Argentine. MDM (1970) no. 1, 1-6.

2346 ROCHAU, Jorge; PERRIDON, Jozef; PEDISIC, Lino. Inmigraciones bolivianos, chilenos y paraguayos en Argentina. B.A., 1969. 24p.

2347 YAMPEY, Nassim. Expatriación y salud mental. RPS 2 no. 4 (1965) 41-48.

2348 ZACARIAS ARZA, Evaristo. ¿El extranjero es factor positivo en el Paraguay? A., Imp. "Efil", 1954. 213p.

IV. GEOGRAPHY

2349 AZARA, Félix de. Geografía física y esférica de las provincias del Paraguay, y misiones guaraníes. Compuesta ... en la Asunción del Paraguay. Año de MDCCXC. (Manuscrito en la Biblioteca Nacional de Montevideo). Bibliografía, prólogo y anotaciones por Rodolfo R. Schuller. Montevideo, Tall. A. Barreiro y Ramos, 1904. cxxxii, 478p. (Anales del Museo nacional de Montevideo, Sección histórico-filosófica, 1)

2350 BAEZ, Cecilio. La Conferencia dada en el Instituto Paraguayo por el Dr. Cecilio Baez sobre los trabajos de demarcación de don Félix de Azara y sus estudios acerca de la geografía del Paraguay, su fauna y su flora. RIP 1897 no. 9, 161-70.

2351 BARROS CAVALCANTI, Mário de. Paraguai. RGIPGH 5-8, no. 13-24 (1949) 105-15.

2352 BELLANI NAZERI, Rodolfo. Ypir ¿Centro de una antiquisima civilización? RGA 26 no. 159 (1946) 297-306.

2353 BERTONI, Guillermo Tell. Bosquejo de geografía humana de América; la antigua Guaranía, el país, los habitantes, primitivos centros de dispersión, su cultura, la conquista, la cruza de razas, la compenetración de culturas. A., Ed. Guarani, 1940. 98p.

2354 BERTONI, Guillermo Tell. Geografía económica nacional del Paraguay. A., Ed. Guaraní, 1940. viii, 235p. (Biblioteca de la Sociedad cientifica del Paraguay, 7)

2355 BERTONI, Guillermo Tell; GORHAM, J. Richard. The geography of Paraguay. *In* no. 474, 9-31.

2356 CAPURRO, Adán. Geografía del Paraguay: 4 curso bachillerato y 5 curso comercial. A., Mimeografía "Alcora", 1955. 124p.

2357 CAPURRO, Adán. Geografía del Paraguay: 1 año del ciclo básico, 4 año bachillerato y 5 año comerical del plan anterior. A., Mimeografía "Alcora", 1957. 135p.

2358 CARNE, Martín. Por tierras paraguayas. RGA 23 no. 141 (1945) 344-48.

2359 DECOUD, Héctor Francisco. Compendio de geografía de la república del Paraguay. A., Escuela Tip. Salesiana, 1901. 47p.

2360 DECOUD, Héctor Francisco. Geografía de la república del Paraguay. B.A., Imp. de P.E. Coni é hijos, 1895. 168p.
2. ed. A., Librería y papelaría nac. de C. Codas, 1896. 170p.
3. ed. A., Escuela Tip. Salesiana, 1900. 132p.
5. ed. Leipzig, Imp. de F.A. Brockhaus, 1906. 127p.
6. ed. Leipzig, Imp. de F.A. Brockhaus, 1911. 131p.

2361 EHRENREICH, Paul. Über seine Reise vom Paraguay zum Amazonas. VGE 16 (1889) 442-62.

2362 EHRMANN, Erik. Paraguay. GFT 19 (1907) 279-94.

2363 FERREIRA GUBETICH, Hugo. Geografía del Paraguay. 4. ed. A., 1960. 252p.
5. ed. 1962. 391p.
8. ed. 1967. 339p.
12. ed. 1975. 397p.

2364 FRANCO VIEDMA, Pablo. El Paraguay; su geografía general, ajustado al programa de estudio vigente del primer curso básico. A., 1972. 119p.

2365 GASPERI, Luis de. Geografía del Paraguay, escrito de acuerdo al plan de estudios y a los programas sintéticos de tercero y cuarto grado de las escuelas graduadas y elementales de la República, aprobados por decreto del P.E. de la nación de 24 de febrero de 1915. B.A., Tall. "Casa Jacobo Peuser", 1920. 305p.

2366 GONZALEZ, Juan Natalicio. Geografía del Paraguay. México, Edit. Guarania, 1964. 816p.

2367 LEVI, Leone. On the geography and resources of Paraguay: a paper read before the Royal Geographical Society, January 12th, 1874. London, W. Clowes, 1874. 15p.

2368 LÜTGENS, Rudolf. Beiträge zur Kenntniss des Quebracho-gebiets in Argentinien und Paraguay. Hamburg, L. Friederichsen, 1911. iv, 70p. (Universität Hamburg. Geographische Gesellschaft. Mittheilungen, Bd. 25. Heft 1)

2369 MAIZ, Fidel. Pequeña geografía para los niños de la escuela de Arroyos y Esteros. A., El Paraguayo, 1876. 196p.
  2. ed. 1890. 196p.

2370 OXIBAR, Cipriano. Apuntes de geografía del Paraguay. 12. ed. A., T. Charitas, 19--. 183p.

2370a RHO, Franco; LEIGHEB, M. Paraguay, une île sans rivage: Paraguay, island without a shore. ATL no. 80 (1973) 24-45.

2371 VILLACRES MOSCOSO, Jorge W. Bolivia y Paraguay: acceso hacía el mar. Madrid, Real Sociedad Geográfica, 1959. 28p. (Publicaciones 405. Serie B)

A. Cartography

2372 COLEGIO DE SAN JOSE, ASUNCION. Mapas corográficos del Paraguay. De acuerdo al Decreto no. 9484 del 10. del jul. de 1945. A., 1946. 18p.

2373 GASPERI, Federico E. de. Atlas general de la república del Paraguay. Aprobado por el Consejo nacional de educación a 5 de febrero de 1919 como texto para las escuelas graduadas elementales. B.A., Papelería, librería e imp. argentina "Casa Jacobo Peuser", F.E. de Gásperi, 1920. 13p.
  2. ed. B.A., Guillermo Kraft, 1939. 13p.

2374 MACHUCA MARTINEZ, Marcelino. Mapas históricos del Paraguay Gigante. A., 1951. 44p.

2375 MÖRNER, Magnus. El mapa del Mariscal. RIB 10 (1960) no. 2, 147-50.

2376 PAN AMERICAN UNION. DEPARTMENT OF ECONOMIC AFFAIRS. Paraguay: Indice anotado de los trabajos aerofotográficos y los mapas topográficos y de recursos naturales. Annotated index of aerial photographic coverage and mapping of topography and natural resources. Washington, 1964. 9p.

2377 PARAGUAY. DIRECCION DE HIDOGRAFIA Y NAVEGACION. Atlas del derrotero paraguayo, Rio Paraguay; cartas de navegación y cartas de los pasos; tramo: confluencia - B. Negra. A., 1950. 10, 29p.

2378 PARAGUAY. INSTITUTO GEOGRAFICO MILITAR. Atlas de la República del Paraguay por departamentos. Preparado conforme al Dcto. no. 1784 de 10 de julio de 1945, que establece la División política del territorio de la república. Preparado y actualizado por el cartografo Alberto da Ponte. A., 1945? 16p.

2379 PONTE, Alberto da. Atlas de la República por departamentos; ajustado al uso de las instituciones de enseñanza. A., 195? 16p.

2380 POZO CANO, Raúl del. Cartografía del Chaco paraguayo. Publicado por orden del sr. ministro de r. exteriores y culto, dr. don Justo Pastor Benitez. A., 1935? 21, 100p.

2381 RAMOS GIMENEZ, Leopoldo. Historia cartográfica del Paraguay con relación al Chaco Boreal. B.A., 1935.
A collection of 12 maps.

2382 SPAIN. ARCHIVO GENERAL DE INDIAS, SEVILLE. Relación descriptiva de los mapas, planos, etc. del Virreinato de Buenos Aires existentes en el Archivo general de Indias, por Pedro Torres Lanzas. 2. ed. B.A., Tall. "Casa Jacobo Peuser", 1921. 171p. (Buenos Aires. Universidad Nacional. Facultad de filosofia y lettres. Publicaciones de la Sección de historia, 7)
Adición ... por José Torre Revello. B.A., Tall. Casa Jacobo Peuser, 1927. 128p. (Buenos Aires. Universidad nacional. Publicaciones del Instituto de investigaciones históricas, 38)

B. Place-names

2383 CADOGAN, León. Carobeni; apuntes de toponimia hispanoguaraní. A., Imp. Paraguay, 1959. 51p.

2384 CADOGAN, León. Ticumberú-Añaretangüé; breve notas sobre la toponimia hispanoguaraní. JIAS 2 (1960) no. 1, 64-76.

2385 DELETANG, Luis Francisco. Contribución al estudio de nuestra toponimia. B.A., Imp. de la Universidad, 1926-31. 2 vols. (Buenos Aires. Universidad nacional. Publicaciones del Instituto de Investigaciones históricas, nos. 29, 58.)

2386 HANSON, Earl Parker. Index to Map of Hispanic America 1:1,000,000. Vol. VIII: Geographical names in

Paraguay and Uruguay. Washington, United States Government Printing Office, 1944. 32p. (American Geographical Society. Map of Hispanic America publication, 5)

2387 UNITED STATES. OFFICE OF GEOGRAPHY. Paraguay; official standard names approved by the United States Board on Geographic Names. Washington, United States Government Printing Office, 1957. ii, 32p. (U.S. Board on Geographic Names. Gazetteer no. 35)

V. ANTHROPOLOGY

A. General studies

2388 La ANTROPOLOGIA en el Paraguay. CS 11 (1951) no. 9, 37-39.

2389 ASOCIACION INDIGENISTA DEL PARAGUAY. Históría del movimiento. RSCP VI (1950) no. 6, 3-50.

2390 BARROS, B.F. Aspectos antropologicos do Paraguai. SSP 6 (1944) 316-20.

2391 BEJARANO, Ramón César. Actividades del Centro de Estudios Antropológicos del Paraguay: 1951. BBAA 14 (1952) no. 1, 133-38.

2392 BERRO DE ESCRIBA, Cristiana. Bio-bibliografía de León Cadogan. SA 8 (1973) no. 1-2, 65-95.

2393 CADOGAN, León. Algunos datos para la antropologia social Paraguaya. SA 2 (1967) no. 2, 429-79.

2394 CADOGAN, León. Sinopsis de la comunicación del Delegado del Paraguay a las Jornadas Internacionales de Arqueología y Etnografía celebradas en Buenos Aires con motivo del Sesquicentenario de la Independencia. BI 21 (1961) no. 2, 144-49.

2395 CADOGAN, León. The urgency of research on the Guayaki and Guarani. BICUAER 5 (1962) 155-58.

2396 CADOGAN según Cadogan. SA 8 (1973) nos. 1-2, 53-64.

2397 CARDOZO, Efraím. El Guaireño León Cadogan. SA 2 (1966) no. 1, 7-26.

2398 COMITATO PRO-BOGGIANI, ASUNCION. Alla ricerca di Guido Boggiani: spedizione cancio nel Ciaco Boreale (alto Paraguay). Relazione e documenti. Publicazione fatta per cura del comitato Pro-Boggiani. Milan, A. Bontempelli, 1903. 108p.

2399 LEHMANN-NITSCHE, Robert. La colección Boggiani di tipos indígenas de Sud-América central. B.A., R. Rosaner, 1904. 100p. (In a portfolio.)
Suplemento. 1940. 8p.

2400 SCHMIDT, Max. Catálogo de la colección etnográfia del Museo de Historia y Etnografía. RSCP 4, no. 5 (1939) 49-62.

2401 SCOTTI, Pietro. La seconda spedizione di Guido Boggiani fra i Dacuvéi (1897). AAE 94 (1964) 31-124.

2402 SCOTTI, Pietro. Tipi di Cultura nel Paraguay. *In* WALLACE, Anthony F.C. Men and cultures: selected papers of the Fifth International Congress of Anthropological and Ethnological Sciences. Philadelphia, 1956. Philadelphia, University of Pennsylvania Press, 1960. p. 501-5.

2403 SUSNIK, Branislava. Guía del Museo etnografía paraguaya. 2. ed. A., Museo Etnográfico Andrés Barbero, 1971. lv, 114p.

2403a VIVIANI, Alberto. Guido Boggiani; alla scoperta del Gran Chaco. Turin, Paravia, 1938. 219p. (I Grandi viaggi di esploraziones)
2. ed. 1951. viii, 156p.

2404 WORKS of Professor Cadogan. BI 21 (1961) 63-65.

B. Archaeology

2405 BERTONI, Moisés Santiago. Resumen de prehistoria y protohistoria de los paises guaraníes; conferencias dadas en el Colegio nacional de segunda enseñanza de la Asunción los días 26 de julio, 8 y 21 de agosto de 1913. A., J.E. O'Leary, director del Colegio nacional, 1914. xiv, 7-162, 2p.

2406 Un FRANÇAIS découvre au Paraguay des inscriptions runiques précolombiennes. AR 56 (1973) 77-78.

2407 Las INSCRIPCIONES rúnicas precolombiennes del Paraguay. B.A., Instituto Ciencia del Hombre, 1972. 43p.

2408 LINNE, S. A sepulchral urn from Paraguay. ETH 5 (1936) 133-36.

2409 SCHMIDT, Max. Nuevos hallazgos pre-históricos del Paraguay. RSCP 1932, Oct., 81-101; 1934, Aug., 132-36.

2410 VELLARD, J. Notes sur la céramique pré-colombienne des environs d'Asuncion. JSA, n.s., 26 (1934) 37-45.

2411 VERA, Robustiano. Arqueología guaraní. El hallazgo de urnas funerarias indígenas. RSCP 2 no. 6 (1930) 275-80.

2412 VERA, Robustiano. Arqueología guaraní. Las urnas funerarias. RAP 2 (1941) 62-67.

C. Physical anthropology

2413 CASTAÑEDA, Leonardo Manrique. Notas sobre la somatometría de los Guayakí. SA 2 (1966) no. 1, 65-74.

2414 JUSTE, Ramón. Aspectos de antropología física Guaraní. SA 4 (1969) no. 1, 165-69.

2415 JUSTE, Ramón. Restos humanos de la zona de Itapuá. SA 2 (1967) no. 2, 485-86.

2416 MORENO AZORERO, Ricardo *and others*. Grupos sanguíneos y otros marcadores genéticos en Indios Chulupies y en Mestizos del Paraguay. SA 4 (1969) no. 1, 7-16.

2417 MORENO AZORERO, Ricardo. Proyecto de investigación: estudios genéticos demográficos antropométricos y métricos y médicos de poblaciones indígenas de la República del Paraguay. SA 1 (1966) no. 2, 315-19.

2418 SAGUIER NEGRETTE, Emilio; MIRAGLIA, Luigi; JUSTE, Ramón; Caracteres primitivos y pigmoides de dos esqueletos guayakí. RSCP, 2. época, 9 (1968) nos. 1-2, 23-39.

2419 URIZAR, Rogelio. Grupos sanguineos de autóctonos del Chaco paraguayo. AI 2 (1942) no. 4, 49-50.

D. Social anthropology and ethnography

1. General

2420 BENITEZ, Justo Pastor. Algunos aspectos de la cultura guaranítica. RL 6 (1961) 21-22, 43-57.

2421 CHASE SARDI, Miguel. Intento de aproximación al problema de la antropología social paraguaya. SA 4 (1969) no. 1, 173-81.

2422 ESPINOLA, Julio César. Valor y límite de los estudios sobre antropología social en el Paraguay. SA 4 (1969) no. 2, 69-131.

2423 MELIA, Bartomeu. El pensamiento "guaraní" de León Cadogan. SA 8 (1973) nos. 1-2, 7-14.

2424 SCHMIDT, Max. El sistema de la etnología; parte primera. Con notas complementarias por Branka J. Susnik. A., 1959. 217p. (Manuales del Museo Etnográfico, Sociedad Científica del Paraguay. Etnografía, 1)

2425 SUSNIK, Branislava. Apuntes de etnografía paraguaya. A., 1961- (Manuales del Museo Etnográfico Andrés Barbero. Etnografía, 2)
3. ed. 1968.
4. ed. 1969.
5. ed. 1970.

2. The Indians

2426 ARNOTT, John. Arte simbolica y decorativá entre los Indios del Chaco. B.A., 1939. xii, 122p.
Also: RGA 12 (1939) 122-28.

2427 ARNOTT, John. La magia y el curanderismo entre los Tobá-Pilagá del Chaco. RGA 2 (1934) 315-26.

2428 ARNOTT, John. La vida amorosa y conyugal de los Indios del Chaco. RGA 4 (1935) 293-303.

2429 ARNOTT, John. Los Tobá-Pilagá del Chaco y sus guerras. RGA 1 (1934) 491-501.

2430 BALDUS, Herbert. Die Guayakí von Paraguay; nach Angaben von F.C. Mayntzhusen und eigenen Beobachtungen. AN 67 (1972) nos. 3-4, 465-529.

2431 BALDUS, Herbert. Ligeiras notas sobre duas tribus tupis da margem paraguaya do Alto Paraná (Guayaki e Chiripá). RMP 20 (1936) 749-56.

2432 BALDUS, Herbert. Indianerstudien in Nordöstlichen Chaco. Leipzig, C.L. Hirschfield, 1931. viii, 230p. (Forschungen zur Völkerpsychologie und Soziologie, 11)

2433 BALDUS, Herbert. Notas complementarias sobre os Indios chamacocos. RMP 17 (1931) 529-51.

2434 BALDUS, Herbert. Os indios chamacocos. RMP 15 (1927) no. 2a, 5-62.

2435 BALDUS, Herbert. Sinopse da cultura guayakí. SSP 5 (1943) no. 2, 147-53.

2436 BARANDIARAN, D. de. Mundo espiritual y shamanismo Sanema. AC 15 (1965) 1-28.

2437 BARTOLOME, Leopoldo J. Movimientos milenaristas de los aborígenes chaqueños entre 1905 y 1933. SA 7 (1972) nos. 1-2, 107-20.

2438 BARTOLOME, Miguel Alberto. Los Guana y sus jefes. SA 4 (1969) no. 1, 135-43.

2439 BARTOLOME, Miguel Alberto. Notas sobre etnografía Apytere. SA 4 (1969) no. 1, 63-75.

2440 BELAIEFF, Juan. El Maccá. A., Ed. Charitas, 1940. 110p.
Also RSCP 4 no. 6 (1940) 1-110.

2441 BELAIEFF, Juan. La caza entre los indios macca. AI 2 no. 3 (1942) 11-14.

2442 BELAIEFF, Juan. Los Indios del Chaco Paraguayo y su tierra. RSCP 5 no. 3 (1941) 1-47.

2443 BELAIEFF, Juan. Los indios del Chaco Paraguayo. RGA 22 no. 130 (1944) 45-54; no. 131 (1944) 89-93.

2444 BELAIEFF, Juan. Some characteristics of the Indians of the Chaco. BI 13 (1953) 161-65.

2445 BELAIEFF, Juan. The Indian as I met him in the Chaco. *In* MISCELLANEA Paul Rivet octogenario dictata. Mexico, Universidad Nacional Autónoma de Mexico, 1958. Vol. II, 43-66. (XXXI Congreso Internacional de Americanistas)

2446 BENITEZ, Leopoldo A. Hipótesis y conjeturas sobre totemismo guaraní. RSCP 4 no. 3 (1937) 116-21.

2447 BERTONI, Guillermo Tell. El indio guayakí; bosquejo etnológico de una raza interesante y mal conocida. A., La Colmena, 1927. 11p.

2448 BERTONI, Moises Santiago. Aperçu ethnographique préliminaire du Paraguay Oriental & du Haut Parana. En égard surtout aux nations ou partialités indiennes les moins connues. ACP 2 no. 6 (1920) 466-544.

2449 BERTONI, Moises Santiago. La civilización guaraní. Parte I. Etnología; origen, extensión y cultura de la raza karaí-guaraní y protohistoria de los Guaraníes. Puerto Bertoni, Imp. y edición "Ex Sylvis",

1922. 546p. (Descripción física, económica y social del Paraguay. División 4: Antropología, numeración 46: 1)

2450 BERTONI, Moises Santiago. La civilización guaraní. Parte III. La higiene guaraní, sus métodos especiales, importancia cientifica y práticos resultados. Puerto Bertoni, 1927. 231p.

2451 BERTONI, Moises Santiago. Los Guayakíes: caracteres antropológicos, razas etnológicas y reseña cultural (Apuntes póstumos). A., Imp. Guaraní, 1941. 62p.

2452 BIRO DE STERN, A. La artesania en las tribus indigenas del Chaco. RED 3 (1958) 183-91.

2452a BLANCO VILLALTA, Jorge Gaston. Mitos tupiguaranies. B.A., Ediciones Culturales Argentinas, Ministerio de Cultura y Educación, Secretaria de Estado de Cultura, Subsecretaria de Cultura, 1975. 95p.

2452b BOGGIANI, Guido. I caduvei; studio intorno ad una tribú indigena del l'alto Paraguay nel Matto Grosso (Brasile). MSGI 5 (1895) 237-93.

2452c BOGGIANI, Guido. Compendio de etnografía Paraguaya moderno. A., Tall. nac. de H. Kraus, 1900. 135p.

2453 BOGGIANI, G. Etnografía del Alto Paraguay. BIGA 18 (1897) 613-25.

2454 BORGOGNON, Juan Alfonso. Aborígenes guaraníes del Chaco paraguayo. SA 1 (1966) no. 2, 264-84.

2455 CADOGAN, León. Algunos textos guayakí del Yñaro. JSA 65 (1965) no. 1, 93-115.
Also: BSCP 4, Etnografía 4 (1960). 53p.

2456 CADOGAN, León. Animal and plant cults in Guarani lore. RASP 14 (1966) 105-24.

2457 CADOGAN, León. Aporte a la etnografía de los guaraní del Amambái, Alto Ypané. RASP 10 (1962) 43-91.

2458 CADOGAN, León. Apuntes de medicina popular guairena. A., Imp. nac., 1957. 57p.

2459 CADOGAN, León. Arandú Porä ogueno' ä va' e Jakairá gui (los que reciben la buena ciencia de los jakairá). BSCP 1, Etnografía 2 (1957) 41-62.

2460 CADOGAN, León. Aves y almas de difuntos en la mitología guaraní y guayakí. AN 50 (1955) 149-54.

2461 CADOGAN, León. Ayvu rapyta; textos míticos de los mbyá-guaraní del Guairá. Sao Paulo, 1959. 217p. (Universidade de Sao Paulo. Faculdade de Filosofia, Ciencias e Letras. Boletim no. 227. Antropologia, no. 5)

2462 CADOGAN, León. Baiô Kará Wachú y otros mitos guayakíes. AI 22 (1962) 39-82.

2463 CADOGAN, León. Chonó Kybwvrá: aporte al conocimiento de la mitología Guaraní. SA 3 (1968) no. 1-2, 55-158.

2464 CADOGAN, León. Chonó Kybwvrá: aves y almas en la mitología guaraní. RASP 15-16 (1967-68) 133-47.

2465 CADOGAN, León. Como interpretan los Chiripá (Avá Guaraní) la danza ritual. RASP 7 (1959) 65-99. Also: A., Artes gráf. Zamphirópolos, 1959. 39p.

2466 CADOGAN, León. Las creencias religiosas de los Mbyá-Guaranies. BF 5 no. 40-42 (1949) 671-83.

2467 CADOGAN, León. El culto al árbol y a los animales sagrados en la folklore y las tradiciones guaraníes. AI 10 (1950) no. 4, 327-33.

2468 CADOGAN, León. La encarnación y la concepción: la muerte y la resurreción en la poesía sagrada "esotérica" de la Jeguakáva Tenondé Poragüe-i (Mbyá-guaraní) del Guairá, Paraguay. RMP n.s., 4 (1950) 233-46.

2469 CADOGAN, León. Datos para el estudio de algunas particularidades del guaraní familiar paraguay. SA 8 (1973) no. 1-2, 15-49.

2470 CADOGAN, León. En torno al BAI ETE-RI-VA y el concepto guaraní de nombre. SA 1 (1965) no. 1, 3-13.

2471 CADOGAN, León. En torno a dos plantas y un animal sagrado de los guaraníes. SA 2 (1967) no. 2, 299-314.

2472 CADOGAN, León. En torno a la aculturación de los Mbya-Guaraní del Guairá. AI 20 (1960) no. 2, 133-50.

2473 CADOGAN, León. En torno al nombre Querandí. SA 2 (1967) no. 2, 315-20.

2474 CADOGAN, León. Especulaciones en torno al bai eté ri vá guayakí. AI 25 (1965) no. 3, 303-19.

2475 CADOGAN, León. The eternal pindó palm and other plants in Mbyá-Guaraní myth and legend. *In* MISCEL-

LANEA Paul Rivet octogenario dictata. Mexico, Universidad Nacional Autónoma de México, 1958. Vol. II, 87-96. (XXXI Congreso Internacional de Americanistas)

2476 CADOGAN, León; COLLEVILLE, Maxence de. Les Indiens Guayakí de l'Yñaro (Paraguay). TILAS 3 (1963) 439-58; 4 (1964) 21-54.

2477 CADOGAN, León. Los indios Jeguakáva Tenondé (Mbyá) del Guairá, Paraguay. AI 8 (1948) no. 2, 131-39.

2478 CADOGAN, León. La lengua Mbyá-guaraní. BF 5 no. 40-42 (1949) 649-70.

2479 CADOGAN, León. Los leyendas guaraníes. BI 7 (1947) no. 4, 378-82.

2480 CADOGAN, León. Mitología en la zona guaraní. AI 11 (1951) no. 3, 195-207.

2481 CADOGAN, León. Ñane ramói jusú papá ñengareté. Canto ritual de nuestro abuelo grande primigenio (el Creador). SA 3 (1968) no. 1-2, 425-50.

2482 CADOGAN, León. Nuevas observaciones acerca del origin de los Guayakí en base de su onomástica y su mitología. *In* JORNADAS internacionales de arqueología y etnografía, II, Buenos Aires, 1960. La arqueología y etnografía argentina y sus correlaciones continentales y extracontinentales. B.A., 1962. p. 33-45.

2483 CADOGAN, León. Paraguay: notas acerca de los guayakí. BI 17 (1957) 252-57.

2484 CADOGAN, León. Las reducciones del Tarumá y la destrucción de la organisación social de los Mbyá-guaraníes del Guairá. (Ká ygüa o Monteses). *In* ESTUDIOS Antropologicos publicados en homenaje al doctor Manuel Gamio. Mexico, Universidad Nacional Autónoma de México, 1956. p. 295-303.

2485 CADOGAN, León. El problema de la población Mbyá-guaraní del departamento de Guairá. BI 11 (1952) no. 1, 74-92.

2486 CADOGAN, León. La religión guaraní de acuerdo a las tradiciones conservadas por los Mbyá-apyteré del Guairá. RAP 19 (1947-48) 25-28; 20 (1947-48) 31-34.

2487 CADOGAN, León. Síntesis de la medicina racional y mistica Mbyá-guaraní. AI 9 (1949) no. 1, 21-35.

2488 CADOGAN, León. Some plants and animals in Guaraní and Guayakí mythology. *In* no. 474, 97-104.

2489 CADOGAN, León. Ta-ngy puku. Aportes a la etnobotánica de algunas especies arbóreas del Paraguay Oriental. SA 7 (1972) no. 1-2, 7-59.

2490 CADOGAN, León. Las tradiciones religiosas de los indios Jeguaká Ténondé Pora-gué í del Guairá comúnmente llamados Mbyá, Mbyá-Apyteré o Ka'ynguá. AAIP 2 (1946) 15-47.

2491 CADOGAN, León. El valor cientifico de nuestros mitos autóctonos. BF 7 no. 49-51 (1952) 463-72.

2492 CADOGAN, León. Ywyra ñe'ery: fluye del árbol la palabra, sugestiones para el estudio de la cultura guaraní. A., Centro de Estudios Antropológicos de la Universidad Católica de Nuestra Señora de la Asunción, 1971. 132p.
Also: SA 5 (1970) no. 1-2, 7-111.

2493 CAMBAS, Anibal. Maintzhusen y los Indios Guayakíes. SA 2 (1967) no. 2, 293-98.

2494 CAMPANA, Domenico del. L'arte plumario dei Mundurucú. AAE 34-35 (1906) 177.

2495 CAMPANA, Domenico del. Contributo all'etnografia del Matacco. AAE 43 (1913) 305-25.

2496 CAMPANA, Domenico del. Contributo all'etnografia dei Toba. AAE 33 (1903) 287-322.

2497 CAMPANA, Domenico del. Notizie in torno ai Ciriguano. AAE 32 (1902) 17-139.

2498 CARIDE, V.P.; VIVANTE, A. Los comunicaciones entre los tupí-guaraní. RGA 17 no. 101 (1942) 72-81.

2499 CARNE, Martin. 24 horas entre los chulupics. RCA 25 no. 148, (1946) 1-8.

2500 CHASE-SARDI, Miguel. Breves notas de campo sobre algunos deportes nivaklé. SA 7 (1972) nos. 1-2, 153-62.

2501 CHASE-SARDI, Miguel. El concepto nivaklé del alma. SA 5 (1970) nos. 1-2, 201-21.

2502 CHASE-SARDI, Miguel. La concepción nivaklé del mundo. SA 7 (1972) no. 1-2, 121-30.

2503 CHASE-SARDI, Miguel. La cosmovisiones dei Mak'a. TA 7 no. 23-24 (1972) 33-37.

2504 CHASE-SARDI, Miguel. Cosmovisión Mak'a. SA 5 (1970) no. 1-2, 239-46.

2505 CLASTRES, Hélène. Rites funéraires Guayaki. JSA 57 (1968) 63-72.

2506 CLASTRES, Pierre; SEBAG, Lucien. Cannibalisme et mort chez les Guayakis (Aché). RMP n.s. 14 (1963) 174-81.

2507 CLASTRES, Pierre. Chronique des Indiens Guayaki: ce que savent les Aché, chasseurs nomades du Paraguay. Paris, Plon, 1972. 366p.

2508 CLASTRES, Pierre. La civilisation Guayaki: archaisme ou regression? SA 2 (1966) no. 1, 55-64.

2509 CLASTRES, Pierre. Compte rendu de mission chez les indiens Guayaki, Paraguay. HM 4 (1964) no. 2, 122-25.

2510 CLASTRES, Pierre. Eléments de démographie amérindienne. HM 13 (1973) no. 1-2, 23-36.

2511 CLASTRES, Pierre. Ethnographie des Indiens guayaki (Paraguay-Brésil). JSA 57 (1968) 9-61.

2512 CLASTRES, Pierre. Ethnologie des indiens Guayaki: la vie sociale de la tribu. HM 7 (1967) no. 4, 5-24.

2513 CLASTRES, Pierre. Mission au Paraguay et au Brésil. HM 7 (1967) no. 4, 101-8.

2514 DOBRITZHOFER, Martin. An account of the Abipones, an equestrian people of Paraguay. From the Latin of Martin Dobrizhoffer. London, J. Murray, 1822. 3 vols.

Reprinted: N.Y., Johnson Reprint Corp., 1970. 3 vols in 1. (Landmarks in anthropology)

2515 DOBRITZHOFER, Martin. Geschichte der Abiponer, einer berittenen und kriegischen Nation in Paraguay. Bereichert mit einer Beobachtungen über die wilden Völkerschaften, Städte, Flüsse, vierfüssigen Thiere, Amphibien, Insekten, merkwürdigsten Schlangen, Fische, Vögel, Bäume, Pflanzen und andere Eigenschaften dieser Provinz. Aus dem Lateinischen übersetzt von A. Kreil. Vienna, Joseph Edlen von Kurzbeck, 1783-84. 3 vols.

2516 DOBRITZHOFER, Martin. Historia de Abiponibus, Equestri, Bellicosaque, Paraquariae Natione, Locupletata, Copi osis Barbarorum Gentium, Urbium, Fluminum, Ferrarum, Amphibiorum, Insectorum, Serpentium Praecipiorum, Piscium, Avium, Arborum, Plantarum, Aliarumque Eiusdem Provinciae Propietatum Observationibus. Vienna, Typis Josephi Nob. de Kurzbeck, 1784. 3 vols.

2517 DOBRITZHOFER, Martin. Historia de los abipones. Traducción de Edmundo Wernicke. Advertencia editorial del professor Ernesto J.A. Maeder. Noticia biográfica y bibliográfica del padre Martín Dobritzhofer por Guillermo Furlong. Resistencia, Universidad Nacional del Nordeste, Facultad de Humanidades, Departamento de Historia, 1967-70. 3 vols.

2517a DOMINGUEZ, Ramiro. Cervantes, olvidado: el lenguaje popular paraguayo. CH 302 (1975) 432-40.

2518 DOMINGUEZ, Ramiro. La tradición oral en Paraguay: forma y contexto. SA 8 (1973) no. 1-2, 101-7.

2519 EHRENREICH, P.M.A. Neue Mitteilungen über die Guayaki (Steinzeitmenschen) in Paraguay. GL 73 (1898) 73-78.

2520 ESPINOLA, Julio César. A proposito del mesianismo en las tribus Guaraní. AI 21 (1961) no. 4, 307-26.

2521 FALKENHAUSEN, Olga. The Payaguá Indians. ETH 14 (1949) no. 2-4, 105-17.

2522 FEICK, Karl. Die Caraguatabast-Knüpfereien der Chamacoco und Tumanahá: ein Beitrag zur Ethnographie des Chaco Boreal. Giessen, A. Töpelmann, 1917. viii, 154p.

2523 FERNANDEZ, Florestan. A analise funcionalista da guerra: possibilidades de aplicaçao a sociedade tupinamba. RMP n.s. 3 (1949) 7-128.

2524 FERNANDEZ, Florestan. La guerre et le sacrifice humain chez les Tupinamba. JSA n.s. 46 (1952) 139-220.

2525 FLURY, Lorenzo. Danzas, costumbres y creencias de los Indios del Gran Chaco. AI 16 (1956) 111-21.

2526 FLURY, Lorenzo. Tres leyendas guaraníes. BI 8 (1948) no. 3-4, 206-16.

2527 GANCEDO, Omar Antonio. Cestería guayaquí. RMLP 7 no. 42 (Antropología) (1971) 67-78.

2528 GANCEDO, Omar Antonio; CIGLIANO, E.M. Un prestamo cultura entre los guayaquí: la cerámica. RMLP 7 no. 46 (Antropología) (1972) 211-24.

2528a GOMEZ-PERASSO, José Antonio. Contexto socio-economico del indio en el Paraguay Oriental. RPS 13 no. 37 (1976) 37-48.

2528b GOMEZ-PERASSO, José Antonio. Los pueblos de indios y su desintegración en el siglo XIX. SA XI no. 1-2 (1976) 125-38.

2528c GOMEZ-PERASSO, José Antonio. Vocabulário Aché-Guajakí. Enfoque etnolográfico. SA X no. 1-2 (1975) 93-134.

2529 GONZALEZ, Gustavo. Entre los Guaraní-Chané (o Ñanaguai) del Noroeste Chaqueño. SA 3 (1968) no. 1-2, 259-339.

2530 GONZALEZ, Gustavo. Más sobre Kurupí. RAP 4 (1969) no. 1, 99-113.

2531 GONZALEZ, Gustavo. Mitos, leyendas y supersticiones guaraníes del Paraguay. SA 2 (1967) no. 2, 321-80.

2532 GONZALEZ, Gustavo. Ñanduti. SA 2 (1966) no. 1, 77-142.

2533 GONZALEZ, Gustavo. Ñanduti. A., Artes Gráf. Zamphirópolos, 1967. 92p. (Biblioteca del Centro de Estudios Antropológicos del Ateneo Paraguayo)

2534 GONZALEZ, Juan Natalicio. Ideología Guaraní: prólogo de Angel Ma. Garibay K. Mexico, Instituto indigenista interamericano, 1958. 86p.

2535 GRABER, Christian L. The coming of the Moros; from spears to pruning hooks. Scottdale, Pa., Herald Press, 1964. 91p.

2536 GRADIN, Carlos J. Contribución al estudio de la zona misionera del alto Paraguay. CINA 5 (1964-65) 68-90.

2537 GRÜNBERG, Georg; GRÜNBERG, Friedl. Los Chiriguanos (Guaraní occidentales) del Chaco Central Paraguayo: fundamentos para una planificación de su desarrollo comunitario. SA 9 (1974) no. 1-2, 7-109.
Also: A., Centro de Estudios Antropologicos, 1975. 109p.

2538 HANKE, Wanda. Aus dem Mythenzyklus um Yaguarón. ZE 83 (1958) no. 1, 69-82.

2539 HANKE, Wanda. Creencias religiosas de algunas tribus indigenas del Paraguay. RGA 12 no. 72, (1939) 181-91.

2540 HANKE, Wanda. En los bosques virgenes del Paraguay. RGA 13 no. 76 (1940) 47-54.

2541 HANKE, Wanda. Indianersprachen im Gran Chaco. LA 5 (1938) no. 9, 565-68.

2542 HANKE, Wanda. Chiripá y tembecuá en las selvas del Paraguay. RIM 20 no. 80 (1960) 95-106.

2543 HANKE, Wanda. Los indios guayaqui. RGA 10 no. 59 (1938) 117-22.

2544 HANKE, Wanda. Niñez y juventud del indio. RGA 11 no. 66 (1939) 193-98.

2545 HANKE, Wanda. Wieder in Paraguay. LA 7 (1940) 654-58.

2546 HAWTREY, S.H.C. The Lengua indians of the Paraguayan Chaco. JAI 31 (1901) 280-99.

2547 HENRY, Jules; HENRY, Zunia. Doll play of Pilagá Indians, an experimental and field analysis of the behavior of the Pilagá Indian children. N.Y., American orthopsychiatric association, 1944. xiii, 133p. (Research monographs, 4)

2548 HENRY, Jules. The economics of Pilagá food distribution. AAN 53 (1951) 187-219.

2549 HENRY, Jules. Some cultural determinant of hostility in Pilagá children. AJO 10 (1940) 111-19.

2550 HEREDIA, José Ramón. Caribes y guaraníes: una sola y misma raza. A., Emasa, 1962. 21p.

2551 JUSTE, Ramón. Nuevas observaciones sobre antropología Guayakí. SA 2 (1966) no. 1, 75-76.

2552 JUSTE MARTELL, Ramón. Antropogénesis del hombre guaraní. Bogotá, Universidad Católica Javeriana, 1957. 96p.

2553 KARSTEN, Rafael. Indian dances in the Gran Chaco. Helsinki, Societas Scientiarum Fennica, 1915. 35p. (LVII. 1914-15. B:6)

2554 KERSTEN, L. Die Indianerstämme des Gran Chaco bis zum Ausgange des 18. Jahrhunderts. IAE 17 (1905) 1-75.

2555 KRIEG, Hans. Chaco-Indianer: ein Bilderatlas. Stuttgart, Strecker & Schroeder, 1934. 29p. (Wissenschaftliche Ergebnisse der deutschen Gran Chaco expedition)

2556 LA HITTE, C. de; KATE, H. ten. Notes ethnographiques sur les Indiens Guayaquis. AMLP, Sección Antropología, 2 (1897). 38p.

2557 LEHMANN-NITSCHE, Robert. Relevamiento antropologico de una Indio Guayaqui. RMLP 15 (1908) 91-101.

2558 LEHMANN-NITSCHE, Robert. Quelques observations nouvelles sur les Indiens Guayakis du Paraguay. RMLP 9 (1899) 399-408.

2559 LIND, Ulf. Die Medizin der Ayoré-Indianer in Paraguay. Ed., Arbeitgemeinschaft Ethnomedizin. Munich, In Kommission K. Renner, 1974. 326p. (Beiträge zur Ethnomedizin, Ethnobotanik und Ethnozoologie, 5)

2560 LOEWEN, Jacob A. The anatomy of an unfinished crisis in Chulupi culture change. SA 2 (1966) no. 1, 231-34.

2561 LOEWEN, Jacob A. From nomadism to sedentary, Chaco Indians. AI 26 (1966) 28-43.

2562 LOEWEN, Jacob A. Los Lengua y su mundo espiritual. SA 4 (1969) no. 1, 115-33.

2563 MAHIEU, Jacques de. L'agonie de Dieu-Soleil; les Vikings en Amérique du Sud. Paris, R. Laffont, 1974. 227p. (Les Enigmes de l'univers.)

2564 MAHIEU, Jacques de. Des Sonnengottes Todeskampf: die Wikinger in Paraguay. Tübingen, Grabert Verlag, 1973. 270p.

2565 MARILUZ URQUIJO, José M. Los guaraníes después de la expulsión de los jesuítas. EA 6 no. 25 (1953) 323-30.

2566 MATALLANA, Baltasar de. La constelación de Temekán. BAV 5 no. 18 (1938) 144-57.

2566a MATSON, G.A. *and others*. Distribution of hereditary blood groups among Indians in South America. Part 6: In Paraguay. AJPA 29 (1968) 81-98.

2567 MAYNTZHUSEN, F.A. Guayaki-Forschungen. ZE 57 (1925) 315-18.

2568 MAYNTZHUSEN, F.C. Los Indios Matacos del Sudeste de Paraguay. RUBA 15 (1911) 333-44.

2569 MEANS, Philip Ainsworth. A note on the Guarani invasions of the Inca Empire. GR 4 (1917) 482-84.

2570 MELIA, Bartomeu. Aportas para una recopilación de textos de los chiripá. SA 7 (1972) no. 1-2, 75-84.

2570a MELIA, Bartomeu. Guaraníes y jesuitas; ruinas de una civilización distinta. A., Ediciones Loyola, 1969. 32p.

2570b MELIA, Bartomeu; GRÜNBERG, Georg; GRÜNBERG, Friedl. Etnografía guaraní del Paraguay contemporaneo: Los Pai-Tavytera. SA XI no. 1-2 (1976) 151-295.

2571 MELIA, Bartomeu; MÜNZEL, Cristiana. Ratones y jaguares: reconstrucción de un genocidio a la manera del de los Axé-Guayakí del Paraguay Oriental. SA 6 (1971) no. 1-2, 101-47.

2572 METRAUX, Alfredo. La civilisation matérielle des tribus Tupi-guarani. Paris, P. Geuthner, 1928. xiv, 331p.

2573 METRAUX, Alfredo. A myth of the Chamacoco Indians and its social significance. JAF 56 no. 220 (1943) 113-19.

2574 METRAUX, Alfredo. Etudes d'ethnographie Toba-Pilaga (Gran Chaco). AN 32 (1937) 171-94.

2575 METRAUX, Alfredo. Le shamanisme chez les Indiens du Gran Chaco. SSP 7 (1945) 157-68.

2575a MIRAGLIA, Luigi. Caza, recolección y agricultura entre indígenas del Paraguay. SA X no. 1-2 (1975) 9-91.

2576 MIRAGLIA, Luigi. Gli Acce o Guayakí, Pigmoidi del Paraguay. AAE 91 (1961) 83-128.

2577 MIRAGLIA, Luigi. Gli Avá, i Guayakí ed i Tobas (Indegeni del Paraguay e regioni limitrofe). ALT 5 (1941) 253-378.

2578 MIRAGLIA, Luigi. Gli ultimi Acce-Guayakí (aborigeni del Paraguay.) TA 8 no. 26-28 (1972) 67-73.

2579 MIRAGLIA, Luigi. Los Guayakí: raza trepadora. SA 4 (1969) no. 2, 133-37.

2580 MIRAGLIA, Luigi; SAGUIER NEGRETE, Emilio. Observaciones somáticas y serológicas en la raza guayakí. SA 4 (1969) no. 2, 139-59.

2581 MIRAGLIA, Luigi; SAGUIER NEGRETE, Emilio. Osservazioni somatiche e sierologiche sulla razza Guayakí. BSN 74 (1965) 375-95.

2582 MIRANDA BORELLI, José I. Notas sobre cerámica moscoví. RAP 4 no. 2 (1969) 203-26.

2583 MORENO, Fulgencio R. Algunos datos sobre la geografía etnografía del Paraguay y del Alto Perú. RCGH 37 (1921) 135-207.
See also no. 1067a

2584 MORENO AZORERO, R.; GINI, L. Reproducción, matrimonio y familia de los aborígenes del Paraguay. SA 9 (1974) no. 1-2, 169-203.

2585 MÜLLER, Franz. Beiträge zur Ethnographie der Guaraní-Indianer im östlichen Waldgebiet von Paraguay. AN 29 (1934) 177-208, 441-60, 695-702; 30 (1935) 151-64, 433-50, 767-83.

2586 MÜNZEL, Mark. Kawre veja puku - "Dejamos lejos al gran oso hormiguero": notas preliminares sobre cinco canciones Axé. SA 6 (1971) no. 1-2, 177-259.

2587 NIMUENDAJU UNKEL, Kurt. Die Sagen von der Erschaffung und Vernichtung der Welt als Grundlagen der Religion der Apapocuva-Guaraní. ZE 46 (1914) 284-403.

2588 NORDENSKIÖLD, Erland. Indianerleben im Gran Chaco, Erlebnisse und Beobachtungen. Berlin, Ullstein, 1925? 125p.

2589 NORDENSKIÖLD, Erland. Indianerleben, El Gran Chaco (Südamerika). Leipzig, A. Bonnier, 1912. viii, 343p.
Also: Leipzig, G. Merseburger, 1913.

2590 NORDENSKIÖLD, Erland. Indianlif; el Gran Chaco (Syd-Amerika). Stockholm, A. Bonnier, 1910. 319p.
Also: Stockholm, Ahlén & Akerlund, 1926. 251p.

2591 NORDENSKIÖLD, Erland. La vie des Indiens dans le Chaco. RG 6 (1912) no. 3. 277p.

2592 NUÑEZ, Cándido. Historia de la raza guaraní; su antepasado hasta la actualidad. Concepción, 1946. 123p.

2592a OLIVEIRA CEZAR, Filiberto de. Leyendas de los Indios Guaraníes. B.A., 1892. 195p.

2593 PALAVECINO, Enrique. Con los indios macca. RGA 12 no. 74 (1939) 309-16.

2594 PALAVECINO, Enrique. Los Indios Chulupi del Chaco Boreal. RGA 5 (1936) 231-38.

2595 PAULOTTI, Osvaldo L. Alfarería guarayo. RSAAT 3 (1942) 173-88.

2596 PAULOTTI, Osvaldo L. La alfarería de los guarayo. RGA 15 no. 89 (1941) 97-104.

2597 PEÑA, Enrique. Etnografía del Chaco: manuscrito del Capitan de Fragata don Juan Francisco Aguirre (1793). BIGA 19 (1898) 464-510.

2598 PLA, Josefina. The pirates of Paraguay. APAU 15 (1963) no. 3, 31-38.
The Payaguá tribe.

2599 PREDA LLAMOSAS, Alberto. Paraguay: panorama of the Indian population. BI 20 (1960) no. 1, 50-63.
Text in English and Spanish.

2600 PROYECTO Marandú: informe. SA 9 (1974) nos. 1-2, 205-33.

2601 ROA BASTOS, Augusto. El génesis de los guaraníes. Leyenda de la creación y destrucción del mundo tomada de Nimuendajú Unkel. RAP 6 no. 20 (1948) 13-22.

2602 ROLON MEDINA, Anastacio. Raíces de la nación paraguaya. A., Imp. La Humanidad, 1968. 251p.

2603 ROTTER, F.P. Vida y cultura de los Indios Guaranís. A., Univ. Católica de la Asunción, 1972. 55p.

2604 SAMANIEGO, Marcial. Algunos conceptos y mitología de los Abá de Ibypyté. SA 3 (1968) no. 1-2, 407-23.

2605 SAMANIEGO, Marcial. Textos míticos Guaraníes. SA 3 (1968) no. 1-2, 373-405.

2606 SCHMIDT, Max. Los Chiriguanos e Izozós. RSCP 4 no. 3 (1938) 1-115.

2607 SCHMIDT, Max. Los Paressís. RSCP 6 no. 1 (1943) 1-296.

2608 SCHMIDT, Max. Los Payaguá. RMP n.s. 3 (1949) 129-269.

2609 SCOTTI, Pietro. Medicina indigena paraguayana. Genoa, Libr. degli studi, 1955. 68p.

2610 SCOTTI, Pietro. Les indiens Moro du Chaco, Paraguay. *In* CONGRESO internacional de Americanistas, XXXVI, Sevilla, 1964. Actas y memorias. Seville, Edit. Católica Española, 1966. Vol. 3, 223-27.

2611 SEBAG, Lucien. Compte rendu de mission chez les indiens Ayoré du Paraguay et de Bolivia. HM 4 (1964) no. 2, 126-29.

2612 SEBAG, Lucien. Le chamanisme Ayoréo. HM 5 (1965) no. 2, 92-122.

2613 SEELWISCHE, José. La organización socio-económica de los indigenas frente a los sistemas coloniales. SA 9 (1974) no. 1-2, 153-67.

2614 SEELWISCHE, José. ¿Terminarán las culturas indígenas? Apuntes sobre la situacion cultural de los Chulupies. SA 2 (1966) no. 1, 235-45.

2615 SHERZER, Joel. La parole chez les Abipone: pour une ethnographie de la parole. HM 10 (1970) no. 1, 40-76.

2616 SHPRINTZIN, N.G. Indeitsy guaiaki. SET 1952 no. 4, 114-27.

2616a SMITH, Robert J. La vida en la muerte de los Aché-Guayaquí. SA X no. 1-2 (1975) 135-76.

2617 SOUTHEY, Robert. Martin Dobrizhoffer, history of the Abipons. QR 26 (1822) 277-323.

2618 STEWARD, Juan Haynes. Handbook of South American Indians; prepared in cooperation with the United States Department of State as a project of the Interdepartmental Committee on Cultural and Scientific Cooperation. Washington, Government Printing Office, 1946-59. 7 vols. (U.S. Bureau of American Ethnology, Bulletin 143)
Reprinted: N.Y.: Cooper Square, 1963.
Vol. I: (i) Ethnography of the Chaco, by Alfred Metraux, p. 197-370. (ii) The present-day Indians of the Gran Chaco, by Juan Belaieff, p. 371-79. (iii) The Guayaki, by Alfred Metraux and Herbert Baldus, p. 435-44.
Vol. III: The Guarani, by Alfred Metraux, p. 69-94.

2619 STRELNIKOV, I.D. Religioznye predstavleniia indeitsev guarani basseina y Verkhnei Parany (Paragvai i Braziliia). SMAE 9 (1930) 293-339.

2620 SUSNIK, Branislava. Catálogo de los objetos recogidos entre los Guayakíes y los Chiripás. BSCP 6 (1962) no. 3, 69-104.

2621 SUSNIK, Branislava. Chiriguanos. A., Museo Etnográfico Andrés Barbero, 1968-

2622 SUSNIK, Branislava. Chulupí; esbozo gramatical analitico. A., Museo Etnográfico Andrés Barbero, 1968. 90, 69p.

2623 SUSNIK, Branislava. Chamacocos. A., Museo Etnográfico Andrés Barbero, 1969. 2 vols.

2623a SUSNIK, Branislava. Dimensiones migratorias y pautas culturales de los pueblos del Gran Chaco y de su periferia. Enfoque etnológico. Resistencia (Chaco), Instituto de historia, Faculdad de humanidades, Universidad nacional de Nordeste, 1972. 32p.

2623b SUSNIK, Branislava. Dispersión Tupí-Guaraní prehistórica: ensayo analitico. A., Museo Etnográfico "Andrés Barbero", 1975. 171p.

2624 SUSNIK, Branislava. Estudios chamacocos. A., Sociedad científica del Paraguay, 1957. 153p.

2625 SUSNIK, Branislava. Estudios Emok-Toba. A., 1962- (Boletín de la Sociedad científica del Paraguay y del Museo etnográfico, 7. Etnolinguistica, 7)

2625a SUSNIK, Branislava. Estudios Guayaki. A., Boletín de la Sociedad Científica del Paraguay, Museo Etnográfico Andrés Barbero, 1960-61. 2 vols.

2626 SUSNIK, Branislava. El Indio colonial del Paraguay. A., Museo Etnográfico "Andrés Barbero", 1965-71. 3 vols.

2627 TAYLOR, J.; TAYLOR, A. Nove contos contados pelos Kaiwas e Guaranis. RASP 14 (1966) 81-104.

2628 TOMASINI, Alfredo. Contribución al estudio de los indios Guayakí. RMA 1 (1969) 75-102.

2629 TURATH, Richard. Indianer der Alto Paraná. LA 5 (1937) no. 5, 281-84.

2630 VELLARD, J. Conférence sur les Guayakí. BMNA 10 (1934) no. 1, 71-94.

2631 VELLARD, J. Exploration du Dr. Vellard au Paraguay. JSA n.s., 24 (1932) 215-18.

2632 VELLARD, J. Les Indiens Ayoreo du Chaco. CRAS 274 (1972) sér. D. no. 24.

2633 VELLARD, J. Les indiens guayaki. JSA n.s., 26 (1934) 223-92; 27 (1935) 175-244.

2634 VELLARD, J.; OSUNA, T. Mission du Dr. Vellard au Paraguay. G 61 (1934) no. 3-4, 203-11.

2635 VELLARD, J. Os Guayakis do Paraguay. GE 2 (1936) no. 1, 16-25; no. 2-3, 31-39.
Also (in more detail) JSA n.s., 25 (1933), 293-334.

2636 VELLARD, J. Textes mwihá recueillis au Paraguay. JSA n.s. 29 (1937) 375-86.

2637 VELLARD, J. Una misión de estudios al Paraguay. HU 33 (1933) 83-103.

2638 VELLARD, J. Une civilisation du miel: les indiens guayakis du Paraguay. Paris, Gallimard, 1939. 188p. (Geographie humaine, 13)

2639 VELLARD, J. Une mission scientifique au Paraguay. (15 juillet 1931 - 16 janvier 1933). JSA n.s. 25 (1933) 293-334.

2640 VIVANTE, Armando; GANCEDO, Omar Antonio. Nuevas observaciones sobre el arco y la flecha de los guayaqui. RMLP (Antropología) 7 no. 44 (1972) 109-55.

2641 VIVANTE, Armando; GANCEDO, Omar Antonio. Sobre el arco y la flecha de los Guayakí. RMLP (Antropología) 7 no. 40, (1968) 39-52.

2642 VOGT, P. Fr. Material zur Ethnographie und Sprache der Guayakí Indianer. ZE 34 (1902) 30-45, 849-74.

2642a WAVRIN, Robert, *marquis de*. Les derniers Indiens primitifs du Bassin du Paraguay. Paris, Larose, 1926. 107p.

2643 WICKE, Charles R.; CHASE-SARDI, Miguel. Análisis componencial de la terminologia de parentesco Chulupí (Ashluslay). SA 4 (1969) no. 2, 185-202.

2644 WICKE, Charles R.; CHASE-SARDI, Miguel. Componential analysis of Chulupi (Ashluslay) kinship terminology. ET 8 (1969) no. 4, 484-93.

2645 YAMPEY, Nasim. Análisis de los mitos sudamericanos Kurupí y Yasiyataré. RAP 4 (1969) no. 1, 77-98.

2645a ZAVALA, Silvio. Las Indias del Paraguay. RHA no. 84 (1977) 7-27.

a) The present-day situation of the Indians

2645b ARENS, Richard. The forest Indians in Stroessner's Paraguay: survival or extinction? London, Survival International, 1978. 13p. (Survival International Document, IV)

2646 ARENS, Richard. Genocide in Paraguay. Philadelphia, Temple University Press, 1976. xvii, 171p.
Contains: Mark Münzel: Manhunt; Eric R. Wolf: Killing the Aches; Norman Lewis: The Camp at Cecilio Baez; Frances R. Grant: Paraguayan realities; Monroe C. Beardsley: Reflections on genocide and ethnocide; Chaim F. Shatan: Genocide and bereavement; Richard Arens: A Lawyer's summation; Elie Wiesel: Now we know.

2646a BAEZ, Julio. Panorama de la situación indígena en Paraguay: Quechas, Aymaras, Guaraníes, Chulupíes, Tobas, Kollas, Macuiritares, Parixis, Matacos. CLA 16 no. 195 (1976) 66-74.

2647 BEJARANO, Ramón César. Consulta indígena latinoamericana. Crítica a Barbados. A., Ed. Toledo, 1972. 67p.

2648 BEJARANO, Ramón César. ¿Genocidio en el Paraguay? A., Ed. Toledo, 1974. 56p. (Serie Estudio antropológicos, 5)

2649 BEJARANO, Ramón César. El problema indígena en el Paraguay y su posible solución. SA 1 (1965) no. 1, 39-48.

2649a BEJARANO, Ramón César. Solucionemos nuestro problema indígena con el I.N.D.I. A., Edit. Toledo, 1976. 236p.

2649b BEJARANO, Ramón César. Solucionemos nuestra problema indígena con el I.N.D.I., homenaje al VIII Congreso Indigenista Interamericano, 24 al 29 de octubre de 1977, Caracas, Venezuela. 2. ed. A., Edit. Toledo, 1977. 255p. (Serie Estudios Antropológicos, 6)

2649c BELSHAW, C.S. Call for help: Miguel Chase Sardi imprisoned in Paraguay. CUA 17 (1976) 541-43.

2650 CADOGAN, León. La tragedia Guaraní. SA 2 (1967) no. 2, 269-91.

2651 CHASE-SARDI, Miguel. La situación actual de los indígenas del Paraguay. SA 6 (1971) no. 1-2, 9-99.

2652 CHASE-SARDI, Miguel. La situación actual de los indígenas del Paraguay, con un ensayo de carta de localización de las tribus indígenas, sobre el mapa del Instituto Geográfico Militar. A., Centro de Estudios Antropológicos, Universidad Católica, 1972. 111p.

2653 GRÜNBERG, Georg; GRÜNBERG, Friedl. Informe sobre los guaraníes Occidentales del Chaco Central Paraguayo. Fundamentos para una planificación de su desarrollo. A., Centro de Estudios Antropológicos, Universidad Católica, 1972. 138p.

2654 HOLDEN JARA, R. Concerning the Indian problem in Paraguay. BI 18 (1958) no. 1, 67-71.

2655 The INDIAN problem in the north of the country. BI 17 (1957) 301-5.

2655a MELIA, Bartomeu; MIRAGLIA, Luigi; MÜNZEL, Mark; MÜNZEL, Christine. La agonía de los Aché-Guayakí: história y cuentos. A., Centro de Estudios Antropológicos, Universidad Católica "Nuestra Señora de la Asunción", 1973. 165p.

2656 MIRAGLIA, Luigi. Dos capturas de Aché-Guayakí en el Paraguay en Abril 1972: diario de viaje. Nuevos aportes para la antropología física y cultural de los Aché-Guayakí. SA 6 (1971) no. 1-2, 149-71.

2657 MÜNZEL, Mark. The Aché Indians: genocide in Paraguay. Copenhagen, IWGIA, 1973. 80p. (IWGIA document 11)
Supplement: The Aché: genocide continues in Paraguay. 1974. 32p.

2657a MÜNZEL, Mark. The manhunts: Aché Indians in Paraguay. *In* CASE studies on human rights and fundamental freedoms: a world survey; ed. by Willem A. Veenhoven. The Hague, Martinus Nijhoff for the Foundation for the Study of Plural Societies, 1975. vol. 4, 351-403.

2658 POBLACION indígena censada en todo el país, según raza, sexo, 1950. A., 1952. 15p.

2658a PROYECTO MARANDU. Por la liberación del indígena, documentos y testimonios, compilación del Proyecto Marandu; prólogo y notas de Adolfo Colombres. B.A., Ediciones del Sol, 1975. 295p.

2658b RODRIGUEZ DOLDAN, Sinforiano. Proyecto "Marandu". Informe de actividades sanitarias. SA XI no. 1-2 (1976) 297-303.

2658c SUPPLEMENT to *Survival International Review*, vol. 3 no. 1/no. 21 (1978). 15p.

2659 SYMPOSIUM ON INTER-ETHNIC CONFLICT IN SOUTH AMERICA, BRIDGETOWN, BARBADOS. The situation of the Indians in South America: contributions to the study of inter-ethnic conflict in the non-Andean regions of South America, ed. by W. Dostal. Geneva, World Council of Churches, 1972. (Publications of the Department of Ethnology, University of Berne, 3).
Contains: Miguel Chase-Sardi: (1) The present situation of the Indians in Paraguay, p. 173-217. (2) Indian Groups of Paraguay, p. 420-424.

2659a TEMPLE, Dominique. Paraguay: the two directions of indigenism. SIR 2 no. 4/no. 20 (1977) 12-15.

b) Folklore

2660 AGRUPACION FOLKLORICA GUARANI. BUENOS AIRES. Concierto de la Agrupación Folklórica Guaraní, institución cultural paraguaya, domingo, 15 de setiembre, a los 10 horas de la mañana. José Asunción Flores, Ariel Ramírez, Emilio Vaesken. Programa. B.A., n.d. 12p.

2661 AGUAYO, Samuel. Bajo el cielo del Paraguay: album de cinco hermosas melodias del folklore paraguaya. B.A., Fermata, 1941. 11p.

2662 AGUIRRE, Andrés. Curuzú infante. A., Dpto. Nac. de Prensa y Propaganda, 1944. 16p.

2663 AYALA, José de la Cruz. Leyenda Guarani. *In* no. 3776, p. 9-17.

2664 BEJARANO, Ramón César. Caraí vosá: elementos para el estudio del folklore paraguayo. A., Edit. Toledo, 1960. 119p. (Serie Estudios antropológicos, 1)

2665 BENITEZ, Justo Pastor. El colorido folklore paraguayo. HP 8-10 (1963-65) 31-38.

2666 BENITEZ, Justo Pastor. El folklore paraguayo. RL 6 no. 25 (1964) 103-09.

2667 CADOGAN, León. Caaguazu: 1952-53 - algunos de su problemas vistos a través del folklore regional. SA 2 (1967) no. 2, 429-63.

2668 CADOGAN, León. Fragmentos del folklore guaireño. CINIF 3 (1962) 87-109.

2669 CADOGAN, León. Fragmentos del folklore guaireño. SA 1 (1966) no. 2, 65-125.

2670 CADOGAN, León. Guahí Rataypy. A., Edit. Guarania, 1948. 78p.
Tales from Guairá.

2672 CARVALHO NETO, Paulo de. Un ejemplo de invención de "folklore". La leyenda del Ñanduty. HBA 3 (1958) no. 11, 120-31.

2673 CARVALHO NETO, Paulo de. Folclore da guerra do Paraguai. JIAS 3 (1961) no. 2, 273-80.

2674 CARVALHO NETO, Paulo de. Folklore del Paraguay: sistemática analítica. Quito, Edit. Universitaria, 1961. 475p.

2675 CARVALHO NETO, Paulo de. Folklore y estadística. TR 7 no. 19-20 (1955-57) 54-58.

2676 CARVALHO NETO, Paulo de. "La Rúa": una danza dramática de moros y cristianos en el folklore paraguayo. *In* MISCELLANEA Paul Rivet octogenario dictata. México, Universidad Nacional Autónoma de Mexico, 1958. Vol. II, 617-44. (XXXI Congreso Internacional de Americanistas)

2677 CHAVES, María Concepción Leyes de. Río lunado; mitos y costumbres del Paraguay. B.A., Ediciones Peuser, 1951. 237p.

2678 GOMEZ SERRATO, Dario. Del folclore paraguayo: la malavisión. FAM 17-18, no. 16 (1969-70) 78-93.

2679 GOMEZ SERRATO, Dario. Folklore paraguayo. FAM 14 (1966) 207-09.

2679a JOVER PERALTA, Anselmo. Cancionero del mate; folklore de Argentina, Brazil, Chile, Uruguay y Paraguay, recogido, ordenado y anotado por Luzán del Campo. 2. ed. B.A., Edit. Tupa, 1944. 123p.
New ed. 1950. 96p.

2680 LAME, Machú. Ñane rembi'ú; alimentación folklórica paraguaya. A., Casa Edit. Toledo, 1960. 93p. (Serie Estudio antropológicos, 3)

2680a MARTINEZ-CROVETTO, Raúl. Folklore toba oriental. I Los tabues menstruales. SA XI no. 1-2 (1976) 139-49.

2680b MARTINEZ-CROVETTO, Raúl. Folklore toba oriental. Relatos fantásticos de origen chamanico. SA X no. 1-2 (1975) 177-205.

2680c MORALES, Ernesto. Leyendas guaraníes. B.A., El Ateneo, 1925. 201p.
Another ed. 1929. 241p.
4. ed. B.A., Ed. Futuro, 1946. 241p.
Also: B.A., Ed. Futuro, 1960. 91p.

2680d RAMALLO, José Antonio C. Cuentos y leyendas de la selva guaraní. B.A., Plus Ultra, 1975. 121p.

2681 ROLLA, José Cruz. Folklore, ritos y costumbres del pueblo guaraní. B.A., 1954.

2681a SOLE RODRIGUEZ, Oriol. Leyendas guaraníes; impresiones, tradiciones, anécdotas. Montevideo, Dornaleche y Reyes, 1902. 177p.

c) Other aspects

2682 CACERES L, Domingo Antonio. Dos palabras sobre historia política y social del Paraguay. JIAS 7 (1965) no. 3, 357-62.
On the racial mixture in Paraguay.

2683 HOLLANDA, Güy de. Los españoles y las castas. HP 1 (1956) 69-76.

2684 CARVALHO NETO, Paulo de. Antología del negro paraguayo, primera series. AUCE 91 no. 346 (1962) 37-66.

2685 CARVALHO NETO, Paulo de. Contribución al estudio de los negros paraguayos de acampamento Loma. AL 5 (1962) no. 1-2, 23-40.

2686 PLA, Josefina. La esclavitud en el Paraguay: el rescate del esclavo. RPS 11 no. 31, (1974) 29-49.

2687 PLA, Josefina. Hermano negro: la esclavitud en el Paraguay. Madrid, Paraninfo, 1972. 273p.

2687a WILLIAMS, John Hoyt. Black labor and state ranches: the Tabapí experiences in Paraguay. JNH 62 (1977) 162-66.

2688 WILLIAMS, J.H. Tevegö on the Paraguayan frontier: a chapter in the Black history of the Americas. JNH 56 (1971) no. 4, 272-83.

E. Linguistics

1. General studies

2689 BOGGIANI, Guido. Cartografía lingüística del Chaco por el Dr. Daniel G. Brinton. RIP 2 no. 16 (1899) 106-37.

2690 BORGOGNON, Juan Alfonso. Panorama indígena Paraguayo. SA 3 (1968) no. 1-2, 341-71.

2691 BRINTON, Daniel G. The linguistic cartography of the Chaco region. PAPS 37 (1898) 178-205.

2692 CADOGAN, León. En torno al bilingüismo en el Paraguay. RASP 6 (1958) no. 1, 23-30.

2693 CASSANO, Paul V. The substrat theory in relation to the bilingualism of Paraguay: problems and findings. ALS 15 (1973) no. 9, 406-26.

2693a CORVALAN, Grazziella. El bilingüismo en el Paraguay. RPS 13 no. 37 (1976) 7-35.

2694 DIAZ, Juan C. Diccionario de nombre propios de persones y apellidos castellanos y algunos extranjeros más usuales en el Río de la Plata; ortografía, ortología silábica y prosodia de dichos nombres y apellidos; apéndices. A., 1949. 100p.

2695 EGUIA RUIZ, Constantino. España en América. Lenguas y lingüistas en el antiguo Paraguay español. RIM 6 (1945) no. 4, 445-80.

2696 FERNANDEZ AREVALOS, Evelio. Presupuestos para una "política lingüistica" en el Paraguay. CMHL 14 (1970) 23-29.

2697 GIMENEZ CABALLERO, Ernesto. El yopará en Paraguay. *In* CONGRESO de Academias de la Lengua Española, IV, Buenos Aires, 1964. Actas y labores. B.A., Academia Argentina de Letras, 1966. p. 124-36.

2698 GONZALEZ, Antonio E. Hispanismos en el Guaraní. BF 6 (1950) 58-65.

2699 LIVIERES BANKS, L.; DAVALOS, J.S. Las lenguas del Paraguay. MN 35 (1969) mai, 15-22.

2699a MANRIQUE CASTAÑEDA, Leonardo. Algunas observaciones sobre el bilingüismo del Paraguay. Montevideo, Universidad de la República, Facultad de Humanidades y Ciencias, Departamento de Lingüistica, 1969. 28p.

2700 MELIA, Bartomeu. Diglosia en el Paraguay o la comunicación desequilibrada. SA 8 (1973) nos. 1-2, 133-40.

2700a MELIA, Bartomeu. Hacia una "tercera lengua" en el Paraguay. EP 2 no. 2 (1974) 31-72.

2701 PENKERT, E. Paraguay-Spanisch und Guarani. LS 11 (1966) nos. 6, 172-74.

2702 POTTIER, Bernard. Aspectos del bilingüismo paraguayo. SA 4 (1969) no. 1, 189-93.

2703 POTTIER, Bernard. La situation linguistique du Paraguay. CMHL 14 (1970) 43-50.

2704 RUBIN, Joan. Bilingual usage in Paraguay. *In* FISHMAN, Joshua A. Readings in the sociology of language. The Hague, Mouton, 1968. p. 513-30.

2705 RUBIN, Joan. Bilingualism in Paraguay. ALS 4 (1962) no. 1, 52-58.

2706 RUBIN, Joan. Language and education in Paraguay. *In* FISHMAN, Joshua A.; FERGUSON, Charles A.; GUPTA, Jyotirindra das. Language problems of developing nations. N.Y., Wiley, 1968. p. 477-88.

2707 RUBIN, Joan. Lenguaje y educación en el Paraguay. SA 2 (1967) no. 2, 401-14.

2708 RUBIN, Joan. National bilingualism in Paraguay. The Hague, Mouton, 1968. 136p. (Janua linguarum. Series practica, 60)

2709 RUBIN, Joan. Toward the use of formal methods in the detection of cultural change. SA 4 (1969) no. 1, 45-62.

2. Spanish

2710 ACADEMIA PARAGUAYA DE LA LENGUA ESPAÑOLA. Guaranismos en el diccionario de la Real Academia. A., 1973. 125p. (Boletín de la Academia Paraguaya de la Lengua Española, 1)

2711 CASSANO, Paul V. Retention of certain hiatuses in Paraguayan Spanish. LI 109 (1973) 12-16.

2712 CASSANO, Paul V. Substratum hypothesis concerning the Spanish of Paraguay. NP 55 (1971) 41-43.

2713 FOGELQUIST, D.F. Bilingualism of Paraguay. H 33 (1950) 23-27.

2714 GASPERI, Luis de. Presente y futuro de la lengua española en el Paraguay. *In* CONGRESO de Instituciones Hispánicas, I, Madrid, 1963. Presente y futuro de la lengua española. Actas de la Asamblea de Filología del I Congreso de Instituciones Hispanicas. Madrid, Ediciones Cultura Hispanica, 1964. Vol. I, 127-33.

2715 LEZCANO, Gustavo Adolfo. Consideraciones sobre la enseñanza del castellano. Por qué seguimos el método que hemos adaptado, y cómo debe ser entendido y aplicado. La Academia-Bello-Chamorro. A., La Colmena, 1945. 47p.

2716 LEZCANO, Gustavo Adolfo. La defensa del método y los programas de don Delfín Chamorro. A., La Humanidad, 195? 232p.

2717 LEZCANO, Luís A. Actualidad de Andrés Bello y Delfín Chamorro. A., La Colmena, 1946. 67p.

2718 MENDOZA, Manuel de. El lector paraguayo. A., 1885. 221, iii p.
Spanish language reader.

2719 MORINIGO, Marcos A. Review of B. Malberg's notas sobre la fonética del español en el Paraguay. NRFH 2 no. 3 (1948) 283-85.

2719a USHER DE HERREROS, Beatriz. Castellano paraguayo: notas para una gramatica contrastiva castellano-guaraní. SA XI no. 1-2 (1976) 29-123.

3. Guarani

a) Dictionaries and grammars

2719b ALMEIDA NOGUEIRA, Baptista Caetano de. Vocabulario (guaraní-española) dos palabras Guaranís usadas pelo traductor da "Conquista Espiritual" do P.A. Ruiz de Montoya. ABNRJ VII (1880). 603p.

2720 BERTONI, Guillermo Tell. Diccionario guayakí-castellano. Precedido de una reseña analitica de los trabajos hasta ahora publicada. RSCP 4 no. 5 (1939) 3-49.
Also: A., Ed. Guaraní, 1939. 48p.

2721 BERTONI, Moises Santiago. Diccionario botánico; latino-guaraní y guaraní-latino con un glosario de vocablos y elementos de la nomenclatura botánica. A., Ed. Guaraní, 1940. 156p.

2722 BIANCHETTI, Juan de. Gramática guaraní (avá ñeé) y principos de filología; ortografia y fonética, analogía, sintaxis, construcción de oraciones, literatura (prosa y verso). B.A., Edit. argentina, Arístides Quillet, 1944. 180p.

2723 BOTTIGNOLI, Justo. Diccionario guaraní-castellano y castellano-guaraní. Turin, Sociedad editora internacional, 1926. 114p.

2724 BOTTIGNOLI, Justo. Gramática razonada de la lengua guaraní; con un prólogo del director de la Sección de filología y fonética experimental, dr. Adolfo Berro García. Montevideo, A. Monteverde, Palacio del libro, 1940. 108p. (Instituto de estudios superiores. Sección de filología y fonética experimental. Publicaciones de la sessión, 1)

2725 BOTTIGNOLI, Justo. Gramática razonada de la lengua guaraní. Turin, Sociedad editora internacional, 1926. 93p.
Also: BF 2 (1938) no. 6-7, 65-76; no. 8-9, 251-87.

2726 CADOGAN, León. Diccionario guayakí-español. Avant-propos de Pierre Clastres. Paris, Musée de l'Homme. 1968. 196, 30p.

2727 COLMAN, Narciso Ramón. Mil refranes guaraníes (ñe'ẽngá); diccionario paramiológico que contiene una colección de refranes, adagios, máximas, pensamientos, aforismos, consejos, comparaciones, exclamaciones, interjecciones, modismos, epitetos, apóstrofes, frases célebres, proverbios, y dichos populares, seguido de otra colección de supersticiones y recetas muy originales del mismo caracter. A., Imp. El Arte, 1928. 100p.

2728 FLORES, I. Mario. Alfabeto; grafía; gramática guaraní. BF 5 no. 37-39 (1948) 417-30.

2729 GATTI, Carlos; ROJAS, Teodoro; BERTONI, A. de Winkelried. Vocabulario guaraní-español para uso medico. A., Tall. Nocito y Raño, 1947. 164p.

2730 GRANADO, Juan G. Pequeño ensayo de la gramática del idioma guaraní, seguido de algunas conversaciones familiares por los padres del seminario. A., El Paraguayo, 1891. vi, 136p.

2731 GREGORES, Emma; SUAREZ, Jorge A. A description of colloquial Guaraní. The Hague, Mouton, 1967. 248p. (Janua Linguarum, series practica, 27)

2731a GUASCH, Antonio. Diccionario guaraní precedido de una síntesis gramatical y de la fauna y flora guaraníticas. 3. ed. B.A., 1948. 656p.

2732 GUASCH, Antonio. Diccionario castellano-guaraní y guaraní-castellano sintáctico, fraseológico, ideológico. 4. ed. Seville, 1961. 788p.

2732a GUASCH, Antonio. El idioma guaraní; gramatica, vocabulario doble, lecturas. A., Imp. nac., 1944. 322p.

2732b GUASCH, Antonio. El idioma guaraní; gramatica, lectura, vocabulario doble. 2. ed. B.A., J. Torres, 1947. 536p.

2733 GUASCH, Antonio. El idioma guaraní (gramatica y antologia de prosa y verso). 3. ed. A., Casa América-Moreno, 1956. 430p.

2733a HANDEL, P. Abaneéme: guía práctica para aprender el idioma guaraní; Practical guide for learning the Guarani tongue: Praktischer Führer zur Erlernung des Guarani. Stuttgart, 1890. iv, 74p.

2734 JOVER PERALTA, Anselmo; OSUNA, Tomas. Diccionario guaraní-español y español-guaraní. 2. ed. B.A., Edit. Tupi, 1950. xxvi, 515p.
2. ed. 1951.

2735 JOVER PERALTA, Anselmo. El Guaraní en la geografía de América: diccionario de Guaranismos. B.A., Edit. Tupa, Artes gráf. de Vinne, 1950. 272p.

2735a MUNIAGURRIA, Saturnino. El guaraní; elementos de gramática guaraní y vocabulario de las voces mas importantes de este idioma. B.A., Casa Editora "Coni", 1947. 250p.

2736 OBELAR, Raimundo D. Vocabulario guaraní. A., Tall. tip. del Estado, 19--. 46p.
2. ed. A., Ariel, 1914. 46p.

2737 ORTIZ MAYANS, Antonio. Breve diccionario guaraní-castellano, castellano-guaraní; contiene esta obra más de 10,000 palabras, incluídas muchas voces de la flora y de la fauna. B.A., Imp. "Abaco", 1941. 250p.

2738 ORTIZ MAYANS, Antonio. Diccionario, castellano-guaraní. A., Tall. "El Arte", 1935. 67p.

2739 ORTIZ MAYANS, Antonio. Diccionario guaraní-castellano; castellano-guaraní, con un compendio gramatical. 5. ed. Edit. Tupa, 1945. 190p.
6. ed. B.A., 1949. 261p.
For earlier ed., see no. 2737.

2740 ORTIZ MAYANS, Antonio. Diccionario español-guaraní; guaraní-español. Nombres de la toponimia, de la flora y la fauna, voces de la mitología, de la leyenda y del folklore. Apéndice de voces regionales con un compendio gramatical. 8. ed. B.A., Manantial, 1961. 356p.
9. ed. 1962.

2740a ORTIZ MAYANS, Antonio. Nuevo diccionario español-guaraní, guaraní-español; nombres de la toponimia, de la flora y de la fauna, voces de la mitología, de la leyenda y del folklore. Apéndice del voces regionales, un compendio gramatical. 10 ed. B.A., Librería Platero Edit., 1973. 986p.

2741 RUIZ DE MONTOYA, Antonio. Arte Bocabulario de la Lengua Guaraní. Dedicado a la Soberana Virgen Maria. Madrid, Iuan Sanchez, 1640. 376, 234p.

2742 RUIZ DE MONTOYA, Antonio. Arte Bocabulario tesoro y catecismo de la Lengua Guaraní. Publicado nuevamente sin alteración alguna por Julio Platzmann. Leipzig, Teubner, 1876. 4 vols.

2743 RUIZ DE MONTOYA, Antonio. Arte de la lengua guaraní escrita para el uso de los pueblos de Misiones por el P. Antonio Ruiz de Montoya, natural de Lima, misionero en la antigua Reducción de Loreto junta al Rio Paranápanema del Brasil, Superior en otras, y Rector del Colegio de la Asunción del Paraguay. Edición publicada en obsequio y conservación del mismo idioma por el R.P. Ex-Definidor Fray Juan M. Alegre de la Orden Seráfica. B.A., Imp. de Pablo E. Coni, 1876. 95p.
Also: Nueva ed. más correcta y esmerada que la primera, y con las voces indias en tipo diferente. Vienna, Faesy y Frick; Paris, Maisonneuve, 1876. iv, 100p.

2744 RUIZ DE MONTOYA, Antonio. Arte de la lengua Guaraní por el P. Antonio Ruiz de Montoya de la Compañía de Jesús con los Escolios, Anotaciones del P. Paulo Restivo de la misma Compañía sacados de los papeles de P. Simon Bandini y de otros. En el Pueblo de S. Maria La Mayor, 1724. 256p.

2745 RUIZ DE MONTOYA, Antonio. Breve noticia de la lengua guaraní sacada del Arte y Escritos de los PP. Antonio Ruiz do Montoya y Simón Bandini. n.p., 1718. 103p.

2746 RUIZ DE MONTOYA, Antonio. Brevis linguae Guaraní Grammatica Hispanice a Reverendo Patre Jesuita Paulo Restivo secundum libros Antonii Ruiz de Montoya et Simonis Bandini in Paraquaria anno MDCCXVIII composita et Breve Noticia de la Lengua Guaraní inscripta sub auspiciis Augustissimi Domini, Petri II, Brasilae Imperatorii ex unico, qui notus est, Suae Majestatis Codice Manuscripto edita et publici juris facta, necnon praefatione instructa opera et studiis Christiani Frederici Seybold Doctoris philosophiae. Stuttgart, G. Kohlhammer, 1890. xii, 87p.

2747 RUIZ DE MONTOYA, Antonio. Lexicon Hispano-Guaranicum Vocabulario de la lengua Guaraní inscriptum a Reverendo Patre Jesuita Paulo Restivo secundum Vocabularium Antonii Ruiz de Montoya anno MDCCXXII in Civitate

S. Mariae Majoris denuo editum et adautum sub auspiciis Augustissimi Domini Petri Secundi Brasiliae Imperatorii posthac curantibus Ylustrissimis Ejusdem Haeredibus ex unico qui noscitur Imperatoris Beatissimi exemplari redimpressum necnon praefationes notisque instructum opera et studiis Christiani Frederici Seybold Doctoris philosophiae. Stuttgart, G. Kohlhammer, 1893. x, 545p.

2748 RUIZ DE MONTOYA, Antonio. Linguae Guaraní Grammatica Hispanice e Reverendo Patri Jesuita Paulo Restivo secundum libros Antonii Ruiz de Montoya, Simonis Bandini aliorumque adjecto particularum lexico anno MDCCXXIV in Civitate Sanctae Mariae Majoris edita et Arte de la lengua Guaraní inscripta sub auspiciis et impensis Illustrissimi Domini Petri Principis Saxo-Coburgensis Gothensis ex unico quod in Europa noscitur ejusdem Serenissimi Principis exemplari redimpressa necnon praefatione notisque instructa opera et studiis Christiani Frederici Seybold Doctoris Philosophiae. Stuttgart, G. Kohlhammer, 1892. 330p.

2749 RUIZ DE MONTOYA, Antonio. Tesoro de la lengua Guaraní compuesto por el Padre Antonio Ruiz, de la Compañía de Jesús. Dedicado a la Soberana Virgen Maria. Madrid, Iuan Sanchez, 1639. 406p.

2750 RUIZ DE MONTOYA, Antonio. Vocabulario de la lengua Guaraní compuesto por el Padre Antonio Ruiz de la Compañía de Jesús. Revista y augmentado por otro Religioso de la misma Compañía. En el Pueblo de S. Maria La Mayor, 1722. 589p.

2750a SAGUIER, Eduardo. El idioma Guaraní: etodo pratico para su enseñanza elemental. 3. ed. B.A., Gurfinkel Hijos Impresores, 1951. 125p.

2750b SOLARI, Benjamin T. Ensayo de filología; breve vocabulario español-guaraní, con las relaciones etimológicas del idioma americano. B.A., Coni, 1928. 189p.

2750c SOLARI, Benjamin T. Ensayo de filología; breve vocabulario español-guaraní, con las relaciones etimológicas del idioma americano, con una noticia biográfica del autor, por Juan Antonio Villoldo. 2. ed. B.A., Coni, 1944. lxxxiv, 189p.

2751 STORNI, Julio Juan de Mata Santiago. Hortus guaranensis; toponimias, alimentos, elementos, instituciones. Tucumán, M. Violetto, 1939-48. (Universidad Nacional de Tucumán. Publicación no. 250, 462)

b) Texts

2751a ALMEIDA NOGUEIRA, Baptista Caetano de. Primera cathechese dos indios selvagens feyta pelos Padres da Companhia de Jesus originariamente scripta em hespanhol (em lingua europea) pelo Padra Antonio Ruiz, antigo instructor do gentis e depois vertida en abaneenga (em lingua indigena) por outra Padre da mesma Companhia. 1733. ABNRJ VI (1878-79) 90, 366p.

2751b AYALA AQUINO, Gumersindo. Apitu'u poti. Prólogo de Bacon Duarte Prado. México, 1949. 71p.

2752 CABALLERO IRALA, Basiliano. Ñane reta cu'i cuemí; ensayos en lengua guaraní. A., 1971. 515p.

2753 CADOGAN, León. La literatura de los guaraníes. Versión de textos guaranies por León Cadogan. Introd., selección y notas por Alfredo López Austin. México, Edit. Joaquin Mortiz, 1965. 168p. (El Legado de la América Indígena).

2754 CENTRO YBYTYMIENSE DE ASUNCION. Ofrendas láureas al poeta paraguaya Narciso R. Colmán (Rosicrán) con un apéndice que contiene "Canciones de juventud" y cuarenta relaciones para El Pericón. A?, 1950. 112p.

2755 COLMAN, Narciso Ramón. Ñande ipi cuéra (Nuestros antepasados). Poema guaraní etnogenético y mitológico. Protohistoria de la raza guaraní, seguida de un estudio etimológico de los mitos, nombres y voces empleados. A., "El Arte", 1929. 96p. (Biblioteca de la Sociedad Científica del Paraguay, 3)

2756 COLMAN, Narciso Ramón. Genesis de la raza Guaraní. Nuestros antepasados (Ñande ipi cuéra). Versión castellana del mismo autor. Poema etnogenético y mitológico; seguida de un estudio etimológico de los mitos, nombres y voces empleados. San Lorenzo, Imp. y edit. Guaraní, 1937. 148p.
Also: San Lorenzo, Imp. y edit. Guarani, 1936. 59p. (Biblioteca de la Sociedad Cientifica del Paraguay, 6)

2757 COLMAN, Narciso Ramón. Ocára potÿ (cantares de "Rosicran"). Con un apéndice que contiene producciones poéticas de otros bardos guaraníes. A., 1917. 145p.

2758 COLMAN, Narciso Ramón. Ocára potÿ (Flores silvestres) Prólogo de Juan E. O'Leary. A., Ariel, 1921. 2 vols.

2758a DECOUD LARROSA, Reinaldo J. Jopare Pyahu: Mbohasambyre guaranime geresiaygua ne'egui. A., Instituto de Estudios Biblicos de Asunción, 1963. 491p.

2759 GOMEZ SERRATO, Darío. Yasîyatepé. Mîtüjhë jha ämbú ra'î cue mí. A., Imp. Zuruc'á, 1929. 126p.

2760 GONZALEZ, Juan Natalicio. Poesia guaraní. CA 16 (1944) no. 4, 137-60.

2761 GUASCH, Antonio. Tupä rape mbo'e renda avañe'eme. Catecismo de la doctrina cristiana: bilingüe, en guaraní y español. Dibujos de tapa y viñetas de Juan Font. A., 1952. 192p.

2762 INSAURRALDE, José de. Ara poru aguiyey haba: conico, quatia poromboe ha marångåtu. Madrid, J. Ibarra, 1759-60. 2 vols.

2763 RUIZ DE MONTOYA, Antonio. Catecismo de la lengua guaraní. Madrid, Por Diego Diaz de la Carrera, 1640. 336p.
Reprinted: Leipzig, B.G. Teubner, 1876.

2764 YAPUGUAY, Nicolás. Sermones y exemplos en lengua guaraní. Con dirección de un religioso de la Compañía de Jesús. Edición facsimilar de la edición principe del año 1727. B.A., Guaranía, 1953. 165p.

c) Studies

2765 ACADEMIA CORRENTINA DEL IDIOMA GUARANI. Sistema de numeración decimal en guaraní. BF 6 no. 43-45 (1950) 232-36.

2766 ACADEMIA CORRENTINA DEL IDIOMA GUARANI. Sistema de signos para representar los fonemas del idioma guaraní. BF 6 no. 43-45 (1950) 237-38.

2767 ATENEO DE FORTINES CORRENTINOS. Intento de una numeración decimal en guaraní. BF 6 nos. 44-45 (1950) 239-56.

2768 ATENEO DE FORTINES CORRENTINOS. Representación gráfica de fonemas propios de la lengua guaraní. BF 6 no. 44-45 (1950) 257-60.

2768a ACADEMIA DE LA LENGUA Y CULTURA GUARANI. Homenaje a la memoria de su fundador y su presidente vitalicio Don Guillermo Tell Bertoni. A., 1969. 31p.

2769 BENITEZ, Leopoldo A. El problema de la grafía guaraní. BF 5 no. 24-26 (1947) 226-34.

2770 BERTONI, Arnaldo de Winkelried. Vocabulario zoológico guaraní. Con etimologia y nomenclatura técnica. *In* CONGRESOS Científicos Latinoamericanos, 3d, Rio de Janeiro. Actas e memorias referentes ás secçoes de pedogogia, anthropologia, agronomia e zootechnica. Rio de Janeiro, Imprensa nac., 1909. Vol. 6, 541-603.

2771 BERTONI, Guillermo Tell. Análisis glotológico de la lengua tupi-guaraní. RSCP 5 no. 2 (1941) 59-95.
Also: A., Imp. Guaraní, 1941. 36p.

2772 BERTONI, Guillermo Tell. Fonología, prosodia y ortografia de la lengua guaraní. RSCP 2 (1923) no. 2, 1-23.
Also: A., Imp. Sudamericana, 1926. 23p.

2773 BERTONI, Guillermo Tell. Importancia cultural del guaraní en los países bilingues de la América Iberoguaraní. BF 6 no. 43-45 (1950) 84-97.

2774 BERTONI, Guillermo Tell. La lengua guaraní: importancia histórica y actual. La lengua, parte integrante del alma de los pueblos, es un factor de civilización. La conjugación del verbo y la existencia del verbo "ser". San Lorenzo, Edit. Guaraní, 1936. 16p.

2775 BERTONI, Guillermo Tell. Reglas de prosodia guaraní. BF 5 no. 40-42 (1949) 579-85.

2776 BERTONI, Guillermo Tell. El uso de la jota por la ye en el alfabeto guaraní. BF 7 no. 49-51 (1952) 442-48.

2777 BERTONI, Moisés Santiago. Influencia de la lengua guaraní en Sud América y Antillas. A., H. Kraus, 1916. 120p.

2778 BERTONI, Moisés Santiago. La lengua guaraní como documento histórico. BF 3 no. 20-21 (1942) 436-56.

2779 BERTONI, Moisés Santiago. La lengua guaraní como documento histórico. Aperçu ethnographique préliminaire du Paraguay oriental et haut Parana. Puerto Bertoni, Imp. y edicion "Ex sylvis", 1920. 434-582p.
Also: ACP 2 no. 6 (1920) 434-528.

2780 BERTONI, Moisés Santiago. La lengua guaraní; estructura, fundamentos gramaticales y clasificación (apuntes póstumos). A., Edit. guaraní, 1940. 35p.

2781 BERTONI, Moisés Santiago. Ortografia guaraní sobre la base de la ortografia internacional adoptada por

los congresos de zoología y botánica, con arreglo á la ortografía lingüística adoptada por el Congreso científico internacional de Buenos Aires (1910) y á la generalmente seguida por los lingüistas norteamericano. A., M. Brossa, 1914. 22p.
3. ed. Puerto Bertoni, Ex Sylvis, 1927.

2782 CABALLERO, Ramón V. Contribution à la connaissance de la phonétique guaraní. RP 1 (1911) 138-62.

2783 CABRERA, Gaspar Natalicio. Carácter peculiar de la cultura Guaraní. A., Instituto Paraguayo de Investigaciones Históricas, 1963. 52p.
Also: A., Imp. Zamphirópolos, 1965.

2784 CABRERA, Gaspar Natalicio. Guarañỹrö. A., Edit. El Gráfico, 1961. 3 vols.

2785 CADOGAN, León. Aporte al estudio de la función de las "partículas" (P. Antonio Ruiz de Montoya) o "sufijos átonos" (P. Antonio Guasch) en el guaraní. BF 9 no. 58-60 (1962) 17-39.

2786 CADOGAN, León. Aporte al estudio de la onomástica guaraní. BF 8 no. 55-57 (1959) 33-58.

2787 CADOGAN, León. Aporte para la interpretación de un apellido guaraní. RASP 5 (1957) no. 2, 189-92.

2788 CADOGAN, León. Breve contribución al estudio de la nomenclatura guaraní en botánica. A., Ministerio de Agricultura y Ganaderia, 1955. 49p. (Boletín no. 194).
2. ed. 1957. 49p. (Boletín no. 196)

2789 CADOGAN, León. En torno al "guaraní paraguayo": o "coloquial". CMHL 14 (1970) 31-41.

2790 CADOGAN, León. Mil apellidos guaraníes; aporte para el estudio de la onomástica paraguay. Homenaje a la II Semana Folklórica Paraguaya, 13/22 de agosto de 1960. A., Edit. Toledo, 1960. 76p. (Estudios antropológicos, 2)

2791 CADOGAN, León. Mil apellidos Guaraníes de las misiones y reducciones de Paraguay. BF 10 no. 61-63 (1964) 7-28.

2792 CADOGAN, León. Registro de algunos voces internas del "Tesoro de la lengua guaraní" del P. Antonio Ruiz de Montoya, S.J. TILAS 3 (1963) 517-32.

2793 CADOGAN, León. A search for the origins of "Ojeo", "Ye-jharú" or Tupichuá. AN 60 (1965) 209-19.

2794 CAETANO DO ALMEIDA NOGUEIRA, Batista. Vocabulario dos palavras guaranís usadas pelo tradutor "Conquista Espiritual" do Padre A. Ruiz de Montoya. ABNRJ 7 (1879) 7-608.

2795 CODAS, Cipriano. Manual elemental de ortografía guaraní, trabajo presentado a consideración de las autoridades de la Academia en noviembre de 1943. A., 1944. 24p.

2796 DALL'IGNA RODRIGUES, Aryon. A nomenclatura na familia Tupí-guaraní. BF 6 no. 43-45 (1950) 98-104.

2797 DECOUD LARROSA, Reinaldo J. Ortografía guaraní. RAP 4 no. 16 (1946) 17-19.

2798 DECOUD LARROSA, Reinaldo J. Teogonía guaraní. RAP 4 no. 13 (1946) 13-15.

2799 EDELWISS, Frederico G. Tupís e guaranís. Estudio de etnonimia e lingüística. Bahia, Secretaria de Educaçao e Saúde, 1947. v, 220p.

2800 FERNANDEZ GUIZZETI, Germán. La marcas aspecto-temporales en el guaraní común del Paraguay. TILAS 9 (1969) 501-18.

2801 FERNANDEZ GUIZZETI, Germán. Sentido, distribución y significado en el análisis funcional de las estructuras idiomáticas indoamericanas. RASP 6 (1958) no. 2, 189-207.

2802 FIEBRIG-GERTZ, C. Guarany names of Paraguayan plants and animals. RJB 2 for 1923 (1930) 100-49.

2803 GARVIN, Paul L.; MATHIOT, Madeleine. The urbanization of the Guarani language - a problem in language and culture. *In* (1) WALLACE, Anthony F.C. Men and cultures. Selected papers of the Fifth International Congress of Anthropological and Ethnological Sciences. Philadelphia, 1956. Philadelphia, University of Pennsylvania Press, 1960. p. 783-90. (2) FISHMAN, Joshua A. Readings in the sociology of language. The Hague, Mouton, 1968. p. 365-74. (3) TILLY, Charles. An urban world. Boston, Little, Brown, 1974. p. 152-59.

2804 GEZ, Juan Wenceslao. Disquisiciones filológicas sobre la lengua guaraní. Corrientes, Imp. del Estado, 1915. 64p.

2805 GONDRA, Manuel. El idioma Guaraní. HP 4-5 (1960) 20-30.

2806 GONZALEZ, Antonio E. Fonética y ortografía guaraníes. BF 5 no. 44-45 (1950) 15-65.

2807 GUIZETTI, German Fernandez. La polisemia del símbolo lingüistico y otras falacias acerca de la indole del significado. SA 2 (1966) no. 1, 175-209.

2808 KAHLE, G. Das Guaraní als paraguayische Volkssprache. BVF 1965, 105-17.

2809 MAYNTZHUSEN, F.C. Die Sprache der Guayakí. ZFE 10 (1919-20) 2-22.

2810 MELIA, Bartomeu. Fuentes documentales para el estudio de la lengua Guaraní de los siglos XVII y XVIII. SA 5 (1970) no. 1-2, 113-61.

2811 MELIA, Bartomeu; RUBIN, Joan. El guaraní dominante y dominando. SA 8 (1973) no. 1-2, 119-31.

2812 MORINIGO, Marcos Augusto. Hispanismos en el guaraní; sobre la penetración de la cultura española en la guaraní, según se refleja en la lengua. B.A., Tall. s.a. Casa J. Peuser, 1931. 432p. (Facultad de filosofía y letras de la Universidad de Buenos Aires. Instituto de filología. Colección de estudios indigenistas, 1)

2813 MORINIGO, Marcos Augusto. Influencia del español sobre el léxico del guaraní. FBA 8 (1962) 3-220.

2814 MORINIGO, Marcos Augusto. Influencia del español en la estructura lingüística del Guaraní. FBA 5 (1959) 235-48.

2815 MORINIGO, Marcos Augusto. Unidad y deferenciaciones del guaraní. SA 8 (1973) no. 1-2, 109-18.

2815a PHILIPSON, J. La enseñanza del guaraní como problema de bilingüismo. BF 6 (1950) 184-95.
Also: JFI 1 (1953) 45-58.

2816 RECALDE, Juan Francisco. Nuevo método de ortografía guaraní. Sao Paulo, Tip. del "Diario español", 1924. 101p.

2817 RECALDE, Juan Francisco. Vocabularios designativos de relaçoes e contactos socias nas linguas tupís ou guaraní. RAMSP 39 (1937) 59-68.

2818 SAGUIER, Eduardo. La acuentación del vocablo guaraní. BF 5 no. 37-39 (1948) 406-16.

2819 SAGUIER, Eduardo. La numeración guaraní. BF 6 no. 43-45 (1950) 66-73.

2820 SCHADEN, Egon. Aspectos fundamentais da cultura guaraní. 2. ed. Sao Paulo, Difusá Européia do Livro, 1962. 190p. (Coleçao Corpo e alma do Brasil, 6)

2821 STORNI, Julio C. Nombres guaraníes de tribus (interpretaciones y comentarios). BF 3 no. 15 (1940) 177-84.

2822 VILLAGRA DE GARCIA, Sara Delicia. La palabra: sus clases morfológicas en la lengua Guaraní. SA 5 (1970) no. 1-2, 163-200.

d) Other indigenous languages

2823 ADAM, Lucien. Matériaux pour servir á l'établissement d'une grammaire comparée des dialectes de la famille Tupi. Paris, J. Maisonneuve, 1896. 134p. (Bibliothèque linguistique américaine, 18)

2824 ADAM, Lucien. Matériaux pour servir à l'établissement d'une grammaire comparée des dialectes de la famille guaicurú (abipone, moscoví, toba, mbaya). Paris, J. Maisonneuve, 1899. 168p. (Bibliothèque linguistique américaine, 20)

2825 BELAIEFF, Juan. El vocabulario Chamacoco. RSCP 4 (1937) no. 1, 10-47.

2826 BELAIEFF, Juan. El vocabulario Maccá; clave y apuntes gramaticales. RSCP 3 (1934) no. 4, 124-30.

2827 BELAIEFF, Juan. Vocabulario Maccá. RSCP 3 (1931) no. 2, 53-67.

2828 DUCCI, Zacarias. Los tobas y su lengua. BIGA 21 (1904) 165-214.

2829 FAMILIA Guaycurú; por Branislava Susnik; José Sanchéz Labrador. A., Museo Etnográfico Andrés Barbero, 1971- (Lenguas chaqueñas, 1)

2830 GARCIA, Rodolfo. Nomes de aves em lingua tupi. BMNB 5 (1929) no. 3, 34-78.

2831 JUNKER, Paulino; WILKSKAMP, Juan; SEELWISCHE, Jose. Manual de la gramática Chulupí. SA 3 (1968) no. 1-2, 159-247.

2832 LOWES, R.H.G. Alphabetical list of Lengua Indian words with English equivalents. JSA n.s., 43 (1954) 85-109.

2833 MACHONI, Antoni, *de Cerdeña*. Arte, y Vocabulario de la lengua lule y tonocote, compuestos con facultad de sus superiores. Madrid, Por los Heredores de Juan Garcia Infanzón, 1732. 9, 97, 135, 17, 1p.
Reprinted: Ed. by Juan Mariano Larsen. B.A., P.E. Coni, 1877. 361p.

2834 METRAUX, Alfred. The linguistic affinities of the Enimagá; Cochaboth group. AAN 44 (1942) no. 4, 720-21.

2835 PETTAZZONI, Rafaelle. In memoria di Guido Boggiani. Cestmir Loukota: Suplementi al vocabulario ciamacoco estratti dai manoschritti inediti di Guido Boggiani. Rome, 1941. 31p. (Centro italiano di studi americani. Comitato etnologico, 1)

2836 RICE, Frederick John Duval. O idioma Tombé. JSA n.s. 26 (1934) 109-80.

2837 SANCHEZ, L.J. Vocabulario Eyiguayegi: según el manuscrito del siglo XVIII. A., 1972. 482p.

2838 SCHADEN, Egon. Vocabulario de la lengua maká. RSCP 4 (1937) no. 2, 68-85.

2839 SCHMIDT, Max. Vocabulario de la lengua chulupí. RSCP 5 (1940) no. 1, 73-97.

2840 SUSNIK, Branislava. Algunos palabras culturales en el area chaqueña. BSCP 6 (1962) no. 3, 33-68.

2841 SUSNIK, Branislava. Chulupí: esbozo gramatical analitico. A., Museo Etnográfico Andrés Barbero, 1968. 90, 69p.

2842 SUSNIK, Branislava. Estructura de la lengua chamacoco-ebitoso. A., 1957. 186p. (BSCP, v. 1)

2843 SUSNIK, Branislava. Familia zamuko: Čamakoko, Ayoweo. A., Museo Etnográfico "Andrés Barbero", 1972. 134p. (Lenguas chaqueñas, 4)

2844 SUSNIK, Branislava. La lengua de los Ayoweos-Moros; estructura gramatical y fraesario etnográfico. 2. ed. A., Museo Etnográfico "Andrés Barbero", 1973. 147p. (Lenguas chaqueñas, 5)

2845 SUSNIK, Branislava. Vocabulario Ace-Guayakí. BSCP 6 (1962) no. 3, 105-220.

2846 SUSNIK, Branislava. Vocabularios inéditos de los idiomas emok-toba y choroti, recogidos por el doctor Max Schmidt. BSCP 6 (1962) no. 3, 1-32.

2847 YAPUGAY, Nicolás. Historia da Paixao de Cristo e taboa dos parentescos em lingua tupí com una resenha dos impressos acerca da dita lingua. Vienna, 1876. xv, 43p.

VI. ECONOMICS

A. General

2848 AIRALDI, Julio César. Apuntes de economía política, 5 y 6 curso comercial, 5 curso bachillerato. A., Mimeografía "Bachero", 1961. 75p.

2848a ARRIAGADA, Juan Carlos. Investieren in Lateinamerika; Investitionsbedin gungen in Argentinien, Bolivien, Brasilien, Ekuador, Kolumbien, Mexiko, Paraguay, Peru, Uruguay, Venezuela; hrsg. von Ibero-Amerika Verein E.V. u HWWA-Inst. für Wirtschaftsforschung Hamburg. Hamburg, Verlag Weltarchiv, 1976. 393p.

2849 ASPECTS récents de l'économie du Paraguay. NED 2415 (May 22, 1958) 1-22.

2850 ASUNCION. EXPOSICION NACIONAL, 1892. Primera exposición nacional de la República del Paraguay, 12 de octubre de 1892; resumen de los trabajos por Ricardo Brugada, secretario de la Comisión Central. Contiene también el catálogo y adjudiciación de premios. Publicación oficial. A., La Democracia, 1892. 88p.

2851 AYLMER, Richard Grenfell. Argentine and Plate republics. Banbury, the author, 1974. 34p.

2852 BAER, Werner. Las condiciones económicas paraguayos: los obstáculos pasados y presentes a la modernización economica. RPS 12 no. 32 (1975) 159-69.

2853 BAER, Werner. The Paraguayan economic condition: past and current obstacles to economic modernization. IAEA 29 (1975) 49-63.

2854 BAEZ ACOSTA, Pedro. Paraguay ¿un país que muere? Hacia una economía heróica, la intervención extranjera. B.A., Edit. 14 de Mayo, 1953. 158p. (Colección Autores paraguayos)

2855 BAEZ ACOSTA, Pedro. Trabajando también se construye una nación; estudios económicas sobre el Paraguay. B.A., 1956. 95p.
2. ed. Santa Fé, Librería y Edit. Colmagna, 1965. 162p.

2856 BANCO DEL PARAGUAY. Plan de ajusto de cambio y disposiciones normativas. A., 1949. 1 vol. (unpaged).

2857 BANCO CENTRAL DEL PARAGUAY. Cuentas nacionales del Paraguay: período 1962-1967. A., Depto de Estudios Económicos, 1968. 65p.

2858 BANCO CENTRAL DEL PARAGUAY. DEPARTAMENTO DE ESTUDIOS ECONOMICOS. Producto e ingreso nacional del Paraguay, 1955. A., 1957. 42p.

2859 BARBOSA, J. Tornás. Cooperativas en el Paraguay. RCECE 2 no. 16 (1940) 333-39.

2860 BARRIENTOS, César. Discurso del Ministro de Hacienda en el agasajo al presidente del Banco Interamericano del Desarrollo, Dr. Felipe Herrero. A., 1961. 7p.

2861 BARRIENTOS, César. Paraguay: economía y desarrollo, exposición del ministro de hacienda y miembro de la Junta de Gobierno del Partido Colorado Gral. (S.R.) don César Barrientos en la Jornada de Capacitación Politica realizada en la ciudad de Paraguarí el 31 de mayo de 1969. A., Imp. de la Dirección General de Estadística y Censos, 1969. 63p.

2862 BASIC data on the economy of Paraguay. WTISER pt. 1 no. 58-48 (1958). 20p.

2863 BENITEZ GONZALEZ, Manuel. Reforma agraria e industrialización; conferencia dictada en el curso de capacitación política en la Universidad Popular "Humberto Garcete" en los días 11 y 13 de septiembre de 1964. A., Partido Revolucionario Febrerista, 1964? 67p.

2864 BERTONI, Guillermo Tell. Bosquejos sobre política económica del Paraguay. San Lorenzo, Imp. y ediciones Guaraní, 1936- (Instituto de investigaciones informes y publicidad. Museo, archivo y biblioteca Bertoni. Boletín no. 1)

2865 BLANCO SANCHEZ, Jesús L. El Paraguay como fuente energética; el Kanendiyá Guasú o Gran Salto del Guayra, su aprovechamiento hidroeléctrico según los proyectos brasileños. Anotaciones y comentarios sobre los mismos. A., 1968. 52p.

2866 BRADFORD, William E.; AYALA, Oscar Aníbal. Recommended procedures for improvement of Paraguayan foreign trade statistics. A., USAID, 1955. 20p.

2867 BUENO DE LOS RIOS, Eliado R. Paraguay, presente y futuro, bajo el gobierno del general de ejército don Alfredo Stroessner y de la Asociación Nacional Republicana (Partido Colorado): informaciones políticas, económicas y financieras. Obras llevadas a cabo durante los años 1959-60. A., 1961. 334p.

2868 CANTARELLI, Davide. La tecnologia del Paraguay. Indagine finanziata del Consiglio nazionale delle ricerche. Padua, CEDAM, 1969. xii, 218p. (La Tecnologia del'America latina)

2869 CASTILLO, Alberto P. Las caracteristicas sobre-salientes de la estructura y evolución económica y social del Paraguay. EPA 4 no. 7 (1965) 5-28.

2870 CEUPPENS, Henry D. Paraguay año 2000. A., Artes Gráf. Zamphirópolos, 1971. 285p.

2871 CODAS, Cipriano. Cuestiones económicas relacionadas con la guerra del Chaco. A., 1934. 25p.

2872 CONGRESO DE DELEGADOS DE GOBIERNO, 2d., ASUNCION, 1963. II Congreso de Delegados de Gobierno, julio 21/29 de 1963. A., 1963. 85p.

2873 CRESPO, Eduardo. El Paraguay y su futuro económico. A., Imp. Nac., 1940. 10p.

2874 CRISTALDO, Julio César. Manual estadístico del Paraguay, 1941-1961. Preparado por la Sección Economía Agrícola, Servicio Técnico Interamericano de Cooperación Agrícola. A., 1963. 114p. (Servicio Técnico Inter-Americano de Cooperación Agrícola. Publicación no. 254)

2874a ENRIQUEZ GAMON, Efrain. La economia paraguaya: una introducción al estudio de la realidad ecónomia. EP 3 (1975) 41-54.

2875 FADLALA, Emilio. El Paraguay ante el Acuerdo sub regional andino surgido de la 2a conferencia de cancilleras de la ALALC. EPA 6 (1968) 6-14.

2876 FADLALA, Emilio. El Paraguay en la integración económica. AP 12 (1969) 25-46.

2877 FEPRINCO. Primer Congreso de entidades económicas del Paraguay. A., 1952. 224p.

2878 FEPRINCO. II Congreso de entidades económicas. A., 1965. 230p.

2879 FERNANDEZ MONTALVO, A. Guía comercial e industrial del Paraguay. A., El Paraguay, 1900. 48p.

2880 FIAT DELEGACION PARA LA AMERICA LATINA. OFICINA DE ESTUDIOS PARA LA COLABORACION ECONOMICA INTERNACIONAL. Sintesis económica y financiera no. 1, Paraguay. B.A., 1959. 4p.
No. 2. 1965. 94p.

2881 FISCHER-TREUENFELD, Richard Friedrich Eberhard von. Paraguay in Wort und Bild. Eine Studie über den wirtschaftlichen Fortschritt des Landes. Hrsg. von L. Rehwinkel. Berlin, E.S. Mittler, 1903. 81p.
2. ed. 1906. 379p.

2882 FLECHA, Agustín Oscar. Cuenca del Plata y el desarrollo del Chaco paraguayo. A., Edit. El Gráfico, 1969. 52p.

2882a FLECHA, Agustín Oscar. Distribución de ingreso y subdesarrollo: un modelo matemático: impacto del gasto de inversión de ITAIPU en la economía nacional. A., Instituto Desarrollo Integral y Armonico, 1975. 121p.

2882b FLECHA, Agustín Oscar. Ingreso rural y desarrollo económico. EP 3 no. 1 (1975) 55-61.

2883 FONSECA NASCIMENTO, Ulpiano. Elementos para la formulación de una política de desarrollo económico en la América latina; el caso del Paraguay; ES 14 (1965) July/Dec., 7-31.
Also: TE 35 (1968) Jan/Mar., 87-127.

2884 FORO de la libre empresa. A., Edit. Emasa, 1967. 142p.

2885 FRETES VENTRE, Daniel. Algunas consideraciones sobre la estructura socioeconómica. AP 12 (1969) 7-23.
Also A., 1968. 42p.

2886 GAONA, Francisco. La hegemonía argentina en el Paraguay. B.A., 1954. 53p.

2886a GARCIA, Emilio. Economia política, analisis de los fenómenos economicos del Paraguay. Vol. 1. A., La Colmena, 1942. 119p.

2887 GERMANY, FEDERAL REPUBLIC. BUNDESSTELLE FÜR AUSSENHANDELSINFORMATION. Südamerikanische Entwicklungsgebeite: Bolivien, Ecuador, Paraguay, Peru. Cologne, 1959. unpaged.

2888 GIMENEZ, Juan; SOLER, Petronila A. Inventario en las estadisticas del Paraguay. EPA 3 (1963) no. 4, 7-36.

2889 GOLZE, W. Paraguay vom Standpunkt der Wirtschaft und Wirtschaftspolitik. Hamburg, 1926? 72p.

2890 GONZALEZ RECALDE, Maria Teresa. La libre empresa en el Paraguay. A., 1972. 42p.

2891 GONZALEZ VIERA, Mauro. Paraguay frente a futuro. A., 1972. 149p.

2892 GRAFICOS de los recursos y gastos de la nación, ejercicio 1912 a 1929-30. A., Imp. nac., 1939. 21p. (Boletín del tesoro, año 25, número especial)

2893 GREAT BRITAIN. COMMERCIAL AND EXPORTS DEPARTMENT. Paraguay; economic and commercial conditions in Paraguay. 1921- London, H.M.S.O., 1921-
Title varies.

2893a GRUNBERG, Georg. Dos modelos de economia rural en el Paraguay: Pai-Tavytera y Koygua. EP 3 no. 1 (1975) 31-39.

2894 INSTITUTO DE BIENESTAR RURAL. Información estadística. A., 1963. 26p.

2895 INSTITUTO INTERAMERICANO DE ESTADISTICA. Actividades estadisticas de las naciones interamericanas, no. 18: Paraguay. 2. ed. Washington, OEA, 1959. vi, 44p.

2896 INTER-AMERICAN DEVELOPMENT COMMISSION. Report presented to the Conference of commissions, by the Paraguayan Commission of Inter-American Development, on economic problems of Paraguay. Washington, 1944? 20p.

2897 JUTKOWITZ, Joel M.; POROY, Ibrahim. Padrones de participación política y cambio económico. A., Centro Paraguayo de Estudios Sociológicos, 1970. 17p.

2898 KERRILIS, L. L'Uruguay et le Paraguay - leurs ressources et leur situation actuelle. JE 4 ser., 1 (1878) 220-39.

2898a LEIVA, Ramón. Paraguay subdesarrollado: sugerencias para un programa de liberación nacional. B.A., 1975. 309p.

2899 LOPEZ FRETES, Reynaldo. Lo que he visto en el Alto Paraguay. A., Imp. nac., 1946. 144p.

2899a MARTINEZ, Benigno T. El Paraguay; memoria bajo el punta de vista industrial y comercial en relación con los países del Plata. Edición oficial. B.A., Establecimiento tip., 1882. 73p.
Also: A., 1885.

2900 MENDEZ FLEYTAS, Epifanio. El mensaje de acero. A., Edit. El País, 1953. 40p.

2901 MENDEZ FLEYTAS, Epifanio. Psicología del colonialismo; imperialismo yanqui-brasilero en el Paraguay. B.A., Instituto Paraguayo de Cultura Pane Garay, 1971. 100p.

2902 MERCADO ALDER, W. Paraguay y el Plan Kennedy. C 3: 18 (1961) 26-32.

2903 MERIDA, C. La conjoncture économique au Paraguay. ERM 1955, Oct., 98-100.

2903a MIRANDA, Aníbal. Efecto de las inversiones extranjeras en la economía paraguaya. EP 4 no. 1 (1976) 129-60.

2904 MONTE DOMECQ', Raúl. Un decenio de progreso (los últimos 10 años). Centenario de la epopeya nacional, 1964-1970. A., 1969. 299p.

2905 MORALES, Juan Félix. Paraguay; su evidente expansión económica y progreso cultural y social en los últimos diez años. Perspectivas promisorias para inversionistas. A? 1967. 114p.

2906 NITOBURG, Eduard Lvovich. Paragvai: ekonomiko-geograficheskiie ocherki. Moscow, Mysl, 1964. 92p.

2906a ORGANIZACION DE LOS ESTADOS AMERICANOS. Cuenca del Río de la Plata: estudio para su planificación y desarrollo - República del Paraguay, Región Nororiental. Washington, OAS, 1976. 230p.

2907 ORGANIZACION DE LOS ESTADOS AMERICANOS. DEPARTAMENTO DE DESARROLLO REGIONAL. Cuenca del Plata; estudio para su planificación y desarrollo, República del Paraguay, Proyecto Aquidaban, desarrollo de la región Nororiental. Washington, OAS, 1975. 197p.

2907a ORGANIZACION DE LOS ESTADOS AMERICANOS. Seminario sobre prioridades para el desarrollo cientifico y tecnológico de Paraguay. Washington, OAS, 1977. 174p. (Estudios sobre el Desarrollo Científico y Tecnológico, 29)

2908 ORGANIZACION SINDICAL. DEPARTAMENTO DE COMISIONES MIXTAS Y MISIONES COMERCIALES. Paraguay. Madrid, 1966. 38p.

2908a ORGANIZATION OF AMERICAN STATES. The economic and social development of Paraguay: characteristics, policies and perspectives. Washington, OAS, 1974. ii, 108p.

2909 PAEZ, José E. Estructura económica y financiera del Paraguay. A., 1972. 28p.

2910 PARAGUAY. Rome, Instituto italo-latino americano, Vice-segretario economica-soziale, 1971. 35p. (Quaderni dell'I.I.L.A., 18)

2911 PARAGUAY, hoy! Informaciones útiles sobre la actualidad económica y sobre sus posibilidades industriales. B.A., Edit. Problemas, 1941. 128p.
Issued by the Comité Central del Partido Comunista del Paraguay.

2912 PARAGUAY, oportunidad de inversión. n.p., 1974. 97p.

2913 PARAGUAY. COMITE NACIONAL DE COORDINACION DE LA ASISTENCIA TECNICA. Programa nacional de asistencia técnica presentado al programa de las Naciones Unidas para el desarrollo, 1972. A., 1973. 108p.

2914 PARAGUAY. DEPARTAMENTO DE ESTADISTICA Y CENSOS. Censos económicos, 1963: Paraguay. A., 1966. 281p.

2915 PARAGUAY. DIRECCION GENERAL DE ESTADISTICA. Estadistica de la propiedad rural de la república del Paraguay. A., Imp. nac., 1921. 33p.

2916 PARAGUAY. DIRECCION GENERAL DE ESTADISTICA. La république du Paraguay; resumé statistique. A., Fischer & Quell, 1888. 16p.

2917 PARAGUAY. MINISTERIO DE ECONOMIA. Paraguay, datos y cifras estadísticas: población, producción, importación, exportación, industrias, vialidad, comercio, instrucción pública. Publicación oficial. A., 1939. 30p.

2918 PARAGUAY. SECRETARIA TECNICA DE PLANIFICACION. Paraguay: principales proyectos de inversión y programas del sector público. A., 1967. Various pagings.

2918a PARAGUAY. SECRETARIA TECNICA DE PLANIFICACION. Plan nacional de desarrollo económico y social, 1977-1981. A., 1976. 2 vols.

2919 PEREZ URIBE, Oscar. Problemas económicos del Paraguay. RCECE 7 no. 68 (1945) 9-32.

2920 PETIT, R.L. El programa de crédito agricola supervisado en el Paraguay. TE 18 (1951) Jan.-Mar., 117-41.

2921 PINCUS, Joseph. The economy of Paraguay. N.Y., Praeger, 1968. xxviii, 517p.
The best study on the Paraguayan economy.

2921a PRIETO, Daniel. Modernización de una economia. PR 1975, Jan.-Feb., 24-28.

2922 RECALDE, Facundo. El Paraguay en cifras, obra de divulgación económica. A., Edit. Antequera, 1946. 183p.

2923 RICCA, Serafim J. Los ministerios para el desarrollo: sus funciones y competencias. A., División de Administración para el Desarrollo, Secretaria Técnica de Planificación del Desarrollo Económico y Social, 1968. 102p.

2923a RIPPY, James Fred. British investments in Paraguay, Bolivia and Peru. IAEA 6 (1953) no. 4, 38-48.

2924 SCHURZ, William L. Paraguay: a commercial handbook. Washington, United States Government Printing Office, 1920. 195p.

2925 SEYNAVE, Maurice. Le Paraguay; monographique économique. Brussels, Office belge du commerce extérieur, 1964. 43p.

2926 SITUATION économique du Paraguay. BFIASEE (1970) Jul.-Sept., 2-21.

2927 SOUZA, Paulo R.; TOKMAN, Victor E. Características y funcionamiento del sector informal: el caso de Paraguay. RPS 11 no. 31 (1974) 51-63.

2928 STATISTICAL sketch of Paraguay. BTJ 5 (1888) 454-57.

2929 TEIJEIRO MARTINEZ, Benigno. El Paraguay; memoria bajo el punto de vista industrial y comercial en relación con los países del Plata. B.A., Establécimiento tip., 1882. 73p.
Also: A., 1885. 73p.

2930 TORRENTS, Santiago. Ensayos de economia dirigida en el Paraguay. RCECE 3 no. 20, 647-54; no. 21, 689-99.

2930a UNITED NATIONS DEVELOPMENT PROGRAMME IN PARAGUAY. Today's challenge, tomorrow's hope. A., 1973. 79p.

2931 UNITED STATES. DEPARTMENT OF AGRICULTURE. Agricultural development in Paraguay: report of a survey team representing the U.S. Department of Agriculture, Land Grant Colleges, and the Agency for International Development. Washington?, 1964. 61p.

2932 UNITED STATES. INTERNATIONAL COOPERATION ADMINISTRATION. Paraguay: fact sheet; aid in action. Washington, Office of Public Services, Bureau of Public Affairs, 1961. 9p. (Department of State publication 7265. Inter-American series, 71)

2933 UNITED STATES. OPERATIONS MISSIONS TO PARAGUAY. Some aspects of the Paraguayan economy as of the end of 1955. Prepared by Frederic R. Fisher, assisted by Miguel Cardona. A., 1956. Unpaged.

2934 UNIVERSIDAD CATOLICA, ASUNCION. CONSEJO DE PLANIFICACION. Antecedentes estadísticos. A., 1973. 94p. (Informe preliminar de discusión, 8)

2935 UNIVERSIDAD CATOLICA, ASUNCION. CONSEJO DE PLANIFICACION. El desarrollo económico y social paraguayo. A., 1973. 119p. (Informe preliminar de discusión, 3)

B. Demography

2936 AMMATUNA CARRUBBA, Juan. Estudio demográfico del Paraguay. RCECE 5 no. 55 (1944) 495-502.

2937 ARDITI, Nasim. El problema de la población en el Paraguay. RCECE 12 no. 105 (1950) 47-77.

2938 ARRIAGA, Eduardo E. Paraguay: tablas de mortalidad. RPS 6 no. 15 (1969) 124-32.

2938a BEHM, Hugo; BRIZUELA DE RAMIREZ, Fulvia. La mortalidad en los primeros años de vida en países de la América Latina: Paraguay 1967-1968. San José, Centro Latino-americano de Demografía, 1977. xi, 52p.

2939 BENITEZ, Manuel. El Paraguay; estudio comparativo de su población; artículo del doctor Manuel Benitez; reproducido en la Revue mensuelle du Paraguay. Nueva ed., anotada con arreglo el último censo. A., Imp. "El País", 1901. 55p.

2940 CONFERENCIA EPISCOPAL PARAGUAYA. El problema de la población en el Paraguay. A., 1974. 20p.

2941 La ENSEÑANZA de la demografía en el Paraguay. RPS 6 no. 16 (1969) 134-36.

2942 ESTIMACIONES de la población del Paraguay para 1968. RPS 5 no. 12 (1968) 129-35.

2943 FERREIRO, Oscar. Explosión demográfica. A., Péndulo, 196? 55p.

2944 HOCHSZTAJN, B. Paraguay: estudio de la migración interna; utilización de una muestral censal, 1962. Santiago, Latin American Demographic Centre, 1973. iii, 66p.

2945 INSFRAN, José V. Mortalidad de los niños menores de 12 meses en el partido de Itá en los años 1924 a 1928. Itá, Unidad Sanitaria de Itá, 1929. 29p.

2946 INSTITUTO DE DESARROLLO INTEGRAL Y ARMONICO. Actitudes y opiniones de los lideres paraguayos acerca de las politicas poblacionales y familiares. A?, 1971. 148p. (Desarrollo y demografía, 2)

2947 INSTITUTO DE DESARROLLO INTEGRAL Y ARMONICO. Implicancias económicas y sociales del crecimiento poblacional paraguayo. A?, 1971. 215p. (Desarrollo y demografía, 1)

2948 LOPEZ, Arquimedes; LOPEZ, Berta H. de. Paraguay: estudio de la migración interna paraguaya; utilización de una muestra censal, 1962. A., Centro Paraguayo de Estudios Sociológicos, 1971. 71p.

2949 LOPEZ, Berta H. de. Estudio de la migración interna Paraguaya: utilización de una muestra censal, 1962. RPS 9 no. 24 (1972) 73-127.

2950 MELLON, Roger; SILVERO, Arnaldo. Proyección de la población del Paraguay (1960-1970). RPS 5 no. 12 (1968) 17-33.

2950a ODRIOSOLA, Ricardo. Materno mortalidad en el Paraguay. BIIAPI 16 (1942) 253-78.

2950b ODRIOSOLA, Ricardo. Mortalidad infantil en Paraguay. BIIAPI 12 (1938) 28-55.

2951 PARAGUAY. COMITE NACIONAL DE ESTADISTICAS VITALES Y SANITARIAS. Proyecto programa de mejoramiento de las estadísticas vitales, años 1962-1965. A., 1962. 74p.

2951a PARAGUAY. DIRECCION GENERAL DE ESTADISTICA Y CENSOS. Algunas caracteristicas demograficas y socio-económicas de los migrantes internos del Paraguay. 1972. A., 1977. 36p.

2952 PARAGUAY. DIRECCION GENERAL DE ESTADISTICAS Y CENSOS. Censo nacional de población y vivienda, 1950. A., Ministerio de Hacienda, 1953. 3 vols.

2953 PARAGUAY. DIRECCION GENERAL DE ESTADISTICAS Y CENSOS. Resumen definitivo de la población del Paraguay, urbana y rural: Asunción y departamentos. Datos obtenidos en el censo de población y viviendas del 28 de octubre de 1950. A., 1954. 13p.

2954 PARAGUAY. DIRECCION GENERAL DE ESTADISTICAS Y CENSOS. Censo de población y vivienda, 14 de Octubre de 1962. A., 1966. i, 53p.

2955 PARAGUAY. DIRECCION GENERAL DE ESTADISTICAS Y CENSOS. Censo nacional de población y viviendas, 1972. A., La Dirección, 1975. xxiii, 561p.

2956 PARAGUAY. DIRECCION GENERAL DE ESTADISTICAS Y CENSOS. Censo nacional de población y vivienda, 1972: formulario. A., Ministerio de Hacienda, 1972. 4p.

2957 PARAGUAY. DIRECCION GENERAL DE ESTADISTICAS Y CENSOS. Censo nacional de población y vivienda (cifras provisionales). A., Ministerio de Hacienda, 1973. 32p.

2958 PARAGUAY. DIRECCION GENERAL DE ESTADISTICAS Y CENSOS. Información sobre el censo de población y vivienda. A., 1972. 7p.

2959 PARAGUAY. MINISTERIO DE RELACIONES EXTERIORES. Paraguay; demonstrative tables of its population. A., Tall. nac. de H. Kraus, 1901. 12p.

2960 PARAGUAY. MINISTERIO DE RELACIONES EXTERIORES. Paraguay; tableaux démonstratifs de sa population. A., Tall. nac. de H. Kraus, 1901. 12p.

2961 PARAGUAY. MINISTERIO DE SALUD PUBLICA Y BIENESTAR SOCIAL. Población según el censo nacional de 1962 y cómputos de población y viviendas para 1970. A., 1970. 8p.

2962 PARAGUAY. SECRETARIA TECNICA DE PLANIFICACION. Algunos aspectos de la población en el Paraguay. A., 1965. 88p.

2963 PARAGUAY. SECRETARIA TECNICA DE PLANIFICACION. Evalución de los censos de población levantados en la República del Paraguay en 1950 y 1960. (Estudio demográfico) A., 1965. 52p. (Estudio demográfico, 1)

2964 PARAGUAY. SECRETARIA TECNICA DE PLANIFICACION. La población económicamente activa del Paraguay (1960-70) (estudio demográfico). A., 1965. 55p. (Estudio demográfico, 3)

2965 RICCARDI, Riccardo. Carta della densitá di popolazione nel Paraguay. BSGI serie 6, 12 (1935) no. 5-6, 391-93.

2965a RIVAROLA, Domingo M. *and others*. La población del Paraguay. A., Centro Paraguayo de Estudios Sociológicos, 1974. 194p.

2966 SILVERO, Arnaldo. Paraguay: resúmen demográfico. SA 2 (1967) no. 2, 481-83.

2967 SILVERO, Arnaldo. Aspectos demográficos del Paraguay. RPS 3 no. 5, (1966) 39-46.

2968 UNITED STATES. BUREAU OF THE CENSUS. Paraguay, summary of biostatistics. Maps and charts, population, natality and mortality statistics. Washington, 1944. 66p.

2969 VALLEJOS, Rafael C. Album de familia. A., 1893. 6p.

2970 VIDAL L., Jorge. Paraguay: proyección de la población, por sex y grupo de edades, 1960-2000. RPS 7 no. 17 (1970) 80-106.
Also: (1) Santiago (Chile), Centro Latinoamericano de Demografía, 1969. 29p.
(2) A., Centro Paraguayo de Estudios Sociológicos, 1969? 29p.

C. Land and agriculture

2971 ACUÑA, Narciso M. La ganadería en el Paraguay. A., Tall. nac. de H. Kraus, 1904. 22p.

2972 ANDRE, Floyd, *and others*. Desarrollo agrícola del Paraguay. A., USAID, 1964. 58p.

2973 ARAD, Irene Szumsztjn de. La ganadería en el Paraguay: periodo 1870-1900. RPS 10 no. 28 (1973) 183-223.

2974 ARNOLD, Adlai F.; ESPINOSA B., Aristides. Estructura y funcionamiento del sector agropecuario y forestal del Paraguay. RPS 6 no. 14 (1969) 102-31.

2975 ARNOLD, Adlai F.; ESPINOSA B., Aristides. Estructura y funcionamiento del sector agropecuario y forestal del Paraguay, 1956-1967, con implicaciones para la política del desarrollo. A., Ministerio de Agricultura y Ganaderia, 1968. ii, 53p.

2976 ARNOLD, Adlai F. Structure and performance of Paraguayan agriculture 1956-1967: with implications for development policy. A., U.S. Agency for International Development, 1968. 45p.

2977 ARNOLD, Adlai F. Foundation of an agricultural policy in Paraguay. N.Y., Praeger, 1971. xx, 294p.

2978 ARNOLD, Adlai F. Reforma agraria y colonización en el Paraguay. A., Centro Paraguayo de Estudios Sociológicos, 1966. 10p.
Also: RPS 3 no. 6 (1966) 58-67.

2979 AVALOS, César. El problema azucarero en el Paraguay. RCECE no. 60-61 (1944) 275-90.

2980 AYALA, Nelson C. Estudio del tabaco en el Paraguay. RCECE 12 no. 109 (1951) 27-39.

2981 BAEZ, Cecilio. Dictamen sobre las tierras de Barranquera de Uriarte. A., Tip. de El Cívico, 1909. 36p.

2982 BANCO AGRICOLA DEL PARAGUAY. Ley y decretos referentes a la "Sección hipotecaria" del Banco agricola del Paraguay con el reglamento interno de la misma. A., Tall. nac. de H. Kraus, 1896. 36p.

2983 BENITEZ, Leopoldo A. Algunas sugestiones sobre producción y comercio de la naranja del Paraguay. A., Tall. Gráf. del Estado, 1916. 26p.

2983a BERTHOLD, T. Agrarreform und Kleinbauernfrage in Paraguay. ZAL 16 (1977) 72-84.

2984 BERTONI, Guillermo Tell. Colección de folletos sobre organización y fomento de agricultura. A., 1924-28. 2 vols.

2985 BERTONI, Guillermo Tell. La estructura del costo de producción y el salario real de agricultor paraguayo. RCECE 14 no. 126, (1954) 5-20.

2985a BORSDORF, Roe. Evaluation and suggested initiatives for the development of local marketing of agricultural commodities in Paraguay, prepared for the Agency for International Development, United States Department of State, at the Food and Feed Grain Institute, Kansas State University, by Roe Borsdorf, Cornelius Hugo, and Elwyn Holmes. Manhattan, Kansas State University, 1977. vi, 67p.

2986 CAMARA DE COMERCIO, ASUNCION. Primera exposición de industria doméstica que realizá el Centro Comercial del Paraguay. A., Tip. La Tribuna, 1901. 28p.

2987 CAMPOS, Alfonso V. El latifundio y minifundio en el Paraguay: situación-problemas. RCECE 8 no. 81 (1946) 24-41.

2987a CARAVIAS, José Luis. Liberación campesina; ligas agrarias de Paraguay. Bilbao, Zero; Madrid, ZYX, 1975. 200p.

2988 CRISTALDO, Julio César. Tres proposiciones para el desarrollo agricola regional del Paraguay. EPA 4 (1965) 29-36.

2989 DEMERSAY, L.M. Alfred. Etude économique sur la maté ou thé du Paraguay. Paris, Ve Bouchard-Husard, 1867. 48p.

2990 DOMINGUEZ, Manuel. El algodón: su producción en el Paraguay. A., Tall. nac. de H. Kraus, 1900. 23p.

2991 DOMINGUEZ, Manuel. Le coton: la production au Paraguay. A., Revue commerciale, 1903. 10p.

2992 DOMINGUEZ, Manuel. Cotton: its production in Paraguay. A., H. Kraus, 1903. 15p.

2993 ESPINOSA B., Aristides. El maíz en el Paraguay: estudio económico preliminar de los problemas de su producción y comercialización. A., STICA, 1959. 16p.

2994 ESTABROOK, Leon. Agricultural survey of South America: Argentina and Paraguay. Washington, Government Printing Office, 1926. 91p. (U.S.A. Department of Agriculture. Bulletin no. 1409)

2995 FERREIRA, Jorge E.; DUERST, Elvin A. Costo de producción del arroz en el Paraguay, cosecha 1948-1949. Estudio sobre diez arroceros comerciales de la región oriental del Paraguay. A., Servicio Técnico Interamericano de Cooperación Agrícola, 1950. 4p.

2995a FOOD AND AGRICULTURE ORGANIZATION. Informe al gobierno del Paraguay sobre servicios de extensión y educación agropecuarias. Rome, FAO, 1974. 23p.

2996 FRANCO, Rafael. La reforma agraria de la revolución paraguaya con un exordio del doctor Bernardino C. Howe; apéndice decreto-ley no. 1060. B.A., Tall. gráf. Damiano, 1938. 36p.

2997 FRIEDMANN, Eugenio. Historia del azúcar en el Paraguay. A., Edit. El Arte, 1966. 300p.

2997a FRUTOS, Juan Manuel. De la reforma agraria al bienestar rural y otros documentos concernientes a la marcha de la reforma agraria. A., Instituto de Bienestar, 1976? 177p.

2998 FRUTOS, Juan Manuel. Proyección social de la doctrina agrarista del coloradismo; conferencia dictada en la Casa de los Colorados, 25-agosto-61. A?, 1961? 28p.

2999 GALEANO ROMERO, Luis A. Las explotaciones agricolas en el Paraguay. Hacia una interpretación sociologica de las características regionales. RPS 11 no. 31 (1974) 167-98.

3000 GALEANO ROMERO, Luis A. Unidades productivas agropecuárias y estructuras de poder en Paraguay, 1811-1870. RPS 9 no. 23 (1972) 91-115.

3000a GILES, Antonio *and others*. Contribución al planeamiento para la consolidación de la Colonia "Repatriación" Caaguazú, Paraguay. Bogota, I.I.C.A.-C.I.R.A., 1966. (Materiales de enseñanza para reforma agraria, 11)

3001 GONZALEZ, Emeterio; CARRERAS, Cayetano A. La tierras de Barranquera Uriarte ó sea Puerto Max. La sentencia de 1 instancia. A., "Ariel" Tall. tip. y encuadernación, 191-? 71p.

3002 GONZALEZ, Teodosio. Informe juridico presentado al p.e. por el fiscal general del estado "ad-hoc", doctor Teodosio Gonzalez, en las demandas del fisco contra el doctor Alejandro Audibert. A., Imp. de "La Democracia", 1899. 50p.

3003 GONZALEZ ALSINA, Ezequiel. La pequeña agricultura: serie de editoriales del diario "Patria" sobre un discurso del presidente del Banco Mundial, Robert S. Macnamara. A., Ediciones del C.E.C., 1974. iii, 124p.

3003a GRABISCH, W. Die Landwirtschaft Paraguays. BL 41 (1963) 156-90.

3003b HECHT, Alfred. The agricultural economy of the Mennonite settlers in Paraguay. GC 6 (1975) no. 4, 14-23.

3003c HECHT, Alfred. The agricultural economy of the Mennonite settlers in Paraguay: impact of a road. EK 42 no. 248 (1976) 42-47.

3003d HERZBERG, J. Staatlich landliche Beratungsdienste als Instrument der Entwicklungsföderung in Sudamerika. Eine Untersuchung am Beispiel Argentiniens, Ecuadors und Paraguays. Materialsammlung, ZAL, no. 26 (1975). xi, 231p.

3004 INSTITUTO DE BIENESTAR RURAL. El gobierno, el pueblo y el Partido Colorado, unido a través de una obra nacional. A., Departamento de Divulgación y Prensa, 1963. 48p.

3005 INSTITUTO DE BIENESTAR RURAL. 10 años de reforma agraria con Stroessner. A., 1964. 48p.

3006 INSTITUTO DE REFORMA RURAL. La reforma agraria en marcha. A., Departamento de Divulgación y Prensa, 1961. 40p. (Folleto, 2)

3007 INSTITUTE OF INTER-AMERICAN AFFAIRS. FOOD SUPPLY DIVISION. Agricultural progress in Paraguay. Summary report, 1942-1949, of the Servicio Técnico Interamericano de Cooperación Agricola (STICA) and the IIAA Food Supply Mission to Paraguay. Washington, 1949. 29, xi p.

3008 INTER-AMERICAN COMMITTEE FOR AGRICULTURAL DEVELOPMENT. Inventory of information basic to the planning of agricultural development in Latin America, Paraguay. Washington, Pan American Union, 1963. 57p.

3009 INTER-AMERICAN COMMITTEE FOR AGRICULTURAL DEVELOPMENT. Inventario de la información básica para la programación del desarrollo agrícola en la América Latina: Paraguay. Washington, Pan American Union, 1963. 57p.

3010 INTER-AMERICAN DEVELOPMENT COMMISSION. Technical mission to Paraguay. Reports on the forests, the forest industries, and trade in forest products, hides and leather industries, edible vegetable oils industries of Paraguay, 1945. Washington, 1947. 116p.

3011 KEMSKI, Karl E. Die Landwirtschaft in paraguayischen Chaco. B.A., Druck von Imp. "Mercur", 1931. 148p.

3012 KONINKLIJK INSTITUUT VOOR DE TROPEN. Paraguay. 2. ed. Amsterdam, 1966. 36p. (Landesdocumentie, 94)

3013 LANGE, F. Landwirtschaft in Paraguay. TP 32 (1929) no. 8, 317-34.

3013a LATERZA, Gustavo. Políticas del estado sobre tierra y vivienda. A., Centro Paraguayo de Estudios Sociológicos, Sociedad Interamericana de Planificación, 197? 84p.

3014 LOPEZ, Adalberto. The economics of yerba mate in seventeenth-century South America. AH 48 (1974) no. 4, 493-509.

3015 LYNCH, John Vincent. Paraguay's agricultural situation and outlook. Washington, U.S. Department of Agriculture, 1962. 11p.

3016 MARTINEZ DIAZ, Nicasio. Breve reseña de política agraria en el Paraguay. VE 13 no. 157 (1943) 364-67.

3017 MARTINEZ DIAZ, Nicasio. La reforma agraria. B.A., Colección Economía Paraguayo, 1963. 143p.

3018 MENDARO, Ernesto. Paraguay. A., Centro de Información Agricola-Ganadera, STICA, 1960. 50p. (Boletín 235)

3019 MITCHELL, Glen H.; BARRON, Theodore. A development view of the Paraguayan beef industry: an independent examination of a traditional industry in a traditional society with a recommended innovational pathway for economic development. Las Cruces, New Mexico State University, 1974. vi, 49p.

3020 NETTO, Gabriel S. El problema de la tierra en el Paraguay. RCECE 3 no. 20 (1941) 595-603.

3021 PAMPLIEGA, Luís; MARTINEZ, Leonardo. Estudio de la colonia "Gral Stroessner". A., Instituto Interamericano de Ciencias Agrícolas de la OEA (I.I.C.A.), 1966. 86p.

3022 PARAGUAY. DIRECCION DE AGRICULTURA Y DEFENSA AGRICOLA. Primer computo censal completo de la estadística agrícola y factores económicos de la producción; tierra - población - valor de la propiedad - costo del bracero - mercados y cotizaciones - fletes y transporto. Organisado por primera vez bajo la dirección inmediata de Guillermo Tell Bertoni. A., La Colmena, 1927. 32p.

3023 PARAGUAY. DIRECCION GENERAL DE AGRICULTURA. Plan agrícola, 1944-1945. Desarrollo anual del plan quinquenal del gobierno. A., Ed. La Nación, 1944. 34p.

3024 PARAGUAY. FISCALIA GENERAL. Jactancia. Juez competente. Vista del fiscal gral. del estado, dr. don César Gondra, en el juicio seguido por los drs. Herrera Vegas, Roberts, don Ricardo Lavalle y don Cárlos

Rodríguez Larreta contra don Francisco Cordero sobre competencia de jurisdicción. Publicación oficial. A., Imp. de El Paraguayo, 1889. 18p.

3025 PARAGUAY. MINISTERIO DE AGRICULTURA Y GANADERIA. Censo agropecuario por muestreo, 1961. A., 1964. 46p.

3026 PARAGUAY. MINISTERIO DE AGRICULTURA Y GANADERIA. Censo agropecuario, 1956. A., 1961. xxiii, 697p.

3027 PARAGUAY. MINISTERIO DE AGRICULTURA Y GANADERIA. Principales enfermedades del tabaco en el Paraguay y las medidas de control. A., 1972. 21p.

3027a PARAGUAY. MINISTERIO DE AGRICULTURA Y GANADERIA. Proyecto de educación agropecuaria, Ministerio de Agricultura y Ganaderia, Banco Interamericano de Desarrollo, Instituto Interamericano de Ciencias Agrícolas. A., 1977. 5 vol.

3028 PARAGUAY. MINISTERIO DE AGRICULTURA Y GANADERIA. Programa de 5 años para el mejoramiento agrícola del Paraguay. A., 1962? 34p.

3029 PARAGUAY. MINISTERIO DE AGRICULTURA Y GANADERIA. Resultantes preliminares del censo agropecuario de 1956. A., Imp. nac., 1958. 24p.

3030 PARAGUAY. MINISTERIO DE AGRICULTURA Y GANADERIA. DIRECCION DE PLANIFICACION Y ASESORTA. Plan de desarrollo agropecuario y forestal, 1969-1973. A., 1968. 3 vols.

3031 PARAGUAY. MINISTERIO DE AGRICULTURA Y GANADERIA. SECRETARIA DE COORDINACION TECNICA. Manual estadístico del Paraguay, 1962-1969. A., 1970. iv, 150p.

3032 PARAGUAY. MINISTERIO DE HACIENDA. DIRECCION DE AGRICULTURA. Primer computo censal completo de la estadística agrícola y factores económicos de la producción. A., La Colmena, 1927. 32p.

3033 PASTORE, Carlos. Origines, evolución y estado actual del latifundio y el minifundio en Paraguay. AP 2 (1966) 106-12.

3033a PASTORE, Carlos. Origines, evolución y estado actual del latifundio y minifundio en el Paraguay. EP 3 no. 1 (1975) 115-21.

3034 PATTY, Gordon Enoch. Agriculture and trade in Paraguay. Washington, U.S. Department of Agriculture,

Economic Research Service, 1961. 15p. (ERS-foreign, 6)

3035 PEÑA, Jaime, R. La agricultura en el proceso económico nacional. A., 1969-75. 3 vols.

3036 PFANNENSCHMIDT, Ernst August Julian. Die Landwirtschaft in Paraguay. Berlin, Verlagsbuchhandlung P. Parey, 1914-15. 2 vols. (Berichte über Land- und Forstwirtschaft im Auslande. Mitgeteilt vom Auswärtigen Amt. Buchausgabe Stück, 21, 22)

3036a PHILLIPS, R., BORSDORF, Roe. Evaluation of the market system and potential for agricultural products in Paraguay. Manhattan, Kansas State University, 1976. 188p. (Kansas State University; Grain Storage, Processing and Marketing Report, 61)

3036b La REFORMA agraria en el Paraguay: pautas políticas y administrativas, 1963-1973. A., Instituto de Bienestar Rural, 1974? xxvi, 256p.

3036c RIVAROLA, Domingo. Freins et obstacles à la reforme agraire au Paraguay. CIV 25 (1975) no. 3-4, 286-93.

3036d ROMERO, Claudio. Review of land tenure situation in Paraguay and an integrated land reform program. *In* LAND tenure, ed. by Kenneth H. Parsons and others. Proceedings of the International Conference on Land tenure and related problems in world agriculture held at Madison, Wisconsin, 1951. Madison, University of Wisconsin Press, 1956. pp. 257-63.

3037 ROMERO, Luis Armando Galeano. Unidades productivas agropecuarias y estructura de poder en Paraguay (1811-1870). RPS 9 no. 23 (1972) 91-105.

3038 SAMANIEGO, José D. Situación actual y proyecciones de las inversiones en obras de infraestructura ganadera en el Paraguay. EPA 7 (1968) 5-11.

3039 SANTOS, Carlos R. Apuntes relativos al porvenir de la agricultura y de la ganadería en el Paraguay. 2. ed. A., Tall. tip. del estado, 1912. 67p.

3040 SCHOOLCRAFT, C. Donald. Agricultural marketing in Paraguay. A., Ministry of Agriculture and Livestock and the United States Overseas Mission to Paraguay, 1961. 58p.

3040a SERVICIO EUROPEO DE UNIVERSITARIOS LATINOAMERICANOS. Paraguay: represión contra las ligas agrarias cristianas. SEUL 7 no. 59-60 (1975) 13-24.

3041 STAHL, Wilmar. Cinco establecimientos agrícolas indígenas en el Chaco Central: un estudio de cambio social guiado. SA 9 (1974) no. 1-2, 111-52.

3042 STEWART, Norman R. Cultural conservatism and the farm dwelling: the mark of the pioneer. LN 15 (1965) no. 1, 24-28.

3043 VASCONSELLOS, Arsenio. La explotación ganadera. EPA 5 (1966) 33-38.

D. Banking. Money. Finance

3044 ACOSTA, César R. 10 años de estabilidad monetaria. EPA 5 (1966) 21-31.

3045 ACOSTA, César R. 10 años de establización monetaria en el Paraguay: política del Banco Mundial y sus organismos auxiliares en relación a América Latina y las Filipinas durante 1965/66. A., Banco Central del Paraguay, 1966. 38p.

3046 ACOSTA, César R. La materia bancaria en el Paraguay (tesis) presentada para optar el título de dr. derecho y ciencias sociales. A., Imp. nac., 1928. 71p.

3047 AHRENSDORF, Joachim. Central bank policies and inflation: a case study of four less-developed economies, 1949-57. IMFSP 7 (1959) no. 2, 274-301.

3048 ANTEZANA PAZ, Franklin. La reforma monetaria paraguaya. EB 1 no. 2 (1943) 26-32.

3049 ARRIOLA, José Tomás. La tribulación y el desarrollo económico. El sistema impositivo paraguaya. EPA 7 no. 11 (1969) 5-52.

3050 ASOCIACION LATINOAMERICANA DE LIBRE COMERCIO. Lista nacional del Paraguay. n.p., 1966. 73p.

3051 AVALOS, César. Sistema del papel moneda en el Paraguay. RCECE 5 no. 44 (1943) 683-701.

3052 BAEZ, Cecilio. Curso de finanzas. 2. ed. A., Imp. nac., 1938. 157p.

3053 BANCO AGRICOLA DEL PARAGUAY. El banco agrícola del Paraguay en la Exposición internacional de agricultura de Buenos Aires. A., Tall. nac. de H. Kraus, 1910. xxiii, 277p.

3054 BANCO AGRICOLA DEL PARAGUAY. Carta orgánica del Banco agrícola del Paraguay, noviembre de 1940. A., La Colmena, 1940. 32p.

3055 BANCO AGRICOLA DEL PARAGUAY. Ley orgánica del Banco agrícola del Paraguay, noviembre 29 de 1915. A., Tall. de Zamphirópolos, 1916. 23p.

3056 BANCO AGRICOLA DEL PARAGUAY. Leyes de creación y reorganización del Banco agrícola, con sus modificaciones; decretos sobre fomento de agricultura; reglamento interno y reglamento de las agencias departamentales del mismo. A., Tall. nac. de H. Kraus, 1899. 66p.

3057 BANCO AGRICOLA DEL PARAGUAY. Leyes de la creación y reorganización del Banco agrícola con sus modificaciones. Reglamento interno y reglamento de las agencias departamentales del mismo, Asunción del Paraguay. A., Imp. de H. Kraus, 1895. 42p.

3058 BANCO AGRICOLA DEL PARAGUAY. Reglamento para la Oficina de propagandas, informaciones y estadísticas del Banco agrícola del Paraguay. A., Tall. nac. de H. Kraus, 1896. 7p.

3059 BANCO AGRICOLA DEL PARAGUAY. Sección hipotecaria del Banco agrícola del Paraguay para agricultores, industriales y ganaderos. Ley de 26 de agosto de 1899 y su reglamentación. A., Tall. nac. de H. Kraus, 1899. 27p.

3060 BANCO DE COMERCIO. Estatutos del Banco de comercio y la ley de concesión promulgada por el poder ejecutio el 6 de marzo de 1886. A., Imp. de "El Orden", 1886. 21p.

3061 BANCO CENTRAL DEL PARAGUAY. Ley orgánica del Banco Central del Paraguay. A., El Arte, 1952. 48p.

3062 BANCO DEL PARAGUAY. Fondo gandero: antecedentes y funciones. A., Gráf. Asunceña, 1971. 73p.

3063 BANCO DEL PARAGUAY. Ley orgánica del Banco del Paraguay y Ley de bancos. A., La Colmena, 1944. 145p.

3064 BANCO DEL PARAGUAY Y RIO DE LA PLATA. Estatutos y ley del Banco del Paraguay y Rio de la Plata. B.A., Imp. La Nación, 1889. 30p.

3065 BANCO DE LA REPUBLICA DEL PARAGUAY. Carta orgánica de Banco de la República. A., Tall. gráf. "La Colmena", 1915. 64p.

3066 BENITEZ S., Jorge. La situación monetaria actuel del Paraguay. RCECE 2 no. 18 (1941) 474-81.

3067 CAMPOS, A.R. La question monétaire du Paraguay. Paris, Librairie de François, 1918. 180p.

3068 CARDONA, Miguel. Régimen financiero de las comunas Paraguayas. RCECE 2 no. 15 (1940) 273-96; no. 16 (1940) 348-58.

3069 CARDOZO, Efraím. La primeras monedas en el Paraguay. *In* SEGUNDO congreso internacional de historia de América reunido en Buenos Aires en los dias 5 a 14 de julio de 1937. B.A., 1938. Vol. 5, 490-501.

3070 CROCKETT, Joseph P.; COSTA, Jasper S. Los impuestos internos del Paraguay. n.p., 1952. 62p.

3071 GONZALEZ, Fernando A. El impuesto inmobiliario en el Paraguay. VE 2 no. 136 (1942) 471-72.

3072 GONZALEZ ERICO, Miguel Angel. Desarrollo de la banca en el Paraguay (1870-1900). A., Centro Paraguayo de Estudios Sociológicos, 1971. 33p.
Also: RPS 9 no. 25 (1972) 133-54.

3072a GONZALEZ GARCIA, Leovigildo. Las actividades bancarias y de seguros en el Paraguay (década de 1957 a 1966). A., Ediciones Nizza, 1969. 393p.

3073 La INSTALACION de una sucursal del banco en el Paraguay. RBNA 3 (1939) no. 2, 79-90.

3074 JACQUET, Alfredo J. La contratación de técnicos extranjeros. A., Puigbonet, 1935. 154p.

3075 JACQUET, Alfredo J. Los planes bancarios y monetarios de la transguerra. B.A., Socrates, 1943. 7p.

3075a KRAGH, Börje. En not om inflationen i Bolivia, Chile och Paraguay. *In* 25 economic essays in English, German and Scandinavian languages in honour of Erik Lindahl, 21 November 1956. Stockholm, Ekonomisk Tidskrift, 1956. pp. 175-85.

3076 MANSFIELD, Charles Y. Elasticity and buoyancy of a tax system: a method applied to Paraguay. IMFSP 19 (1972) no. 2, 425-46.

3077 MARTINEZ DIAZ, Nicasio. La moneda y la política monetaria en el Paraguay. A., La Colmena, 1951. 190p.

3078 MARTINEZ DIAZ, Nicasio. El sistema impositivo paraguayo. RCE serie 2, 31 no. 258 (1943) 27-44.

3079 MORENO, Fulgencio Ricardo. La cuestión monetaria en el Paraguay. Exposición del Ministro de Hacienda, don Fulgencio R. Moreno, hecha en defensa de sus proyectos en la hon. Cámara de Diputados (sesiones de los días 22 y 27 de Agosto de 1902). A., H. Kraus, 1902. 125p.

3080 OLASCOAGA, Ramón de. El comercio internacional y la moneda nacional. A., H. Kraus, 1895. 56p.

3081 OLASCOAGA, Ramón de. La commerce international et la monnaie nationale, avec une introduction de Charles Gide. Paris, Librairie de la Société du recueil des lois et des arrêts et du Journal du palais ancienne Mon L. Larose & Forcel, 1896. viii, 3-49p.

3081a PANGRAZIO, Miguel Angel. Derecho y finanzas. A., Tall. Gráf. Casa América, 1969-

3082 PARAGUAY. COMISION PARA LA REVISION DE LAS LEYES IMPOSITIVAS. Informe sobre la contribución territorial, por el dr. Rodolfo Ritter. A., Tall. gráf. del estado, 1912. 106p.

3083 PARAGUAY. COMISION PARA LA REVISION DE LAS LEYES IMPOSITIVAS. Informe sobre impuestos internos, por Fulgencio R. Moreno. A., Tall. gráf. del estado, 1912-.

3084 PARAGUAY. COMISION PARA LA REVISION DE LAS LEYES IMPOSITIVAS. Informe sobre la legislación aduanera, por el Dr. Francisco Gubetich. A., Tall. gráf. del estado, 1914. 3-290p.

3085 PARAGUAY. CONTADURIA GENERAL. Disposiciones sobre fiscalización, inspección y otras relativas a los sociedades anónimas y fianza de sociedades de seguro. A., Imp. nac., 1939. 36p.

3086 PARAGUAY. FISCALIA GENERAL. El fiscal general del estado con el Banco del Paraguay y Río de la Plata por devolución de un bono de cuatrocientas mil libras esterlinas. A., Tall. nac. de H. Kraus, 1899. 88p.

3087 PARAGUAY. MINISTERIO DE HACIENDA. El esfuerzo nacional y las necesidades de financiamiento externo. A., 1974. 225p.

3088 PARAGUAY. MINISTERIO DE HACIENDA. Reforma tributaria. A?, Imp. nac., 1964. 77p.

3089 PARAGUAY. PRESIDENTE (1902-1904). Mensaje y proyectos financieros del p.e. á hh. cc. 11. Refundición de la Sección comercial de la Caja de conversión y del Banco agrícola en una institución cue se denominará Banco de la república del Paraguay. Autorización al Banco de la república del Paraguay para contratar un crédito á oro por $2.500.000. Conversión del papel moneda al 900 mediante el crédito ó las economías. Modificación de la ley de la Caja de conversión. A., Imp. y enc. de "El País", 1904. 44p.

3090 PARAGUAY. SECRETARIA TECNICA DE PLANIFICACION. Paraguay: requerimientos financieros externos en el bienio 1965-66. Informe preparado el Comité Interamericano de la Alianza para el Progreso, CIAP. A., 1964. 2 vols.

3091 PEÑA VILLAMIL, Manuel. La concesión de servicios públicos: doctrina y legislación. A., Edit. Lapacho, 1957. 246p.

3092 POUMAILLOU, Paul. Study on investment and planning in the economic development of Paraguay. A., U.S. AID Mission to Paraguay; Central Bank of Paraguay, 1962. 113p.

3093 El REGIMEN monetario orgánico de la república del Paraguay. A., Ed. Guaranía, 1943. 43p.

3094 RIVAS DE ZAZZI, O.; DUARTE VERA, K.E.; QUIÑONEZ ZARZA, M. Planeamiento, organización y administración de la División de Bienestar Social. RPS 4 no. 10 (1967) 24-93.

3095 SANCHEZ MASI, Luis. El mercado de capitales en el Paraguay. Con la colaboración de economistas del CEPADE. Mexico, Centro de Estudios Monetarios Latinoamericanos para el Banco Interamericano de Desarrollo, 1972. 224p.

3096 SOLER, Carlos A. La producción total del Paraguay en 1946 y su valor neto. Ensayo sobre la renta nacional. A., La Colmena, 1948. 32p.

3097 TAYLOR, George R. Paraguay, with particular reference to price control. *In* HARRIS, Seymour E. Economic problems of Latin America. N.Y., McGraw-Hill, 1944. p. 391-419.

3098 TOMAS ARRIOLA, J. La tributación y el desarrollo económico - el sistema impositivo paraguayo. EPA 7 no. 11 (1969) 5-52.

3099 TRIFFIN, Robert. Monetary and banking reform in Paraguay. Washington, Board of governors of the Federal Reserve System, 1946. 170p.

3100 UNITED STATES. BUREAU OF FOREIGN COMMERCE. Investment in Paraguay; conditions and outlook for United States investors. Washington, 1955. v, 110p.

3101 UNITED STATES. FEDERAL RESERVE SYSTEM. BOARD OF GOVERNORS. New monetary and banking measures in Paraguay. Washington, 1944. 10p.

3102 UNITED STATES. OFFICE OF PRICE ADMINISTRATION. FOREIGN INFORMATION BRANCH. LATIN AMERICAN SECTION. Paraguay: a study of price control, cost of living and rationing. Washington, 1943. vi, 40p.

3103 WALLACE, Donald O. Paraguay income tax service. Centerport, N.Y., Foreign Tax Law Association, 1955. 1 vol. (loose-leaf)

3104 WAMOSY SOSA, Juan B. Saneamiento monetario de nuestro papel moneda. A., 1956. 29p.

E. Industry

1. *General studies*

3105 BANCO AGRICOLA DEL PARAGUAY. El Banco Agrícola del Paraguay en la Exposición Internacional de Agricultura de Buenos Aires. A., Tall. nac. de H. Kraus, 1910. xxiii, 277p.

3106 CABALLERO, Carlos Roger. Land of opportunities. A., Ministry of Industry and Commerce, 1966. 39p.

3107 CABALLERO, Carlos Roger. Paraguay, tierra de oportunidades. A., Ministerio de Industria y Comercio, 1966. 48p.
For earlier ed., see no. 3123.

3108 CERNAK, F. L'industrie du sciage au Paraguay. BFT 1959 (Nov.) 39-49.

3109 CHAMORRO, Blás R. Estudio sobre la estrategia y política de desarrollo industrial en países pequeños. A., 1974. 57p.

3110 CONGRESO DE ENTIDADES ECONOMICAS PRIVADAS, 2d., ASUNCION, 1965. Resoluciones y recomendaciones. A., Federación de la Producción, la Industria y el Comercio, 1965. 230p.

3110a ENRIQUEZ GAMON, Efraín. Itaipú, aguas que valen oro. B.A., Gráf. Guadalupe, 1975. 786p.

3111 FALETTO, E. El empresario industrial en el Paraguay. RPS 2 no. 4 (1965) 32-40.

3112 LATINOCONSULT PARAGUAY; LATINOCONSULT ARGENTINA. Estudio de factibilidad para el desarrollo de la industria turística en el Paraguay; preparado para el Ministerio de Obras Públicas y Comunicaciones. A., 1970. 343p.

3113 LIEBIG'S EXTRACT OF MEAT COMPANY. Liebig's en el Paraguay; libro de homenaje en el centenario de la fundación de la Liebig's Extract of Meat Company Limited, 1865-1965. Paraguay, Zeballos-Cue, 1965. 238p.

3114 LOPEZ, Adalberto. Shipbuilding in sixteenth-century Asunción del Paraguay. MM 61 (1975) 31-37.

3115 MARTINEZ DIAZ, Nicasio; RECALDE, Facundo. Hombres de negocios del Paraguay. A., La Colmena, 1950. 294p. (Colección Economía paraguaya)

3116 OLMEDO, Natalicio. Vida y actividades en el alto Paraguay; histõria, crítica, relato de hechos desconocidos, descripción fiel de las poblaciones industriales, ilustraciones interesantes, año 1946. A., Edit. El Gráfico, 1946. 161p.

3117 PARAGUAY: oportunidades de inversión en la industria. A., 1972. 71p.
Text in English and Spanish.

3118 PARAGUAY. COMISION NACIONAL DEL PRIMER CENSO INDUSTRIAL DEL PARAGUAY, 1955. Paraguay: primer censo industrial. A., 1958. 221p.

3119 PARAGUAY. DEPARTAMENTO DE ESTADISTICA Y CENSOS. Censo industrial del Paraguay, 1963. Totales por departamentos, resultados preliminares sujetos a rectificaciones. A., Ministerio de Industria y Comercio, 1965. 33p.

3120 PARAGUAY. DEPARTAMENTO DE ESTADISTICA Y CENSOS. Censo industrial del Paraguay, 1963; resultados preliminares de la República por departamento, sujeto a rectificaciones. A., Ministerio de Industria y Comercio, 1965. 51p.

3121 PARAGUAY. DEPARTAMENTO DE TIERRAS Y COLONIAS. Posibilidades del desarrollo de la industria hidroeléctrica en el Paraguay. A., Imp. sudamericana, 1925. 15p.

3122 PARAGUAY. MINISTERIO DE INDUSTRIA Y COMERCIO. Paraguay: land of opportunities. A., 1965. 39p.

3123 PARAGUAY. MINISTERIO DE INDUSTRIA Y COMERCIO. Paraguay: tierra de oportunidades. A., 1965. 63p.
For later eds., see no. 3107.

3124 PARAGUAY. SECRETARIA TECNICA DE PLANIFICACION. Análisis y programa industrial. A., 1971. 69p.

3124a PEREIRA, Osny Duarte. La seudo-rivalidad argentino-brasileña, pro y contra de Itaipu. B.A., Corregidor, 1975. 328p.

3125 RIVAROLA, D.M. Los empresarios en el Paraguay. RPS 5 no. 11 (1968) 123-28.

3126 RUIZ, Gabriel J. Desenvolvimiento de la industria y el comercio del Paraguay desde la independencia hasta el gobierno de Don Carlos A. López. RCECE (1939) no. 8, 621-32.

3126a SCHILLING, Paulo R. *and others*. Una situación explosiva, la cuenca del Plata. B.A., Tierra Nueva, 1974. 138p.

3127 TENE, Ilmar. Informe sobre el uso de la madera de construcción de viviendas. A., FAO; Naciones Unidas, 1970. 8p. (Documentos de trabajo, no. 9. FAO/SF/PAR. 150)

3128 UNION INDUSTRIAL DEL PARAGUAY. Primera guía industrial, 1973. A., 1973. 343p.

3129 UNITED NATIONS. El desarrollo industrial del Paraguay. Santiago (Chile), 1966. 54p. (ST/ECLA/Conf. 23/L.51)

3130 VAEKSEN, A. Réalités et perspectives de l'industrie du Paraguay. RSBEE no. 207 (1963) 535-40.

2. Labor

3131 CANNON, Mary M. Women workers in Paraguay. Washington, United States Department of Labor, Women's bureau, 1946. 16p.

3132 CHARTRAIN, François. El mundo del trabajo en Paraguay entre 1870 y 1936. (Reflexiones sobre el estudio histórico). RPS 10 no. 27 (1973) 93-100.

3133 CODAS, Cipriano. Las vacaciones pagadas en el Paraguay; resolución de la Union Industrial Paraguaya, sus antecedentes y comentarios. A., Edit. El País, 1951. 50p.

3134 MARIN IGLESIAS, Alejandro. La organización del trabajo en nuestro país. A., Imp. nac., 1940. 12p.

3134a MAS GARCIA, A. Promoción profesional de trabajadores en Paraguay; un desafío, una respueta. A., Centro de Promoción Profesional de Trabajadores, 1972. 143p.

3135 MELLON, Roger; SILVERO, Arnaldo. Población económicamente activa del Paraguay. RPS 3 no. 7 (1966) 30-42.

3136 O.I.T.-P.R.E.A.L.C. La situación y perspectiva del empleo en Paraguay 1973. A., Programa Regional del Empleo para América Latina y Caribe, 1973. 100p.

3136a SERVIN, Santiago. Semblanza de los obreros del norte paraguayo. B.A., Ed. Impulso, 1961. 174p.

3137 THULLEN, Peter. Estudio sobre el régimen de los salarios mínimos en el Paraguay. A., El Arte, 1952. 42p.

F. Trade and commerce

3137a ASOCIACION LATINOAMERICANA DE LIBRE COMERCIO. Importación de productos incluidos en el programa de liberación, Paraguay, 1962-1965. Montevideo, ALALC, 1965? 151p.

3138 BERTONI, Guillermo Tell. Estudio sobre el intercambio mercantil y sobre las demás vinculaciones económicas paraguayas-argentinas. San Lorenzo, Guarani, 1936. 16p. (Instituto de investigaciones y publicidad - Museo, archivo y biblioteca Bertoni, Boletín, no. 3)

3139 BRAZIL. EMBAIXADA (PARAGUAY). SETOR DE PROMOÇAO COMERCIAL. Como exportar para o Paraguai. Brasilia, Ministerio das Relaçoes Exteriores, Divisao de Informaçao Comercial, 1973. 49p.

3140 CALVET, A. Mission de M. Calvet dans l'Amérique du Sud. Rapport au Ministre du commerce, sur l'immigration européenne, le commerce et l'agriculture à la Plata Argentine, Paraguay, Uruguay, 1886-1888. Paris, Sceau Impr. Charaire et fils, 1889. 180p. & atlas of 25 pl.

3141 CENTRO DE ESTABLECIMIENTOS FORESTALES Y GANADEROS DEL PARAGUAY. La capitales argentinos en la república del Paraguay. B.A., Imp. G. Krieger, 1912. 12p.

3141a CENTRO INTERAMERICANO DE PROMOCION DE EXPORTACIONES. Perfiles de la oferta exportable de maderas de Bolivia, Brasil, Chile y Paraguay. Bogota, CIPE, 1970? 157p.

3142 CORPORACION Paraguaya de alcoholes. A., Tall. gráf. de Zamphirópolos, 1944. 99p.

3143 DEMERSAY, A. De l'avenir des relations commerciales entre la France et le Paraguay. JE 1 ser., 37 (1853) 382-89; 2 ser., 8 (1855) 251-61.

3144 The DIPLOMATIST. Survey on Paraguay and its links with Great Britain. London, Diplomatist Publications, 1963. 34p.

3145 FADLALA, Emilio; DUERST, Elwin A. Tendencias de las exportaciones durante los últimos 14 años (1938-1951). A., 1951. 50p.

3146 The FATE of Paraguay. FM 81 (1870) 166-84.

3147 FISHER, Frederic. Recomendaciones y sugerencias sobre el problema del trigo en el Paraguay. A., STICA, 1953. 45p.

3148 GONZALEZ ERICO, Miguel Angel. Estructura y desarrollo del comercio exterior del Paraguay: 1870-1918. RPS 12 no. 34 (1975) 125-55.

3149 GRUPO ASESOR DE PLANIFICACION EN EL PARAGUAY. Síntesis del estudio sobre evolución histórica y perspectivas del comercio exterior. A., 1965. 119p.

3150 MISION ESPAÑOLA DE HOMBRES DE NEGOCIOS A BRASIL Y PARAGUAY. Memoria. Madrid, Departamento de Comisiones Mixtas y Misiones Comerciales, 1967. 300p.

3151 PAN AMERICAN UNION. Foreign trade of Paraguay for 1940 and 1941. Washington, 1942. 8p.

3152 PARAGUAY. ASESORIA TECNICA ADUANERA. Estadísticas del comercio de importación de la república del Paraguay durante años especificadas entre 1926 y 1940. Import trade statistics of the republic of Paraguay for selected years between 1926 and 1940. Washington, 1942. 4 vols.

3153 PARAGUAY. DIRECCION GENERAL DE ESTADISTICA. Comercio exterior del Paraguay. Años 1921-1927. Estadística retrospectiva de 1879 a 1927. A., Imp. nac., 1928. 32p.

3154 PARAGUAY. LAWS, STATUTES, ETC. Tarifa de avalúos y leyes para las aduanas de la república del Paraguay para 1890. A., Imp. de "El Paraguayo", 1889. 206p.

3155 PARAGUAY. LAWS, STATUTES, ETC. Tarifa de avalúos de importación y exportación para las aduanas de la república del Paraguay, 1906. A., Tall. nac. de H. Kraus, 1906. 181p.

3156 PARAGUAY. LAWS, STATUTES, ETC. Tarifa de avalúos de exportación para las aduanas de la república del Paraguay, 1909. A., Tall. nac. de H. Kraus, 1909. 11p.
Also: A., Tall. gráf. del estado, 1913. 10p.

3157 PARAGUAY. SECRETARIA TECNICA DE PLANIFICACION. Evolución histórica y perspectivas del comercio exterior paraguayos. A., 1965. 119p.

3158 PASTOR, F.S.; YUBERO, L.B. El comercio paraguayo. A., 1899. 120p.

3159 PERU. República del Peru. Bolivia. República de Bolivia. Paraguay. República del Paraguay; Külkereskedelmi utmutato. Budapest, Közgazdaségi és fogi Kk., 1957. 154p.

3160 SANABRIA, Julio. Paraguay, a country open to trade and investment. A., 1968? 57p.

3160a SANABRIA, Julio. Paraguay país abierto para el comercio y las inversiones. A., 1969. 58p.

3161 UNITED STATES. DEPARTMENT OF COMMERCE. Paraguay: a commercial handbook, by W.L. Schurz. Washington, Government Printing Office, 1920. 195p.

3162 UNITED STATES. DEPARTMENT OF STATE. Trade agreements with Paraguay, signed at Asunción, September 12, 1946.

Analysis of general provisions and reciprocal benefits. A., 1946. 31p.

3163 UNITED STATES. TARIFF COMMISSION. The foreign trade of Latin America. Part II. Commercial policies and trade relations of individual Latin American countries. Section 7. Paraguay. Washington, 1940. 44p.

3164 WOOD, Bryce. The Department of State and the non-national interest: the cases of Argentine meat and Paraguayan tea. IAEA 15 (1961) no. 2, 3-32.

G. Transport and communications

3165 BEJARANO, Ramón César. Vías y medios de comunicaciones del Paraguay, 1811-1961. A., Edit. Toledo, 1963. 262p.

3166 BENITEZ, Justo Pastor. Mensaje de un Paraguay. *In* no. 1903, p. 94-101.
On radio.

3167 BOSE, Walter B.L. Las orígenes del correo en el Paraguay, 1769-1811. AHA (1939) 143-70; (1940) 695-98.

3168 CARDONA, Miguel. La marina mercante paraguaya. BNAP 2 no. 13 (1946) 43-61.

3169 ESTRADA DE FERRO INTERNACIONAL BRASIL-PARAGUAY. Memorial de "Estrada de Ferro Internacional Brasil-Paraguay". Rio de Janeiro, "America Editora" P.A. Rodas, 1914. 90p.

3170 FLECHA, Agustín Oscar. La ruta Trans-Chaco como factor de integración en el proceso de desarrollo económico y social. EPA 5 (1966) 7-19.

3171 HEISECKE, Christian; BERTHET, Justin. Informe de los señores Heisecke y Berthet á la Comisión de hacienda del honorable Senado, 31 de agosto de 1893. A., Tall. nac. de H. Kraus, 1896. 12p.
On the Paraguay Central Railway Company.

3172 INAUGURACION del Puente Internacional sobre el Río Paraná. A., 1961. 79p.

3173 LIBRE navegación: el Acta de Buenos Aires y el Acta adicional de Asunción; su ejecución. A., Ministerio de Relaciones Exteriores, 1965. 68p.

3173a LONG, W.R. Railways of South America, pt. 2, Bolivia, Colombia, Ecuador, the Guianas, Paraguay, Peru, Uruguay, and Venezuela. Washington, USGPO, 1927. xii, 420p.

3174 MARINA mercante nacional; consideraciones sobre su organización. Recopilación de trabajos, por José Bozzano (h.) and others. A., Imp. Naval, 1947. 1 vol. (various pagings)

3175 MONTORFANO, Victor. La radio y el estado; por una transmisora oficial de onda corte y larga. A., Imp. nac., 1943. 141p.

3176 ORTEGA, Néstor F. El trafico fluvial entre Buenos Aires y Paraguay a fines del siglo XVIII. TC 1949, 129-41.

3177 (PARADIZ, Antonio). Empresa de navegación del alto Paraguay y esplotación de la vía carretera abierta al interior de Bolivia en virtud de las concesiones otergadas por el gobierno de aquella república al empresario coronel d. Antonio Paradiz. Organización definitiva de la asociación llamada a fomentar los intereses comerciales del alto Perú y los estados del Río de la Plata. B.A., Imp. de "La Union argentina", 1875. 38p.

3178 PARAGUAY. Contrato ad-referendum; mensaje del gobierno y proyecto de ley sobre pago del servicio de la deuda externa y garantía del Ferrocarril en títulos de deuda pública. 20 de setiembre de 1892. A., Tall. nac. de H. Kraus, 1896. 10p.

3179 PARAGUAY. Mensaje del gobierno y bases de arreglo de la garantía del Ferro-carril, 17 de junio de 1896. A., Tall. nac. de H. Kraus, 1896. 9p.

3180 PARAGUAY. Mensaje del gobierno y proyectos de ley relativos al arreglo de la garantía del Ferro-carril central. 24 de mayo de 1893. A., Tall. nac. de H. Kraus, 1896. 15p.

3181 PARAGUAY. Protocolo de venta del Ferro-carril nacional á favor de la sociedad anónima the Paraguay central railway company, limited. 12 de junio de 1889. A., Tall. nac. de H. Kraus, 1896. 17p.

3182 PARAGUAY. ADMINISTRACION NACIONAL DE TELECOMUNICACIONES. Normas técnicas para el servicio de televisión. A?, n.d. 9p.

3183 PARAGUAY. CONGRESO NACIONAL. La cuestión ferrocarrilera en el Congreso nacional. A., Tall. nac. de H. Kraus, 1907. 682p.

3184 PARAGUAY. DIRECCION GENERAL DE CORREOS Y TELECOMUNICACIONES. Convención telegráfica entre la Dirección general de correos y telégrafos y la Empresa del ferrocarril central del Paraguay. A., Imp. de la Dirección general de correos y telégrafos, 1905. 8p.

3185 PARAGUAY. INTERVENTOR DE FERROCARRILES. Informe del Interventor de ferro-carriles, don Esteban Rojas, sobre las cuentas de garantía del Ferro-carril central del Paraguay. 16 de enero de 1895. A., Tall. nac. de H. Kraus, 1896. 8p.

3186 PARAGUAY. SUBSECRETARIA DE INFORMACIONES Y CULTURA. Ruta III: síntesis de su importancia económica. A., Imp. nac., 1958. 14p.

3187 PARAGUAY. SECRETARIA TECNICA DE PLANIFICACION. Síntesis del estudio sobre el transporte en el Paraguay. A., 1964. 20p.

3188 PARAGUAY CENTRAL RAILWAY COMPANY, LIMITED. Contestación del señor director gerente del Ferro-carril al Informe del señor interventor don Esteban Rojas. 18 de julio de 1896. A., Tall. nac. de H. Kraus, 1896. 16p.

3189 PARAGUAY CENTRAL RAILWAY COMPANY, LIMITED. Protesta del señor director gerente del Ferro-carril, 12 de enero de 1894. A., Tall. nac. de H. Kraus, 1896. 9p.

3190 PARAGUAY CENTRAL RAILWAY COMPANY, LIMITED. Offer of £200,000 6 per cent prior lien debenture stock. London, 1909? 3p.

3191 PARAGUAY CENTRAL RAILWAY COMPANY, LIMITED. Réplica del director gerente de la Empresa del ferro-carril al Informe de los señores Heisecke y Berthet, 26 de setiembre de 1893. A., Tall. nac. de H. Kraus, 1896. 16p.

3192 PARAGUAY CENTRAL RAILWAY COMPANY, LIMITED. Report of proceedings at meetings of prior lien debenture stock holders and 6 per cent. three-year old note holders held at Winchester House, Old Broad Street, London, E.C., on Friday, July 20th, 1917. B.H. Binder esq., F.C.A., receiver and manager, in the chair. London, 1917. 20p.

3193 RAMIREZ, Juan Isidro. El estado y el ferro-carril nacional; sus cuestiones ante el derecho, conferencia leida en el Instituto Paraguayo el 1º de setiembre de 1905. A., Tip. y enc. "El País", 1905. 36p.

3194 SAMANIEGO, Marcial. El plan quinquenal de los transportes nacionales como factor determinante en el proceso de desarrollo socio-económico de nuestro país. A., Ministerio de Obras Públicas y Comunicaciones, 1970. 13p.

3195 SEPULVEDA WHITTLE, Tomás. Transporte y comercio exterior del Paraguay. B.A., Banco Americano de Desarrollo; Instituto para la Integración de América Latina, Asociación Latinoamericana de Libre Comercio, 1967. 85p.

3196 STEWART, William. Contestación al folleto del señor don H.L. White, por el Dr. Stewart. Asuntos del Paraguay central railway co. ltd. A., Imp. de La Democracia, 1893? 31p.

3197 UNITED NATIONS. Estudio integrale del transporte: informe final (Paraguay transport survey, final report). Paris; Rio de Janeiro, BOEOM-ENECOM, 1973. 4 vols.

3198 WARREN, Harris Gaylord. The Paraguay Central Railway, 1856-1889. IAEA 20 (1967) no. 4, 3-22.

3199 WARREN, Harris Gaylord. The Paraguay Central Railway, 1888-1907. IAEA 21 (1967) no. 1, 31-48.

VII. SOCIOLOGY AND SOCIAL ADMINISTRATION

A. General studies

3200 ANGEL PANGRAZIO, Miguel. Indicadores de la estructura social del Paraguay. A., 1973. 370p.

3201 ASPECTOS generales de la situación social del Paraguay: población, educación, salud y vivienda. RPS 5 no. 12 (1968) 109-28.

3201a BAADE, Perla. La vivienda en el Paraguay: situación y perspectivas. A., Centro Paraguayo de Estudios Sociológicos, Sociedad Interamericana de Planificación, 1976. 49p.

3202 BAREIRO SAGUIER, Ruben. Le Paraguay, nation de métis. RPP 18 (1963) no. 4, 442-63.

3203 CAMPO, Luis del. Cositas del Paraguay. B.A., Edit. Impacto, 1963. 54p.

3204 CENTRO PARAGUAYO DE ESTUDIOS SOCIALES. Programa 1972-1973. A., CPES, 1972. 121p.

3205 CENTURION MORINIGO, Ubaldo. Juventud, patria y justicia social. A., Artes Gráf. Zamphirópolos, 1970. 51p.

3206 CONFERENCIA EPISCOPAL PARAGUAYA. El problema social paraguayo. Pastoral colectiva del Episcopado Paraguayo. A., Secretariado Permanente de la CEP, 1963. 31p.

3206a DURAN, Margarita. Historia de los pobres del Paraguay. A., El Gráfico, 1972. 89p. (Colección Oñondivepa, 2)

3207 FOGEL, Gerardo. Estudio del departamento de Itapúa; proyectos prioritarios de promoción socio-económico de la Zona de Encarnación. A., Instituto de Desarrollo Integral y Armonico, 1970. 67p.

3208 FOGEL, Gerardo. Programa integrado urbano-rural de desarrollo de la comunidad en Encarnación, Itapúa (Paraguay). RPS 6 no. 14 (1969) 5-69.

3208a FRETES VENTRE, Daniel. Evolución y perspectivas de la estructura social y economica del Paraguay. EP 3 (1975) no. 1, 87-113; no. 2, 45-137.

3209 INSTITUTO DE DESARROLLO INTEGRAL Y ARMONICO. Estudio del departamento Kaáguasú. A., 1972. 132p.

3210 LEDERMAN, Esteban; SILVERO, Arnaldo. La planificación de los recursos humanos en el Paraguay. RPS 5 no. 12 (1968) 53-108.

3211 MENDOZA A., Raúl. Desarrollo y evolución de la población Paraguaya. RPS 5 no. 12 (1968) 5-16.

3211a PANGRAZIO, Miguel Angel. Indicadores de la estructura social del Paraguay. A., Tall. Gráf. de Edit. La Voz, 1973. 370p.

3212 PARAGUAY. CONSEJO NACIONAL DE PROGRESO SOCIAL. Programa integrado de desarrollo rural: zona del Paraná 1974-1979. A., CNPS, 1973. 200p.

3213 La POBLACION paraguaya. RPS 5 no. 12 (1968) 5-140.

3214 RIVAROLA, Domingo M. Bases preliminares para el estudio de la movilidad social en el Paraguay. RPS 1 no. 1 (1964) 9-29.

3215 RIVAROLA, Domingo M.; HEISECKE, Guillermo. Población, urbanización y recursos humanos en el Paraguay. A., Centro Paraguayo de Estudios Sociológicos, 1969. 215p.
2. ed. 1970. 263p.
An important collection of essays.

3215a RIVAROLA, Domingo M.; MORINIGO, José M. La vivienda en el Paraguay: sus condicionantes socio-económicos. A., Centro Paraguayo de Estudios Sociológicos, Sociedad Interamericana de Planificación, 1976. 86p.

3216 SAMANIEGO, Roque. Progresar o perecer. A., Ariel, 1919. 35p.

3217 SANCHEZ QUELL, Hipolito. Datos para un esbozo de sociología paraguaya. RPS 3 no. 6 (1966) 68-76.

3218 SIMPSON, James R. Población, carne y bienestar económico en el Paraguay dentro de los proximos 50 años. RPS 11 no. 31 (1974) 65-78.

3219 UNIVERSIDAD CATOLICA DE ASUNCION. CONSEJO DE PLANIFICACION. Los recursos humanos y el desarrollo nacional. A., 1973. 58p. (Informe preliminar de discusión, 4)

B. The family

3220 BANCO CENTRAL DEL PARAGUAY. Encuesta sobre presupuestos familiares; manual de instrucciones para la crítica y codificación. A., 1963. 45p.

3220a CASTAGNINO, Darío. La mujer en el contexto socioeconómico y jurídico del Paraguay, Darío Castagnino, colabaran Juan Andrés Cardozo and others. A., Centro Paraguayo de Estudios de Población, 197? 152p.

3220b CENTRO PARAGUAYO DE ESTUDIOS DE POBLACION. Perfil estadístico de la mujer paraguaya. A., 1975. 28p.

3221 CENTRO PARAGUAYO DE ESTUDIOS DE POBLACION. Planificación familiar. A., 1971. 74p.

3222 CENTRO PARAGUAYO DE ESTUDIOS DE POBLACION. Población y planificación familiar en el Paraguay. A., 1971. 161p.
"Trabajos presentada el segundo Seminario Nacional de Planificación."

3223 CENTURION, Carlos R. La mujer paraguaya a través de la historia. A., Imp. Ariel, 1939. 13p.

3224 CERISOLA, M.I. Elsa. Fecunidad diferencial en la República del Paraguay según condición de ruralidad y nivel de instrucción de la mujer. RPS 5 no. 12 (1968) 34-52.

3225 CHAVES, Maria Concepción de. La condición social de la mujer guaraní. RGA 15 no. 89 (1941) 105-08.

3226 CONSEJO NACIONAL DE PROGRESO SOCIAL; UNICEF. Congreso nacional, infancia y juventud: documento final. A., 1971. 120p.

3227 DUARTE PRADO, Bacón. Función cultural y política de la juventud. A., Cultura, 1951. 55p.

3228 ESCARDO Y ANAYA, Víctor. Programa de UNICEF en el Paraguay. La colaboración de nuestro instituto. BIIAPI 24 (1950) no. 2, 149-56.

3228a GASLONDE, Santiago; CARRASCO, Enrique. Una encuesta modelo para evaluar la eficacia de los programas de planificación familiar: su aplicación a cinco ciudades de Paraguay. Santiago de Chile, Centro Latinoamericano de Demografía, 1973. v. 235p. (Publications. Serie A no. 119)

3229 HELMS, N.W. Matrilocality, social solidarity and culture contact: three case studies. SJA 26 (1970) no. 2, 197-212.

3230 IBARRA, Enrique, and others. Implicancias económicas y sociales del crecimiento poblacional paraguayo. A., Instituto de Desarrollo Integral y Armónico, 1971? 214p. (Serie desarrollo y demografia, 1)

3230a MICKELWAIT, Donald R.; RIEGELMAN, Mary Ann; SWEET, Charles F. Women in rural development: a survey of the roles of women in Ghana, Lesotho, Kenya, Nigeria, Bolivia, Paraguay and Peru. Boulder, Colo., Westview Press, 1976. xvii, 224p.

3231 MOVIMIENTO FAMILIAR CRISTIANO. Matrimonio y cambio social. A., 1972. 87p.

3232 NUÑEZ CARVALLO, Gabriel. La familia en el Paraguay; organización y función. BFDCS 26 (1962) no. 4, 161-75.

3232a PANE, Ignacio Alberto. Apuntes de sociología; Geografía social; La mujer guaraní. A., Instituto Colorado de Cultura, 1976. 361p.

3233 PARAGUAY. SECRETARIA TECNICA DE PLANIFICACION. Familia, infancia y juventud. Investigación de la secretaría de planificación. A., 1969. 58p.

3233a RIOS VELAZCO DE CALDI, Ramona Luisa. Diccionario de la mujer guaraní. A., Edit. Siglo Veintiuno, 1977. 327p.

3234 RIVAROLA, Domingo M. Apuntes para el estudio de la familia en el Paraguay. RPS 8 no. 21 (1971) 84-104.

3234a SANTOS CASTRO, Asunción. La escritora domada, crítica polémica. A., 1975. 146p.

3235 URBIETA ROJAS, Pastor. La mujer paraguaya; esquema historiográfico. Prólogo de Juan Boggino. Xilografías de Lotte Schulz. A., Colección Paraguay, 1962. 79p.

C. Urban sociology

3236 ASUNCION. INTENDENCIA MUNICIPAL. Plan de viviendas. A., 1961. 16p.

3237 ASUNCION. INTENDENCIA MUNICIPAL. Supermercados; planes, costo y mantenimiento. A., Edit. "El País", 1961. 11p.

3238 DOCUMENTO: programa integral de desarrollo de la comunidad del Barrio "Luis Alberto de Herrera". RPS 4 no. 10 (1967) 126-32.

3239 ESCOBAR, Julio César. Algunos indicadores del asentamiento en un sector del area metropolitana de Asunción. RPS 9 no. 25 (1972) 155-69.

3240 GAIGNARD, R. Les villes de sous-développement, le cas du Paraguay. RGPS 43 (1972) no. 4, 399-426.

3241 HICKS, Frederic; PICCHIONI, Egidio. Algunos aspectos de la industrialización en una comunidad paraguaya. SA 2 (1966) no. 1, 31-54.

3242 LALIBERTE, Marcos; PENTOCARRERO, Alfonso. Lineamientos generales del programa integral de desarrollo de la Comunidad del Barrio Luis Alberto de Herrera. A., 1967. 18p.

3243 MITCHELL, Glen H. Notas sobre hábitos de compra y consumo de comestibles en familias de clase trabajadora en Asunción. RPS 8 no. 22 (1971) 132-61.

3244 PARAGUAY. COMISION POPULAR ENCARGADA DE LOS FESTEJOS DEL DIA 17 DE DICIEMBRE DE 1910. "Fulgencio Yegros" en el 19 aniversario de su fundación; publicación iniciada por la Comisión popular encargada de los festejos del día 17 de diciembre de 1910. A., Imp. Grabow & Schauman, 1910. 36p.

3245 RATINOFF, Luís. La urbanización en América Latina: el caso Paraguay. RPS 2 no. 4 (1966) 17-42.

3246 RIVAROLA, Domingo M. La estratificación social en Asunción. RPS 3 no. 5 (1966) 23-38.

3247 SERVICE, Elman R.; SERVICE, Helen S. Tobatí, Paraguayan town. Chicago, 1954. 337p.

3248 TONESS, Odin. Migración a Yaguarón 1870-1909. A., 1971. 6p.

3249 TONESS, Odin. Tobatí: uno pueblo en el Paraguay. RPS 6 no. 14 (1969) 132-37.

3250 TONESS, Odin; TONESS, Catalina. Matrimonio en Yaguarón, costumbres y clases en la elección de esposo y esposas. A., 1971. 9p.

D. Rural sociology

3251 ACOSTA, César R. La población rural del Paraguay. *In* PAN AMERICAN UNION. SOCIAL SCIENCE SECTION. Materiales para el estudio de la clase media en la América Latina; ed. by Theo R. Crevenna. Washington, Unión Panamericana, 1950-51. Vol. 3 (1950), p. 93-108.

3253 BECKER, Wilhelmus L. Análisis social del primer proyecto piloto integral de desarrollo rural en el eje norte de colonización. RPS 6 no. 14 (1969) 70-101.

3253a BECKER, Wilhelmus L. Análisis socio-económico del Distrito de Atyrá. RPS 6 no. 16 (1969) 116-31.

3254 CODAS PAPALUCA, Alcides. Cuestiones rurales del Paraguay, ensayo (estudio sociológico). Santos, Sao Paulo, Instituto D. Escolastica Rosa, 1939. 309p.
2. ed. B.A., Ediciones Tupá, 1949. 157p. (Colección Amerindia)

3255 DOMINGUEZ, Ramiro. El valle y la loma; comunicación en comunidades rurales. A?, Edit. Emada, 1966. 142p. (Biblioteca del Centro de Estudios Antropológicos del Ateneo Paraguayo)
Also: SA 1 (1966) no. 2, 127-242.

3256 ESPINOLA, Julio César. Encuesta social de la Colonia "Pte Stroessner". A., 1967. 20p.

3257 FOGEL, G. El desarrollo regional y el cambio rural en el Paraguay. RPS 5 no. 11 (1968) 96-122.

3258 FOGEL, Ramón. Análisis de una pequeña comunidad rural: estudio de la Colonia Piraretá. RPS 4 no. 8 & 9 (1967) 5-39.

3259 FOGEL, Ramón. Determinantes negativos de la movilización en los sistemas sociales rurales del Paraguay. A., CPES, 1970. 22p.
Also: RPS 9 no. 24 (1972) 149-62.

3260 FOOD & AGRICULTURE ORGANIZATION. Estudio analítico sobre los servicios de extensión rural de Argentina, Ecuador y Paraguay. Rome, 1973. 137p.

3261 INTERNATIONAL LABOUR OFFICE. Development Programme: Technical Assistance Sector (Paraguay). R. 7. Informe al gobierno del Paraguay sobre una misión preliminar en el campo del desarrollo rural, con referencia particular a la capicitación campesina y a la organización cooperativa. Geneva, 1967. 49p. (OIT/TAP/Paraguay/R. 7)

3262 MANDELBURGER, Federico. La planificación social y el desarrollo del medio rural. RPS 5 no. 11 (1968) 86-90.

3263 ORTIZ, José Concepción. Aportes para una historia del campesino paraguayo. A., Tall. Gráf. de la Escuela Técnica Salesiana, 1968. 120p.

3264 PARAGUAY. CONSEJO NACIONAL DE PROGRESO SOCIAL. Programa integrado de desarrollo rural, eje norte de colonización 1972-1976. A., 1972. 84p.

3265 PARAGUAY. CONSEJO NACIONAL DE PROGRESO SOCIAL. Programa integrado de desarrollo rural, eje norte de colonización plan de acciones. 1974-1975. A., Oficina Nacional de Progreso Social, 1974. 132p.

3266 PARAGUAY. CONSEJO NACIONAL DE PROGRESO SOCIAL. Programa integrado de desarrollo rural, zona del Paraná, 1974-79. Tomo 1: Diagnóstico. A., 1973. 200p.

3267 PARAGUAY. DIVISION DE SANEAMIENTO AMBIENTAL. Programa nacional de saneamiento básico rural. A., 1958. 174p.

3268 PARAGUAY. MINISTERIO DE SALUD PUBLICA Y BIENESTAR SOCIAL. Paraguay. Area del programa integrado del desarrollo rural. Región del Alto Paraná. Año 1973. A., 1973. 42p.

3269 REY DE CASTRO, Carlos. La clase rural paraguaya; conferencia dada en el Instituto paraguayo el 28 de julio de 1902, aniversario de la independencia del Perú. Con un prólogo del dr. Manuel Dominguez. A., Tall. nac. de H. Kraus, 1903. ix, 64p.

3269a REY DE CASTRO, Carlos. Las clases rurales en el Paraguay. B.A., Edit. Tupa, 1947. 60p. (Opúsculos febreristas, 2)

3270 RIVAROLA, Domingo M.; SUSNIK, Branislava. La movilidad social y el medio agrario paraguayo. A., El Arte, 1964. 74p.

3271 La SOCIEDAD rural en el Paraguay. RPS 4 no. 11 (1968) 75-134.

E. Social administration

3272 INTERNATIONAL LABOUR OFFICE. Informe al Gobierno del Paraguay sobre la situación financiera del Instituto de Previsión Social. Geneva, 1965. ii, 54, 13p.

3273 MONOGRAFIAS nacionales de seguridad social: Paraguay. SS 12 no. 24 (1963) 87-91.

3274 ODRIOSOLA, Ricardo. El niño y la seguridad social. RISS 5 no. 4 (1956) 1005-14.

3275 PARAGUAY. Dispensarios médicos ambulantes e higiene municipal rural. A., Tall. gráf. del estado, 1917. 32p.

3276 PARAGUAY. DELEGACION A LA CONFERENCIA SANITARIA INTERNACIONAL DE LAS REPUBLICAS AMERICANAS. 5th, SANTIAGO DE CHILE, 1911. Higiene internacional. Las conferencias sanitarias internacionales de las repúblicas americanas; informe presentado al gobierno de la república del Paraguay, por el doctor R. Urízar, delegado oficial a la V Conferencia Sanitaria internacional de las repúblicas americanas, celebrada en Santiago de Chile, del 5 al 12 de noviembre de 1911. A., Tall. gráf. del estado, 1912. 464, vi p.

3277 PARAGUAY. DEPARTAMENTO DE EDUCACION SANITARIA. Diversas nociones de medicina general del programa de conferencias y audiciones radiales del Departamento de Educación Sanitaria. A., Tall. gráf. de la Edit. El País, 1943. 64p.

3278 PARAGUAY. DEPARTAMENTO NACIONAL DE HIGIENE Y ASISTENCIA PUBLICA. Reglamentación del ejercicio de la farmacia y petitorio. A., Imp. de F. Jordán, 1908. 39p.

3279 PARAGUAY. INSTITUTO DE PREVISION SOCIAL. Homenaje al Dr. Emilio Cubas en el XIX aniversario de la fundación del Instituto de Previsión Social, con motivo de sus 19 años de servicios en la Institución. A., 1962. 49p. (Folleto, 25)

3280 PARAGUAY. INSTITUTO DE PREVISION SOCIAL. IPS: 19 años, 1943-1962. A., 1962. 20p. (Folleto, 23)

3281 PARAGUAY. INSTITUTO DE PREVISION SOCIAL. Instituto de Previsión Social: XXI aniversario. A., 1964. 37p. (Folleto, 26)

3282 PARAGUAY. MINISTERIO DE SALUD PUBLICA Y BIENESTAR SOCIAL. Plan de desarrollo de los servicios sanitario-asistenciales del Ministerio del Salud Pública y Bienestar Social y de regionalización sanitaria de la República. A., 1957. 128p.

3283 PARAGUAY. SERVICIO NACIONAL DE ERRADICACION DEL PALUDISMO. Manual del rociador. A., 1966. 29p.

3284 PARAGUAY. SERVICIO NACIONAL DE ERRADICACION DEL PALUDISMO. Plan de erradicación del paludismo. A., 1964. 2 vols.

3285 PARAGUAY. SERVICIO NACIONAL DE ERRADICACION DEL PALUDISMO. Manual del rociador geográfico. A., 1966. 1 vol. (various pagings)

3286 PECCI, J.M. Los seguros españoles de enfermedad y accidentes del trabajo y la seguridad social en el Paraguay. Madrid, Instituto Cultura Hispanica, 1954. 132p.

3287 SEGURO social de Paraguay. SS 2 no. 7 (1953) 128-51.

3288 Los SEGUROS sociales en el Paraguay. RISS 10 (1961) no. 2, 283-324.

VIII. GOVERNMENT AND POLITICS

A. General studies

3289 ALDEN, Joseph. La ciencia de gobierno en relación con las instituciones americanas, por José Alden, traducida del inglés al español, por José Segundo Decoud, con apéndices que contienen la Constitución de la república del Paraguay, la ley de jurados, los reglamentos internos de ambas cámaras, etc. A., Imp. de "La Reforma", 1887. 117p.

3290 ALONSO CRIADO, Matías. La penitenciaría de Asunción. Informe sobre sistemas carcelarios, presentado al Sr. D. Eduardo Fleytas, Ministro del Interior en el Paraguay. Montevideo, Imp. Latina, 1904. 14p.

3291 AYALA, Manuel. La elección presidencial. A., Imp. Ariel, 1921. 31p.

3292 BAEZ, Cecilio. Ensayo sobre la libertad civil. A., Imp. de La Democracia, 1893. 65p.

3293 BENITEZ, Justo Pastor; SERAFINI, Rodolfo. Labor parliamentaria: cinco años de acción en la Cámara de Diputados, 1968-1972. A., 1972. 325p.

3294 BENITEZ, Justo Pastor. Sentido y alcance de la constitución de Estigarribia & Post-Escriptum. *In* no. 1903, 36-56, 57-72.

3295 BORDON, J. Rodolfo. La penetración imperialista y la cuestión social en el Paraguay. B.A., 1932. 38p.

3296 BRUNINI, José. Urugvai i Paragvai. Moscow, TSK MOPR SSSR, 1930. 32p.

3297 BURGOS, Abelardo. El policía, la policía y las relaciones públicas. A., 1971. 221p.

3297a CACERES DE THOMAS, Carmen. Domingo Robledo, narración biográfica de su vida y sus obras. A., Artes Gráficas Zamphirópolos, 1973. 74p.

3298 CARDUS HUERTA, Gualberto. Discurso político. A., 1922. 40p.

3299 CHAVES, Federico. Discurso pronunciado en la concentración civica pro-reelección presidencial, realizada en el estudio "Comuneros" el 12 de febrero de 1953. A., 1953. 10p.

3299a CHIRIFE, Alberto César. El lenguaje en la función pública. A., El País, 1959. 104p.
2. ed. 1960.

3299b CUBILLA, Oscar Zacarías. Estrategia politica: estudio introductorio. A., 1975. 253p.

3300 DECOUD, Héctor Francisco. La Convención nacional constituyente y la carta magna de la república. B.A., Tall. gráf. argentinos L.J. Rosso, 1934. 406p.

3301 DOMINGUEZ, Manuel. La Constitución del Paraguay: conferencias leídas en la clase de derecho constitucional. A., H. Kraus, 1909. 174p.

3301a DOMINGUEZ, Manuel. No se matan a puñaladas las ideas. *In* no. 203, 107-12.

3302 ESTECHE FANEGO, Juan; JACQUET, J. Eugenio. Manual electoral; compaginación de la ley no. 600, comentarios y recomendaciones sobre su mejor aplicación. A., 1972. v, 36, 17p.

3303 FERREIRA GUBETICH, Hugo. Educación cívica y moral. 3er año, de acuerdo a los programas vigentes. A., La Colmena, 1960. 106p.

3303a GONZALEZ, Juan Natalicio. El estado servidor del hombre. Mexico, Edit. Guarania, 1960. 326p.

3304 GONZALEZ, Juan Natalicio. El paraguay y la lucha por su expresión. A., Edit. Guarania, 1945. 94p.

3305 GROSS-BROWN, Sigfrido V. First principles and the Paraguayan constitution. RPOL 6 (1944) 94-102.

3306 GVOZDAREV, Boris Ivanovich; KROPOTOV, Viktor Anatolievich. Gosudarstvennyi stroi Paragvaia. Moscow, Gos. izd-vo yurid. lit-ry, 1962. 76p.

3307 LOTT, Leo B. Paraguay. *In* NEEDLER, Martin C. Political systems of Latin America. Princeton, N.J., Van Nostrand, 1964. p. 381-401.
2. ed. N.Y., Van Nostrand Reinhold, 1970. p. 428-51.

3308 INSTRUCCION sobre los obligaciones más principales de un verdadero ciudadano reimpresa en la Asunción del Paraguay. A., Imp. nac., 1863. 73p.

3309 MAHN, Liliana B. Algunos aspectos de la evolución política en el Paraguay. A., Centro Paraguayo de Estudios Sociológicos, 1970. 48p.

3310 NICHOLS, Byron A. La cultura política del Paraguay. RPS 8 no. 20 (1971) 133-58.

3311 NICHOLS, Byron A. Las espectativas de los partidos políticos en el Paraguay. RPS 5 no. 13 (1968) 22-61.

3312 OLMEDO JIMENEZ, María Elina; RAMIREZ RUSSO, Manfredo; CESPEDEZ C., Aníbal A. Nociones generales de educación cívica. 4 curso bachillerato, normal y comercio. 3. ed. A., El Arte, 1961. 165p.

3313 OLMEDO JIMENEZ, María Elina; RAMIREZ RUSSO, Manfredo. Nociones fundamentales de organización social. 3. curso ciclo básico, bachillerato, comercio y normal. 4. ed. corr. y actualizada. A., El Arte, 1961. 212p.

3314 PARAGUAY. DIRECCION GENERAL DE ESTADISTICA. Censo electoral. Elecciones ordinarias de senadores y diputados verificadas el 4 de marzo de 1917. A., Tall. gráf. del estado, 1917. 44p.

3315 PARAGUAY. DIRECCION GENERAL DE PRESUPUESTO. Anexo del personal de la administración central, ejercico fiscal, 1971. A., Imp. nac., 1971. 263p.

3316 PARAGUAY. LAWS, STATUTES, ETC. Obligaciones generales de los sargentos, cabos y guardias civiles. A., Tall. nac. de H. Kraus, 1898. 14p.

3317 SALVINI, G. Situazione política e religiosa in Paraguay. AS 23 no. 12 (1972) 727-38.

3318 SANABRIA, Salustiano. Organización política del Paraguay. A., Imp. López, 1946. 163p.

3319 SANCHEZ, Ranulfo. Constitución de la República del Paraguay; su exegesis. Algunas leyes que le reglamentan. n.p., 195-? 109p.

3320 STEFANICH, Juan. Nacionalismo. A., 1929. 19p.

3321 UNIVERSIDAD NACIONAL, ASUNCION. ESCUELA PARAGUAYA DE ADMINISTRACION PUBLICA. Manual del gobierno paraguayo. A., 1963. vii, 95p.
2. ed. 1965. vii, 90p.

3322 25 de noviembre en Arroyos y Esteros, 1870-1889. A., Imp. de "La Razón", 1889. 43p.

3323 YNSFRAN, Edgar Linneo. Segundo Congreso de delegados de gobierno. A., Ministerio del Interior, 1963. 85p.

B. Official documents

3324 18 años de progreso nacional con el presidente Stroessner. Colaboración del Ministerio de Hacienda. A., 1972. 164p.
Texts of national constitution and statutes of the Partido Colorado.

3325 MARIN IGLESIAS, Alejandro. Comisión redactora del anteproyecto de constitución nacional: discurso del Ministro de Gobierno y Trabajo. A., Imp. nac., 1940. 8p.

3326 MARIN IGLESIAS, Alejandro. El Ministro de Gobierno y Trabajo expone los fundamentos para un nuevo régimen municipal. A., Imp. nac., 1940. 7p.

3327 PARAGUAY. COMISION DE REFORMA CONSTITUCIONAL. Bases de un ordenamiento constitucional para la República del Paraguay: anteproyecto elevado por la Comisión de Reforma Constitucional a la Junta Ejecutiva Nacional del Partido Demócrata Cristiano. A., Edit. El Gráf, 1967. 34p.

3328 PARAGUAY. CONGRESO NACIONAL. Actas de las sesiones de los Congresos de la República, desde el año 1811 hasta la terminación de la guerra. A., Tip. del Congreso, 1908. 65p.

3329 PARAGUAY. CONGRESO NACIONAL. Diario de sesiones del Congreso. Versión taquigráfica (período extraordinario - octubre 1938 - febrero 1939). A., Imp. nac., 1939. 475p.

3330 PARAGUAY. CONGRESO NACIONAL. CAMARA DE DIPUTADOS. Reglamento interno de la honorable Cámara de diputados de la república del Paraguay. A., Imp. de "El Pueblo", 1871. 19p.
2. ed. A., Tip. del Congreso, 1897. 26p.

3331 PARAGUAY. CONGRESO NACIONAL. CAMARA DE DIPUTADOS. Reglamento interno de la Cámara de diputados y constitución de la república del Paraguay. A., Tip. "La Union", 1906. 111p.

3332 PARAGUAY. CONGRESO NACIONAL. CAMARA DE DIPUTADOS. Reglamento interno de la H. Cámara de representantes. A., Imp. nac., 1949. 36p.

3333 PARAGUAY. CONGRESO NACIONAL. SENADO. Reglamento de la Cámara de senadores de la república del Paraguay. A., Tip. y encuadernación de "La República", 1891. 30p.
2. ed. A., Tip. del Congreso, 1905. 28p.

3334 PARAGUAY. CONGRESO NACIONAL. SENADO. Reglamento de la Cámara de senadores y constitución de la República del Paraguay. A., Tall. Gráf. del Estado, 1917. 61p.
Also: A., Imp. nac., 1926. 97p.

3335 PARAGUAY. CONSTITUTION. Ante-proyecto de reformas de la constitución, por el doctor Luis de Gásperi. Precedido del parecer del doctor Cecilio Báez. A., Imp. nac., 1931. 62p.

3336 PARAGUAY. CONSTITUTION. Constitución de la República del Paraguay y sus antecedentes; constituciones de 1844, 1870 y 1940. Proyectos de Constitución de los partidos políticos. Proyecto de la Comisión redactora de la Convención Nacional Constituyente. Ed. por Juan Carlos Mendonça. A., EMASA, 1967. 409p. (Colección cultura paraguaya)

3337 PARAGUAY. CONSTITUTION. Las Constituciones paraguayas y los Proyectos de Constitución de los partidos políticos. Edición corregida por Juan Carlos Mendonça. A., EMASA, 1967. 316p. (Colección cultura paraguaya)

3338 PARAGUAY. CONSTITUTION. Constitución de la república del Paraguay sancionada por la honorable Convención constituyente en sesión de 18 de noviembre de 1870. A., Imp. de "La Voz del pueblo", 1871. 27p.
Also: B.A., Imp. de "La Unión", 1872. 32p.
A., Tip. de "El Paraguayo", 1890. 28p.
A., Tall. "Espana", 1916. 47p.
A., Tall. Gráf. "La Colmena", 1917. 39p.
A., Imp. nac., 1925. 37p.
A., 1928. 38p.
A., La Colmena, 1934. 30p.

3339 PARAGUAY. CONSTITUTION. Constitución de la república del Paraguay y Ley n. 1357. A., Imp. nac., 1934. 35p.

3340 PARAGUAY. CONSTITUTION. Constitución de la república del Paraguay. A., Imp. nac., 1940. 39p.

Also: A., Imp. nac., 1953. 23p.
A., Imp. nac., 1957. 14p.
A., Imp. nac., 1960. 20p.

3341 PARAGUAY. CONSTITUTION. Constitution of the Republic of Paraguay, 1940. Washington, Pan American Union, 1963. iii, 12p.

3342 PARAGUAY. CONSTITUTION. Constitución de la República del Paraguay; su exégesis, algunas leyes que la reglamentan. Ed. augmentada y mejorada. A., 1964. 127p.

3343 PARAGUAY. CONSTITUTION. La nueva Constitución de la República. Sancionada por la Convención Nacional Constituyente de 1967 y promulgada por el Poder Ejecutivo de la Nación el 25 de agosto de 1967. A., Sub-Secretaria de Informaciones y Cultura de la Presidencia de la República, 1967. 48p.

3343a PARAGUAY. CONSTITUTION. Constitución de la República del Paraguay: sancionada por la Comisión Nacional Constituyente el 25 de Agosto de 1967 y promulgada por el Poder Ejecutivo en la misma fecha. A., 1977. 51p.

3344 PARAGUAY. CONSTITUTION. Constitution of the Republic of Paraguay, 1967. Approved by the National Constituent Convention on August 25, 1967, and promulgated by the executive power on the same date. Washington, Pan American Union, 1969. ii, 33p.

3345 PARAGUAY. CONVENCION NACIONAL CONSTITUYENTE, 1870. Actas de la Convención Nacional Constituyente del año 1870. A., Tip. del Congreso, 1897. 158p.

3346 PARAGUAY. CONVENCION NACIONAL CONSTITUYENTE, 1967. Convención Nacional Constituyente; diario de sesiones, 23 de mayo al 25 de agosto de 1967. A., Imp. nac., 1973-74. 2 vols.

3347 PARAGUAY. DECLARACION DE LA INDEPENDENCIA. Acta de independencia de la república del Paraguay. A., 184? 4p.

3348 PARAGUAY. DECLARACION DE LA INDEPENDENCIA. Acta de independencia y Constitución de la república del Paraguay. A., Tall. nac. de H. Kraus, 1896. 39p.

3349 PARAGUAY. MINISTERIO DE RELACIONES EXTERIORES. SECCION BIBLIOTECA, ARCHIVO Y EXPEDICION. Lista de ministros de relaciones exteriores del Paraguay desde la época de su independencia. Confeccionada por la Sección Biblioteca, Archivo y expedición del Ministerio de relaciones exteriores, bajo la dirección del sr. Abdón P. Alvarez. A., Imp. nac., 1943. 8p.

3350 PARAGUAY. MINISTERIO DE RELACIONES EXTERIORES. Proyecto de reglamento que establece al ceremonial diplomático de la república del Paraguay. (Cabinete del ministro). A., Tall. gráf. del estado, 1912. 40p.

3351 PARTIDO COLORADO. Proyecto de Constitución nacional para la República del Paraguay, elaborado y aprobado por la honorable Junta de Gobierno del Partido Colorado, y que será presentado a la Convención Nacional Constituyente. A., 1967. 24p.

C. Political parties

1. *General studies*

3352 CORVALAN, Grazziella. Ideologias y origen social de los grupos políticos en el Paraguay. RPS 9 no. 23 (1972) 106-18.

3353 GOMEZ FLEYTAS, José Gaspar. Ubicación histórica de los partidos tradicionales en el Paraguay. RPS 7 no. 19 (1970) 144-64.

3354 HICKS, Frederick. Interpersonal relationships and "caudillismo" in Paraguay. JIAS 13 (1971) no. 1, 89-111.

3355 ORTIZ MOLINA, Pedro. Clarinada de alerta; conferencia auspiciada por el Centro Anti-Comunista "General Rogelio R. Benitez", Asunción, Paraguay, 22 de junio de 1962. A., Ministerio de Defensa Nacional, 1962. 12p.

2. *Partido Colorado*

3356 ALBERTO, Carlos. El coloradismo paraguayo, su unidad ideológica y moral. A., 1951. 193p.

3357 ALMEIDA ROJAS, Ricardo. Guía de la Asociación Nacional Republicana. A., 1951. 272p.
2. ed. A., 1951. 272p.

3357a ARGAÑA, Luis María. Perfiles políticos; perfiles doctrinarios e ideologicos de los partidos y de los movimientos políticos en el Paraguay. A., Departamento de Prensa e Información de la Junta de Gobierno del Partido Colorado, 1977. 234p.

3358 ASOCIACION NACIONAL REPUBLICANA. Acta de Fundación del Partido Colorado. Estatutos, declaraciones de principios y programa. A., 1947. 24p.

3359 ASOCIACION NACIONAL REPUBLICANA. Estatutos y programa (abropado por la convención del 2 de marzo de 1938). A., Imp. Patria, 1938. 17p.

3360 ASOCIACION NACIONAL REPUBLICANA. Memoria de la junta de gobierno. A., 1963. 29p.

3361 DUARTE PRADO, Bacón. Fundamente doctrinarios del coloradismo. A., El Arte, 1959. 214p.

3362 FRUTOS, Juan Manuel. Aspectos de la tarea revolucionaria del coloradismo. A., Biblioteca Colorado, 1969. 94p.

3363 GAGLIADIORNE, César R. Plan de organización política del Partido Colorado. B.A., López, 1968. 146p.

3364 El GOBIERNO, el pueblo y el Partido Colorado, unidos a través de una obra nacional. A., 1963. 48p.

3365 GONZALEZ, Juan Natalicio. El Partido Colorado de Paraguay: teoría y fundamento de la libertad. RABC 1948, mayo, 152-70.

3366 GONZALEZ, Juan Natalicio. Por la unidad del Coloradismo. A., Edit. Guarania, 1947. 7p.

3367 JUVENTUD COLORADA. Manifiesto de la Juventud Colorada. A., 1951. 31p.

3368 MENDEZ FLEYTAS, Epifanio; CATALDI, J. Virgilio. El coloradismo no será destruído. A., "El Demócrata", 1948. 43p. (Comité de Defensa del Coloradismo, Folleto no. 2)

3369 MENDEZ FLEYTAS, Epifanio. El orden para la libertad: fundamentos del coloradismo. A., Edit. Cultura, 1951. 156p.

3370 PARAGUAY. MINISTERIO DE HACIENDA. OFICINA DE PRENSA. Exposición del Ministro de Hacienda y miembro de la junta de gobierno del Partido Colorado, Cesar Barrientos, en la Jornada de Capacitación Politica realizada en la ciudad de Paraguari el 31 de Mayo de 1969. A., 1969? 63p.

3371 PARTIDO COLORADO. Convención Nacional Constituyente - periodo preconstituyente. A., Asociación Nacional Republicana, 1967. 19p.

3372 PARTIDO COLORADO. Mensaje de la Junta de Gobierno al pueblo colorado de la República. A., Asociación Nacional Republicana, 1956. 12p.

3373 RAMIREZ, Isidro; SALOMONI, Tomás A. Ideales políticos; presentados a la Comisión directiva del Partido Nacional Republicano. A., Ariel, 1916. 49p.

3374 RAMIREZ, Juan Isidro. Una jornada del pensamiento democrático; la orientación y actuación del Partido Colorado ante la verdad y ante su propria reponsabilidad moral y política. Montevideo?, Casa América, 1959. 49p.

3375 REFLEXIONES republicanos. A., 1968-

3. *Partido Comunista*

3376 PARTIDO COMUNISTA DEL PARAGUAY. Manifesto of the Paraguayan Communist Party. IB 37 (1965) April 14, 39-46.

3377 PARTIDO COMUNISTA DEL PARAGUAY. Paraguay hoy! Unión de todos los paraguayos en defensa de la libertad y de la independencia de la Patria! Puntos de vista del Comité Central del Partido Comunista del Paraguay. B.A., Ed. Problemas, 1941. 128p.

3378 RAMOS, Dionisio Bejarano; SOLER, Miguel Angel. Building up strength. WMR 16 (1973) no. 3, 95-100.

3379 TANIS, Aquiles. El comunismo en Paraguay. ESC 3 (1955) July/Sept., 51-56.

3380 VASQUEZ, Pedro. An anti-dictatorial front in the making. WMR 17 (1974) no. 4, 82-87.

3381 VASQUEZ, Pedro. Unity against the dictatorship. WMR 18 (1975) no. 6, 32-37.

4. *Partido Democrata Cristiano*

3382 PARTIDO DEMOCRATA CRISTIANO. Documentos desde la Convención Ordinaria del 2 de julio de 1971, hasta la Convención Nacional Extraordinaria de marzo de 1972. A., Departamento de Propaganda y Relaciones Publicas del P.D.C., 1972. 64p.

3383 JUVENTUD DEMOCRATA CRISTIANA. Geografía electoral. A., Ediciones Revolución, 1967. 56p.

3384 MOVIMIENTO SOCIAL DEMOCRATA CRISTIANO. Acta fundacional y declaración de principios. A., 1960. 19p.

5. *Partido Liberal*

3385 AYALA, José Antonio. Liberalismo y bienestar social; trabajos presentados y aprobados en el primer Congreso Doctrinario del Liberalismo Paraguayo. Prólogo de Justo Prieto. B.A., Edit. Ayacucho, 1953. 79p.

3386 AYALA ALBERTINI, Julio César. Esquema ideológico de la juventud liberal. A., Edit. "Alon", 1964. 28p.

3387 BENITEZ, Justo Pastor. Ensayo sobre el liberalismo paraguayo. A., 1932. 126p.

3388 BENITEZ, Justo Pastor. Ideario político, exposición de ideas de la juventud radical. A., Ariel, 1921. 50p.

3389 BENITEZ, Justo Pastor. El liberalismo como fuerza renovadora. *In* no. 1903, p. 9-25.

3390 BENITEZ, Justo Pastor. Una presentación al directorio del Partido Colorado. *In* no. 1903, p. 31-35.

3391 BORDON, F. Arturo. La verdad en su lugar; lo que hizo el Partido Liberal en el Gobierno, legionarismo y antilopizmo, fundadores de los partidos tradicionales del Paraguay. A., 1972. 28p.

3392 BORDON, F. Arturo. Verdades del barquero; misión política del Partido Liberal del Paraguay; campaña periodística de reivindicación de la verdad histórica. A., Edit. "El Gráfico", 1962-

3393 CODAS, Cipriano. Proyecto de programa sintético; sometido a consideración de la Asamblea de la Juventud Liberal celebrada al 31 de octubre de 1937 en el Teatro Nacional. A., 1937. viii, 8p.

3394 El PARTIDO Liberal frente a la historia; balance de un régimen de traiciones al destino paraguayo, por D.G.F. A., 1957. 22p.

3395 PARTIDO LIBERAL. Estatutos, programa. A., Tip. C. Zamphirópolos, 1916. 64p.

3396 PARTIDO LIBERAL. Manifiesto. n.p., 1947. 16p.

3397 PARTIDO LIBERAL. Memorias y documentos, 1911-1913. A., Tall. de Zamphirópolos, 1914. 62p.

3398 PARTIDO LIBERAL. Programa del Partido Liberal. A., 1935. 42p.

3399 PASTORE, Carlos. Temas del Congreso del Liberalismo Paraguayo. Montevideo, Edit. Antequera, 1951. 14p.

3400 PRIETO, Justo. Manual del ciudadano liberal paraguayo. B.A., Edit. Asunción, 1953. 170p. (Biblioteca del Club Liberal Alón)

3401 PRIETO, Justo. El partido político en la constitución social; la tradición liberal en el Paraguay. B.A., Tall. gráf. Lucania, 1960. 61p.

6. Partido Liberal Radical

3402 DOCUMENTOS para la historia. A., Centro de Documentación de Clarín Republicano, 1971-

3403 PARTIDO LIBERAL RADICAL. Hacia la libertad y la integración paraguaya. A., 1972. 8p.

7. Partido Revolucionario Febrerista

3404 LEWIS, Paul H. Leadership and conflict within the Febrerista Party of Paraguay. JIAS 9 (1967) no. 2, 283-95.

3405 LEWIS, Paul H. The politics of exile; Paraguay's Febrerista Party. Chapel Hill, University of North Carolina Press, 1968. xxv, 209p.

3406 PARTIDO REVOLUCIONARIO FEBRERISTA. Bases para un programa de liberación nacional; movimiento "Unidad y Revolución". B.A., 1957. 47p.

3407 PARTIDO REVOLUCIONARIO FEBRERISTA. Farsa y realidad; respondo a un cuestionaria del diario "La Mañana", el vice presidente en ejercicio de la presidencia del Partido Revolucionario Febrerista don Roque Gaona. A., Departamento de Cultura de P.R.F., 1961. 31p.

3408 PARTIDO REVOLUCIONARIO FEBRERISTA. Ideario, declaración de principios y programa de gobierno. 2. ed. A., Comité Ejecutive Nacional, 1959. 48p.

3409 PARTIDO REVOLUCIONARIO FEBRERISTA. Por qué somos febreristas. A., Partido Revolucionario Febrerista, Dpto. de Cultura, 1959. 22p. (Publicación, 2)

3410 PARTIDO REVOLUCIONARIO FEBRERISTA. Qué es el febrerismo; ideario, declaración de principios y programa del Partido de Revolucionario Febrerista. A., 1953. 48p.

3411 PARTIDO REVOLUCIONARIO FEBRERISTA. Realidad y mentira; el febrerismo ante los problemas nacionales. A?, Dpto. de Prensa del P.R.F., 1955. 78p.

3412 PARTIDO REVOLUCIONARIO FEBRERISTA. DEPARTAMENTO DE ASUNTOS FEMENINOS. Ideario de la mujer febrerista. B.A., 1962. 17p. (Publicación, 3)

3413 SPERATTI, Juan. Los partidos políticos; orientaciones, esfuerzos y realidades del adoctrinamiento febrerista. A., Emasa, 1967. 44p.

3414 STEFANICH, Juan. El estado solidarista; estructura y funciones del estado en el nuevo sistema continental americano. Una nueva democracia ha nacido en América. B.A., El Mundo Nuevo, 1952. 168p.
Rev. ed. B.A., Edit. Arayú, 1955. 243p.

3415 STEFANICH, Juan. Fundamentos del mundo nuevo; hacia la libre ordenación de un mundo de naciones libres. B.A., El Mundo Nuevo, 1944. 241p.

3416 STEFANICH, Juan. El mundo nuevo: una nueva teoria de la democracía. B.A., El Mundo Nuevo, 1945. 210p.

3417 UNION NACIONAL REVOLUCIONARIA. La Unión Nacional Revolucionaria. Su constitución y su programa. A., 1939. 10p.

3418 VANGUARDIA REVOLUCIONARIA FEBRERISTA. Tesis políticas e ideológicas de la revolución nacional. A., 1971. 16p.

8. *Movimiento Popular Colorado*

3419 CHAVES, Osvaldo. Contribución a la doctrina de la revolución paraguaya. Prólogo de Mario L. Mallorquín. B.A., Ediciones Canendiyú, 1971. 318p.

9. *Unión Nacional Paraguaya*

3420 UNION NACIONAL PARAGUAYA. JUNTA CENTRAL COORDINADORA DEL EXILIO. Un pueblo en lucha por la libertad. B.A., 1960. 31p. (Publicación, 1)

D. Armed Forces

3421 ARANDA G., Bernardo. La fuerzas armadas y las problemas nacionales. A., 1945. 2 vols. (Biblioteca de la Revista de las FF. AA. de la Nación)

3422 BEJARANO, Ramón César. Nociones de geografía militar. A., Imp. Militar, 1953. 156p.

3423 BEJARANO, Ramón César. Contribución de las FF. AA. al bienestar y programa del país. A., Edit. Toledo, 1959. 111p.

3424 BEJARANO, Ramón César. Guía para la instrucción téorica en un cuerpo de tropa; G.I.T. 2. ed. A., Imp. nac., 1954. 526p.

3425 DELGADO, Nicolás. Manual del soldado paraguayo; educación guerrera basada en los principios fundamentales del reglamento para la infantería. A., Imp. de la "Escuela militar", 19--. 55p.

3426 DIAZ LEON, Carlos. El servicio de sanidad militar francés durante la guerra actuel. Informe al ministro de la guerra de la república del Paraguay. Con prefacio del profesor Vincent. Paris, Le François, 1916. 250p.

3427 ESCUELA MILITAR, ASUNCION. Reglamento orgánico y plan de estudios de la Escuela militar. A., Tall. gráf. del estado, 1920. 23p.

3428 GONZALEZ MERZARIO, Américo. Política y ejército; consideraciones sobre problemas político-militares del Paraguay. B.A., Edit. Yegros, 1955. 145p.

3429 MASI, Cayetano. Nociones de higiene militar. A., Imp. militar, 1921. 155p.

3430 PARAGUAY. DIRECCION DE SANIDAD MILITAR. Proyecto de reglamento de servicio de enfermeros y camilleros para la sanidad del Ejército. A., Imp. y librería La Mundial, 1919. 24p.

3431 PARAGUAY. EJERCITO. ESCUELA MILITAR. Manual del sub-oficial paraguayo; arreglado para la instrucción téorica de las tropas del Ejército Nacional, por los oficiales de la Escuela Militar. A., 1917. 208p.

3432 PARAGUAY. EJERCITO. ESCUELA MILITAR. Reglamento orgánico y plan de estudios de la Escuela militar. A., Tall. gráf. del estado, 1920. 23p.

3433 PARAGUAY. INTENDENCIA DEL EJERCITO. Exposición de trabajos y proyectos presentados al Ministerio de guerra y marina por el intendente del Ejército, sr. Teófilo Medina. A., Imp. La Mundial, 1917. 56p.

3434 PARAGUAY. MINISTERIO DE GUERRA Y MARINA. Programas de exámenes para los guardia marinas en comisión y efectivos de la Marina nacional. A., Imp. y libreria La Mundial, 1919. 14p.

3435 PARAGUAY. MINISTERIO DE GUERRA Y MARINA. Programas de exámenes para los S.S., J.J. i O.O. mayores de sanidad. A., Tall. gráf. El Arte, 1920. 32p.

3436 PARAGUAY. MINISTERIO DE GUERRA Y MARINA. Programas para la Escuela de enfermeros i camilleros. A., Tall. gráf. El Arte, 1920. 19p.

3437 PARAGUAY. MINISTERIO DE GUERRA Y MARINA. Reglamento de dotación de paz del Ejército y Armada. A., Tall. gráf. del estado, 1915. 38p.

3438 PARAGUAY. MINISTERIO DE GUERRA Y MARINA. Reglamento de dotación de paz del Ejército y Marina nacionales. Abreviatura: R.D.P. A., 1920. 32p.

3439 PARAGUAY. MINISTERIO DE GUERRA Y MARINA. Reglamento de ejercicios para la Caballería. Abreviatura: Regl. ej. cab., no. 7. A., Tall. nac. de H. Kraus, 1909. xv, 217p.

3440 PARAGUAY. MINISTERIO DE GUERRA Y MARINA. Reglamento de ejercicios para la Infantería. Abreviatura: Regl. ej. inf., no. 6. A., Tall. nac. de H. Kraus, 1909. viii, 162p.

3441 PARAGUAY. MINISTERIO DE GUERRA Y MARINA. Reglamento de servicio en campaña; Abreviatura: Regl. s. en c., no. 7. A., Tall. nac. de H. Kraus, 1909. v, 163p.

3442 PARAGUAY. MINISTERIO DE GUERRA Y MARINA. Reglamento de tiro para la Infantería. Abreviatura: R.T.I. no. 7. A., Tall. nac. de H. Kraus, 1915. 146p.

3443 PARAGUAY. MINISTERIO DE GUERRA Y MARINA. Reglamento orgánico del Ejército y servicio de las oficinas militares. R.O.E. n:1. A., Tall. gráf. del estado, 1915. 33p.

3444 PARAGUAY. MINISTERIO DE GUERRA Y MARINA. Reglamento para la conservación y limpieza del fusil y carabina "Mauser". A., Tall. gráf. del estado, 1912. 13p.

3445 ROLON, Raimundo. Ni militarismo ni antimilitarismo. A?, 19--? 8p.

3446 ROLON, Raimundo. Proyecto de ideario del Partido Nacional Republicano en cuanto a las FF. AA. de la nación. A., 1947. 16p.

3447 ROMERO DIAZ, Antonio. Puesto fronterizo; relato. A., Edit. Emasa, 1966. 218p. (Colección Cultura Paraguaya)
2. ed. A., Edit. La Voz, 1970. 263p.

3448 SAMANIEGO, Roque. Nuestro problema militar: los datos del problem, organización militar, educación militar. A., Imp. "El Liberal", 1919. 29p.

3448a SPERATTI, Juan. Política militar Paraguaya; esbozo de temas y cuestiones de la instrucción y educación del mando. B.A., 1955. 116p.

3449 VILLASBOA BARBOSA, Mutshuito. Hacia la guerra total y los problemas de las fuerzas armadas. A., 194-?- (Biblioteca de las FF. AA. de la Nación, v. 11)

IX. LAW

A. Collections of laws

3450 PARAGUAY. COMISION NACIONAL DE CODIFICACION. Antecedentes del ante proyecto del Código civil paraguayo (por) Luis de Gásperi. A., Colegio de Abogados, 1962. 85p.

3451 PARAGUAY. CONGRESO. Colección de leyes sancionadas por el Congreso de la Nación en sus sesiones extraordinarias de 1877. A., Imp. La Reforma, 1877. 18p.

3452 PARAGUAY. CONGRESO. CAMARA DE DIPUTADOS. Banco de la República del Paraguay: leyes y decretos pertinentes. A., La Colmena, 1936. 88p.

3453 PARAGUAY. CONTADURIA GENERAL Y DIRECCION DEL TESORO. Compilación de disposiciones legales referentes a la organización administrativa y financiera de la nación. 1. Leyes y decretos-leges. 2. Decretos, y 3. Resoluciones. Junio de 1937. A., Imp. nac., 1937. 152p.

3454 PARAGUAY. CORTE SUPREMA DE JUSTICIA. Fallos y disposiciones del Superior Tribunal de Justicia correspondientes al año 1899. Publ. por Emeterio González. A., Tip. El País, 1962. 549, xlix p.

3455 PARAGUAY. LAWS, STATUTES, ETC. Antecedentes de la reforma de la Ley no. 915. Texto de los anteproyectos. A., 1954. 105p.

3456 PARAGUAY. LAWS, STATUTES, ETC. Anteproyecto de código civil. A., Edit. "El Gráfico", 1964. 1050p.

3457 PARAGUAY. LAWS, STATUTES, ETC. Anteproyecto de código procesal civil, por Juan Carlos Mendonça. A., 1970. 147p.

3458 PARAGUAY. LAWS, STATUTES, ETC. Anteproyecto de código procesal penal para el Paraguay, por Victor B. Riquelme. A., 1952. 288p.

3458a PARAGUAY. LAWS, STATUTES, ETC. Código de comercio y leyes complementarios; anotado por Oscar Paciello. A., Ediciones Comuneros, 1977. 551p.

3459 PARAGUAY. LAWS, STATUTES, ETC. Código de procedimientos y arancel nacional de derechos de la República del Paraguay, sancionada por el honorable Congreso Nacional en 14 de agosto de 1876. A., Imp. de la Reforma, 1876. 60p.

3460 PARAGUAY. LAWS, STATUTES, ETC. Código de procedimientos de la República del Paraguay con las leyes de modificación interpretado por las Cámaras de Apelación, 1899-1912, por Jorge Klug. A., Tall. Gráf. del Estado, 1912. 336p.

3461 PARAGUAY. LAWS, STATUTES, ETC. Códigos de procedimientos civiles y penales. A., Est. Tip. de El Cívico, 1908. 319p.

3462 PARAGUAY. LAWS, STATUTES, ETC. Códigos de procedimientos en materia civil, comercial y penal. A., Imp. nac., 1921. 2 vols. in 1.

3463 PARAGUAY. LAWS, STATUTES, ETC. Código de procedimientos penales. A., El Paraguayo, 1890. 119p.

3464 PARAGUAY. LAWS, STATUTES, ETC. Código de procedimientos penales; sus modificaciones. Ley de decentralización judicial, Ley de represión de los delitos de contrabando y Constitución nacional. A., 195-? 196p.

3465 PARAGUAY. LAWS, STATUTES, ETC. Código paraguayo del trabajo; leyes y decretos reglamentarios con indice alfabético sumariado y concordancias. Compiladores: Jorge Darío Cristaldo M. y José Kriskovich P. A., Ediciones Fides, 1964. 257p.

3466 PARAGUAY. LAWS, STATUTES, ETC. Código penal de la república del Paraguay. Publicación oficial. A., Imp. de La Reforma, 1880. 4, 87, 112p.
Includes "Apuntes de derecho penal" por el Manuel Obarrio.

3467 PARAGUAY. LAWS, STATUTES, ETC. Código penal de la República del Paraguay. Publicación oficial. A., "La República", 1892. 88p.

Also: A., Tall. nac. de H. Kraus, 1903. 134p.
A., Tall. nac. de H. Kraus, 1910. 114p.
2. ed. oficial. A., Tall. Gráf. del Estado, 1913. 102p.
A., Tall. gráf. del Estado, 1914. 132, ii p.

3468 PARAGUAY. LAWS, STATUTES, ETC. Código penal de la República del Paraguay. A., 1960. 81p. (Revista del Ministerio de Justicia y Trabajo, 2 época, 5)

3469 PARAGUAY. LAWS, STATUTES, ETC. Código penal paraguayo y leyes complementarias. A., 1965. 29p. (Revista del Ministerio de Justicia y Trabajo, 5, no. 47)
Reprinted: 1968.

3469a PARAGUAY. LAWS, STATUTES, ETC. Código penal de la República del Paraguay y leyes complementarios, anotado por Oscar Paciello. A., Ediciones Comuneros, 1975. 215p.

3470 PARAGUAY. LAWS, STATUTES, ETC. Código procesal paraguayo del trabajo, comentado. Con 700 jurisprudencias del Tribunal de Apelación de Trabajo de la Capital, dictadas hasta el 31 de mayo de 1968; indice alfabético sumariado y concordado; Constitución nacional, leyes, decretos, reglamentos, y acordadas; por Jorge Darío Cristaldo Montaner y José Kriskovich Prevedoni. A., Ediciones Fides, 1968. 323p.

3471 PARAGUAY. LAWS, STATUTES, ETC. Código rural de la república del Paraguay. A., Imp. de "El Paraguayo", 1877. 37p.
Also: A., Imp. de "La Reforma", 1884. 23p.

3472 PARAGUAY. LAWS, STATUTES, ETC. Código rural con los adiciones, supresiones y modificaciones introducidas hasta la fecha. Recopilación completa y ordenada, por Genaro Romero. A., Tall. gráf. de "La Rural", 1929. 53p. (Biblioteca de "La Rural", 1)

3473 PARAGUAY. LAWS, STATUTES, ETC. Código rural vigente en la República del Paraguay, promulgada el 8 de agosto de 1877, conteniendo todas las modificaciones, supresiones y adiciones hechas hasta la fecha. A., Tip. "La Tribuna", 1900. 37p.

3474 PARAGUAY. LAWS, STATUTES, ETC. Colección de leyes que entienden con la Oficina de deuda pública, 1899. A., Tall. nac. de H. Kraus, 1899. 37p.

3475 PARAGUAY. LAWS, STATUTES, ETC. Compilación de disposiciones aduaneras del Paraguay, por Juan P. Caceres y Justo G. Cañete. A., Imp. nac., 1956. 2 vols.

3476 PARAGUAY. LAWS, STATUTES, ETC. Compilación de disposiciones gubernativas de organización administrativa y financiera de la nación. A., Imp. nac., 1963. 408p.

3477 PARAGUAY. LAWS, STATUTES, ETC. Compilación de disposiciones legales que rigen la organización y funcionamiento de entidades qutárquicas, autónomas y de economía mixta; leyes y decretos-leyes, decretos, resoluciones y apéndice. A., Imp. nac., 1963. 435p.

3478 PARAGUAY. LAWS, STATUTES, ETC. Compilación de disposiciones legales sobre el seguro social. A., Instituto de Previsión Social, 1966. 96p. (Folleto, 28)

3479 PARAGUAY. LAWS, STATUTES, ETC. Compilación de disposiciones vigentes de impuesto a la renta, por Félix R. Talavera y Justo Pastor Bello. A., 1959. 206p.

3480 PARAGUAY. LAWS, STATUTES, ETC. Compilación de leyes y decretos, ordenada por Carlos A. Pastore, presidente del departamento, ejecutada por Carlos A. Rolon. 1. Bosques. 2. Colonias. 3. Inmigración. 4. Yerbales. A., Imp. nac., 1939. 325, vi p.

3481 PARAGUAY. LAWS, STATUTES, ETC. Indice cronológico de leyes, acuerdos del Congreso y de cada Cámara Legislativa de los años 1870-1921. A., Imp. nac., 1924. 144p. (Paraguay. Diario oficial, no. 862)

3482 PARAGUAY. LAWS, STATUTES, ETC. Indice de jurisprudencia del trabajo, 1962-1966. Compiladores: Enrique B. Bordenave y Arminda González Gini. A., Edit. Gráf., 1967. 188p.

3483 PARAGUAY. LAWS, STATUTES, ETC. Instrucciones y formularios para la indagación sumaria ante los juzgados de paz; por José W. Benites. Publicación oficial. A., Tall. nac. de H. Kraus, 1903. 116p.

3484 PARAGUAY. LAWS, STATUTES, ETC. Legislación bancaria paraguaya; compilación de disposiciones vigentes. Anexo: relaciones con organismos internacionales; indice de disposiciones bancarias derogados; por Segundo Udagawa. A., 1962. 195p.
4. ed. A., 1975. 405p.

3485 PARAGUAY. LAWS, STATUTES, ETC. Legislación fiscal del Paraguay, compilada por los doctores Carlos A. Mersán y Joaquín A. Burgos. A., Edit. Guarania, 1944. 447p.

3486 PARAGUAY. LAWS, STATUTES, ETC. Legislación fiscal del Paraguay. Con la legislación bancaria, y las normas del Convenio de Unión Económica Paraguayo-Argentino. 2. ed. por Carlos A. Mersán. A., 1954. 804p.
3. ed. A., 1968. 722p.

3486a PARAGUAY. LAWS, STATUTES, ETC. Legislación fiscal del Paraguay: legislación aduanera y portuaria; Carlos A. Mersán. 4. ed. A., Escuela Técnica Salesiana, 1976. 2 vol.

3486b PARAGUAY. LAWS, STATUTES, ETC. Legislación Paraguaya. A., Facultad de Ciencias Jurídicas y Diplomáticas de la Universidad Católica de Asunción, 1974-

3487 PARAGUAY. LAWS, STATUTES, ETC. Ley orgánica de los tribunales. A., Tall. nac. de H. Kraus, 1898. 54p.

3488 PARAGUAY. LAWS, STATUTES, ETC. Ley orgánica de los tribunales. Arancel de los actuarios judiciales. A., Imp. nac., 1923. 88p.

3489 PARAGUAY. LAWS, STATUTES, ETC. Leyes no. 729 y 742: Códigos del trabajo y procesal del trabajo de la República del Paraguay. Decreto no. 20.884 de reorganización del Departamento Nacional del Trabajo. A., "El Diario Juridico" y Edit. "El Gráfico", 1962. 74p.

3490 PARAGUAY. LAWS, STATUTES, ETC. Leyes de impuestos internos de la república del Paraguay. A., Tall. de "El Diario", 1906. 59p.

3491 PARAGUAY. LAWS, STATUTES, ETC. Leyes de inmigración y de colonización y hogar. A., Tall. nac. de H. Kraus, 1905. 42p.

3492 PARAGUAY. LAWS, STATUTES, ETC. Leyes de inmigración, colonización y reducción de tribus indígenas. A., Tall. gráf. del estado, 1913. 27p.

3493 PARAGUAY. LAWS, STATUTES, ETC. Leyes de organización y de procedimientos para la justicia nacional, con arreglo á las adiciones y modificaciones sancionadas hasta el año 1902. Concordadas y anotados por Emetrio González. A., Tip. El País, 1902. 769p.

3494 PARAGUAY. LAWS, STATUTES, ETC. Leyes y decretos de aduana, república del Paraguay. A., Tall. nac. de H. Kraus, 1898. 123p.

3495 PARAGUAY. LAWS, STATUTES, ETC. Leyes y decretos relativos a los municipalidades: ordenanzas de la municipalidad de la Asunción constituida por la H.J.M. de la capital. A., 1928. 663p.

3496 PARAGUAY. LAWS, STATUTES, ETC. El nuevo Código penal y su exposición de motivos, por el Dr. Teodosio González. A., Tall. nac. de H. Kraus, 1911. 278p.

3497 PARAGUAY. LAWS, STATUTES, ETC. Ordenanza militar y código penal y de procedimientos de la República del Paraguay. Publicación oficial. A., Imp. de "El Paraguayo", 1887. xi, 147, 47, 36, 8p.

3498 PARAGUAY. LAWS, STATUTES, ETC. Plan económico, presentado por el poder ejecutivo; colección de leyes sancionadas por el h. Congreso de la nación en sus sesiones extraordinarias de noviembre de 1890. A., Tip. y encuadernación "El Paraguayo", 1891. 31p.

3499 PARAGUAY. LAWS, STATUTES, ETC. Proyecto de Código de procedimientos civiles. A., Tip. y enc. "El País", 1906. 186p.

3500 PARAGUAY. LAWS, STATUTES, ETC. Proyecto de Código de procedimientos penales, presentado al p. legislativo por el senador dr. Teodosio González. A., Tip. "El País", 1905. 175p.

3501 PARAGUAY. LAWS, STATUTES, ETC. Proyecto de Código de procedimientos penales, presentado por el diputado nacional Dr. Carlos R. Centurión. A., Imp. nac., 1935. 129p.

3502 PARAGUAY. LAWS, STATUTES, ETC. Proyecto de un nuevo Código penal y su exposición de motivos, por el dr. Teodosio González. A., Tall. nac. de H. Kraus, 1906. 278p.

3503 PARAGUAY. LAWS, STATUTES, ETC. Proyecto de un nuevo Código rural para la república del Paraguay, por el dr. Teodosio González. A., Tall. nac. de H. Kraus, 1906. 174p.

3504 PARAGUAY. LAWS, STATUTES, ETC. Recopilación de leyes, decretos y reglamentos: jurisprudencia nacional; publicación dirigada por el dr. Juan B. González. n.p., 19--. 228p.

3505 PARAGUAY. LAWS, STATUTES, ETC. Recopilación de leyes en las materias civil, comercial, rural, penal, militar y de procedimientos de la república del Paraguay, con arreglo á los modificaciones, adiciones y derogaciones introducidas en ellas hasta el año de 1892, por Rafael C. Vallejos. A., Imp. de El Independiente, 1892. 600p.

3506 PARAGUAY. LAWS, STATUTES, ETC. Recopilación de leyes y disposiciones fiscales de la República del Paraguay, con arreglo á las modificaciones, anotaciones y adiciones introducidas en ellas hasta al presente periodo legislativo, por Rafael C. Vallejos. A., Tip. de "La República", 1891. iv, 396p.

3507 PARAGUAY. LAWS, STATUTES, ETC. Régimen de cambios de la república del Paraguay y reglamentación de las operaciones de cambio del mercado oficial. A., La Colmena, 1945. 39p.

3508 PARAGUAY. LAWS, STATUTES, ETC. Régimen legal de la falencia comercial y civil en el Paraguay, por Horacio Gabriel Lebrón. A., Tall. de Artes Gráf. Zamphiropolos, 1967. 174p.

3509 PARAGUAY. LAWS, STATUTES, ETC. Registro del estado civil; su organización. Edición oficial. A., Tall. nac. de H. Kraus, 1899. 91p.

3510 PARAGUAY. LAWS, STATUTES, ETC. Reglamentos internos y orgánicos y decretos referentes á la Escuela de agricultura y granja modelo. A., Santisima Trinidad, 1898. 43p.

3511 PARAGUAY. LAWS, STATUTES, ETC. Repertorio de jurisprudencia, por Arquimedes Laconich. A., 1948. 752p.
Suplemento, 1- A., 1952-
Reprinted: A., 1968. 636p.

3512 PARAGUAY. LAWS, STATUTES, ETC. Vademecum del ganadero: código rural y convenios, leyes, decreto-leyes, decretos, resoluciones y circulares de las distintas reparticiones públicas referentes a ganado, por Juan del Rosario Martinez. A., Imp. nac., 1957. 371p.

3513 PARAGUAY. MINISTERIO DE HACIENDA. Indice alfabético por materia y concepto de las leyes impositivas. A., Imp. nac., 1938. 65p.

3514 PARAGUAY. SUPERIOR TRIBUNAL DE JUSTICIA. Acordadas sobre abstención de los fiscales en l criminal en los procesos. A., 1924. 5p.

3515 PARAGUAY. TRIBUNAL DE APELACION EN I CIVIL Y CRIMINAL. Jurisprudencia comercial; fallos de la Cámara de apelación en l. comercial (desde su fundación en 1899 hasta 1916) extractados y recopilados por Jorge Klug. A., Imp. de El Liberal, 1916. 110p.

B. Treatises

3516 ACOSTA, César R. Social legislation in Paraguay. ILR 50 (1944) July, 40-46.

3517 APUNTES de derecho constitucional y administrativo. 6 curso comercial. A., Mimeografía "Bachero", 1961. 60p.

3517a AQUINO DE ORTIZ, Marina. Recurso de amparo. A., Tall. Gráf. de la Escuela Salesiana, 1969. iv, 213p.

3518 ARBO, Higinio. Ciudadanía y naturalización. B.A., P. Garcia, 1926. 186p.

3519 ARBO, Higinio. Derecho internacional convencional: junta internacional de jurisconsultos: informe de la Delegación del Paraguay sobre las sesiones de Rio de Janeiro del año 1927. A., Imp. nac., 1928. 223p.

3520 ARBO, Higinio. Libre navegación de los ríos; régimen juridico de los ríos de la Plata, Paraná y Paraguay. B.A., Librería y edit. "El Ateneo", 1939. 214p.

3521 ARGAÑA, Luís María. El amparo; su fundamentación parliamentaria - su antecedentes - Ley no. 340. A., El Gráfico S.R.L., 1972. 81p.

3522 ARGAÑA, Luís María. La propiedad horizontal por pisos o por departamentos en el Paraguay; necisidad de la reforma del artículo 2617 del Código civil. B.A., Ediciones Nizza, 1960. 149p.

3523 ARGAÑA, Luís A. Tratado de derecho mercantil. A., La Colmena, 1936-37. 3 vols.

3524 BAEZ, Cecilio. Conferencias dadas en la Universidad Nacional de la Asunción sobre el derecho constitucional. A., La Mundial, 1917. 86p.

3525 BAEZ, Cecilio. Curso de derecho internacional privado americano. A., Imp. Nac., 1926. 157p.

3526 BERTONI, Guillermo Tell. Derecho y administración rural del Paraguay: régimen legal e institucional de la administración rural paraguaya. A., Cultura Guaraní, 1943. 88p.

3527 CARONI, Carlos A. Derecho del trabajo; estudios de su desarrollo en el Paraguay. B.A., Edit. 14 de Mayo, 1954. 15p.

3528 CODAS, Cipriano. Organización municipal, contiene la exposición y comentarios a la ley orgánica de las municipalidades del 2 de febrero de 1909. A., Imp. La Mundial, 1917. 118p.

3529 CREYDT, Oscar A. El derecho de expulsión ante el derecho internacional, constitucional, administrativo y penal. Con prólogo del Dr. Alfredo L. Palacios. A., 1927. 178p.

3529a FRESCURA Y CANDIA, Luís P. Curso de legislación del trabajo. A., La Colmena, 1940. 282p.

3529b FRESCURA Y CANDIA, Luís P. Derecho paraguayo del trabajo y de la seguridad social: estudio de doctrina y legislación. 2. ed. B.A., Edit. Heliasta, 1975. 868p.

3529c FRESCURA Y CANDIA, Luís P. La legislación del trabajo en la república del Paraguay. B.A., Ed. Jurídica Argentina, 1941. 67p.

3530 FRUTOS VAESKEN, Alexis. Honorarios; análisis y crítica de la ley 110. Su reforma. A., Emasa, 1969. 208p.

3531 GASPERI, Luis de. Curso de derecho civil. A., Imp. nac., 1929-35. 2 vols.

3532 GASPERI, Luis de. De la igualdad civil de los sexos en el derecho comparado; explicación y crítica de la ley no. 236. B.A., 1957. 243p.

3533 GASPERI, Luis de. El derecho de expulsión ante el derecho internacional, constitucional, administrativo y penal. A., 1927. 178p.

3534 GASPERI, Luis de; MORELLO, Augusto M. Tratado de derecho civil. B.A., Tip. Edit. Argentina, 1914. 4 vols.

3535 GASPERI, Luis de. Tratado de las obligaciones en el derecho civil paraguayo y argentino. B.A., Ed. Depalma, 1945. 3 vols.

3536 GIRALA, Salim A. Un proyecto de ley de impuesto a la renta y sus aberraciones jurídicas. A., Zamphirópolos, 1964. 180p.

3537 GONZALEZ, Teodosio. Derecho penal, tratado bajo el doble aspecto científico y legislativo; contiene la explicación y comentario del Código penal paraguayo. A., La Colmena, 1928. 3 vols.

3538 GONZALEZ, Teodosio. Ligeras observaciones al Proyecto de reformas del Código penal. A., Tall. nac. de H. Kraus, 1896. 112p.

3539 GONZALEZ TORRES, Dionisio. Medicina legal. A., El Arte, 1956. 296p.

3540 GROSS-BROWN, Sigfrido V. Administrative justice in Paraguay. 18 TLR (1944) 610-18.

3541 GROSS-BROWN, Sigfrido V. Labor legislation of Paraguay. MLR 58 (1944) no. 4, 796-803.

3541a IRALA BURGOS, Jerónimo. La extradición: su régimen juridico en el Paraguay. EP 2 no. 1 (1974) 23-48.

3542 LACONICH, Arquimedes. Ochenta años de vida tribunalicia. A., 1951. 154p.

3543 LARA CASTRO, Mariano Luis. Aspectos del derecho: desarrollados y adaptados al programa de educación civica y moral 4 curso, bachillerato, normal, comercial. A., La Colmena, 1960. 130p.

3544 MARIN IGLESIAS, Alejandro. Derecho paraguayo y filosofia del derecho. VRU 3 (1970) no. 1, 75-86.

3545 MARTINEZ MILTOS, Luis. La responsabilidad penal de las personas jurídicas (historia, doctrina, legislación). A., Edit. América-Sapucai, 1956. 206p. (Colección jurídica)

3546 MENDONÇA, Juan Carlos. La reforma legislativa en Paraguay y la renovación del proceso civil. IALR 6 (1964) no. 2, 313-46.

3546a MENDONÇA, Juan Carlos. Legislative reform in Paraguay and the renovation of civil procedure. IALR 6 (1964) no. 2, 347-78.

3546b MERSAN, Carlos A. Derecho tributario. A., 1969. 328p.
2. ed. A., 1976. 408p.

3547 MERSAN, Carlos A. El impuesto a la renta en el Paraguay. A., Edit. Guarania, 1946. 228p.

3548 MERSAN, Carlos A. Manual de legislación y jurisprudencia del trabajo. A., El Arte, 1954. 148p.

3548a MERSAN, Carlos A. Nuevo régimen legal del impuesto a la renta; textos comentados. A., 1971. 76p.

3549 MONTE, Juan. Juicio ejecutivo seguido por la razón social Gatti y cía, contra la municipalidad de la capital; informe in-voce del doctor Juan Monte ante la Superior Cámara de apelación en 1 civil, sosteniendo la improcedencia de las excepciones opuestas por la institución deudora. A., Tall. de "Ariel", 1917. 29p.

3550 MONTEALEGRE, Eduardo. Anotaciones sobre la ley orgánica del Banco del Paraguay. TE 12 (1945) no. 1, 46-68.

3551 MOOSMAYER, Peter. Das Staatsangehörigkeitsrecht von Argentinien, Uruguay und Paraguay. Frankfurt am Main. A. Metzner, 1972. 159p. (Sammlung geltender Staatsangehörigkeitsgesetze, 33)

3552 NUÑEZ CARVALLO, Gabriel. El estado de sitio y el habeas corpus en el derecho constitucional paraguayo. A., El Arte, 1962. 113p.

3553 PAIVA, Félix. Estudio de derecho constitucional; la independencia del poder judicial. A., "Ariel", 1915. 170p.

3554 PAIVA, Félix. Estudio de la Constitución del Paraguay. A., Imp. nac., 1926-27. 2 vols.

3555 PARAGUAY. CORTE SUPREMA DE JUSTICIA. Programa de derecho civil. A., Imp. de "La Nación", 1887-88. 2 vols.

3556 PARAGUAY. CORTE SUPREMA DE JUSTICIA. Programa de derecho comercial. A., Imp. de "La Nación", 1887. 19p.

3557 PARAGUAY. CORTE SUPREMA DE JUSTICIA. Programa de derecho mercantil. A., Imp. de "La Nación", 1887. 18p.

3558 PARAGUAY. CORTE SUPREMA DE JUSTICIA. Programa de derecho penal. A., Imp. de "La Nación", 1887. 21p.

3559 RIQUELME, Benigno. Código de procedimientos penales en concordancia con el derecho penal. A., 1897. 410p.

Also: A., Imp. F. Jordan, 1908. iii-viii, 332p.

3560 RIQUELME, Victor B. Instituciones de derecho procesal penal; prólogo del doctor Niceto Alcalá-Zamora y Castillo. B.A., Edit. Atalaya, 1946-49. 2 vols.
Also: A., Alcora, 1955. 2 vols.

3561 RIQUELME, Victor B. El proceso penal en mi anteproyecto (Exposición de motivos) 1 parte. A., 1954. 105p.
See also no. 3458.

3562 ROLON, Francisco. Contestación de Quebrachales fusionados, el fisco y Cramer, Weyer & Müller á la demanda de reivindicación de 12 leguas de campo én "Puerto Max", promovida por H. Uriarte y otros. A., Imp. Grabow & Schauman, 1909. 115p.

3563 ROLON, Francisco. Lecciones dé derecho procesal, primer curso. A., Imp. nac., 1939. 279p.

3564 ROLON, Francisco. Legislación inmobiliaria; el registro Torrens. A., Tall. "España", 1916. 38p.

3565 SAGUIER ACEVAL, Emilio. Compendio de derecho político. A., El País. 1967. 337p.

3566 SAPENA PASTOR, Raúl. A statement of the laws of Paraguay in matters affecting business. Washington, Pan American Union, 1953. 138p.
2. ed. by Raúl Sapena Pastor and Raul Sapena Brugada. 1962. xiv, 284p.
3. ed. rev. by Gustavo Gatti and Jorge H. Escobar. 1973. xiv, 297p.

3567 SILVA, Ramón. La protección del adquiriente de buena fé en el derecho civil paraguayo. A., Imp. Juan Bravo, 1960. 154p.

3568 SOLER, Juan José. Introducción al derecho paraguayo. Madrid, Ediciones Cultura Hispanica, 1954. 577p.
2. ed. A., La Colmena, 1959. xv, 609p.

3569 SOLER, Juan José. Ley de extranjéria; proyecto del señor senador doctor Juan José Soler y exposición de motivos. A., Imp. nac., 1926. 35p.

3570 SOLER, Juan José. Un palique en la Comisión Nacional de Codificación. A., El Arte, 1962. 218p.

3571 SOLER, Juan José. Técnica jurídica; abogacía. A., El Arte, 1963. 284p.

3572 SOSA, Enrique A. La misión del abogado como profesional del derecho; tesis para optar al título de doctor en derecho y ciencias sociales. A., Imp. nac., 1941. 138p.

3573 UNIVERSIDAD NACIONAL, ASUNCION. FACULTAD DE DERECHO Y CIENCIAS SOCIALES. Programa de derecho internacional. Profesor: Carlos R. Centurión. A., El Arte, 1946. 14p.

3573a VILLAGRA MAFFIODO, Salvador. Régimen legal de la empresa pública en el Paraguay. EP 2 no. 1 (1974) 185-93.

3574 VELAZQUEZ, Eliado. La prueba en la filiación natural. A., Tall. de tip. "El País", 1910. 62p.
Reprinted: 1951. 70p.

3574a VICTOR Simón, una vida rauda y fecunda; edición de sus amigos en el 1er aniversario de su tránsito. A., Casa América, 1977. 78p.

3575 ZULEIZARRETA, Ramón. Elementos de derechos civil. Lecciones dictadas en la Universidad Nacional de la Asunción. A., H. Kraus, 1899-1900. 2 vols.

X. EDUCATION

A. General studies

3576 BAEZ ALLENDE, Amadeo. El Instituto internacional de educación de Nueva York y el Comité permanente internacional de educación del Paraguay. A., Imp. nac., 1942. 19p.

3577 BENITEZ, Leopoldo A. Instrucciones para los maestros de escuela sobre el cultivo del algodonero. A., Imp. "El Arte", 1920. 27p.

2577a BORDENAVE, Enrique B. La legislación paraguaya sobre educación de 1869 a 1946. EP 2 no. 1 (1974) 67-110.

3577b BRUGADA GUANES, Alejandro. Pedro Aguilera: su vida y sus obras. A., Casa América, 1976. 141p.

3578 CABALLERO IRALA, Basiliano. Preparación integral de la juventud paraguaya. B.A., Edición particular del autor, 1945. 180p.

3578a CARDOZO, R.I. La instrucción pública en el Paraguay. Washington, USGPO, 1929. ii, 10p. (Pan American Union. Serie sobre educación, 54)

3578b CARDOZO, R.I. Public instruction in Paraguay. Washington, USGPO, 1929. ii, 10p. (Pan American Union. Education no. 10)

3579 CARDOZO, Ramón I. Por la educación común. A., Imp. nac., 1928. 192p.

3580 CENTURION, Juan Crisóstomo. Conferencia dada en el Ateneo paraguayo en la noche de 28 de enero de 1885. A., Imp. de "La Democracia", 1885. 16p.

3581 CENTURION, Juan Crisóstomo. Conferencia dada en el Ateneo paraguayo en la noche de 28 de enero de 1885 y otros publicaciones relativas á instrucción pública en tiempo de los Lopez. 2. ed. A., Imp. de "La Democracia", 1886. 39p.

3582 CHAVES, Manuel Wenceslao. Informe a la Dirección S. de escuelas. A., Imp. La Tribuna, 1891. 56p.

3582a DAHLQUIST, Juan R. Páginas de un maestro, colección de artículos conferencias y discursos; con un prólogo del dr. Manuel Dominguez. A., Tall. tip. del estado, 1912. 215p.

3583 DOMINGUEZ, Manuel. Las escuelas en el Paraguay; conferencia dada en el Instituto Paraguayo de la Asunción el 25 de setiembre de 1897. A., Tall. nac. de H. Kraus, 1897. 56p.

3584 DOMINGUEZ, Manuel. Historia de la enseñanza nacional; conferencia dada en el Instituto Paraguayo. RIP 1 no. 10 (1897) 217-70.

3585 DURAN, Juan Agustín. Gimnasia de educación conforme al programa aprobado por el Consejo secundario y superior. A., Imp. de la Democracia, 1895. 176p.

3586 GONZALEZ, Juan Natalicio. La instrucción pública y la vida intelectual durante el coloniaje. RAP 1 no. 3 (1941) 13-35.

3587 HEISECKE, Guillermo. Aspectos estructurales de la educación en el Paraguay. AP 12 (1969) 86-110.

3588 MARIN IGLESIAS, Alejandro. Cartas a la juventud paraguaya. Prólogo del doctor Justo Prieto. B.A., Sebastian Amorrortu e hijos, 1937. 198p.

3589 MASSARE DE KOSTIANOVSKY, Olinda. La instrucción pública en la época colonial. A., Imp. Salesiana, 1968. 275p.
2. ed. A., 1975. 396p.

3589a MENENDEZ, Elisa Amparo. Punctualizaciones; venturas y desventuras de mi vida en el Paraguay. B.A., Tall. Gráf. Claridad, 1949. 260p.

3590 PARAGUAY. CENTRO DE DOCUMENTACION PEDAGOGICA. El desarrollo educativo en el Paraguay. A., 1965-66. 38p.

3591 PARAGUAY. CONSEJO NACIONAL DE EDUCACION. Plan de enseñanza adoptado por el h. Consejo nacional de educación para las escuelas rurales de la república, 1920. A., Imp. "El Arte", 1920. vi, 18p.

3592 PARAGUAY. CONSEJO NACIONAL DE EDUCACION. Reglamento orgánico y disciplinario de las escuelas graduadas de la república. Publicación oficial. A., Tall. nac. de H. Kraus, 1898. 16p.

3593 PARAGUAY. DIRECCION GENERAL DE ESCUELAS. Liquidación de haberes y sistema de pagos á los maestros de escuelas de la campaña. A., Imp. "El Arte", 1920. 12p.

3594 PARAGUAY. DIRECCION GENERAL DE ESCUELAS. Reglamento de las academias de corte y confección, aprobado por el Consejo nacional de educación en su sesión del 8 de octubre de 1919. A., Imp. "El Arte", 1920. 7p.

3595 PARAGUAY. DIRECCION GENERAL DE ESTADISTICAS. Ensayo sobre analfabetismo en el Paraguay, 1951; by Leovigildo González Garcia. A., 1952. 89p.

3596 PARAGUAY. MINISTERIO DE EDUCACION Y CULTO. La educación paraguaya: estado actual y programas de innovaciones educacionales. A., 1972. 22p.

3597 PARAGUAY. MINISTERIO DE EDUCACION Y CULTO. Estadísticas educativas, 1950-1960; enseñanza pre-escolar y primaria, enseñanza medio y normal. Editado con la cooperación del Sev. Coop. Int. de Educación. A., 1961. 50p.

3598 PARAGUAY. MINISTERIO DE EDUCACION Y CULTO. La experiencia de Itapúa: estudio de rendimiento escolar en computadoras. A., Instituto Superior de Educación, 1973. 67p.

3599 PARAGUAY. MINISTERIO DE EDUCACION Y CULTO. Informe oficial sobre educación, ciencia y cultura a la III Reunión Interamericana de Ministros de Educación. Bogotá-Colombia, 4, agosto, 1963. A., 1963. 390p.

3600 PARAGUAY. MINISTERIO DE EDUCACION Y CULTO. Nuevo plan de actividades educativas para la enseñanza media, decreto no. 24.063. A., 1967. 68p.

3601 PARAGUAY. MINISTERIO DE EDUCACION Y CULTO. La educación y la justicia en los años 1932-33. A., Imp. nac., 1934. 105p.

3602 PARAGUAY. SUPERINTENDENTE INTERINO DE INSTRUCCION PUBLICA. Primera memoria que sobre educación común aparece en la nación, presentada al Consejo superior de educación por el Superintendente interino de instrucción pública Atanasio C. Riera. A., Tip. de "El Paraguayo", 1890. 134p.

3602a RIVAROLA, Domingo M. Educación y desarrollo en el Paraguay. La enseñanza básica. RPS 14 no. 39-40 (1977) 245-350.

3603 RIVAROLA, Domingo M. Influencia de los factores sociales en la irregularidad escolar. A., Centro Paraguayo de Estudios Sociológicos, 1971. 94p.

3604 RODRIGUEZ ALCALA DE GONZALEZ ODDONE, Beatriz. Rosa Peña. A., Academia Paraguaya de Historia, 1970. 30p.

3605 SALCEDO CACERES, Epifanio; ORTIZ DE SALCEDO, Margarita. Perfiles de la educación Paraguaya. RPS 7 no. 18 (1970) 143-91.

3606 SANCHE, Santiago. Estadística educacional del año 1955. A., Ministerio de Educación y Culto, 1957. 84p.

3606a SCHIEFELBEIN, Ernesto. Relaciones entre educación y empleo en el Paraguay. RPS 14 no. 39-40 (1977) 7-29.

3607 SPERATTI, Juan. Carapeguá: proceso y realidad cultural. A., 1969. 97p.

3607a UZCATEGUI GARCIA, Emilio. Panorama de la educación paraguaya. 2. ed. A., Imp. nac., 1959. 229p.

3608 VELAZQUEZ, Rafael Eladio. Educación paraguaya en el siglo XVII. HP 8-10 (1963-65) 75-95.

3609 VOCATIONAL education in Paraguay. Washington, Pan American Union, Division of Education, 1951. 169p. (Vocational education, series N, no. 13)

B. Primary education

3610 BADIE, Gerardo. Mi Manual. (4. grado). Coordinador: Gerardo Badie. Artes del languaje: Clemente Rodriguez. Estudios sociales: Miguel Rigual y Rafael Silva. Ciencia, salud, agricultura, música: Gerardo Badie. Aritmética y geometría: Pedro Cardozo. A., Colegio de San José, 1961. 480p.

3611 BARRIOS, M. Virgilio. Táctica escolar: obra aprobada por el h. Consejo nacional de educación. A., Casa editorial "La Prensa", 1919. 25p.

3612 CENTRO PARAGUAYO DE ESTUDIOS SOCIOLOGICOS. Educación en los barrios populares. Exploración del rendimiento escolar. Resultados de la muestra de rendimiento. A., CPES, 1971. 11p.

3613 CENTRO PARAGUAYO DE ESTUDIOS SOCIOLOGICOS. Educación en los barrios populares. III etapa. Validación de los test de rendimiento. A., CPES, 1972. 26p.

3614 FERREIRA GUBETICH, Hugo. Auxiliar paraguayo de segundo (-sexto) grado. B.A., Tall. Gráf. Luman, 1959. 5 vols.

3615 KREIDER, L. Emil. Crecimiento de la población: un aspecto en la educación primaria en el Paraguay. RPS 7 no. 18 (1970) 129-42.

3616 PARAGUAY. CONSEJO NACIONAL DE EDUCACION. Plan de estudios de las escuelas primaria. A., Tip. de El País, 1902. 47p.

3617 PARAGUAY. CONSEJO NACIONAL DE EDUCACION. Reglamento orgánico de las escuelas normales elementales. A., Tip. de Cándido Zamphirópolos, 1918. 23p.

3618 PARAGUAY. DIRECCION GENERAL DE ESCUELAS. Proyecto de reforma escolar (enseñanza primaria) por Ramón I. Cardozo. A., Imp. nac., 1923. 94p.

3619 PARAGUAY. MINISTERIO DE EDUCACION Y CULTO. Enseñanza primaria: planes de estudio y programas. A., 1950. 50p.

3620 PARAGUAY. MINISTERIO DE EDUCACION Y CULTO. Programa para las escuelas primarias del Paraguay: grados inferiores. A., Imp. nac., 1961. 250p.

3621 PARAGUAY. MINISTERIO DE JUSTICIA, CULTO E INSTRUCCION PUBLICA. Plan de estudios y programas sintéticos para las escuelas primarias de la república. A., Tall. gráf. del estado, 1915. 143p.

3622 PEREZ, Isidro. Literatura del quinto curso: la lírica y la épica. A., Imp. de la Penitenciaria Nacional, 1961? 121p.

3623 SERAFINI, Oscar; ODDONE, Hugo Barbosa. Inteligencia y creatividad en una muestra de niños residentes en barrios populares de Asunción. Su relación con el remedimiento. RPS 10 no. 28 (1973) 153-81.

3624 STIMSON, James; LABELLE, Thomas J. The organizational climate of Paraguayan elementary schools: rural-urban differentiations. EUS 3 (1971) no. 3, 333-49.

C. Secondary education

3625 BENITEZ, Luis G. Lecciones de historia americana para ciclo básico, bachillerato y normal. 2. ed. A., La Colmena, 1959. 222p.

3626 CATECISMO político y social para uso de los alumnos de la Escuela Normal del Paraguay. A., Imp. nac., 1855. 15p.

3627 GOMEZ RIOS, Emiliano. Elementos de historia general de América, para el 2 curso del ciclo básico, bachillerato y normal. 6. ed. B.A., Ediciones Nizza, 1961. 244p.

3627a GUGGIARI, José Patricio; BENITEZ, Justo Pastor. La reforma de la enseñanza secundaria. A., Imp. nac., 1931. 52p.

3628 OSUNA, Tomás. Ensayo sobre un plan de estudios para la enseñanza secundaria. A., Tall. gráf. del Estado, 1968. 155p.

3629 PARAGUAY. CONSEJO NACIONAL DE EDUCACION. Programas analíticos de acuerdo con el nuevo plan de estudios para las escuelas medias y superiores de la república del Paraguay. A., La Colmena, 1925. 99p.

3630 PARAGUAY. MINISTERIO DE EDUCACION Y CULTO. Reforma de la educación secundaria en el Paraguay. A., Imp. nac., 1957. 105p.

3631 PARAGUAY. MINISTERIO DE JUSTICIA, CULTO E INSTRUCCION PUBLICA. Reforma del plan de estudios de la enseñanza secundaria. A., 1919? 5p.

D. Higher education

3631a AGUINAGA, Samuel. El Paraguay en el exterior. Congreso científico de Montevideo. Conclusiones aprobadas, informes y datos biográficos de los delegados del Paraguay. Montevideo, Imp. de "El Siglo", 1901. 56p.

3632 APMANN, Robert. Engineering education in Paraguay. JDA 8 (1974) no. 2, 257-70.

3633 APSTEIN, Theodore; CREVENNA, Theo R. The universities of Paraguay and Uruguay. Washington, Pan American Union, Division of Intellectual Cooperation, 1947. iv, 68p.

3634 BAEZ ALLENDE, Amadeo. Reseña histórica de la Universidad Nacional. A., Imp. nac., 1939. 189p.

3634a BLAIR, Calvin Patton; SCHAEDEL, Richard P.; STREET, James H. Responsibilities of the foreign scholar to the local scholarly community: studies of U.S. research in Guatemala, Chile, and Paraguay; edited and with an introduction by Richard N. Adams. N.Y., Council on Educational Cooperation with Latin America, 1969. 112p.

3635 CARDOZO, Efraím. Origines de la enseñanza superior en el Paraguay. HP 2 (1957) 68-81.

3636 CENTRO PARAGUAYO DE ESTUDIOS SOCIOLOGICOS. Curso regional de ciencias sociales. A., CPES, 1971. 33p.

3636a EDUCATION AND WORLD AFFAIRS. COUNCIL ON EDUCATIONAL COOPERATION WITH LATIN AMERICA. Survey of U.S.-Paraguayan educational relations at the university level. N.Y., Education and World Affairs, 1967. 22p.

3637 La ESCUELA paraguaya de administración pública. DAI 44-45 (1961) Aug.-Sept., 66-69.

3638 FALUCHO (BAMBILL, Julio). Antecedentes históricos sobre la fundación de la Universidad Nacional de la Asunción y los Colegios Nacionales de Villa Rica, Villa Concepción, Villa del Pilar y Villa Encarnación. A., El País, 1903. 60p.

3639 FEDERACION UNIVERSITARIA DEL PARAGUAY. III Congreso Universitario del Paraguay, 1967. A., 1967. 47p.

3640 GUTIERREZ, Asir P. Educational planning for the National University of Asunción, Paraguay. Washington, 1970. 41p.

3641 INTERNATIONAL STUDENT CONFERENCE. RESEARCH AND INFORMATION COMMISSION. Paraguay (1961/62) a report. Leiden, COSEC, 1962? 56p.

3642 MARESKI, Sofia. Organización y programa de trabajo del Centro Paraguayo de Documentación Social. RPS 6 no. 16 (1969) 132-33.

3642a PAN AMERICAN UNION, OFICINA DE CIENCIA Y TECNOLOGIA. Guía de instituciones y sociedades científicas Latinoamericanos: primera parte, Bolivia, Paraguay, y Uruguay. Washington, 1951. x, 30p.

3643 PARAGUAY. CONSEJO NACIONAL DE EDUCACION. Reglamento orgánico de las escuelas normales de la nación. Publicación oficial. A., Tall. Mons. Lasagna, 1903. 24p.

3644 PARAGUAY. DIRECCION GENERAL DE ESCUELAS. Programas sintéticos para las escuelas normales elementales de la república. Aprobado por el honorable Consejo nacional de educación. A., Tall. gráf. del estado, 1919. 15p.

3645 PARAGUAY. MINISTERIO DE JUSTICIA, CULTO E INSTRUCCION PUBLICA. Programas de los colegios nacionales; curso académico de 1896-1897. A., Tall. nac. de H. Kraus, 1896. 5 vols.

3646 PARAGUAY. MINISTERIO DE JUSTICIA, CULTO E INSTRUCCION PUBLICA. La reforma de la enseñanza normal. A., Imp. nac., 1933. 57p.

3647 PARAGUAY. MINISTERIO DE JUSTICIA, CULTO E INSTRUCCION PUBLICA. Reglamento interno y plan de estudios de la Escuela nacional de agricultura. A., Establecimiento tip. del El Cívico, 1907. 33p.

3648 PEREZ ACOSTA, Juan Francisco. Núcleos culturales del Paraguay contemporáneo, confraternidad y cultura; homenaje al Instituto Paraguayo en su cincuentenario (1895- 10 de julio - 1945). B.A., 1959. 145p.

3649 PRIETO, Justo Pastor. Sentido social de la cultura universitaria. B.A., Plantié, 1942. 378p.

3650 La REFORMA universitaria. A., Imp. nac., 1929. 61p.

3651 RESUMEN de las actividades desarrollados por la Sociedad Bolivariana del Paraguay en el decenio 1960-1970. BSBP 6 (1970) 117-28.

3652 RIQUELME GARCIA, Benigno. El Colegio Seminario Conciliar de San Carlos. RNCP 1 no. 1 (1957) 42-46.
Established 1783, closed 1822.

3653 RIVAROLA, Domingo M. Universidad y estudiantes en una sociedad tradicional. AP 12 (1969) 48-84.

3654 SOLER, Juan José. El problema económico de la Universidad. A., El País, 1948. 30p.

3655 UNITED NATIONS EDUCATIONAL, SCIENTIFIC AND CULTURAL ORGANIZATION. SCIENCE COOPERATION OFFICE FOR LATIN

AMERICA. Scientific institutions and scientists in Latin America: Paraguay. Montevideo, 1959. 93p.

3656 UNIVERSIDAD CATOLICA, ASUNCION. CONSEJO DE PLANIFICACION. El plan decenal de desarrollo de la Universidad Católica. A., 1973. 36p. (Informe preliminar de discusión, 1)

3657 UNIVERSIDAD NACIONAL, ASUNCION. Guía. A., El Arte, 1947. 121p.
Also: A., 1969. 383p.

3658 UNIVERSIDAD NACIONAL. ASUNCION. Plan general de desarrollo de la Universidad Nacional de Asunción. A., 1973. 122p.

XI. THE ARTS AND MUSIC

A. General studies

3659 ALBORNOZ, Pablo. Arte jesuítico de las Misiones hispano-guaraní. A., Guaraní, 1941. 32p.

3660 BAEZ, Jorge. Artes y artistas paraguayos. Periodo renacentista. A., Edit. "El Liberal", 1941. 88p.

3661 BAREIRO SAGUIER, Rubén. Speaking of Paraguay: a survey of recent cultural trends. APAU 14 (1962) no. 2, 32-36.

3662 DE BRITO, Fernando Saturnino. Las artes en las Misiones jesuíticas del Paraguay y necesidad de creación de un organismo técnico de protección de nuestra acervo de arte e historia. RY 2 no. 7 (1963) 11-22.

3663 DOCUMENTOS de arte argentina. Cuaderno XX. Las misiones guaraníes. Escultura, pintura, grabados y artes menores. Texto de Miguel Solá. B.A., 1946. 34p. 80pl. (Publicación de la Academia nacional de bellas artes).

3664 FERNANDEZ, Miguel Angel. L'art moderne au Paraguay. E 48 no. 494 (1970) 146-55.

3665 FERNANDEZ, Miguel Angel. La plástica paraguaya moderna. CA 21 (1962) no. 1, 91-103.

3666 GAMARRA DOLDAN, Pedro. Le surréalisme au Paraguay. E 46 no. 475-476 (1968) 254-57.

3667 INSTITUTO PARAGUAYO DE CULTURA HISPANICA. Cuatro años de labor del Instituto Paraguayo de Cultura Hispanica, 1958-1963. A., Tall. Gráf. Emasa, 1963. 49p.

3668 PLA, Josefina. Las artes plásticas en el Paraguay: breve esquema historico. AIAAIE 19 (1966) 79-96.
Also: B.A., Universidad Nacional de Buenos Aires, Facultad de Arquitectura y Urbanismo, 1966. 22p.

3669 PLA, Josefina. Las artesanías en el Paraguay. A., Ediciones Comuneros, 1969. 91p.

3670 PLA, Josefina. La baroque hispano-guaraní. E 48 no. 494 (1970) 142-46.

3671 PLA, Josefina. El barroco hispano-guaraní. CH 58 no. 173 (1964) 345-53.
Also: A., Imp. nac. del Boletín Oficial del Estado, c. 1964. 9p.

3671a PLA, Josefina. El barroco hispano-guaraní. A., Edit. del Centenario, 1975. 274p.

3671b PLA, Josefina. The Hispano-Guarani baroque. APAU 28 (1976) Supplement to no. 11/12, 1-16.

3672 PLA, Josefina. Historia y catálogo del Museo de Bellas Artes. A., 1970. 61p.
2. ed. A., Casa América, 1975. 175p.

3673 PLA, Josefina. Treinta y tres nombres en las artes plásticas paraguayas. A., Edit. Cultura, 1973. 59p.

3674 PLATTNER, Felix A.; LUNTE, E. Kunst in "Jesuitenstaat" von Paraguay. DM 12 (1959) no. 11-12, 407-14.

B. Fine arts

3674a CALZADA, Isidoro. Aurelio García: pintor del Mariscal. A., Edit. Don Bosco, 1970? 12p. (Galería de paraguayos ilustres, 12. Celeste)

3675 PLA, Josefina; FERNANDEZ, Miguel Angel. Arte moderno del Paraguay; muestra retrospectiva. Misión Cultura Brasileña con la colaboración del Sepro, Asunción, agosto 1964. A?, 1964. 20p.

3675a PLA, Josefina. La cerámica popular paraguaya. SA XI no. 1-2 (1976) 7-28.

3675b PLA, Josefina. El espíritu del fuego: biografía de Julian de la Herrería. A., Imp. Alborada, 1977. 207p.

3676 PLA, Josefina. El grabado en el Paraguay. A., Alcor, 1962. 39p.

3677 CAMPOS CERVERA, Andrés. Julián de la Herreria; recuento de arte. Explicación final de Josefina Plá. A., Diálogo, 1957. a-hp. (Cuadernos de la Piririta, 2)

3678 ORTELLADA ROJAS DE FOSSATI, Maria Antonia. Aurelio García. A., Artes Gráf. Zamphirópolos, 1969. 179p.

3679 PAOLI, Arnaldo. Un artista paraguayo en Europa: labor artística y cultural de Arnaldo Paoli en Alemania, Bélgica, España, Escocia, Francia, Inglaterra, Italia, Países Bajos, Suiza y Santa Sede. A., El Arte, 1957. 83p.

C. Architecture

3679a ALBORNO, Pablo. A colonial church in Paraguay. BPAU 66 (1932) no. 10, 700-09.

3679b BRUGADA GUANES, Alejandro. Paracuaria, obras arquitectonicas de la era jesuítica en el Paraguay. A., Offset Comuneros, 1975. 89p.

3680 BUSANICHE, Hernán. La arquitectura en las misiones jesuíticas guaraníes. Santa Fé, Arg., Castellví (El Litoral), 1955. 204p.

3681 BUSCHIAZZO, Mario José. La arquitectura en madera de las misiones del Paraguay, Chiquitos, Mojos y Maynas. *In* INTERNATIONAL CONGRESS OF THE HISTORY OF ART, XX, NEW YORK, 1961. Acts, Studies in Western Art. Vol. 3. Latin American Art ... Princeton, Princeton University Press, 1963. p. 173-90.

3682 DOCUMENTOS de arte argentino. Cuaderno XIX. Las misiones guaraníes. Arquitectura. Texto de Miguel Solá. B.A., 1946. 33p. 110pl. (Publicaciones de la Academia bellas artes).

3683 FURLONG CARDIFF, Guillermo. La arquitectura en las misiones Guaraníes. EBA 57 (1937) 81-100.

3684 FURLONG CARDIFF, Guillermo. La arquitectura de las misiones guaraníticas. EALP 1937, jun.-agosto, 86-100.

3685 GIURIA, Juan. La arquitectura en el Paraguay. B.A., Universidad de Buenos Aires, Instituto de Arte Americano e Investigaciones Estéticas, 1950. 137p.

3685a GUTIERREZ Z., Ramón. Evolución urbanística y arquitectónica del Paraguay, 1537-1911. Corrientes, Arg., Departamento de Historia de la Arquitectura, Universidad Nacional del Nordeste, 197? 412p.

3686 PLA, Josefina. Apuntes historico-descriptivos sobre algunos templos Paraguayos. Area no misionera. AIAAIE 21 (1968) 9-31.

3687 PLA, Josefina. El templo de Yaguarón; una joya barroca en el Paraguay. A., Edit. del Centenario, 1970. 48p. (Colección "Paraquaria", 4)

3688 SEBASTIAN, Santiago. Plano inédito de Candelaria, misiones jesuíticas del Paraguay. AEAR 30 no. 119 (1957) 245-51.

D. Theatre

3689 ASUNCION. DEPARTAMENTO DE CULTURA Y ARTE. IV. Departamento de Cultura y Arte: su organización y desarrollo; y, Cuatro siglos de teatro en el Paraguay, por Josefina Plá. A., Casa América, 1966. 244p. (Publicaciones de la Asesoría Financiera de la Municipalidad de la Capital)

3690 BANNER, J. Worth. Ildefonso Bermejo, iniciador del teatro en el Paraguay. RI 17 no. 33 (1951) 97-107.

3691 CAILLET-BOIS, Julio. El teatro en la Asunción a mediados del siglo 16. RFH 4 (1942) no. 1, 72-76.

3691a DREDEMIE, Oscar J. Los orígenes del teatro en las regiones del Rio de la Plata; la obra de los Jesuítas de la provincia del Paraguay. EBA 57 (1937) 61-80.

3691b FRANCO VERA, Optaciano. Rufo Galeano y el teatro luqueño. A., Casa América, 1975. 94p.

3692 JONES, Willis Knapp. Paraguay's theater. BKA 15 (1941) Jan., 40-42.

3693 MAY-GAMBOA, C. Tiempoovillo: Paraguayan experimental theatre. LATR 8 (1975) no. 2, 75-83.

3694 PLA, Josefina. El teatro en el Paraguay (1554-1870). CA 24 no. 4/vol. 141 (1965) 201-22.

3695 PLA, Josefina. El teatro en el Paraguay. 2. ed. A., Diálogo, 1967- (Colección Camalote, 1)
First ed. is no. 3689.

3695a PLA, Josefina. Teatro religioso medieval: su brote en Paraguay. CH no. 291 (1974) 666-80.

3695b PLA, Josefina. En torne al personaje teatral contemporáneo. CA 12 (1953) no. 4, 276-91.

3696 RIVAROLA MATTO, José Maria. Julio Correa et le théatre Guaraní. E 48 no. 494 (1970) 139-42.

3696a TERCERA muestra paraguaya de teatro. LATR 9 (1976) no. 2, 79-80.

E. Music

3696b BACCAY, Dalmidio Alberto. Vitalidad expresiva de la música guaraní. B.A., 1961. 108p.

3697 BOETTNER, Juan Max. La música en tiempo de los López. HP 1 (1956) 38-48.

3698 BOETTNER, Juan Max. Música y músicos del Paraguay. Edición de Autores Paraguayos Asociados. A., El. Gráf., 1957. 294p.

3699 BOZZANO BAGLIETTO, Deolinda. Manual de canciones escolares. A., La Colmena, 1958. 68p.

3699a CARDOZO OCAMPO, Mauricio. Mis bodas de oro con el folklore paraguayo: memorias de un Pychai. A., Offset comuneros, 1972. 319p.

3700 DOMINGUEZ, R. Aristóbulo. Aires nacionales paraguayos; arreglados para piano. n.p., 1928. 111p.

3701 DOMINGUEZ, Ramiro. Ditirambos para fluto y coro. A., Péndulo, 1964? 1 vol. (unpaged)

3702 FLORES, J. Muzykalnaia zhizn' v Paragvae. SMU 17 (1953) no. 4, 101-02.

3703 FURLONG CARDIFF, Guillermo. Domenico Zipoli, músico eximio en Europa y América, 1688-1726. AHSJ 17 (1955) 418-28.

3704 KAMPRAD, Alfredo. Con el violín entre los indios lenguas y la música de ellos. RSCP 3 no. 5 (1934) 139-42.

3705 KAMPRAD, Alfredo. La música entre los indios lenguas. RGA 3 no. 17 (1935) 129-33.

3705a RIERA, Federico. Homenaje a Félix Perez Cardozo: su vida, su obra y sus canciones. A?, 195? (unpaged)

3705b RIERA, Federico. Recuerdos musicales del Paraguay. B.A., Edit. Perrot, 1959. 53p.

XII. LITERATURE

A. General studies

3706 ALVAREZ GONZALEZ, Aurora; ARMENDARIZ AGORETTA, Rosario. Panorama de la literatura paraguaya. A., Ediciones Loyola, 1967? 214p.

3706a AMARAL, Raúl. Las generaciones en la cultura paraguaya: ensayo de investigación bibliográfica. A., Centro Paraguayo de Estudios Sociológicos, 1976. 19p.
Also: RPS 13 no. 35 (1976) 141-55.

3707 AMARAL, Raúl. El modernismo literario en el Paraguay. (De la etapa precursora a la iniciación formal) CA no. 187 (1973) 205-22.

3708 AMARAL, Raúl. El novecentismo paraguayo, linea biográfico y doctrinal de una generación. B.A., Instituto Judío Argentino de Cultura e Información, 1968. 19p. (Cuadernos de Comentario)
Also: CM 15 no. 16 (1968) 27-42.

3709 AMARAL, Raúl. El romanticismo paraguayo. B.A., 1966. 8p.
Also: CM 13 no. 47 (1966).

3710 AMARAL, Raúl. Rubén Darío, Valle Inclan y el modernismo paraguayo. CA no. 189 (1973) 195-210.

3711 BAEZ, Jorge. La torre del silencio, y otros ensayos. A., Imp. nac., 1955. 115p.

3712 BAREIRO SAGUIER, Rubén. El criterio generacional en la literatura paraguaya. RI 30 no. 58 (1964) 293-303.

3713 BAZAN, Juan F. Un hueco en la literatura paraguaya. *In* no. 152, p. 42-48.

3714 BENITEZ, Justo Pastor. Algunos aspectos de la literatura paraguaya. (Disertación leida en la Academia Brasilera de Letras) Rio de Janeiro, 1935. 16p.

3715 BENITEZ, Justo Pastor. Noticias sobre la literatura Paraguaya actual. BAAL 1937 (April-June) 227-36.

3716 BENITEZ, Justo Pastor. Panorama de la literatura paraguaya en el siglo XX. RNC 17 no. 111 (1955) 25-37.

3717 BENITEZ, Justo Pastor. El proceso literario en el Paraguay. AMH 1944, Dec., 37-45.

3718 CENTURION, Carlos R. Actuales tendencias de la literatura paraguaya. RIB 16 (1966) 383-97.

3719 CENTURION, Carlos R. La generación intelectual del 23. RAP 2 no. 7 (1943) 15-43.

3720 CENTURION, Carlos R. Historia de las letras paraguayas. B.A., Edit. Ayacucho, 1947-51. 2 vols.

3721 CENTURION, Carlos R. Historia de la cultura paraguaya. A., Patronato de Leprosos del Paraguay, 1961. 2 vols. (Biblioteca "Ortiz Guerrero")
2. ed. of no. 3720. The most thorough account of Paraguayan literature.

3722 DECOUD, José Segundo. La literatura en el Paraguay; conferencia leida en el Ateneo paraguayo en sesión del 28 de noviembre de 1884. 2. ed. B.A., La Plata, Imp. lit., libreria y encuadernación de J. Peuser, 1889. 18p.

3723 LITERATURE du Paraguay. E 48 no. 494 (1970). 282p.

3724 FOGELQUIST, Donald F. Paraguayan literature of the Chaco war. MLJ 33 (1949) no. 8, 603-13.

3725 GONZALEZ, Juan Natalicio. Evolución política y literaria del Paraguay. RABA 1935, 5-18.

3726 IBANEZ GUTIERREZ, Carlos. Sentido de la literatura paraguaya en el siglo XX. RJ 47 no. 232 (1957) 77-91.

3727 JONES, Willis Knapp. Literature of the Chaco War. H 21 (1938) 33-46.

3728 LANTEUIL, Henri de. O Paraguai e a sua literatura. F 1944, Nov., 33-41.

3729 MORINIGO, Mariano. Capitulo antimodernista en la literatura Paraguaya. RNC 26 no. 165 (1964) 31-66.

3730 PANE, Ignacio Alberto. Ensayos paraguayos; selección y reseña de la historia cultura del Paraguay, por J. Natalicio González. B.A., W.M. Jackson, 1945. lxxiv, 382p. (Colección panamericana, 24)
2. ed. 1946.
3. ed. 1957.

3731 PEREZ, Isidro. Literatura del cuarto curso, adaptado al programa del cuarto curso del nuevo plan de estudios. A., El País, n.d. 128p.

3732 PEREZ-MARICEVICH, Francisco. La poesía y la narrativa en el Paraguay. A., Edit. del Centenario, 1969. 72p. (Colección Ensayos, no. 1)

3733 PLA, Josefina. A literatura paraguaya. CB 4 (1962) no. 1, 40-51.

3734 PLA, Josefina. Aspectos de la cultura paraguaya: literatura paraguaya en el siglo XX. CA no. 120 (1962) 67-103.

3734a PLA, Josefina. La literatura paraguaya en una situación de bilinguismo. EP 2 no. 2 (1974) 5-30.

3735 PLA, Josefina. Literatura paraguaya en el siglo XX. 2. ed. A., Ediciones Comuneros, 1972. 60p.

3735a PLA, Josefina. Obra y aporte femeninos en la literatura nacional. A., Centro Paraguayo do Estudios Sociológicos, 1976. 51p.

3736 RIVAROLA-MATTO, Juan Bautista. Algunas ideas acerca de la literatura paraguaya. CA 30 (1972) 1, 225-35.

3737 ROA BASTOS, Augusto. Pasión y expresión de la literatura paraguaya. U 44 (1960) abril/jun., 157-76.

3738 RODRIGUEZ ALCALA, Hugo. Historia de la literatura paraguaya. Mexico, Ediciones de Andrea, 1970. 196p. (Colección Studium, 63)
Also: Asunción, Colegio de San José, 1971. 202p.

3739 RODRIGUEZ ALCALA, Hugo. La literatura paraguaya. B.A., Centro Editor de América Latina, 1968. 64p. (Enciclopedia literaria, 59. España e Hispanoamérica)
Also: A., Ediciones Comuneros, 1971. 98p.

3740 El ROMANTICISMO paraguayo. CM 47 (1966) 66-73.

3741 SANCHEZ QUELL, Hipólito. Comentarios: actualidad anuncena; cosas del tiempo ído; al vibrar del cable; quien es quien?; horizontes lejanos; lo que debe hacer. A., El Arte, 1953. 207p.

3742 VALLEJOS PEREZ GARAY, Roque. La literatura paraguaya como expresión de la realidad nacional. A., Edit. "Don Bosco", 1967. 63p. (Colección "Ñandutí literario, 3)
2. ed. 1971. 108p.

3743 XXX (CARRANZA, Adolfo P.) Las letras en Paraguay. RNBA 12 (1890) 343-59.

1. *Poetry*

3744 ANTHOLOGIE poétique. E 48 no. 494 (1970) 34-63.
French translations of Paraguayan poetry.

3745 ARANDA, Santiago Dimas; GONZALEZ FRUTOS, Maria Hedy. 15 testimonios de la poesía paraguaya, 1920-1970. A., 1972. 53p.

3746 BAREIRO SAGUIER, Ruben. Joven poesía paraguaya. CMHL 14 (1970) 153-60.

3747 BAREIRO SAGUIER, Ruben. Poesía Paraguaya del presente siglo. *In* no. 272, 80-82.

3748 BEBAN, Mercedes. Poesía y paisaje del Paraguay. B.A., 1947. 44p.

3748a BEYOND the river: an anthology of Paraguayan poetry; trans. by Charles R. Carlisle. Berkeley, Calif., Thorp Springs Press, 1977. ix, 72p.

3749 BOBADILLA, Julian. Ca'aguy poty; poesias seleccionadas en guaraní y castellano. A., Trujillo, 1962. 72p.

3750 BUZO GOMES, Sinforiano. Indice de la poesía paraguaya, presentado y anotado por Sinforiano Buzo Gomes. A., B.A., Edit. Tupâ, 1943. 384p.
2. ed. B.A., Edit. Indoamericana, 1952. 335p.
3. ed. A., Ediciones Nizza, 1959. 343p.

3750a CARLISLE, Charles R. Lo contemporaneo de diez poetas paraguayas. EP 1 no. 2 (1974) 141-54.

3751 CEA, José Roberto. Notas sobre el mundo poético de los guaraníes. CSS 36 (1955) abril-jun., 79-88.

3752 DE VITIS, Michael Angelo. Parnaso paraguayo, selectas composiciones poéticas coleccionadas. Barcelona, Maucci, 1926. 271p.

3753 ESCULIES, Oscar. Tres poetas del Paraguay. RAP 3 (1970) no. 1, 32-41.

3753a MARCOS, Juan Manuel. El ciclo romántico modernista en el Paraguay. A., Ediciones Criterio, 1977. 147p.

3754 OCHO poetas paraguayos: Josefina Plá and others. A., Diálogo, 1963. 18p. (Colección Styles)

3755 PANE, Ignacio Alberto. Don Eusebio Lillo i el Paraguai. A., Imp. univ. de S.A. Garcia V., 1902. 15p.

3756 PEREZ-MARICEVICH, Francisco. Poesía y conciencia de la poesía en el Paraguay. A., Ediciones Epoca, 1967. 20p. (Cuadernillos de ensayos breves ser. A., no. 1)

3757 PLA, Josefina. Antología de poesía paraguaya. Madrid, Imp. nac. del Boletín oficial del Estado, 1966. 45p.

3758 PLA, Josefina. Antología de poesía paraguaya: recuento de una lírica ignorada. CH 68 (1966) 281-325.

3759 PLA, Josefina. Poesía femenina en el Paraguay. EC 85 (1962) 63-69.

3760 PLA, Josefina. Poesía de hoy en el Paraguay. EC 110 (1970) 25-31.

3761 PLA, Josefina. Poesía paraguaya actuel. JIAS 9 (1967) no. 4, 529-40.

3762 ROBERTS, W.H. Hacia una tradición indígena en la poesía paraguaya. HF 5 (1961-62) 13, 33-43.

3763 ROBERTS, W.H. Paraguayan poetry of social protest. KFLQ 9 (1962) 45-51.

3764 RODRIGUEZ ALCALA, Hugo. Un clásico y un superrealista, o dos visiones de una misma realidad: el Paraguay. HR 33 (1965) no. 1, 40-51.

3765 RODRIGUEZ ALCALA, Hugo. La promoción poetica paraguaya de 1950. CA no. 165 (1969) 170-89.

3766 RODRIGUEZ ALCALA, Hugo. Sobre la poesía paraguaya de los últimos veinte años. RHM 23 (1957) no. 3-4, 305-14.
Also in no. 4129, 199-211.

3767 RODRIGUEZ ALCALA, José. Antolojia paraguaya. A., Casa editora: Tall. nac. de H. Kraus, 1910. viii, vii, 163p.

3768 ROMERO, Elvio. La poésie paraguayenne dans la cité. E 48 no. 494 (1970) 19-33.

3769 SANCHEZ QUELL, Hipolito. Los nuevos en la actual poesía paraguaya. LL 14 (1939) 374-85.

3770 SANCHEZ QUELL, Hipolito. Triángulo de la poesía rioplatense. B.A., Edit. Américalee, 1953. 126p.

3770a SOCIEDAD BOLIVARIANA DEL PARAGUAY. Cantos paraguayos a Bolívar. A., 1957. 39p.
2. ed. 1959.

3771 VALLEJOS PEREZ GARAY, Roque. Antologia crítica de la poesía paraguaya contemporánea. A., Edit. Don Bosco, 1968. 195p. (Colección "Ñanduti literario", 4)

3772 VALLEJOS PEREZ GARAY, Roque. Tres generaciones de poetas. MN 33 (1969) 54-59.

3773 WEY, Walter. La poesía paraguaya; historia de una incógnita. Traducción del portugués por Haydée Lagomarsino y Gladys Torres. Montevideo, Biblioteca Alfar, 1951. 109p.

3774 WIEZELL de ESPINOLA, Elsa. Seven paraguayan poets. APAU 19 (1967) no. 6, 31-36.

2. *Prose*

3775 ARANA, Oswaldo. El hombre en la novela de la guerra del Chaco. JIAS 6 (1964) no. 3, 347-65.

3776 ATENEO PARAGUAYO. Composiciones literarias leídas en la velada celebrada en conmemoración del 2 aniversario de su fundación. B.A., Imp. de M. Biedma, 1888. 69p.

3777 BAREIRO SAGUIER, Rubén. Documento y creación en las novelas de la guerra del Chaco. AP 8 (1968) 89-98.

3778 BAREIRO SAGUIER, Rubén. El tema del exilio en la narrativa paraguaya contemporánea. CMHL 14 (1970) 79-96.

3778a BAZAN, Juan F. Narrativa paraguaya y latinoamericana. A., 1976. 642p.

3779 CENTURION, Carlos R. Origenes del periodismo Paraguayo. *In* no. 272, p. 77-79.

3780 CODINA DE GIANNONI, Iverna. Paraguay en una voz. *In her* América en la novela. B.A., Cruz del Sur, 1964. p. 165-70.

3781 COTELA, R. La novela paraguaya: subdesarrollo y literatura. T 14 (1967) 14-20.

3782 FERNANDEZ DECAMILLI, Evaristo. Apuntes sobre el periodismo en Villarrica. Villarrica, Tall. EMASA, 1958. 28p.

3783 LIVIERES ARGAÑA, Juan I. Antología de la oratorio paraguaya, 1811-1967. A., Escuela Técnica Salesiana, 1968. xvi, 430p.
2. ed. A., Edit. La Voz, 1970. 485p.

3784 MEBA (ARGUELLO, Manuel E.B.); BAREIRO SAGUIER, Rubén. Cuento y novela. A., El Arte, 1960. 94p. (Escuela Municipal de Arte Escéncio. Colección Manuales)

3785 NAGY, Arturo. La Princesa de Salerno y otros relatos. A., Edit. del Centenario, 1971. 123p. (Colección "Paraquaria", 6)
"Selección de articulos aparecidos en periódicos asuncenos."

3786 PEREZ-MARICEVICH, Francisco. Breve antología del cuento paraguayo. A., Ediciones Comuneros, 1969. 199p.

3787 PLA, Josefina. Crónicas del Paraguay. Prólogo del Francisco Pérez Maricevich. B.A., J. Alvarez, 1969. 174p.
An anthology of short stories.

3788 PLA, Josefina. Contenido humano y social de la narrativa. PA 2 no. 8 (1964) 83-99.

3789 PLA, Josefina; PEREZ-MARICEVICH, Francisco. Narrativa paraguaya (recuento de una problemática). CA 27 no. 4, no. 159 (1968) 181-96.

3790 PLA, Josefina. La narrativa en el Paraguay de 1900 a la fecha. CH 77 no. 231 (1969) 641-54.

3791 RODRIGUEZ ALCALA, Hugo. La narrativa paraguaya desde 1960 a 1970. NNH 2 (1972) 1, 39-58.
Also: ROMF 84 (1972) 517-45.

3792 RODRIGUEZ ALCALA, Hugo. La narrativa paraguaya desde comienzos del siglo XX. CHML 14 (1970) 51-78.

3793 TEATRO breve: Historia de un numeró (por Josefina Plá); Cantata heroica (por Ramiro Domínguez). A., Diálogo, 1969. 50p. (Colección Dionisos)

3794 VILLARINO, María de. La novela de la guerra chaqueña. SUR 8 (1938) 58-66.

B. The period before 1935: individual writers

Arturo ALSINA

3795 La marca de fuego, drama en tres actos. A., 1926. 57p.

José ALSINA CANALS

3796 El arpa bohemica: poesias. 2. ed. A., Imp. sudamericana, 1924. 115p.

Cecilio BAEZ

3797 Composiciones poéticas. Paris, J. Peyronnet, 1926. 46p.

3798 Composiciones - en prosa y verso. A., Imp. "España", 1918. 49p.

Jorge BAEZ

3799 La canción de la epopeya y Las leyendas. Poesías y prosas. A., Imp. M. Brossa, 1928. 22p.

3800 Iris de gesta: poesias y prosas. A., Edit. Heraldo, 1929. 36p.

3801 La ofrenda de Leuconoe. A., Paraguaya, 1940. 75p.

Rafael BARRETT

3802 Cuentos breves. Madrid, Edit. América, 1919. 182p. (Biblioteca Andrés Bello, 59)

3803 Ideas y críticas. Montevideo, O.M. Bertani, 191-? 202p.

3804 Al margen: críticas literarias y cientificas. Montevideo, O.M. Bertani, 1912. 185p.

3805 Mirando vivir. Montevideo, O.M. Bertani, 191?

3806 Moralidades actuales. Madrid, Edit. América, 1919. 301p. (Biblioteca Andrés Bello, 58)

3807 Obras completas. B.A., Edit. Americalee, 1943. 688p.
2. ed. 1954. 3 vols.

3807a BENITEZ, Justo Pastor. Un pensador en el trópico. *In* no. 162, 2. ed., 143-48.

3807b DOMINGUEZ, Manuel. Rafael Barrett. *In* no. 203, 184-88.

3807c FORTEZA, Jorge R. Rafael Barrett: su obra, su predica, su moral. B.A., Edit. Atlas, 1927. 124p.

Héctor L. BARRIOS

3808 Guijarros; composiciones serias y humoristicas, publicadas en diversas épocas en órganos de la prensa nacional, prosa y verso con un apéndice titulado "Enciclopedias", comedia presentado por el autor en el primer concurso de este genero. A., El País, 1906. 86p.

Clodobe BAZAN

3809 Monólogos, versos y escritos. A., M. Brossa, 1923. 79p.

José S. BAZAN

3810 El dictador Francia y otras composiciones en verso y prosa. Madrid, R. Fé, 1887. vii, 442p.

Ildefonso Antonio BERMEJO

3811 Un paraguayo leal, drama en dos actos y en verso. A., Tall. nac. de H. Kraus, 1898. 83p.

Jaime BESTARD

3812 La ciudad florida (memorias de un bohemio). B.A., Fanetti, 1951. 224p.

Juan Andrés CARDOZO

3813 De pie frente al dolor. A., Asedio, 1966. 49p. (Colección Umbral, 1)

Manuel D. CARDOZO

3814 Agua mansa y ycuá caaguy; poesías. A., Zurucu'a, 1927. 64p.

Jean CASABIANCA

3815 Oda al Paraguay. A., Tall. nac. de H. Kraus, 1903. 22p.

Fermín DOMINGUEZ

3816 Hilachas. A., Tall. tip. del Estado, 1912. 175p.

Oscar ESCULIES

3817 Rumor de agua. Prólogo de Juana de Ibarbourou. Montevideo, Impresora uruguaya, 1936. 74p.

Eloy FARIÑA NUÑEZ

3818 Canto secular (poema). B.A., Tall. gráf. de la Cía. gral. de fósforos, 1911. 38p.

3819 Carmenes. B.A., Gráf. Argentino, 1922. 90p.

3820 Conceptos estéticas; mitos guaranies. B.A., Tall. Gráf. M. Pastor, 1926. 318p.

3821 El jardín del silencio; ensayos filosóficos. A., H. Kraus, 1925. 148p.

3822 Las vértebras de pan; cuentos. B.A., Biblioteca Selecta Americana, 1914. 137p.

3822a BENITEZ, Justo Pastor. El payé de la raza. *In* no. 162, 2. ed., 114-18.

3823 URBIETA ROJAS, Pastor. Eloy Fariña Nuñez: su vida y su obra. B.A., Lucania, 1972. 30p.

Heriberto FERNANDEZ

3824 Sonetos a la hermana; compilados por Miguel Angel Fernández. A., Diálogo, 1957. 15p. (Cuadernos de la Piririta, 1)

3825 Visiones de eglogas: poemas. Retrato del pinto Holdenjara. Paris, E. Chassaing, 1925. 33p.

3826 Voces de ensueño; poemas. Paris-Mexico, Bouret, 1926. 31p.

Luis Fernán FERNANDEZ DE LA PUENTE

3827 Solar guaraní: poesías. B.A., Biblioteca Selecta Americana, 1913. 126p.

Federico GARCIA

3827a Mosaico. Proemio de Viriato Díaz Perez. A., 1918. 162p.

Juan Natalicio GONZALEZ

3828 Baladas guaranies. Paris, Indias, 1925. xiv, 58p.

3829 Cuento y parabolas. B.A., Ediciones Monte Domecq', 1922. 127p.

3830 Elegías de Tenochtitlán. Mexico, Edit. Guaranía, 1953. 80p. (Colección Nezahualcoyoti, 8)

3831 Motivos de la tierra escarlata. Mexico, Edit. Guaranía, 1952. 174p. (Colección Nezahualcoyoti, 3)

3832 La raíz errante. Mexico, Edit. Guaranía, 1953. 280p. (Colección Nezahualcoyoti, 6)

Carlos GROSSO SOSA

3833 Mimbipá; o, La ciudad misteriosa guaraní, novelita histórica. Prólogo de Fortunato Toranzos Bardel, Concepción del Paraguay, 1928. 116p.

Alejandro GUANES

3834 De paso por la vida, poesías. A., Imp. nac., 1936. 119p.

3834a BENITEZ, Justo Pastor. Alejandro Guanes. *In* no. 162, 2. ed., 118-21.

3835 RODRIGUEZ ALCALA, Hugo. Alejandro Guanes, vida y obra. RHM 14 (1948) 1-2, 1-50, 173-84.
Also in no. 4127, p. 113-62.

3836 RODRIGUEZ ALCALA, Hugo. Alejandro Guanes, 1872-1920: vida y obra, bibliografía, antología. N.Y., Hispanic Institute in the United States, 1948. 68p. (Autores modernos)

3837 RODRIGUEZ ALCALA, Hugo. Los 'recuerdos' de Alejandro Guanes. RHM 13 (1947) 3-4, 249-62.

Teresa LAMAS CARISIMO DE RODRIGUEZ ALCALA

3838 La casa y su sombra. Formosa, Arg., Edit. America-Sapucai, 1955. 125p.

3839 Tradiciones del hogar. Segunda serie. Dibujos de Sorozábal y R. Rodríguez Alcala. A., La Mundial, 1928. 163p. (Biblioteca paraguaya de La Mundial)

Arturo D. LAVIGNE

3840 Amor en prosa. A., Imp. de El País, 1903. 30p.

3841 Loca: poema. A., 1902. 23p.

3842 Trinos matinales; poesías. A., 1904. 157p.

Eusebio Aveiro LUGO

3843 La chala, drama en tres actos. A., 1917. 57p.
Also: A., 1927? 30p.

3844 La epopeya del mariscal Francisco Solano López; drama histórico en 3 actos y 4 cuadros. Concepción, Tall. gráf. Minerva, 1948. 54p.

Epifanio MENDEZ FLEYTAS

3846 Bajo la verde arboleda: ensayos literarios en prosa y versos. 2. ed. A., Tall. de la edit. "Trujillo", 1940. 151p.

Silvano MOSQUEIRA

3847 Impresiones sobre los Estados Unidos. Una actitud hidalga del Perú. Homenaje a Colombia. Fiesta en el Museo Godoi. A., Tall. nac. de H. Kraus, 1926. 162p.

Juan Emiliano O'LEARY

3848 A Verdi, poesía declamada por el autor en la velada celebrada en el Teatro nacional el 18 de abril de 1901. A., Tall. nac. de H. Kraus, 1901. 15p.

3849 A la memoria de mi hija Rosita. Paris, Monte Domecq', 1918. 157p.

3850 Canciones de ultramar. Un prólogo en dos etapas por H. Sánchez Quell. A., Edit. Crisol, 1971. 50p.

3851 Sonetos. Selección y prólogo de Raúl Amaral. A., Tall. gráf. de Casa América-Moreno Hnos., 1964. 18p.

Fausto ORTIZ

3852 Presente divino; poesías en castellano y guaraní. n.p., n.d. 44p.

Manuel ORTIZ GUERRERO

3853 Arenillas de mi tierra. B.A., Tall. Gráf. Lumen, 1969. 63p.

3854 La conquista; drama de la conquista española en tierra y alma guaraní. A., Edit. paraguaya, 1926. iv, 63p.

3855 Eireté: comedia en un acto. Villarrica, 1920. 56p.

3856 Nubes del Este. A., Edit. Paraguaya Zurucu'á, 1928. 89p.

3857 Obras completas (éditas). Prólogo de Arturo Alsina. Ilus. de Andrés Guevara. A., Edit. Indoamericana, 1952. 328p.
Also: A., Edit. Manuel Guerrero, 1969. 383p.

3858 Pepitas. A., Edit. Paraguaya Zurucu'á, 1930. 79p.

3859 Surgente. A., 19--. viii, 73p.
2. ed. A., Imp. nac., 1943. 73p.

3860 RECALDE, Facundo. Evocación de Ortíz Guerrero. Oración a la paz. Eva Perón. A., El Arte, 1952. 51p.

Juan de Dios PEZA

3861 El canto al Paraguay. A., La Patria, 1902. 16p.

Leopoldo RAMOS GIMENEZ

3862 Alas y sombres. B.A., La Edit. novísima, 19--. 102p.

Facundo RECALDE

3863 El jugete roto; comedia dramática en tres actos. A., 1925. 90p.

3864 Virtutes celestes; versos. A., n.d. 106p.

José RODRIGUEZ ALCALA

3865 Ecos del alma. Con un prólogo de Daniel Jiménez Espinosa. A., Imp. de "El País", 1903. 109p.

Anastasio ROLON MEDINA

3866 El arbol de embrujo; novela corta del ambiente paraguayo. A., Ed. El Arte, 1948. 43p.

3867 Búcaros rotos; poesías. A., 1929. 35p.

3868 Estampas de mi terruño. Prólogo del Dr. Juan Stefanich. A., 1930. 140p.

Luis RUFFINELLI

3868a Soprendidos y desconocidos; comedia en tres actos, estreñada en el teatro Granados por la compañía Roberto Ribelli, en su función de despedida, el 14 de octubre de 1924. A., Imp. Ariel, 1924. 51p.

Ricardo SANTOS

3868b El hombre de la selva; novela original. Iturbe, Imp. "El Liberal", 1920. 119p.

Juan STEFANICH

3869 Aurora. A., Libr. La Mundial, 1920. 331p. (Biblioteca Paraguaya del Centro Estudiantes de Derecho, 9)

3870 Hacia la cumbre. A., H. Kraus, 1914. ix, 200p.

3871 Horas trágicas; prosas de paz y de dolor. A., Librería La Mundial, 1922. 30p.

Francisco TAPIA

3872 El origen de la tierra; editado por El Paraguayo ilustrado. A., Tall. nac. de H. Kraus, 1896. 12p.

Benigno TEIJEIRO MARTINEZ

3872a Independencia y tiranía, o El doctor Francia. Drama histórico con tres actos y un epílogo, en prosa y verso. Representado por primera vez en el Teatro Nacional de la Asunción el 14 de setiembre de 1874. A., Imp. y lit. de la Floresta americana, 1874. 125p.

Arnaldo M. VALDOVINOS

3873 Cosecha cultura. A., Imp. Esc. Charitas, 1930. 39p.

3874 El mutilado del agra. A., La Mundial, 1935. 8p.

C. The period after 1935: individual writers

Carlos Waldemar ACOSTA

3875 Nandé (nosostros). Dibujos tapa: Hebe Manicone. B.A., Ediciones Asociación Interamericana de Escritores, 1958. 130p.

Mariela de ADLER

3876 La endemoniada; historias de amor, fantasmas y curas. A., Edit. Don Bosco, 1966. 115p. (Colección Nandutí literario, 2)

3877 De otro modo; historias en voz baja. A., Escuela Técnica Salesiana, 1968. 146p.

José de Jesús AGUIRRE

3878 15 poemas hacia la luz. A., Libreria y Edit. "El Ateneo", 1968. 55p.

César ALONSO DE LAS HERAS

3879 Qué cercano tu recuerdo; poemas. A., Edit. F.V.D., 1970. 74p.

3879a San Blas; misterio dramático en tres cuadros, el último dividido en dos tiempos. A., El Arte, 1945. 60p.

Raúl AMARAL

3879b Carta civil al Paraguay. A., Diálogo, 1960. 30p. (Cuadernos de la Piririta, 5)

3880 La voz; elegía paraguaya. A., Artes Gráf. Zamphirópolos, 1967. 16p.

José Luis APPLEYARD

3881 Aquel 1811 (escenas de la Independencia); la acción, en cinco actos, en Asunción, 1811. A., Ediciones Comuneros, 1971. 174p.

3882 Entonces con siempre; poemas. A., Ediciones Trapiche, 1963. 58p. (Colección Viento norte)

3883 Imágenes sin tierra; novela. A., Edit. EMASA, 1965. 114p. (Colección Cultura paraguaya)

3884 Los monólogos. A., Ediciones Oñondivepa, 1973. 124p. (Colección Oñondivepa, 5)

3885 El sauce permanente y Tres motivos. A., Ediciones Péndulo, 1965. 46p. (Poesía)

Santiago Dimas ARANDA

3886 Antología del silencio; selección 1958-68. A., Edit. Manuel Ortiz Guerrero, 1970. 122p.

3887 Metal es la fragancia. B.A., Ediciones Universitarias "Criterio", 1972. 72p.

3888 Palo verde; poesía. A., Artes Gráf. "Didot", 1966. 37p.

Ramón C. ARAUJO

3889 Noche en el corazón. A., Edit. Dagre, 1955. 246p.

Marialuisa ARTECONA DE THOMPSON

3890 Canción de navidad. A., La Garza, 1963. 6p.

3891 Canción para dormir a una rosa. A., Emasa, 1964. 38p.

3892 Cartas al señor sol. A., Edit. Emasa, 1965. 27p.

3893 Grito en los Andes; poemas. Prólogo de R. Antonio Ramos. A., Sociedad Bolivariana del Paraguay, 1964. 26p.

3894 El metal y la espuma. A., 1965. 27p.

3895 Ronda de la amistad. A., 196-. 7p.

3896 Viaje al país de las campañas. A., Emasa, 1965. 80p.

O. BARCENA ECHEVESTE

3897 El polvo de mil caminos; cartas del viaje. A., Edit. America-Sapucai, 1962. 236p.

Rubén BAREIRO SAGUIER

3898 Biografía de ausente. Madrid, Alcor, 1964. 47p.

3898a Ojo por diente. Caracas, Monte Avila Editores, 1973. 147p.

3899 Pacte du sang: récits du Paraguay. Traduit de l'espagnol par Anne-Marie Métailié. Paris, Les Editions du Cerf, 1971. 120p. (Terres de feu)
A translation of no. 3898a.

3900 Ronde de nuit. E 48 no. 494 (1970) 112-16.

3900a Caso Rubén Bareiro Saguier. HAM 2 no. 4/5 (1973) 72-101.

Diógenes BARRETO MARECO

3901 Hilario, el cantor de su patria el Paraguay; poesías novelizadas. A., Imp. Ñande Purajhéi, 1955. 61p.

Rogelio BARRIOS S.

3902 El cielo fué testigo; novela. A., Edit. Ariel, 1950. 218p.

Juan F. BAZAN

3903 Del surco guaraní, novela. B.A., 1949. 265p.

3904 Divagaciones literarias, esbozos criticos, ensayos, artículos. A., Edit. El Liberal, 1934. 155p.

3905 Espejo lírico. A., Edit. "Dagre", 1953. 132p.

3906 Polen al viento; cuentos de ambiente paraguayo. A., Ed. de Agencia de Librerías S. Nizza, 1954. 171p.

3906a El valle de las tormentas: novela. A., 1975. 251p.

Ovidio BENITEZ PEREIRA

3907 Como la voz de muchas aguas; fantasío dramática. A., Radio Charitas, 1965? 80p. (Ediciones Charitas, 1)

3908 La otra mitad del sueño. A., Diálogo, 1966. 22p. (Cuadernos del colibri, 6)

Egidio BERNARDIER

3909 Antología poética. B.A., Edit. Sísifo, 1969. 79p.

3910 La danza del verano; versos. A., Edit. Sísifo, 1966. 61p. (Colección Cronos)

3911 El regreso en la huída. A., Edit. Sísifo, 1965. 43p. (Colección Cronos)

3912 Suplicio de silencio, 1963; poemas. A., Edit. Sísifo, 1965. 59p. (Colección Cronos)

José Antonio BILBAO

3913 El claro arrobo. B.A., Edit. Difusión, 1946. 75p.

3914 Cuaderno de bitácora (1954-1958). B.A., López, 1961. 55p.

3915 La estrella y la espiga (sonetos) 1953-1958. B.A., López, 1959. 80p.

3916 Itinerario de amor. A., 1970. 52p.

3917 La saeta en el arco, 1964-1965. B.A., Imp. López, 1966. 69p.

3918 Verde umbral. B.A., Difusión, 1953. 90p.

Esteban CABAÑAS

3919 Los monstruos vanos. A., Diálogo, 1964. 16p. (Cuadernos del colibrí, 3)

Fernando CABALLERO

3919a El río del este. Mexico, Edit. Diógenes, 1971. 362p.

3919b FOSTER, David William. Novela autobiográfica de joven paraguayo. NNH 3 (1973) 304-07.

Carlos CABALLERO FERREIRA

3920 Sangre en el surco. Montevideo, Edit. "Goes", 1958. 108p.

Miguel Angel CABALLERO FIGUN

3920a Del tiempo gris. A., Edit. Mayo, 1977. 35p.

3920b Los fuegos. A., Edit. Mayo, 1977. 33p.

Isidoro CALZADA

3921 Acá Carayá; novela histórica de la Caballería paraguaya en la guerra contra la Triple Alianza. A., Ediciones Comuneros, 1969. 206p.

3921a Alvar Núñez Marangatú; novela histórica del gran explorador de la conquista Alvar Núñez Cabeza de Vaca.

A., Edit. Don Bosco, 1970. 122p. (Colección Ñanduti literario, 5)

3921b Campeador de América; biografía novelada de Juan de Garay, fundador de Santa Fe y Buenos Aires. A., Edit. Don Bosco, 1971. 313p. (Colección Ñanduti literario)

3921c La estrella de las Navas. A., 1970. 387p.

3921d Itapúa (La roca que emerge), primera biografía novelada sobre la vida del misioneri paraguayo beato Roque González de Santa Cruz. A., Edit. Don Bosco, 1970. 106p. (Colección Ñanduti literario, 6)

3921e Tacuara jhacuava (lanza tacuara): historia de la heroica montonera guaraní, que comandado por el legendario caudillo Andresito Guacurarí, detuvo en las riberas del río Uruguay al imperio luso-brasileño; novela histórica. A., Edit. Don Bosco, 1971. 167p. (Colección Ñanduti literario, 8)

Luis del CAMPO

3923 Aromita. A., 1962. 197p.

Hérib CAMPOS CERVERA

3924 Ceniza redimida; poemas. B.A., Edit. Tupa, 1950. 117p.

3925 Hombre secreto. A., Diálogo, 1966. 19p. (Cuadernos del colibri, 7)

3926 RODRIGUEZ ALCALA, Hugo. Hérib Campos Cervera, poeta de la muerte. RI 17 no. 33 (1959) 61-79.
Also in no. 4129, 149-69.

Jorge CANESE

3926a Mas poesía. A?, Ediciones Criterio, 1977. 88p.

Roberto CAÑETE

3926b Habitante. n.p., 1971? 36p.

Gladys CARMAGNOLA

3927 Navidad; diciembre de jazmín y mbocayá. A., El Arte, 1966.

3928 Ojitos negros; poemas a mi sobrino. A., 1965. 58p.

Gabriel CASACCIA

3929 La babosa. B.A., Losada, 1952. 322p.
2. ed. B.A., Losada, 1960. 298p. (Novelistas de nuestra época)

3930 El bandolero; voces dramáticas. B.A., Atlántida, 1932. 130p.

3931 Los exiliados. B.A., Edit. Sudamericana, 1966. 303p. (Colección "El Espejo")

3932 Le faux pas de Felipa. E 48 no. 494 (1970) 72-78.

3933 El guajhú; cuentos paraguayos. B.A., Proventas, 1938. 170p.

3933a Los herederos. Barcelona, Edit. Planeta, 1975. 287p.

3934 Hombres, mujeres y fantoches (novela). B.A., El Ateneo, 1930. 239p.

3935 La limace; tr. par E. Frois. Paris, Gallimard, 1959. 368p. (Croix Sud)

3935a La llaga. B.A., Edit. G. Kraft. 1964. 188p.

3936 Mario Pareda. B.A., Librería del Colegio, 1939. 130p.

3937 El pozo; cuentos. B.A., Ayacucho, 1947. 156p.
2. ed. B.A., J. Alvarez, 1967. 185p. (Colección Narradores americanos)

3938 El secreto de los hermanos Franco. CMHL 14 (1970) 141-46.

3939 CASE, Thomas E. Paraguay in the novels of Gabriel Casaccia. JIAS 12 (1970) 1, 76-83.

3940 COLLMER, Robert G. The displaced person in the novels of Gabriel Casaccia. RAL 3 ii (1970) 37-46.

3940a FEITO, Francisco E. Un cuento desconocido de Gabriel Casaccia. HAM 4 no. 11-12 (1975) 63-67.

3940b FEITO, Francisco E. El Paraguay en la obra de Gabriel Casaccia. B.A., F. García Cambeiro, 1977. 185p. (Colección Estudios Latinoamericanos, 23)

3940c PECCI SAAVEDRA, Miguel. Una valiosísima novela paraguaya: La babosa. B.A., El Ateneo, 1953. 31p.

3941 RODRIGUEZ ALCALA, Hugo. Introducción al estudio de la novelistica de Gabriel Casaccia. NNH 4 (1974) 91-103.

Nilsa CASARIEGO DE BEDOYA

3942 Poema. A., Asedio, 1972. 18p. (Colección "La Garza". Seria menor, 1)

Augusto CASOLA

3943 El laberinto. A., Escuela Técnica Salesiana, 1972. 107p.

Juan M. CASSANELLO

3944 Alma y sentimiento de un poeta paraguayo; selección de poesías del R.P. Dr. Juan M. Cassanello, salesiano. A., Edit. Don Bosco, 1966. 117p. (Colección Ñanduti literario, 1)

María Concepción Leyes de CHAVES

3945 Madame Lynch, evocación. B.A., Ediciones Peuser, 1957. 660p.

3946 Madame Lynch, evocaçao. Trad. de Manuel Campos. Rio de Janeiro, Livraria Freitas Bastos, 1960. 440p.

3946a Madame Lynch y Solano Lopez. B.A., 1976. 590p.

3947 Tava'í. A., La Colmena, 1942. 138p.
B.A., Ediciones Peuser, 1954. 170p.

Ana Iris CHAVEZ DE FERREIRO

3948 Crónica de una familia. A., Edit. Emasa, 1966. 139p. (Colección Cultura paraguaya)

Julio CORREA

3949 Cuerpo y alma; poesías. B.A., Difusión, 1943. 86p.

3950 Ñane mba'era'in; sainete en tres actos, y su traducción al castellano por Antonio Ortiz Mayans. Prólogo de Arturo Alsina. A., Edit. Ortiz Guerrero, 1965. 82p. (Teatro guaraní)

3951 Sombrero Ka'a y cuentos. Estudio preliminar de Francisco Pérez-Maricevich. A., Edit. de Centenario, 1969. 96p. (Biblioteca de autores paraguayos, 1)

Francisco CRISTALDO

3951a Rosa braña; poesías, prosas en castellano y guaraní, inéditas, seleccionadas y traducciones. A., 1965. 72p.

René DAVALOS

3952 Buscar la realidad. A., Diálogo, 1966. 21p. (Cuadernos del colibrí, 8)

Rodrigo DIAZ-PEREZ

3953 Astillas de sol. Palma de Mallorca, Mosséu Alcover, 1971. 40p.

3954 El minuto de cristal. A., Tall. de artes gráf. de la Escuela Técnica Vocacional, 1969. 24p.

3955 Los poros del viento. Palma de Mallorca, 1970. 26p.

Ramiro DOMINGUEZ

3956 Las 4 fases del luisón. A., Escuela Técnica Salesiana, 1967. 48p.

3957 Salmos a deshora. A., La Colmena, 1963? xvi p.

3958 Zumos. Madrid, Ediciones Alcor, 1962? unpaged.

Rodolfo DUARTE TROCHE

3958a Hogueras crepitantes. B.A., Ediciones Tiempo de Hoy, 1975. 42p.

Efraín ENRIQUEZ GAMON

3958b La agonía del héroe, año del sesquicentenario del natalicio del Mariscal Francisco Solano López. A., 1977. 143p.

Modesto ESCOBAR

3958c Don Juan Pitogue. A., 1974? 21p.

3959 Siete en punto. A., Artes Gráficas Zamphirópolos, 1972. 33p.

Miguel Angel FERNANDEZ

3960 A destiempo. A., Diálogo, 1966. 27p. (Cuadernos del colibrí, 5)

3961 Oscuros días. A., Diálogo, 1960. 13p. (Cuadernos de la Piririta, 3)

Renee FERRER ALFARO

3962 Hay surcos que no se llenan. A., 1965. 48p.

3963 Voces sin réplica. A., 1967. 35p.

Rigoberto FONTAO MEZA

3964 Infierno y gloria. A., 1934. 108p.

Víctor I. FRANCO

3964a El afortunado hijo de Andalucia. A., Instituto Paraguayo de Cultura Hispanica, 1976. 184p.

Eugenio FRIEDMANN

3965 En busia de una destino: memorias de Emilio Carlins. Prólogo por Mario Halley Mora. A., Edit. La Voz, 1972. 170p.

Carlos GARCETE

3966 L'arbre fourchu. E 48 no. 494 (1970) 126-32.

3967 La caja de fósforos (Farsa en un tiempo). Aumento de sueldo (monodrama breve en un acto). Teatro. B.A., Edit. Futuro, 1964. 44p.

3968 La muerte tiene color; cuentos. B.A., Edit. Futuro, 1958. 122p.

Amador GARCIA ACEBO

3969 Olas sin playa. A., Edit. El Arte, 1966. 38p.

Gustavo Carlos GATTI CARDOZO

3970 Livia; poemas. Montevideo, Barreiro y Ramos, 1965. 52p.

Dora GOMEZ BUENO DE ACUÑA

3971 Barro celeste. A., Imp. nac., 1943. 52, xii p.

3972 Flor de caña: poesias. A., Imp. nac., 1940. 108p.

3973 Luz en el abismo. Proemio de Augusto Roa Bastos. A., Edit. Indoamericana, 1954. 158p. (Ediciones indoamericanas, 5)

3973a Vivir es decir; proemio de José Luis Appleyard. A., 1977. 89p.

Enriqueta GOMEZ SANCHEZ

3974 Ofrendas. A., El Arte, 1939. 64p.

3975 Oro y acera. B.A., Tall. gráf. de la Edit. Araujo, 1936. 134p.

Antonio E. GONZALEZ

3976 Yasíh Rendíh; novela. A., Edit. El Gráf., 1960. 310p.

Ezequiel GONZALEZ ALSINA

3977 El gran rival; comedia en cuatro actos. A., Rigran, 1951.

Aurelio Bienvenido GONZALEZ CANALE

3977a Carta a un poeta. A., 1967. 32p.

3978 Grito entre las venas; poemas de amor. A? 1968. 28p.

3979 Pureza. Lima, Edit. "Amauta", 1970. 18p.

Alicibíades GONZALEZ DELVALLE

3980 El grito del luisón. A., Ediciones del Pueblo, 1972. 99p. (Colección Blás Garay, 2)

Juan T. GONZALEZ F.

3981 Acosta Ñú; homenaje a los mártires de la batalla de Acosta Ñú en el centenario de la epopeya nacional, años 1869-1969. A., 1969. 64p.
Poetry.

Fernando GUERRA

3982 Rumor de muchedumbre y grito de amor. B.A., 1955. 96p.

Miguel Angel GUILLEN-ROA

3983 Caminos, poemas. A., Asedio, 1961. 18p.

3984 Inminencia terrena. A., 1964. 55p.

3985 Romancero serrano. A., 1966. 62p.

3986 Siete cuentos de paz. A., Edit. Emasa, 1970. 112p.

3987 Tierra y horizonte. B.A., López, 1960. 56p.

Mario HALLEY MORA

3988 Cuentos y anticuentos. A., Edit. El País, 1971. 110p. (Colección El País, 1)

3988a Cuentos y microcuentos. A., The author, 1976. 124p.

3989 Piel adentro. A., Ediciones Diálogo, 1967. 23p.

3990 La quema de Judas; novela breve. A., 1965. 86p.

3991 Teatro de Mario Halley Mora. A., El País, 1971-
Vol. 2 (1971) has the title: Teatro paraguayo de Mario Halley Mora.

3992 Un traje para Jesús; comedia en tres actos. A., Ediciones Juvi, 1958. 54p.

Alfredo Andrés JACQUET

3993 Ensueños matinales; poesías. A., La Colmena, 1940. 146p.

3994 Interludios. A., 1972. 84p.

3995 Lágrimas furtivas. A., El Arte, 1961. 76p.

3996 Petalos de una flor celestial; principales pasajes de la vida de Sta. Teresita del Niño Jesús; poemas. B.A., Cruz del Sur, 1941. 58p.

3997 Voces del alma, cantos líricos. B.A., Libro de Edición Argentina, 1955. 105p.

Lidia KALLSEN DE TORRES

3997a Voces del camino. A., Imp. Ipora, 1939. 72p.

Marta Diana KANIUKA

3998 Una voz en el abismo; poemas. A., Impresa en los Tall. Gráf. de la Penitenciaría Nacional, 1962. 74p.

Vicente A. LAMAS

3999 La senda escondida; poesía. A., El Arte, 1956. 138p.

Henri de LESCOET

4000 Misericordia. A., Diálogo, 1964. 12p. (Cuadernos del colibrí, 2)

LOURDESPINOLA

4000a Monocorde amarillo. A., Tall. gráf. de Ocara Poty Cue Mi, 1976. 21p.

Myrtha LIBSTER

4001 Noches y día. A?, 1964. 53p.

Juan Manuel MARCOS

4002 Poemas. A., Ediciones Universitarias Criterio, 1970. 15p. (Colección Koeti)

Luis María MARTINEZ

4003 Ardes, es la palabra: 1959-1961. A., 1966. 57p.

4004 Armadura fluvial; A., Asedio, 1961. 76p. (Colección "La Garza", 2)

4005 Desde abajo es el viento. B.A., Imp. López, 1970. 122p.

4006 El jazmin azorado. B.A., Ediciones "Epoca", 1969. 106p.

4007 Poesías. A., Casa América, Morena Hnos. 1960. 7p.

4008 Rafagas de la tierra, 1956-1958; poemario. A., Asedio, 1962. 80p. (Colección "La Garza")

Reinaldo MARTINEZ

4009 Juan Bareiro. A., El Arte, 1957. 298p.

Sindulfo MARTINEZ

4010 Por los caminos del viejo mundo, visión de un periodista paraguayo. A., Edit. El Arte, 1964. 180p.

Ricardo MAZO

4011 La segunda soledad; Nueva York, 1969-1970. A., Fondo Editor Paraguayo, 1971. 28p. (Colección poesia)

Juan Carlos MENDONÇA

4012 Notas. A., Edición de Autor, 1954. 161p.

4013 Rosario lirico; poesías. A., El Gráfico, 1952. 95p.

Elly Esther MERCADO DE VERA

4013a Vendimia de sueños. n.p., 197? 43p.

Victor MONTORFANO

4014 Después del ocaso negro, los que nacerán mañana; fantaciencia de la era atómica. 2. ed. A., Edit. El Arte, 1961. 133p.

4015 El Paraguay libertado, homenaje a la revolución nacional, libertadora del Paraguay, 1931/1945. A., Imp. nac., 1945. 77p.
A drama.

Pierre Moraviah MORPEAU

4016 Breve antología de las antologías de los poemas de Pierre Moraviah Morpeau (Piermoraviamorpo). A., Edit.-Tall. Gráf. Zamphirópolos, 1959. 34p.

Juberli MUSTO SIAN

4016a Aljofar de ensuenos (versos). A., América-Sapucai, 1956. 110p.

4016b Suspiros (versos). A., Imp. nac., 1944. 141p.

Noemi NAGY

4017 Rogelio; cuentos y recuerdos. A., Edit. del Centenario, 1972. 95p.

Lilian de NAPOUT

4017a En la distancia de la flecha. A., Liquen Edit., 1977. 34p.

José Concepción ORTIZ

4018 Amor de caminante (verso). B.A., Ayacucho, 1943. 86p.

Julio PANIAGUA TORRES

4019 Dimensión y destello. A., 1965. 14p.

4020 Simiente y flor en 15 primaveras. Sao Paulo, Gráf. Biblos, 196-. 69p.

Miguel PECCI-SAAVEDRA

4021 Boceto renacentista y Monna Lisa y Leonardo. B.A., El Ateneo, 1949. 116p.

4021a Eleonor y manos blancas. B.A., El Ateneo, 1952. 122p.

4021b Etópolis. 2. ed. B.A., El Ateneo, 1950. 117p.

Hernan del PEÑON Y TRINIDAD

4021c La cruz del amor eterno. A., Edit. El Grafico, 1955. 326p.

Angel PERALTA ARELLANO

4022 Estampa de Asunción. A., 1967. 77p.
3. ed. A., 1970. 107p.

Emilio PEREZ CHAVES

4022a El fénix del recuerdo. A., Ediciones Criterio, 1976. 49p.

Francisco PEREZ-MARICEVICH

4023 Axil. A., 1960. 12p.

4024 Paso de hombre; poemas. A., Ediciones Comuneros, 1963. 43p. (Colección La Garza, 8)

4025 Souvenir de Pascual Ruiz. E 48 no. 494 (1970) 123-26.

Josefina PLA

4026 Aquí no pasado nada: comedia en 3 actos por Josefina Plá y Roque Centurion Miranda. A., Imp. nac., 1945. 46p.

4026a Antología poética, 1927-1977. A., Ediciones Cabildo, 1977? 97p.

4027 Invención de la muerte. A., Diálogo, 1965. 24p. (Colección del colibrí, 4)

4028 La mano en la tierra. A., Alcor, 1963. 32p.

4029 El polvo enamorado. A., Diálogo, 1968. 21p. (Colección del colibrí, 11)

4030 Le phono. E 48 no. 494 (1970) 79-88.

4031 La raíz y la aurora. A., Ediciones Diálogo, 1960. 23p. (Cuadernos de la Piririta, 4)

4032 Rapsodia de Eurídice y Orfeo: poema. A., 1949. 8p.

4033 Rostros en el agua. A., Diálogo, 1963. 15p. (Cuadernos del colibrí, 1)

4034 Satelites oscuros. A., Diálogo, 1966. 30p. (Cuadernos del colibrí, 9)

4035 RODRIGUEZ ALCALA, Hugo. Josefina Plá, española de América y la poesía. CA 27 no. 4 (1968) 73-101.

4036 RODRIGUEZ ALCALA, Hugo. Josefina Plá y la poesía. PSA 172 (1970) 19-64.

4037 ROA BASTOS, Augusto. La poesía de Josefina Plá. RHM 32 (1966) no. 1-2, 56-61.

Maria Gloria RAMIREZ-PANE CATALDO

4037a Recordando. A., Edit. Arte Nuevo, 1977. 35p.

4037b Viviendo, once poemas. A., 1976. 12p.

R. Antonio RAMOS

4038 Recuerdos de Sevilla. A., Instituto Paraguayo de Cultura Hispánica, 1966. 31p.

J.A. RAUSKIN

4039 Casa perdida. A., Fondo Editor Paraguayo, 1971. 12p. (Colección Poesía)

4040 Linceo. A., Péndulo, 1965. 45p.

4041 Oda. A., Ediciones Péndulo, 1964. 11p.

Augusto César RECLADE BLANCO

4042 Canto de esperanza. A., 1972. 20p.

L. Oscar RELOS, pseud.

4043 Canto juvenil; prólogo de Luis Resquín Huerta. A., Edit. Trujillo, 1953. 71p.

Luis RESQUIN HUERTA

4044 Acuarelas concepcioneras. A., Edit.-Tall. Gráf. Zamphirópolos, 1960. 88p.

4045 Cantos a Sulamita. A., El Arte, 1951. 48p.

4046 Ritos paganos. A., 1949. 94p.

Yula RIQUELME DE MOLINAS

4046a Los moradores del vortice, poemas. A., Artes Gráf. Zamphirópolos, 1976. 77p.

Jorge Rodolfo RITTER

4047 La hostia y los jinetes. A., La Colmena, 1969. 245p.

4048 El pecho y la espalda; novela. B.A., Nizza, 1962. 316p.

4049 La poitrine et le dos. E 48 no. 494 (1970) 89-96.
A fragment from no. 4048.

4049a La tierra ardia: novela sobre la Guerra del Chaco. A., Escuela Técnica Salesiana, 1974. 395p.

José Maria RIVAROLA MATTO

4050 The fate of Chipí González. *In* Men and angels; three South American comedies; trans. and with an intro. by

Willis Knapp Jones. Carbondale, Southern Illinois University Press, 1970. xlvi, 191p.

4051 Feuillage dans les yeux (fragment). E 48 no. 494 (1970) 104-09.
A fragment from no. 4054.

4052 El fin de Chipí González; comedia en tres actos. A., 1953. 68p.
A., Diálogo, 1965. 61p. (Colección Dionisos)

4053 Le fin de Chipí González (fragment). E 48 no. 494 (1970) 109-11.

4054 Follaje en los ojos; los confinados del Alto Paraná. B.A., A., 1952. 181p.

4054a Mi pariente el cocotero. A., Ediciones Comuneros, 1974. 34p.

4055 Yvypóra; el fantasma de la tierra. B.A., S. Rueda, 1970. 284p. (Rueda literaria)

Augusto Antonio ROA BASTOS

4056 El baldío. B.A., Edit. Losada, 1966. 152p. (Novelistas de nuestra época)

4057 Crónica paraguaya. SUR 293 (1965) marzo-abril, 102-12.

4058 Cuando un pájaro entierra sus plumas. CMHL 14 (1970) 147-52.

4059 Cuerpo presente y otros textos. B.A., Centro Editor de América Latina, 1972. 119p. (Narradores de hoy, 30)

4060 Entretiens. CMHL 17 (1971) 207-18.

4061 Le feu et la lèpre. Traduit de l'espagnol par J.-F. Reille. Paris, Gallimard, 1968. 319p. (La croix du sud)

4062 Filho de homem; romance. Traduçao de Aníbal da Silva Tello. Lisbon, Publicacoes Europa-America, 1968. 382p.

4063 Hijo de hombre. B.A., Edit. Losada, 1960. 270p. (Novelistas de nuestra época)
Also: Havana, Casa de las Américas, 1970. xx, 400p. (Colección Literatura latinoamericana, 54)

4063a Hijo de hombre. Madrid, Alfaguara, 1977. 388p.

4064 Madera quemada. Cuentos. Santiago de Chile, Edit. Universitaria, 1967. 168p. (Colección letras de América, 6)

4065 Menschensohn. Roman. Aus dem Span. von Curt Meyer-Clason. Munich, Hanser, 1962. 309p.

4066 Moriencia. Caracas, Monte Avila Editores, 1969. 170p.

4067 Los muertos son muy débiles. CMHL 19 (1972) 181-85.
A fragment from no. 4075.

4068 Die Nacht der treibenden Feuer. Erzählungen. Aus dem Span. von Ulla H. de Herrero. Munich, Hanser, 1964. 255p.

4069 El naranjal ardiente, nocturno paraguayo; poemas. A., Diálogo, 1960. 26p. (Cuadernos de la Piririta, 6)

4070 Los pies sobre el agua. B.A., Centro Editor de América Latina, 1967. 158p. (Libros de mar a mar, 6)

4070a El pollito de fuego. B.A., Ediciones de la Flor, 1974. (unpaged) (Colección Libros de la florcita)

4071 El ruiseñor de la aurora y otros poemas. A., Imp. nac., 1942. 146p.

4072 Son of man; trans. by Rachel Caffyn. London, V. Gollancz, 1965. 256p.

4073 El trueno entre las hojas. B.A., Edit. Losada, 1953. 226p.
Also: B.A., G. Kraft, 1958. 246p. (Colección Cupula)
B.A., Losada, 1968. 249p.

4073a El trueno entre las hojas. Barcelona, Bruguera, 1977. 252p.

4074 Les visages sombres. E 48 no. 494 (1970) 96-103.

4075 Yo el supremo. B.A., Siglo XXI Argentina Edit., 1974. 467p.

4076 AGOSTI, Héctor P. La problemática de Roa Bastos. *In his* La milicia literaria. B.A., Ediciones Sílaba, 1969. p. 133-37.

4076a ALDANA, Adelfo L. La cuentistica de Augusto Roa Bastos. Montevideo, Ediciones Geminis, 1975. 218p.

4076b ALDANA, Adelfo L. Lo universal en la cuentistica de Augusto Roa Bastos. ETL 4 (1975-76) no. 1, 53-60.

4077 ALEGRIA, Fernando. Cigarrillos Máuser. *In* no. 4089, 15-18.

4077a ANDREU, J.L. 'Hijo de hombre': fragmentación y unidad. RI no. 96-97 (1976) 473-84.

4077b AUGUSTO Roa Bastos; Juan Benet. Amsterdam, Revista Hispanica de Amsterdam, 1976. 140p. (Cuaderno de Norte)

4078 BAREIRO SAGUIER, Rubén. Noción del personaje en "Hijo de hombre". NNH 4 (1974) 69-74.

4078a BAREIRO SAGUIER, Rubén. Roa Bastos y la nueva narrativa paraguayo. *In* Actual narrativa latinoamericana: conferencias y seminarios. Havana, Casa de las Americas, 1970. pp. 71-101.

4079 BENEDETTI, Mario. Roa Bastos entre el realismo y la alucinación. *In his* Letras del continente mestizo. Montevideo, Edit. Arca, 1967. p. 88-92.
Also in no. 4089, 21-24.

4080 BORDELOIS, Ivonne. Augusto Roa Bastos. "Hijo de hombre". SUR no. 268 (1961) 131-33.

4081 BOREL, Jean-Paul. Apuntes para un análisis sociológico de la narrativa paraguaya: A. Roa Bastos y R. Bareiro Saguier. CMHL 25 (1975) 39-56.

4082 CAMPOS, Jorge. Una novela paraguaya. "Hijo de hombre". IN 168 (1968) 13.

4082a CARDOSO, Heber. Augusto Roa Bastos: entrevista. HAM 4 no. 11-12 (1975) 49-58.

4083 CASTILLO, Abelardo. "Hijo de hombre", novela de A. Roa Bastos. EOR no. 2 (1961) 33.

4083a CRUZ-LUIS, A. Dimensión histórica de "Yo el Supremo". CLA 95 (1976) 118-30.

4084 ESCUDERO, Alfonso M. Fuentes de información sobre: Ernesto Sabato, Juan Rulfo, Augusto Roa Bastos, Carlos Droguett. TL no. 1 (1971) 110-18.

4084a FOSTER, David William. Augusto Roa Bastos' I, the Supreme: the image of a dictator. LALR 4 no. 7 (1975) 32-35.

4085 FOSTER, David William. The figure of Christ crucified as a narrative symbol in Roa Bastos' "Hijo de hombre". BKA 37 (1963) 16-20.

4086 FOSTER, David William. La importancia de "Hijo de hombre" de Roa Bastos en la literatura paraguaya. DHR 3 (1964) 95-106.

4087 FOSTER, David William. The myth of Paraguay in the fiction of Augusto Roa Bastos. Chapel Hill, University of North Carolina Press, 1969. 88p. (University of North Carolina. Studies in the Romance languages and literatures, no. 80)

4088 FOSTER, David William. Una nota sobre el punto de vista narrativa en "Hijo de hombre" de Roa Bastos. RI no. 73 (1970) 643-50.
Also in no. 4089, 155-67.

4088a FOSTER, David William. 'La pensée sauvage' in A. Roa Bastos' recent fiction. CHA 4 no. 2 (1975) 29-34.

4089 GIACOMAN, Helmy F. Homenaje a Augusto Roa Bastos: variaciones interpretativas en torno a su obra. N.Y., Las Américas, 1973. 294p.

4090 GURZA, Esperanza. El exito del fracaso en "El trueno entre las hojas" de Augusto Roa Bastos. *In* KRAFT, Walter C. Proceedings: Pacific Northwest Conference on Foreign Languages. 25th annual meeting, April 19-20, 1974, Eastern Washington State College. Corvallis, Oregon State University, 1974. Vol. XXV, Pt. 1: Literature and Linguistics. p. 168-72.

4091 GURZA, Esperanza. Gaspar ha muerto. Viva el Cristo! PH no. 43 (1967) 499-505.

4092 HERZENHORN, Jaime. Reflexiones sobre la temática de los cuentos de Augusto Roa Bastos. *In* no. 4089, 253-66.

4093 KLEINBERGS, Andris. Estudio estructural de "Hijo de hombre" de Roa Bastos. AT 166 no. 240 (1968) 155-67.
Also in no. 4089, 187-201.

4094 LECHNER, Jan. Apuntes para el estudio de la prosa de Roa Bastos. NR 12 (1971) 2, 28-34.

4095 LEHNHERDT, Urte. Ensayo de interpretación de "Hijo de hombre" a través de su simbolismo cristiano y social. RI 34 no. 65 (1968) 67-82.
Also in no. 4089, 169-85.

4096 LORENZ, Günter W. Augusto Roa Bastos. *In his* Diälog mit Lateinamerika. Tübingen, Horst Erdman, 1970. p. 401-59.
Also: Diálogo con América latina. Barcelona, Edit. Pomaire, 1972. p. 271-310.

4096a LORING, Salvador. Tan tierra son los hombres. Glosario a un soneto de Augusto Roa Bastos. EP 1 no. 1 (1974) 177-84.

4097 LUCHTING, Wolfgang. Time and transportation in "Hijo de hombre". RSW 41 (1973) 98-106.

4098 MAGNOLO, Marta. "Hijo de hombre". LD no. 14 (1963) 4-9.

4099 MALDAVSKY, David. Autocrítica: reportaje a Augusto Roa Bastos. LB no. 12 (1970) 11-12.

4100 MALDAVSKY, David. Un enfoque semiótico de la narrativa de Roa Bastos: "Hijo de hombre". *In* no. 4089, 79-95.

4101 MARTINEZ, Mary. "Hijo de hombre" por Augusto Roa Bastos. EBA no. 520 (1960) 821-22.

4102 MENTON, Seymour. Realismo mágico y dualidad en "Hijo de hombre". RI 33 no. 63 (1967) 55-70.
Also in no. 4089, 203-20.

4102a MONTERO, J.L. Realidad y ficción en 'Hijo de hombre'. RI 42 no. 95 (1976) 267-74.

4103 PASSAFARI DE GUTIERREZ, Clara. Entrevista con Augusto Roa Bastos. LD no. 2 (1960) 32-34.

4104 PASSAFARI DE GUTIERREZ, Clara. La condición humana en la narrativa de Roa Bastos. U no. 46 (1960) 137-61.
Also in no. 4089, 25-45.

4105 PICCINI, Mabel. "El trueno entre las hojas" y el humanismo revolucionario. *In* no. 4089, 239-49.

4105a PINO MENDEZ, Antonio. 'Yo el Supremo': dictadura y polémica. PH 17 (1976) 70-80.

4106 PUEBLA, Manuel de la. El estilo de la narrativa de Augusto Roa Bastos. *In* no. 4089, 47-62.

4106a RAMA, Angel. Los dictadores làtinoamericanos. Mexico, Fondo de Cultura Economica, 1976. 63p. (Testimonios del Fondo, 42)
Includes a study of 'Yo el Supremo'.

4107 ROBLES, Humberto E. El círculo y la cruz en "Hijo de hombre". NNH 4 (1974) 193-219.

4107a RODRIGUEZ ALCALA, Hugo. A. Roa Bastos y el bilingüismo paraguayo. CA 25 (1976) 198-207.

4108 RODRIGUEZ ALCALA, Hugo. Augusto Roa Bastos y 'El trueno entre las hojas'. RI 20 no. 39 (1955) 19-45.

4108a RODRIGUEZ ALCALA, Hugo. Dos cuentos de Augusto Roa Bastos. *In* no. 4111, 40-81.

4109 RODRIGUEZ ALCALA, Hugo. "Hijo de hombre" de Roa Bastos y la intrahistoria del Paraguay. CA no. 121 (1963) 221-34.
Also in no. 4089, 65-78.
See also no. 4113.

4110 RODRIGUEZ ALCALA, Hugo. Jorge Luis Borges en 'La excavación' de Augusto Roa Bastos. *In* PUPO-WALKER, Enrique. El cuento hispanoamericana ante la crítica. Madrid, Ed. Castalia, 1973. pp. 179-94.
Also in no. 4089, 223-35.

4111 RODRIGUEZ ALCALA, Hugo. Narrativa hispanoamericana. Güiraldes-Carpentier-Roa Bastos-Rulfo: estudios sobre invención y sentido. Madrid, Edit. Gredos, 1973. 217p.

4112 RODRIGUEZ ALCALA, Hugo. "Official truth" and "True truth": Augusto Roa Bastos' "Borrador de un informe". SSF 8 (1971) 141-54.

4113 RODRIGUEZ ALCALA, Hugo. El sentido universalista del "Hijo de hombre" de Roa Bastos o la intrahistoria del Paraguay. *In* no. 4132, 75-97.
The same essay as 4109.

4114 RODRIGUEZ ALCALA, Hugo. Verdad oficial y verdad verdadera: "Borrador de un informe" de Augusto Roa Bastos. CA 27 no. 1 (no. 156) (1968), 251-67.
Also in no. 4089, 279-94.

4114a RODRIGUEZ ALCALA DE GONZALEZ ODDONE, Beatriz; DOMINGUEZ, Ramiro; IRALA BURGOS, Adriano; PLA, Josefina. Comentarios sobre Yo el Supremo. A., Ediciones Club del Libro No. 1, 1975. 67p.

4115 RODRIGUEZ GARAVITO, Agustín. El mundo del libro: "Hijo de hombre". BCB 4 (1961) no. 4, 293-99.

4116 RODRIGUEZ RICHART, J. "Mano cruel", narración picaresca de Roa Bastos. BBMP 45 (1969) 239-54.

4117 RUIZ, Marco E. La introspección auto-crítica en "Contar un cuento". *In* no. 4089, 269-76.

4118 STORNI, Eduard Raúl. "Hijo de hombre" por Augusto Roa Bastos. U no. 45 (1960) 356-57.

4118a TEIXEIRA DE OLIVEIRA ZOKNER, Cecília. A palavra tierre e o vocabulário socio-hierárquico en 'Hijo de hombre': relaçoes. LC 23 (1975) 71-80.

4118b TEIXEIRA DE OLIVEIRA ZOKNER, Cecília. Céspedes e Roa Bastos, duas visoes da Guerra do Chaco: unidade. LC 21-22 (1973-74) 89-96.

4119 TREVISAN, L.O. Literatura de una tierra joyosa; su novelista: Augusto Roa Bastos. RLM 6 (1967) 79-107.

4119a UNIVERSITY OF POITIERS. CENTRE DE RECHERCHES LATINO-AMERICAINES. Seminario sobre 'Yo el Supremo' de Augusto Roa Bastos; organizado en Abril de 1976. Poitiers, Centre de Recherches Latino-Américaines, 1976. 182p.

4120 VALDES, Adriana; RODRIGUEZ, Ignacio. "Hijo de hombre": el mito como fuerza social. TL no. 1 (1971) 75-95.
Also in no. 4089, 97-154.

José Carlos RODRIGUEZ

4121 Poemas de la hermana. A., Ediciones Criterio, 1967. 7p. (Colección Coeti)

Guido RODRIGUEZ ALCALA

4122 Apacible fuego. A., Ediciones Epoca, 1966. 17p.

4123 Ciudad sonámbula. A., Ediciones Criterio, 1968. 16p. (Colección Koeti)

4124 Viento oscuro; poesía. A., Ediciones Universitarias Criterio, 1969. 24p. (Colección Koeti)

Hugo RODRIGUEZ ALCALA

4125 Abril, que cruz al mundo. Mexico, Edit. Estaciones, 1960. 45p.

4126 A la sombra del pórtico y poemas de la guerra del Chaco. A., Edit. "El País", 1942. 60p.

4126a El canto del aljibe; presentación de Manuel Durán. Mexico, UNAM, Dirección General de Publicaciones, 1973. 118p.

4126b Cuentos nuevos del sur: Argentina, Chile, Paraguay, Uruguay; ed. by Hugo Rodríguez Alcalá and Sally Rodríguez Alcalá. Englewood Cliffs, N.J., Prentice-Hall, 1967. xii, 234p.

4127 Ensayos de Norte a Sur. Prólogo de Francisco Romero. Seattle, University of Washington Press; Mexico, Ediciones de Andrea, 1960. 214p. (Colección Studium, 27)

4128 Estampas de la guerra (poesías) con prólogo del doctor Cecilio Baez. A., Imp. Candido Zamphirópolos, 1939. 61p.

4129 Korn, Romero, Güiraldes, Unamuno, Ortega, literatura paraguaya y otros ensayos. Mexico, Ediciones de Andrea, 1958. 239p. (Colección Studium, 19)

4130 Palabras de los dias; poemas. Apunte liminar de Augusto Roa Bastos. Maracaibo, Universidad del Zulia, Facultad de Humanidades y Educación, 1972. 94p. (Arte y letras, 47)

4131 Poemas: horas líricas. A., Imp. nac., 1939. 120p.

4132 Sugestión e ilusión; ensayos de estilística e ideas. Xalapa, Universidad Vera-cruzeña, 1967. 272p.

4132a CORREAS DE ZAPATA, Celia. Hugo Rodríguez-Alcalá: poeta del exilio. PSA 83 (1976) 115-33.

Claudio ROMERO

4133 El terruño; novela social. A., 1952. 208p.

Elvio ROMERO

4134 Antología poetica; 1947-1964. B.A., Losada, 1965. 210p. (Biblioteca clásica y contemporánea, 157)

4135 Da cara al corazón, 1955. B.A., Losada, 1961. 74p.

4135a De caminante. B.A., Edit. Papeles de Buenos Aires, 1976? 18p.

4136 Despiertan las fogatas, 1950-1952. B.A., Losada, 1953. 134p.

4137 Destierro y atardecer. B.A., Losada, 1975. 96p. (Poetas de ayer y de hoy)

4138 Días roturados; poemas de la guerra civil, Paraguay, 1947. B.A., Lautaro, 1948. 126p.
Also: Havana, Ediciones Nuevo Mundo, 1963. 121p.

4139 Doce poemas. Quito, Casa de la Cultura Ecuatoriana, 1962. 71p.

4140 Esta guitarra dura; libro de guerrilleros, Paraguay 1960. B.A., Lautaro, 1961. 94p.
Also: Havana, Imp. nac. de Cuba, 1961. 77p.

4141 Los innombrables, 1959-1964. B.A., Edit. Losada, 1970. 110p. (Biblioteca clásica y contemporánea, 360)

4142 Nosotros los innombrables. Havana, La Tertulia, 1962. 17p. (Colección Laura, 5)

4143 Un relámpago herido; poesía amorosa, 1963-1966. B.A., Edit. Losada, 1967. 70p. (Poetas de ayer y de hoy)

4144 Resoles áridos (1948-1949). B.A., Lautaro, 1950. 114p.

4145 Romancero español, 1936-1939. Selección de Elvio Romero. B.A., Edit. Quetzal, 1967. 132p.
A selection of Spanish poetry.

4146 S etoi surovoi gitaroi. Stikhi. Moscow, Khudozh. lit., 1968. 207p.
Russian trans. of no. 4140.

4147 El sol bajo las raíces, 1952-1955. B.A., Edit. Losada, 1956. 137p. (Poetas de España y América)

4148 Stikhi. Moscow, Izd-vo inostrannaia literatura, 1961. 63p.

4149 Zemnoi znoi; stikhi. Moskva, Pravda, 1966. 30p.

4150 DARMANGEAT, P. Elvio Romero. LLN 58 (1964) 1, 117-19.

4151 RODRIGUEZ ALCALA, Hugo. Elvio Romero, poeta del campo. *In* no. 4129, 213-35.

4152 SASSONE, H. Un relámpago herido. CUN 96-97 (1967) 217-19.

Nelson ROURA

4153 Poemas. A., Ediciones Péndulo, 1965. 71p.

Jesús RUIZ NESTOSA

4154 Las musarañas. B.A., Centro Editor de América Latina, 1973. 147p.

Eduardo SAMMAT

4155 Abono y simiente, cuentos y narraciones. A., La Colmena, 1969. 95p.

Hipólito SANCHEZ QUELL

4156 El minuto fugitivo; 3 juicios críticos y 24 poemas. A., Edit. La Voz, 1970. 64p.

4157 Por las calles de París y tierras de sol. A., Emasa, 1966. 125p.

Elena SCHUSTER

4157a Tres anillos de Isis. A., Artes Gráf. Zamphirópolos, 1955. 60p.

Francisco Javier SERVIAN

4158 Caminando por el mundo. A., Imp. Guaraní, 1951. 46p.

Lincoln SILVA

4159 Rebelión después. B.A., Edit. Tiempo Contemporáneo, 1970. 127p. (Colección Ficciones)

Otto SKELL

4159a Poemas. A., Fondo Editor Paraguayo, 1976. 30p.

Ida TALAVERA DE FRACCHIA

4160 Esto de andar; poesías. A., Ediciones Péndulo, 1966. 29p.

Fortunato TORANZOS BARDEL

4161 Alma guaraní. A., América-Sapucai, 1964? xxxii, 172p.

Víctor María TARRUELLA

4162 Miradas rotas. A., Instituto Paraguayo de Cultura Hispánica, 1954. 47p. (Colección "Poesía", 1)

Teresita TORCIDA DE ARRIOLA

4163 Se hace teatro. A., Edit. C.N.N., 1972. 58p. (Colección Schola vitae, 1)
(Preludio, por Mariela de Adler; Farsa de una farsa, por T. Torcida de Arriola)

Arnaldo VALDOVINOS

4164 Cruces de quebracho; relatos de un combatiente en la guerra del Chaco Boreal. B.A., Claridad, 193? 134p. (Colección Claridad. Novelas de la guerra)

Marcelino VALIENTE

4164a El sembrador. A., 1959. 104p.

Roque VALLEJOS PEREZ GARAY

4165 Los arcangeles ebrios. A., Asedio, 1964. 37p. (Colección La Garza, 10)
2. ed. Montevideo, Aquí, Poesía, 1964. 20p.

4166 Palabras al viento. A., Ediciones del Pueblo, 1972. 142p.

4167 Poemas del Apocalipsis. A., Diálogo, 1969. 23p. (Cuadernos del colibrí, 14)

4167a Pulso de sombra. A., Diálogo, 1961. 15p. (Cuadernos de la Piririta, 7)

Manuel VERON DE ASTRADA

4168 Banderas en el alba; poemas. Sao Paulo-A., Ricardo Granda, 1955. 138p.

4169 Intermedio lírico. A., Imp. Zamphirópolos, 1972. 36p.

Benigno VILLA

4170 Casilda; comedia dramática en tres actos y un prólogo. A., Ediciones Juvi, 1958. 46p. (Teatro, 1)

Carlos VILLAGRA MARSAL

4171 Mancuello y la perdiz; novela corte. Prólogo de Julio César Troche. A., Edit. Emasa, 1965. 73p. (Colección Cultura paraguaya)

4172 Montagnard du nord. E 48 no. 494 (1970) 116-22.

José VILLAREJO

4173 Cabeza de invasión, novela. B.A., Edit. Ayacucho, 1944. 190p.

4174 Hooohh la Saiyoby. A., Edán, 1935. 64p.

4175 Ocho hombres; novela de la guerra del Chaco. B.A., Atlántida, 1934. 187p.

Elsa WIEZELL

4176 Barro de estrellas. B.A., Indo-americana, 1951. 138p.

4177 El canto y la luz. A., Bellas Artes Miserere, 1964. 37p.

4177a El duendo fugitivo. A., Tall. Gráf. de la Escuela Técnica Salesiana, 1976. 41p.

4178 Eco tridimensional. Montevideo, 1968. 19p.

4179 Lirondela. A., 1953. 59p.

4180 Mensaje para hombres nuevos. A., Edit. Emasa, 1966. 67p.

4181 Orbita de visiones. A., 196-. 22p.

4182 Palabras para otro planeta. A., Ediciones Colección Paraguaya, 1967. 19p.

4183 Poema ciego. A., El Arte, 1956. 63p.

4184 Poemas de un mundo en brumas. A., Edit. Indoibérica, 1950. 98p.

4185 Poema ultrasónico. A., 1969. 36p.

4186 Por las calles de Cristo. A., Asedio, 1961. 12p.

4187 Puente sobre el Tapecué. A., Ocara Poty Cué Mí, 1968. 23p.

4188 Sembradores del sol. A., Tall. gráf. de Ocara Poty Cué Mí, 1970. 38p.

4189 Tiempo de amor. n.p., n.d. 15p.

4190 Temblor de acacias. A., Ocara Poty Cué Mí, 1966. 47p.
3. ed. 1972.

4191 Tronco al cielo. A., Ediciones Nizza, 1960. 64p.

4192 Virazón. A., 1972. 17p.

4193 SABAT ERCASTY, Carlos. Una musa paraguaya: Elsa Wiezell. RNM 50 no. 148 (1951) 55-68.

Aníbal ZOTTI

4193a Eramos cinco, novela. B.A., Zotti, 1975. 181p.

Carlos ZUBIZARRETA

4194 Crónica y ensayo. A., Edit. Emasa, 1969. 208p. (Colección Cultura paraguaya)

4195 Los grillos de la duda; cuentos. A., Edit. Emasa, 1966. 140p. (Colección Cultura paraguaya)

José R. ZUBIZARRETA PERIS

4195a Dos historias en el cielo, novela. Lima, Edit. Juridica, 1973. 102p.

XIII. SCIENCE

A. Earth sciences

4196 BERTONI, Moisés Santiago. Descripción física y económica del Paraguay. A., M. Brossa, 1918. 174p.

4197 BERTONI, Moisés Santiago. Estudio de las periodicidades diarias aparentes o reales de las lluvias y tempestades. Puerto Bertoni, Imp. "Ex sylvia", 1918. 58p. (*His* Descripción física y económica del Paraguay. Div. 2: Meteorología y climatología. Sección 24: Prognosia del tiempo, Núm. 24:2)

4198 BLANCO SANCHEZ, Jesús L. El río Paraguay; monografía hidrográfica. A., Lumen, 1962. 22p.

4199 BOETTNER, Ricardo. Geología, con nociones de geología del Paraguay de acuerdo al programa oficial de segundo año del ciclo básico. 3. ed. A., La Colmena, 1960. 129p.

4200 BOETTNER, Ricardo. Reflections on the geology of Paraguay. *In* no. 474, 61-64.

4201 ECKEL, Edwin B. Geology and mineral resources of Paraguay - a reconnaissance. With sections on igneous and metamorphic rocks, by Charles Milton and Edwin B. Eckel. Soils by Pedro Tirado Sulsona. Washington, 1959. 110p. (United States Geological Survey. Professional Paper, 327)

4202 FARIÑA SANCHEZ, T. Climate. *In* no. 474, 331-38.

4203 FARIÑA SANCHEZ, T. Investigación estadística de las precipitaciones pluviométricas en Asunción del Paraguay. RM 5 no. 18 (1946) 78-88.

4204 FARIÑA SANCHEZ, T. Rasgos climatológicos del este del Paraguay. BSAB 11 (1971) Supl., 111-19.

4205 GONZALEZ, Teodosio. Una gira por el Pacífico, el Congreso científico de Santiago, la hospitalidad chilena; impresión de un delegado paraguayo. A., Tall. gráf. La Unión, 1909. 45p.

4206 HARRINGTON, Horacio J. Geología del Paraguay oriental. B.A., 1950. 82p. (Universidad Nacional. Facultad de Ciencias Exactas, Físicas y Naturales Científicas. Serie E. Contribuciones Geología, 1)

4207 MAACK, Reinhard. Arenito Caiuá no Paraguai. Curitiba, 1959. 14p. (Curitiba, Paraná, Brasil. Instituto de Biologia e Pesquisas Tecnológicas. Notas preliminares e estudos. Série Geologia e mineralogia, 2)

4208 MAACK, Reinhard. Neue Forschungen in Paraguay und am Rio Paraná. Die Flussgebiete Monday und Acaray. ER 93 (1962) 4-48.

4209 MARBAIS DU GRATY, Alfred Louis Hubert Ghislain, *baron*. Minerales del Paraguay. (De la História del Paraguay) por Alfredo du Graty. A., Tall. nac. de H. Kraus. 1902. 20p.
Also: RIP 4 no. 33 (1902) 266-82.

4210 MINERAL resources of Paraguay. MJ 253 no. 6481 (1959) 444-45.

4211 MIRAGLIA, L. Vulcani postpliocenici spenti fiancheggianti il fiume Paraguay (fra il 25 e il 26 lat. Sud). BSNN 74 (1965) 267-77.

4212 PUTZER, Hannafrit. Die Geologie von Paraguay. Berlin, Gebrüder Borntraeger, 1962. x, 182p. (Beiträge zur regionalen Geologie der Erde, 21)

4213 RAMOS GIMENEZ, Leopoldo. La riqueza del Paraguay en energia hidraulica inexplotada. RGA 3 no. 25 (1936) 247-54.

4214 REBAUDI, Ovidio. Apuntes sobre mineria paraguaya. Trabajo presentado al "Tercer Congreso científico panamericano", efectuado en Lima en Diciembre de 1924. A., 1924. 46p.

4215 REBAUDI, Ovidio. Artículos y trabajos. A., 1910. 152p.

4216 RIVAS RODRIGUEZ, Serafín. Contribución al estudio del clima del Paraguay. A., Tip. de "El Paraguayo", 1890. 33p.

4217 RIVAS RODRIGUEZ, Serafín. Etude sur le climat du Paraguay. Dédiée à l'Association rurale uruguayenne comme preuve de la grande estime qu'a pour elle son membre honoraire, Serafin Rivas. A., Typ. de "El Paraguayo", 1890. 38p.

4218 ROMERO, Genaro. Nuestra riqueza minera. A., Imp. nac., 1930. 70p. (República del Paraguay. Cartilla informativa, 18)

4219 SERVICIO TECNICO INTER-AMERICANO DE COOPERACION AGRICOLA. PARAGUAY. A reconnaissance soil and land classification of Paraguay, by Pedro Tirado-Sulsona, Joseph B. Hammon, José Rosa Ramírez. A., 1954. 109p.

4220 SOCIEDAD CIENTIFICA DEL PARAGUAY. Conferencias. A., 1962. 89p.

4221 SOSA ESCALADA, E. Influencia de desmontes en el régimen de las aguas. RIP 10 no. 61 (1909) 778-88; no. 63, 968-77.

4222 STOLTENBERG, Ida. Landschaftskundliche Gliederung von Paraguay. MGG 38 (1927) 69-130.

4223 TERUGGI, M.E. Bosquejo geológico del Paraguay y la provincia de Corrientes. BSAB 11 (1971) Supl., 1-16.

4224 TOSSINI, Luis. El río Paraguay. ASCA 132 (1941) no. 3, 118-34; no. 5, 218-25; 133 (1942) no. 6, 502-22.

4225 VILLALBA, Porfirio. Apuntes sobre la riqueza hidrográfica del Paraguay. orografía y climatología. A., La Colmena, 1961. 56p.

4226 WRIGHT, C.W.; GLOVER, R.G. Mineral resources, production and trade of Uruguay and Paraguay. FMQ 3 (1940) no. 4, 1-37.

B. Life sciences

4227 ARATA, Pedro de. Botánica médica Americana. Los herbarios de las Misiones del Paraguay. B 7 (1898) 419-48; 8 (1898) 185-92.

4228 ATTENBOROUGH, David. Djurfångst i Paraguay. Övers. av. Stina Hergin. Stockholm, Tiden, 1962. 205p.

4229 ATTENBOROUGH, David. Zoo quest in Paraguay. London, Lutterworth, 1959. 168p.

4230 AZARA, Félix de. Apuntamientos para la historia natural de los páxaros del Paraguay y Río de la Plata.

Madrid, Imp. de la viuda de Ibarra, 1802-05. 3 vols.
Also: B.A., 1942. 5 vols.
See also: HARTLAUB, Gustav. Systematischer Index zu don Felix de Azaras "Apuntamientos para la Historia natural de los páxaros del Paraguay y Rio de la Plata". Bremen, Druck von C. Schünemann, 1847. vi, 29p.

4230a AZARA, Felix de. Apuntamientos para la historia natural de los quadrupedos del Paraguay y Río de la Plata. N.Y., Arno Press, 1978. 3 vols.
Reprint of 1802 ed.

4231 AZARA, Félix de. Essais sur l'histoire naturelle des quadrupèdes de la Province du Paraguay par don Félix d'Azara Capitaine de Vaisseau de la Marine Espagnole; Commissaire de Sa Majesté Catholique pour les Limites Espagnoles et Portugaises de l'Amérique Méridionale: Citoyen de la ville de l'Assomption capitale du Paraguay, etc. Ecrit depuis 1783 jusqu'en 1796 (an 4 de la République Française). Avec une Appendice sur quelques Reptiles, Et formant suite nécessaire aux Oeuvres du Buffon; traduits sur le Manuscrit inédit de l'auteur. Paris, Charles Pougens, An XI (1801). 2 vols.

4232 AZARA, Félix de. The natural history of the quadrupeds of Paraguay and the River La Plata: translated from the Spanish of Don Félix de Azara with a memoir of the author, a physical sketch of the country, and numerous notes, by W. Perceval Hunter. Vol. 1. Edinburgh, Adam & Charles Black; London, Longman, Orme, Brown, Green & Longman, 1838. xxxii, 340p.

4233 BERTONI, Arnaldo de Winkelried. Aves nuevas del Paraguay. Contribución á Azara. Descripción de las aves nuevas descubiertas por el autor y contribución al estudio de la avifauna paraguaya. Materiales recogidos desde 1890 hasta fines de 1900. A., Tall. nac. de H. Kraus, 1900. 216p.

4234 BERTONI, Arnaldo de Winkelried. Catalogos sistemáticos de los vertebrados del Paraguay. RSCP 4 no. 4 (1939) 1-58.

4235 BERTONI, Arnaldo de Winkelried. Contribución á la biología de las avispas y abejas del Paraguay (hymenoptera). Edición del autor. B.A., Imp. y casa editora "Juan A. Alsina", 1911. 97-146p.
Also: AMNBA 22 (ser. 3, t. 15) 97-146.

4236 BERTONI, Arnaldo de Winkelried. Fauna paraguaya. Catálogos sistemáticos de los vertebrados del Paraguay. Peces, batracios, reptiles, aves y mamiferos conocidos hasta 1913. A., M. Brossa, 191-. 86p. (Moisés S. Bertoni. Descripción física y económica del Paraguay. Numeración novenal, 59: 1)

4237 BERTONI, Moisés Santiago. Condiciones generales de la vida orgánica y división territorial. Puerto Bertoni, Imp. y edición "Ex sylvis", 1918. 174p. (*His* Descripción física y económica del Paraguay. Div. 1: Introducción y gen; sección 12: Condiciones generales, núm. 12:1)

4238 BERTONI, Moises Santiago. The conditions of animal life in Paraguay. *In* no. 474, 65-69.

4239 BERTONI, Moisés Santiago. Las plantes usuales del Paraguay y países limítrofes; caracteres, propiedades y aplicaciones con la nomenclatura guaraní, portuguesa, española y latina y la etimología guaraní, incluyendo un estudio físico e industrial de las maderas. A., Establecimiento gráfico M. Brossa, 1914- (*His* Descripción física y económica del Paraguay. Num. novenal 31)

4240 BERTONI, Moises Santiago. Plantas usuales del Paraguay; Alto Paraná y Misiones. A., H. Kraus, 1901. 122p.

4241 CABRERA, A.L. La vegetación del Paraguay en el cuadro fitogeográfico de América del Sur. BSAB 9 (1971) Supl., 121-31.

4241a CATALDO, Javier. La flora medicinal paraguaya. A., Rolon, 1968. 460p.

4242 CHODAT, Robert. Plantas Hasslerianae ou soit énumération des plantes récoltées au Paraguay par le Dr. Emile Hassler, d'Aarau (Suisse) et déterminées par le Prof. Dr. R. Chodat, avec l'aide de plusieurs collaborateurs. Première partie. Geneva, Imprimerie Romet, 1898. 203p.

4242a CHODAT, Robert; VISCHER, Wilhelm. La végétation du Paraguay. Vaduz, J. Cramer, 1977. 558p.
Reprint of articles from the Bulletin de la Société Botanique du Génève.

4243 GORHAM, J. Richard. The history of natural history in Paraguay. *In* no. 474, 1-8.

4244 HASSLER, Emile. Enumeración preliminar de las plantas usuales del Paraguay. RIP 3 no. 29 (1901) 161-70.

4245 LAUBMANN, Alfred. Die Vögel von Paraguay. Stuttgart, Strecker & Schröder, 1939. xvi, 334p. (Wissenschaftliche Ergebnisse der deutschen Gran Chaco Expedition)

4246 MICHALOWSKI, Miguel. Géneros de los árboles leguminosos del Paraguay; Guía para los especialistas forestales. A., Centro de Información Agrícola Ganadera de STICA, 1957. 21p. (Servicio Técnico Interamericano de Cooperación Agrícola. Boletín, 209)

4247 MORONG, T.; BRITTON, N.L. An enumeration of the plants collected by Dr. Thomas Morong in Paraguay, 1888-1890. ANYAS 7 (1892-93) 45-280.

4248 PARODI, Domingo. Contribuciones á la flora del Paraguay. Fasc. 1-4. B.A., Imp. de Pablo E. Coni, 1877-79. 159p.

4249 PARODI, Domingo. Contribuciones á la flora del Paraguay. Familia de las amarantáceas. B.A., Imp. de "La Nación", 1892. 183p.

4250 PARODI, Domingo. Notas sobre algunas plantas usuales del Paraguay, de Corrientes y de Misiones. B.A., Imp. de P. Coni, 1886. xxvii, 123p.

4250a PAYNTER, Raymond A.; CAPERTON, Alastair M.G. Ornithological gazetteer of Paraguay. Cambridge, Mass., Bird Department, Museum of Comparative Zoology, Harvard University, 1977. iv, 43p.

4251 PEREYRA, José M. La obra ornitológica de Azara. Apuntamientos para la historia natural de los pájaros del Paraguay y Rio de la Plata. Comentada y actualizada por José A. Pereyra. B.A., 1945. 140p.

4252 RENGGER, Johann Rudolph. Naturgeschichte der Saeugethiere von Paraguay. Basel, Schweighausersche Buchhandlung, 1830. xvi, 394p.

4253 RODRIGUEZ, Pedro Miguel. Plantas medicinales del Paraguay, redactado en presencia de libros y revistas, aumentado con observaciones y datos farmacológicos. A., Imp. La Mundial, 1915. 141p.

4254 RODRIGUEZ BARBOSA, Nemesio. Pojhá naná; recetario de plantas medicinales del Paraguay. 2. ed. A., Zamphirópolos, 1966. 104p.

4255 SAINT-HILAIRE, Augustin François César Prouvencal de. Esquisse de mes voyages au Brésil et Paraguay, considérés principalement sous le rapport de la botanique (with an introductory essay by Anna E. Jenkins). Waltham, Mass., The Chronica botanica co.; N.Y., G.E. Stechert, 1946. 61p. (Chronica botanica, v. 10, n. 1)

4255a SANCHEZ LABRADOR, José. Peces y aves del Paraguay natural ilustrado, 1767; manuscrito preparado bajo la dirección de Mariano N. Castex. B.A., Compañía General Fabril, 1968. 511p.

4256 SCHADE, Francisco; MASI PALLARES, Rafael. Las aves del Paraguay. RPM, 2 (1967) no. 1, 72-85; 3 (1968) no. 1, 86-105; 4 (1969) no. 1, 77-96; 5 (1970) no. 1, 33-58; 6 (1971) no. 1, 103-28.

4257 SCHADE, Francisco. The ecology and control of the leaf-cutting ants of Paraguay. *In* no. 474, 77-95.

4258 SCHADE, Francisco. The snails and mussels of the state of Guairá, Paraguay. *In* no. 474, 71-76.

4259 SCHROTTKY, C. Blumen und Insekten in Paraguay. ZWI 3 (1907) 47-53, 73-78.

4260 SPEGAZZINI, Carolus. Fungi guaranitici. Pugillus I. B.A., P.E. Coni, 1886. 177p.

4260a WETMORE, Alexander. Observations on birds of Argentina, Paraguay, Uruguay and Chile. Washington, USGPO, 1926. iv, 448p. (National Museum, Bulletin, 133)

C. Agriculture and forestry

4261 ALONSO CRIADO, Matías. El cultivo del café como remedio de la crisis económica del Paraguay. Montevideo, Tip. de Escuela nacional de artes y oficios, 1897. 102p.

4262 ALONSO CRIADO, Matías. El cultivo de la vid como remedio de la crisis agrícola del Paraguay. Montevideo, Imp. y litografía "La Razón", 1896. 78p.

4263 BENITEZ GONZALEZ, Manuel. La situación de la agricultura en el Paraguay. RPS 1 no. 1 (1964) 49-74.

4264 BERTONI, Guillermo Tell. El porvenir del cultivo del algodonero en la cuenca del Río Paraguay. A., Ariel, 1923. 52p.

4265 BERTONI, Moisés Santiago. Agenda y almanaque agrícola paraguayo. A., Tall. nac. de H. Kraus, 1903. 360p.

4266 BERTONI, Moisés Santiago. Agenda y mentor agrícola. Guía del agricultor y colono con el calendario de todos los trabajos rurales. Puerto Bertoni, Ex Sylvis, 1926. 448p.

4267 BERTONI, Moisés Santiago. Almanaque agrícola paraguayo y agenda del agricultor. A., H. Kraus, 1901. 248p.

4268 BERTONI, Moisés Santiago. Calendario agrícola. A., Ministerio de Agricultura y Ganaderia, 1971. 64p.

4269 BERTONI, Moisés Santiago. La orientación de la agricultura Paraguaya y los cultivos tropicales. ACP no. 5 (1919) 394-407.

4270 CHACON, Teodoro. Compendio elemental de agricultura práctica para el uso de las escuelas de la República del Paraguay. A., Imp. y lit. de "La Reforma", 1896. 107p.

4271 CENTURION, Cirilo and others. Estudio de adaptación de dos variedades de algodón seleccionadas en Africa Central, REBA B-50 y REBA BTK-12 en el Paraguay. A., Ministerio de Agricultura y Ganaderia, 1972. 8p.

4272 CIANCIO, Pedro N. La soja y el problema alimentario del Paraguay. A., El Gráfico, 1950. 502p.

4273 COMITE EJECUTIVO DE LOS ESTABLECIMIENTOS INDIGENAS. Informe sobre los establecimientos agrícolas de los indigenas en el area de las colonias Mennonitas, Chaco Central (Paraguay). A., CEEI, 1973. 42p.

4274 DEMERSAY, Alfred. Du tabac du Paraguay, culture, consommation et commerce avec une lettre sur l'introduction du tabac en France par Ferdinand Denis. Paris, Guillaumin, 1851. v, 30, xliii p.

4275 DOUBLET, R.N.A. Le maté. Paris, 1885. 91p.

4276 EPERY, R.P. Essai sur le maté (thé du Paraguay). Paris, 1883. 59p.

4277 FOGEL, Ramón Bruno. La medición del ingreso en unidades agrícolas de subsistencia en el Paraguay. Resultados de un ensayo metodológico. RPS 11 no. 31 (1974) 121-65.

4278 FOREST resources of Paraguay; presented by the Delegation of Paraguay. UN 2 (1948) no. 3, 129-32.

4279 FRUTOS, Juan Manuel. El Instituto de Bienestar Rural y la ganadería nacional. A., Asociación Rural del Paraguay, 1970. 190p.

4280 GIROLA, Carlos D. La yerba mate (Ilex paraguayensis St. Hil.) B.A., Universidad Buenos Aires, Facultad de Agronomia y Veterinaria, 1931. 26p.

4281 GONZALEZ ALSINA, Ezequiel. La pequeña agricultura: serie de editorales del diario "Patria" sobre un discurso del presidente del Banco Mundo, Robert S. MacNamara. A., Ediciones del C.E.C., 1974. iii, 122p.

4282 HAMILL, Edward B. Posibilidades de los bosques del Alto Paraná para producir pulpa. A., Instituto de Asuntos Interamericanos, 1955. 39p.

4282a HAWKES, John Gregory; HJERTING, J.P. The potatoes of Argentina, Brazil, Paraguay and Uruguay: a biosystematic study. Oxford, Clarendon Press, 1969. xxiv, 527p.

4283 HOLDRIGE, Leslie R. Estudio ecológico de los bosques de la Región Oriental del Paraguay. *In* Documento de trabajo, no. 1. SF/PAR, FAO/Naciones Unidas. A., 1973. 15-19p.

4284 INSTITUTE OF INTER-AMERICAN AFFAIRS. Crop development in Paraguay, by R. Howard Porter. Washington, Food Supply Division, Institute of Inter-American Affairs, 1947. 94p.

4285 INSTITUTE OF INTER-AMERICAN AFFAIRS. The forest resources of Paraguay, a special report by Morton A. Klein. Washington, Food Supply Division, Institute of Inter-American Affairs, 1946. 112p.

4286 INTER-AMERICAN DEVELOPMENT COMMISSION. The forest resources of Paraguay and their possible industrial utilization, by Eugene C. Reichard. Washington, Inter-American Development Commission, 1946. 26p.

4287 KERR, George A. The quebracho forests of South America: personal notes and observations in Argentina and Paraguay. BPAU 54 (1922) 9-34.

4288 KOTSCHWAR, A. Proyecto de desarrollo forestal y de industrias forestales, silvicultura y ordenación forestal. Rome, Programa de las Naciones Unidas para el Desarrollo; FAO, 1973. 173p. (UNDP Proyecto PAR/ 66/515 - Technical Report no. 2)

4289 LANGER, Alexander. Die Baumwollkultur in Paraguay. TP 51 (1928) no. 9, 340-60.

4290 MENGUAL G., Lorenzo. El cultivo del té en el Paraguay. A., El Arte, 1958. 85p.

4291 MERRIAM, L.C. Informe preliminar sobre el potencial de parques y reservas naturales y areas de recreación en el Paraguay. A., FAO/Naciones Unidas, 1972. (Documento del trabajo, 10)

4292 MICHALOWSKI, Miguél. Arboles y arbustos del Paraguay. A., Centro de Información Agrícola Ganaderia - STICA, 19--. 183p. (Servicio Técnico Inter-Americano de Cooperación Agricola, 231)

4293 MIRAGLA, Luigi. Foreste del Paraguay. RFMSN 12 (1938) 393-99; 470-84.

4294 MULHALL, Michael G. The cotton fields of Paraguay and Corrientes; being an account of a tour through these countries, preceded by annals of cotton planting in the River Plate territories from 1862 to 1864. B.A., Imp. de The Standard, 1864. 120p.

4295 NICASTRO, Carlo. Il mate o té del Paraguay (Ilex paraguariensis St. Hil.). ACO 22 (1928) no. 11, 403-17; no. 12, 465-69; 23 (1929) no. 1, 19-29; no. 2, 67-74; no. 5, 221-30; no. 7, 324-34; no. 8, 369-81.

4295a PADILLA, Napoleón. Plan de desarrollo tabacalero del Paraguay. A., Banco interamericano de desarrollo, 1964. 106p.

4296 PARAGUAY. DIRECCION GENERAL DE AGRICULTURA. Plan mínimo de cultivos obligatorios y de racionalización agrícola, año agrícola 1943/44. A., La Colmena, 1943. 63p.

4297 PARAGUAY. MINISTERIO DE AGRICULTURA Y GANADERIA. Censo de Agricultura del Paraguay para los años 1942-43 y 1944. A., Servicio Técnico Inter-Americano de Cooperación Agricola, 1948. 272p.

4298 PARAGUAY. MINISTERIO DE AGRICULTURA Y GANADERIA. Tres años de ensayos con variedades de trigo en el Paraguay. A., 1970. 24p.

4299 PARAGUAY. MINISTERIO DE RELACIONES EXTERIORES. Le maté; ou Thé du Paraguay. A., "Ariel", 1914. 20p.

4300 PENA VILLAMIL, Manuel. Breve historia de la ganaderia Paraguaya. HP 13 (1968-70) 83-97.

4301 PETERSON, Lyall N. Forest products of Paraguay. JF 46 (1948) no. 1, 20-26.

4302 ROMERO, Genaro. Nuestra riqueza forestal. A., Imp. nac., 1929. 46p.

4303 ROMERO, Genaro. El porvenir de la yerba mate. A., La Mundial, Montevideo y Estrella, 1915. 28p.

4303a SAMANIEGO, César C. Caña de azúcar. Tacua rhe-he y caña paraguaya. A., Imp. nac., 1936. 120p.

4304 SAMANIEGO, César C. "Ilex paraguayensis" yerba-mate "caá". A., Paraguay, 1927. 124p.
2. ed. A., Imp. nac., 1937. 146p.

4305 SIMS, Harold D. Japanese agriculturists in Brazil and Paraguay: a review of the literature. PSN 3 (1974) no. 2, 13-19.

D. Engineering. Technology. Nutrition

4306 APONTE BENITEZ, Leandro. Cincuento años de aeronáutica en el Paraguay. A., El Arte, 1957. 355p.

4307 APONTE BENITEZ, Leandro. Tte I Silvio Pettirossi; sus bodas de plata con la gloria. A., Imp. nac., 1942. iv, 187p. (Biblioteca de la "Revista de las FF. AA. de la Nación", 3)

4308 PARAGUAY. COMISION DEL PARAGUAY EN LA EXPOSICION UNIVERSAL DE BARCELONA. Catálogo de los objetos que la República del Paraguay exhibe en la Exposición Universal de Barcelona. Barcelona, Imp. de los Sucesores de N. Ramirez, 1888. 66p.

4309 INSTITUTE OF INTER-AMERICAN AFFAIRS. Paraguayan rural life, survey of food problems, 1943-1945. Washington, 1946. 130p.
Reprinted: Westport, Conn., Greenwood Press, 1975. 130p.

4309a MAY, Jacques Meyer; McLELLAN, Donna L. The ecology of malnutrition in Eastern South America: Venezuela, Guyana, Surinam (and the Netherlands Antilles), French Guiana, Brazil, Uruguay, Paraguay and Argentina. N.Y., Hafner Press; London, Collier Macmillan, 1974. x, 558p.

4310 MOLINA, Raúl Alejandro. El consumo del vino en el primitivo Buenos Aires, el vino de Castilla y de la tierra. RJEHM 1 no. 7 (1972) 367-73.

4311 MONTALTO, Francisco Américo. Un aspecto de la acción educativa del Departamento de nutrición, la Escuela de idóneos en alimentación y el "Instituto dr. Andrés Barbero". A., Imp. Ariel, 1943. 41p.

4312 MONTALTO, Francisco Américo. Aspectos fundamentos del problema de la nutrición en el Paraguay; síntesis crítica y fundamentada de la labor realizada en el ex-Departamento de Nutrición. B.A., Impresora Oeste, 1956. xiv, 485p.

4313 MONTALTO, Francisco Américo. La situación alimentaria de la población ante el problema del desarrollo económico-social del país. A., 1962. 18p.

4314 MONTALTO, Francisco Américo. Valor del "enriquecimiento" de las harinas en la solución de los problemas de la nutrición en el Paraguay. A., 1958. 14p.

4315 STORNI, Pablo Duarte de. Human nutrition in Paraguay. *In* no. 474, 141-207.

4315a UNITED STATES. PUBLIC HEALTH SERVICE. HEALTH, EDUCATION AND WELFARE DEPARTMENT. Republic of Paraguay, nutrition survey of Armed Forces, May - Aug. 1965, report from Nutrition Program, Health Services and Mental Health Administration. Washington, USGPO, 1968. v, 99p.

4316 VELILLA de AQUINO, Josefina. Tembí u paraguai. Comida paraguaya. A., Ediciones Primer Instituto de Arte Culinario, 1971. 138p.

XIV. MEDICINE

4317 BERTONI, Moisés Santiago. Contribución al estudio de la malaria (chucho) y su tratamiento, observaciones hechas en el Alto Paraná y Paraguay. A., Kraus, 1900. 29p.

4318 El CUERPO médico del Paraguay, reconociendo al doctor Guillermo Stewart, los servicios que como profesional ha prestado al país en el transcurso de cincuenta años, le ofrece el testimonio de su respetuosa consideración. A., Tall. de "El Diario", 1906. 37p.

4318a CONLY, Gladys N. The impact of malaria on economic development: a case study. Washington, Pan American Health Organization, Pan American Sanitary Bureau, Regional Office of the World Health Organization, 197? viii, 117p. (Scientific Publication, no. 279)

4319 GONZALEZ, Gustavo; VELAZQUEZ, Carlos J. Enfermedad de Chagas. A., Facultad de Ciencias Médicas, Catedra de Semiología Médica, 1964. 98p. (Biblioteca de enfermedades rurales del Paraguay y regiones vacinas)

4320 GONZALEZ, Gustavo. La medicina Guaraní-Tupí precolonial. SA 1 (1965) 1, 27-38.

4321 GONZALEZ, Gustavo. La medicina Guaraní-Tupí colonial, primera parte. HP 2 (1957) 36-49.

4322 MIGONE, L.E. Apuntes de climatología y nosografía médica del Paraguay. RSCP 2 no. 5 (1929) 203-22.

4322a MONTENEGRO, Pedro de. Materia médica misionera; noticia preliminar de Raúl Quintana. B.A., Biblioteca Nacional, 1945. xlviii, 469p.

4323 PARAGUAY. DEPARTAMENTO DE LEPRA. Plan de control de lepra en el Paraguay. A., Ministerio de Salud Pública y Bienestar Social, 1957. 1 vol. (various pagings)

4324 PARAGUAY. DEPARTAMENTO NACIONAL DE HIGIENE Y ASISTENCIA PUBLICA. Nomenclatura de las causas de fallecimiento para los certificados de defunción, aprobada por el superior gobierno con fecha 29 de abril de 1905. A., Tall. nac. de H. Kraus, 1905. 16p.

4325 PARAGUAY. DEPARTAMENTO DE HIGIENE Y ASISTENCIA PUBLICA. Sobre las lombrices intestinales con algunas instrucciones para curarlas. A., Tall. nac. de H. Kraus, 1903. 7p.

4326 PARAGUAY. SERVICIO NACIONAL DE ERRADICACION DEL PALUDISMO. Anteproyecto de presupuesto, 8 años; plan de erradicación del paludismo. A., 1964. 1 vol. (various pagings)

4327 PEREZ MARICEVICH, Blás Rafael. La medicina empírica en el Paraguay. SA 7 (1972) 1-2, 61-73.

4328 RECALDE, Juan Francisco. La buba; colaboración científica aparecida en La Tribuna con fecha 15 de noviembre de 1917. A., 1917. 16p.

4328a SANCHEZ LABRADOR, José. La medicina en el Paraguay natural (1771-1776); exposición comentada del texto original por Anibal Ruiz Moreno. Tucumán, Universidad de Tucumán, 1948. 348p. (Universidad de Tucumán, publ. 423)

4329 STEWARD, Guillermo. La peste. A., Tall. nac. de H. Kraus, 1899. 22p.

XV. SELECT LIST OF PARAGUAYAN PERIODICALS

The following select list of Paraguayan periodicals is arranged by title. Where a periodical is issued by a ministry, society, or similar organization, the name of the organization is given, being separated from the title by a dash. The year in which the periodical was first issued is also given; where the periodical is numbered other than by year, then the date when the first volume was published is given in brackets.

4330 Acción. Revista Paraguaya de educación y del hogar - Colegios Religiosos del Paraguay. 1 (196?) -

4331 Agricultura, comercio e industrias - Ministerio de Agricultura, Comercio e Industrias. 1 (1941) -

4332 Album paraguayo. 1955 -

4333 Alcor. 1956 -

4334 Almanaque nacional del Paraguay. 1896 -

4335 Anales - Asociación Indigenista del Paraguay. 1 (1945) -

4336 Anales - Instituto Nacional de Parasitología. 1 (1928) -

4337 Anales - Universidad Nacional del Paraguay. 1 (1899) -

4338 Anales - Universidad Nacional del Paraguay, Facultad de Ciencias Médicas. 1 (1927) -

4339 Anales - Universidad Nacional del Paraguay, Facultad de Odontología. 1 (1937/38) -

4340 Anales Cientificos Paraguayos. Puerto Bertoni, 1 (1901) -

4341 Anales del Paraguay. Revista editorial de ciencias, arte, literatura y crítica. 1 (1936) -

4342 Anuario - Instituto Femenino de Investigaciones Históricas. 1 - 1970/71 (1971) -

4343 Anuario - Ministerio de economia. 1938/39 (1939) -

4344 Anuario estadístico de la república del Paraguay. 1888 (1896) -

4345 Anuario hidrográfico - Dirección de Hidrografía y Navegación. 1 (1940) -

4346 Archivo diplomático y consular del Paraguay. 1 (1908) -

4347 Asi es. 1 (1962) -

4348 Boletín - Departamento de Tierras y Colonias. 1 (1920) -

4349 Boletín - Departamento Nacional de Fomento. 1 (1913) -

4350 Boletín - Ministerio de Hacienda. 1 (1920) -

4351 Boletín - Ministerio de Relaciones Exteriores. 1 (1913) -

4352 Boletín de aduanas - Dirección General de Aduanas. 1 (1949) -

4353 Boletín de educación paraguaya. 1 (1956) -

4354 Boletín de meteorológica agrícola - Estación Meteorológica e Hidrométrica. Puerto Bertoni, 1 (1910) -

4355 Boletín del tesoro - Contaduria General y Dirección del Tesoro. 1 (1913) -

4356 Boletín estadístico de comercio exterior - Dirección General de Estadistica y Censos. 1963/64 (1966) -

4357 Boletín estadistico del Paraguay - Dirección General de Estadística y Censos. 1 (1957) -

4358 Boletín estadístico mensual - Banco Central del Paraguay. 1958 -

4359 Boletín mensual - Dirección de Economia Rural. 194? -

4360 Boletín naval - Armada Paraguaya. 1 (1944) -

4361 Boletín oftalmológico - Centro de Prevención de la Ceguera. 1 (1957) -

4362 Boletín sanitario - Ministerio de Salud Pública y Previsión Social. 1 (1942) -

4363 Boletín semestral - Dirección General de Estadística. 1 (1915) -

4364 Boletín trimestral - Dirección General de Estadística. 1 (1906) -

4365 Cartilla agropecuaria - Ministerio de Agricultura. 1 (1938) -

4366 Comercio - Cámara y Bolsa de Comercio del Centro de Importadores. 1 (1968) -

4367 Comunidad. 1956? -

4368 Criterio; revista Universitaria de Cultura. 1 (1966?) -

4369 Crítica y análisis. 1 (1963) -

4370 Cuadernos republicanos. 1 (1967) -

4371 Cultura - Centro de Cultura Paraguaya "General Bernardino Caballero". 1 (1943) -

4372 Diálogo; Revista Paraguaya de noticias. 1 (1971) -

4373 Dinamica - Centro de Economistas Colorados. 1 (1966) -

4374 Economista Paraguayo - Colegio de Doctores en Ciencias Económicas. 1 (1961) -

4375 Encuesta industrial - Departamento de Estadística y Censo. 1958 -

4376 Enfoques paraguayos; visión gráfica de todos los tiempos. B.A., 1957 -

4377 Estudios Paraguayos; revista de la Universidad Católica "Nuestra Señora de la Asunción". 1 (1973) -

4378 Etnografía - Museo de História Natural y Etnografía. 1 (1957) -

4379 Etnolingüistica - Museo de História Natural y Etnografía. 1 (1957) -

4380 Folleto - Ministerio de Salud Pública. 1 (1943) -

4381 Guaraní; guía de tráfico aéreo, maritimo, fluvial, terrestre y de hoteles. 1 (1961) -

4382 Guía general del Paraguay; anuario. 1906 -

4383 Hacienda pública - Ministerio de Hacienda. 1 (1957) -

4384 História paraguaya - Academia Paraguaya de la História. 1 (1956) -

4385 Industria y comercio - Ministerio de Industria y Comercio. 1 (1969) -

4386 Industrialia; tribuna del desarrollo industrial. 1 (1973) -

4387 Memoria - Banco Central del Paraguay. 1 (1952) -

4388 Memoria - Dirección general de estadística. 1925/26 (1927) -

4389 Memoria - Instituto "Doctor Andrés Barbero". Escuela de Visitadores de Higiene. 1940/41 (1941) -

4390 Memoria - Ministerio de Hacienda. 1882 -

4391 Memorial del ejército. 1 (1915) -

4392 Minerva. 1 (1967) -

4393 Opinión; sobre problemas nacionales e internacionales del Paraguay. B.A., 1 (196?) -

4394 Panorama. 1 (1969) -

4395 Paraguay. 1 (1912) -

4396 Paraguay - Agrupación Folklórica Guaraní. B.A., 1 (1943) -

4397 Paraguay histórico. 1 (1959) -

4398 Paraguay industrial y comercial - Ministerio de industria y comercio. 1 (1944) -

4399 Paraguay review. Revue du Paraguay - Dirección general de inmigración y colonización. 1 (1901) -

4400 Revista - Centro de Estudiantes de Medicina. 1 (1920) -

4401 Revista - Centro de Importadores. 1 (1940) -

4402 Revista - Centro Estudiantes de Ciencias Económicas de la Universidad Nacional del Paraguay. 1 (1939?) -

4403 Revista - Centro Estudiantes de Odontologia. 1 (1939) -

4404 Revista - Circulo Odontológico del Paraguay. 1 (1955) -

4405 Revista - Instituto Paraguayo. 1 (1896) -

4406 Revista - Ministerio de Salud Pública y Previsión Social. 1 (1946) -

4407 Revista - Museo de Históría Natural y Jardín Botánico-Zoológico. 1 (1921) -

4408 Revista - Sociedad Científica del Paraguay. 1 (1921) -

4409 Revista - Universidad Nacional del Paraguay, Facultad de Quimica y Farmacia. 1 (1945) -

4410 Revista de administración militar. 1 (1936) -

4411 Revista de agricultura y ganaderia - Ministerio de Agricultura. 1 (1944) -

4412 Revista de agronómia - Estación Agronómica de Puerto Bertoni. Puerto Bertoni, 1 (1897) -

4413 Revista de derecho y ciencias sociales. 1 (1927) -

4414 Revista de instrucción primaria. 1903 -

4415 Revista de las fuerzas armadas de la nación. 1 (1940) -

4416 Revista de sanidad militar - Dirección Superior de Sanidad Militar. 1 (1927) -

4417 Revista de turismo - Dirección General de Turismo. 1 (1942) -

4418 Revista del Paraguay. 1 (1913) -

4419 Revista del Paraguay; ciencias, literatura y artes. B.A., 1 (1891) -

4420 Revista histórica; publicación quincenal de documentos relativos al Paraguay. 1 (1899) -

4421 Revista médica del Paraguay - Sociedad de Medicina y Cirugia y Especialidades. 1 (1935) -

4422 Revista médica del Paraguay - Circulo Paraguayo de Médicos. 1 (1955) -

4423 Revista mensual; publicación de datos é informaciones sobre el país. 1 (1896) -

4424 Revista militar. 1922 -

4425 Revista municipal; órgano oficial de la Municipalidad de la capital. 1 (1957) -

4426 Revista odontológica - Centro de Odontológia de Paraguay. 1 (1946) -

4427 Revista Paraguaya. 1 (1925) -

4428 Revista Paraguaya de Sociologia - Centro Paraguaya de Estudios Sociológicos. 1 (1964) -

4429 Revue du Paraguay. 1 (1888) -

4430 Suplemento Antropológico - Universidad Católica. 1 (1966) -

4431 Tribuna Universitaria - Centro de Estudiantes de Medicina. 1 (1940) -

INDEX

Numbers refer to items, not to pages. Names of authors are in capital letters.